old testament history

old testament history

by

CHARLES F. PFEIFFER

BAKER BOOK HOUSE
Grand Rapids, Michigan

Contents

CONTENTS

CONTENTS

CONTENTS

List of Maps

Illustration Credits

Aleppo Museum, 43, 215
Alva Studios, 207
Ashmolean Museum, 40
Boston Museum of Fine Arts, 130, 140
The British Museum, 22, 23, 26, 27, 29, 42, 84, 118, 132, 147, 290,
    308 (top), 318, 333, 334, 338, 339, 341 (top & bottom), 346, 347, 348,
    353, 377, 419, 433, 435, 446, 505, 517, 519, **525**
The Brooklyn Museum, 293, 539
The Cairo Museum, 134, 157, 161, 193
Drew-McCormick Archaeological Expedition, 212, 559
Ecco Homo Orphanage, Jerusalem, 588
Jack Finegan, 200
Ewing Galloway, 79
Nelson Glueck, 323
H. Gokberg, 521
Israel Information Service, 68, 245
Israel Museum, Jerusalem, 71, 72, 313
Paul Lapp, 77
Gerald Larue, 590
Levant Photo Service, 56, 97, 126, 234, 246, 254, 269, 321, 347, 356,
    417, 561, 584, 587
The Louvre Museum, 41 (top & bottom), 65 (top), 70, 75, 87, 94, 112, 135,
    280, 287, 312, 327, 420, 494, 531 (bottom)
Matson Photo Service, 38, 54, 59 (bottom), 182, 202, 206, 209 (top), 216,
    249, 251 (top), 308 (bottom), 360, 367, 380, 405, 471, 547
H. H. McWilliams, 412
The Metropolitan Museum of Art, 127, 131, 136, 139, 153 (top), 159, 518,
    527 (top & bottom)
Oriental Institute of the University of Chicago, 31, 39, 44, 60, 82, 110, 113,
    142, 145, 218, 277 (top), 314, 335, 336, 345, 349, 354, 425, 428,
    459, 500, 522, 523, 528, 530, 531 (top), 535, 552, 558
Palestine Archaeological Museum, 598 (top & bottom), 599, 600
Palestine Institute, Pacific School of Religion, 243
Charles F. Pfeiffer, 170, 209 (bottom), 268, 311, 382, 430, 589 (bottom),
    591, 592

(Continued on next page)

Preface

The history of Israel, the major part of Old Testament history, touches every facet of human experience. The joys and sorrows and the victories and defeats of men and nations confront us on every page. We believe that the Bible has its origin in God, but we also insist that it is the most human of books. Its greatest heroes sinned against God, and suffered as a result. David's experience with Bathsheba left its mark on the remainder of his life. Love and lust — self-sacrificing devotion and selfish greed — stare at us from the Biblical portraits of both saints and sinners.

For many centuries, practically all that was known of history prior to the Greeks came from the pages of the Old Testament. A century and a half of archaeological discoveries have changed that to the point where learned volumes have been written about the Hittites, the Arameans, the Babylonians, the Assyrians, and just about every other people mentioned in the Old Testament. Biblical patriarchs can be understood against the background of their own age, and annals of later Assyrian and Babylonian kings can be read along with the Biblical passages that describe their deeds.

The purpose of this book is a very simple one. The author has tried to draw on the abundance of archaeological, historical, and linguistic studies now available to help in the understanding of the events described in the Old Testament. The Old Testament itself remains its principal source. We still must acknowledge that often it remains our only source. Especially in the period prior to 1000 B.C., we must usually be satisfied with light that archaeological and historical studies throw on the general history of the times. We meet Abraham, Moses, and the men of their generation only in the Bible, but we have considerable information about the times in which they lived from extra-Biblical sources. This in itself is an important asset to the serious student of Scripture. During the period of Israel's monarchy, the quantity of archaeological material becomes greater. Hebrew kings such as Jehu and Hezekiah and foreign rulers such as Pharaoh Shishak and Sennacherib of Assyria left records which bear their names.

It is now possible to take the Biblical records and read them with the assistance of those texts and artifacts from the Biblical world which provide the historical and cultural setting of the major events of Old Testament history.

The Bible as History

The faith of the ancient Israelites, to whom later Judaism and Christianity trace their roots, was based on historically verifiable fact. Israel's patriarchs and prophets, her kings and priests lived in time and performed deeds that might be praiseworthy or blameworthy. Israel as a nation lived in a historical setting and interacted with Egyptians, Assyrians, Babylonians, as well as closer Canaanites, Moabites, Ammonites, and many other peoples. This statement might seem unnecessary, but many have taken the historical elements of the Bible as of little import. A subjectivism affirms that God's presence in the hearts of his people now is important, but what God did through a Moses or an Isaiah can be dismissed as so much "ancient history."

Unlike her Canaanite neighbors, Israel's faith was built on the memory of historical events: "By strength of hand, the Lord brought us out of Egypt, from the house of bondage" (Exod. 13:14). Baal was a Canaanite fertility god who would disappear during times of drought and reappear with the coming of rain. Yahweh, Israel's God, brought the rains from heaven to parched lands, but he intervened in other ways on behalf of his people, and much of the Old Testament is a record of those interventions.

The Old Testament historical records are as important to the Christians as to the Jew. The opening verses of Matthew link Jesus Christ to David and Abraham (Matt. 1:1). Jesus refers to events described in the Old Testament as historical fact (cf. Matt. 19:8; Mark 2:25; John 3:14). He does not argue for the historicity of the Old Testament records; He takes that for granted. Similarly Paul, in looking back on the Christian affirmation of resurrection, asserts that the resurrection of Jesus is an all-important fact: "If Christ has not been raised, then our preaching is in vain, and your faith is in vain" (I Cor. 15:14). While in no sense minimizing the necessity of an inner work of the Holy Spirit within the individual, the Biblical faith affirms that there have been events of history which have proved decisive for man in his relationships to time and eternity.

These events are recorded in the Bible, which affirms that the God whose acts it records is "the Living God" (Josh. 3:10). While every age has found encouragement and correction in the study of God's dealings with Israel, no age has had better opportunities to read the sacred texts in the light of the history of the ancient world than our own.

Our study must begin, of course, with the Bible text itself. In as far as possible we should let the Bible speak for itself. As a rule figures of speech are clearly identifiable. When, speaking of deliverance from Egypt, God says to Israel, "I bore you on eagles' wings" (Exod. 19:4), we know that we have a poetic description, specifically a metaphor describing the power and the loving care of God for his people. Normally, however, Biblical history is described in terms of people living and acting at specific times and places. When we read that Joseph went down to Egypt (Gen. 39:1) we must take that as a fact. We may be concerned with the circumstances — the behavior of the jealous brothers, the providence of God in watching over Joseph during very trying times, and the ultimate happy outcome of the whole episode — but we do not honor the Biblical text by reading into it a typology in which Egypt has some mystic, hidden meaning. The Joseph story is so wonderful in its own right that it is a tragedy to spoil it by dragging in completely extraneous material.

On the other hand, historical study can do much to help us understand the story in its context. The tomb paintings from Beni Hasan in Egypt depict Semites coming to Egypt. They date from around 1900 B.C., so we have a pretty good idea of the way the patriarchs would have looked to the Egyptians. A comparison of Biblical with Egyptian chronology may help us to see Joseph in relation to the Egyptian rulers of his day. A knowledge of Egyptian schools, literature and customs will help us to understand Joseph's behavior in Egypt.

Beginning with the Bible, then, we supplement our study with other historical sources:

Hieroglyphic Egyptian texts: Since the discovery of the Rosetta Stone by scholars who accompanied Napoleon to Egypt, and its decipherment by Champollion in the 1820's, a science of Egyptology has developed into a major discipline. We know of Egyptian religion through reading the Pyramid Texts, the Coffin Texts, and the Book of the Dead. Stories such as the Sinuhe Tale help us to envision the relationship between Egypt and Palestine during the time of the Biblical patriarchs. The adventures of Wen-amun provide comparable material during the time of the judges, when Egyptian prestige had suffered. Wisdom literature, comparable to the Biblical Proverbs; hymns, including a hymn to the Sun god from the time of the rebel Pharaoh Akhenaton, and a great variety of other texts have enabled us to trace the history of Egypt from before 3000 B.C. to Roman times.

Cuneiform texts from Mesopotamia: Beginning with the Sumerians, before 3000 B.C., and continuing through the Semitic Akkadians, Babylonians, and Assyrians, a wealth of material in the cuneiform script challenges the historian. It was not until the middle of the nineteenth century that cuneiform could be read, but now we have numerous law codes (including early Sumerian codes, the Babylonian Hammurabi Code, and Assyrian codes) and historical annals of Assyrian and Babylonian kings. We can read, for example, Sennacherib's own account of his siege of Jerusalem.

The Gilgamesh Epic gives us the Babylonian account of the flood. Other texts provide legends of creation, hymns to the gods and goddesses, and the more prosaic letters and contracts which help us to visualize the daily life of the people of ancient Mesopotamia.

Hittite Literature: Excavations at the Hittite capital of Boghazkoi, in central Turkey, provide the texts which describe the once powerful Hittite empire which was defeated by the Peoples of the Sea (an Aegean people) around 1200 B.C. Hittite states continued in northern Syria for several centuries after the fall of the Empire, and we read of a Hittite in David's army (II Sam. 11:3). Hittite literature appears in a hieroglyphic form (but unlike Egyptian hieroglyphs) and a cuneiform type, similar to the cuneiform of Sumer and Babylon. Historical records, legends, historical texts, and a law code provide documentation for our study of the Hittites.

Canaanite Literature: Most of our knowledge of the Canaanites comes from Ras Shamra, ancient Ugarit, located on the coast of Syria, just opposite the point of the island of Cyprus. The literature, discovered in 1929, describes in considerable detail the religion of which Baal was the favorite god. Myths and legends illustrate the ideas of the Canaanites, rivals of Israel for possession of the Promised Land. Economic texts give us a means of understanding the daily life of the Canaanites.

Other ancient Semitic Texts: The Gezer Agricultural calendar, from the time of Solomon, and the Siloam Inscription, describing the completion of a tunnel for water in Hezekiah's day, are examples of isolated Hebrew inscriptions. The Mesha Inscription was written in a sister language, Moabite, to describe victories of the Moabites over the Israelites. Collections of ostraca (broken pieces of pottery used as writing material) from Samaria and Lachish provide useful pictures of life in the two cities in critical times.

Aramaic became the *lingua franca* during Persian times, and numerous letters and documents have been identified. The Jewish colony of mercenary soldiers at Elephantine, at the first cataract of the Nile in Egypt, has left correspondence which describes their problems. We even have a collection of Aramaic magical texts produced by a not so orthodox Jewish community.

Classical historians: By the end of Old Testament history we find classical sources which can be compared with the Biblical texts. Herodotus visited in Asia Minor, Babylon, and Egypt, and his observations are always interesting — even if the information he was given is not always accurate. Josephus, the Jewish historian who fought in the war between the Jews and the Romans, A.D. 66-70, wrote his *Antiquities of the Jews*, but that volume is not as valuable as his later *Jewish War* of which he was an eyewitness. Josephus provides a valuable description of the Judaism of his day.

In addition to written materials, the historian draws heavily on the discoveries of the archaeologist — the temples and palaces, the city walls and private houses, the pottery and coins, and other artifacts. It is only as a result of painstaking work by many dedicated individuals that we have an adequate picture of life as it was lived in Old Testament times. Every new year discoveries are made, providing fresh material to aid us in our efforts to understand the Bible in its Near Eastern setting.

When the Lord identified Himself to Moses from the burning bush, He said, "I am . . . the God of Abraham, the God of Isaac, and the God of Jacob" (Exod. 3:6). Although the experience of the Exodus and the precepts of the Mosaic Law were focal points of later prophetic thought, the earlier events in the lives of the patriarchs served as a continuing challenge throughout the history of Israel—as they continue to do today.

Genesis is the "Book of Beginnings," and it gives considerable attention to the beginnings of Israel. The tribal organization is traced to the twelve sons of Jacob-Israel. He, in turn, is described as the son of Isaac, and the grandson of Abraham. It was divine election which had called Abraham from Ur of the Chaldees, and which subsequently chose Isaac instead of Ishmael, and Jacob instead of Esau. The patriarchal records are interesting as literature, but the author clearly wanted us to be more than entertained. He saw in the history of the patriarchs the accomplishment of divine purposes. Man might lie and cheat—and suffer the consequences of sin—but God was ever in the shadows "keeping watch above His own."

In brief compass Part One seeks to examine the faith and institutions of the Patriarchal Age. Some attention has been given to the political and religious life of the world in which they moved. Although archaeological discoveries contain no explicit reference to the patriarchs, they yield much material on the life of the people who were contemporary with the patriarchs

No attempt has been made to work out an exact chronology for the period. For practical purposes Part One covers the period between 2000 and 1500 B.C., except that it discusses the history of Israel only as far as the settlement of Jacob and his sons in Egypt.

The essential historicity of the Biblical record and the essential reliability of the Biblical text are presuppositions in this book. This does not preclude the recognition of epic features in the narrative; but it does presume that the Biblical writers sought to communicate a body of factual material which, with due regard to form and style, can be objectively studied.

PART ONE

The Patriarchal Age

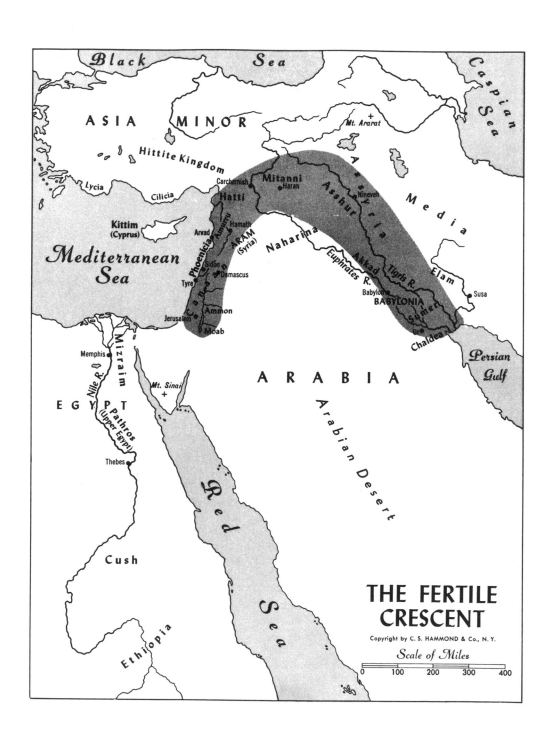

1

Before Abraham

Although the focus of Biblical history is on Abraham and his descendants, the people we call Israel, the earliest chapters of Scripture deal with mankind as a whole. The Bible begins with the simple, majestic statement, "In the beginning God created the heavens and the earth" (Gen. 1:1). All things come into being as a result of the creative Word of God. The Biblical historians were not concerned with chronology, and they give no hint as to the date of creation. Scholars of a later age would add together the figures given in the Biblical genealogies and come up with a variety of dates for creation, including Archbishop Ussher's date of 4000 B.C. and the Jewish reckoning which makes the year 1973 of our era begin in the year 5732 after creation. The Biblical writers were content to affirm that when the world as we know it began, it was God who brought it into being.

Man, the crown of creation, is related to the world of nature, of which he is a part, and to God, whose image he bears. The Lord God formed man "of dust from the ground" (Gen. 2:7), thus reminding him of his relationship to the material universe. God also "breathed into his nostrils the breath of life" (Gen. 2:7b), designating man as a creature uniquely related to God. Man, created in the likeness and image of God, was to rule the rest of God's creation (Gen. 1:26), multiplying and using (not abusing) all that God had made (Gen. 1:28-30).

Man's paradise was short-lived, however. Adam and his wife Eve yielded to the Tempter, disobeyed God, and brought sin, misery, and death upon the human race (Gen. 3). The Biblical record tells us that God's creation was good, but sin soon entered and spoiled the universe that God had made. With sin came a break in fellowship with God, and man's alienation from his fellow man. Cain, a son of Adam, murdered Abel his brother, and the long history of murder and bloodshed which was to mark the pages of history began. The Biblical record affirms that early in human history man rebelled against his Creator and became the rebel against God that only God's grace could overcome and save.

The development of human culture is given in outline form in the fourth chapter of Genesis. Man, in the days of Cain and Abel, lived the life of the farmer and the herdsman. Cain's son Enoch, however, built a city which bore his name (Gen. 4:17). Arts and crafts flourished. Bronze and iron were used for weapons and implements of various kinds (Gen. 4:22). Man devised musical instruments and experiments with various types of music (Gen. 4:21). Israel's neighbors thought of arts and crafts as direct gifts of the gods. The Greek Prometheus was friendly to man, showing mankind the way to use fire. The Egyptian Ptah was a god of the crafts, using a forge at Memphis for the manufacture of swords, shields, and other implements. In contrast, the Biblical record sees the arts and crafts as human developments among the descendants of Cain.

Man has a new beginning following a destructive flood which destroyed the earlier civilization. Sumerian and Babylonian versions of the flood story have survived, and in important details they are parallel to the Biblical account. They are polytheistic, however, and they lack the moral element in the Biblical records. The Bible depicts God as angered at man's incorrigible conduct. Every imagination of the thoughts of man's heart is evil continually (Gen. 6:5). Judgment must come upon a wicked race, but one family, that of Noah, is spared. Following the flood, Noah's sons provide the nucleous for subsequent history.

In the Table of Nations (Gen. 10) we trace the three branches of the family of Noah. Japheth (10:2) is the ancestor of peoples whom we usually designate as Indo-European. They include the Greeks, designated as Javan, or the Ionians.

The Hamites are largely found in northern Africa, including Ethiopia (Cush) and Egypt (Mizraim) (Gen. 10:6-8). Canaan, ruled by the Egyptians in this early period, is included, as is a Mesopotamian ruler named Nimrod, who ruled Babel, Erech, and Akkad (Gen. 10:10) and who moved northward to colonize Assyria, building Nineveh and other cities there. (Gen. 10:11).

While Nimrod has not been positively identified, the places associated with him are among the earliest mentioned in the records of ancient Mesopotamia. Babylon (Babel) had a long history, including the Old Babylonian Empire with the great

Tablet inscribed with a part of the Babyonian account of the Creation.

lawgiver Hammurabi, and the New Babylonian Empire of Nebuchadnezzar. Erech gives us our first written documents shortly before 3000 B.C. Akkad was the capital of a great ruler, Sargon of Akkad, who conquered the Sumerian city states, moved northward to the region later known as Assyria, and finally reached the Mediterranean Sea in his conquests. Some scholars actually identify Sargon, who ruled around 2400 B.C., with the Biblical Nimrod.

The descendants of Canaan in the Table of Nations include Heth, father of the Hittites whose empire in Asia Minor during the second millennium B.C. actually challenged the Egyptian empire. The Jebusites, a Canaanite people that occupied Jerusalem prior to the Israelite conquest of the city in David's time, Amorites, and others are also related to the line of Ham.

Part of a clay tablet inscribed in cuneiform with the Assyrian account of the Deluge.

The principal interest of the Table of Nations is the line of Shem, father of the Semites (Gen. 10:21-31). We find the Elamites and the Aramaeans here, and Eber, father of the Hebrews, is a Semite. Actually the term Eber is more inclusive than Israel, since Eber had descendants not of the line of Abraham. The family of Shem, however, has provided us with the genealogical background for Abraham, whose family produced the nation of Israel.

The Table of Nations is concerned with the relationships which existed between Israel and her neighbors. Modern historians make language the means of distinguishing Semites from those of other biological and cultural backgrounds. We call Sargon of Akkad a Semite because he spoke a language which is related to Hebrew, Arabic, and the other Semitic languages.

End view of a Sumerian carved limestone drinking trough, probably from the temple of the goddess Inanna at Uruk, southern Iraq.

We should remember that mankind had had a long history before Abraham appeared on the scene. Egypt had become unified under Pharaoh Nar-Mer (or Menes) and its great pyramids which tourists marvel at today were constructed at least five hundred years before the time of Abraham. In Mesopotamia, Sumerians had developed a system of writing over a millennium before Abraham. When Biblical history records the journeys of Abraham, it gives us a picture of folk migrations which had been going on for centuries. Abraham's journey from Ur to Haran, and then to Canaan and Egypt, follows the route of the Fertile Crescent, the route that traders and soldiers took from time immemorial.

The Biblical Patriarchs:

History or Fancy?

Biblical scholars have frequently been skeptical concerning the existence of the men who are presented in Scripture as the physical and spiritual progenitors of Israel and, in a wider sense, the spiritual fathers of all who trust the God of Israel, and his Son, Jesus Christ. It has become accepted procedure to begin the history of Israel with the Exodus from Egypt, and to make a few allusions to the patriarchs in an introduction or preface.[1]

William F. Albright, who has a high respect for the historicity of the patriarchs, has written, "Until recently it was the fashion among biblical historians to treat the patriarchal sagas of Genesis as though they were artificial creations of Israelite scribes of the Divided Monarchy or tales told by imaginative rhapsodists around Israelite campfires during the centuries following their occupation of the country."[2] It was thought that varying traditions, representing the different ethnic groups which formed the nation of Israel had been fused into one continuous narrative. It has been suggested, for example, that an "Abraham tradition" existed at the cult center of Hebron, and that an "Isaac tradition" had its center at Beer-sheba. A fusion of the two took place, and Isaac was regarded as the son of Abraham.

In the writings of G. A. Danell,[3] we are told that Abraham, the cult-hero of the Hebron region, was taken over by the nation of Israel at the time of the monarchy. The same ideas are propounded in the writings of J. Pedersen[4] of Copenhagen, who suggested that the stories of the patriarchs had a utilitarian pur-

---

1. e.g. Martin Noth, *The History of Israel* and Bernhard W. Anderson, *Understanding the Old Testament.*
2. W. F. Albright, "The Biblical Period," in *The Jews: Their History, Culture, and Religion,* edited by Louis Finkelstein.
3. G. A. Danell, *Studies in the Name Israel in the Old Testament,* pp. 34-35.
4. J. Pedersen, *Israel, III-IV,* pp. 666-669.

pose: "to prove the right of Israel to Canaan." Pedersen observes that "no one disputed this right in pre-exilic times," and therefore gives an intolerably late date to the patriarchal narratives. His conclusion was that "all the main features of the stories about Abraham are coloured by the time after the regal period."

This attitude is basically that of the nineteenth century Old Testament scholar whose famous *Prolegomena to the History of Israel* marked a landmark in Biblical scholarship. Living before the day of archaeological discovery, Wellhausen could write in all good conscience, "We attain to no historical knowledge of the patriarchs, but only of the time when the stories about them arose in the Israelite people; this latter age is here unconsciously projected, in its inner and its outward features, into hoary antiquity, and is reflected there like a glorified image."[5]

Although Wellhausen is still respected for his contribution to Biblical studies, his modern disciples have had to modify many of his conclusions. Archaeological discoveries during the past half century show us that the patriarchal narratives fit in the period in which the Bible places them, and in no other. The clay tablets from Nuzi and Mari have helped us to visualize the political and the social world in which the patriarchs moved. The conjectures of Wellhausen made sense in the years before the discovery of vast quantities of literature from a period contemporary with the patriarchs. We are less dependent on hypothetical reconstructions of history now that we have actual historical records.

It should not be assumed, however, that current Old Testament scholarship has reverted to a "pre-critical" attitude toward the patriarchal narratives (Gen. 12-50). Albright speaks of the "substantial historicity of patriarchal tradition," although he does not insist on accuracy in detail.

A contemporary writer in the field of Biblical Theology, Gerhard Von Rad, rejects the higher critical principles associated with Wellhausen. In their place he studies the "units" of narration, a procedure known as "Form Criticism" which is applied to both Old Testament and New Testament studies. Von Rad and the form critics consider that each story in the Biblical text forms a "unit" which had a separate history of its own.[6] In the process of time individual units were incorporated into great

The tablet above records measures of surface and length and weights. The bottom tablet shows measures of capacity. The measures are from one of the earliest centers of Mesopotamian culture, Nippur, Babylon, founded about 4000 B.C.

5. Julius Wellhausen, *Prolegomena to the History of Israel,* (English Translation) pp. 318-319.
6. Gerhard Von Rad, *Theologie des Alten Testaments,* Band I, p. 7 ff.

Game board from Ur.

blocks of traditional material. As the final stage of the process these "blocks" were incorporated into the books of our Bible.

The results of Form Criticism may become quite arbitrary, however. John Bright in his recent book, *A History of Israel*,[7] sounds a warning against the results which may be expected from Form Criticism: "To pick and choose from the traditions . . . according historicity to this, while denying it to that, is a most subjective procedure, reflecting no more than one's own predelections. Nor is there any objective method by which the history of the traditions may be traced, and historical worth assayed by examination of the traditions themselves. Form Criticism, indispensable as it is in understanding and interpreting the traditions cannot, in the nature of the case, pass judgment on historicity in the absence of external evidence."

Aside from the Scriptures themselves, the only objective way of testing the historicity of the patriarchal records is to examine them in the light of the facts which archaeology has made available to us. We will have to admit that the patriarchs themselves are not mentioned in any non-Biblical document, but we have no reason to believe they should be so mentioned. Abraham, Isaac, and Jacob, according to Scripture dwelt "in tents," having separated themselves from the centers of urban life. If we can find non-Biblical texts which describe the kind of life presented in the Biblical account of Genesis 12-50 (which varies in a marked degree from the situation after the tribes entered Canaan under Joshua), we have at least presumptive evidence that the Biblical text reflects genuine history.

The verdict of Albright, quoted above, is that archaeology has provided such materials. In the Introductory Volume to *The Interpreter's Bible,* James Muilenberg wrote, "Archaeology has revealed an extraordinary correspondence between the general social and cultural conditions portrayed in Genesis and those exposed by excavations. Discoveries from such sites as Nuzi, Mari, and elsewhere, provide the geographical, cultural, linguistic, and religious background against which the stories of the patriarchs are laid."[8]

Although the tendency of modern Biblical scholarship has been to have a higher regard for the historicity of the patriarchal records than that held by many writers a generation or two ago, the theological use of that fact varies considerably. The con-

---

7. John Bright, *A History of Israel,* p. 69.
8. James Muilenburg, "The History of the Religion of Israel," *Interpreter's Bible,* I, p. 296.

The standard of Ur above presents scenes of peace. In the one below, scenes of war are shown.

servative may feel that his doctrine of verbal inspiration has been made intellectually respectable because the views of the Wellhausen school have been so rudely upset. The liberal, however, will see the similarity between religious institutions of ancient Israel and her neighbors of the Fertile Crescent as a reason for denying any uniqueness to the faith of the Old Testament. The neo-orthodox will be content with the "essential" historicity of the Biblical records and stress the importance of a personal divine encounter as embodying the true "word of God." In a very real sense theologians interpret the facts of archaeology, as they do the facts of Scripture, in accord with their basic presuppositions. Aside, however, from the overtones which may be read into the facts, we can now assert without fear of contradiction that the Biblical patriarchs need not be regarded as demigods or characters from the realm of folk-lore. They appear as real men, living in a real world which is now well-known because of the work of modern archaeology.

3

Patriarchal Organization

The term "patriarch" is expressive of the social structure under which the earliest Israelites lived. The father was recognized as both legal and spiritual head of the family. Wives and children were dependent upon the father, or patriarch, of the family, who also served as its governor, priest, and magistrate. The family, including its slaves, was subject to the patriarch, who represented the sole authority, under God.

It was the absence of any constituted government that caused the patriarch to rule without external restraint. As the head of the family, the patriarch assumed responsibility for its welfare. When Joseph, in Egypt, sent word through Reuben that Benjamin should be sent to Egypt, aged Jacob was understandably concerned. In anguish he exclaimed, "You have bereaved me of my children: Joseph is no more and Simeon is no more, and now ye would take Benjamin . . . " (Gen. 42:36) . Thereupon Reuben, the eldest of the brothers and their spokesman, stated, "Slay my two sons if I do not bring him back to you" (Gen. 42:37) . This offer was in accord with principles which we meet in the Code of Hammurabi. There we read that a man who causes the death of another's daughter is made to suffer by having his own daughter slain. It was a matter of the rights of one father against the rights of another father.

The patriarchal records in the Bible presuppose the absolute power of a father over the very lives of his children. The record of Abraham's preparation to offer Isaac on Mount Moriah (Gen. 22) emphasizes the feelings of the father and his obedience to God. The thought that Isaac should have been consulted is foreign to the spirit of the record. Abraham, as the patriarch, had full control over the life of his son. When Jacob, under pressure of famine, decided to send Benjamin to Egypt, the patriarch alone made the decision: "Take also your brother," he said to his older sons with the observation, "If I am bereaved of my children, I am bereaved" (Gen. 43:13-14). Both Abraham and Jacob dearly loved their children. Their welfare was a major concern, but the concern was in terms of a patriarchal type of society.

Similar control was exercised by the patriarchs over their daughters. Lot was embarrassed when the men of Sodom wanted to have homosexual relations with two "men" to whom he had accorded the hospitality of his home. Rather than breach the laws of hospitality, which guaranteed protection to the visitor while under one's roof, Lot said to the men of Sodom, "Behold, I have two daughters who have not known man; let me bring them out to you and do to them as you please, only do nothing to these men, for they have come under the shelter of my roof" (Gen. 19-8). Lot's sense of the demands of hospitality caused him to offer to sacrifice his daughters to mob violence. As patriarch of his family, Lot considered that he had the right to dispose of the girls as he wished.

Emphasis on patriarchal authority might produce situations which would seem to us inhuman. The Biblical records make it clear, however, that true love existed among the members of patriarchal family groups. Abraham's love for Ishmael (Gen. 17:18), and subsequently for Isaac (Gen. 22:2), form an important factor in the life of the patriarch. The love, however, was always expressed within the framework of patriarchal life.

The patriarch of the family, or tribe, had not only the right of absolute control, but also the duty to punish those guilty of crime. When Laban pursued Jacob, complaining because of the theft of the *teraphim,* or household gods, Jacob protested innocence, and added: "Any one with whom you find your gods shall not live" (Gen. 31:32). It was Jacob's duty, as head of the household, to enforce principles of right-doing.

The family unit included not only the father, his wives and their children, but also the sons and their wives. Levirate marriage customs brought the wives into a permanent relationship with the family of their husbands. When Judah learned that Tamar, his widowed daughter-in-law, was pregnant, he demanded, "Bring her out and let her be burned" (Gen. 38:24). Tamar had been married, successively, to two sons of Judah, and she was expected to await the third. When Judah withheld his third son, Tamar disguised herself as a prostitute in order to entice Judah, himself, to father a child. In demanding the death of a daughter-in-law who had violated the laws of chastity, Judah was within his rights. In this instance, however, Tamar

A bronze foundation figurine with an inscription of Warad-Sin, king of Larsa.

was spared in view of the fact that the patriarch himself was equally guilty.

Concepts of patriarchal authority are reflected in the Mosaic Law. Not only do we read, "Honor your father and your mother that your days may be long in the land which the Lord your God gives you" (Exod. 20:12) but we also read of the punishment meted out to the one who shows contempt for his parents: "Whoever strikes his father or his mother shall be put to death" (Exod. 21:15); "Whoever curses his father or his mother shall be put to death" (Exod. 21:17).

A procedure is outlined for the treatment of a rebellious son: "If a man has a stubborn and rebellious son, who will not obey the voice of his father or the voice of his mother, and, though they chastise him, will not give heed to them, then his father and his mother shall take hold of him, and bring him out to the elders of his city at the gate of the place where he lives, and they shall say to the elders of his city, 'This our son is stubborn and rebellious, he will not obey our voice; he is a glutton and a drunkard.' Then all the men of the city shall stone him to death with stones; so they shall purge the evil from your midst; and all Israel shall hear, and fear" (Deut. 21:18-21).

The patriarch maintained his position throughout life, being succeeded, normally, by his eldest son. Another successor might be chosen, however. Jacob set aside the principle of primogeniture when he called Reuben "unstable as water," and said to him, "You shall not have the pre-eminence" (Gen. 49:4). Judah was designated as the one who would bear the scepter over the sons of Jacob (Israel) (Gen. 49:8-12).

In the course of a few generations, the patriarchal family would grow unwieldy. Instead of a family, it should then be called a clan, and it would often be wise for it to break up into smaller units. We read that Esau "went into a land away from his brother Jacob, for their possessions were too great for them to dwell together" (Gen. 35:6-7). Judah appears to have started a separate family when he "went down from his brothers" (Gen. 38:1) and married a Canaanite girl. A number of clans with common ties of family and tradition might function together as a tribe.

The social structure of family (sometimes called "father's house"), clan, and tribe finds its fullest expression in Scripture during the period following the Exodus. Gideon, we are told, was a member of a family in the clan of Abiezer (Judg. 6:11) of the tribe of Manasseh. When called to lead Israel against the Midianite oppressors, he objected: "Behold, my clan is the

Bronze figure of a four-faced god, from the Old Babylonian period (ca. 1800 B.C.).

weakest in Manasseh, and I am the least in my family" (Judg. 6:15).

In a patriarchal society with no external authority, some means must be found to insure law and order among various tribal groups. The most basic of these among the ancient Semitic peoples was the concept of blood revenge. Murder was regarded as a tribal matter, and the family of a slain man sought vengeance on the murderer or his tribe. It was considered a tribal obligation for members of a tribe to avenge the wrong done to one of their fellows.

4

Men and Tribes

It has often been suggested that the descriptions of the Biblical patriarchs are actually records of the movements and activities of whole tribes. Terms such as "son" and "beget" may be used metaphorically, and in some instances the Biblical writers use them to show the relationships of ethnic groups. When, for instance, we read that Canaan became the father of Sidon, his firstborn (Gen. 10:15) we understand that the city of Sidon was the first of the great Canaanite cities, although later surpassed by Tyre. That the author of Genesis was thinking of Sidon as a city is clear, for he continues, "and the territory of the Canaanites extended from Sidon, in the direction of Gerar, as far as Gaza" (10:19). We also read in Genesis 10 that Canaan was the father of "the Jebusites, the Amorites, the Girgashites, the Hivites, the Arkites, the Sinites, the Arvadites, the Zemarites, and the Hamathites" (Gen. 10:16-18) — all ethnic groups or city-states of Canaan. Among the descendants of Keturah, Abraham's second wife, we find Midian and Shuah (Gen. 25:1), both of whom appear later as tribes (cf. Exod.2:15; Job 2:11). Genealogical tables often are used to show relationships among peoples. Those who compiled them did not hesitate to omit generations when it suited their purpose to do so and, on occasion, to use tribal designations.

In the records of the patriarchs themselves, however, there is no hint that we are dealing with large tribal groups. We may explain the mobility of Abraham in terms of ethnic movements during the early second millennium B.C., but the Scripture makes it clear that the particular movement of which we are reading is that of the man Abraham. This is evident in the care that is taken to insure that the sons of the patriarchs will marry the right type of girls. Great effort was expended to send back to Paddan-aram in order to secure a bride for

Isaac. Abraham received specific promises which were to be fulfilled in his son.

We must recognize, however, that the movements of Abraham and his household do involve more than a few people. The covenant promise was limited to a blood relationship, but the larger "household" of the patriarch was such that he could muster three hundred and eighteen trained men to rescue his nephew Lot (Gen. 14:14). The rite of circumcision was performed on the entire household: "he that is born in your house and he that is bought with your money" (Gen. 17:13).

In spite of the efforts of the patriarchs to keep their line free from the corrupting influences of paganism, an early breakdown in family distinctiveness is carefully recorded in Scripture. Isaac and Rebekah were grieved because Esau married Hittite girls (Gen. 26:34-35). Although Jacob married wives from Paddan-aram, his son Judah married a Canaanite (Gen. 38:2). Joseph, in Egypt, was married to the daughter of Potiphera, the priest of On (Gen. 41:45), and Moses, while in the wilderness, married the daughter of a Midianite priest (Exod. 2:15-22).

The Israelites, like other peoples of both ancient and modern times, developed a heterogeneous society and culture. We read of Hobab in the wilderness (Num. 10:29-32): Rahab at Jericho (Judg. 6:25), the Gibeonites (Josh. 9); and Ruth the Moabitess being incorporated into the people of Israel. Many of these people could claim no blood relationship with Abraham, but they shared his faith and entered into the promises which God had given him. The patriarchs were men. They gave birth to tribes which soon incorporated varying ethnic elements

The name Israel, rather than Abraham, is the term used to describe those who trace their history back to the patriarch who first entered Canaan. Israel is presented to us in Scripture as an alternate name for Jacob. The concept of Israel the man is merged into that of Israel the nation in Genesis 46:3-4. Jacob had learned that his son Joseph was alive and prospering in Egypt. The aged father had reached Beer-sheba, but he was still hesitant about moving farther. God spoke to him, however, in a theophany, saying, "I am God, the God of your father; do not be afraid to go down to Egypt; for I will there make of you a great nation. I will go down with you to Egypt, and I will also bring you up again; and Joseph's hand shall close your eyes." Here the man Jacob was told that he would die in Egypt — his son Joseph would close his eyes in death. The nation Jacob-Israel, would become great in Egypt, and God would bring them back into Canaan. This fact is given to Jacob as a means of assurance. His concern would not be with his own future life. As a mortal he would go "the way of all the earth" (cf. I Kings 2:2), but he could feel that his life had not been wasted, his posterity would be multiplied and brought back to the land which God had promised to Abraham.

Near Beersheba, a truck transports a section of the conduit that will carry water from Galilee to the Negeb.

5

The Patriarchs:

Abraham, Isaac, Jacob

The lives of the patriarchs are depicted in realistic terms. They were men of faith, but not always faithful men. Yet Scripture does emphasize the sovereignty of God in their lives. Abraham lied concerning the identity of Sarah, and Jacob cheated his brother and deceived his father. In each instance, however, God used the hour of spiritual defeat to impart lessons which would result in growth in grace.

It is with good reason that Abraham is esteemed the father of the faithful of all ages (Gal. 3:7). In the great "faith chapter" we read, "By faith Abraham obeyed when he was called to go out to a place which he was to receive as an inheritance; and he went out, not knowing where he was to go" (Heb. 11:8). Believing God, Abraham left Ur together with his father (Gen. 11:31; Acts 7:1-4); then left Haran and went toward Canaan, a land both unknown to him and lacking in the high civilization of the Mesopotamian cities which were left behind.

Abraham was a man of "like passions" with ourselves, however. He seems to have delayed in Haran when he should have moved on into Canaan (Gen. 11:31 — 12:5). His decision to go to Egypt for food in a time of famine need not be interpreted as a lack of faith (Gen. 12:10), but his conduct there certainly was unbecoming a child of God (Gen. 12:11-16). Abraham decided to lie, or tell a half truth (which is just as bad), in order to protect himself from Pharaoh. By stating that Sarah was his sister, Abraham placed her in a compromising position, and Pharaoh had no hesitancy in taking her for his harem (Gen. 12:15). It is true that Abraham expected to be honored as Sarah's brother, whereas he might have been killed as her husband (Gen. 12:12, 16). Nevertheless the action was contrary to human decency as well as the demand for truthfulness on the part of those who bear the name of God. Pharaoh learned the

*Ruins of the ziggurat at Ur,
which towered eighty feet above
the Sumerian plain.*

truth, and Abraham was ushered out of Egypt in disgrace (cf. Gen. 12:17-20).

Abraham's impatience in awaiting an heir is understandable, but it also indicated a lack of faith. The expedience of having a child by Hagar, Sarah's maid, was in accord with the customs of the day, but it was contrary to the purpose of God (Gen. 16:2; 17:19). In due time a son was born to Sarah, and Abraham's plans for Ishmael had to be seriously altered.

The lapses of Abraham, however, do not eclipse his greatness. It took both courage and faith to leave the comforts of Ur and embark on a spiritual pilgrimage. Suffering through a famine in a strange land was, itself, a sore trial. The greateartedness of Abraham was never more manifest than in his dealings with Lot. The very fact that differences should arise between the herdsmen of the two men reminds us of the conflict of interests inherent in all human relationships. Age and position would have justified Abraham in deciding matters unilaterally. Instead, however, he gave Lot his choice of the land (Gen. 13:8-13), whereupon the Lord renewed the promise that Canaan would one day be the inheritance of Abraham's descendants (Gen. 13:14-17).

The supreme test of Abraham came, however, after his son Isaac had reached maturity. God had said that Isaac would be the heir to the promises given to Abraham. Now all this appeared to be canceled. God gave the strange command to take the lad to the mountains of Moriah and there offer him as a sacrifice (Gen. 22:1-2). There is no hint of hesitancy in the actions of the patriarch. He went, with the full assurance of faith that "God was able to raise men even from the dead" (Heb. 11:19). And God did intervene. A ram was offered instead of Isaac, for Abraham had proved himself worthy of the title, Father of the Faithful.

The apostle Paul consistently regarded Abraham as the supreme example of faith: "He staggered not at the promise of God through unbelief; but was strong in faith, giving glory to God; and being fully persuaded that, what he had promised, he was able also to perform. And therefore, it was imputed to him for righteousness" (Rom. 4:20-22). James showed that the faith of Abraham was manifest in his works: "You see that faith was active along with his works, and faith was completed by works" (James 2:22).

Isaac's life is largely associated with that of his father, Abraham, and his son, Jacob. The twin sons of Isaac and Rebekah differed in temperament. Esau was an outdoor man who par-

*A restoration of the ziggurat of
Ur-nammu at Ur.*

ticularly pleased Isaac, but Jacob stayed closer to home and became the darling of Rebekah.

Obedient in not going down to Egypt (Gen. 26:2), Isaac nevertheless followed the pattern of Abraham in lying about his wife to Abimelech, king of the Philistine state of Gerar. Much of Isaac's life was spent in southern Canaan in the vicinity of Gerar, Rehoboth, and Beer-sheba.

The rivalry between Jacob and Esau, abetted by the attitude of their parents, forms a regrettable chapter in the patriarchal history. Neither brother, and neither parent, was blameless. Jacob took unfair advantage of Esau in demanding the birthright — the right of the firstborn to pre-eminence in the tribe — but Esau also showed lack of faith in God by accepting the bargain (Gen. 25:29-34). Like many another, he was willing to sacrifice the future on the altar of the present. He argued with himself that the birthright would be meaningless if he were to die of starvation and thus, in the words of Scripture, he "despised his birthright" (Gen. 25:34). Esau's marriage to Hittite girls (Gen. 26:34) was further proof that the wishes and ideals of his parents were remote from his thoughts. The verdict of history is that Esau was a "profane person" (Heb. 12:16 A.V., R.S.V. renders "irreligious"), a man given wholly to the things of time and sense.

Rebekah and Jacob connived to deceive Isaac. The act cannot be justified morally or ethically, even though Rebekah may have sensed spiritual qualities in Jacob which were missing in Esau. The father had determined to bestow the birthright on Esau, his favored son, but Rebekah was equally determined that it should fall on Jacob. The boys were twins, but Esau had been born first and the law of primogeniture was observed in Israel under normal circumstances. When, as in the case of Jacob and, subsequently, Reuben (Gen. 49:3-4), primogeniture is not observed, the reason is given. It is clear that these are exceptional cases, and as such they demand explanation.

Isaac is presented in Hebrews 11 as a man of faith because of his confidence that God would work in the lives of his sons (and their descendants). "By faith," we read, "Isaac invoked future blessings on Jacob and Esau" (Heb. 11:20). The blessing of Esau did not compare with that of Jacob (Gen. 27:27-40), nevertheless it was prophesied that Esau-Edom would become a great people and would one day break the yoke of Jacob and lead an independent existence (Gen. 27:40).

Jacob, the deceiver, had a long, tortuous road before he became a respected patriarch and tribal father. With the two-fold purpose of escaping the wrath of Esau and finding a wife for himself, he went northward to Haran where he remained for twenty years (Gen. 27:41-44; 31:38). During his flight he dreamed of a ladder reaching to heaven, and heard the voice of God renewing the covenant earlier made with Abraham and Isaac to the effect that his descendants would one day inherit all of Canaan (Gen. 28:12-14). Jacob made a vow there, at Bethel, promising to serve the Lord if He should bring him back in peace (Gen. 28:20).

The years at Haran were not marked by spiritual progress, although the blessing of God was evident in material things. Laban had outwitted Jacob by making him serve seven years for Leah, when actually Rachel was the desired wife. An additional seven years of labor were required for Rachel, but Jacob did not hesitate to spend that time in the service of her father (Gen. 29:9-30). In due time, Jacob was blessed with a large family and, in spite of Laban's craftiness, his flocks and his herds also prospered.

It was only when difficulties arose with the sons of Laban (Gen. 31:1), that Jacob determined to migrate back to Canaan with his wives, children, and possessions. Fearful of an encounter with Esau, Jacob sent his retinue across the Jabbok while he remained alone on the northern shore. There he had an experience with a nameless assailant which was to have important spiritual results. Jacob and "a man" wrestled throughout the night, but neither could down the other. The man then touched the joint of Jacob's thigh, causing him to go limp, but Jacob fought on. In some way the patriarch sensed that his mysterious assailant was God Himself, and Jacob insisted, "I will not let you go unless you bless me" (Gen. 32:26). The blessing came in the form of a new name — expressive of a new relationship — "Israel," meaning "He who strives with God," or "God strives." Jacob called the place of this encounter, "Peniel," for, he observed, "I have seen God face to face, and yet my life is preserved" (Gen. 32:24-30).

Jacob and Esau were amicably reunited, although they soon went their several ways, Esau to the region of Mount Seir, and Edom (Gen. 33:16), but Jacob to Shechem in Canaan (Gen. 33:18). After a sad experience at Shechem where Dinah, a daughter of Jacob, was defiled by one of the youths of the city and her brothers retaliated by killing its inhabitants and

The Jabbok River (Wadi Zerka).

Cult statutes of a god and goddess, from the square temple of Abu, Tell Asmar, Iraq.

plundering their property, Jacob and his family moved on to Bethel. Jacob insisted that the idols which his household had accumulated be put away (Gen. 35:1-4), as they turned toward the city where God had first appeared to him twenty years before. Here, again, God confirmed the covenant (Gen. 35:9-15).

The latter years of Jacob were beset with much grief. Rivalries among his sons caused them to sell Joseph, the eldest son of his favorite wife Rachel, into slavery. Rachel herself had died in giving birth to a second son, Benjamin, and Jacob's love for Rachel was now showered on her two sons (Gen. 35:16-19; 37:3). Years later, during a time of famine, Jacob learned that Joseph was alive, and the family group was reunited. Before that, however, there were years of bitter grief.

The faith of Jacob, like that of his father, is associated, in Hebrews, with his blessing: "By faith Jacob, when dying, blessed each of the sons of Joseph, bowing in worship over the head of his staff" (Heb. 11:21). Jacob had not only uttered patriarchal blessings on his own sons (Gen. 49:1-28), but he adopted the sons of Joseph, giving Ephraim and Manasseh, each, a tribal portion (Gen. 48:17-20).

6

The Peoples Among
Whom the Patriarchs Lived

Although we cannot assign positive dates to the Biblical patriarchs, their lives appear to span the opening half of the second millennium before Christ — roughly 2000 to 1500 B.C. Before the rise of modern archaeological studies, these years were a complete blank except for the events described in Scripture. Now, however, we are able to trace the movements of peoples in the ancient world as far back as 3000 B.C. with an amazing degree of accuracy. Abraham, instead of being at the beginning of history, now appears rather late in the history of the lands of the Fertile Crescent — the name assigned by the Egyptologist James H. Breasted to the fertile valley of the Tigris and Euphrates rivers and the coastlands of Syria and Palestine. Abraham journeyed through the Fertile Crescent and had contacts with its peoples. His descendants Isaac, Jacob, and Joseph likewise moved from Canaan northward to Paddan-aram and southward to Egypt. The culture of the patriarchs is described as seminomadic, but it was touched by some of the most advanced civilizations the world has ever seen.

1. Sumerians

By the time of the Biblical patriarchs, Sumerians had lived for more than a millennium in southern Mesopotamia in the land known to Bible students as Shinar. The Sumerians built a number of city-states including Ur, the birthplace of Abraham, Erech (Uruk) fifty miles northwest of Ur, and Lagash, fifty miles due north of Ur. The cities were ruled by men who bore the title *ensi* and served as viceroys for the gods of Sumer. The *ensi* was expected to act as "shepherd" over the flock of the patron deity of the city which he ruled. The god himself was regarded as the real king. The *ensi* had charge of practical

The Sumerian king list gives the earliest tradition of rulers who reigned before the flood, and of later rulers whose reigns reached to historical times.

matters such as the maintenance of the canals which made irrigation possible and the defense of the city on the field of battle.

Gudea of Lagash in sitting position.

Occasionally an *ensi* sought power beyond that of his own state and dreamed of empire. Such a ruler was Urukagina of Lagash (*ca.* twenty-fourth century B.C.) who, through conquest, became king, or *lugal* "of Lagash and Sumer." Although we do not have a law code from Urukagina, he is known as the first reformer in history. He relieved the people by reducing the fees which were charged by greedy priests and lowered prices in general throughout his realm.

The system of city-states in use by the Sumerian *ensis* was not able to meet the challenge of a dedicated empire-builder such as Sargon of Akkad. Sargon's origins are obscure. He was a Semite who rose to power in Kish, conquered all of Sumer, and then embarked on a series of conquests which took him westward to Syria. The dynasty of Sargon (*ca.* 2360-2180 B.C.) introduced the Semitic Akkadian language in place of the Sumerian tongue which had been spoken in southern Mesopotamia from the dawn of history. The tents in which the earlier Sumerians lived were replaced by huts of sun-dried brick.

Sargon's greatest successor was Naram-sin whose Victory Stele is one of the great monuments of antiquity. It commemorates a victorious campaign against a mountain people known as the Lullubi. The king's light-armed soldiers are seen advancing up the slope of a mountain with lances and standards. High in the hills, towering above them, is the king himself, wearing the horned helmet of a god and carrying a war axe and bow and arrow. His enemies are seen beneath his feet, one with an arrow piercing his throat, and another with raised hands begging for life.

Shortly after the conquests of Naram-sin, however, Akkadian power collapsed (*ca.* 2200 B.C.) under the impact of invaders from the mountain country to the northeast known as Gutium. The century of Gutian rule was one of cultural sterility, and few records of the period have survived. The defeat of the Akkadian dynasty did, however, make possible the emergence of a Sumerian renaissance which took place under the Third Dynasty of Ur.

The first king of the Third Dynasty of Ur was Ur-nammu, whose law code is the oldest currently known. Another important ruler of the period was Gudea, viceroy under one of the Ur III kings in the city of Lagash. Statuary and objects of art from the

The victory stele of Naram-sin, grandson of Sargon of Akkad.

A Sumerian steatite bowl carved with human figures and animals, from central Iraq.

period of Gudea's rule are considered among the finest examples of Sumerian craftsmanship.

The distinction between Sumerian and Akkadian (Semite) tended to break down during the Third Dynasty of Ur (*ca.* 2060-1950 B.C.). Akkadian became the spoken language of southern Mesopotamia, with Sumerian surviving as the language of the learned, particularly in the temple. Semites became the predominant element in the population and many of the Sumerian kings of Ur actually had Semitic names and, doubtless, Semitic blood.

Abraham left Ur during the period when Sumerian culture was in the decline. Its golden period was long in the past. The people of southern Mesopotamia had known the art of writing for over a millennium and had developed social and political institutions of a high order.

2. Amorites

We read of invasions of "barbarians" into the lands of the Fertile Crescent about 2000 B.C., particularly into northern Syria and Mesopotamia. The Babylonians called these people "Amorites," a name meaning "westerners." Palestine and Syria were known as the land of the Amorites, and the Scriptures indicate that they occupied large portions of Canaan. On occasion the terms Canaanite and Amorite appear to be interchangeable.

Before entering the fertile lands of the Tigris-Euphrates valley and Palestine, Amorites lived as Bedouins in the Arabian desert. In times of weakness among the lands of the Fertile Crescent, or during periods of famine resulting from a greater scarcity of food than usual in the desert areas, nomads have emerged from the desert and conquered the more civilized peoples. Not only the Amorites, but also the Aramaeans and, in the seventh century A.D., the Islamic Arabs emerged from the desert to challenge the settled peoples in neighboring lands.

Many of the Amorite names are strikingly similar to those we meet among the Biblical Hebrews. Documents from the Amorite city of Mari, on the middle Euphrates, mention an Abam-ram (Abraham), and a Jacob-el (Jacob) as well as people known as Benjaminites. Cities include Til-Turakhi (Terah), Sarugi (Serug) and Phaliga (Peleg). They are all located in the neighborhood of Haran, the district known in the Bible as Paddan-aram ("the fields of Aram").

During the period of disorder following the end of the Third Dynasty of Ur, the Sumerian city-states were replaced by Amorite kingdoms. One of our early law codes was produced by an Amorite king of Isin named Lipit-Ishtar. He used the classical Sumerian language rather than his Amorite tongue, however.

Assyria was also ruled by an Amorite, Shamshi-adad I (*ca.* 1748-1717 B.C.), who pursued a policy of conquest, occupying the territory from the Zagros mountains to northern Syria. Shamshi-adad set up a stele to commemorate his conquest and took upon himself the grandiose title "King of the World."

Although Shamshi-adad was able to conquer the state of Mari, on the middle Euphrates, Assyrian power was ephemeral. Yasmah-adad, the son of Shamshi-adad, ruled Mari for sixteen years, but his dynasty was ousted by a native of Mari named Zimri-lim (1730-1700 B.C.) under whose leadership Mari became a major power. The borders of Mari reached from the frontiers of Babylon to the neighborhood of Carchemish. A defensive alliance was made with Babylon, and diplomatic correspondence was carried on with numerous states in Syria. The kings of the leading powers of the Mari age — Babylon, Larsa, Eshnunna, Qatna, and Aleppo — all had Amorite names with the exception of Rim-sin of Larsa.

A French expedition under André Parrot excavated the mound known as Tell el-Hariri which marks the spot of ancient Mari, on the middle Euphrates. The 20,000 clay tablets found there deal with military, diplomatic, and administrative matters, and provide primary source material for the study of life during the Patriarchal Age.

Mari boasted a magnificent temple to Ishtar which has been studied by the archaeologists. Ishtar was believed to have given a staff and ring, emblems of authority, to the king of Mari. The palace of Zimri-Lim is one of the best preserved structures in the Near East. It covered more than fifteen acres and was equipped with vast courts, suites of rooms, a bathroom, kitchen, and chapel. The throne room was adorned with frescoes such as appear in the great palaces of the later Assyrian rulers. The Mari palace not only made provision for the royal family and the state officials, but it also contained a school for the scribes who served as royal secretaries.

The Mari age was one of great mobility. Traders journeyed to Anatolia in Asia Minor, to Byblos and Ugarit on the Mediterranean coast, and overseas to Cyprus and Crete.

A fertility goddess, which was excavated at Mari.

The power of Mari waned, however, before another Amorite ruler, Hammurabi of Babylon (1728-1686 B.C.). Hammurabi was forceful on the field of battle as well as efficient in affairs of government. He annexed the states of Isin and Larsa, brought Assyria into subjection, and then turned his attention to Mari. Zimri-lim, the last king of Mari, was defeated by Hammurabi (1697 B.C.) and a few years later his capital was completely destroyed. Mari never arose from the ashes.

Many empires of antiquity covered more territory than that of Hammurabi, but few have been culturally more significant. Hammurabi's Babylon has left us a legacy of literature in a variety of areas: common letters and contracts, major epics dealing with the creation of the world and the flood, mathematical treatises, astronomical texts, grammars, dictionaries, and — most famous of all — the law code of the king, himself.

Although the dynasty of Hammurabi persisted for a century and a half after the death of the great lawgiver, its day of real power was short lived. Conquered states began to assert their independence during the reign of Hammurabi's successor, Samsu-iluna (1685-1648 B.C.) Trouble also came from without when a little-known people who are termed Kassites (or Cossaeans) appeared in southern Mesopotamia and challenged the power of Babylon.

A bronze statuette of King Ur-nammu, depicting the king as a humble basket carrier during the building of a temple.

3. Hurrians

During the Patriarchal Age large numbers of people known as Hurrians (Biblical Horites) entered the Fertile Crescent, presumably from the mountains of Armenia. By the sixteenth century B.C., Hurrians had large settlements in Upper Mesopotamia, Syria, and Palestine. The town of Nuzi, southeast of Nineveh, was almost solidly Hurrian. From the cuneiform tablets discovered at Nuzi we learn something of the language and customs of the Hurrians, although they seem to have adopted much of the older Amorite culture of the area. These tablets, written in the Semitic Akkadian language, illustrate many of the social customs and attitudes which find expression in Hammurabi's law code and in the daily life of the Biblical patriarchs.

Late in the sixteenth century a kingdom known as Mitanni dominated northern Mesopotamia between the Mediterranean and Media. The state had a predominantly Hurrian population, although its rulers bore Indo-Aryan names. The Indo-Aryans, who appear to have been associated with the Hurrians in their tribal movements, introduced the chariot into the techniques of warfare. A class of chariot-warriors known as *maryannu* occupied the upper strata of society.

The Hurrians and the Indo-Aryans appear to have intermarried with the result that the two peoples became, for all practical purposes, one. About 1500 B.C. their state of Mitanni held the balance of power between the Hittite Empire and Egypt.

4. Hapiru

A people known as Hapiru (sometimes written ʿApiru or Habiru) appear in many parts of the Near East during patriarchal times. They are mentioned in tablets from the Third Dynasty of Ur, from Babylon, and from the Hittite territory of Asia Minor. We read of them in nineteenth century Anatolia, eighteenth century Mari, fifteenth century Nuzi, and fourteenth century Ras Shamra (Ugarit). They are frequently mentioned in the Tell el-Amarna tablets from fourteenth century Egypt and in numerous other Egyptian writings of the Empire Period — the fifteenth to the twelfth centuries B.C.

The Hapiru not only turn up in a variety of places; they serve in many different capacities. In times of peace they are found working in the widely scattered communities of the Near East. Sometimes they appear as clients to men of the upper classes and, in times of adversity we read of Hapiru selling themselves into slavery. The Nuzi tablets show that the status of slave might be preferred to that of a free man because of the economic security it brought. Hapiru in Egypt served as slaves on the royal building projects, as did the Biblical Hebrews (cf. Exod. 1:11).

In unsettled periods the Hapiru usually appear as a semi-nomadic people who stage periodic raids on the settled communities. The Amarna Letters contain appeals from kings of Canaanite city states (including Jerusalem) for help from Egypt to repel the invading Hapiru. Sometimes the Hapiru served as mercenary soldiers, hiring themselves out to the highest bidder.

Who were these Hapiru? Most of their names are Semitic, but there are numerous exceptions. They do not conform to the pattern of an ethnic group. George Mendenhall, of the University of Michigan, suggests that the term Hapiru designates a people living beyond the bounds of a given community (i.e. a people without citizenship). They were not subject to the laws and mores of the settled peoples, hence were regarded as outsiders. The Near East had developed a highly organized social structure, but the Hapiru were not a part of it. Sometimes they made their peace with the ruling society, and sometimes they were outlaws.

The similarity of the name Hebrew to Hapiru may not be accidental. Although in modern usage the words Hebrew and Israelite are synonymous, this is not uniformly true in Scripture. The term Hebrew is rarely used, and then usually in contexts in which Israelites identify themselves to foreigners, or by foreigners in referring to Israelites. In the book of Genesis the term is used once of Abraham and several times in the account of Joseph in Egypt. When a confederacy of kings from the East defeated the king of Sodom and his allies, one of those who had escaped brought word of the capture of Lot to "Abram the Hebrew" (Gen. 14:13). Potiphar's wife, in falsely accusing Joseph, exclaimed, "See, he has brought among us a Hebrew to insult us" (Gen. 39:14, 17). In stating his case before Pharaoh, Joseph identified himself with the statement, "For I was indeed stolen out of the land of the Hebrews . . ." (Gen. 40:15). When Pharaoh's daughter looked upon the infant Moses, she exclaimed, "This is one of the Hebrews' children" (Exod. 2:6).

The word Hebrew continued in use down to the time of the wars with the Philistines. When the Israelites brought the sacred ark to the battlefield at Aphek, the Philistines heard the shout of the warriors and asked, "What does this great shouting in the camp of the Hebrews mean?" (I Sam. 4:6). Encouraging their own forces to renewed efforts to resist the Israelites, the Philistine leaders exclaimed, "Take courage and acquit yourselves like men, O Philistines, lest you become slaves to the Hebrews, as they have been to you" (I Sam. 4:9).

When the prophet Jonah was confronted by his angry shipmates with the demand that he identify himself, he replied, "I am a Hebrew, and I fear the Lord of heaven, who made the sea and the dry land" (Jonah 1:9). Such usage becomes rare, however, in the latter part of the Old Testament.

We cannot identify the Biblical Hebrews with the Hapiru of the ancient cuneiform literature but there are evident relationships between the two peoples. The Israelites in their early history were looked upon as an alien people, and from the standpoint of Canaanites and Egyptians they were doubtless looked upon as Hapiru. The Israelite conquest of Canaan was certainly regarded as an Hapiru invasion, although chronological considerations argue against identification of the events of the book of Joshua with the invasions described in the Amarna Letters. Among the Hapiru who were slaves in Egypt during the reign of Pharaoh Ramesses II there may have been many whom we know as Hebrews or Israelites.

5. Egypt

Our knowledge of ancient Egypt parallels that of Sumer. Although located at opposite ends of the Fertile Crescent and differing in cultural inheritance, Egyptians and Sumerians both made their appearance in history about 3000 B.C.

As in the case of the Sumerians, we are unable to say much concerning the racial affinities of the Egyptians. Mizraim, the son of Ham in the Biblical Table of Nations (Gen. 10), gives us our Hebrew name for Egypt. This causes us to speak of Egyptians as Hamites, whereas we speak of the Israelites and many of their neighbors as Semites. In modern usage the terms Hamitic and Semitic are used to describe languages rather than racial characteristics. People who spoke Semitic languages are termed Semites, although we know that many non-Semitic peoples were incorporated into the Semitic cultures of the ancient world. Similarly the peoples which we term Hamites have a variety of racial strains. Earlier historians thought of the Egyptians as negroid, but this view has been abandoned. J. H. Breasted in his monumental *History of Egypt* observed, "At most, he [the Egyptian] may be slightly tinctured with negro blood."[1] The language of ancient Egypt is usually termed Hamito-Semitic.

At the time when hieroglyphic writing first appeared (*ca.* 3000 B.C.), Egypt was already a highly cultured country. We do not learn of its past from the excavation of mounds, as in ancient Sumer, but from the study of tombs and burial chambers built in the desert which stretches interminably on both sides of the Nile valley. The dryness of the desert made it unsuitable for cultivation, but it was an ideal climate for the preservation of the bodies and artifacts of the ancient Egyptians. Mummified bodies of Pharaohs and their servants, along with quantities of jewelry, stone vases, copper vessels and other objects have been found there. Even wood, which would normally have rotted away centuries ago, has been preserved in the dry desert.

The period between the twenty-ninth and the twenty-third centuries B.C. is known as the Old Kingdom, a period when the Pharaoh reigned with absolute power as god and king.

---

1. James Henry Breasted, *A History of Egypt*, p. 26.

One of Egypt's great pyramids, with sphinx in the foreground.

Records indicate that many of these rulers were educated men. They could read and write, direct mining operations in the Sinai peninsula and dispatch orders to their military commanders at Nubia, south of Egypt, and Punt on the Red Sea. Ministers and engineers sought audience with the Pharaohs to discuss the needs of the land. Since Egypt has no rainfall, but is dependent for irrigation on the annual floods resulting from the overflow of the Nile River, considerable attention had to be given to irrigation problems. This dependence of all the Egyptians on the Nile doubtless helps to account for the strength of the government. Only through collective effort could the people hope to survive.

The Pharaohs, however, had personal concerns and frequently employed architects to plan extensive royal estates. During the twenty-sixth and the twenty-fifth centuries a series of immense pyramids was built at great expense of material and labor. These pyramids are esteemed among the wonders of the ancient world. They had been standing for five hundred years when Abraham sojourned in Egypt, and they are standing today.

The first pyramid was designed by Imhotep, a renowned priest who served as architect for Pharaoh Djoser. The step pyramid which he constructed at Saqqara is the earliest large stone structure in history. It comprises a large stone burial vault (known as a mastaba) on which five successive layers were built in the form of steps. The terraced monument which resulted was one hundred ninety feet high.

The largest of the pyramids was built by a Pharaoh named Khufu, or Cheops, founder of the Egyptian Fourth Dynasty. The square base of his pyramid covered thirteen acres. It was 481 feet high and contained 2,300,000 blocks of yellow limestone, each averaging two and one-half tons. Herodotus, the Greek historian, claimed that the laborers worked in groups of 100,000 men. The precision with which the building was erected amazes even the mind steeped in precision instruments and exact formulae.

A second pyramid at Giza was built by Khafre (Chephren), the successor of Khufu, near which was a sphinx with the representation of Khafre's head on the body of a reclining lion. Later Pharaohs continued to build pyramids, but the size and grandeur gradually diminished. The pyramids were built as tombs for the Pharaohs, and the energy expended on them proved to be an unproductive drain upon the national economy. The pyramids were luxuries which the nation could ill afford.

The twenty-second and twenty-first centuries B.C. mark a period of Egyptian history known as the "First Intermediate Period." Our sources of information for this time are scanty, but it appears that the nobles grew in power at the expense of the central government. Resentment against oppression found expression in the desecration of the tombs of Old Kingdom Pharaohs. Temples were pillaged and their works of art were subjected to systematic and determined vandalism. One of the nobles boasted, "I rescued my city in the day of violence from the terrors of the royal house."[2]

Although Egyptian Pharaohs were never again to have the absolute power which they enjoyed during the Pyramid Age, a strong central government was established in the twenty-first century. This government, known as the Middle Kingdom, lasted until the eighteenth century when Egypt was overrun by the Hyksos invaders from Asia.

The patriarch Abraham is not mentioned by name but there is abundant evidence of contacts between Egyptians and Semites during the age of the Middle Kingdom. A tomb painting at Beni Hasan, 169 miles south of Cairo, depicts a powerful noble of the Middle Kingdom, Khnumhotep, welcoming a group of desert Semites who are bringing gifts and seeking trade. The inscription which accompanies the painting reads, "The arrival, bringing eye-paint, which thirty-seven Asiatics bring to him." The leader of the Semites is identified as, "Sheik of the highlands, Ibshe."

During the Middle Kingdom, the god of Thebes, the capital city, lost his provincial character and became the god of the whole land. He was identified with the sun god, Re, and bore the combined title, "Amon-Re, King of the Gods." A massive temple to Amon-Re was built at Karnak, near Thebes. Construction was continued for a period of over two millennia — from the Middle Kingdom of Egypt until Roman times. Ultimately the priests of Amon-Re achieved a power which compared with that of the Pharaoh, himself.

In the interest of greater efficiency, the capital of Egypt was moved from Thebes to Memphis at the head of the Delta. In this way more effective control could be maintained over the "two Egypts" — Lower Egypt, or the Delta, and Upper Egypt, the Nile Valley to the borders of Nubia at the First Cataract. Efficient palace schools were maintained there in order to train officials for their political posts.

---

2. James Henry Breasted, *Ancient Records of Egypt,* I, p. 690.

Bronze became a basic metal in the Egyptian economy, and the Pharaohs of the Middle Kingdom again exploited the copper mines in the Sinai region. Beautiful pieces of feminine jewelry date from this period. Although not as original in design as the work of the Old Kingdom masters, Middle Kingdom artists maintained an excellent standard of work.

Of more utilitarian value was the program of Middle Kingdom Pharaohs to expand the amount of cultivable land in the area southwest of Memphis known as the Faiyum. A huge embankment was built there to serve as a catch basin for the waters of the Nile at the time of the annual inundation. In this way an estimated twenty-seven thousand acres of cultivable land were added to the Faiyum district.

Middle Kingdom Egypt produced some of the great masterpieces of world literature. One of these is the tale of Sinuhe, an Egyptian who fled to Canaan and prospered there. The land of Canaan was barbaric, however, in comparison with Egypt, and Sinuhe was happy to return to his home country that he might die there and be buried in a pyramid!

Another Middle Egyptian story recounts the adventures of the sole survivor of a storm at sea. The Shipwrecked Sailor, who gives his name to the story, was cast ashore on a magical island ruled by a giant serpent who had superhuman power and wisdom. The story relates how the serpent was kind to the sailor and sent him home in a ship which materialized according to the serpent's prophecy. The serpent also told the sailor that he would never see the island again, ". . . it will have become water." The island, the story tells us, disappeared, and no one could ever disprove the sailor's yarn. This is regarded as one of the earliest examples of the short story.

A third Middle Kingdom work, of an entirely different variety, is the Tale of the Eloquent Peasant. A wronged farmer presented his case before the magistrate with such eloquence that a decision was deferred. The peasant's eloquent appeals for justice were recorded for the amusement of the king — and of the modern reader!

Although the ancient Egyptians were a religious people, skepticism was not lacking. The Song of the Harper tells of the minstrel who sang about the vanity of life to the guests at a banquet. Since we cannot take our possessions with us when we leave the world, the harper suggests that we eat, drink, and be merry.

Before the end of the eighteenth century, Egyptian power was again in decline. The contention for power on the part of rival dynasties opened the way for invasion by foreigners from Asia known as the Hyksos.

The name Hyksos, long thought to have meant "shepherd kings," is now taken to be a contraction of words meaning "rulers of foreign lands." They worshiped the Canaanite gods, notably Baal, and are thought to have been Canaanite and Amorite princes from Syria and Palestine. The Hyksos rulers established their capital at Avaris (Tanis), in the Delta near the northeastern frontier. In this way they were close to their Asiatic domains as well as the land of Egypt.

The Hyksos were hated by the native Egyptians, with the result that monuments of their rule were destroyed. Josephus, the Jewish historian of the first century A.D., records a passage from Manetho, an Egyptian historian of about 300 B.C., who wrote of the Hyksos conquerors:

> In his reign (i.e. Pharaoh Titimaeus), for what cause I know not, a blast of God smote us; and, unexpectedly, from the regions of the east, invaders of obscure race marched in confidence of victory against our land. By main force they easily seized it without striking a blow; and having overpowered the rulers of the land, they then burned our cities ruthlessly, razed to the ground the temples of the gods, and treated all the natives with a cruel hostility.... Finally they appointed as king one of their number whose name was Salitis.

Hated as the Hyksos rulers were, they brought important changes into Egyptian life. Egypt had thought of itself as the center of culture and refinement, and looked with disdain on foreign "barbarians." The Hyksos, by humiliating Egypt, made the Egyptians conscious of the fact that there were other people in the world and that they must, in one way or another, be reckoned with. The Hyksos introduced the war chariot into Egypt. Within a few years Egyptian chariots would be turned against the Asiatics.

The Hyksos were expelled from Egypt about 1570 B.C. The liberator was Amosis (1570-1546) whose brother Kamose had succeeded in raising an army and pushing the Hyksos into the eastern Delta where they consolidated their forces at Avaris, their capital. Kamose did not live to see the final defeat of the Hyksos, but his brother carried on the fight, seized Avaris, and drove the Hyksos from Egypt. Amosis pursued them to southern Palestine where he laid siege to their fortress at Sharuhen. After a three year siege, Sharuhen fell and the Hyksos threat to Egypt was over.

With Amosis the New Kingdom, or Empire period of Egyptian history began, the period graphically described in the title

The gigantic cliff temple at Abu Simbel, in Nubia, one of the many monuments built by Ramesses II.

of a book by George Steindorff and Keith Seele, *When Egypt Ruled the East.* After his victory at Sharuhen, Amosis turned his attention to Nubia, the land south of Egypt. The Hyksos had never been able to subdue Nubia, but Amosis did so, and the Egyptian Empire was begun. Before the end of the Empire Period, (*ca.* 1100 B.C.), Egyptian power reached the Euphrates, and Egyptian armies were a familiar sight in Syria and Palestine.

The descent of Joseph and, later, of his father and brothers, had important repercussions in later Israelite history. The Pharaoh under whom Joseph served as Prime Minister is not named, however, and we have no means of positive identification. Many scholars consider the period of Hyksos rule to be the logical time to place the account of another Semite, Joseph, rising to power in Egypt. The fact that so little is known about the Hyksos period makes it impossible for us to be certain.

It is, of course, also possible that Joseph entered Egypt during the latter years of the Middle Kingdom. The Beni Hasan inscription indicates that Semites were not strangers in Egypt, and it is conceivable that Joseph came there at that time. The fact that shepherds were described as an abomination to the Egyptians (Gen. 46:34) and that the Egyptians would not eat with the Hebrews (Gen. 43:32) may suggest that we are dealing with a native dynasty. On the other hand, the Hyksos rulers probably adopted many of the customs and attitudes of the people they conquered. The fact that the Pharaoh lived fairly close to Goshen, where Joseph's family was permitted to settle (Gen. 46:31; 47:10), appears to argue for a time when the capital was in the Delta, as it was during the Hyksos period.

7

The Cities

of the Patriarchs

The Biblical patriarchs spent most of their lives "in tents" living a seminomadic life. Their wealth was in herds and flocks rather than real estate.

If Abraham and his descendants lived in the Palestinian Negev rather than the cultural centers of the Fertile Crescent, it was from choice rather than necessity. The Biblical record tells us that the father of the Israelite nation left Ur of the Chaldees with his father, Terah. Subsequently they sojourned in Haran before Abraham began the seminomadic life in Canaan.

1. Ur of the Chaldees

The Sumerian city of Ur, in southern Mesopotamia, was first excavated by the British consul at Basra, J. E. Taylor, in 1854. At that time all that was left of the once great city was a mound known in Arabic as *al Muqayyar* ("the mound of pitch"). Excavations were resumed by H. R. Hall in 1918, and again by Sir Leonard Wooley in 1922.

Gold helmet of Mes-Kalam-Dug, from Ur.

The title "Ur of the Chaldees" identifies the city as having been located in the land which was later called Chaldaea. One of the Chaldaean, or Neo-Babylonian kings, Nabonidus, (555-539 B.C.) actually gave attention to rebuilding the city of Ur which had been in ruins for centuries.

The Ur of the book of Genesis was a thriving cultural center of Sumerian life. Its history is known to go back to the Early Bronze Age (3000-2100 B.C.). Several hundred clay tablets discovered at Ur represent the culture of the Classical Sumerian period (2800-2700 B.C.).

An ancient Sumerian document, known as the King List, lists rulers who lived both before and after the flood, described in another cuneiform tablet. The third dynasty of kings after the

Ruins at Ur of the Chaldees, Abraham's early homeland.

flood, according to the King List, came from Ur. Mes-anni-padda was the name of the first of these kings.

Our appreciation of the art of ancient Ur has been greatly increased since the discovery, by Woolley, of the so-called royal cemeteries which are thought to date about 2500 B.C. A noble lady, popularly named Queen Shubad, was buried there along with her impressive head attire, jewelry, a gold tumbler and cup. There was a tragic side to the royal tombs, however. The evidences of Sumerian culture and refinement were countered by evidence that attendants were sacrificed at the time of the funeral of their masters. It was evidently felt that faithful servants should accompany their earthly masters into the next world.

The Sumerians of Ur shared the fate of others of their race when Sargon of Akkad founded a Semitic dynasty in southern Mesopotamia (2360-2180 B.C.). Although Ur was no longer a major political center, Woolley did find remains of the city dating from the time of Sargon's rule.

A brief Sumerian renaissance (2070-1960 B.C.) brought Ur to the fore again. Ur-nammu is accounted first king of the Third Dynasty of Ur which lasted until an Amorite from Mari on the middle Euphrates, Ishbi-irra by name, overran the Sumerian territory and occupied Isin (1960-1830 B.C.). At the same time a group of Elamites crossed the Tigris and established their vassal, Naplanum, on the throne of Larsa.

During the Third Dynasty of Ur a number of important buildings were erected. The moon god Nanna (Semitic, Sin), the patron deity of Ur was honored with a beautiful temple built on a specially constructed temple tower known as a ziggurat. Another temple was built for Nanna's consort, Nin-gal. A treasury building and a palace for the high priestess also adorned the city during the Ur III period.

The Elamites who had seized Larsa extended their power over Ur in the years which followed the Third Dynasty of Ur. Subsequently Rim-sin of Larsa was conquered by the sixth king of the first dynasty of Babylon, (1728-1686 B.C.), the great lawgiver Hammurabi. Ur rebelled, however, during the reign of Samsu-illuna, Hammurabi's son. The city was destroyed and, in spite of the efforts of Nabonidus to rebuild it over a millennium later, it never again became a place of importance.

It would be interesting to know just when "the God of glory appeared unto our father Abraham when he was in Mesopotamia, before he dwelt in Haran," but we do not have exact chronologies before the days of the Israelite kingdom (*ca.* 1000 B.C.). Some Biblical scholars suggest that Ur-nammu was the ruler of Ur during the time of Abraham. Did Abraham look upon the great Ziggurat which Ur-Nammu built? Did he know anything of the law code of this ruler who called himself "king of Sumer and Akkad?" We cannot know for sure.

Even if the Ur of Abraham's lifetime was earlier or later than Ur-Nammu, it was a cultural and religious center of considerable importance. Jewish tradition suggests that Abraham's ancestors had been idol-makers at Ur. Scripture, while silent on such details, does make it clear that the ancestors of the Biblical patriarchs served "other gods" before they came to know the true God. Abraham turned his back on a highly civilized environment when he left Ur in obedience to the command of the Lord.

2. Haran

Travelers between southern Mesopotamia and Palestine did not journey through the desert but took the longer route around the Fertile Crescent. Abraham, with Terah, his father set out along the familiar road northward from Ur.

The migration from Ur took Abraham and his father to Haran, a northern Mesopotamian city on the Bilikh River about sixty miles from its entrance into the Euphrates. The word Haran means "road" and the city was located on an important caravan route connecting Nineveh and Babylon with Damascus, Tyre, and Egypt. Haran, like Ur, was devoted to the worship of the Moon God. People from Ur would feel at home there, and the temptation was great to forego the uncertain journey into Canaan. Terah, Abraham's father, got no farther than Haran, but Abraham himself moved on to Canaan.

Shortly before and after 2000 B.C., a nomadic people known as Amorites ("westerners") invaded the settled areas of the Near East. The Aramaeans, to whom Laban was related (Gen. 31:20), are thought to have been an Amorite people. The Israelites, too, acknowledged their Aramaean origin in the confession, "A wandering Aramaean was my father" (Deut. 26:5). It is of interest that Haran is known to have been an Amorite state shortly after 2000 B.C.

The region around Haran was subsequently thought of as the ancestral home of Abraham's family. It is known as Paddan-aram ("Field of Aram") or Aram-naharaim ("Aram of the Two Rivers" or "Mesopotamia"). To this area Abraham sent a

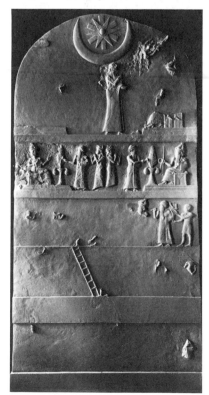

The Ur-nammu stele depicts the king receiving directions for building a ziggurat. In successive registers he completes the task assigned by his god.

trusted servant to secure a suitable bride for Isaac, and here Jacob fled to escape the wrath of Esau and to marry a daughter of Laban. Actually he was married to both Leah and Rachel, and remained about twenty years before returning to Canaan.

3. The Cities of Canaan

Abraham moved on from Haran into the land of Canaan. He first pitched his tent under the oak (or terebinth) of Moreh at Shechem. The site of Shechem (modern *Tell Balatah*) is known to have been an important Canaanite city between 2000 and 1800 B.C., and again between 1400 and 1200 B.C. Water was a perennial problem in Canaan, and the fact that "Jacob's well" was in the Shechem area made it a particularly attractive site.

Water pots produced by the potters at Hebron.

Tell Balatah was excavated in recent years by the Drew Mc-Cormick Expedition which was heir to the work of German scholars who conducted seven campaigns there between 1913 and 1934. Palaces and streets were discovered which date to the eighteenth, and the first half of the seventeenth centuries B.C. In his report in the *Biblical Archaeologist*, Edward F. Campbell, Jr., observed: "The one hundred years which immediately preceded the coming of the Hyksos to Shechem appear to have seen lively building activity indeed. Who knows but that the patriarch Joseph saw these now ruined palaces when they were dominating the western edge of the city?"[1]

Beer-sheba is also noted for its wells. The city is still the market center for the Negev, a position which it doubtless had since patriarchal times. Abraham, Isaac, and Jacob all spent some portion of their lives in Beer-sheba. The mound Tell Beer Sheva, east of the modern city, is being excavated by the University of Tel Aviv.

The Tell el-Amarna tablets from fifteenth century Egypt speak of the city of *Rubuti* ("the four") which seems to be the equivalent of the Biblical Kirjath-arba ("city of four," or "tetrapolis"). This city in southern Palestine, nineteen miles southwest of Jerusalem, is best known to us as Hebron ("the league") a city which, according to Numbers 13:22 was built "seven years before Zoan in Egypt."

Zoan, known at different times as Avaris and Tanis, was rebuilt by the Hyksos rulers of Egypt about 1700 B.C. George

---

1. Edward F. Campbell, Jr., "Excavation at Shechem, 1960," *The Biblical Archaeologist* XXIII, 4, p. 110.

A boy and his donkey at the site of Mamre, near Hebron.

Ernest Wright of Harvard suggests that this was the date which the sacred historian had in mind when describing the age of Hebron. If this is so, the city of Hebron was built after the time of Abraham, which would agree with the fact that the Patriarch was associated with Mamre, a plain near Hebron, rather than the city itself.

Twelve miles north of Jerusalem was the city of Luz, subsequently named Bethel (Gen. 28:19). Here Abraham built his first altar when he arrived in Canaan (Gen. 12:8) and, later, the fugitive Jacob dreamed of an open heaven and a ladder with angels bringing a message of divine encouragement (Gen. 28:11-13, 22).

The site of Bethel was excavated in 1934 by an expedition directed by Professor W. F. Albright. Pottery evidence indicates that the city was occupied during the twenty-first century B.C. The most interesting discoveries, however, come from the period subsequent to that of the patriarchs. Remains of a city wall from the sixteenth century B.C. have been found. The quality of the masonry of these walls and the houses of the period, is higher than that of any other Palestinian structures.

Both Abraham and Isaac had important dealings with the king of the Philistine city-state known as Gerar, identified with *Tell el-Jemmeh* in southern Palestine. Like Haran, Gerar was situated along a rich caravan route and, for that reason, had a thriving economy. Excavations by Sir Flinders Petrie have shown the diversity of objects used by the citizens of Gerar from the sixth to the fourth centuries B.C. Its importance during patriarchal times is indicated in the Biblical record (Gen. 20:1-18; Gen. 26:1-22).

8

Canaan During

Patriarchal Times

The land to which Abraham migrated is known in the Pentateuch as the land of Canaan. The peoples of the land, although of varying ethnic backgrounds, are frequently given the collective name of Canaanites. Our knowledge of these people and the culture they represent has been greatly increased as a result of modern archaeological work. Our prime source of first hand information has been the literature from Ras Shamra, ancient Ugarit, discovered and deciphered in the years since 1929.

The etymology and significance of the name Canaan has been the subject of considerable speculation. George Adam Smith in his classical *Historical Geography of the Holy Land* relates the word Canaan to the Hebrew root *kanan* which means "to be humbled" or "to be made low." In this sense, Canaanites would be "lowlanders."

Others derive the word Canaan from the word for "purple dye" for which Canaan, especially the northern part, was once famous. Justification for this viewpoint comes from the Greeks who called the people *Phoinikes,* plural of *Phoinix;* and their land *Phoinike,* words which appear to be related to the word *phoinios,* "blood-red." This appears to refer to the reddish-purple dye which the Phoenicians extracted from the murex shellfish and made their principal article of export.

As a matter of fact the Phoenicians considered themselves Canaanites throughout their history in Syria, and their Carthaginian descendants did so in Africa as late as the fifth century A.D. Augustine states that in his time the Carthaginian peasants, when questioned concerning their race, answered, *"Chanani."*

The identification of the Canaanites with "lowlanders" as opposed to the Amorites, and, later, the Israelites who settled in the "highlands," is attractive, but the Greek usage seems to argue for a name which developed from the commercial side of Canaanite life. It is possible, of course, that folk etymology has been at work, and that the meaning of the name Canaan has been variously interpreted at different periods of history. W. F. Albright suggests that Phoenician sailors were given their name because of their sunburned skin.

Jericho as seen from the old Roman road.

1. Pre-historic Canaanites

Some of the earliest of human remains come from caves near Mount Carmel. Relics discovered there include roughly chopped and irregularly flaked flints which were used as fist hatchets. Fragments were chipped from a core of flint to make the hatchet easy to grasp for cutting or pounding. Artistic ability is seen in a head of a bull carved in bone which was discovered in one of the caves.

During the two millennia before the dawn of history (*ca.* 5000-3000 B.C.) there is evidence that the inhabitants of Canaan had begun to settle in towns and villages. Permanent houses with red painted floors were found by the Jericho expedition of 1935-36. At Teleilat el-Ghassul, four and one-half miles north of the Dead Sea, houses of the same period had foundations of uncut stone and walls of mud brick. Pottery was usually hand made, but there is evidence that the potter's wheel was known. Pavements were made of stone. Numerous flint implements, including polished axes, were discovered, but we know that copper was also in use before the beginnings of Canaanite history.

Ruins of Jericho, including the remains of an ancient city wall (lower right in photo).

The relationship of these prehistoric peoples to the historic Canaanites is, of course, problematical. The land of Canaan witnessed a variety of ethnic movements, and the Scriptures speak not only of Canaanites but also of Jebusites, Hittites, Girgashites, Horites, Hivites, Amorites, and many others.

2. Early Cities of Canaan

Early in the Patriarchal Age (the nineteenth century B.C.) we read of many cities of considerable size in Canaan. Gezer was surrounded by strong walls and seems to have been an Egyptian outpost during patriarchal times. Egyptian statues and other objects were discovered there.

Another great city was Megiddo, which guards the strategic pass from the Plain of Sharon through the Valley of Esdraelon to the Jordan valley. A "high place" of Megiddo was used for the offering of sacrifices to the gods of Canaan about the time Abraham was bearing testimony to the faithfulness of the Lord as a sojourner in Shechem, Bethel, and Beer-sheba.

The mound of Megiddo (modern *Tell el Mutesellim*) has been excavated, first by the Deutsche Orientgesellschaft and, since 1925, by the Oriental Institute of the University of Chicago. A city is known to have been situated there as early as 3500 B.C. A brick wall and gate are dated to about 1800 B.C., when the city was occupied by Canaanites. It was not until the time of Solomon that Megiddo became an Israelite stronghold (I Kings 9:15).

During the patriarchal period the towns of Transjordan and the valley of the Jordan were also flourishing. Nelson Glueck, the noted Palestinian archaeologist and president of Hebrew Union College, made a survey of the area east and south of the Dead Sea during the years 1932 to 1939. His studies indicated that the nomadic peoples of that area had lived in villages prior to 2000 B.C., but that the villages were abandoned during the twentieth or nineteenth centuries. This appears to be a historical reflection of the events described in the book of Genesis when Sodom, Gomorrah, and the cities of the plain were destroyed. The area seems to have suffered from a tremendous earthquake about that time.

W. F. Albright has shown that Sodom, Gomorrah, and Zoar are probably beneath the shallow waters at the southern tip of the Dead Sea. Two sites nearby were excavated, and Albright concluded that they were abandoned about the twentieth century B.C. Before the destruction of Sodom and Gomorrah the area was a flourishing center of civilization. Lot felt it to be the most desirable portion of Canaan (Gen. 13:5-13).

3.   An Egyptian in Canaan

From the Patriarchal Age we have a first-hand account of Canaan as it appeared to an Egyptian refugee named Sinuhe. How much of the Sinuhe story is fact and how much fiction we may never know. If it was written by a stay-at-home Egyptian, he had an excellent knowledge of both the geography and the social structure of Canaan.

The events of the story begin about 1950 B.C. when King Amenemhet died and his eldest son, Sesostris, took the throne. Sinuhe never quite explains why he had to leave Egypt, but leave it he did. After some harrowing experiences in Egypt itself, Sinuhe reached the "Walls of the Ruler," built to protect

An ivory game board from Megiddo (ca. 1350-1150 B.C.)

the northeast frontier of Egypt from invasion by the Asiatics. This seems to be the wall ("Shur") to which Hagar was fleeing after she left the home of Abraham. The Israelites at the time of the Exodus were directed southward into the Sinai peninsula so that they would not be attacked on the heavily traveled coastal route.

An individual, such as Sinuhe, would be better able to elude the Egyptian garrison than would the Israelite encampment. Sinuhe states that he crouched under a bush during the day and eluded the watch at the wall under cover of night.

Once he had escaped the Egyptian garrisons, Sinuhe had no serious problems. He was hospitably received by a Bedouin sheikh who had been in Egypt. Refreshments of water and boiled milk were offered the weary traveler.

Sinuhe spent some time at Byblos, on the Phoenician coast and in a land known as Kedem. The word itself means "east" and it is thought to refer here to the desert region east of Damascus. After spending a half year there he was invited to come to Upper Retjenu, evidently a name for the mountainous part of Palestine. There he soon achieved high rank. The local king gave his eldest daughter to Sinuhe in marriage and allowed him to choose some of the country for himself.

Waxing eloquent concerning this "land of Ya'a," Sinuhe exclaimed:

> It is a good land, Ya'a by name, figs and grapes are in it; it has more wine than water, it has much honey and olive oil in plenty; all fruits are upon its trees; limitless barley and spelt are there, and all kinds of herds and flocks.

A tribe was assigned to Sinuhe, who became a petty ruler in Canaan. He describes his food: wine, boiled meat, roast fowl, and the game of the desert. Milk, he says, was used in cooking. This diet, we should observe, was hardly typical of patriarchal Canaan. Sinuhe was a chieftain and a royal favorite, so he was provided with special fare.

Before long Sinuhe gained a reputation for his prowess on the field of battle. He was challenged, however, by the local Goliath but Sinuhe's reputation was vindicated. An arrow hit the assailant in the neck and Sinuhe killed the challenger with his own battle axe.

Sinuhe's successes in Canaan did not dim his love for Egypt, however. When he received a letter inviting him to return home, he eagerly prepared to leave for Egypt. He turned over his property to his children and, accompanied by attendants, started on the long journey. At the Roads of Horus, near modern Kantara, he met the frontier patrol which sent word to the Pharaoh that Sinuhe had arrived. The Bedouins who had accompanied Sinuhe to Egypt were given gifts and sent home. Sinuhe, himself, was impressed by all that he saw. Egypt was a land of efficiency: "Every serving-man was at his task."

Egyptian clothes were exchanged for the rough Bedouin garments which Sinuhe was wearing. He says: "A burden was given back to the desert — my clothes to the Sandfarers. I was clothed in fine linen, and anointed with fine oil; I lay down at night upon a bed. I gave the sand to those who dwell on it, and wood oil to him who would anoint himself with it."

In connection with this transformation, designed to make Sinuhe a good Egyptian again, we read, "I was shaved and my hair was combed." Some centuries later before an audience with the reigning Pharaoh we read of Joseph: ". . . they brought him hastily out of the dungeon, and he shaved himself, and changed his raiment" (Gen. 41:14). Semites were normally bearded, but Egyptians were clean shaven. Joseph also was given "vestures of fine linen" (Gen. 41:42) in keeping with the post which was assigned to him in Egypt.

The crowning achievement of Sinuhe's return to Egypt was the stone pyramid which was built for him. Burial in Canaan was quite simple. The body was placed in a cloth and buried in the ground. Egypt, however, made a great to-do over funerals. Draughtsmen designed the pyramid, sculptors carved it, and builders took the responsibility of seeing that everything was done properly. Sinuhe can be considered a success, according to Egyptian standards. He was buried in a pyramid.

The desire to be buried in one's homeland was not exclusively Egyptian, of course. Jacob had charged his sons: "Bury me with my fathers in the cave that is in the field of Ephron the Hittite" (Gen. 49:29). Joseph, too, said to his fellow-Israelites, "God shall surely visit you, and ye shall carry up my bones from hence." (Gen. 50:25). Jacob's remains were taken to Canaan shortly after he died, but Joseph was embalmed (or mummified) and "put in a coffin in Egypt" (Gen. 50:26) until the time of the Exodus.

4. Agriculture

Agriculture is dependent upon fertile soil. In Canaan this poses a problem because of the long periods when there is no rain. Throughout the summer the fields are parched, but the "former rains" begin late in September or early in October. This makes possible a time of planting and ploughing in the fall of the year. The winter is wet with occasional snow as far south as Bethlehem. In March and April a series of heavy showers known as the "latter rains" soak the fields and fill empty cisterns. Following the latter rains the dry summer begins.

Compared with the fertile Nile valley and the lands drained by the Tigris and Euphrates, Canaan was a land which held little promise. The Biblical records speak of numerous famines, often accompanied by migrations of people in search of food. During the time of Joseph the Israelites migrated to Egypt because they could not produce enough food in Canaan.

Those who had recently come from the Arabian Desert, however, found Canaan to be in truth a land "flowing with milk and honey." Food could not be produced there without effort, but when the population was willing to labor hard it usually was able to maintain itself. The Egyptian, Sinuhe, boasted about the figs, dates, and other products of Canaan.

Grains, vines, and olives were the basic agricultural products of ancient Canaan, as of other Mediterranean lands. Wheat, oats and barley were raised, along with beans, vetch, figs, pomegranates and nuts.

The cities of northern Phoenicia had an abundance of water flowing from the Lebanon mountains to the Mediterranean. To prevent erosion and to extend the amount of arable land, a system of terracing and irrigation was developed. In this way both summer and winter cultivation was possible to provide for the large population along the coast.

Terracing was not limited to Phoenicia, however. The mountainsides of Syria and Palestine were terraced by means of walls built a few yards apart to protect the soil and make farming possible. Vineyards, orchards, and gardens could be maintained in this way. Grains were raised with greater efficiency along the coastal plains and in the Esdraelon Valley.

In the excavations at Jericho, John Garstang and his associates unearthed storage jars containing wheat, barley, oats, millet, and lentils. We know that flax was raised at Jericho during the time of Joshua, for Rahab hid the Israelite spies on her roof and concealed them with "stalks of flax which she laid in order upon the roof" (Josh. 2:6). The "pottage" for which Esau exchanged his birthright (Gen. 25:29-34) was made of red lentils and water or milk. Other vegetables and meat or suet were sometimes

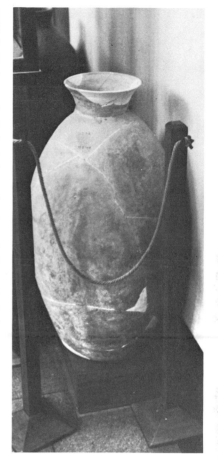

Calciform-type storage jar from about 2000 B.C., discovered in the Jordan Valley region.

added. Bread was dipped into the pot and used to convey the pottage to the mouth.

Reference is made to mandrakes (Gen. 30:14-18) which were gathered by Reuben at the time of wheat harvest and brought to his mother, Leah. The mandrake is a root, related to the potato and tomato, with a fruit resembling the plum. It grows wild and can be seen all over Palestine in May of each year.

W. F. Albright suggests that lettuce was grown in Palestine from the third and fourth millennium B.C. Egypt, Syria, and the Middle East in general also produced cucumbers at an early date (Num. 11:5; Isa. 1:8).

The instrument used for harvesting grain was the sickle which, before 2000 B.C., was made of flint teeth which were fastened with plaster into a bone or wooden handle. Later, iron was introduced. In the process of reaping, the harvester grasped a number of stalks with one hand, and with the other cut them off about a foot below the ears of grain. The remaining stubble was subsequently burned to fertilize the soil. The reapers were followed by binders who bound the grain into sheaves.

The so-called calendar, discovered during the excavations of Gezer by R. A. S. Macalister working with the British Palestine Exploration Fund (1902-08), describes the agricultural seasons of Palestine. Although the "calendar" probably should be dated about 925 B.C., the pattern of life it describes was doubtless pursued for centuries before that time:

> His two months are (olive) harvest,
> His two months are planting (grain),
> His two months are late planting;
> His month is hoeing up of flax,
> His month is harvest of barley
> His month is harvest and feasting;
> His two months are vine tending,
> His month is summer fruit.

5. The Cloth Industry

Spinning and weaving were carried on by the Canaanites during the third millennium before Christ. Archaeologists have discovered whorls of stone and of bone from this period. The industry was carried on in the home with wool as the earliest fabric. Canaanite wool is mentioned in the Nuzi documents (fifteenth century B.C.).

Flax grew in hot, low sections of Canaan such as the Jordan Plain near Jericho, where Scripture notes flax was used at the time of the conquest (Josh. 2:6). Loom weights used in making linen have been discovered at Teleilat el-Ghassul, northeast of the Dead Sea, dating back to the fourth millennium B.C.

6. The Alphabet

Chief among the debts which the West owe to the Canaanites is the alphabet. According to Greek tradition the art of writing was learned from a man named Cadmus. Actually Cadmus is but a Grecianized form of the Semitic word *Kedem,* which means "the East." The Greek word for *book, biblion,* from which our word "Bible" is derived, is the name of the Syrian city of Byblos, also known as Gebal.

Among the clay tablets discovered since 1929 at Ras Shamra, ancient Ugarit on the northern coast of Syria, were hundreds of documents dating from the fifteenth and fourteenth centuries B.C. written in a cuneiform alphabet which had not been previously known. The cuneiform used by the Sumerians, Babylonians and Assyrians was a cumbersome means of writing in which hundreds of syllables were represented by as many combinations of wedges. The alphabet at Ugarit comprised thirty-one alphabetic signs which were used in the production of a variety of literary and business documents.

By 1200 B.C. when the Canaanites felt pressure from the Philistines who had settled along the southern coastal plain and from the Israelites who had invaded the land from the east and conquered much of the interior hill country, the Canaanites were largely confined to the coastal territories north of Mount Carmel known as Phoenicia. From Tyre and Sidon, the great Phoenician cities, traders and colonists sailed to the islands of the Mediterranean and northern Africa. It was from contacts with these Phoenicians that the alphabet was introduced into Greece.

Ugarit (Ras Shamra).

An adz inscribed with the Ugaritic alphabet.

9

An Episode
in World Politics

The patriarchal records place the focus of attention upon a man, Abraham, and the providence of God by which a sovereign purpose was fulfilled through his descendants, Isaac and Jacob. Although mention is made of surrounding peoples, we look to extra-Biblical sources to gain information concerning their history.

On one occasion, however, Abraham became involved in the politics of the Fertile Crescent. In that instance, described in Genesis 14, Abraham was called upon to rescue his nephew Lot, who had been taken captive by a confederation of kings from the East.

Four kings from Mesopotamia had demanded tribute of the city-states of Canaan. The eastern kings are mentioned by name: Amraphel, king of Shinar; Chedorlaomer, king of Elam; Arioch, king of Ellasar; and Tidal, king of Goiim (or "nations"). The leader of the confederacy appears to be the Elamite, Chedorlaomer (Gen. 14:4). The name of this king is authentically Elamite and we know that, during the Patriarchal Age, Elamites controlled a large area. About 1950 B.C., Elamites conquered the city of Ur, once the center of a thriving Sumerian civilization. The kings of Elam desired to control the whole of Sumer and, about 1770 B.C. the Elamite ruler Kudur-mabuk conquered the important state of Larsa.

The name of "Amraphel, king of Shinar," was once popularly identified with the great Babylonian lawgiver, Hammurabi (*ca.* 1728-1686 B.C.), but this is ruled out by both linguistic and chronological considerations. The name, however, is Semitic, as we would expect of a king of Babylon. Several Mesopotamian kings bore the name Arriwuk ("Arioch"), a fact known from the Mari tablets. We do not know the identity of the state which he ruled, although Ellasar may be a variant of Larsa. Several Hittite kings bore the name Tudhalias, which may be the Biblical "Tidal king of Nations." The "nations" may have been a confederacy, the nature of which is unknown to us.

The eastern kings fought and rendered tributary the kings of Sodom, Gomorrah, Admah, and Zeboiim in the Valley of Siddim, the southern portion of what is now the Dead Sea. This area subsequently was submerged as a result of a cataclysmic judgment (Gen. 19).

We are told that the Canaanite kings from the Dead Sea area paid their tribute faithfully for twelve years. In the thirteenth year they rebelled, but it was evidently too late in the season for the eastern alliance to do anything about it. The following year, however, Chedorlaomer and his allies marched west.

The eastern confederates followed the route of the Fertile Crescent into northern Syria. They probably marched through Damascus and then took the main road through eastern Palestine. The towns of Ashteroth-karnaim, Ham, and Shaveh-kiriathaim were inhabited by Rephaim, Zuzim, and Emim, aboriginal inhabitants of Canaan who lost their tribal identity before the time of the Israelite conquest. The east-Jordan country was explored by Nelson Glueck, who concluded that there were large cities in the region during the time of Abraham, but that it was largely uninhabited for about four centuries beginning about 1700 B.C.

Chedorlaomer journed southward as far as to El-paran, probably the ancient name of Ezion-geber at the head of the Gulf of Aqabah. In the southern part of the country the eastern confederacy defeated the Horites, or Hurrians who had settled at Mount Seir (Edom). On the northward march they went to En Mishpat — Kadesh, in the Amalekite country southeast of Beer-sheba, and then to Hazezon-tamar (En-gedi) which was occupied by Amorites.

The king of Sodom and his allies fought Chedorlaomer in the Valley of Siddim, with disastrous results. In their flight some of the men of Sodom and Gomorrah fell into the slime pits, while others escaped to the mountains. The enemy was able to take as booty all of the property which had to be left behind, and a number of men, including Lot.

One of the men who had escaped alive brought word of the defeat of the men of Sodom and the capture of Lot to Abraham. The patriarch then gathered his personal army of three hundred eighteen men and pursued the enemy to Dan, later to become

Signpost at Sodom.

the northern frontier of Israel, and then, after defeating them in battle, followed them to Hobah, north of Damascus. Abraham was able to rescue Lot and those who were with him along with the property of the men of Sodom which had been taken.

The "kings" involved in these battles were rulers of city-states, rather than "kings" in the later sense of the term. The fact that Abraham was able to defeat them is still no mean achievement. He probably harassed them by repeated attacks and retreats until they were weakened. Then he made the final thrust which liberated Lot and his companions.

Abraham and the other patriarchs attempted to live in peace with the peoples of Canaan. It was only through the attempt of Lot to make common cause with the men of Sodom that Abraham became involved in this bit of international politics.

10

The Religion

of the Canaanites

The pernicious effect of Canaanite religion on Israel was not felt until the days of the judges (cf. Judg. 2:11-13) , but it became one of the greatest sources of temptation to the covenant people in the years between the conquest of Canaan and the Babylonian exile.

The reader of the Old Testament is familiar with Baal, the infamous "high places," and other aspects of a religion which was constantly denounced by the prophets of the God of Israel. Further clues to the nature of Canaanite religion were gathered from the writings of the ancient Egyptians, Phoenician records, and Greek literature. The latter were, at best, fragmentary, and frequently far removed from the historical situation in which Baalism was a vital force. Discoveries made since 1929 at Ras Shamra, however, have completely changed the picture. Ras Shamra, ancient Ugarit, is a small Arab village near modern Latakia, opposite the "point" of the island of Cyprus. The site was probably occupied since the first settlements of man in Syria. The lowest level of the mound is believed to date from the fifth millennium B.C. It is thought that Amorites and Semitic Canaanites pushed northward from the Arabian Desert and settled in the area during the third millennium B.C., bringing about important ethnic changes in Ugarit. Early in the second millennium an alliance was made with Egypt. Discoveries at Ugarit have shown strong Egyptian influences along with artifacts from the Minoan, Cretan civilization during this period.

During the heyday of Ugaritic prosperity — the fifteenth and fourteenth centuries B.C. — the poetic epics and myths of the ancient Canaanites were recorded on clay tablets in a cuneiform script. The Ugaritic alphabet is one of the earliest known to man. Our interest in the tablets arises from the relatively complete picture they present of Canaanite religion. We are no longer dependent on second hand accounts of the creed and cult of the Canaanites. Those who worshiped Baal and his associates have left us a first hand witness to their faith.

The nominal head of the Canaanite pantheon was El, a "remote, high god," who interfered little in the affairs of the world. El may be thought of as a mild old gentleman who delegated authority to his children, only reserving the right to be final arbiter in the event of disputes among them.

In a slightly different form, the word Il, or Ilu is the Akkadian word for "god." The cuneiform sign *il* is regularly prefixed to signs representing the popular deities of the Akkadian Semitic world. We read, then, of "the god Ishtar," "the god Ea," and "the god Baal." In this sense, *il* is the equivalent of our "god."

Gold pendant depicting Asherah, the Canaanite fertility goddess.

Just as we have one word for God or the gods, so the Hebrew Elohim served a dual purpose. It may speak of God, creator of heaven and earth (Gen. 1:1). When, however, Jacob asked his family to "put away the strange gods" which were in their midst (Gen. 35:2), or the rebellious Israelites asked Aaron to make gods to lead them from Sinai (Exod. 32:1), Elohim is also used. Depending on its context, Elohim in the Bible may refer to the God of Israel, or the gods of the surrounding nations. Similarly El, or Il in the ancient Near East may be a distinct personal being — the El of Ugaritic mythology — or simply a generic term for deity. The fact that El was the father of the gods may account for their bearing his "name."

El, in the Canaanite mythology, presided over the assembly of the gods who gathered in the farthermost reaches of the north. The north, Mount Saphon, was an area concerning which little was known by the ancient Semites, and it became to them what Mount Olympus became to the Greeks.

The consort of El in the Ugaritic texts was named Asherat, "Lady of the Sea." In the form Asherah, the name appears about forty times in the Old Testament, especially in the books of Kings and Chronicles. In Ugarit the name Elat ("the goddess" — a feminine form of El) is also used of Asherat.

When not the name of a goddess, the term Asherah, and its plural, Asherim, denote the wooden poles which stood at Canaanite places of worship. In the Authorized Version of the Bible the word is regularly translated "grove." The terms "sacred tree" or "Asherah image" would better convey the thought of the original. The Asherah is thought to have been the trunk of a tree with the branches chopped off. It was erected beside the altar of Baal (Judg. 6:25, 28) in the fertility cult which was scathingly denounced by the Israelite prophets.

El and his wife Asherah produced a family of seventy Elim, gods and goddesses, best known of whom was Baal (meaning "master," "lord"), who was identified with the storm god, Hadad. Baal was the god of fertility responsible for the germination and growth of crops, the increase of flocks and herds, and the fecundity of human families.

Baal worship was the most degrading aspect of Canaanite civilization. Devotees brought wine, oil, first fruits, and firstlings of the flocks to the "high places." Near the rock altar was a *mazzebah* or sacred pillar which represented the male element in the fertility cult, corresponding to the Asherah, or female element. Chambers were maintained for sacred prostitution by *kedeshim* ("male prostitutes") and *kedeshoth* ("sacred harlots") (cf. I Kings 14:23, 24; II Kings 23:7). It should be noted that the language of the prophets who describe unfaithfulness to the Lord as adultery, and speak of those who forget the God of Israel as going "whoring after idols," is more than figure of speech.

Silver figurine of a female deity (ca. 1800-1600 B.C.), discovered at a temple in Nahariyya, Israel.

We first read of the appeal of Baalism to Israel before Joshua brought his people into Canaan. Numbers 22 records an incident in which a Babylonian soothsayer named Balaam played the principal role. Balak of Moab was frightened at reports of the defeat of powerful Amorite kings at the hands of Israel. In concert with the elders of Midian he sent for Balaam, trusting that he could pronounce a potent curse on Israel and thus insure its defeat. Unable to do this, Balaam devised a fiendish plan. He proposed that the Midianites invite the Israelites to the worship of Baal at Peor, knowing that this would mean apostasy from the God of Israel. The Hebrew historian writes:

> And Israel abode at Shittim, and the people began to commit harlotry with the daughters of Moab. And they called the people unto the sacrifices of their gods; and the people did eat and bowed down to their gods. And Israel joined himself unto the Baal of Peor; and the anger of the Lord was kindled against Israel. (Num. 25:1-3).

It has been suggested that the term "joined himself," related to the noun *tsemed,* "a couple," "a pair," might be rendered, "they paired off" — an Israelite and a Moabitess — in the worship of the Baal of Mount Peor.

While Baal, "rider of the clouds," is in essence one god, at the sound of whose voice the mountains rock, the earth shakes, and all his enemies flee in terror, in actual cult he is identified with each locality in which he is worshiped. In addition to the

Baal of Peor we read of Baal-gad (Josh. 11:17), Baal-hazor (II Sam. 13:23), Baal-zephon (Num. 33:7) and others. The New Testament mentions Beelzebul (Matt. 12:24 R.S.V., a variant of Beel-zebub), a name which may be associated with Baal-zebul of the Ugaritic texts. In Ugarit Baal-zebul signifies "Prince Baal," and was a term of high honor. The gods of the heathen were regarded as evil spirits by the Biblical writers, and Beelzebub or Beel-zebul became a name for Satan.

Baal-zebub was the name of the god of Ekron, according to II Kings 1:2, 3, 6, 16. The original may have been Baal-zebul, which was changed in contempt by the Israelites who considered a name meaning "Lord of flies" more fitting. The name of Saul's son Esh-baal (I Chron. 8:33), meaning "man of Baal," was changed to Ish-bosheth, "man of shame" (II Sam. 3:14). Similarly Jonathan's son Mephibosheth (II Sam. 4:4) is also named Merib-baal (I Chron. 8:34). Equating Baal with shame, the author of Kings felt justified in changing "Baal" names in order to eliminate a reference to religious ideas which had proved a stumbling-block to Israel for so many years. Saul and Jonathan, in giving their sons "Baal" names doubtless used the term as a synonym for Israel's God, their true "Lord," or "Master." The word, however, while having an innocent use, later was so associated with the evils of Canaanite Baalism that it was deemed obnoxious for a loyal Israelite.

The sister and spouse of Baal in the Ugaritic texts is known as Anat. Although bearing the epithet "the virgin," Anat was the goddess of passion, destructive as well as positive. Love and fertility were her domain, although Baal himself occupied the leading role in the cult. The lewd side of Anat worship may be noted from the figurines and pottery plaques of the nude Anat which have been dug from various Palestinian sites dating to the second millennium B.C.

Anat is goddess of war as well as sex. She fights Baal's enemies, smiting them and wading in their blood, even washing her hands in it! She attacked Mot, the god of death, and forced him to give back her brother, Baal. She cleaved Mot with her sword, ground him up and planted him in the ground.

The goddess Anat may appear in the name of the Israelite judge Shamgar, ben (son of) Anat(h). Either Anat(h) is the name of a parent of Shamgar, a fact which would be consistent with the religious syncretism of those days, or it may simply mean "warrior" — i.e. a "son" of the goddess of war! Anat may also be identified with the "queen of heaven" to whom Jews of

Figurine of a seated deity, from Hazor, eleventh century B.C.

Jeremiah's time burned incense (Jer. 44:19). We cannot be positive about such identifications, however, because the three principal Canaanite, goddesses are constantly confused and it is often impossible to identify the activities of a goddess unless she is specifically named.

Like Asherah and Anat, Astarte (Ashtaroth) was primarily concerned with sex. According to Philo, the Phoenicians attributed to Astarte two sons, Pothos ("sexual desire") and Eros ("sexual love"). In Egypt, Anat and Astarte were fused into one goddess, Antart. Theodore Gaster suggests that the three goddesses represent three aspects of womanhood:

> Ashterah was the wife and mother, sedate and matronly mistress of the home and female head of the family. Ashtarth (Astarte) was the sweetheart and mistress, a glamorous and voluptuous embodiment of sexual passion and therefore also the genius of reproduction and of fecundity in general. Anath was the young girl, a beautiful and virginal creature, full of youthful zest and vigor and addicted especially to the thrills of battle and the excitement of the chase. Since, however, all of them were *au fond* but aspects of the same thing, they naturally shared several qualities and attributes in common, and were not infrequently confused with one another.[1]

The Canaanite pantheon included a host of deities which served as the deification of natural phenomena. Shemesh, the sun, received considerable attention. Four towns in Scripture bear the name Beth-shemesh, and there is another named En-Shemesh. Such names indicate that the town was devoted to the worship of the deity whose name it bears. The Israelites, of course, occupied towns which had been settled by earlier Canaanites, and the names continued in use.

Jericho is named for Yareah, the moon god, as is Beth-yerah south of Tiberias. Under another name, Sin, the moon god had been worshiped in Ur and Haran at the time of Abraham.

Sedeq, "right," and Mishor, "equity," were attendants of the sun god who, because he surveys all things, was also regarded as a god of justice. Dawn and sunset were deified in the persons of Shahar and Shalem, "the celestial ones," who have been equated with Castor and Pollux of Greek and Roman mythology.

One of the Ugaritic texts speaks of an offering to "Queen Shapash (the sun) and to the stars." Shapash was a feminine manifestation, at Ugarit, of Shemesh, or Shamash, the sun god. Another text speaks of "the army of the sun and the host of the day," in connection with a ceremony performed on a rooftop. In the days preceding the captivity of Judah, Jeremiah com-

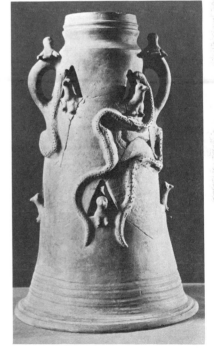

Cult object depicting snakes and birds, from the southern temple at Beth-shan, level five.

---

1. Theodore Gaster, "The Religion of the Canaanites," *Forgotten Religions* V. Ferm, ed., p. 125.

These two jar fragments, from Beth-shan of the Late Bronze Age, show the faces of a Canaanite man (top) and a Canaanite woman (bottom).

plained, "because of all the houses upon whose roofs they have burned incense unto all the host of heaven..." (Jer. 19:13).

Dagon of the Old Testament finds his counterpart in the Ugaritic Dagan, the god of grain and the genius of the crops. He was worshiped by the Philistines who built temples to him at Gaza and Ashdod (Judg. 16:23-30; I Sam. 5:1-7). Following the battle of Mount Gilboa, during which Saul and Jonathan died, the Philistines took the head of Saul and fastened it "in the temple of Dagan" at Beth-shan (I Chron. 10:10). At least two Beth-Dagons are known — one in the lowlands of Judah near the Philistine border (Josh. 15:33, 41), and another in Asher on the frontier toward Zebulon, near Mount Carmel.

The divine smith of the Canaanite pantheon was Koshar (or Kauthar) who also bore the name Hasis. Gaster translates the compound name, "Sir Adroit and Cunning." Koshar is the craftsman and inventor of tools and weapons. He finds his counterpart in the Egyptian Ptah, and the classical Hephaestus and Vulcan. Koshar was also the discoverer and patron of music. Philo of Byblos considers him (under the name Chusor) the originator of magical incantations. The Book of Genesis, by contrast, traces the arts and crafts to human origins. Jubal, a son of Lamech and Adah "was the father of all such as handle the harp and pipe." Tubal-cain, son of Lamech and Zillah was "the forger of every cutting instrument of brass and iron" (Gen. 4:21-22).

The nether world and the barren places of earth were the realm of Mot (the Canaanite god of death). Mot is the particular enemy of Baal, and the fertility cult in general, as death is the enemy of life. In his manifestation as Resheph, "the ravager," he is the god of plague and pestilence. One of the Karatepe inscriptions (8th century B.C.) calls him "Resheph of Birds," perhaps alluding to vulture-like characteristics. Mot also appears of Horon, "He of the Pit." The Book of Joshua (10:8-11) mentions a Beth-horon in the valley of Aijalon.

The sea was controlled by Yam, another enemy of Baal. "Prince Sea," as Gaster calls him, contended with Baal for mastery over the earth. Yam also appears under the name Lotan, the seven-headed monster of the deep. The name appears in the Old Testament as Leviathan. The Psalmist praises God for His power:

Thou didst shatter the heads of the sea-monsters in the waters. Thou didst crush the heads of Leviathan. (Psalm 74:13-14).

The Biblical writers did not, of course, accept the Canaanite mythology. They were prepared, as pious Israelites, to fight it to the death. Poetic forms and figures of speech, however, were used as a means of expressing the power of the God of Israel. Writing before the discovery of the Ugaritic texts, John Davis said, "Leviathan may be merely a creation of the popular fancy, an imaginary sea monster; the inspired poets and prophets of Israel subsidizing fable to serve in the illustration of truth."[2]

Molech or Milcom is mentioned in Scripture as the national God of Ammon (I Kings 11:5, 33). In the third millennium before Christ, the god Malik appears in the Assyro-Babylonian pantheon. The excavations at Mari on the middle Euphrates show that Muluk was worshiped in that region around 1800 B.C. In II Kings 17:31 we are told that the gods of the area of Sepharvaim — from which the Assyrians transplanted colonists to replace the men of Israel who had been taken into captivity — were named Adrammelech and Anammelech. The Tyrians worshiped Melkarth — the Melk (king) of the city.

Molech worship was expressly forbidden in the Mosaic law (Lev. 18:21; 20:1-5). Nevertheless it was popularly observed in times of apostasy. Solomon built an altar to Molech in the Valley of Hinnom at Tophet (I Kings 11:7). Both Ahaz and Manasseh offered their sons in sacrifice to Molech (II Kings 16:3; 21:6). Josiah, in his attempt to establish the Law of the Lord, desecrated the Hinnom Molech center in order to render it useless for pagan religious practices (II Kings 23:10). The Molech cult was revived, however, and the prophecies of Jeremiah and Ezekiel afford evidence that it continued to the time of the Exile (Jer. 7:29-34; Ezek. 16:20-21; 20:26, 31; 23:37-39).

The term Molech is related to the Semitic word for king (Hebrew *melech*). It originally signified a counsellor. Its meaning is not far removed from Baal, "master." The Palmyrenes had a deity whom they worshiped as Malach-baal. Milch-baal is a Phoenician personal name, and it is certain that the Baal whom Elijah challenged was the Baal of Tyre, otherwise known as Melcharth.

According to Albright, the concept of *Mulku,* or kingship, gave rise to the concept of *mulkana* which means "promise" in Syriac. The deity Molech became the god of vows and solemn promises, and children were sacrificed to him as the harshest and most binding pledge of the sanctity of a promise.

A god from Ugarit, wearing a high crown similar to the white crown of Upper Egypt. The figure is made of bronze, covered with gold and silver, and dates from the fifteenth or fourteenth century B.C.

2. John Davis, *A Dictionary of the Bible,* pp. 449-50.

Molech worship included a practice which is described in Scripture as making a son or daughter pass through the fire. Some scholars have thought of this as a harmless rite of purification from which the child emerged unscathed. The testimony of Scripture, however, indicates that the child died as a result of this hideous rite. Ezekiel complains, "...thou hast taken thy sons and thy daughters...and these hast thou sacrificed...to be devoured...thou hast slain my children and delivered them to cause them to pass through the fire" (Ezek. 16:20-21. cf 23:37). The evidence is clear that children were slaughtered and burnt like other sacrificial victims. Josephus says of Ahaz, "He also sacrificed his own son as a burnt offering to the idols according to the custom of the Canaanites." Archaeologists have found hundreds of urns containing the bones of children of from four to twelve years of age who had been burned alive.

The Greek writers who touched upon the subject of the history and customs of the Phoenicians and their colonies note with disgust the practice of child sacrifice. It was an established and prominent part of the religion of Carthage to burn children in a pit of fire. Albertus Pieters observes:

> It is interesting to note the statement in Josephus that the grand niece of Jezebel, about 20 years after the death of Jezebel's father, founded the city of Carthage in Northern Africa, the forces of which, under Hannibal, nearly overwhelmed Rome....Had Jezebel succeeded in Palestine and Hannibal in Italy, this faith might have overspread the world. The sword of Scipio Africanus and the faith of Elijah the Tishbite were strange allies, but the Lord used them both to save the world from such a fate.[3]

It is known that human sacrifices were offered by the Phoenicians during times of calamity, although there is no specific reference to them in Tyre itself. The annual Melkart festival at Tyre had much in common with Baal worship in other Canaanite communities. When the prolonged heat of the summer would burn everything up, Melkarth would offer himself a sacrifice to the sun in order to win the favor of heaven. During the month Peritius (February-March) the festival of the awakening, or resurrection of Melkarth was observed. Elijah's comment, "Cry aloud...peradventure he is sleeping and must be awaked" (I Kings 18:27) may be a reference to this belief.

Classified as a mystery cult by modern students of religion is the worship of Adonis, which became popular in Hellenistic times. Adonis was the son of Cinyras, mythical king of Byblos. He was the husband of Astarte or Ashtoreth. The legend relates that Adonis was hunting wild boar in the Lebanon mountains

A Phoenician deity.

3. Albertus Pieters, *Notes on Old Testament History*, p. 97.

when the animal which he was pursuing turned upon him and so gored his thigh that he died of the wound. From that time on he was mourned annually. At the time of the summer solstice, the anniversary of his death, all of the women of Byblos went in a wild procession to Aphaea in the Lebanon where his temple stood. There they wept and wailed on account of his death. The river which his blood had once stained turned red to show its sympathy with the mourners, and was thought to flow with his blood afresh. After the weeping had continued for a definite time, an image of the god was buried in the sacred temple precinct, bringing the mourning to an end. On the next day Adonis was supposed to return to life. His image was disinterred and carried back to the temple with music and dances. Wild orgies accompanied the rejoicing. Adonis at Byblos was the Phoenician counterpart of Tammuz, or Dumuzi, the Babylonian god of pasture and flocks, whose worship had reached Jerusalem (Ezek. 8:14). In the Babylonian epics, Tammuz dies in the autumn, when vegetation withers, departs to the underworld, and is recovered by the mourning Ishtar in time to return in the springtime to the fertilized upper-world.

Astarte figurine mold with a modern cast.

Cyrus H. Gordon, observing that Baal is god of dew as well as rain, asserts that there is no Canaanite seasonal pattern wherein Baal spends part of each year in the netherworld.[4] He sees, rather, a pattern in which years of plenty are followed by a year or more of famine. It is during the time of drought that Baal is presumed to be in the clutches of Mot (death). In either instance, however, the Biblical record stands out in marked contrast to the mythological interpretation of fertility which characterized the thought of ancient Canaan.

---

4. Cyrus H. Gordon, "Canaanite Mythology," in *Mythologies of the Ancient World,* edited by Samuel N. Kramer, pp. 183-217.

11

The Daily Lives
of the Patriarchs

Although the patriarchs are described as tent-dwellers, Scripture also makes it clear that Abraham had come from a city, Ur of the Chaldees in the Hebrew text of Genesis 11:31. Cyrus H. Gordon has suggested that Abraham was actually a merchant trader from a city of nothern Mesopotamia named Ura.[1] The merchants of Ura are known to have engaged in trade with Ugarit, along the Mediterranean coast.

When the Shechemites sought to form an alliance with the Israelites, they mentioned trade as part of the alliance terms: "You shall dwell with us, and the land shall be open to you; dwell and trade in it, and get property in it" (Gen. 24:10). Similarly Joseph, while testing the brothers who had sold him into slavery, asked them to bring Benjamin to him in Egypt, adding "then I shall know that you are not spies but honest men, and I will deliver to you your brother [i.e. Simeon], and you shall trade in the land" (Gen. 42:34).

Gordon summarizes the life of Abraham as follows: "Abraham comes from beyond the Euphrates, plies his trade in Canaan, visits Egypt, deals with Hittites, makes treaties with Philistines, forms military alliances with Amorites, fights kinglets from as far off as Elam, marries the Egyptian Hagar, etc. His contacts and freedom of movement reflect a sophisticated milieu where an international order . . . made such a career and such enterprise possible."

The patriarchs lived in tents, or "houses of hair" as they are called by desert Bedouin today. Goat's hair was hand-woven by the women into a very satisfactory cloth. Narrow strips were made on small looms, and then sewn together. Following the

---

1. Cyrus H. Gordon, "Abraham and the Merchants of Ura," *Journal of Near Eastern Studies,* XVII, 1, p. 30.

time of the shearing of the goats, old tents might be patched and new tents set up.

Tents varied in size, depending upon the number of people they were designed to accommodate. An average tent might cover a ten by fifteen foot area. It would be supported by nine poles, arranged in three rows. The middle row might be seven feet high, and the outer rows only six feet, creating a slope from the center.

The inside of the tent was divided into two compartments. The one used by the men served also as a reception room for guests. An inner room, used as the women's apartment, served also as a storage room for cooking pots and other utensils.

A wealthy family might have several tents. This would be of particular advantage in a family with more than one wife. It was probably from the seclusion of her own tent that Sarah heard the incredible report that she would bear a son in her old age (Gen. 18:10). When Isaac married Rebekah, the young lady who had come from Paddan-aram to be his bride, he took her into the tent of Sarah, his deceased mother (Gen. 24:67). Jacob seems to have had a large number of tents for his wives and servants. When Laban had overtaken Jacob seeking the idols which Rachel had stolen we read, "So Laban went into Jacob's tent, and into Leah's tent, and into the tent of the two maidservants, but he did not find them" (Gen. 31:33).

The interior of the tent had very simple furnishings. The soil itself was the floor of the tent. A few straw mats or woolen rugs would imply a degree of luxury. A sheet of metal or a few stones set up at the tent door would serve as a stove for cooking the daily supply of bread. Necessary items for preparing and storing food would include earthen vessels and goat-skin bottles for water, wine, and milk. When Abraham dismissed Hagar and Ishmael he, "rose early in the morning, and took bread and a skin of water, and gave it to Hagar" (Gen. 21:14).

During the day most of the activities of the household were conducted at the door of the tent. Abraham is depicted as sitting "at the door of his tent in the heat of the day" (Gen. 18:1) when three strangers approached. With characteristic Bedouin hospitality he ordered that water be brought to wash their feet and suggested that they rest under a nearby tree. Then the patriarch entered Sarah's tent, asking her to "Make ready, quickly, three measures of fine meal, knead it, and make cakes" (Gen. 18:6). He next chose a calf from the herd, and ordered a servant to prepare it. Abraham also took curds and milk and gave a hearty meal to his visitors (Gen. 18:1-8).

Bedouin tent encampment near the Dead Sea.

Milk was an important article in the diet of the patriarchs. We read of the milk of cows, sheep (Deut. 32:14), goats (Prov. 27:27), and camels (Gen. 32:15). The milk of camels is rich and strong, but not very sweet. It is prized today among nomadic Arabs.

The word which the Revised Standard Version renders "curds" in Genesis 18:8, has been traditionally translated "butter." Scripture usage, however, makes it clear that curdled milk is meant. This is still considered a delicacy among the Arabs. Milk is poured into a skin bottle which still contains sour clots from the previous milking. It is then shaken, and the result is the beverage which is known in Hebrew as ḥem'ah, "curds."

In addition to the meat of the calf which Abraham prepared for his guests, the patriarchs ate bullocks, lambs, kids (Gen. 27:8-9), and the flesh of game animals (Gen. 25:28). These might be boiled, roasted on hot stoves, or made into a stew. The food was served in the containers in which it was cooked.

The fruits of the land — figs, grapes, and dates — formed staple articles of diet in patriarchal times as they did later. Honey was also regarded as a delicacy, and it was so plentiful that Canaan was called the land "flowing with milk and honey" (Exod. 3:8). Honey was produced by bees from fruits and flowers and placed in the cells of a comb (cf. Psalm 19:10). Wild honey might be found in rocks (Deut. 32:13), in trees (I Sam. 14:25) and even in the carcass of an animal (Judg. 14:8). The term honey (Arabic *dibs*) is applied not only to the product of bees, but also to a man-made syrup produced from dates and grapes. Honey in both forms took the place of sugar (cf. Exod. 16:31).

When Jacob wished to send "the choice fruits of the land" to Egypt, we read that he gave to his sons, "a little balm and a little honey, gum, myrrh, pistachio nuts, and almonds" (Gen. 43:11). These were "luxury items" sent to Egypt in the hope that the rulers there would provide much needed grain for famine-stricken Canaan.

Although the patriarchs moved about the land of Canaan, the Scripture records make it clear that they practiced agriculture or, at least, maintained close relations with those who did. Bread ("cakes") was an essential item in the diet of the patriarchs (Gen. 19:3; 21:14; 27:17). As a matter of fact the patriarchs spent considerable periods of time in several of the places where they settled. Jacob is pictured as settled in the Hebron area at the time his sons pasture the flocks as far away as Shechem and Dothan (Gen. 37:12-17). Isaac sojourned in Gerar long enough to sow his seed and reap the harvest (Gen. 26:12). It was lack

A street scene in Hebron.

of grain that forced Jacob to send his sons to Egypt (Gen. 42:1-2).

Small quantities of grain could be prepared by the use of a pestle in a stone mortar (Lev. 2:14). For larger amounts, a mill was made, consisting of two circular stones, the upper of which could be rotated by hand while the lower remained stationary. This process produced the fine flour which was prized by the conscientious host (cf. Gen. 18:6). To make unleavened bread the flour was mixed with water and salt in a wooden kneading bowl (Exod. 8:3; 12:34).

The dough was formed into flat cakes, twelve to sixteen inches in diameter and one-eighth to one-quarter inch thick. To bake the bread a fire was built on a flat stone. When the stone was heated, the embers were raked off and the cake placed on the stone and covered with the embers and ashes. When one side was baked, the cake was turned over and the process repeated (cf. Hosea 7:8). Leavened bread was made by adding to the dough a lump saved from the previous baking. Many nomads carry a metal plate for baking which is placed over a fire built in a hole in the ground or over a fireplace in the corner of the tent.

For centuries the dress of the patriarchs was largely a matter of conjecture based upon the attire of nomadic Arabs who were observed in Bible lands in recent centuries. It was inferred that, since life in the East had not drastically changed over many centuries, Abraham probably looked very much like a modern sheikh of the desert.

Archaeology sometimes confirms the truthfulness of traditional ideas, and sometimes it gives them a rude jolt. The latter has been true of the concepts of dress during patriarchal times. We now have an actual painting, in color, from the tomb of an Egyptian nobleman at Beni Hasan, depicting a nomadic chieftain from Palestine with his retinue. It is dated during the nineteenth century B.C. and gives us an authentic picture of the way in which Canaanites dressed during patriarchal times.

Egyptians in the painting are wearing white linen loincloths, but the Asiastics are clothed in ornate embroidered garments. A number of the men wear striped skirts which reach from the waist to the knee. Other men, and all of the women wear a single piece garment, fastened at one shoulder, which reaches well below the knee. A little boy wears red shorts. The men wear sandals, but the women have a more substantial "boot." The clothing is made of wool which has been woven in many colors.

Paintings (ca. 1890 B.C.) from the Tomb of Khnemhotep, in Beni Hasan, Egypt, show the migration of Asiatics into Egypt.

The men in the painting are bearded, and most of them have throw-sticks or javelins. One has a bow and arrow and one, interestingly, a lyre (the Biblical "harp"). On a donkey they carry two pairs of goat-skin bellows which indicates that these traders also did metal work. A water-skin is on the back of the man playing the lyre.

The women have long hair and are clustered together. They are close to the children, two of whom are riding a donkey and one following behind.

12

Social and Business Life
in Patriarchal Times

Our most detailed description of life during patriarchal times comes from the city of Nuzi, or Nuzu, southeast of Nineveh. Clay tablets discovered there were written by Hurrian scribes in the Akkadian language about 1500 B.C. They reflect patterns of life which were characteristic of northeastern Mesopotamia during the period when the patriarchs and members of their families lived in Haran and the Paddan-aram area.

A large number of Nuzi documents deal with adoption. As in Israel, land could not be permanently alienated at Nuzi. A legal fiction could be devised, however, so that a man with money and insufficient land could be adopted by a man with land who needed money. Through the fiction of adoption, land could be transferred within the new "family." One Nuzi family amassed an enormous estate by means of these fictitious adoptions.

There were, of course, real adoptions at Nuzi. A childless family might adopt a son to insure the continuity of the family. The adopted son would show filial respect to his new parents during their lifetime, and care for the funeral rites at the time of their death. Adoption tablets carefully outline the duties and responsibilities of each party to the contract.

On occasion the Nuzi tablets mention the adoption of a beloved family servant, or slave. Such seems to have been the relationship between Abraham and Eliezer who apparently was "the elder of his house that ruled over all that he had" (Gen. 24:2). God made it clear to Abraham, however, that his heir would be a natural son, and not the servant Eliezer.

Adoption contracts usually provided for the possibility of the birth of a natural son into the family. In such cases the adopted son took a subordinate position to the natural son. After the birth of Ishmael, Eliezer would lose his priority in Abraham's family.

The conduct of Sarah in urging her husband to have sexual relations with Hagar (Gen. 16:2) is inexplicable by modern standards. The Nuzi tablets make it clear, however, that this was not true in ancient Mesopotamia. The prime purpose of marriage, at least from the legal point of view, was the procreation of children, and marriage contracts specified that a wife who did not provide her husband with offspring was obligated to provide a handmaid who would be able to do so. The position of the wife was often protected by a provision in the contract which stated that the handmaid was to continue as her slave. This provision was also part of the law code of Hammurabi of Babylon. The handmaid and her child were also protected, however. The lawful wife had no right to dismiss them from her household. After Hagar knew that she had conceived a child of Abraham, she showed a spirit of contempt for her mistress, but she was still reckoned the handmaid of Sarah (Gen. 16:6). Being harshly treated she fled from Sarah and headed toward Shur (a word meaning "wall," which probably refers to the wall which had been built by the Egyptians at the frontier of their country to keep out the Asiatic Bedouins). The Angel of the Lord met Hagar by a well and urged her to return home and submit herself to her mistress, Sarah. She did so, and in due time Ishmael was born and became Abraham's heir. God, however, appeared to Abraham and assured the patriarch that he would have a son by Sarah, his wife (Gen. 17:15-19). Ishmael, the prophecy stated, would become a great people, but the covenant blessing would continue through the line of Isaac (Gen. 17:20-21), the son who would be born to Sarah. After the birth of Isaac, Sarah wanted to expel Ishmael and his mother (Gen. 21:9, 10), but Abraham was grieved at the thought and only complied with his wife's request when God gave him a direct command to do so (Gen. 21:12).

That Sarah's action in providing Hagar as a handmaid for Abraham is not unusual in patriarchal times is clear from the subsequent conduct of Rachel and Leah. Unable to bear children herself, the beautiful Rachel suggested that Jacob have children by Bilhah, her maid (Gen. 29:3). In fact the children of Jacob (Israel) trace their ancestry to four mothers: Leah, Rachel (who subsequently bore two sons), and the two maids, Bilhah and Zilpah. Preference was shown to the sons of wives rather than handmaids. One of the prime causes of factions among Jacob's sons was the fact that they had different mothers. Joseph and Benjamin, the children of the beloved Rachel, were always their father's favorites.

Stone weights used by ancient tradesmen in Nineveh.

The relations between Jacob and Laban are also illustrated in the Nuzi tablets. At the time when Jacob arrived at Paddan-aram, Laban does not appear to have had any sons of his own. A man with daughters, but no sons, frequently adopted his son-in-law, who would assume filial obligations and become heir to the property of his wife's father. Laban appears to have adopted Jacob who had married his two daughters, Leah and Rachel. Later, however, we read of sons in the household of Laban, a fact which would remove Jacob from the favored position. When friction arose, Jacob, who had been cheated by Laban several times, determined to return to Canaan with his wives and property. While preparing to leave, Rachel, without Jacob's knowledge, stole the *teraphim*, or family idols, of Laban's household (Gen. 31:19, 34, 35). When he learned what had happened, Laban pursued the caravan indignantly asking, "Wherefore hast thou stolen my gods?" (Gen. 31:30). The significance of these "gods," or *teraphim,* is illustrated in the Nuzi tablets. They were not only regarded as "good luck" charms, but they also insured to their possessor rights to the family inheritance. Rachel, evidently, determined to secure for her husband the right to be Laban's chief heir in place of her brothers who would normally have taken the *teraphim*.

Inheritance was subject to transfer within the family at Nuzi. We read of a man who transferred a grove which he had inherited to his brother in return for three sheep. This forms a striking parallel to the conduct of Esau and Jacob. When hungry Jacob exclaimed, "Give me, I pray thee, some of that red pottage to eat . . . ," Jacob countered by demanding, "Sell me first thy birthright" (Gen. 25:30-34). Considering his birthright of little value, Esau exchanged it for the "mess of pottage" (cf. Heb. 12:16).

We also learn that oral blessings were considered binding in the courts at Nuzi. The sanctity of the word was highly regarded among the Israelites, who honored their word even when they were tricked into making pronouncements contrary to their real intent. After Jacob succeeded in fooling his father about his true identity, Isaac gave him the blessing intended for Esau. When the truth was learned, Isaac realized that he had given his blessing and would not go back on his word (Gen. 27:23). At a later time, Joshua honored his covenant with the Gibeonites even though he had been fooled by them into thinking that they had come from a distant land (Josh. 9). Court proceedings from Nuzi contain the record of an oral blessing similar to those pronounced by Jacob as he gathered his sons

This basalt panel from Beth-shan of the Late Bronze Age is an excellent example of Hittite workmanship.

at his deathbed (cf. Gen. 49). The blessing was mentioned, and the Nuzi court upheld it as legally binding.

Abraham's purchase of a burial plot from Ephron the Hittite has been explained as a result of a study of the Hittite Law Code by Manfred R. Lehman. The code, discovered at the ancient Hittite capital at Boghazkoy dates back to the fourteenth century B.C., but the laws it embodies are evidently much older. The law states that certain feudal services must be performed by the owner of a piece of real estate. If the land is transferred, the new owner must assume the feudal obligation. If, however, the new owner purchases only a portion of the property, feudal obligations continue for the former owner. Abraham specified that he wished to purchase only the cave at the edge of Ephron's field (Gen. 23:9). Ephron insisted, however, "I sell you the field, and I sell you the cave which is in it" (Gen. 23:11). He evidently saw the possibility of ridding himself of feudal obligations, and insisted that Abraham purchase the entire field, or none of it. Hittite business documents list the exact number of trees in each real estate transaction. The mention of the trees (Gen. 23:17) in connection with Abraham's purchase of Ephron's field conforms with this custom.

In making payment for the field we read that Abraham weighed out the price (coinage of money had not been invented), with the added note that the silver was "current money with the merchant" (Gen. 23:16). During the Patriarchal Age commercial men traveled extensively throughout the Fertile Crescent and in Asia Minor. Silver as a medium of exchange had to meet certain specifications to be "standard" for such business transactions.

With the spiritual concept of a covenant with God which included not only the individual but his "seed" or posterity, marriage was a solemn institution in the eyes of the Biblical patriarchs. The father would assume the responsibility for arranging a suitable marriage for his son. Particular care was taken that marriage with the idolatrous inhabitants of Canaan be avoided. Thus Abraham sent his servant to distant Paddan-aram to find a suitable bride for Isaac (Gen. 24). There were, of course, sons who did not submit to parental discipline in this respect. Esau grieved his father and mother by marrying, obviously without their consent, two native Hittite girls (Gen. 26:34). His brother Jacob, on the other hand, personally went to the Paddan-aram area where he chose his own bride — the lovely Rachel — although the crafty Laban tricked him into taking her less attractive sister first.

The father of a prospective bride was given a *mohar* (usually fifty shekels) which served as compensation for the loss of his daughter. This *mohar* was not necessarily paid in silver, for Jacob was able to exchange fourteen years of labor for Leah and Rachel (Gen. 29:20, 27, 30). Although the *mohar* was not, strictly speaking, regarded as a "bride price" in Israel, the custom evidently goes back to a time when brides were purchased. The law code of Eshnunna specified that a prospective groom pay "bride money" with the stipulation that it be returned to him with 20 percent interest in the event that the bride died.

Frequently the father of the bride bestowed gifts upon his daughter which would, practically speaking, result in a return of part of the *mohar*. Rebekah, Leah, and Rachel all brought female slaves with them when they left their father's home (Gen. 24:61; 29:23, 29).

The purpose of marriage in the ancient Near East was not to provide companionship, but rather to insure the survival of the family by the provision of male descendants. This is evident both in the Nuzi marriage contracts with their stipulation that a childless wife must provide an handmaid for her husband, and in the concept of levirate marriage where the next of kin must father a child for the man who died without issue.

The wife was an important member of the family, both as mother and worker. The romantic account of the choice of a bride for Isaac actually hinges on the willingness of the young lady to work hard. The sign which Abraham's servant posited as the means by which he would recognize the young lady of God's choice was simple and direct:

> Behold, I am standing by the spring of water, and the daughters of the men of the city are coming out to draw water. Let the maiden to whom I shall say, "Pray let down your jar that I may drink," and who shall say, "Drink, and I will water your camels" — let her be the one whom thou hast appointed for thy servant Isaac (Gen. 24:14).

Camels, of course, travel long without water, and when they are watered they drink large amounts. Rebekah took an exceptionally hard manual chore upon herself when she offered to bring water for the camels. This was interpreted as the sign that she was the girl for Isaac.

The settlement of the *mohar* payment was a decisive element in betrothal. Abraham's servant provided costly gifts for Rebekah's brother and her mother (Gen. 24:53) as well as the young lady herself. They all enjoyed a banquet (Gen. 24:54) after which the young lady herself was asked if she would go

A deer hunt as depicted in a Hittite relief.

to Canaan to become the wife of Isaac (Gen. 24:57). This may
not have been legally necessary but considerate parents then, as
now, would not ride roughshod over the desires of their children
in so important a matter.

Betrothal in antiquity was a more serious arrangement than
the modern concept of engagement. A woman who was found
to be unfaithful after betrothal was punished as an adulteress
(Deut. 22:23-27). If the bridegroom died before marriage could
be consummated, the girl was regarded as a member of his family
and had the rights and obligations imposed by the concept of
levirate marriage.

Levirate marriage was designed to perpetuate the name of
the deceased husband in Israel, and to keep his property intact
so that it could be passed on to the next generation. When a
man died without having fathered children, it was the obligation of his brother or next of kin to marry the widow. The first
son of the second marriage was reckoned by law to the first
husband, whose name he bore and whose property he inherited.

A vivid illustration of levirate marriage is presented in
Genesis 38. Judah obtained a girl named Tamar to be the wife
of his firstborn son, Er. When Er died without progeny, Tamar
was married to her husband's younger brother, Onan. He, too,
died childless, and Tamar was sent to her father's house to wait
until Judah's third son, Shelah, reached maturity.

Judah, however, seems to have hesitated to arrange for the
marriage of Shelah to Tamar. Perhaps he felt that she was in
some way responsible for the death of her first two husbands.
When Tamar suspected that Shelah was being withheld from
her, she determined to take things in her own hands. She disguised herself as a prostitute, seduced her father-in-law, Judah,
and in due time bore twin sons.

When Judah learned that his daughter-in-law was pregnant,
he was indignant at her evident infidelity. Confronted with the
evidence of what had actually happened, he had to admit, "She
is more in the right than I" (Gen. 38:26). While not condoning
the means she used in getting a son, he recognized that he had
been in the wrong in keeping Shelah from Tamar. We actually
learn from the Hittite code that when there was no brother-in-
law to perform the levirate duty, the father-in-law was responsible to do so.

Nuzi marriage contracts sometimes specify that the woman
purchased by a man for his son shall, if widowed, pass on to a
second and, if necessary, a third son. The custom also appears in

the Middle Assyrian and the Hittite law codes as well as in the Mosaic law (Deut. 25:5-10). It doubtless goes back to a period when a woman who was purchased in marriage belonged permanently to the family of the man who bought her.

We do not read of any wedding ceremony at the time of the patriarchs. The veiled bride was brought into the tent of her groom and they were regarded as man and wife (Gen. 24:22, 65). At a later time we read that Samson propounded a riddle to be solved within the "seven days of the feast" (Judg. 14:12) which served as a part of the marriage celebration. When responding to Jacob's protest that he had labored for Rachel and had received Leah instead, Laban replied, "Complete the week of this one, and we will give you the other also in return for serving me another seven years" (Gen. 29:27). Evidently Laban wished Jacob to go through with the week of festivities arranged for Leah's wedding, with the assurance that the matter of Jacob's desire for Rachel could then be given due attention. Marriage in patriarchal times, as now, should be a joyful time in which the blessings of God receive due recognition.

13

The God
Whom the Patriarchs Worshiped

The religious concepts of the patriarchs contain the germ of later Israelite and Christian faith. Their attitudes were unsophisticated, and the institutionalized elements of a religion with an established priesthood and a central sanctuary were in the distant future. The Bible teaches us that the ancestors of the patriarchs were idolators (Josh. 24:2, 14). Names such as Terah and Laban (both derived from words for the moon) suggest that the moon god was worshiped at one time. The fact that the Sumerian moon god, Nanna, was the patron deity of both Ur and Haran is consistent with this suggestion.

A variety of names for the God worshiped by the patriarchs appears in the book of Genesis. Sometimes the deity is specifically related to his worshiper. On the basis of this fact, Albrecht Alt has suggested that each of the patriarchs had a separate cult in which the deity had a name compounded with the personal name of his worshiper: The Shield of Abraham (Gen. 15:1); the Fear (*paḥad*) of Isaac (Gen. 31:42, 53; Albright translates "Kinsman of Isaac"); and the Champion (or Strong One) of Jacob (Gen. 49:24). According to Alt these deities were originally regarded as separate entities but they were subsequently fused into the concept of Yahweh, the God of Israel.

Although this scheme is widely followed today, it actually says little about the ancestral faith of the Israelites. The Biblical text itself contains no hint that each Israelite regarded his own deity as one god among many. There are, on the contrary, amazing instances in which the gods of others are identified with the God they worshiped.

After rescuing Lot from a confederation of eastern kings who had conquered and despoiled Sodom, Abraham paid a visit to Salem where he paid tithes to the priest-king of the city, Melchizedek. Although there is no hint that the two had ever met before, Abraham recognized Melchizedek as a true priest. Yet Melchizedek was a priest of El Elyon ("God most high") who, he declared, had given Abraham victory over his enemies (Gen. 14:20). Later, Abraham reported that he had made a vow to Yahweh-El Elyon (Gen. 14:22; R.S.V. renders the name "The Lord God Most High"). This is a clear instance of a fusion of two divine names which Abraham appears to have done consciously because he could identify the two names as representative of one deity. The patriarch could recognize the validity of Melchizedek's ministry even though he used a different name for God from that usually employed by Abraham.

It is quite possible that Abraham shared many of the erroneous views concerning religious matters which characterized the age in which he lived. The fact that he received a revelation from God did not render him omniscient. It was the faith of Abraham, however, augmented by subsequent revelation, which became the basis for all subsequent Jewish, Christian, and even Moslem thought.

The differences between the faith of Abraham, and that of the Canaanites among whom he lived, can hardly be exaggerated, however. Their religion was based on the cult of Baal, a fertility god, and had, as a practical purpose, the insuring of the fertility of the fields, man, and beast. Abraham's faith had a historical basis. God had entered history and issued a call which Abraham was bound to obey.

The relationship between Abraham and the God he worshiped was based on the concept of covenant. It is known that covenant formed an important element in the social and political life of the ancient Near East. In nomadic societies we often find clans regularizing their relations with one another by means of a covenant (cf. Gen. 31:44-54).

George Mendenhall of the University of Michigan has made a study of covenants in the ancient Near East during the second millennium B.C. They are found to fall into two categories: the parity treaty (between equals), and the suzerainty treaty (between a king and his vassals). The treaty between Jacob and Laban, in which each agreed to honor a stated frontier, would be classed as a parity treaty. The covenant between Yahweh and Israel, however, would be a suzerainty treaty. God is recognized as the gracious yet all-powerful King of his people, and they are expected to obey his command.

Genesis 15 contains the record of a ceremony by which God and Abraham entered into solemn covenant relationships. Abraham was instructed to cut in two a number of animals and place the halves opposite one another. After the sun had set, the divine Presence in the form of "a smoking fire pot and a flaming torch" passed between the pieces (Gen. 15:17). In this way God was depicted in the act of ratifying the covenant. The terms of the covenant were actually very simple. God identified himself as the One who had brought Abraham from Ur of the Chaldees to give to him the land of Canaan, and Abraham was promised a progeny comparable in number to the stars in heaven.

The covenant between God and Abraham would be, in Mendenhall's terminology, a suzerainty treaty. It finds its origin in the will of the suzerain (God) who recounts his gracious acts (taking Abraham from Ur) and declares his purposes with reference to Abraham. The patriarch is expected to exercise faith in the divine promise.

Mendenhall's studies have particular reference, however, to the Mosaic Law, which is presented in terms which frequently form an exact parallel to ancient suzerainty treaties. Some scholars, considering the Mosaic formulation the first such covenant in Israelite history, have argued that the Biblical references to covenants in the Patriarchal Age are a retrojection of concepts which were held at a later time. There are important differences between the two, however. The patriarchal covenants are personal in nature, and largely future in fulfillment, demanding only the trust of the worshiper. The Sinai covenant was based on a past act of redemption (the Exodus from Egypt) and embodied a full legal formulation. It was addressed to the entire Israelite people.

Covenant solidarity between God and his people is illustrated by the names used by the Israelites and their northwest Semitic neighbors. Many such names begin with Ab (father), Aḥ (brother) and Amm (people, or family). A name such as Eliezer ("my God is a help") may be compared with Abiezer ("my [divine] Father is a help"). An Israelite prophet actually bore the name Ahijah ("my brother is Yahweh"). A generation which stresses the transcendence of God may find such names unduly familiar, but they do illustrate the conception of kinship between a man and his deity which was characteristic of the patriarchal faith.

14

The Patriarchal Institutions

Formal aspects of patriarchal religion were surprisingly few. The patriarchs are presented to us as men of prayer, and they habitually build altars on which sacrifices are made to God. No details are given concerning the nature of the sacrifices, however, and the head of the family uniformly acted as his own priest. Job, whose life has much in common with the patriarchs, is dipicted as arising early in the morning and offering burnt offerings for his children (Job 1:5).

1. Prayer

Prayer is expressive of an attitude of dependence upon the Lord. The fact that, in the days of Seth, "men began to call upon the name of the Lord" (Gen. 4:26), implies that there have been times and places where prayer and worship have been neglected. Prayer is, in its very essence, fellowship with God. When sin mars that fellowship we find man hiding from his Creator (Gen. 3:10). The absence of prayer marks a secular individual or society.

During the age of the Biblical patriarchs, prayer formed a most important part of life. Although frequently associated with sacrifice (Gen. 12:8; 13:4), prayer was not a formalized rite but rather a free, spontaneous communication between man and his God. It was a dialogue in which we meet argumentation as well as conversation.

Not only was there no set form of words, but the prayers of the patriarchs could be offered from a variety of postures. When Abraham received word of the impending judgment on Sodom he "stood before the Lord" (Gen. 18:22) and talked with Him as a man might talk to his associate. The servant who had been sent to Paddan-aram to find a suitable wife for Isaac, when con-

A worshiper kneels before his god, from Larsa.

scious that God had prospered his journey, "bowed his head and worshiped the Lord" (Gen. 24:26). He showed a spirit of humble thankfulness to the God who had met his need and that of his master.

Sometimes we are surprised at the fact that the patriarchs actually argue or talk back to God. When God addressed Abraham with the words, "Fear not . . . your reward shall be very great," the patriarch replied, "O Lord God, what wilt thou give me, for I continue childless . . ." (Gen. 15:1-2). The promises of God seemed idle to Abraham because he had no heir, and the patriarch did not hesitate to make the fact known to God. Thereupon, we read, the Lord brought Abraham out into the oriental night and said, "Look toward heaven, and number the stars, if you are able to number them. So shall your descendants be," was the assurance which Abraham accepted by faith. God, we are told, "reckoned it to him for righteousness" (Gen. 15:5-6).

Much of the prayer mentioned in the patriarchal records is in the form of intercession. When God told Abraham that Sarah, his wife, would give birth to a son, the patriarch's response was a supplication, "Oh that Ishmael might live before thee" (Gen. 17:18). God made it clear that Ishmael would be blessed in his own way (Gen. 17:20-21), but that the covenant blessing would continue through the line of Isaac (Gen. 17:19).

The declaration that Sodom was to be destroyed, brought a petition from Abraham that it be spared if fifty righteous men could be found in the city (Gen. 18:24-25). Abraham argued that God must do "right" since He is the Judge of all the earth, implying that it would not be "right" for the righteous to perish with the wicked. God replied that the city would be spared if as few as ten righteous men could be found in Sodom (Gen. 18:32). Although ten could not be found, the one righteous family, that of Lot, was removed from the city before destruction came (Gen. 19:15-29). The subsequent tragedies in Lot's experience do not alter the lesson of God's righteousness shown in the deliverance of the family of Lot before the destruction of Sodom.

When Abimelech of Gerar learned that Sarah, whom he had taken for himself, was actually Abraham's wife, he was understandably disturbed. God's comforting word to Abimelech included an assurance of the efficacy of prayer: "Restore the man's wife; for he is a prophet, and he will pray for you, and you shall live" (Gen. 20:7). Abraham is known as the "friend of God" (cf. II Chron. 20:7) and his intercession could be counted on to bring a blessing to Abimelech and his household.

Prayer in the patriarchal records frequently expresses dependence upon God for daily mercies. On his journey to Paddan-aram, Abraham's servant prayed, "O Lord, God of my master Abraham, grant me success today" (Gen. 24:12). Abraham had sent him to find a suitable bride for Isaac, and the servant sought divine wisdom on so important an undertaking. Later, when arrangements were being made to take Rebekah back to Canaan, he testified, "The Lord has prospered my way" (Gen. 24:56).

Vows and prayers were often closely related. At Bethel, Jacob, fleeing from the brother he had wronged, saw a vision of a ladder which reached from earth to heaven, and heard the voice of the Lord saying, "I am the Lord, the God of Abraham your father and the God of Isaac; the land on which you lie will I give to you and to your descendants" (Gen. 28:11-13). The Lord further promised to be with Jacob during his journeys and to bring him back safely to the land of Canaan. Humbled, yet encouraged at this awesome experience, Jacob arose the next morning and vowed, "If God will be with me, and will keep me in this way that I go, and will give me bread to eat and clothing to wear, so that I come again to my father's house in peace, then the Lord shall be my God" (Gen. 28:20-22).

Sometimes fear is a factor in prayer. The consciousness of a lack of ability to cope with the circumstances of life may cause us to seek the face of God in prayer. During the years which Jacob spent in Paddan-aram, Esau, whom he had defrauded, was a hazy memory. As Jacob moved toward Canaan again, the possibility of an encounter with his brother became a fearful prospect. In anguish he prayed, "O God of my father Abraham, and God of my father Isaac, O Lord who didst say to me, 'Return to your country and to your kindred, and I will do you good,' I am not worthy of the least of all the steadfast love and all the faithfulness which thou hast shown to thy servant, for with only my staff I have crossed this Jordan; and now I have become two companies. Deliver me, I pray thee, from the hand of my brother, from the hand of Esau...." (Gen. 32:9-12).

This prayer was in part answered during a strange nocturnal experience on the shore of the Jabbok when Jacob, alone, wrestled with a "man" (Gen. 32:24). During the encounter Jacob sought, and received, a blessing and a new name (Israel) from the stranger whom he identified with God Himself (Gen. 32:30).

2. Sacrifice

The concept of sacrifice, regularized by the Mosaic law, appears on the earliest pages of Scripture. Cain and Abel each offered a *minḥah* ("offering") to the Lord, although only that of Abel was accepted (Gen. 4:3-5). This serves as a reminder that the presentation of a sacrifice was never accounted meritorious in itself. The spirit of the worshiper was most important. Isaiah as the spokesman of God cried out to his generation, "I have had enough of burnt offerings of rams and the fat of fed beasts; I do not delight in the blood of bulls, or of lambs, or of he-goats.... Bring no more vain oblations" (Isa. 1:11-13).

The abuse of sacrifice, however, did not mean that its use was not encouraged under the Old Testament economy. Man, in his sacrifice, presented a portion of his own property to the God who is the author of every perfect gift. In the choice of the sacrifice man chose a gift which he deemed fit to present to God. Under the Levitical laws (Lev. 1:1-7:37) the appropriate sacrifices for various occasions and individuals were prescribed.

Following the flood we read that Noah offered *'oloth*, "burnt offerings" to the Lord. As its name implies, the burnt offering was slain and then totally burned on an altar. The worshiper thus gave a portion of his property and, in a sense, of himself to God. The very death of the victim may be a reminder, as it certainly was on the Day of Atonement (Lev. 16:1-22), that the worshiper is worthy of death, and that God is pleased to accept the life of the slain beast as a substitute for the sinner who has broken the divine law.

Sacrifice was a regular part of the worship of Abraham and the Israelite patriarchs. After the theophany at Shechem, in which God said, "Unto thy seed will I give this land," we read that Abraham "built there an altar unto the Lord" (Gen. 12:7). Later altars were built at Bethel (Gen. 12:8; 13:18).

After his unpleasant experiences with Abimelech of Gerar, Isaac settled at Beer-sheba where again we read of a theophany. God identified himself as "the God of Abraham," and assured Isaac of divine protection and the fact that his "seed" would be multiplied (Gen. 26:24). As his father Abraham had done, Isaac "built an altar there and called upon the name of the Lord" (Gen. 26:25).

Laban was angered at the departure of Jacob from Paddan-aram. He pursued the patriarch as far as to Mizpah where a satisfactory settlement was reached. Laban accepted the fact that Jacob, with his wives, children, and possessions, was returning

Goat eating leaves. This figure from Ur (ca. 2500 B.C.) has been compared to the "ram caught in the thicket" (Gen. 22:13), but it predates the time of Abraham by at least five hundred years.

home to Canaan, and suggested that the two men make a covenant of peace. In concluding the terms of their covenant, "Jacob offered a sacrifice on the mountain and called his kinsmen to eat bread; and they ate bread and tarried all night on the mountain" (Gen. 31:54).

After the sad experience at Shechem, where Simeon and Levi killed the Shechemites because of the defilement of Dinah, their sister, Jacob heard the voice of God saying, "Arise, go up to Bethel, and dwell there and make there an altar to the God who appeared to you when you fled from your brother Esau" (Gen. 35:1). Subsequently Jacob and his sons moved to Bethel where they built an altar which they named, "El Beth-el" ("God of the House of God"). In this way they commemorated the grace of God in bringing them safely back to Bethel.

We subsequently read of an altar built at Beer-sheba where Jacob "offered sacrifices to the God of his father Isaac" (Gen. 46:1). Here God appeared to the patriarch and directed that he go down with his sons to Egypt where Joseph had become Vizier (Prime Minister).

Adolphe Lods, in his work *Israel from its Beginnings to the Middle of the Eighth Century,* says concerning the pre-Mosaic Israelites, "their religion must already have contained, even if in a somewhat barbarous and elementary form, the greater part of the rites which were later codified in the Levitical law."[1] Although the term "barbarous" would be more applicable to the Canaanites than to Israel, the Scriptures make it clear that faith and Law long antedate Moses and Sinai.

Abraham's journey with Isaac to Mount Moriah marks an important chapter in the concept of sacrifice. To Micah's question, "Shall I give my first-born for my transgression, the fruit of my body for the sin of my soul?" (Micah 6:7), the Scripture answers, "No." As late as the time of Jeremiah, the Judaeans, "built the high places of Baal to burn their sons in the fire" (Jer. 19:5). This had been prohibited by the Law (cf. Lev. 20:1-5). When Abraham had taken Isaac to Mount Moriah, ready to offer his own son on a stone altar, God said, "Do not lay your hand on the lad" (Gen. 22:12), and a ram caught in a nearby thicket served as a substitute. Although individuals under pagan influence frequently lapsed into heathen practices, the prophets of Israel consistently denounced human sacrifice.

This reconstructed pillar at Shechem was originally erected in the forecourt of the fortress-temple that dates back to the fifteenth century B.C., the time of the Patriarchs.

---

1. Adolphe Lods, *Israel from its Beginnings to the Middle of the Eighth Century,* p. 277.

Just as there are certain points which the moral law of the Old Testament has in common with contemporary law codes of the Fertile Crescent lands, so we find certain ceremonial laws in use at ancient Ugarit which have a resemblance to those of the Mosaic Law. The Ugaritic documents (15th and 14th centuries B.C.) speak of a Burnt Offering, a Whole Burnt Offering, a Guilt Offering, and a Peace Offering.

It should be remembered, however, that the Mosaic law did not originate the concept of sacrifice in Israel. As in the instance of the moral law, much of the ceremonial law recorded in Exodus and Leviticus is actually a codification of practices which had been observed from much earlier times. Sacrifice was in use at the earliest levels of Biblical history and was a normal occurrence during the Patriarchal Age.

3. Circumcision

The rite of circumcision became the sign of the covenant between the Lord and Abraham. Physically it involved the removal of the foreskin of the male organ of reproduction. Spiritually it became the sign which designated the individual who had associated himself with the people of Israel.

The rite of circumcision was practiced by many peoples of antiquity, usually at the time of puberty. The fact that it was often regarded as a preparation for marriage may be inferred from the fact that the Semitic word for bridegroom (ḥathen) literally means "circumcised," and the corresponding word for father-in-law (hothen) literally means "he who circumcises." Among the neighbors of Israel who practiced circumcision in ancient times were the Edomites, Ammonites, Moabites, and Egyptians. The "uncircumcised Philistine" was, of course, an exception.

Among the Israelites, circumcision was practiced on the eighth day of a child's life (Gen. 17:12). All male Israelites, including slaves, were circumcised, as were any foreigners who might wish to be associated with Israel in the observance of the Passover (Exod. 12:48). Thus circumcision became the external mark of citizenship in Israel.

Circumcision marked Israel as the covenant people of the Old Testament economy. It was established as a covenant sign to Abraham who was to become, according to divine promise, "a great nation" and through whom, it was stated, "all the families of the earth will bless themselves" (Gen. 12:2-3). The practice of the rite from generation to generation served as a continuing reminder of the promises of God and of his constant faithfulness.

Circumcision, like sacrifices, could be rendered meaningless if it was reduced to a mere ritual. Jeremiah complained of his generation that "all the house of Israel is uncircumcised in heart" (Jer. 9:26). Similarly the book of Deuteronomy, after recounting the fearful consequences of disobedience to the Law of the Lord, speaks of a day when Israel will be restored: "And the Lord your God will circumcise your heart and the heart of your offspring, so that you will love the Lord your God with all your heart and with all your soul, that you may live" (Deut. 30:6).

15

The Theology
of the Patriarchs

The Bible student who reads the patriarchal records (Gen. 12-50) is aware of the fact that the men whose lives it records were not given to philosophical speculation. There is no hint of a "systematic theology" in the sense in which that term is now used. The concern of the patriarchs was with a God who had revealed himself to them, and with their response to that revelation. God was not a remote "first cause" to be believed or rejected, but a Person who was as real as any member of the family.

Although God was in a very personal sense "the God of Abraham," the patriarch saw in Him a God whose interests far exceeded any tribal limitations. He was "maker of heaven and earth" (Gen. 14:19) and he purposed to bring blessing to "all the families of the earth" (Gen. 12:3). Abraham thought in terms of the laws of nature when he questioned the possibility of having a son because of his own advanced age and that of Sarah, his wife. When Sarah incredulously exclaimed, "Shall I indeed bear a child now that I am old?" (Gen. 18:13), God replied with a question, "Is anything too hard for the Lord?" (Gen. 18:14).

God's omnipotence was also evident during Abraham's sojourn in Egypt. The patriarch had lied concerning the true identity of Sarah with the thought that he might save his own life by so doing (Gen. 12:10-16). When Pharaoh took Sarah, purposing to add her to his harem, "the Lord afflicted Pharaoh and his house with great plagues" (Gen. 12:17). The patriarchs learned that God was omnipotent, and that his purposes were sure because there was no limit to his power.

The omniscience of God is also constantly before us in the patriarchal records. He knows the future, and can tell in advance of the birth of Isaac to Sarah (Gen. 17:19). Although, in

4 8636

the language of anthropomorphism, God is pictured as coming down to investigate the sins of Sodom and Gomorrah (Gen. 18:21), it is clear that He does this because of His knowledge that "their sin is very grave" (Gen. 18:20). The "investigation" does not reflect upon his knowledge, but rather emphasizes his justice. As a human judge must secure all the facts before passing sentence, so the "Judge of all the earth" will surely "do right" (Gen. 18:25).

The judgment on the city of Sodom reflects the holiness and justice of God. This was not an act of impatience, or a severe punishment for a minor offense. The record states that "the outcry against Sodom and Gomorrah is great, and their sin is very grave" (Gen. 18:20). When Lot provided hospitality for the two "angels" who came to Sodom, we read that "the men of the city . . . both young and old, all the people to the last man, surrounded the house" (Gen. 19:4) and sought carnal relations with them.

The justice of God is tempered, however, with mercy. Had there been ten righteous men in Sodom, the city would have been spared (Gen. 18:32). God appeared to the fugitive Jacob at Bethel with the assurance, "Behold, I am with you and will keep you wherever you go, and will bring you back to this land" (Gen. 28:15). When he was about to offer his son as a sacrifice, Abraham heard the voice of God saying, "Do not lay your hand on the lad or do anything to him" (Gen. 22:12). The ram in the thicket became the offering, and Isaac was set free.

When Abraham's servant met Rebekah by a well in distant Paddan-aram, he testified saying, "The Lord has led me in the way to the house of my master's kinsmen" (Gen. 24:27). The patriarchs were conscious of a God who directed their every step. This did not result in a neglect of attention to secondary causes. It is clear that Jacob had to flee from Canaan because of the wrath of Esau, whom he had defrauded of the birthright (Gen. 27:41-45). Yet Jacob was assured of the continuing presence of God in his journeys (Gen. 28:15).

Cause and effect are clearly seen in the story of Joseph. The fact that Joseph was the favored son quite understandably made his brethren jealous. The jealousy reached a climax when they determined to murder him and then, through the counsel of Judah, sold him into slavery instead. From the human point of view, Joseph went to Egypt because of the jealousy of his brothers and their sinful determination to get rid of him.

Parallel to the story of the sinful purposes of the brethren is the story of the gracious purposes of God: "The Lord was

with Joseph, and he became a successful man" (Gen. 39:2).
God's providence was frequently hidden, however. After arising
to a place of trust in Potiphar's household, Joseph was the object of false witness, accused of immorality, and consigned to
prison. Even this, however, is interpreted as a part of the sovereign purposes of God, and we still read, "the Lord was with
him, and whatever he did, the Lord made it to prosper" (Gen.
39:23).

When called upon to interpret Pharaoh's dream, Joseph provided the counsel which made it possible for Egypt to have food
during a time of famine. Other peoples, including Joseph's own
brethren, looked to Egypt for deliverance from starvation. In
making himself known to his brethren, Joseph said, ". . . do not
be distressed or angry with yourselves, because you sold me here;
for God sent me before you to preserve life. . . . So it was not you
who sent me here, but God. . . ." (Gen. 45:4-8). Joseph was able
to look behind the sinful intent of his brothers and see his presence in Egypt as part of the purpose of an all-powerful, all-gra-
cious God.

Although the patriarchal period antedates the Mosaic Law,
there is no lack of concern about the heinousness of sin. The
destruction of Sodom (Gen. 19) illustrated God's attitude
toward sin.

An important principle concerning sin is expressed at the
time of the ratification of God's covenant with Abraham (Gen.
15:7-21). The descendants of Abraham would one day possess
the land of Canaan, but the patriarch, himself, would not live
to see that time. The reason for the delay in giving the land
to Abraham is stated in the words, ". . . the iniquity of the
Amorites is not yet complete" (Gen. 15:16). The statement is
prophetic, implying that one day (and, in the context, specifically, in "the fourth generation"), the sins of the inhabitants
of Canaan will be such that God will drive them out and give
their land to Israel. The further principle that expulsion would
result only when the sin proved incorrigible illustrates the long-
suffering of God with sinful mankind.

Man, in the patriarchal records, is a creature wholly dependent
on and subject to God. The command to Abraham was, "Walk
before me and be blameless" (Gen. 17:1). This meant that the
patriarch had to leave home and loved ones, and wander in a
foreign country (Gen. 12:1). Abraham had to dismiss the beloved Ishmael (Gen. 17:18; 20:10-14), and, subsequently, he was
directed to offer Isaac as a sacrifice on Mount Moriah (Gen.
22:1-14).

The promises to the patriarchs were largely of a material nature. God promised to Abraham countless descendants (Gen. 15:5) who would have great possessions (Gen. 15:14), including the entire land of Canaan (Gen. 13:14-17). This is called "the land of promise" (Heb. 11:9), because Abraham did not personally live to see his descendants possess it. Abraham was but a sojourner, looking with the eye of faith to the time when God's purposes would be fulfilled.

Little is said concerning the attitude of the patriarchs to life beyond the grave. Of Abraham we read that he "died in a good old age, an old man and full of years, and was gathered to his people" (Gen. 25:7). When Jacob received evidence that convinced him of the death of Joseph, he said, ". . . I shall go down to Sheol, to my son, mourning" (Gen. 37:35). Not until the death and resurrection of Christ do we find the full-orbed doctrine of resurrection which elicited the confident outcry of Paul, "To me to live is Christ, and to die is gain" (Phil. 1:21).

The faith of the patriarchs was oriented toward the future. Although promised the entire land of Palestine, Abraham owned no real estate except the parcel of ground which he purchased from Ephron the Hittite (Gen. 23:3-16).

Promises concerning the future were related to the idea of a "seed" or descendants through whom blessing would flow to all families of the earth (Gen. 12:1-3). There is, indeed, within the patriarchal records both a particularistic and a universalistic strain. The particularistic was immediate — the line of the faithful must not intermarry with the wicked Canaanites (Gen. 24:1-4). The grounds were religious, however, and not racial. If Israel felt an obligation to maintain separation from her neighbors it was, ideally at least, because she was conscious of a God-given mission which required absolute separation from idolatry and all forms of heathen religious life. During the later Exodus period this was made explicit: "You shall not do as they do in the land of Egypt, where you dwelt, and you shall not do as they do in the land of Canaan, to which I am bringing you" (Lev. 18:3). Pre-exilic Israel tended to forget this injunction, until things became so bad that Jeremiah cried out, ". . . as many as your cities are your gods, O Judah" (Jer. 2:28).

The universalistic strain of patriarchal faith is an advance beyond anything we know in the ancient world. We not only meet the general statements of blessings to the families of the earth, but we read specifically of blessings upon non-Israelite peoples. When God made it clear that Isaac, not Ishmael, would be the child of the covenant line, a blessing was also pronounced upon Ishmael: "I will bless him and make him fruitful and multiply him exceedingly; he shall be the father of twelve princes, and I will make him a great nation" (Gen. 17:20).

The blessing which Isaac meant for Esau fell, by trickery, on Jacob, with the result that little was left for Esau. Yet even here we read a kind of negative blessing: "By your sword you shall live, and you shall serve your brother; but when you break loose you shall break his yoke from your neck" (Gen. 27:40). Esau would be subject to Jacob, or, translated into later political history, Edom would be subject to Israel (later to Judah, the southern kingdom), but the Edomites would regain their freedom. The prophet Obadiah describes the way in which proud, independent Edom stood aloof while the Babylonians plundered Judah and Jerusalem.

The covenant line of the patriarchs — Abraham, Isaac, and Jacob — was distinct, but Ishmael and Esau became great peoples. From Jacob our covenant line breaks into twelve parts, one of which (Levi) becomes the priestly tribe and another (Judah) becomes the tribe of King David. Each of the tribes is considered a part of Israel, however, and the covenant made at Mount Sinai embodies all.

It is beyond even these, however, that the blessings of Abraham ultimately reach. The patriarchs did not fill in the details concerning the nature of their hope. Their descendants would go to Egypt (Gen. 15:13), but they would return and, in some future day, the "seed" of Abraham would bring blessing which would transcend all tribal boundaries and reach to all mankind.

It was this patriarchal blessing which was in the mind of the New Testament writers who stressed the relationship of Jesus to Abraham. In Matthew's genealogy, Jesus is linked with David, the king, and with Abraham, to whom the promise of blessing was first given (Matt. 1:1). Jesus is thus presented as the Messianic king and the promised "seed of Abraham."

The apostle Paul insists that "in Christ Jesus the blessing of Abraham [has] come upon the gentiles" (Gal. 3:14). He looks upon the promise of blessing through Abraham's "seed" as finding its ultimate fulfillment not simply in the large number of descendants of Abraham, but in the one "seed" of Abraham — Jesus Christ — through whom blessings were mediated to "all families of the earth." Indeed the non-Jew may actually, by faith, be blessed with Abraham, the man of faith (Gal. 3:9). In this latter sense it is the spiritual relationship of the individual to

Abraham that is meaningful, and all "families of the earth" may actually account themselves one with Abraham on the basis of faith in the promises of God.

16

The Patriarchs
and Divine Revelation

The Epistle to the Hebrews begins with the assertion that it was "at sundry times and in divers manners" that God spoke to the fathers (Heb. 1:1). The writer was stressing the fact that Jesus is God's final revelation, and that the revelations of the Old Testament economy were, of necessity, incomplete. He affirms, however, that the partial revelations through the prophets were, indeed, the Word of God.

The patriarchal records consistently presuppose a God who speaks to his children. Stephen, testifying before a Jewish High Priest, said, ". . . the God of glory appeared to our father Abraham, when he was in Mesopotamia, before he lived in Haran, and said to him, Depart from your land and from your kindred and go into the land which I will show you" (Acts 7:2).

Often the patriarchal narrative mentions the fact of revelation, with no clue as to the means by which it is accomplished. When we read that, "the Lord said to Abram, go from your country and your kindred, and your father's house" (Gen. 12:1), we are not told whether God spoke in a dream, a vision, an audible voice, or a theophany. The fact, rather than the means, of revelation is stressed.

Subsequently, however, we read that the Lord "appeared" to Abraham (Gen. 12:7). Such appearances were sometimes associated with visible manifestations. In ratifying the covenant with Abraham, we read, "behold, a smoking fire pot and a flaming torch passed between these pieces" (Gen. 15:17). God, in the form of fire, consumed the sacrifice which Abraham had offered to seal the covenant.

The close relationship between Abraham and his God is reflected in the description of the patriarch as "the friend of God" (James 2:23). The Arabs have named him *El-Khalil* ("the friend").

The term theophany is frequently used in describing visible appearances of God to man. In Genesis 17:1 we read that the Lord "appeared" to Abram, changed his name to Abraham, promised the land of Canaan as an inheritance to his descendants, and established circumcision as the sign of the covenant. He further declared that Sarai, whose name was changed to Sarah, would bear a son who would become Abraham's heir. The account of the theophany closes with the words, "When he had finished talking with him, God went up from Abraham" (Gen. 17:22). The episode presupposes that Abraham and his God speak face to face.

The appearance of three "men" at the door of Abraham's tent (Gen. 18:2), caused the patriarch to make elaborate preparation for their entertainment. He was not aware, of course, that the Lord was appearing in this way (Gen. 18:1). One of these "men" prophesied that Sarah would give birth to a son (Gen. 18:10). Before leaving, the Lord (evidently to be identified as one of the "men"), told Abraham of impending judgment upon Sodom (Gen. 18:17). Thereupon Abraham interceded on behalf of the wicked city, praying that it might be spared if as few as ten righteous men might be found there (Gen. 18:22-32). Then we read, "And the Lord went his way when he had finished speaking to Abraham, and Abraham returned to his place (Gen. 18:33).

We read of subsequent appearances of God to Isaac, warning him not to go to Egypt (Gen. 26:2) and assuring him of protection and blessing (Gen. 26:34). When Jacob was sleeping at Bethel, he dreamed of a ladder which reached from earth to heaven. Above the ladder he saw a theophany. The One who spoke identified himself as the God of Abraham and Isaac, and assured Jacob that the land of Canaan would become the inheritance of his descendants (Gen. 28:13). Many years later, Jacob testified, "God almighty appeared to me at Luz in the land of Canaan, and blessed me" (Gen. 48:3).

The term "angel of the Lord" is frequently used to describe the characteristic form of theophany during the patriarchal period. When Hagar was fleeing from Sarah she met the Angel of the Lord, who commanded her to return to her mistress. The angel told Hagar she would give birth to a son, Ishmael, who would be a strong, outdoor man (the term "wild ass of a man" is not an insult). Hagar identified the Angel with God himself, and returned as she had been commanded (Gen. 16:1-14).

After Abraham had shown his willingness to offer Isaac on Mount Moriah, we read that "the angel of the Lord called to him from heaven" (Gen. 22:11), commanding him to spare the lad. Abraham offered a ram which had been found caught in a nearby thicket, and Isaac was set free. Then, we read, "the angel of the Lord called to Abraham a second time from heaven" (Gen. 22:15) assuring him that his descendants would be a means of blessing to "all the nations of the earth."

Jacob's years at Paddan-aram are not marked by any communication with God but, at the close of that period, when concerned about problems rising from the jealousy of Laban's sons, we read that the "angel of the Lord" spoke to him in a dream, identifying Himself as the God of Bethel, and commanding Jacob to return to the land of his birth (Gen. 31:11-13). In old age, looking back over the joys and heartaches of life, Jacob spoke of "the God who has led me all my life long to this day, the angel who has redeemed me from all evil" (Gen. 48:15-16).

The term "angel of the Lord" or "angel of God" appears to be used, in some contexts at least, as a synonym for God Himself. Geerhardus Vos in his *Biblical Theology* suggests: "If the Angel sent were Himself partaker of the godhead, then He could refer to God as his sender, and at the same time speak as God, and in both cases there would be reality back of it. Without this much of what we call the Trinity, the transaction could not but have been unreal and illusory."[1] Vos makes it clear that he does not consider the disclosure of the Trinity an Old Testament phenomenon. He sees, however, intimations of the Trinity in the patriarchal revelations through the Angel of the Lord.

G. W. Bromiley suggests another explanation of the term Angel of the Lord and its evident reference to God. Bromiley emphasizes the angel as the vehicle of revelation and suggests that, through the angel God speaks so clearly and fully that He, Himself can be said to speak.[2] This, Bromiley feels, better accounts for the usage of the term "Angel of the Lord" in Luke 2:9 where the angel actually heralds the birth of Jesus.

The messages to the patriarchs mediated by the Angel of the Lord, and those in which God himself appears or speaks, are not essentially different. In each instance the authority behind the communication is clearly God Himself.

---

1. Geerhardus Vos, *Biblical Theology*, pp. 86-87.
2. Geoffrey W. Bromiley, "Angel," *Baker's Dictionary of Theology*, pp. 42-43.

17 | Law in Patriarchal Times

The laws which govern the common life of a people afford insights into the values which they hold dear. A legal system which seeks to protect the helpless from the potential despot is itself evidence of a moral sense in the society which avows it. Conversely, a law code which regards wives and slaves as the property of the head of a household reflects a culture in which even the fiction of personal equality is denied.

Ancient law codes, like their modern counterparts, were not always binding. The code represented the ideal, but all evidence indicates that judges had the right to make independent decisions when confronted with specific problems. There is no hint that rulers were expected to master the legal systems of their predecessors, although a legal tradition existed in the Near East from Sumerian times which found expression in the Babylonian code of Hammurabi. Although Biblical law, which deals with moral principles as well as specific infractions, has a different point of reference (the sovereign will of Yahweh who has entered into covenant with His people), there are enough parallels to show that the history of Israel was not isolated from the culture of her neighbors.

I. Ur-nammu

Ur-nammu was the Sumerian ruler who founded the Third Dynasty of Ur, about 2050 B.C. His code, written three centuries before that of the great Babylonian lawgiver, Hammurabi, has been partially preserved in two fragments of a clay tablet now in the Istanbul Museum of the Ancient Orient. The obscure Sumerian writing on the tablet was deciphered by Samuel Noah Kramer of the University of Pennsylvania. It tells how Ur-

Standing male figure in the act of worship, from Tell Asmar (ca. 2800 B.C.).

nammu was chosen by the moon god, Nanna, to rule Ur as his earthly representative.

The first responsibility of Ur-nammu was to defend the boundaries of Ur against encroachments by neighboring Lagash. Having accomplished this, he turned his attention to reforms which were needed within the city-state of Ur. Ur-nammu determined that his government would be marked by justice. The widow and the orphan were not to be neglected. Honest weights and measures were prescribed for the mercantile class of Ur.

The Ur-Nammu law code is in a poor state of preservation, so that only a small fraction of its contents is known. One law seems to refer to the ordeal by water, later mentioned in the Hammurabi code. A woman accused of immorality is cast into the river, which acts as her judge. If the river receives her (i.e., she drowns), her guilt is considered self-evident. If, on the other hand, she swims to shore, she is deemed innocent.

Three of the laws which can be read with a fair degree of accuracy deal with instances of the mutilation of the body. If a man has cut off another man's foot, he is to pay ten shekels. In the Code of Hammurabi such payments are often prescribed when injury is to one of an inferior social status. There the penalty for injury to someone of the same class corresponds to the pattern, "an eye for an eye, and a tooth for a tooth."

The institution of slavery was firmly rooted in the ancient Near East. The victor on the battlefield would normally enslave the conquered army. Slavery, of course, brings many problems with it, and Ur-nammu had to prescribe legislation to deal with the run-away slave, a problem also dealt with in detail in Hammurabi's Code.

2. Eshnunna

Another ancient law code comes from the city-state of Eshnunna which flourished from the end of the Third Dynasty of Ur to the time of the Babylonian king, Hammurabi. Two tablets containing the Eshnunna code were discovered at Tell Abu Harmal, in the Diyala region east of Baghdad by archaeologists from the Iraq Directorate of Antiquities in 1945. Unlike the Ur-nammu code, these tablets were written in the Akkadian language, the Semitic tongue spoken in ancient Assyria and Babylonia. Although we are not certain concerning the date of the Eshnunna code, it is thought to have been promulgated during the reign of Bilalama, about 2000 B.C. Albrecht Goetze, of Yale University, translated them into English.

The code begins with a brief prologue which tells how Tishpak, the chief god of Eshnunna, bestowed upon some ruler (whose name has not been preserved) "the kingship over Eshnunna." It is Goetze's suggestion that the ruler was probably Bilalama.

Sixty paragraphs of the code have been preserved. They deal with such varied subjects as the price of commodities, the wages of labor, the hire of wagons and boats, assault and battery, marriage, divorce, and adultery.

The behavior of oxen and the responsibility of their owners is discussed in the Eshnunna code, in the Code of Hammurabi, and in the Bible.

The Eshnunna Code states:

> If an ox gores an (other) ox, and causes (its) death, both ox owners shall divide (among themselves) the price of the live ox, and also the equivalent of the dead ox. (53)

An exact parallel occurs in the Mosaic law:

> And if one man's ox hurt another's, that he die; then they shall sell the live ox, and divide the money of it; and the dead ox also they shall divide (Exod. 21:35).

It was the responsibility of the owner of oxen to take steps to prevent this from recurring. The Eshnunna code adds:

> If an ox is known to gore habitually, and the authorities have brought the fact to the knowledge of its owner, but he does not have his ox *dehorned,* it bores a man and causes (his) death, then the owner of the ox shall pay two-thirds of a mina of silver. (54)

3. Lipit-Ishtar

During the expedition of the University of Pennsylvania at Nippur in Iraq (1889-1900) fragments of a Sumerian law code were discovered. It was almost a half century later (1947) when the fragments were seriously studied. Samuel N. Kramer announced the discovery of a new Sumerian code in the *Journal of the American Oriental Society,* and Francis Rue Steele, in cooperation with Dr. Kramer, published the edited text in the *American Journal of Archaeology.*[1]

The four fragments found at Nippur were found to be part of the law code of Lipit-Ishtar, the fifth king of the Sumerian city-state of Isin, who reigned for eleven years beginning about 1868 B.C. The code begins with a prologue of almost one hundred lines, most of which have been poorly preserved. It tells

---

1. Vol. VII, No. 3, July-Sept. 1948.

how Lipit-Ishtar was chosen by the gods Anu and Enlil as the one to "establish justice in the land" and "bring well-being to the Sumerians and the Akkadians."

The code contains thirty-eight paragraphs dealing with such practical matters as the hire of boats, rental of oxen, inheritance, marriage, and tax default. Fines were imposed for damages:

> If a man cut down a tree in the garden of another man, he shall pay one-half mina of silver. (10)
>
> If a man rented an ox and damaged its eye, he shall pay one-half of its price. (35)

The desire for children, so basic to the thought of the Old Testament, is inherent in the Lipit-Ishtar code:

> If a man's wife has not borne him children (but) a harlot (from) the public square has borne him children, he shall provide grain, oil, and clothing for that harlot; the children which the harlot has borne him shall be his heirs, and as long as his wife lives the harlot shall not live in the house with his wife. (27)
>
> If a man married a wife (and) she bore him children and those children are living, and a slave also bore children for her master (but) the father granted freedom to the slave and her children, the children of the slave shall not divide the estate with the children of their (former) master. (25)

Although the Bible never condones consorting with an harlot, it does mention the fact that both Abraham and Jacob had children by female servants in the household. The Nuzi tablets tell us that a barren wife was actually required to provide an handmaid for her husband in order that he might have children. Abraham appears to have given Hagar her freedom after the birth of Isaac (Gen. 21:14), and Scripture makes it clear that Ishmael, her son, did not divide the estate with Isaac, Abraham's son by Sarah (Gen. 17:19-21).

A further provision in the Lipit-Ishtar code states:

> If a man has turned away from his first wife... (but) she has not gone out of his (house), his wife which he married *as his favorite* is a second wife, he shall continue to support his first wife.

Leah, the first wife of Jacob, took a second place in his affections. There was never any thought, however, that she should be divorced in favor of the beloved Rachel. In fact the twelve "children of Israel" (Jacob) had four mothers, Leah, Rachel, and their two handmaids, Bilhah and Zilpah.

Lipit-Ishtar closes his law code with a blessing on those who will not damage the stele on which it was written, and a curse on any who would presume to harm it.

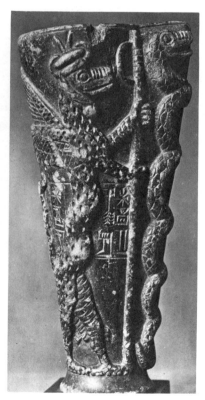

Goblet for libations from Lagash.

4. Hammurabi

The second year of the reign of the Amorite king of Babylon, Hammurabi, was given the name, "the year when he established justice." Hammurabi built upon the work of his predecessors, but his code is the fullest and best known.

The laws of Hammurabi were inscribed on a black diorite stele, six feet in height, which is now in the Louvre. The stele was discovered by the French archaeologist, Jacques de Morgan, during excavations at the Persian city of Susa (Biblical Shushan) in 1901. Elamites are thought to have taken the stele during one of their many raids on ancient Babylonia.

At the top of the stele is a bas-relief showing Hammurabi standing before the Semitic sun-god, Shamash who, because he encircles the crest of heaven, is also the god of law and justice. The god is depicted with a ring and staff, symbols of royalty, in his right hand. Before him stands Hammurabi, ready to receive the royal authority which will enable him to transmit the laws to his people.

The text of the code, written in Akkadian cuneiform, is written in fifty-one columns on the stele. In its prologue, written in poetry, Hammurabi claims to have been chosen by the gods to bring justice to the land. The poetic epilogue reaffirms the desire of Hammurabi to prevent the strong from oppressing the weak and to protect the interests of the orphan and the widow. Hammurabi directed that the stele be set up in a public place so that his subjects would know their rights.

The laws themselves exhibit a social structure with three classes: an upper class of free-born nobles, an intermediate class of plebeians or commoners, and the lowest class made up of slaves. Priests, merchants, and soldiers were found among the two upper classes. Even slaves, however, had rights which had to be respected, although penalties to those who had wronged them were not as severe as for the upper classes. A monetary value was assigned to slaves; some of whom, however, were free to engage in business. A noble was equal in value to two commoners, and a commoner to two slaves, in the eyes of the law.

These distinctions made in Hammurabi's Code may be contrasted with the Biblical attitude toward various levels of society. Slavery existed in ancient Israel, but it was not a normal part of the social structure and provision was made whereby the Hebrew slave was set free at the sabbatical year (Exod. 21:1-6). Of particular interest is the Biblical attitude toward "strangers"

A model of the stele that records the code of Hammurabi. The original is in the Louvre, Paris.

in Israel. The covenant sign of circumcision was given not only to the physical sons of Abraham, but extended to all:

> ...whether born in your house or bought with your money from any foreigner who is not your offspring, both he that is born in your house and he that is bought with your money, shall be circumcised (Gen. 17:12-13).

When it is remembered that Abraham was able to gather a personal army of three hundred and eighteen trained men, "born in his house" to rescue his nephew Lot (Gen. 14:14), we gain a fresh appreciation of the part that non-Israelites played in the patriarchal history.

At the time of the Exodus we read of a "mixed multitude" (Exod. 12:38; Num. 11:4; Josh. 8:35) which accompanied the Israelites. No certain identification can be given to this group, but they appear to have included the children of marriages between Israelites and Egyptians and various groups of non-Israelites who chose to associate themselves with the covenant people.

The time of bondage in Egypt was never forgotten by Israel, and the responsibility for kind treatment of strangers was frequently reinforced by the reminder that Israel had been "strangers in Egypt" (cf. Exod. 23:9; Lev. 19:34). The sympathetic attitude toward strangers is illustrated by the law of the sabbath which specifically mentions them as exempt from work, along with the Israelites (Exod. 20:10).

An important principle of Israelite law states: "Ye shall have one manner of law, as well for the stranger as for the home-born" (Lev. 24:22). This involved responsibility as well as privilege: "He that blasphemeth the name of the Lord, he shall surely be put to death, all the congregation shall certainly stone him, as well the stranger as the home born" (Lev. 24:16).

The Hammurabi law code was purely civil in application. Although mention is made of religious functionaries, and the law itself is traced to the appointment of Hammurabi by the gods, the code itself pertains entirely to the regulation of human conduct on the ethical plane. Conversely the Mosaic law has both moral and religious (ceremonial) aspects as well as those of a strictly civil nature. Comparisons between the Biblical and the Hammurabi code can be made on the level of the regulations which both impress on society. Only the Israelite code has a specific religious motivation.

Even at the level of human relationships, there are great differences between the Israelite code and that of Hammurabi's

Babylon. Until the time of David, Israel was primarily an agricultural people. She was, in fact, less advanced technologically than her neighbors. The Philistines had a monopoly on iron as late as the time of Saul (I Sam. 13:19-22). Babylon, however, was a land with important commercial ventures. A system of canals, connecting the Tigris and the Euphrates Rivers, required the co-operation of many people if the land was to be properly irrigated. All this found expression in the Code of Hammurabi. Even the veterans from the Babylonian wars were granted a kind of "G.I. Bill of Rights."

There are, of course, significant areas of life which the Babylonians shared with the Biblical Hebrews, and numerous places where the two laws overlap. The Biblical principle

> life for life, eye for eye, tooth for tooth, hand for hand, burning for burning, wound for wound, stripe for stripe (Exod. 21:23-25).

is basic in the Hammurabi code. This is spelled out in such detail that a builder who builds a house which collapses and kills the son of the owner of the house is made to suffer by having one of his own sons killed! If a slave is killed under similar circumstances it is enough for the builder to provide another slave of equal value.

According to Deuteronomy 19:18-19, a false witness was to be punished with the penalty he intended to bring upon the other man. In similar vein the Code of Hammurabi states:

> If a (man) came forward with false testimony in a case and has not proved the word which he spoke, if that case was a case involving life, that man shall be put to death. (3)

Several points of parallel may be observed between Babylonian and Israelite law as it pertains to marriage and divorce. In both codes adultery was punishable by death for both parties (Lev. 20:10; Deut. 22:22; Code of Hammurabi, 129).

A woman whose chastity was suspected could have a trial by ordeal according to both the Biblical and the Hammurabi codes, although the nature of the ordeal differed. The Babylonian code (132) provided that the wife who was suspect should be cast into the river which acted as the judge, a method which was earlier mentioned in the Ur-nammu Code. In Numbers 5:11-28 a different ordeal is prescribed. There the priest gives to the woman water in which dust from the sanctuary has been placed and the woman is counted innocent if she does not swell up and die.

Although there is no parallel in Israelite law, the provisions of the Code of Hammurabi whereby a maid servant may be provided by a barren wife so that her husband may have children is illustrated by Sarah's suggestion that Abraham have children by Hagar (Gen. 16:3). The wife is protected by the provision that the slave who bears children does not gain equality with her mistress, and the slave is protected in that she cannot be sold after giving birth to a child of her master (paragraphs 144-147).

Not only were men, under certain circumstances, permitted to divorce their wives, but the aggrieved wife could divorce her husband according to the Babylonian laws (paragraphs 138-141). In the Biblical record mention is only made of the husband divorcing his wife (Deut. 24:1-4).

Proper respect for parents was insisted on in both codes. The Code of Hammurabi reads:

> If a man has struck his father, one shall cut off his hands. (195)

In this instance the Biblical penalty is even more severe:

> He that smiteth his father or his mother shall be surely put to death (Exod. 21:15).

Kidnapping brought the death penalty:

> If a man has stolen the young son of a freeman, he shall be put to death. (14)
> He that stealeth a man, or if he be found in his hand, he shall surely be put to death (Exod. 21:16).

Assault on a pregnant woman was considered a heinous crime both in the Code of Hammurabi and the Bible:

> If a man has struck the daughter of a person of the upper class and caused her to drop what is in her womb . . . if that woman has died, one shall put to death his daughter. (209-10)
> If men strive, and hurt a woman with child, so that her fruit depart from her, and yet no mischief follow: he shall be surely punished . . . and if any mischief follow, then thou shalt give life for life (Exod. 21:22).

We have seen that the problem of the goring ox had been met as early as the Eshnunna code. The Code of Hammurabi has a similar provision:

> If a (man's) ox was a gorer and his city council made it known to him that it was a gorer, but he did not pad its horns (or) tie up his ox, and that ox gored to death a member of the aristocracy, he shall give one-half mina of silver (251)

Under similar circumstances the Biblical law states:

> If an ox gore a man or a woman that they die: then the ox shall be surely stoned, and his flesh shall not be eaten; but the owner of the ox shall be quit. But if the ox were wont to push with his horn in time past, and it hath been testified to his owner, and he hath not kept him in, but that he hath killed a man or woman; the ox shall be stoned and his owner also shall be put to death (Exod. 21:28-29).

5. The Hittite Code

Our knowledge of Hittite law comes from texts discovered at Boghazkoy, the ancient Hittite capital in Asia Minor. Although dated during the fourteenth century B.C., there can be no doubt that the legal tradition embodied in the code goes back centuries before that time.

Two tablets of a series of Hittite laws have been preserved, and it is known that there was at least one other tablet. The formula "if anyone" is used in introducing each paragraph.

We may infer from the Hittite code that blood revenge was not practiced among the Hittites as it was among the Semites. We read:

> If anyone kills a man or a woman in a quarrel, he has to make amends for him/her. He shall give four persons, man or woman, and pledge his estate for security. (1)

The Hittites did not use the *lex talionis* ("an eye for an eye"), for we are told:

> If anyone blinds a free man or knocks out his teeth, he shall give twenty shekels of silver and pledge his estate as security. (7)

Both blood revenge and the *lex talionis* were marks of a patriarchal society, such as that of the fathers of Israel. With the development of the institutions of government, they tend to be replaced by judicial processes.

Hittites are known to have been in Canaan during patriarchal times, and it is of interest to note that certain principles of Hittite law were observed there. One such provision states:

> If in a village anyone holds fields under socage as inheritance — if the fields have all been given to him, he shall render the services; if the fields have been given to him only to a small part, he shall not render the services. They shall render them from his father's house. (46)

Grants of land were made under Hittite law on condition that the user perform certain military services to the state. When Abraham sought to purchase a burial plot for Sarah in the corner of a field belonging to Ephron, the Hittite (Gen. 23:4), Ephron insisted that he purchase the entire field (Gen. 23:11). Had Abraham purchased only a small part of the field, Ephron would still have had to meet his feudal obligations. By selling the entire field, the obligation passed to Abraham.

The principle of levirate marriage (cf. Deut. 25:5-10) is also reflected in the Hittite law:

> If a man has a wife, and the man dies, his brother shall take his wife, then his father shall take her. If in turn also his father dies, one of his brother's sons shall take the wife whom he had. There shall be no punishment. (193)

A Hittite soldier is pictured on a sculptured slab, from Carchemish.

This actually goes farther than the Israelite law, for the Hittites made provision for the father of the deceased to take the widow, after the brother. Tamar, in seeking a child by Judah (Gen. 38:12-19), was acting in accord with this principle.

The Biblical patriarchs lived before the codification of Israelite law. Theirs was not a lawless society, however. Our earliest law code, that of Ur-nammu, certainly antedates Abraham. Other codes from Sumer, Babylon, Assyria, and the Hittite lands reflect a legal tradition which bears witness to a highly developed civilization. Certain of the elements of these earlier codes were adapted to the requirements of Israel, and others were repudiated. The patriarchs did not live in a legal vacuum, and an examination of the laws of their neighbors throws much light on their own lives.

18

The Literature
of the Patriarchal Age

We have no records of any written documents among the Israelites prior to the time of Moses. There was a time when men questioned whether the art of writing existed as long ago as the time of Moses (mid-second millennium B.C.). For centuries we thought of ancient history as beginning with Greece. With the discovery of advanced cultures dating back almost two millennia before Moses, doubts concerning the writing ability of the Hebrew lawgiver have been removed.

Another question impresses itself upon us, however. Was there any Israelite literature in the pre-Mosaic era. How did Abraham and his sons pass on to their children the rudiments of their faith?

In some respects the questions are unanswerable. We would suspect that some form of communication existed. Other cultures had developed epic literature which embodied the traditions of the earliest days of the tribe or nation. Since Israel was a part of the environment of the ancient Near East, it probably followed patterns similar to those which are known to have existed in the Tigris-Euphrates valley and at Ugarit.

We are not left entirely to conjecture, however. The reader of the Old Testament is soon aware that the Bible does not contain all of the ancient literature of Israel. In Numbers 21:14 we find a poetic quotation from a book bearing the name, *The Book of the Wars of the Lord*. In Joshua 10:13 and again in II Samuel 1:17, 18, reference is made to a *Book of Jasher,* (or *Book of the Upright*).

All that we actually know about these books is contained in the Scriptures that mention them. A fraudulent *Book of Jasher* which has been published in recent years was probably written about A.D. 1750. E. J. Goodspeed in his small volume entitled

Modern Apocrypha exposes the volume sold as *The Book of Jasher* as one of sixteen famous "Biblical" hoaxes.

The fact that the Biblical quotations from both the *Book of Jasher* and the *Book of the Wars of the Lord* are all poetic in nature leads us to examine other poetry in the Old Testament historical books to determine whether or not the Biblical writers quote from other poetic works.

Semitic poetry is characterized by a structure known as parallelism. In one form of parallelism, a statement is made in one line and the same idea is repeated in other words in the next. Such a pattern occurs in Genesis 4:23-24:

> Adah and Zillah, hear my voices;
>   You wives of Lamech, hearken to what I say:
> I have slain a man for wounding me,
>   a young man for striking me.
> If Cain is avenged sevenfold,
>   truly Lamech seventy-seven fold.

This boastful "Song of Lamech" is an excellent example of Semitic poetry. Adah and Zillah mentioned in the first line form a parallel to "you wives of Lamech" of line two. "Hear" and "hearken" are also synonymous.

There are many other bits of poetry in the book of Genesis. Jacob's blessing of his sons (Gen. 49:2-27) is probably the longest. They each possess the parallelism which particularly attracted the Semites of the ancient Near East. Poets from Assyria and Babylonia, and even non-Semitic Egypt, regularly used this means of expression.

Before the ability to read and write became prevalent there was a strong motivation to produce national and religious literature in poetic form. Poetry can be memorized more readily than prose, and there is evidence that the Greek Iliad and Odyssey were memorized and recited by ancient bards long before Homer reduced them to writing. The Sumerian and Babylonian accounts of the flood are in poetic form, and without doubt had a similar history.

The Biblical doctrine of inspiration defines the end product — the records contained in Scripture — as inspired of God. It does not preclude the use of source material. The later historical books of the Old Testament quote a large number of records which were used by inspired writers — "Chronicles of the Kings of Israel" (I Kings 14:19), "The History of Nathan the Prophet," "The Prophecy of Ahijah the Shilonite," and "The Visions of Iddo the Seer" (II Chron. 10:29).

The Biblical statement that Moses went to school in Egypt (Acts 7:22) implies that the Israelite lawgiver had a wealth of information at his disposal. During the years when he was being raised by his devout mother, Moses certainly was told about the great acts of God in Israel's past. He must have heard about the call of Abraham, the birth of Isaac, the journeyings of Jacob and the descent into Egypt of the tribes while Joseph was Prime Minister. Both at his mother's knee and in the schools of Egypt Moses was prepared for his great work.

Recent scholarship has come to appreciate the accuracy with which oral tradition was transmitted before writing became commonplace. In modern life we do not need to depend upon memory because we can record all information which we deem vital. The multiplicity of our daily reading may actually hinder the process of memory. The Brahmins of India, however, in a culture which is totally different from ours, memorize the 153,826 words of their holy book, the Rigveda. We need not think of the materials of the book of Genesis as passed on in a unit in the age of the patriarchs, but we have every reason to believe that the patriarchs passed on the traditions which they received, and that these, later, under the guidance of the Holy Spirit, were incorporated into our Bible as the Book of Genesis.

Ancient Israel confessed, "Yahweh heard our voice, and saw our affliction, our toil, and our oppression; and Yahweh brought us out of Egypt with a mighty hand and an outstretched arm, with great terror, with signs and wonders" (Deut. 26:8). Each year at the Passover season Israel remembers God's mighty acts which brought deliverance to a people enslaved by Egypt's pharaoh. Few people wish to be perpetually reminded of their humble origins, but Israel is ever mindful of the admonition: "You shall remember that you were a slave in the land of Egypt, and Yahweh your God brought you out thence with a mighty hand and an outstretched arm" (Deut. 5:15).

Apart from the Biblical text, however, we possess no documentation for the period of Israel's sojourn in Egypt and her subsequent wilderness experience. The corpus of Egyptian texts is enormous, and scholars try to understand the Biblical events in the light of known facts about Egypt. The reader should be aware of the fact, however, that the Bible mentions no pharaoh of the Exodus period by name, and Egyptian documents do not mention Israel until she is in the land of Canaan.

These facts do not encourage a skeptical attitude, however, for the events described in the Bible tally perfectly with what we know about Egypt. Many of the Biblical names of the Exodus period—including Moses himself—are clearly Egyptian, and Semites are known to have settled in the eastern Delta region of Egypt in very ancient times. Even the plagues visited upon Egypt have a distinctly local coloring. While contemporary Biblical scholars differ concerning many of the details of interpretation, they agree that at least a part of the people that came to be known as Israel experienced the Exodus.

The covenant between Yahweh and Israel at Sinai forms the basis for an understanding of later Biblical history. Prophets denounced Israel for breaking that covenant, and heralded the day when Yahweh would write a new covenant on the fleshy tables of human hearts (Jer. 31:31-35). The Tent of Meeting in the wilderness gave way to the Temple in Jerusalem, and that, ultimately, to the Word made flesh who dwelt (lit. "tabernacled") among us (John 1:14).

PART TWO

Egypt and the Exodus

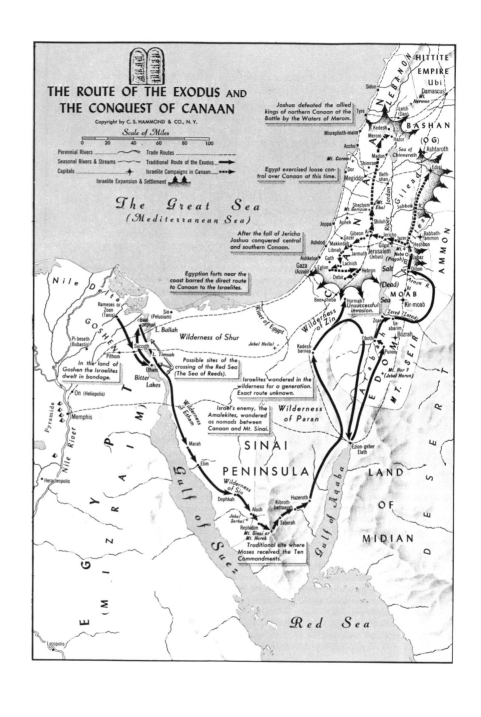

THE ROUTE OF THE EXODUS AND
THE CONQUEST OF CANAAN

Copyright by C. S. HAMMOND & CO., N.Y.

Scale of Miles

0   20   40   60   80   100

Perennial Rivers ....   Trade Routes ....

Seasonal Rivers & Streams ....   Traditional Route of the Exodus ➤

Capitals ....   Israelite Campaigns in Canaan ➤➤

Israelite Expansion & Settlement ▲▲▲

The Great Sea
(Mediterranean Sea)

Joshua defeated the allied kings of northern Canaan at the Battle by the Waters of Merom.

Egypt exercised loose control over Canaan at this time.

After the fall of Jericho Joshua conquered central and southern Canaan.

Egyptian forts near the coast barred the direct route to Canaan to the Israelites.

In the land of Goshen the Israelites dwelt in bondage.

Possible sites of the crossing of the Red Sea (The Sea of Reeds).

Israelites wandered in the wilderness for a generation. Exact route unknown.

Israel's enemy, the Amalekites, wandered as nomads between Canaan and Mt. Sinai.

Unsuccessful invasion.

Traditional site where Moses received the Ten Commandments.

Nile Delta

River of Egypt

Wilderness of Shur

Wilderness of Zin

Wilderness of Paran

Wilderness of Sin

Wilderness of Etham

SINAI PENINSULA

Gulf of Suez

Gulf of Aqaba

LAND OF MIDIAN

Red Sea

HITTITE EMPIRE
Ubi
Damascus
Mt. Hermon

BASHAN
(O G)
Ashtaroth
Edrei

LEBANON

Sidon
Tyre
Kedesh
Merom
Misrephoth-maim
Accho
Mt. Carmel
Dor
Megiddo
Madon
Shimron
Hazor
Sea of Chinnereth

Gilead
Jabbok R.
Rabbath-ammon
AMMON

Shechem
Mt. Gerizim
Mt. Ebal
Shiloh
Joppa
Aphek
Gibeon Ai
Gezer
Jericho
Jazer
Heshbon
Nebo (Pisgah)
Jahaz
Dibon

Ashdod
Makkedah
Jerusalem (Jebus)
Jarmuth
Libnah
Ashkelon
Gath
Lachish
Eglon
Gaza (Azzah)
Debir
Hebron
Beer-sheba
Hormah?

Salt (Dead) Sea
Arnon R.
Ar
MOAB
Kir-moab
Zered (Zared)
Zoar
Ije-abarim
Oboth
Bozrah
Punon
Mt. Hor? (Jebel Harun)
EDOM
MT. SEIR

DESERT

Kadesh-barnea
Jebel Hellal

Ezion-geber Elath

Rameses or Zoan (Tanis)
Baal-zephon
Sin (Pelusium)
L. Ballah
Pi-beseth (Bubastis)
Pithom
Succoth
L. Timsah
Etham
Bitter Lakes
GOSHEN
On (Heliopolis)
Pyramids
Memphis
Heracleopolis
Lycopolis

EGYPT (MIZRAIM)

Marah
Elim
Dophkah
Alush
Kibroth-hattaavah
Hazeroth
Taberah
Jebel Serbal
Rephidim
Mt. Sinai or Mt. Horeb

Arabah

19

The Land of Egypt

Stretching a distance of six hundred miles from Aswan (ancient Syene) at the First Cataract of the Nile, northward to the Mediterranean, is the narrow strip of cultivable land that comprised ancient Egypt.[1] The Greek historian Herodotus stated that Egypt is the gift of the Nile, for the strip of fertile land produced by the flooding of the Nile is the only break in the Sahara and Libyan deserts which stretch across North Africa to the Red Sea, and continue beyond it as the Arabian Desert. The deserts which stretch interminably to the east and west of the Nile valley made access to ancient Egypt quite difficult, and explain in part the somewhat isolated history of the country in early times.

The English name "Egypt" is derived from the Greek and Latin forms of the ancient *Ha-ku-ptah,* an earlier name for the city of Memphis, near modern Cairo. When Memphis served as capital of Egypt, its name was apparently used for the whole country, just as the city of Babylon gave its name to the Babylonian Empire. Egypt was also known to its own people as *Ta-meri,* "the beloved land," and *Kemet,* "the black country," a name descriptive of the black soil of the Nile Valley which contrasted with the nearby *Deshret,* or red country, which gives us our word "desert." The Hebrews and other Semites use the name *Misrayim,* which, in the form "Mizraim," appears in the English Bible as the second son of Ham and the Progenitor of the Ludim, Lehabim, Naphtuhim, Casluhim, and Caphtorim (Gen. 10:6, 13).

From Mount Ruwenzori, near the equator, the Nile Valley extends 2,450 air miles northward to the Mediterranean. The actual length of the Nile valley, however, including the numerous twists and turns in its tortuous route, amounts to about

---

1. *Herodotus* ii. 18.

four thousand miles, making it the second longest river valley on earth. The valley was formed as the water cut its way through sandstone and limestone, which is traversed in six places by granite and other hard stones creating cataracts which interfere with navigation and serve as natural boundaries for Nile Valley peoples. The region of the Fourth Cataract was settled by the people known in the Bible as Cushites whose kingdom became known as Cush or Ethiopia. Between the Fourth and Third Cataracts is Jebel Barkal, the southernmost point of Egyptian rule during the New Kingdom, when Cush was under an Egyptian viceroy. The land of Nubia, rich in gold, lay between the Third and First Cataracts. The remains of Abu Simbel, two huge shrines hewn out of living rock by Rameses II, are north of the Second Cataract. Their chapels, stelae, and inscriptions suggest something of the history that passed up and down the Nile.

The Nile Valley from Aswan, at the First Cataract, to the Mediterranean provided Egypt with about 13,300 square miles of cultivable land, roughly equivalent in area to Belgium or the American states of Massachusetts and Connecticut. Only the northern part of the Nile Delta lies within reach of the winter rains of the Mediterranean. Alexandria, in the western Delta, has about eight inches of rain annually, falling during the late autumn and early winter. Cairo, at the head of the Delta, has but one and one-half to two inches, mostly in January, and rain is so rare in Upper Egypt that it is looked upon as a miracle. Often years go by with no rain at all. The only fertility that comes to the land is brought by the flood waters of the Nile which deposit on its banks both moisture and rich alluvial soil washed down from central Africa.

The Egyptians were puzzled concerning the source of the Nile, flowing as it does northward from the central part of Africa. Mythology suggested that the river had its origin in heaven, and that it fell to the earth far to the south of their land. The *Book of the Dead* states that it sprang from four sources at the Twelfth Gate of the netherworld.[2] Legend also suggested that it emerged from the netherworld at the First Cataract, near modern Aswan. Even Herodotus was puzzled at conflicting views concerning the sources of the Nile. One, which he affirms is "most in error," holds that "the Nile flows from where snows melt." This is impossible, according to Herodotus,

Farming in the Egypt delta region.

2. Chapter 146.

for the river flows "from the hottest places to lands that are for the most part cooler." Herodotus, of course, did not know of the snow-capped mountains which actually did provide one of the sources of the Nile.[3]

The main stream, known as the White Nile, flowing from the mountainous region of central Africa provides a steady flow of water throughout the year. This is augmented by the Blue Nile, flowing from Lake Tana in the Abyssinian plateau, which becomes a mountain torrent from June to September as a result of heavy spring rains. Near Khartoum, in the Sudan, the Blue Nile joins the White Nile in its northward course. Two hundred miles farther downstream, the Atbara, the Nile's only significant tributary brings additional flood waters into the Nile from the highlands of Ethiopia. It is the water from the Blue Nile and the Atbara, added to the more steady stream of the White Nile, that bring about the annual inundation on which the economy of Egypt depends.

Although an annual flood was predictable, its extent varied from year to year. Too much water would sweep away dykes and canal banks and destroy the mud brick homes in Egyptian villages. Too little water would result in famine and starvation.

Such a famine is known to have taken place during the reign of Pharaoh Zoser, the builder of the famed Step Pyramid, who reigned about 2600 B.C. An inscription discovered near the First Cataract of the Nile, dating from about 100 B.C. says:

> I was in distress on the Great Throne, and was in affliction of heart because of a very great evil, for in my time the Nile has not overflowed for a period of seven years. There was scarcely any grain; fruits were dried up; and everything which they eat was short. Every man robbed his neighbor....[4]

Zoser lived about a thousand years before Joseph, the Hebrew slave who became Prime Minister of Egypt. Joseph gained the confidence of the Pharaoh by interpreting his dreams and by suggesting a plan whereby food might be stored during the years of prosperity so that there would be ample supplies during the famine years which would follow (Gen. 41:28-57).

The annual inundation usually begins at Aswan at the end of May or the beginning of June, and the Nile continues to rise until early in September. In Memphis, at the head of the

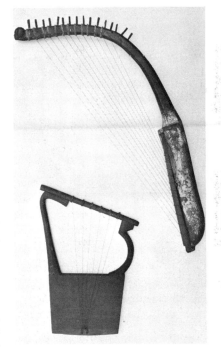

Egyptian musical instruments. The wooden lyre (top) from Thebes dates from the Eighteenth Dynasty. The wooden harp is from approximately the same period.

---

3. *Herodotus* ii. 20-34 contains a full discussion of Greek and Egyptian ideas concerning the source of the Nile. The subject seems to have fascinated him.

4. A translation of the text, first published by H. K. Brugsch in 1891, appears in James A. Pritchard, ed. *Ancient Near Eastern Texts Relating to the Old Testament* (Princeton: University Press, 1955), p. 31.

Symbols of Upper Egypt (papyrus, left) and Lower Egypt (lotus) are featured on these columns.

Delta, the flood stage is reached from one to two weeks later. By building dams, dykes, and canals, the Egyptians were able to control the flooding, and to slow down the rate at which the waters would normally subside. Lake Moeris in the Faiyum, the predecessor of the modern Birket Qarun, was praised by classical writers as the earliest attempt to use the flood waters to provide for irrigation on a prolonged basis. Pharaohs of the Twelfth Dynasty had seen the possibilities of diverting the waters of the Nile into the Faiyum area during the inundation period.

The necessity for control of the Nile was a factor in uniting Egypt and encouraging a tendency toward centralized authority. A strong government could sponsor a program of public construction to make the best use of the Nile. During the inundation season, when agricultural work was at a standstill, the peasant's time could be utilized in building drainage canals and other public works. Herodotus says that the laborers who built the Great Pyramid worked during three month shifts. Pyramid construction probably took place during the inundation season when labor in the fields was impossible. Pyramid building did not harm the economy because the fields were neglected, but because the labor could have been expended in more productive ways. Had effort been made to develop irrigation projects rather than to build tombs for the Pharaohs, the standard of living for the entire people could have been raised significantly. This judgment is a modern one, to be sure. Those who believed that Pharaoh was a god worked on his pyramid with the same devotion that medieval Christians expended on the building of great cathedrals.

Before the beginnings of history, the small states or nomes of ancient Egypt were united into two kingdoms: Lower Egypt comprising the Delta; the Upper Egypt, the Nile Valley from Memphis at the apex of the Delta to Aswan, at the First Cataract. Even in historical times when the states were united under one Pharaoh, Egyptians spoke of their country as "The Two Lands," and the ruler bore the title, "King of Upper and Lower Egypt," and wore a double crown.

The tableland of Upper Egypt is from one to twenty-four miles in width, hugging the shores of the Nile. From his fertile valley the Egyptian could look to the east or the west and see barren desert cliffs as high as 1,800 feet. Quite naturally he regarded Egypt as the one land particularly blessed of the gods. Even the border at the First Cataract was protected by a series of cascades and rapids which served as a natural barrier to the movement of hostile peoples from the south.

The Egyptian Delta area had been a large gulf in remote prehistoric times when the area around Cairo bordered the Mediterranean. As the Nile waters made their way to the sea however, they deposited alluvium in the gulf at their mouth, and the Delta slowly emerged, becoming the Lower Egypt of historical times. As the Nile waters entered the Delta they were diverted into a number of branches, only two of which have persisted into modern times, the others having largely dried up. At its widest extent the Delta extends about 125 miles. Because of its proximity to the Mediterranean, the Delta had contacts with the outside world, and its inhabitants did not enjoy the isolation which characterized the people of Upper Egypt. The Delta was the great reservoir of land in ancient Egypt, with a dozen or so important towns, each of which was surrounded by fertile soil suitable for agriculture or the grazing of cattle. Pharaohs and their nobles enjoyed hunting in the thickets of the Delta where the jackal, fox, hyena, lion, lynx, and leopard were common. The reeds of the Delta marshes were used in making papyrus, the writing material of ancient Egypt which was the forerunner of our paper. Papyrus was also used in making baskets, sandals, small ships, and rope.

Bordering Egypt to the northeast was the Sinai Peninsula, an arid region which served as a buffer zone between Egypt and the nations of Asia. The civilized Egyptians built a wall on their border and sought to keep from their land the nomadic people of the desert, but in times of Egyptian weakness the bedouin were able to enter and settle down. Through the centuries Egypt was invaded by a succession of Hyksos, Assyrians, Babylonians, Persians, and Arabs who crossed the Sinai Peninsula and occupied Egypt. Conversely, during Egypt's Empire Period, she penetrated western Asia as far as the upper reaches of the Euphrates. Nevertheless the Sinai Peninsula discouraged such contacts, and military ventures often had to be supplemented by naval control of the eastern Mediterranean.

Early man lived on the desert plateau which today stretches along both sides of the Nile Valley. Although the Libyan and the Sahara deserts are now barren except for a few oases, there was a time when they received enough rain to make possible life on a relatively large scale. In regions that are now completely barren, strata reveal the presence of hippopotami, buffalo, wild asses, gazelles, and ostriches. At the end of this period African

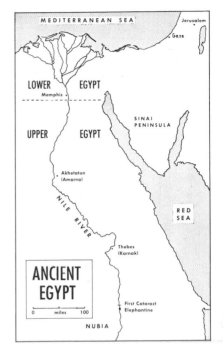

ANCIENT EGYPT

Head of an Egyptian princess in limestone relief from Akhetaton, modern Amarna.

climate changed markedly, for the rain belt shifted, the wells began to dry up, and man and beast had to retreat to regions which afforded a means of livelihood. As bordering lands became desert, the Nile Valley continued to provide fertile ground.

People of differing races moved into the Nile Valley long before the dawn of history. The earliest inhabitants appear to have been a hunting people of the "Brown Mediterranean" type. Their tombs have yielded hunting knives, and the remains of dogs which were domesticated and trained as companions on the chase. After settling in the Nile Valley, the earliest Egyptians domesticated cattle, and subsequently became cultivators of the soil.

Early in historic times the basic Mediterranean population of Egypt was modified by groups of Asiatics of Anatolian and Semitic descent who settled from time to time on the eastern frontier of the Delta. They are known to have been in Egypt at the end of the Sixth Dynasty (*ca.* 2250 B.C.), and the Asiatic Hyksos actually ruled Egypt from about 1720 to 1550 B.C. During the time of Joseph, a Semitic Israelite who became Prime Minister of Egypt, the Israelite tribes settled in the district of the western Delta known as Goshen (Gen. 46).

Characteristically, the ancient Egyptian was tall and thin. He had reddish brown skin and long, curly black hair. Usually he wore a short beard. He had full lips, a long skull, and almond-shaped eyes. His hands were quite small. The ancient Egyptians spoke a Hamito-Semitic language which has been preserved in writing since about 3000 B.C. Its latest form, Coptic, is still used as a liturgical language in the Coptic Church. The Egyptian language seems to have been built on a Hamitic, African base to which numerous Semitic elements were added. These include a considerable amount of vocabulary, as well as prefixes, suffixes, and verb forms. The Egyptian verb, like that of the Semitic languages, is based on a tri-consonantal root.

The alluvium which provided Egypt with excellent soil made it inevitable that her economy would be based on agriculture. Egyptians lived in small villages, which they left each morning to tend their farms. Although theoretically all land belonged to the king, in practice the Egyptians treated their soil, cattle, and homes as private property, paying the required taxes to the government. Barley was the principal agricultural crop, with wheat and emmer occupying a secondary position. Egyptian flax made possible the manufacture of a high grade of linen, for which Egypt became famous. Fruits and melons were also grown in considerable quantity. Although the Egyptian became a food-producer before historic times, the abundance of life in the Nile made it inevitable that he would not abandon hunting entirely. Fish, geese, and ducks supplemented the food grown by Egyptian peasants on their small farms.

The Bible mentions the antipathy felt by the Egyptians of the Nile Valley toward the bedouin who tended flocks of sheep and goats (Gen. 46:34). Not only did Israel settle in the land of Goshen, east of the Delta, but bedouin have kept their flocks in that general area throughout history. Even today, Arab bedouin regularly appear in the Wadi Tumilat area between Lake Timsah and the Delta. The pasture land is covered with clumps of bulrushes, papyrus, and shrubs.

While the Egyptian frowned upon the nomadic bedouin with his sheep and goats, large cattle were raised in Egypt itself, and they were so abundant that their hides became an export commodity. The Hyksos invaders introduced the horse into Egypt (*ca.* 1700 B.C.), and in subsequent years Egypt was noted for its fine horses (cf. I Kings 10:28-29). The donkey was the caravan animal of ancient nomads who entered Egypt, as we know from the Beni Hasan tomb painting which depicts Semitic traders with their retinue. The camel was rare in Egypt until Persian times.

Egypt had a decided advantage over Mesopotamia in her natural supply of stone from nearby cliffs. Whereas Sumer and Babylon built their temples and palaces of mud brick, Egypt could use limestone, alabaster, granite, and basalt in her major buildings. Copper was available from the mines of Sinai, and Nubia was a ready source of gold, which was also mined in the hills between the Nile and the Red Sea. Egypt did not have a native supply of iron, however. With the beginnings of the Iron Age she was at a disadvantage because all her iron had to be imported. Egypt was also poor in wood. Her papyrus and shrubs could serve some minor needs, but good wood had to be imported from Phoenicia. Early in her history, Egypt maintained trade relations with Byblos (ancient Gebel) on the Syrian coast where she secured the famed cedar trees of Lebanon, along with fir and cyprus trees.

The history of Egypt is traditionally divided into thirty dynasties, extending from the time when Upper and Lower Egypt were unified under Menes (*ca.* 2980 B.C.) to Alexander's

Egyptian girls playing a double flute and a seven-stringed lyre, from a copy of the painting in a tomb at Thebes.

conquest (332 B.C.) The first two dynasties, which ruled from This, or Thinis, are known as the Early Dynastic or Thinite Period. Dynasties three to eight (*ca.* 2676-2194 B.C.) comprise the Old Kingdom, or Pyramid Age, when Pharoahs reigned from Memphis with unchallenged control. The absolutism of the Old Kingdom ended in a time of social upheaval known as the First Intermediate Period (*ca.* 2160-1991 B.C.) during which local princes gained power at the expense of the central government. Their rule covers Dynasties nine through eleven. The establishment of the powerful Twelfth Dynasty at Thebes (*ca.* 1991 B.C.) ushered in the brilliant Middle Kingdom (*ca.* 1991-1670 B.C.) during which literature and the arts flourished.

Egypt experienced her most trying hour during the Second Intermediate Period (*ca.* 1670-1568 B.C.), comprising Dynasties fifteen and sixteen, when Asiatic Hyksos seized control and reigned from Avaris in the eastern Delta. Kings of the Seventeenth Dynasty began the liberation of Egypt, and Ahmose, founder of the Eighteenth Dynasty, expelled the Hyksos and ushered in Egypt's New Kingdom, or Empire Period (1568-1085 B.C.) Egyptian armies marched into western Asia and controlled territory as far north as the Euphrates River. Dynasties nineteen and twenty mark the Rameside age, at the end of which a period of decline began from which Egypt never fully recovered. Dynasties twenty-one to twenty-three (1085-718 B.C.) were a period of transition, during which Israel became a monarchy under Saul and David. Solomon married an Egyptian princess, but relations with Egypt subsequently deteriorated, and Jeroboam was able to find a place of asylum there, from which he returned to challenge Rehoboam's right to the throne. Egypt sought to control Palestine through invasions and alliances designed to hold in check the rival Assyrian Empire in the East.

Dynasties twenty-five and twenty-six comprise the Late Period (750-525 B.C.) during which Ethiopian kings from Napata struggled with Assyrians for lordship over Egypt, and Saite kings including Necho and Apries (Hophra) fought on Palestinian battlefields and promised aid to the states of western Asia that would resist Assyria and Babylonia. Dynasties twenty-seven to thirty comprise the Persian Period (525-341 B.C.) following the conquest of Egypt by Cambyses. Egypt tried to throw off the Persian yoke, and was periodically successful until 332 B.C. when Alexander the Great conquered Egypt, whose people looked upon him as a deliverer, and the Hellenistic Age began.

This Egyptian sunk-relief in limestone portrays a young man in the style of Akhenaton and dates from the Eighteenth Dynasty (ca. 1370 B.C.).

20

Egyptian Religion

In the earliest days each village in Egypt looked to its own deity for the blessings of life and protection against hostile powers, human or demonic. The village would boast a shrine to its deity, and the worship of the local god served as a unifying influence within the community and a means of distinguishing one village from another.

Many of the names of these early village gods have been preserved in later traditions. Ptah was the god of Memphis, Atum of nearby Heliopolis. Ancient Thebes was dedicated to the worship of Montu. Khnum had his shrine at Herwer, near the First Cataract, and Min was worshiped at Coptos. Sometimes the god had no name distinct from the village in which he was worshiped. The god of Ombos is simply known as "the Ombite," and "He of Edfu" describes the god of that community.

Goddesses as well as gods claimed the allegiance of the Nile Valley peoples. Hathor was the "Lady of Dendera," and Neith was the goddess of Sais. Her name appears in Asenath (literally "She is of Neith"), the daughter of Potiphera, priest at On (Heliopolis), who married Joseph and was the mother of Ephraim and Manasseh (Gen. 41:45, 50-52; 46:20). The protective goddess of Memphis was Sekhmet, and Sobek was goddess in the Faiyum.

As the small Egyptian communities united to become states, or nomes, local gods gained a wider recognition; and when the two empires of Upper Egypt (the Nile Valley) and Lower Egypt (the Delta) came into being, two of the local gods — Seth of Ombos and Horus of Behdet — became the gods of the two nations. The political situation was explained in terms of a struggle for supremacy among the gods, each of whom took as his share half of Egypt.

About 3000 B.C., when Egypt became a unified state under

The palette of Narmer. The reverse (top) depicts Narmer with mace in hand ready to smite an enemy. The obverse (bottom) contains a circular recess for grinding cosmetics.

Nar-mer (Menes), Upper Egypt emerged as the dominant part of the country and Horus became god of "the two Egypts" — as the combined empire of Upper and Lower Egypt was called. The Pharaoh was considered the incarnation and patron of Horus and was therefore considered a god in his own right.

During the three thousand years of ancient Egyptian history the gods gained and lost popularity and religion itself acquired many nuances which would have been strange to the earliest Egyptians. The vulture goddess of Nekheb (Elkab) and the serpent goddess of Buto became national deities during one of the periods when north and south were divided. The worship of Amon was transferred from Hermopolis to Thebes during the Eleventh Dynasty. Later, Amon was identified with Re and the national god of the New Kingdom became "Amon-Re, King of the Gods."

As people moved from place to place they brought their local gods with them and erected new shrines for their worship. On occasion the god of a particular community gained a reputation for special power as the result of some supposedly potent cure or display of miraculous intervention. As a result, people from neighboring areas would make pilgrimages to the god's shrine, or build him new shrines in their own villages. In some such way, Neith of Sais acquired a shrine at Esna.

At an early date local deities came to be associated with some distinctive characteristic, so that the falcon-shaped Montu was worshiped as a war god and Min of Coptos became a god of fertility and harvest, and patron of desert travelers. Ptah of Memphis, in whose province the distinctive art of Egypt originated, became patron of artists, smiths, and metal workers. As such he may be compared with the Canaanite Kathar-wa-Khassis, the classical Hephaestus, and the Teutonic Vulcan.

Sekhmet of Memphis was a fire goddess who annihilated her enemies, while the more kindly Hathor of Dendera was a goddess of love and joy. The falcon god Horus, identified with the sun, was pictured as a youthful hero in perpetual battle with his evil brother Seth, the storm god. The ibis-headed Thoth, of Hermopolis, was the moon god who had created the divisions of time and order in the universe. Thoth was "lord of divine words," who had invented hieroglyphic writing and was the god of learning in general. Sobek, the crocodile god, had his home in the water.

In addition to the numerous city gods, an ancient Egyptian was concerned with a multitude of lesser gods, demons, and spirits who might either help or injure man. There were gods who assisted women in childbirth, gods of the household, and gods of the harvest. In times of illness, spirits provided healing, and others were particularly active in time of war. Maᶜat was the goddess of truth and justice.

When the people of a district lived in peace and enjoyed fellowship with one another, the local gods shared in this fellowship. Gods might actually be taken to a neighboring city to pay a visit to that city's deity. An outside god might be presented with his own chapel in the temple of the city god, so that eventually the god of a powerful and wealthy city might be surrounded by the images of gods and demigods.

In time certain gods came to be grouped together as family units. In the temple of Karnak at Thebes we meet the god Amon, the goddess Mut, and their son Khonsu (the moon). Similarly at Memphis we find Ptah, Sekhmet and Nefertem. At Abydos we meet the favored family of Osiris, Isis, and Horus.

The outward manifestations of the gods of Egypt were crude, and historians wonder how a people so advanced in many areas of culture could be so crass in matters of religious devotion. Neith was represented as a shield to which a pair of crossed arrows had been nailed, and Busiris was depicted in the form of a pillar with the head and arms of a king. Ptah of Memphis and Min of Coptos were fetishes in semi-human form.

Most common were the representations of deities in animal form. Sobek, the crocodile; Thoth, the ibis; Khnum, the ram; Hathor, the cow; and Buto, the serpent are but a few of the gods depicted as animals.

It was customary to have the wooden statue of a god in its own shrine in the local temple. On feast days the statue would be removed and carried in procession on the shoulders of priests, or transported on the river in a sacred bark. When a particular animal was sacred to a given temple, specimens of that animal were kept in the Temple. Strabo, in the time of Augustus Caesar, mentions the crocodile sacred to Sobek at Arsinoe, capital of the Faiyum:

The Egyptian god Amon.

> It is fed with the bread, meat, and wine brought by the strangers who come to see it. Our host went with us to the lake, taking along a small meal-cake, some meat, and a small flask of wine. We found the animal lying on the bank; the priests approached, and while some of them opened his jaws, another thrust first the cake into his mouth, then the meat, and finally poured the wine after them. Thereupon the crocodile plunged into the lake and swam to the opposite shore.

From very ancient times the Egyptians represented their gods in human forms as well. Gods appeared with human face and figure, wearing the same clothing as the Egyptians. Their head was adorned with a helmet or crown. In their hands were a baton and a scepter, symbolic of authority. The goddess would carry a papyrus blossom with a long stem.

Gods which had been depicted in animal form were transferred into human figures surmounted by the heads of the sacred animals. Thus Sobek might be depicted as a crocodile, or as a man with the head of a crocodile. Khnum became a man with a ram's head; Horus a man with the head of a falcon; Thoth a man with the head of an ibis. The goddess Sekhmet became a woman with the head of a lionness.

In addition to local deities identified with animals, Egypt had several sacred animals which were particularly venerated. Most important was the Apis Bull of Memphis which, according to a legend preserved in Greek sources, was begotten by a ray of sunlight which descended from heaven and impregnated a cow. The Apis Bull was black, with white spots including a white triangle on the forehead and the figure of a crescent moon on the right side. Usually he wore a red cloth on his back. As early as the Old Kingdom, priests were assigned to care for the Apis Bull. Later theological speculation sought to discover a relationship between the Bull and Ptah, the god of Memphis. As a result the Apis Bull was declared to be the son of Ptah, or "the living reincarnation of Ptah."

During New Kingdom times deceased bulls were given elaborate burials in mausoleums at Saqqara near Memphis. Rameses II laid out an elaborate gallery in which bulls were buried in stone sarcophagi. The gallery, known as the Serapeum was carved out of solid rock. It was three hundred fifty feet long with rows of niches for the burial of individual bulls. Many pious pilgrims came to the Serapeum to venerate the bulls as late as the Ptolemaic period.

In addition to the divine Pharaoh, certain other humans were deified by the Egyptians and accorded a place in the pantheon. The famous architect Imhotep who served as chief minister to Pharaoh Zoser was regarded as the son of Ptah and became an Egyptian god of wisdom and medicine. Imhotep's greatest accomplishment was the Step Pyramid which he designed for Zoser at Saqqarah, near Memphis. His fame was known to the Greeks who called him Imouthes and identified him with their god of healing, Asklepios. Divinity was also ascribed to Amenophis, son of Hapu, the minister of the Eighteenth Dynasty Pharaoh Amenhotep III.

Discovered at Thebes, this commemorative scarab was issued in 1422 B.C. on the occasion of the construction of a pleasure lake for Queen Tiy by Pharaoh Amenhotep III.

The phenomena of nature — sun, moon, stars, heaven, earth, the Nile — all had a place in Egyptian religion. The sky god was pictured as a falcon with protective wings spread over Egypt, or over all the earth. The sun and moon were his divine eyes, and the stars were attached to his body. Wind is the breadth of his mouth, and water his perspiration.

In another nature myth the sky was depicted as the goddess Nut. In primordial times she was embraced by the earth god, Geb, until Shu — god of the atmosphere — separated them by elevating Nut high above the earth and placing himself beneath her. From the union of Geb and Nut — earth and heaven — there sprang a son, Re, the sun god and the most popular of all the cosmic gods. He travels by day in his bark across the celestial ocean. When night comes he transfers to another boat, descends to the netherworld and continues his voyage.

Re also was depicted as a falcon soaring through the sky with bright plumage, or as a young hero carrying on a constant struggle with the hostile powers of darkness. As the god of Edfu in Upper Egypt, Re often appears as a sun disk with extended wings, the form in which he regularly appears as a symbol of protection over doors and elsewhere in Egyptian temples. It became customary for Egyptians to present offerings to Re under the open sky. Pharoahs of the Fifth Dynasty considered themselves the children of Re. He had a temple near Memphis which had, as its chief feature, an obelisk erected on a stone substructure.

In the development of Egyptian theology, connections were seen between the local gods and celestial powers. The falcon shaped Horus was identified with the sky god and became Harakhti, "Horus of the Horizon." He in turn was identified with Re, giving the doubly compound name Re-Harakhti, "Re-Horus of the Horizon." In this form Re appears as a king with the head of a falcon surmounted by the sun disk, from which hangs the uraeus serpent, a symbol of royalty.

The crocodile, Sobek, and the ram, Khnum, along with Amon of Thebes were identified with Re and assigned the sun disk and uraeus as signs of rank. Local gods retained their old attributes and myths alongside the newer identifications so that the religion contained many confusing and self-contradicting ideas. There were efforts to distinguish various phases of the sun god, so that Khepri, the sun in the form of a scarab, was worshiped as the morning sun, and Atum as the evening sun.

The female deities tended to become identified with the sky

goddess Nut. When Hathor, the cow goddess was identified with Nut, mythology suggested that the sky was an enormous cow, held fast by numerous gods and supported in position by Shu, god of the atmosphere. The stars were attached to the cow's belly and the sun-god travelled in his bark around her body.

The cat goddess of Bubastis, and the lionesses Sekhmet and Pekhet were identified with Mut, the consort of Amon and mother of the gods. Hathor and Isis were also identified. Amon of Karnak, Min of Coptos, and Khnum of Elephantine were combined into a single deity.

While the confusion produced by the Egyptian religious concepts may seem to defy schematization, the priests at the religious centers did try to work out logical theologies. The best known formulation dates from Fifth Dynasty Heliopolis. Here the priests described the self-engendered Atum emerging from primeval chaos, bringing the cosmos into being. From himself, Atum produced Shu, the god of the air, and Tefnut, goddess of moisture. The union of this couple produced Geb, the earth god, and Nut, the sky goddess. They, in turn, produced four children: Osiris who represented the forces of life, and his wife-sister Isis; Seth, representing the force of destruction, and his wife-sister Nephthys. The nine gods and goddesses: Shu, Tefnut, Geb, Osiris, Isis, Seth, and Nephthys are known as the Ennead.

The priests at Hermopolis taught that eight primordial gods were created from primeval chaos by the voice of Thoth. Four frogs represent the male deities, with four snakes representing the female principle. These deities produced at Hermopolis an egg from which emerged the sun who conquered his enemies, created mankind, and organized the world as we know it.

As early as Old Kingdom times a theology was developed at Memphis which exalted the god Ptah as chief of the pantheon. Ptah made eight other Ptahs, all embodied in himself. Atum was the thought of Ptah, Horus, his heart, and Thoth his tongue.

By historical times the Egyptian local gods, cosmic deities, and gods responsible for some function or aspect of life were so blended that one name bore numerous connotations. Thoth was god of Hermopolis, but he was also the moon god and the god of wisdom. Hathor was goddess of Dendera, a sky goddess, and goddess of love.

Once during the history of Pharaonic Egypt the established religion was challenged by a reformer. The Eighteenth dynasty Pharaoh Amenhotep IV devoted himself to the god Aton, one of the manifestations of the sun god of Heliopolis. After breaking with the Amon priesthood at Thebes, the capital of New Kingdom Egypt, Amenhotep IV took to himself the name Akhenaton and moved his capital to Akhetaton, modern Tell el-Amarna, where he encouraged new concepts of literature and art as well as the new religious emphasis. Akhenaton banned all religious activity except that which was addressed to Aton, and as a result is frequently considered a monotheist. His was not, however, the spiritual monotheism which was represented by Israel's prophets, but rather a monotheism which exalted the disk of the sun to a pre-eminent position. Akhenaton's reforms did not long outlive their chief exponent, and the priests of Amon were able to reassert the religious philosophy of the old regime during the lifetime of Tutankhamon, Akhenaton's son-in-law.

In Old Kingdom times the Pharaoh was theoretically the sole priest, but in practice he delegated authority to the nomarchs and other officials for the performance of the religious rites. It was during the Middle Kingdom that the professional priesthood evolved, and by New Kingdom times the priesthood had developed to the point where four companies of priests served in rotation, a month at a time. Priests were permitted to marry and they engaged in commerce, trade, and other secular activities when not officiating in the temples.

The afterlife was uppermost in Egyptian thought, and much of the energy expended by the inhabitants of the Nile Valley had as its goal the provision for a happy future. Egyptian religion taught that man could live on in the future exactly as he had lived on earth provided the necessities for such existence were available. Tombs were provided with jars of food and drink. Wealthy Egyptians or their relatives established endowments, the income from which was to furnish food for the deceased for all time. Children were expected to provide for their parents' welfare in the next life. Walls of tombs were covered with representations of food, drink, and other objects which might serve the deceased, and it was thought that these pictures might magically be transformed into the actual objects.

The deceased also depended upon the prayers of survivors to guarantee their welfare. Visitors who chanced to pass a tomb were invited to repeat prayers which could magically conjure up all that was needed for the nourishment and enjoyment of the deceased. Food, drink, oils, ointments, cosmetics — all that might be useful to the departed in the next life — could be

A granite statue of Horemhab, the commander of Tutankhamon's armies, who later became a pharaoh in his own right.

made available by the faithful prayers of relatives and friends.

The lavish furnishings of the tombs of Egyptian Pharaohs can best be imagined by viewing the articles discovered by Howard Carter in the tomb of Tutankhamon in the Valley of the Kings, west of Luxor, ancient Thebes. Tutankhamon was a minor Pharaoh who died young, but the wealth of objects discovered in his tomb staggers the imagination. They are the most treasured exhibits in the Cairo Museum today.

The Egyptian thought of man as a creature with a body and a soul (Egyptian *Ba*) which was pictured as a bird which departs the body at death and flies around the world. At night the *ba* might return to the safety of the tomb, but this could take place only if the body of the deceased was properly preserved. To prevent decomposition and enable the soul to recognize the body the Egyptians developed the art of mummification. The *ba* could, by means of magical formulas, transform itself into a falcon, a serpent, a lily, or a crocodile. The Greeks erroneously interpreted this as a doctrine of the transmigration of the soul.

In addition to the *Ba,* the Egyptian also had a *Ka,* a protective spirit or genius who was born simultaneously with the individual and had a close relation to him throughout life. The *Ka* did not die with the individual, but survived the deceased to quicken him with life and strength and protect him from his enemies in the next life.

Domestic gods were also concerned with the well being of departed ones in the grave. Many cities had special mortuary gods, including Khenty-Imentiu, "The first of the westerners". (i.e., the dead) who was represented as a jackall. Such deities early receded in favor of Osiris, the deified king of Busiris who met a tragic death by drowning in the Nile. While Abydos became the chief center for the worship of Osiris, his fame spread throughout Egypt. The saga of his life and death was the most appealing of all the stories of Egypt's gods. Although it has not been preserved in Egyptian texts, it is known from the writings of Plutarch.

Osiris was a good king, but Seth, his wicked brother, had designs on the throne. Seth, by trickery, had his brother lay himself in an artistically wrought chest, whereupon seventy-two henchmen of the usurper sprang upon the chest, closed the lid, and cast it into the Nile River. It was carried by the waters of the Nile to the Mediterranean, then along the Palestinian coast as far as Byblos where it landed. In the meantime Isis, the

This relief, dating back to the Eighteenth Dynasty, shows Hapi, the god of the Nile.

lovely sister and wife of Osiris journeyed throughout the world seeking the body of her husband. After finding it at Byblos, she carried it back to Egypt and mourned for her departed loved one.

Since the wicked Seth was now on the throne of Egypt, Isis had to act with utmost caution. She concealed the coffin and went to Buto, in the Delta marshes, to stay with her son Horus. While on a hunting expedition, Seth came upon the coffin of his hated brother. He divided the body into fourteen pieces and scattered them throughout Egypt. Isis, however, learned of this insult to her dead husband and again went in search of his remains. She discovered them and erected a monument over each. When the lad Horus grew to manhood he avenged the death of his father by winning a victory over Seth. Through the magic of Horus, Osiris was brought back to life and ruled in the west as king of the blessed dead.

By identification with Osiris, the Egyptians hoped to share in his victory and immortality. As Osiris had died, so they knew they must die, but because Osiris had been given life again, so they hoped for a blessed future. The faithfulness of Horus in using the proper formulas to bring his father back to life suggested that faithful sons of all Egyptians might perform the proper rites to insure to their parents a blessed future. In this way the deceased might actually become Osiris.

The entrance into the blessed realm of Osiris depended on the proper use of magical formulas and spells, but they were valueless unless the deceased had lived a virtuous life on earth. At death each individual appeared for judgment in the presence of Osiris who sat with a court of forty-two judges. The deceased sought to convince his judges that he had been innocent of wrong-doing throughout life. After he had given his defense his heart was weighed in the balances before the god Thoth. If his heart was found to be guiltless, the individual entered a blessed future life.

The dwelling place of the dead was in the west — the region of the sunset. The departed might be transferred into shining stars in the heavens or, in mundane fashion, as living in celestial fields of rushes where they cultivated soil, plowed, sowed, and reaped as on earth. There, however, grain grew seven cubits (twelve feet) high — a wonderful paradise for the Egyptian peasant!

Labor, however, did not seem desirable in a heavenly para-

This combination of writing equipment served as the hieroglyph for the word "scribe." A palette, with two circular sections hollowed out, is attached to a writing reed and a water jar. The palette is original; the other objects are reconstructed.

dise, and after the Middle Kingdom we find mummiform figures placed in the tombs of the deceased. They are provided with farm implements and sacred symbols to perform the menial tasks of the future life. These figurines, known as *Ushabtiu*, bore the names of the deceased whom they were to serve. Magical formulas inscribed on the figures could bring them to life and enable them to perform their duties.

The Egyptian "Book of What is in the Netherworld" describes an earth beneath the world of the living, with a stream — a subterranean Nile — flowing through its length. This earth is divided into twelve parts, corresponding to the twelve hours of the night. The parts are separated from each other by great gates. The ram-headed sun god, surrounded by a royal retinue, sails his bark on the stream bringing light and life for a time to those who inhabit the nether regions. The nightly voyages bring joy to the deceased, who become for a time companions of the sun god. At dawn, however, the sun god leaves the subterranean world to enter the upper world and journey across the celestial ocean where the living may behold him.

Earliest Egyptian burials were simple affairs. The body was placed on its left side in a natural sleeping position. Knees were against the body and hands before the face. In Old Kingdom times, the period of the earliest Pharaohs, bodies were stretched out full length and placed in tombs. Mummification was practiced to prevent deterioration of the body. The viscera were removed and the resulting cavity filled with wads of linen cloth. The corpse was saturated with natron and bound with linen wrappings. Cedar oil was used at a later time. Resinous pastes were used to preserve the contour of the body.

The viscera were interred in four vases, protected by four deities responsible for guaranteeing the deceased against hunger and thirst. In rich burials, the vases were placed in chests constructed in the form of a chapel adorned with representations of the gods and religious inscriptions. The process of mummification lasted seventy days, after which the body was laid in its coffin and removed to the tomb. In Old Kingdom times the coffin was a rectangular chest of stone or wood. It was made in the form of a house with doors to symbolize the concept that the coffin was a house for the dead. During the Eighteenth Dynasty the coffin was in the form of a man or woman arrayed in the costume of the time, or in the form of a mummy decorated with religious pictures and inscriptions.

The Egyptian concern with the material aspects of survival — the great concern for proper mummification and the correct magical formulas — has caused many modern students to conclude that their religion was devoid of an element of personal warmth and devotion. It is true that we have little evidence of the personal side of Egyptian religion, but it does appear that Egyptians felt that their gods were near to them and were interested in their welfare. Such names as Meri-Re, "Beloved of Re," and Ptah-em-saf, "Ptah is his protection" show that religion was more than a formality to the devout.

The events preceding the Exodus may be looked upon as a contest between Yahweh, Israel's God, and the numerous gods of Egypt. The element of power is uppermost in the contest: Egypt's gods are powerless, but Yahweh is omnipotent. While Yahweh is specifically the God of Israel, He is concerned that his power be known among the Egyptians: "And the Egyptians shall know that I am Yahweh, when I stretch forth my hand upon Egypt and bring out the people of Israel from among them" (Exod. 7:5). When the Nile became putrid, and the sun (Re) was darkened, the Egyptians could see the impotence of their gods. Centuries later the Greeks and Romans expressed contempt and scorn at finding primitive religious ideas in a race so admirable for its achievements. It is one of the ironics of history that Israel, never a world power and usually a pawn between the larger states, should have been the nation through which the knowledge of the true God came while Egypt, at one time the major power in the East, never matured in religious thinking but worshiped a multitude of gods and entertained crass theories of the universe until the Jew, the Christian, and ultimately the Moslem put the death blow to the religious concepts of ancient Egypt.

21

The Pharaoh
Who Knew Not Joseph

Joseph the Prime Minister! The recollection of the wisdom of this Semitic official who had saved Egypt from the horrors of famine must have lasted long in the memories of his grateful subjects. Yet we do not meet the name of Joseph in any Egyptian record. Ever since scholars began to decipher the hieroglyphic writing of Egypt people have wondered about the strange absence of any mention of Joseph, or Moses, or any phase of the Israelite sojourn in Egypt. Not until the reign of Merneptah (*ca.* 1224-1216 B.C.) do we meet the name of Israel, and then it appears on a stele which boasts of Egyptian victories in Canaan. Nationalistic Egyptians may have chosen to forget the Semite who had saved their land from the consequences of famine.

For centuries, Semites had brought their wares to Egypt and caravans of semi-nomadic peoples bringing articles for trade became commonplace. The nineteenth century B.C. tomb painting from Beni-Hasan depicts a group of Asiatics entering Egypt with their families to trade eye paint for the products of the Nile Valley.

Many Semitic traders eventually found a home in Egypt, particularly in the eastern Delta, the region closest to Syria and Palestine. It was in this area that Joseph encouraged his family to settle when famine conditions had driven them out of Canaan. Scripture calls this district the land of Goshen (Gen. 47:6, 27). Although we are not certain of the exact location of Goshen, it is sometimes called "the land of Ramesses" (cf. Gen. 47:6, 11), suggesting that it was the region adjacent to the city of Raamses in the northeastern Delta.

The Egyptians, always proud of the culture which they had developed in the Nile Valley and Delta, were humiliated during the years which followed the decline of the Middle Kingdom (*ca*. 1991-1786 B.C.). During a time of Egyptian weakness a people known as the Hyksos seized control of the government and ruled much of Egypt. Many of the Hyksos were Semites, but some were Hittites and Hurrians. Manetho, a priest at Heliopolis during the third century B.C., who wrote a history of Egypt, said of the Hyksos:

> In his reign (i.e., Tutimaeus), for what cause I know not, a blast of God smote us; and unexpectedly, from the regions of the East, invaders of obscure race marched in confidence of victory against our land. By main force they easily seized it without striking a blow; and having overpowered the rulers of the land, they then burned our cities ruthlessly, razed to the ground the temples of the gods, and treated all the natives with cruel hostility.... Finally, they appointed as king one of their number whose name was Salitis.[1]

Manetho is giving, to be sure, a biased picture of the Hyksos whose rule was resented by the native Egyptians. The Hyksos invasion probably began with the infiltration of semi-nomadic Asiatics into the eastern Delta. During times when Egypt was not strong enough to defend her frontiers, the Semitic peoples from the east moved toward the lush terrain of the Nile Delta. After establishing a hegemony over the eastern fringes of the Delta, making Avaris their capital, the Hyksos gradually extended their power until the entire Delta, and finally Upper Egypt as well, was subject to their power.

The name Hyksos means "rulers of foreign lands," and in Manetho's list of Egyptian rulers they comprise the Fifteenth and Sixteenth Dynasties. Hyksos rule was well established by 1700 B.C. and continued for about a century and a half. Biblical scholars usually suggest that Joseph and his brothers entered Egypt during Hyksos times on the assumption that the non-Egyptian Hyksos rulers would be more likely than native born Pharaohs to promote a Semite such as Joseph to a position of authority. It is possible that the Pharaoh under whom Joseph ruled was a native Egyptian, however, for prejudices against Semites are mentioned in the Biblical text. We read that "the Egyptians might not eat bread with the Hebrews, for that is an abomination to the Egyptians" (Gen. 43:32) and that the Israelites settled in Goshen instead of the Nile valley because "every shepherd is an abomination to the Egyptians" (Gen. 46:34). Since we have no means of giving positive dates to the descent of Joseph and his family into Egypt, we cannot be certain concerning the dynasty in power when they settled in Goshen. Biblical evidence, however, suggests that Joseph's fam-

The Beni Hasan tomb painting shows Semites entering Egypt during the nineteenth century, B.C.

---

1. Quoted in Josephus, *Against Apion* I, 14.

Amenhotep II is depicted on this limestone relief as standing on his chariot and shooting arrows at a copper target.

ily settled in an area near Pharaoh's court (Gen. 46:28f.), a fact that argues for Hyksos times when the Empire was ruled from Avaris in the Delta.

If Joseph was given his favored position under a native dynasty, it must have been prior to the Hyksos rule. Following the period of Hyksos control, Egyptian life could never be the same. A new nationalism supplanted the older tolerance for foreigners. Egypt determined to rule rather than be ruled. Native rulers of the Eighteenth Dynasty tried to cut out of the monuments every reference to the despised Hyksos, but modern Egyptologists have been able to piece together evidence that their rule was not entirely bad. The Hyksos Empire included both Egypt and Palestine. Trade connections were maintained with Mesopotamia and the island of Crete as we know from inscriptions bearing the name of Khayan, their most famous king.

The horse and chariot were introduced into Egypt by the Hyksos invaders. The particular type of fortification used by the Hyksos has been found in Palestine and Syria as well as Egypt. Huge earth ramparts were built to enclose fortified areas for the housing of chariots. Excavations at Jericho and Shechem have brought to light such fortifications, suggesting that kings of the Palestinian city states owed feudal allegiance to the Hyksos king.

The family of Jacob-Israel that migrated to Egypt during the time of Joseph comprised about seventy people. As the population grew, Israelites probably moved out of Goshen and lived in closer proximity to their Egyptian neighbors. It is also possible that some migrated from time to time back to Canaan, their ancestral homeland. When Jacob died, Joseph and his brothers led a large retinue back to the family burial place at Hebron (Gen. 50:7-14). Through the intervening years there must have been many such caravans traversing the familiar roads eastward from Goshen.[2]

When the Israelites entered Canaan under Joshua they seem to have found some closely related peoples who recognized them as friends. Although neither the books of Joshua nor Judges state this in so many words, there is much circumstantial evidence to show that it was so. Shechem, near the boundary

2. W. F. Albright, BASOR 58 (April 1935), pp. 10-18 and BASOR 74 (April 1939), pp. 11-23 maintains that the Joseph tribes (Ephraim and Manasseh) were in Palestine around 1400 B.C.

between Ephraim and Manasseh (Josh. 17:6), had been associated with Israelite tradition since Abraham had first entered Canaan (Gen. 12:6-7). During the fifteenth century B.C. the *Hapiru* people mentioned in the Amarna Letters occupied the city.[3] The account of the conquest of Canaan by the Israelites includes no record of battles at Shechem, but following the conquest Joshua called all of the tribes to assemble there for renewal of the covenant (Josh. 24:1-28). The people of Shechem were evidently Israelites who were in Canaan prior to the Exodus.

Although Lower and Middle Egypt seem to have become reconciled to Hyksos rule, Thebes in Upper Egypt plotted the revolt which ultimately brought native Egyptians back into power. After several generations of strife, an Egyptian named Ahmose succeeded in capturing the Hyksos capital at Avaris, in the eastern Delta, and driving them out of the country. Ahmose, according to the reckoning of Manetho, was the founder of the Eighteenth Dynasty which ushered in Egypt's New Kingdom or Empire Period. After driving them out of Egypt, Ahmose pursued the Hyksos to their stronghold at Sheruhen in southern Palestine, and spent the next six years trying to dislodge them. The years of Hyksos rule taught the Egyptians that they could not be satisfied with the isolated seclusion which the Nile Valley provided. The path of safety seemed to be in Empire, and Egypt sought to drive the Hyksos rulers from Palestine and rule in her own right.

The "new king over Egypt who did not know Joseph" (Exod. 1:8) must have been one of the New Kingdom rulers who did not trust foreigners in his land. The Egyptians foresaw a time when their own land would be invaded, and they were naturally concerned about the loyalty of resident aliens. A foreign element in the population might side with Egypt's enemies in the event of conflict. From the Egyptian viewpoint it was a matter of self-preservation that dictated a policy of anti-semitism.

The Egyptians, however, did not want to drive the Israelites out of the country. Their flocks and herds could provide dainties for the tables of aristocratic Egyptians, and the Israelites themselves comprised a labor force that could be utilized in the royal building projects.

Amarna letters from governors of city-states in Palestine who appealed for help from Egypt against rebels and the semi-nomadic Hapiru.

---

3. Cf. J. B. Pritchard, ed. *Ancient Near Eastern Texts*, pp. 477, 485-87, 489, 490.

The government decided to build a series of store cities as repositories for provisions and weapons which might be needed in the event of attack upon the eastern Delta. Since the Israelites were living nearby, it seemed wise to put them to work on these cities. Pithom, the first store city mentioned in Exodus (1:11), is the Egyptian *Per-itm,* "house of (the god) Atum," in the Wadi Tumilat, the fertile depression which runs through the desert separating the Delta from Ismailia. Scholars differ concerning the identification of Pithom, suggesting either Tell el-Mashkhuta ("mound of idols") or Tell er-Retabeh.

Raamses, the second store city, is the Egyptian *Per-Raamses,* "the house of Ramesses" where Ramesses II (1290-1224 B.C.) maintained his residence. Since the excavations of Pierre Montet at Tanis, most scholars agree that Raamses was located at or near Tanis, the Zoan of Psalm 78:12, 43, and the Avaris of Hyksos times. A letter of a scribe of the Nineteenth Dynasty reveals the impression Raamses made on an Egyptian:

> I have arrived at Per-Raamses the Beloved of Amon, and find that it is most excellent, a magnificent place that has no equal. The god Re has founded it according to the plan of Thebes. To sojourn there is a benefit to life; its fields are full of every good thing, it has foodstuffs and provisions every day. Its pools are full of fish, its lagoons full of birds, its meadows green with grass ... its fruits have the flavor of honey in the cultivated fields (?). Its granaries are full of barley and grain; they rise up to the sky. It has onions and leeks for foodstuffs (?), pomegranites, apples, and olives and figs from the orchards. Sweet wine from Kenkeme that is more excellent than honey ... the Shi-hor (i.e. the Pelusiac Branch of the Nile) furnishes salt and nitrate: its boats depart and return. Foodstuffs and provisions are there every day. There one enjoys living, and no one exclaims. Ah yes! The lowly are treated there like the great — Arise, let us celebrate its festivities of heaven and its beginning of summer.

The ruling Pharaoh hoped that the forced labor imposed upon the Israelites would weaken them and check their rapid growth. His plans were frustrated, however, for the more they were oppressed the more they multiplied (Exod. 1:12). It became necessary to try a different strategy.

To limit population growth, the Pharaoh instructed the two midwives who attended the Israelite mothers to kill any male children that were born. In preparation for childbirth, women crouched on a pair of bricks or stones, the "birthstools" mentioned in Exodus (1:16). An Egyptian text preserved in the Papyrus Westcar (*ca.* 1700-1600 B.C.) tells how three goddesses delivered a priest's wife of three sons. Each goddess took a child in her arms. In turn they cut the umbilical cord, washed the child, put it on a little brick bench, and went to the waiting husband to announce the birth. If such a ritual was practiced

This bas-relief, from the great cliff temple built by Ramesses II, records prisoners brought in from countries to the north.

in the Israelite homes it would have been between the birth of a son and the announcement of the event to the waiting husband that the midwives were asked to kill the child.

The midwives, however, "feared God" (Exod. 1:17) and refused to commit murder even at the command of the Pharaoh. They gave as their excuse that the strong Hebrew women would give birth to their children before the midwife could arrive. When the Pharaoh learned that he could not work through the midwives to control the Israelite population he determined to go directly to the people. By royal decree it was ordered that every Israelite male child should be cast into the Nile.

A frontal view of the great cliff temple built by Ramesses II. Carved in a mountainside, the work is 210 feet in depth.

22

The Preparation of Moses

Into the home of a pious couple of the tribe of Levi a child was born who, according to Pharaoh's decree, should have been cast into the Nile River to perish. The parents, however, like the pious midwives who had defied the royal edict, determined to save their child. For three months Jochebed watched over her infant son, keeping him from prying eyes, and she came to love him more and more each day. As the boy grew older she knew that she could not keep her secret, so she determined to save him by outwitting the king. She placed him in an ark of bulrushes in the Nile and trusted God to care for the child.

An older sister, Miriam, was watching the child in his strange bed when Pharaoh's daughter came to the river to bathe. Jochebed must have known of her habits, and trusted that her sympathy would be aroused by the helpless child. According to plan the princess saw the child and determined to save him. When Miriam saw the princess' interest she offered to find a nurse to care for the child. And so it happened that, in the providence of God, Miriam arranged for Moses' mother to care for her own son with the blessing of Pharaoh's daughter.

The fascinating story of Moses in the bulrushes has parallels in the literature of other peoples. Sargon of Akkad, the Semitic empire builder who ruled much of western Asia during the twenty-fourth century B.C., had a similar experience. Legend says that he was born of a priestess who placed him in a reed basket on the Euphrates River. Akki, a worker on the canals, found the infant and adopted him as his own. The foundling later became the world conqueror who was the first ruler of the dynasty of Akkad (*ca.* 2360-2180 B.C.).

Although both Sargon and Moses were placed in baskets and taken to rivers, other circumstances of their infancy were quite dissimilar. Sargon's mother wanted to rid herself of an unwanted child, while Moses' mother wished to protect her son from mortal danger. Moses did not, like Sargon, grow up to be a king, but rather became a prophet of God, a deliverer from tyranny, and a lawgiver.

Who was the Pharaoh's daughter who found Moses? The question is related to matters of chronology, and no definite answer can be given. The church historian Eusebius[1] records a tradition that her name was Merris whereas the rabbinical traditions suggest Bityah. Josephus calls her Thermutis.[2]

While there is no evidence to indicate the spot where the child was found, the general locale can be identified with little difficulty. It was near both a royal palace — where Pharaoh's daughter resided — and the place where the Hebrews lived, described elsewhere as the Land of Goshen (Gen. 47:6, 11). This limits the location to the eastern Delta, perhaps near Tanis or Bubastis.

The name Moses seems to be of Egyptian origin. Although the Hebrew form of the word is a play on words, signifying one who is "drawn out" of the water (Exod. 2:10), the Egyptian name goes back to *mes, mesu,* meaning "one born," "a child." A name such as Thothmes means "child (or one born) of Thoth." The name Moses may be a shortened form of a once longer Egyptian word.

Scripture gives no details concerning the youth of Moses. We know that Pharaoh's daughter adopted him and gave him an education such as an Egyptian prince might receive (cf. Acts 7:22). The Egyptian school system was a highly developed one. Sons of tributary princes from the Syro-Palestinian city states were sent to Egypt to study with Egyptian royalty. In this way they became pro-Egyptian in politics, and when a throne was vacant, the rulers of Egypt sought to place one of these Egyptian-trained vassals in the position of power. The boys also served as hostages, for the king of a city state would hardly attack an Egyptian garrison if he thought his own son might suffer as a result. During Moses' period of schooling he may have had classmates from as far north as the Euphrates River, and he may have learned quite a bit about geography and history from them.

Egyptian learning at the middle of the second millennium B.C. was at a high level in such centers as On (Heliopolis) nineteen miles north of the earlier capital, Memphis. The Sep-

---

1. *Praeparatio evangelica* ix. 27.
2. *Antiquities* II. ix. 5.

tuagint actually mentions Heliopolis along with Pithom and
Raamses as cities where the Israelites performed slave labor, and
Manetho, the Egyptian historian, claims that Moses became a
priest at Heliopolis. Herodotus, known in the West as "the
Father of History," observed that the priests at Heliopolis were
well informed concerning historical matters. Some generations
before Moses, Joseph married Asenath, a daughter of Potiphera,
a priest at Heliopolis.

Circumstantial evidence would lead us to think that the
education of Moses would take him to a place such as Heliopolis. Temples were usually the depositories for records and
royal decrees, and the priests would have access to materials
which would not normally be available to laymen.

Probably Moses' first task as a student was the mastery of the
hieroglyphic system of writing. The name hieroglyphic (literally
"sacred writing") is of Greek origin and it suggests that the
priests were the first masters of the art of written communication. Hieroglyphic texts date back well over a millennium and
a half before the time of Moses, but only the educated priest
or scribe had the ability to read and write.

In addition to the hieroglyphs, Moses probably learned to
read the Akkadian cuneiform method of writing on clay tablets.
Akkadian was the lingua franca of the Amarna Age (fifteenth
and fourteenth centuries B.C.). Rulers of the city states in
Syria and Palestine as well as kings from the Tigris-Euphrates
region corresponded with Egyptian Pharoahs in Akkadian cuneiform. Moses also may have become familiar with the proto-
Sinaitic alphabetic script which was used in the turquoise mines
at Serabit el-Khadem near Mount Sinai.

A prince such as Moses would have studied the maxims of
Ptah-hotep and other sages who gave Egypt a reputation for
wisdom in the ancient world. When the Biblical historian
wished to extoll the wisdom of King Solomon he said, "... Solomon's wisdom surpassed the wisdom of all the people of the
east, and all the wisdom of Egypt" (I Kings 4:30). Long
before Solomon, the wise men of Egypt sought to instruct the
younger generation in prudence and decorum so that they
could serve their country in the best possible way.

As an Egyptian prince, Moses would have grown accustomed
to the skillful music of court harpists and the sound of handmaids reading aloud the stories which had become a part of
Egypt's literary heritage. He probably knew by heart the story
of Sinuhe, an Egyptian courtier who left his homeland and

spent years among the bedouin of the Syro-Palestinian country until he reached old age and was welcomed back to the wonderful land of Egypt.

Yet at some time in his life Moses learned that he was not an Egyptian. He grew increasingly resentful of the way in which the Egyptians treated his own people. As he visited royal construction projects he heard the sound of the taskmaster's whip and the cries of his kinsmen. Scripture gives no hint of the struggle that must have gone on in Moses' soul during those years. Should he forget his oppressed people and seek fame and office among the people who had adopted him? As the son of Pharaoh's daughter might he even succeed one day to the throne? While we do not know what went on in Moses' mind, we do know the choice that he made: "By faith, Moses, when he was grown up, refused to be called the son of Pharaoh's daughter, choosing rather to share ill-treatment with the people of God than to enjoy the fleeting pleasures of sin" (Heb. 11:24-25).

The Bible does not tell us if the Hebrews ever resorted to violence in their quarrel with Pharaoh. Perhaps passive resistance was their only weapon besides prayer. Once Moses, however, did resort to violence, and the act changed his whole history and that of his people. Seeing an Egyptian taskmaster mistreating a Hebrew slave, Moses intervened and slew the Egyptian. Whatever questions he had in his mind before that act, afterwards there was no turning back. The slaying of the Egyptian might have passed unnoticed had Moses not later tried to intervene in a dispute between two Israelites. When an angry Israelite challenged Moses' right to intervene, mentioning the episode of the slain Egyptian, Moses knew that it would not be safe for him to stay in Egypt.

In fleeing into the eastern wilderness, Moses probably took the same road as Sinuhe, the hero of the story he had known from youth. Sinuhe had fled Egypt seven centuries before Moses, and his journey took him all the way to Syria, while Moses remained in the territory of the Midianites, probably in the Sinai Peninsula. Both refugees found a welcome among nomadic peoples, and both might well have continued to live in prosperity among an alien people. Here, however, the similarity ends. Sinuhe returned to Egypt because he was desirous of spending his last days in the land of his birth. Moses returned because Yahweh had commissioned him to lead his suffering kinsmen to freedom.

Brickmaking in the time of the Eighteenth Dynasty (ca. 1450 B.C.), from the tomb of Rehkmire, who was Vizier of Upper Egypt.

Brickmaking in Egypt hasn't changed much through the centuries. A wooden frame is still used to form the wet clay into a brick. The frame is lifted and the process repeated for each brick. The bricks, after being sun-dried, provide sturdy building material in a land with a low annual rainfall.

Moses' years in Midian were not wasted. After helping the seven daughters of a Midianite priest to water their flocks, Moses was invited to live with the priest, and ultimately he married one of the daughters (Exod. 2:18; 3:1). Moses seems to have had a happy time with Jethro (or Reuel), his father-in-law. During the years of his sojourn in Midian, Zipporah, Moses' wife, bore two sons — Gershom and Eliezer (Exod. 2:11-22; 18:4).

When the Pharaoh, who had ruled Egypt at the time Moses slew the Egyptian, had died (Exod. 2:23a), Israel hoped for deliverance from the oppression. God heard the prayers of his people and appeared to Moses in the midst of a burning bush, identifying Himself as the God of Abraham, Isaac, and Jacob (Exod. 3). Moses was to become the leader of his people, rescuing them from Egyptian bondage and bringing them back to the land of their fathers. God instructed Moses to demand that Pharaoh permit the Israelites to go a three day journey into the wilderness to sacrifice. When Moses insisted that he did not have eloquence for the task, God stated that Aaron his brother could be his spokesman (Exod. 4:14-16). Moses was also armed with two signs: a rod which could be transformed into a serpent, and a hand which would turn leprous when placed in his bosom (Exod. 4:1-9).

On the way back from Midian to Egypt a strange event took place. At a lodging place along the way the Lord met Moses and, in the words of Exodus 4:24, sought to kill him. Moses was evidently very sick, so his wife Zipporah took a flint and circumcised her son. For some unexplained reason Moses had not performed the rite of circumcision, which was the seal of the covenant made between the Lord and Abraham. After the circumcision, Moses recovered from his sickness and continued the journey.

Aaron joined Moses (Exod. 4:27), and Moses shared with his brother the experience which he had had in the wilderness. Aaron in turn recounted God's mighty acts to the elders of Israel, and they and the people knew that God was about to answer their prayers by sending deliverance.

23

The Ten Plagues
and the Passover

When Moses appeared before Pharaoh, demanding that Israel be permitted to sacrifice in the wilderness, Pharaoh asked contemptuosuly, "Who is Yahweh?" To the proud ruler of Egypt, the God of the Israelites was but one god among many, and certainly inferior to the gods of Egypt. Moses and Aaron identified Yahweh as the God of the Hebrews, affirming that his people were required to offer sacrifices in the wilderness lest their God be displeased and bring a plague upon them.

Pharaoh, however, showed no flexibility. Not only would he not allow them to go to the wilderness, but he insisted that their work load be increased. They would not be provided straw as a binding material for the bricks they produced, but they would still have to produce the same number of bricks each day.

The bad news of Pharaoh's despotism was countered by good news from the God of Israel. God assured his people that deliverance was at hand. Moses and Aaron went before Pharaoh. Aaron cast down the rod which had been given him as a symbol of God's authority and power. The rod became a serpent. Thereupon the Egyptian magicians, traditionally named Jannes and Jambres (cf. II Tim. 3:6-8), performed a similar feat in an attempt to discredit Moses. In imitating this miracle they may have made use of the art of snake charming. When rendered completely insensible, a snake will appear as still as a rod. "But Aaron's rod swallowed up their rods" (Exod. 7:12). In this way the God of Israel demonstrated his power over the wisest of the Egyptians and their gods.

When Pharaoh refused to acknowledge the claims of the God of Israel, he and the entire land of Egypt suffered a series of ten plagues. Except for the last — the death of the first born — none of the plagues was completely strange to Egypt. The

A stele of Ramesses II, which was discovered at Beth-shan.

timing of the plagues — at the word of Moses — and their intensity constituted the miraculous element. The Bible consistently presents Yahweh as sovereign over all creation. The forces of nature are always subject to his control.

The distinction made between the Israelites in Goshen and the Egyptians in the Nile Valley underscored the concern of Israel's God for his people. From one viewpoint the plagues were a chapter in Moses' contest with Pharaoh; from a second viewpoint they represent the challenge of Yahweh to the gods of Egypt.

When Moses, at the command of God, stretched his rod over the Nile waters they became red and putrid (Exod. 7:14-25). This plague reflects conditions brought about by an unusually high Nile, which normally reaches flood stage in August. The waters are then saturated with finely powered red earth from basins of the Blue Nile and Atbara, and they carry along minute organisms which help to color the water and create conditions so unfavorable for the fish that they die in large numbers. It may be that the extreme intensification of this phenomenon as described in Exodus 7:21, occurring at the word of Moses, produced the first plague which lasted seven days. Pharaoh, however, was unmoved by the scourge which should have convinced him of Yahweh's power.

When Moses again approached Pharaoh and he refused to let Israel go, God told Moses to stretch forth his rod over the waters, and there came forth from the waters, an army of frogs which invaded the land in such numbers that they became a national catastrophe (Exod. 8:1-15). Frogs are not unusual in the Nile Valley. The plague of frogs, however, came at the word of Moses and was of such intensity the Pharaoh should have recognized the power of Yahweh. When the frogs died in large numbers the land again was filled with the odor of decaying flesh. But Pharaoh remained unmoved and refused to let Israel go as Moses had requested.

Heaps of decaying frogs and fish provide an ideal breeding ground for insect pests. At the word of the Lord, Moses stretched forth his rod and smote the dust, and there came forth a large number of insects variously described as gnats, lice or mosquitoes (Exod. 8:16-19). This was, as the third plague, God's third warning to Pharaoh and challenge to Egypt's gods.

While the Egyptian magicians had been successful in imitating the first two miracles, we read that when they tried to bring forth lice "They could not" (Exod. 8:14). We can only speculate why this might have been. Nor do we read of the magicians seeking to imitate the subsequent miracles. Instead they give up with the report to Pharaoh "This is the finger of God" (Exod. 8:15).

Next followed the plague of flies (Exod. 8:20-32), probably the *Stomoxys calcitrans* which was an evil itself, and brought disease in its wake. This was the first plague in which God made a distinction between the Israelites and the Egyptians (Exod. 8:19). The Israelites were safe in Goshen, and the plague did not reach them there.

The fifth plague, a plague upon Egypt's cattle (Exod. 9:1-7), had religious as well as economic overtones. The goddess Hathor was represented as a bull, and the Apis Bull had for centuries been one of the objects of veneration throughout Egypt. Yahweh struck at the heart of Egyptian religious life in bringing a plague on the cattle.

The sixth plague (Exod. 9:8-12) struck human beings and animals with boils. These may have been produced by the same carrier flies that spread disease among the cattle. But again the plague was confined to the Egyptians. Yahweh preserved his people from affliction in Goshen.

As the seventh plague God used a disastrous hailstorm (Exod. 10:1-20). "Only in the land of Goshen, where the children of Israel were, was there no hail" (Exod. 9:26). This took place at the end of January or the beginning of February, for the barley and flax were ruined, but the wheat and spelt had not yet grown up (Exod. 9:31-32).

We now read for the first time that Pharaoh acknowledged his sin in not letting Israel go. And, recognizing that Moses was God's intermediary, he asked Moses to entreat Yahweh to cause the storm to cease. Moses "spread abroad his hands to the Lord; and the thunders and hail ceased ..." (Exod. 9:33).

Next, probably in March, locusts in unprecedented numbers swooped into Egypt and ate whatever vegetation had survived the earlier plagues (Exod. 10:1-20). Pharaoh once more acknowledged his sin and begged Moses to "entreat the Lord," and when Moses entreated the Lord, God sent a mighty west wind which swept the locusts into the Red Sea (Exod. 10:18, 19).

In the ninth plague thick darkness (Exod. 10:21-29) covered the land. Dust storms, known as *Khamsin,* are common in Egypt. Masses of earth, brought down the Nile Valley at the time of the annual inundation, dry into a fine powder. Such storms frequently come in March and last about three days (cf. Exod. 10:23). When the *Khamsin* wind comes, dust fills the air.

This limestone relief, from the Great Hall in the Karnak temple, portrays Ramesses II storming Ashkelon. Ladders have been placed against the city wall and a soldier is hacking at a door with an axe.

In the ninth plague the darkness was so intense that the sun itself seemed to be blotted out. "But all the children of Israel had light in their dwellings" (Exod. 10:23).

The plagues represent God's judgment on the gods of Egypt (cf. Exod. 12:12). Ha°pi, the Nile god had brought stench and ruin instead of blessing. Frogs, associated with the gods of fruitfulness, brought disease instead of life. The light of the sun (Re) was blotted out during the plague of darkness. Yahweh desired Egypt as well as Israel to know His power.

The last plague, the death of Egypt's firstborn, was Egypt's darkest hour but it marked the beginning of Israel's deliverance. To protect Israel in time of plague, God ordered the head of each household to slay a lamb (Exod. 12:1-6) and to sprinkle its blood on the lintel and doorposts of the house (Exod. 12:7). The roast lamb was then to be eaten in haste, each Israelite having his loins girded, sandals on his feet, and his staff in his hand (Exod. 12:11). Israel was to be prepared to leave in haste, for this was to be their last night in Egypt.

When the death angel passed through Egypt, the first born of man and beast died, but the blood upon the Israelite houses was a sign which the angel honored. God said, "The blood shall be a sign for you, upon the houses where you are; and when I see the blood, I will pass over you, and no plague shall fall upon you to destroy you when I smite the land of Egypt." (Exod. 12:13). The Passover took place on the tenth day of Abib, or Nisan, which corresponds to our March-April. It was to become an annual festival in which God's people would celebrate their deliverance from Egypt. Passover was a family festival, presided over by the father of the house (Exod. 12:3-4), although in later years it came to be associated with the Jerusalem Temple (cf. II Chron. 30:1-27; 35:1-19). In New Testament times the paschal victim was ritually slaughtered in the Temple but the Passover meal could be eaten in any house within the bounds of Jerusalem. After the destruction of the Temple (A.D. 70), the Passover again became a family festival, observed in Jewish homes throughout the world.

Closely associated with the Passover ceremony was the Feast of Unleavened Bread (Exod. 12:14-20; Lev. 23:5-8), and eventually they became one eight day festival — the twenty-four hour Passover observance followed by seven days of the Feast of Unleavened Bread. The unleavened bread is called "the bread of affliction" in Deuteronomy 16:3, because the Israelites ate it in haste before leaving Egypt.

At the midnight hour when death struck the first-born of Egypt, Pharaoh sent for Moses and urged him to take his people away (Exod. 12:29-32). Moses, the Israelites, a mixed multitude that accompanied them, flocks and herds left Raamses on the first step of the journey to Canaan. They took with them the silver and gold jewelry which their Egyptian neighbors gave them (Exod. 12:35-36) and the bones of Joseph who had asked his brothers to swear that they would carry his bones back to Canaan at the time that God would bring them back to the land of promise (Exod. 13:19; cf. Gen. 50:24, 25).

An Egyptian bronze mirror with a sculptured handle, probably the type of mirror that the Israelite women took with them on the Exodus.

24

From Egypt to Sinai

The Sinai Peninsula, which Israel entered after crossing the Red Sea, comprises the barren wilderness south of the land bridge which connects Egypt with Palestine. The Brook of Egypt, known today as the Wadi El-Arish, flowing northward from the Wilderness of Paran, marks the geographical boundary between the two countries. It is but a short distance from Egypt to Palestine. Kantara, in the eastern Delta is but one hundred seventeen miles from Raphia in southern Canaan. The Roman general Titus took just five days to march his army from Sile in Egypt to Gaza. In 1967 the Israelis reached the Suez Canal in a shorter period of time.

The Peninsula itself is triangular in shape, two hundred sixty miles long and one hundred fifty miles wide at the north, where a belt of sandy soil fifteen miles deep stretches along the Mediterranean Coast. South of this coastal plain is a high gravel and limestone plateau which stretches southward one hundred and fifty miles. Beyond the plateau, at the apex of the Peninsula, is a granite mountain formation with peaks reaching as high as eight thousand feet above sea level. This is the region of the copper and turquoise mines which were exploited by the Egyptians since the third millennium before Christ.

Traffic eastward from Egypt had a choice of three roads, The most direct route was the *Via Maris,* "the way of the sea," which skirted the Mediterranean. It began at the frontier fortress of Sile, near modern Qantara, and reached Canaan at Raphia. Pharaoh Seti I (1308-1290 B.C.) built a series of fortifications along this route which was used by the armies of Egypt when they campaigned in Asia. The Egyptians named the road, "The Way of Horus," but Scripture calls it "The Way of the Land of the Philistines" (Exod. 13:17-18), asserting that the Israelites avoided this direct road into Canaan at the direction of God. Pharaoh's former slaves were in no condition to wage full-scale warfare, which would have been unavoidable had they chosen to use the direct coastal road.

South of the *Via Maris* was the "Way to Shur" over which Hagar had fled from her mistress Sarah during patriarchal times (Gen. 16:7). Hagar, an Egyptian, was evidently on the way home when an angel stopped her and told her to return to Abraham and Sarah. The Egyptians had built a wall at their eastern frontier to control caravan traffic and the migration of nomads. Shur, a name meaning "wall" was probably the name of the town which grew up around the check point garrisoned by Egyptian border guards near modern Ismailia on the Suez Canal. The "Way to Shur" crossed the Sinai Peninsula from southern Canaan where it connected with the important water-parting route from Jerusalem and Hebron to Beer-sheba in the Negeb.

A third route, known in modern times as "the Pilgrim's Way," *Darb el-Haj,* runs across the Peninsula from the head of the Gulf of Suez to Ezion geber (Elat) at the head of the Gulf of Aqaba. The two gulfs — Suez and Aqaba — extend like rabbit ears in a northwesterly and northeasterly direction bounding the Sinai Peninsula.

Although it is clear that the Exodus did not take Israel along any well-traveled road it is difficult for modern geographers to trace the route with any certainty. Scripture calls it the "Reed Sea" or Wilderness Route, but the precise location of the crossing of the Reed Sea is not known. Near the town of Raamses are two bodies of water: the Water of Horus (Shihor in Isa. 23:3) and the Papyrus Marsh, a name similar in meaning to the Biblical "Reed Sea." Scripture states that the Exodus began at Raamses in the eastern Delta (Num. 33:5), a town identified with Egyptian *Per-Ramses,* the capital which Ramesses II built at or near the site of ancient Tanis. It was in this region that the patriarch Jacob had settled some centuries before (Gen. 47:11) when it was described as "the choicest part of the land."

The fleeing Israelites made stops at Succoth, modern *Tell el-Mashkutah,* in the eastern part of the Wadi Tumilat, and at Etham "on the edge of the wilderness" (Exod. 13:20). From Etham, possibly a frontier fortress where they encountered difficulty, the Israelites turned northward to Pi-hahiroth (Exod. 14:2, 9). The Israelite encampment is described as: "at the sea, by Pi-hahiroth, in front of Baal-zephon" (Exod. 14:9). Clear as these geographical references must have been to ancient readers, modern scholarship has had difficulty understanding their

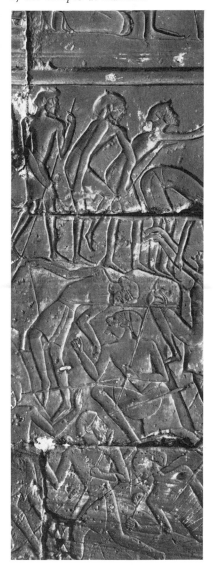

These bearded, Canaanite foes of Seti I are the Shasu-bedouin. The relief is on the north wall of the temple at Karnak.

meaning. Baal-zephon is a Semitic name meaning, "Baal of the North." This deity, originally adopted in Egypt from Canaanite sources, was worshiped in many places in Lower Egypt. A letter from the sixth century B.C. mentions "Baal-zephon and all the gods of Tahpanhes," suggesting to many scholars that a Baal-zephon temple was located at Tahpanhes, modern Tell Defneh, about twenty-seven miles south-southwest of Port Said.[1] W. F. Albright would locate Baal-zephon in the region of the later Egyptian town of Tahpanhes to which Jeremiah fled around 586 B.C. (Jer. 43) along with his countrymen who feared reprisals from Nebuchadnezzar after the slaying of Gedaliah. Herodotus states that Pharaoh Psammetichus I (664-610 B.C.) established a colony of Greek mercenaries there. In Hellenistic times the town boasted a temple to Zeus Casius, the Greek equivalent of Baal-zephon, which stood on the narrow strip of land bordering Lake Sirbonis to the north.

Migdol is a common Semitic place name, meaning "tower." The Egyptian wall must have had many towers, but it is unlikely that many bore Semitic names. We read of a Migdol of Seti later called the Migdol of Merneptah, modern Tell el Heir south of Pelusium in the northern sector of the wall. This seems to be that area from which Israel left Egypt at the Exodus.

The Pharaoh decided to pursue the escaping Israelites before they reached the Reed Sea and came upon them with his chariots in the region of Pi-hahiroth, possibly one of the canals linking the various lakes reaching to the Nile in this region. The approach of Pharaoh's chariots struck terror in the hearts of the escaping Israelites (Exod. 15:10-18). Moses encouraged them to trust the Lord, and he, at God's command, lifted his rod in the direction of the Reed Sea, whereupon God sent a strong east wind which divided the sea so that the people could cross over on dry land. The miracle was one of timing. At the moment Moses raised his rod, the wind drove back the waters of the sea so that Israel could cross over. The Egyptian chariots attempted to follow, but their chariot wheels were clogged and when Moses stretched his hand over the sea a second time, the waters returned and covered Pharaoh's host (Exod. 14:26-31). Moses led the people in a song of triumph (Exod. 15:1-17) and his sister Miriam exclaimed:

> Sing to the Lord for He has triumphed gloriously;
> The horse and his rider he has thrown into the sea. (Exod. 15:21)

A stele of Seti I, which was discovered at Beth-shan.

1. Cf. William F. Albright, BASOR, 109 (1948), pp. 15-16.

Traditionally the name of the sea which Israel crossed in its exodus from Egypt has been known as the Red Sea, although the Hebrew name *Yam Suph* is clearly, "sea of reeds." The term aptly describes the lake region north of the Gulf of Suez comprising the Bitter Lakes and Lake Timsah. It is possible that the Israelites went along the narrow neck of land on which Baal-zephon stood and that the Biblical Sea of Reeds was modern Lake Sirbonis. We are certain that the crossing was in this area because the Israelites found themselves in the Wilderness of Shur after crossing the sea (Exod. 15:22). The Wilderness of Shur is in the northwestern part of the Sinai Peninsula extending from the Wadi el Arish (the Biblical "River of Egypt") to the modern Suez Canal. All of the direct routes from Egypt to Canaan passed through the Wilderness of Shur.

Instead of taking one of the direct routes eastward, the Israelites turned southward into the Sinai Peninsula, taking a route parallel to the Gulf of Suez. A brief stop was made at Marah, an oasis where the water was bitter until Moses threw a tree into the water making it sweet (Exod. 15:22-25). Marah is often identified with ᶜAin Hawara several miles inland from the Gulf of Suez. G. E. Wright prefers ᶜAin Musa, or an unknown spring near the Bitter Lakes since ᶜAin Hawara is hard to reconcile with a three day journey from the Reed Sea (Exod. 15:22). The second stop was at Elim, a word meaning "terebinths" or "oaks." The Israelites were refreshed by its twelve springs and seventy palm trees (Exod. 15:27). Although we cannot be certain concerning its location, it may have been the Wadi Gharandel about forty miles south southeast of Suez along the west side of the Sinai Peninsula. Israel continued to move southward along the Gulf of Suez. The next encampment according to Numbers 33:10 was "by the Sea of Reeds," a term here evidently used of the Gulf of Suez. The fifteenth century Egyptian port of Merkhah, situated five miles south of Ras Abu Zeneimeh has been suggested for the place of encampment.

About six weeks after the Exodus from Egypt, Israel entered the Wilderness of Sin (Exod. 16:1), usually identified with Debbet er-Ramleh, a sandy section of the southwestern Sinai Peninsula (Exod. 16:1). Here the people murmured against Moses and Aaron, and God miraculously provided manna to sustain them (Exod. 16:4-12). The Israelites were instructed to gather an omer apiece for five days, and two omers on the sixth day to provide food for the sabbath (Exod. 16:16-21). The word "manna" means, "What is it?" the question which

The Monastery of Saint Catherine, at Mount Sinai.

the Israelites asked when they first saw it. Scripture states that manna was "like coriander seed, white, and the taste of it was like wafers made with honey" (Exod. 16:31).

Many scholars identify manna with the excretions of insects on tamarisk trees each June. At night drops of the secretion fall to the ground where they remain until ants consume them. These drops are small, sticky, light in color, and sugary sweet. The fact that it was provided but six days a week and that it continued to nourish the Israelites until they arrived in Canaan, after forty years in the wilderness, indicates that manna cannot be explained on purely natural bases. The modern parallel to Biblical manna, still gathered in the Sinai peninsula, can at best suggest the means that God used in feeding his people.

At least twice during the wilderness wandering God provided quail to augment the diet of his people (Exod. 16:13; Num. 11:31). Quail cross the Mediterranean in September and October to winter in Arabia or Africa, and they migrate northward again in the spring. As the quail blew in from the sea, the Israelites "spread them out all around the camp" (Num. 11:32). In describing the customs of the Egyptians, Herodotus notes: "They eat fish uncooked, either dried in the sun or preserved with brine. Quails and ducks and small birds are salted and eaten raw."[2]

In leaving the Wilderness of Sin, the Israelites made a stop at Dophkah (Num. 33:12), near the copper and turquoise mines which were operated by Pharaohs from early dynastic times. In the center of the mining region was the famed temple of the goddess Hathor at Serabit el-Khadem. Hundreds of ancient inscriptions have been identified at the temple and at the entrances to the mines. Although most of them are in hieroglyphic Egyptian characters, about forty are in the so-called Proto-Sinaitic alphabetic script of the fifteenth century B.C. The mines were probably not in use at the time the Israelites passed through Dophkah.

The last stop before Mount Sinai was at Rephidim (Exod. 17:1), possibly modern Wadi Refayid in the Wilderness of Sinai. Here the people murmured against Moses because they lacked water. God instructed him to meet their need by using his rod to strike the rock (Exod. 17:6). He did so and water miraculously flowed from the smitten rock. C. S. Jarvis tells of a camel corps digging for water which had an experience

---

2. Herodotus, *Histories* i. 77.

analagous to that of Moses. A hammer accidentally hit a rock and water came out from the rock itself. The polished hard surface of the limestone covered soft porous rock from which the water flowed. Such parallels may be useful in showing the means that God used in meeting the needs of His people, but they do not diminish the need for God's miraculous intervention to sustain Israel in its wilderness journey.

At Rephidim Israel encountered hostilities for the first time. Nomadic Amalekites attacked the encampment (Exod. 17:8-13), but thanks to the intercession of Moses, assisted by Aaron and Hur, and the valor of Joshua who appears in Scripture for the first time as a mighty warrior, Israel prevailed. The Amalekites continued to be bitter enemies of the Israelites in the period of the Judges (Judg. 3:13) and of the monarchy (I Sam. 27:6; 30:1-20).

Jethro, Moses' father-in-law who had provided a home and a wife for Moses during his years in the wilderness, joined Moses again before the Israelites reached Mount Sinai. Jethro rejoiced in the success of Israel and paid tribute to Moses' God, offering a burnt offering and other sacrifices (Exod. 18:10-12). He also gave practical advice when he noted that Moses was overworked. Moses was attempting to handle all the detail for the encampment, whereas Jethro suggested that he appoint able men to assist in governing the people (Exod. 18:13-27).

Three months after the Exodus, Israel reached the wilderness of Sinai and encamped before the mountain of the same name (Exod. 19:1). Geographers are far from unanimous, however, concerning the identity of Mount Sinai. Tradition since the latter part of the fourth century has located Sinai in the southern part of the Sinai Peninsula. Legend states that Catherine of Alexandria, after her martyrdom, was carried by angels to the top of the mountain that now bears her name. A monastery has been located there continuously since the fourth century, although the Christians have undergone periods of severe persecution. The Moslem conquest brought with it anti-Christian feeling, but the monastery had already undergone persecution in the days of St. Nilus (A.D. 390) and the monk Ammonius (A.D. 373). The present Monastery of Saint Catherine, on the northwest slope of Jebel Musa, a 6,500 foot high mountain, was founded about A.D. 527 under Emperor Justinian who established it on the site where Helena, the mother of Constantine, had erected a small church two centuries earlier.

Approaching Jebel Musa ("Mount Moses") from Serabit el-

View of the rugged terrain from Saint Catherine's Monastery.

Khadem, the traveler enters a wide valley called er-Raha, two miles long and one-third to two-thirds of a mile wide. This would have been a natural place for Israel to have encamped (Exod. 19:1-2; Num. 33:15). Towering above the plain are three summits, Ras es-Safsaf to the northwest, Jebel Musa to the southeast, and, still higher, Jebel Katarin rising 9,000 feet to the southwest. While Jebel Musa is the favored location we cannot be positive concerning the original Sinai. Ras es-Safsaf is closer to the plain and is favored by some scholars for that reason (cf. Exod. 20:18). The church historian Eusebius preferred still another site, Jebel Serbel west of the Wadi Feiran, and some scholars abandon the Sinai Peninsula entirely, suggesting a site in northwestern Arabia or in the vicinity of Kadesh-barnea. The imposing granite formations of the southern Sinai Peninsula are still preferred, however, as the site for Mount Sinai where Moses received the Law.

25

The Encampment
at Sinai

The third month after their departure from Egypt, the Israelites encamped before the sacred mount. Moses commanded
the people to prepare themselves for three days and forbade
anyone to go up the mountain under penalty of death. On the
third day, amidst lightning, thunder, and thick clouds, Moses
ascended the mountain and received the divine Law (Exod.
19:16-20). A second time accompanied by Joshua, he went up
the mountain. Forty days and nights he communed with God,
during which time he received additional commandments
(Exod. 24:1-15).

Upon entering the cloud-covered mountain Moses received
the Book of the Covenant which was to regulate Israel's religious life. When the people expressed their willingness to observe its precepts, Moses sprinkled the blood of sacrificial
animals upon the altar which he had erected and upon the
people. By this act God and Israel were effectually joined together and the Covenant became binding. God would henceforth be Israel's God, and Israel would be His people.

The first of the Ten Commandments specifies that Yahweh is
the God of His people, and that they are to have no other gods
aside from him. This command is not an absolute assertion of
monotheism, but monotheism is germinally present. From the
practical point of view, the commandments had to reckon with
many deities. The Israelites themselves were conscious that
their fathers had worshiped other gods (cf. Gen. 35:2). They
had been in Egypt where a complex polytheism was accepted
as the national religion. They would soon be in Canaan where
the fertility cult would hold sway. In such a context it was
necessary to affirm a strict monolatry — Yahweh, as Israel's God
would not tolerate a rival. The fact that these other "gods"
were in reality idols, the work of man's hands and man's im-

agination would later be asserted as monotheism developed philosophically and theologically. The Decalogue dealt with its practical side — no Israelite might worship any God except Yahweh.

The temptation of the ancients — and of many moderns — is to think of God in visible, tangible form. In Egypt the Israelites daily saw the images of birds, beasts, and humans receiving worship. At Sinai Yahweh made it clear that no "graven image or likeness" would be tolerated in religion. Not only must His people not bow down to images of pagan deities, they must make no image of Yahweh, either. The golden calf (Exod. 32:1-6) was a violation of the command, even though it was designed to represent the God who had brought Yahweh's people from Egypt. The calves that Jeroboam set up at Bethel and Dan (I Kings 12:28) are likewise forbidden. Although the theologically mature leaders may have pictured Yahweh as riding the calves, the tendency of such representations was to cause people to identify the deity with the cult object, and it is just that tendency that the decalogue sought to check.

The commandment against the misuse of God's name lays stress on the attribute of holiness. Yahweh had revealed His name to Moses, and Israel, God's people, was warned against a loose use of the divine Name. Israel must not swear at all in the name of a false god, and she must never swear falsely in the name of her own God, Yahweh. Thoughtless vows (such as that of Jephthah, Judg. 11:30-31), cursing, sorcery, soothsaying were all contrary to the intent of the commandment.

Israel had been prepared for the Sabbath commandment by the miracle of the manna. The basis for the Sabbath commandment of Exodus 20:8-11 is that "in six days Yahweh made heaven and earth, the sea and all that is in them, and rested the seventh day." In the repetition of the commandments in Deuteronomy 5, no mention is made of creation, but rather Israel was commanded, "You shall remember that you were a servant in the land of Egypt, and Yahweh your God brought you out thence with a mighty hand and an outstretched arm; therefore Yahweh your God commanded you to keep the sabbath day." The Sabbath is presented as a day of abstaining from labor, and as such it was to become a mark of Israel's loyalty to Yahweh.

The second "table of the Law" is concerned with man's relations with his fellows: children must obey their parents, the sanctity of life must be recognized, the rights of personal property must be respected, man must maintain his integrity as a citizen ("You shall not bear false witness against your neighbor"). Finally, the source of evil in man is underscored. Man must not desire that which is not rightly his. He must respect the marriage relationship and honor his neighbor's right to a happy home with the possessions that God has entrusted to him.

The ceremony by which the union of Israel and Yahweh was accomplished (Exod. 24:3-8) consisted of a covenant ritual. An altar was erected representing the deity, and the people stood opposite. Sacrificial victims were then slain, and their blood was drained off into bowls. Part of the blood was then thrown over the altar, and the rest flung over the heads of the people. Symbolically the life of the victim was used to cover the two contracting parties — Yahweh and Israel. Since both were united in the blood of a third party they were united to one another.

This relationship between Yahweh and Israel was one of election, or choice. Among many ancient Semitic tribes the tribal members thought of themselves as blood descendants of the deity. Israel, however, remembered a time when she was not the people of Yahweh, when her ancestors had worshiped other gods in Ur of the Chaldees. Religion among the patriarchs was highly personal, but at Sinai it became national. Yahweh had not simply pledged himself to be the god of an individual, but of a people. God set his love upon Israel, and Israel voluntarily accepted that love and the covenant which expressed it.

In addition to the Ten Commandments, Moses gave to Israel a series of laws to clarify the application of the Decalogue to the life of God's people (Exod. 20:22 — 23:19). Instructions were given concerning the proper place of sacrifice, the treatment of slaves, and other applications of the law to the circumstances of daily life.

Mount Sinai as seen from the Sinai Plain.

Professor George Mendenhall of the University of Michigan has shown that the form of the Sinai Covenant is paralleled by treaties made between kings and their vassals in the ancient Near East, particularly among the Hittites. Near Eastern literature affords examples of parity covenants, or covenants between equals. Such covenants appear in the Bible between David and Jonathan (I Sam. 20) and between Shechem and Israel (Gen. 34). When a king covenants with a vassal, however, the treaty takes a different form. Such covenants are mentioned in II Samuel 5:1-5 where David covenants with the people as their king, and in I Kings 20:33-34 where Ahab imposes a treaty on the Syrians.

A view of Moses' Peak from the Rock Cave area.

Mendenhall has shown that a typical Hittite suzerainty treaty has six parts which are paralleled in the Mosaic Law. The treaty begins by identifying the sovereign in a form such as, "Thus says X, the Great King." The Biblical decalogue begins with such a line of identification, "I am Yahweh your God" (Exod. 20:2a; Cf. Josh. 24:2). Secondly, the treaty mentions its historical background, speaking of the benevolent actions of the king. In Exodus 20:2b, Yahweh declares that he brought his people "out of the land of Egypt, out of the house of bondage." It is this act of mercy that forms the basis for the third element in the covenant, its stipulations. A Hittite treaty would spell out the obligations of vassals. They would not be permitted to have treaty relations with foreign powers, particularly such as were unfriendly to the Hittites. Yahweh demands of his people, "You shall have no other gods before me" (Exod. 20:3), and again, "Take heed to yourselves, lest you make a covenant with the inhabitants of the land whither you go, lest it become a snare in the midst of you. You shall tear down their altars and break their pillars, and cut down their Asherim (for you shall worship no other god, for Yahweh whose name is Jealous is a jealous God)" (Exod. 34:12-13).

A Hittite covenant was deposited in the sanctuary of the vassal and publicly read at regular intervals. Yahweh instructed Moses, "And you shall put into the ark, the testimony which I shall give you" (Exod. 25:16). This testimony, or law, was to be read every seven years (Deut. 31:9-13). At the time that Solomon built his temple we read, "There was nothing in the ark except the two tables of stone which Moses put there at Horeb, where the Lord made a covenant with the people of Israel when they came out of the land of Egypt" (I Kings 8:9).

A treaty between a Hittite king and his vassals would continue by invoking the deities of the respective parties as witnesses. Israelite monotheism precludes invoking a pantheon, as the heathen did, and since God "had no one greater by whom to swear, he swore by himself" (Heb. 6:13). At the covenant renewal before the death of Joshua, Moses' successor "took up a great stone, and set it there under the oak in the sanctuary of the Lord, and Joshua said to all the people, 'Behold, this stone shall be a witness against us; for it has heard all the words of the Lord which he spoke to us; therefore it shall be a witness against you lest you deal falsely with your God'" (Josh. 24:26, 27).

The treaty would conclude with a list of blessings which

could be expected by those who would keep the covenant faithfully, and the curses which would fall upon the violator of covenant responsibilities. Such lists of blessings and curses appear in Leviticus 26 and Deuteronomy 27 and 28. As a solemn warning we read, "Cursed be he who does not confirm the words of this law by doing them" (Deut. 27:26).

Immediately following the ratification of the covenant, Israel was commanded to construct a portable Tabernacle, or "tent of meeting" so that God might dwell in the midst of His people (Exod. 25:8). To prepare for the building of this sanctuary, Moses instructed the people to bring free-will offerings of gold, silver, bronze; cloth or yarn of blue, purple, and scarlet color; fine linen; goats' hair; rams' skins; goat skins; acacia wood; spices for anointing oil and incense; and precious stones for the ephod and breastplate of the priest (Exod. 25:1-7). The workmanship was entrusted to a man of the tribe of Judah named Bezalel who was filled "with the Spirit of God, with ability and intelligence, with knowledge and all craftsmanship, to devise artistic designs, to work in gold, silver, and bronze, in cutting stones for setting and in carving wood, for work in every craft" (Exod. 31:1-5). Associated with Bezalel was Oholiab of the tribe of Dan.

The tent of meeting was erected in a court having a perimeter of three hundred cubits (450 feet), surrounded by curtains of fine twined linen hung on bronze pillars, seven and one-half feet high, with silver hooks. The only entrance was at the east end, and through it the Israelites were able to approach the Altar of Burnt Offering (Exod. 27:1-8; 38:1-7). The altar was made of acacia wood covered with bronze, seven and one-half feet square and four and one-half feet high with horns projecting from each corner. Like other parts of the tent of meeting, it was portable and equipped with staves and rings. Beyond the Altar of Burnt Offering was a bronze laver used by the priests for ceremonial washing before officiating at the Altar or in the Tent of Meeting (Exod. 30:17-21; 38:8; 40:30).

In the western half of the court, the Tent of Meeting was located. It was forty-five feet long, fifteen feet wide, and divided into two parts. The Tent of Meeting was built of acacia wood boards overlaid with gold (Exod. 26:1-37; 36:20-38). There were forty-eight boards in all, twenty for each of the sides and eight for the west end. They were fifteen feet high, two and one-quarter feet wide, and held together by bars and sockets. The ceiling was in the form of a curtain of fine twined linen of purple, blue, and scarlet cover ornamented with cherubim. The outer covering was made of goat's hair as protection for the linen, and over this, for added protection, were coverings of rams' skins and goats' skins. Two veils of the same material as the first covering were employed: one at the entrance to the Tent of Meeting (at the east end) and the other to separate the two interior rooms, the Holy Place and the Most Holy Place.

The northern part of the Holy Place was occupied by the Table of Shewbread, made of acacia wood overlaid with gold, with a golden rim around the top. A ring was attached to each leg for carrying (Exod. 25:23-30; 37:10-16). On the table were twelve cakes of unleavened bread which were changed each Sabbath, those of the week before being eaten by the priests (Lev. 24:5-9). Plates for incense were also placed on the table.

The Golden Lampstand was placed in the southern part of the Holy Place. It was beaten or hammered from one piece of pure gold (Exod. 25:31-39; 37:17-24) and had a central stem with three curving branches on each side, making seven lamps in all. Snuffers and trays were also made of gold. Every evening the priests filled the lamp with olive oil which had been furnished by the Israelites (Exod. 27:20-21; 30:7-8).

Before the veil separating the Holy Place from the Holy of Holies was the Altar of Incense, three feet high and one and one-half feet square, made of acacia wood overlaid with gold (Exod. 40:22-28). It had a golden border around the top and was equipped with a horn and ring at each corner (Exod. 30:1-10, 28, 34-37). Each morning and evening as the priests came to attend the Golden Lampstand they took fire from the Altar of Burnt Offering in the court, and offered incense at the Altar of Incense in the Holy Place.

Beyond the veil was the Holy of Holies, the throne room of Yahweh. Its central object was the Ark of the Covenant made of acacia wood overlaid within and without with pure gold. The ark was three and three-quarters feet long, two and one-quarter feet deep and wide, equipped with golden rings and staves for carrying (Exod. 25:10-22; 37:1-9). The cover of the ark, known as the Mercy Seat, served as the base for two golden cherubim which faced each other with wings overshadowing the center of the Mercy Seat. Here on the annual Day of Atonement, the High Priest sprinkled blood for the nation of Israel (Lev. 16:14).

Within the Ark of the Covenant were placed the tablets of

the Law (Exod. 25:21; 31:18; Deut. 10:3-5), a pot of manna (Exod. 36:34), and Aaron's rod that had blossomed in token of his divine election (Num. 17:10). The Ark of the Covenant was looked upon as Israel's most sacred cult object. After the conquest it was temporarily housed at Shiloh (I Sam. 4:3) whence it was taken by the Israelites to the field of battle as a guarantee of victory over the Philistines. This desecration of the Ark was contrary to God's will, and the Philistines defeated Israel at Aphek and captured the Ark, although they later had to return it to the Israelites (I Sam. 4-7).

In patriarchal times the father of the household offered prayer and sacrifices on behalf of himself and his household, but with the establishment of the covenant between Yahweh and his people at Sinai, a specific priestly tribe was set apart to care for the spiritual ministry in Israel. The priests served as mediators between God and man. They officiated at the offerings (Exod. 28:1-43) and, as custodians of the Law, were expected to instruct the people concerning their moral and cultic obligations. By means of Urim and Thummim (Num. 27:1; Deut. 33:8) they sought to discern Yahweh's will and make it known to the people. The priests were to be examples of holy living, and they were expected to be particularly careful in matters of marriage and family discipline (Lev. 21:1 — 22:10).

The priests wore vestments which became the external mark of their office. The basic garment was a long, white, seamless tunic over which they wore a girdle of blue, purple, and scarlet needlework. Breeches of fine linen and a plain, close fitting cap completed the attire of the ordinary priest (Exod. 28:40-43; 39:27-29). The High Priest wore an additional robe, blue in color, extending from his neck to below his knees. Attached to the bottom of the robe was a fringe of alternating bells and pomegranites.

The High Priestly ephod consisted of two pieces of linen, gold, blue, purple, and scarlet in color, joined with shoulder straps. On each shoulder piece was a stone with the names of six of the twelve tribes. Golden borders and chains of gold further adorned the ephod. Linked to the shoulder straps of the ephod was a nine square inch pouch, suspended on chains of pure gold. This formed the breastplate, in which were set twelve stones bearing the names of the twelve Israelite tribes. As his headdress the High Priest wore a turban which bore a golden plate with the words, "Holiness to the Lord."

In a solemn ceremony the sons of Aaron were set apart for

their priestly work. The consecration ceremony began with a ceremonial washing in water, after which the future priests were clothed in the appropriate garments. Moses officiated at the service in which the subjects were anointed with oil, symbolic of their induction into the priesthood. Moses then offered a young ox as a Sin Offering, followed by rams for the Burnt Offering and the Peace Offering. Then sacrificial blood was applied to the right thumb, right ear, and the large toe of the right foot of the priest.

Next Moses took the fat and right leg of his sacrificial victims, along with three pieces of pastry normally alotted to the priest, and presented them to Aaron's sons for a Wave Offering. The breasts were presented as Wave Offerings, then boiled and eaten by Moses and the priests. Before the meal Moses sprinkled anointing oil and blood on the priests and their garments. The ceremony was repeated on each of seven days (Exod. 29:1-37; 40:12-15; Lev. 8:1-36).

26

In the Wilderness

The encampment at Sinai came to an end when the cloud which symbolized God's presence among His people moved northeastward from Mount Sinai. The people followed as far as the Wilderness of Paran (Num. 10:12), a high plateau region composed chiefly of limestone formations. The interminable wastes of Paran are occasionally broken by refreshing oases. Soon after their arrival, the Israelites murmured in disgust against Moses, their leader, remembering the food which they had while in Egypt (Num. 11:1-10). When Moses brought the problem to Yahweh, he was instructed to gather together seventy elders who would share his gift of prophecy and thus aid in administering the affairs of Israel (Num. 11:16-30). When quails were driven into the Wilderness of Paran by a strong wind the people feasted on this delicacy which was a welcome change from the manna which they had come to loathe. No sooner had they begun to eat the quails, however, than a plague broke out in the camp and many died (Num. 11:31-35). The place was named Kibroth-Hattaavah, "graves of craving" because there the people had despised God's provision for their needs and lusted after other food.

Another crisis arose when Miriam and Aaron criticized Moses for marrying an Ethiopian (Heb. "Cushite") woman (Num. 12:1). If the term is taken to mean an Ethiopian, then she was probably one from among the mixed multitude which left Egypt with Israel at the time of the Exodus. Josephus (Antiquities ii.10) preserves a tradition that Moses as commander-in-chief of the Egyptian army had beseiged an Ethiopian city. According to this legend a princess, Tarbis, fell in love with the Hebrew commander and they were married. The story has no historical value but it illustrates the way in which a Jewish historian of the first century A.D. attempted to solve the problem.

Cushite may, however, in this context be derived from Kushu, or Cushan, a tribe associated with Midian (Hab. 3:7). According to the latter hypothesis she was of a tribe closely allied to the people of Jethro and Zipporah. Zipporah was last mentioned after the defeat of Amalek (Exod. 18) and she may have died before Moses took the Ethiopian or Cushite wife. Otherwise Moses had two wives.

The anger of Yahweh was aroused against Miriam and Aaron for speaking against Moses. In punishment for her rebellion, Miriam became leprous and was shut up outside the camp for a week (Num. 12:10-15). Whatever others might think of Moses' marriage, Yahweh made it clear that the lawgiver had done right.

On the northern border of the Wilderness of Paran is Kadesh-barnea, often identified with ᶜAin Qudeis, about fifty miles southwest of Beersheba. Actually the springs at ᶜAin Qudeirat, twelve miles northwest of ᶜAin Qudeis afford much better facilities for an encampment such as that of the Israelites, and modern scholarship suggests that the Israelites encamped in that region, using all of the springs in the area. ᶜAin Qudeirat is the richest spring in northern Sinai flowing between two mountain ranges and irrigating a fertile valley.

Kadesh-barnea served as the headquarters for the Israelite tribes for thirty-eight years (cf. Deut. 2:14). At the beginning of that period Moses chose one man from each of the twelve tribes to go on a spying expedition northward to the land of Canaan. The spies were instructed to survey the land itself, observe the people and note the fortifications (Num. 13:1-20). The spies did as they were told, and returned with enthusiastic reports. It was indeed a land of milk and honey, and they brought a sample of its fruit to back up their glowing report (Num. 13:26-27). While all agreed that the land was all they had hoped for, the majority were so frightened by the walled cities and their powerful defenders that they were not willing to move into Canaan. Caleb, however, urged the people to go up to possess the land, assured that with God's help they could do the otherwise impossible (Num. 13:30). The majority prevailed, however, and a generation of pilgrims became wanderers in the wilderness.

The aftermath of the report of the spies was tragic. The people of Israel seemed to be in a hopeless position, unable to return to Egypt and unable to press on into Canaan. In despair, they said, "Would that we had died in the land of Egypt! Or would that we had died in this wilderness!" When the people actually planned to choose a leader who would take them back to Egypt, Moses interceded before Yahweh. The wrath of Yahweh was turned from his rebellious people, but he declared that the disobedient people would not live to see the promised land (Num. 14:20-25). Only Caleb and Joshua of the people over twenty who had left Egypt would live to see Canaan — the others would perish in the wilderness (Num. 14:26-35).

A group of Israelites, contrary to Moses' wishes, made an abortive attack upon the Amalekites and the Canaanites of the Hill Country of southern Judea, but the Israelites had to flee before them (Num. 14:39-44). A confederation of Canaanite cities under the King of Arad was successful in repulsing the Israelite assault. The attack was contrary to God's will and its results were disastrous. Israel would not attempt to enter Canaan again until after the death of Moses.

A further rebellion broke out against Moses when Korah and a company of other Levites challenged his right to rule. Two hundred and fifty leaders in Israel insisted that all of Yahweh's people were holy, and they resented the fact that Moses was acting like a prince in their midst (Num. 16:3, 13). As a further grievance they reminded Moses that he had not brought them into "a land flowing with milk and honey" although they had followed him from such a land with the promise of better things (Num. 16:12-14). There was also a religious issue, for Korah and the Levites were offended that Aaron's family had been set apart for the privilege of priesthood (Num. 16:8-10).

The revolt came to an end when "the earth opened its mouth and swallowed them up" (Num. 26:9) so that the rebels and their households were destroyed.

The day after Korah and his company had met their death in the awful judgment of Yahweh, the people again complained against Moses for being responsible for the death of their brethren (Num. 16:41). The wrath of Yahweh was again aroused, and fourteen thousand seven hundred people died in a plague (Num. 16:49). As a visual demonstration of God's choice for the priestly office, Moses asked that rods — symbols of authority — be brought by the several tribes. The twelve rods were then deposited in the Tabernacle, and the next day Moses entered the Tabernacle and found that the rod of Aaron "had sprouted and put forth buds and produced blossoms, and it bore ripe almonds" (Num. 17:1-11). In this way the appointment of Aaron was confirmed before all Israel.

Miriam, Moses' sister, died while Israel was encamped at Kadesh (Num. 20:1). She was some years older than Moses, for it is generally agreed that Miriam was the sister who watched the baby Moses in the bulrushes and suggested her mother as his nurse. There is no record that she ever married, although rabbinical tradition says that she was Caleb's wife and the mother of Hur.

When the people again murmured for lack of water, Yahweh instructed Moses to speak to the rock, telling it to yield its water (Num. 20:8). Instead, Moses angrily said to the people, "Hear now, ye rebels, shall we bring forth water for you out of this rock?" Thereupon he took his rod and struck the rock twice. Although he was successful in providing water by that means, Yahweh reprimanded him for his disobedience: "Because you did not believe in me to sanctify me in the eyes of the people of Israel, therefore you shall not bring this assembly into the land which I have given them" (Num. 20:12). Moses, like others of his generation, was destined to die without entering the promised land.

Had Israel accepted the counsel of Caleb and Joshua, her armies would have entered Canaan from the south. Instead she passed a generation in the wilderness, after which she revised her military plans. Canaan would be entered from the east, with a crossing of the Jordan north of the Dead Sea in the region of Jericho. The shortest means of doing this was for the Israelites to go around the southern extremity of the Dead Sea, then through Edomite territory northward to the plains of Moab. From Kadesh, Moses sent a request to the king of Edom, urging him to allow his "brother Israel" to pass through his land up the King's Highway, the direct road running from the Gulf of Aqabah to Syria (Num. 20:14-21). Although the Israelites promised to remain on the road and to pay for any water they would consume, the Edomites refused them permission to travel through their country.

Moses and his people turned southeastward from Kadesh, however, and as they approached the border of Edom, Aaron died and was buried at Mount Hor (Num. 20:22-29). Josephus (Antiquities iv. 4. 7) suggests that it was near Petra, and tradition identifies it with a 4,800 foot peak to the west of Edom. Benno Rothenberg, however, locates Mount Hor on the route from Kadesh-barnea to Arad. Near a holy mountain in the vicinity of Tell Arad is the Wadi Harunia which may preserve the name of Mount Hor.

From Mount Hor, Israel began her long detour around Edom (Num. 21:4), turning southeastward toward Ezion-geber on the Gulf of Aqaba, the eastern extension of the Red Sea.

While in the neighborhood of Mount Hor, a Canaanite king of Arad in the Judean Negeb attacked Israel and took some captives (Num. 21:1). Israel was able to make a counter attack and to destroy the Canaanites of the region.

The people again grew impatient at the delays, and again they complained to Moses about their lack of adequate food and water supplies. This time they encountered a plague of venomous serpents whose bite caused painful inflammation and many people died (Num. 21:6-9). When the people acknowledged their sin and sought mercy, Yahweh commanded Moses to set up a bronze figure of a serpent on a pole, that those bitten might look to it in faith and live.

Israel made its way northward toward Moab, avoiding the Edomite strongholds as she journeyed (Num. 21:10-20). From Ezion-geber she probably advanced through the Arabah Valley as far as the Zered, which enters the Dead Sea at its tip. Going eastward through the Zered Valley, Israel sought to by-pass Moab. She probably turned northward at the edge of the desert, and then westward through the Arnon Gorge which formed the northern boundary of Moab. North of the Arnon was the Amorite territory of Sihon. Israel asked Sihon for permission to use that portion of the King's Highway that went through his country, and he, like Edom, refused. This time, however, there was a battle. Sihon attacked Israel, but Israel gained a decisive victory and took possession of his land from the Arnon Valley, its southern border, to its northern border on the Brook Jabbok (Num. 21:21-32).

The victory over Sihon gave the Israelite armies courage and they went farther north to the territory of Og, king of Bashan. In a battle at Edrei, Og met defeat at the hand of Israel (Num. 21:33-35). The victories over Sihon and Og in Transjordan were to have important consequences. Word of the power of Israel quickly spread throughout the area and counter measures were attempted.

Balak of Moab, fearing that conventional methods of warfare might prove ineffective, sought the help of a foreign seer named

The site of Arad, in the Judean Negeb.

Balaam who had gained a reputation for the potency of his spells. Balaam's home was at Pethor, evidently another form of the name Pitru, a city in the Euphrates Valley near Carchemesh (Num. 22:5; 23:7). Balak wanted Balaam to place a curse upon Israel, but the seer refused to accompany the first group of messengers who sought to purchase his services (Num. 22:7-14). Balak was not discouraged, however. He sent a larger delegation composed of princes of his realm, and finally Balaam was induced to accompany them to Moab.

Balaam did not curse Israel, however. Balak took him to a succession of heights from which he could look upon the Israelite encampment. Instead of uttering curses, however, Balaam pronounced a series of blessings. From the heights overlooking Israel, Balaam spoke of Israel's pre-eminence (Num. 24). Among his prophetic utterances he declared:

> I see him, but not now; I behold him but not nigh:
> A star shall come forth out of Jacob, and a scepter shall rise out of Israel.

Both Jewish and Christian scholars have seen in these words the promise of a coming Messiah who would come from Israel and bring blessing to mankind. The Jewish nationalist leader who defied Rome in the days of Hadrian (A.D. 132-135) was popularly called Bar Kochba, "son of the star." A star heralded the birth of Jesus to the eastern Magi (Matt. 2:2, 9-10) and the resurrected Christ identified himself in the Revelation as "the root and offspring of David, the bright morning star" (Rev. 22:16).

Scripture does not remember Balaam for the prophecies which he reluctantly uttered, but rather for his base desire for gain (II Peter 2:15). He stands as the example of one with God-given abilities who is ready to sell them to the highest bidder. Although restrained by God from cursing Israel by his utterances, it was at his suggestion (Num. 31:16) that the Moabites invited Israel to participate in the licencious worship at Baal-peor which had terrifying results for Israel. Baal, the Canaanite fertility god was worshiped by rites of religious prostitution in which acts which produce human fertility were thought to symbolically transfer power to the earth, causing it to produce. It was to such an orgy that Israel was invited, and the prior warnings against conformity to the religious standards of Canaan went unheeded (Num. 25:3). Baal-peor marks the beginning of that tendency toward idolatry among the Israelites that continued until the destruction of Jerusalem and the exile that followed. Balaam's counsel was fiendishly successful. Israel sinned, and Yahweh's anger was aroused against the people who had earlier vowed to place no other gods before him. Those who had taken part in the Baal-peor worship were killed and in the plague that followed the incident twenty-four thousand people died (Num. 25:4-9).

After the plague, and toward the close of the thirty-eight years in the wilderness, Moses and Eleazar instructed the people to take a census. Those twenty years of age and older numbered 601,730 (Num. 26:2, 51), as compared with 603,550 at the time of the earlier census taken at Sinai (Num. 1:46). These figures do not include the Levites, of whom there were 23,000 in the census taken at Shittim (Num. 26:62). The purpose of the census was twofold. Since major battles were ahead, it was necessary to ascertain the number of available fighting men. Equally important, since Israel would soon enter the land of Canaan, a basis had to be determined for the equitable division of the land (cf. Num. 26:52-56). The generation that had left Egypt forty years earlier was dead (Num. 26:63-65), and the new generation would soon possess the land which had been promised to the Biblical patriarchs.

The large numbers of people who died during the wilderness journey caused the survivors to face serious problems concerning inheritance rites. One of these pertained to the daughters of a man named Zelophehad who left no male heirs. His five daughters argued that their father had not participated in the rebellion which Korah led. Had he done so, there would have been no reason to preserve his family's name in Israel. Since he died a "natural death" — the Bible says "for his own sin" (Num. 27:3), implying that all men so die — his daughters felt that they should inherit their father's property. In general, women did not inherit property in a tribal society, but in this instance Moses saw the justice of their plea and ordered that their father's inheritance should go to them (Num. 27:1-11). From that time on the law of inheritance affirmed that an inheritance should pass to daughters when no sons survive.

As Moses approached the end of his life he consecrated Joshua the son of Nun as his successor (Num. 27:12-23). Joshua was a young man at the time of the Exodus (Exod. 33:11) and had distinguished himself in fighting the nomadic Amalekites (Exod. 17:8-13). He represented his tribe, Ephraim, when the spies conducted their survey of the Promised Land, and stood with Caleb in insisting that Israel should trust God and enter their inheritance (Num. 14:6-10). Joshua may have been about

The view westward from Mount Nebo. This unusual infra red telephoto affords a good view of the Jordan River entering the Dead Sea and a panorama of the Judean Wilderness farther west. On the horizon, the spine of the central range, traces of Jerusalem and Bethlehem are visible.

seventy years of age when he succeeded Moses as leader of the twelve tribes of Israel.

The death of Moses marks the end of the trek from Egypt to Canaan. After blessing his people (Deut. 33), the aged lawgiver went up from the plains of Moab to Mount Pisgah "which is opposite Jericho" (Deut. 34:1). From that vantage point he could see the Promised Land spread out at his feet, but Moses did not live to enter Canaan. At the age of one hundred twenty he died in Moab, leaving Joshua with the challenge to enter and possess the land which Yahweh had promised to the Patriarchs of Israel.

27

Mosaic Religion

The religion of the Patriarchs had been intensely personal. God appeared to Abraham, Isaac, and Jacob, promising them multiplied progeny (cf. Gen. 15:5) and ultimate inheritance of the land of Canaan (Gen. 13:14-15). By the time of the Exodus, the family had been replaced by the tribe as the self-conscious social unit, but the patriarchal promises were not forgotten. The tribes were returning to the home that God had given them. Joseph, in faith, had refused burial in Egypt, assured that God would one day bring his people back to their homes in Canaan (Gen. 50:24-26). The bones of Joseph which the Israelites took with them when leaving Egypt (Exod. 13:19) provided a link with the Patriarchs and the God who had revealed himself to them.

Under Moses, however, the Israelite tribes took the first steps toward nationhood, and collectively entered into covenant with Yahweh who would henceforth be known in a unique sense as Israel's God. Israel's election was of pure grace. Moses reminded them, "It was not because you were more in number than any other people that Yahweh set his love upon you and chose you, for you were the fewest of all peoples; but it is because Yahweh loves you, and is keeping the oath which he swore to your fathers, that Yahweh has brought you out with a mighty hand, and redeemed you from the house of bondage, from the hand of Pharaoh, king of Egypt" (Deut. 7:7-8).

It was God's purpose that the twelve tribes should develop a national consciousness centered in his revelation. The focus of Old Testament history would henceforth be upon Israel, although the promise that one day all nations would bless themselves in Abraham's seed (Gen. 12:1-2) was never abrogated. Israel had the honored position of the firstborn (Exod. 4:22), but was in no sense the only son.

Yahweh's choice of Israel did not imply that he would bless her under all circumstances. Blessing was conditioned on obedience, and rebellion brought with it strict retribution (cf. Exod. 32:25-29; Num. 11:33; 14:20-38; 17:6-15; 21:6; 25:6-9). Conversely when the heathen obeyed his word, blessing came upon them. The book of Jonah tells how the most wicked city of its day, Nineveh, was spared the wrath of God when it turned to him in penitence. Rahab of Jericho was saved from destruction because she believed in the power of Israel's God and demonstrated her faith by protecting the spies who sought refuge in her house. (Josh. 2).

When God appeared to him in the burning bush (Exod. 3), Moses was concerned that he be able to identify the One who had commissioned him to deliver Israel from Egypt. The Egyptians and their neighbors worshiped many gods, and the Israelites would be expected to question the source of the commission Moses professed to have received from God. God, Hebrew *Elohim,* is a generic name which may be used of the God of Israel or the gods of other peoples. The question of Moses was one of identity: "Who are you?" "How do you identify yourself?"

Many scholars translate God's reply (Exod. 3:14) as a perfect or a future tense of the verb "to be": "I am who I am," "I am what I am," or "I will be what I will be." God would thus be giving a cryptic answer, involving a play on the verb "to be" and the name Yahweh which is derived from that verb. God identified himself to Moses as Yahweh, who had earlier appeared to the Patriarchs (Exod. 3:15).

Israel's God claimed not only to be self-existent but also to be the author of all that exists. The name Yahweh is translated by W. F. Albright,[1] "He causes to be what comes into existence," identifying Israel's God with the Creator and moving power in all things. Israel's neighbors worshiped gods who were identified with the phenomena of nature — sun, moon, River Nile — but Israel's God claimed to be the creator of all things. He showed his control over nature in the plagues which he inflicted upon the rebellious Egyptians (Exod. 7-10), in parting the waters of the Reed Sea (Exod. 15:21) and in providing quails, manna, and water for his people's needs during their long journey. He produced lightning, thunder, and smoke, and

---

1. *From the Stone Age to Christianity* (Garden City, N.Y., Doubleday Anchor Books), pp. 259-261.

caused the very mountains to quake when he gave his Law at Sinai (Exod. 19:16-19; 20:18) .

According to a popular reconstruction of the religion of Israel, Moses introduced a new deity, or at least a new name for the deity, to the Israelite tribes after his contacts with Jethro. Yahweh, adherents to this view claim, was originally a mountain god worshiped by Kenites and Midianites in the Sinai peninsula. During Moses' forty years in the wilderness he is thought to have become a worshiper of Yahweh, whom he later identified with the God of Israel's Patriarchs. There is no *a priori* reason why Jethro might not have known the true God before his contacts with Moses, as Melchizedek (Gen. 14) did before the visit of Abraham, but the book of Exodus makes it clear that the history and religion of the Mosaic era is a continuation of that of the Patriarchs. Changes affect the externals of religion, but its essence is the same in Mosiac and Patriarchal ages

Another view, popularized by Sigmund Freud, would derive Mosaic monotheism from the solar monotheism of Akhenaton, the rebel Pharaoh who renounced the traditional Egyptian polytheism and devoted himself to the worship of Aton, the sun disk. While most scholars will agree that Akhenaton's theology was an advancement over that of his predecessors, his reforms were short lived, and their influence on succeeding generations seems to have been slight. Even if Moses had heard of Akhenaton's reforms, he showed no sympathy for sun worship. To Israel, all the gods of Egypt — including Aton — were defeated by Yahweh in the events associated with the Exodus.

The God who revealed himself through Moses to Israel forbade the use of images or pictures. As One who is in essence Spirit, he insisted that no attempt be made to depict him in the likeness of any created object (Exod. 20:4) . He might appear to men in any form he chose, but his Person was not to be confused with his manifestations. He appeared to Moses in a flame of fire (Exod. 3:2) and went before his people in the wilderness in a pillar of cloud by day, and a pillar of fire by night (Exod. 13:21-22) .

Yahweh consistently presents himself to Israel as a holy God upon whose Person mortal man could not look and live (Exod. 33:20) . Even Moses covered his face in God's presence (Exod. 3:6) . As a holy God, he demanded holiness of those who worship him (Exod. 19:6) . When Nadab and Abihu dishonored God's holiness they died (Lev. 10:1-3) .

The power of Yahweh was demonstrated in the wonders which Moses wrought in Egypt, and in the act of Israel's deliverance. God's power provided sustenance for Israel during its years in the wilderness, and when Moses himself questioned God's ability to meet an extremity, Yahweh asked him, "Is Yahweh's hand shortened?" (Num. 11:23). The seer Balaam tried to curse Israel at the instigation of Balak of Moab, but the power of Yahweh turned his curse into a blessing. When Balak reprimanded Balaam for not following directions, the seer answered, "Must I not take heed to speak what Yahweh puts in my mouth?" (Num. 23:12).

In no sense is Yahweh restricted as to place. He hears the cry of his persecuted people in Egypt and calls Moses in the wilderness to become their deliverer. The Holy of Holies in the sacred Tabernacle is his throne room, but from the highest heaven he smells the sweet-smelling savor of sacrifices offered by the penitent. He is the God of Mount Sinai, but leads his people to Canaan, the land of their inheritance.

No Israelite could question the extent of God's knowledge. He knew of the affliction of his people, but he also knew of Pharaoh's intentions: "I know that the king of Egypt will not let you go unless compelled by a mighty hand" (Exod. 3:19). Yahweh anticipated Pharaoh's every move, and in announcing the last plague said to Moses, "Afterwards he will let you go hence; when he lets you go he will drive you away completely" (Exod. 11:1). Through prophets, God could foretell events of the future (cf. Num. 24:15-24), and through the mysterious Urim and Thummim the High Priest could declare God's will to leaders (Num. 27:21) and people (Deut. 33:8, 10).

The Urim and Thummim were kept in the breastplate of the High Priest (Exod. 28:30; Lev. 8:8) which was attached to the ephod, a garment which reached from the breast to the hips, held in place by two shoulder bands and tied around the waist (Exod. 39:1-26). The inquirer asked questions which could be answered, "Yes" or "No." An answer could not be forced, however. When Saul sought information concerning the impending battle at Mount Gilboa, the Urim gave him no answer (I Sam. 28:6).

The exact nature of the Urim and Thummim is not known, but it has been suggested that they were flat stones, each of which had one side marked Urim (from 'arar, "to curse") and the other marked Thummim (from tamam, "to be perfect"). The stones were either thrown or ceremonially drawn by the priest from the pouch. When both stones displayed the Urim side, a negative answer was given, when both stones showed the Thummim, the answer was positive, and when one Urim and one Thummim appeared, no reply could be given to the question.

Yahweh is consistently presented as a God who is just in his ways, judging the Egyptians when they resist his will, but also judging disobedient and rebellious Israel. Although Balaam as a prophet uttered God's message, the fact that he sought to help Balak in cursing Israel brought divine judgment on his head (Num. 31:8, 16). God's judgments are just, but he delights in mercy. Yahweh describes himself as "a God merciful and gracious, slow to anger and abounding in steadfast love and faithfulness, keeping steadfast love for thousands, forgiving iniquity and transgression and sin, but who will by no means clear the guilty, visiting the iniquity of the fathers upon the children and the children's children to the fourth generation" (Exod. 34:6 7). Yahweh showed his love to Israel by carrying her "on eagles' wings" (Exod. 19:4) to himself.

The mercy of Yahweh is particularly shown in the provision of the Tabernacle, or "Tent of Meeting," at which the sinner could present his offering and receive pardon. He who had spoken amidst the thunderings and lighting of Sinai, directed the sinner to come with a sacrifice to the door of the Tent of Meeting (Lev. 1:1-3). The sanctity of the Tabernacle with its provision that no Israelite save the High Priest, and he only once a year, might enter the Holy of Holies stressed the holiness and inaccessibility of Israel's God. The sacrificial system, the Altar of Burnt Offering at the gate of the Tabernacle, and the laver for the cleansing of the priests, emphasize the corresponding truth — the all-holy God delights in showing mercy to his penitent people.

Although sacrifices had existed from the beginnings of Biblical history (cf. Gen. 4:1-7), they were codified for the first time in the Mosaic legislation. Four kinds of sacrifice involving bloodshed are mentioned in the book of Leviticus: Burnt Offerings, Peace Offerings, Sin Offerings, and Trespass Offerings. The animals had to be ceremonially clean, and offerings were limited to such animals as the Israelites themselves were permitted to eat. These included sheep, goats, and oxen. In certain of the sacrifices either male or female animals might be offered, and in case of poverty, pigeons might be substituted for the more expensive animals.

When sacrifices were made on behalf of the nation, the High Priest officiated. Individuals, however, might bring their own sacrifices to the Altar of Burnt Offering, place their hands on the head of the victim, and kill it. An officiating priest would then sprinkle the blood and burn the sacrifice.

In the Burnt Offering the entire sacrifice was consumed upon the altar (Lev. 1:5-17; 6:8-13), signifying the complete consecration of the offering (cf. Rom. 12:1). The Peace Offering was voluntarily given (Lev. 3:1-17; 7:11-34), and emphasized concepts of communion or fellowship. The fat of the Peace Offering was burned, a part of the remaining meat was assigned to the priest, and the worshiper and his guests feasted on the rest. Atonement for sins committed unwittingly was made through the Sin Offering (Lev. 4:1-35; 6:24-30), and trespasses in which the offender might make restitution were provided for in the Trespass Offering which insisted that the offender repay his debt with an additional double tithe (Lev. 5:14 — 6:7).

Besides the animal sacrifices, provision was made for a Meal Offering (A.V. "Meat Offering," R.S.V. "Cereal Offering") which often accompanied the Burnt Offerings or the Peace Offerings. The offering might be of fine flour mixed with oil, frankincense, and salt, or of flour prepared in the oven in the form of bread, cakes, or wafers (Lev. 2:1-16; 6:14-23). Honey was rigidly excluded from the Meal Offerings.

Before the giving of the law at Sinai, the Sabbath was set apart as a day of solemn rest (Exod. 16:22-30). Festivities also marked the beginning of each month (the "new moon," Num. 10:10) and, in particular, the beginning of the seventh month which was known in Old Testament times as the Feast of Trumpets (Lev. 23:23-25; Num. 28:11-15; 29:1-6). The Passover Feast, commemorating the Exodus, was associated with the Feast of Unleavened Bread which immediately followed it (Exod. 10:2; 12:8, 14; Num. 28:16-25). As an agricultural festival it commemorated the beginning of the barley harvest, but its prime religious interest centered in the celebration of deliverance from Egyptian bondage. Fifty days after the Passover, Israel celebrated another agricultural festival, marking the beginning of the wheat harvest. This festival, known in the Old Testament as the Feast of Weeks (Exod. 23:16; 34:22) was later known as Pentecost (Acts 2). Prescribed offerings were presented to Yahweh, and Israel was reminded of the necessity of remembering the poor (Lev. 23:22).

The tenth day of the Seventh month was the Day of Atonement, the most solemn day of the year (Exod. 30:10; Lev. 16:1-34; 23:26-31). In elaborate ceremonies, propitiation was made for Aaron and his sons, for the Holy Place itself, for the Tent of Meeting, for the Altar of Burnt Offering, and for the whole people of Israel. It was on the Day of Atonement that the High Priest entered the Most Holy Place to perform his sacred rite of sprinkling blood. In another of the colorful rituals of the day, two goats were set apart as a Sin Offering for the people. The High Priest sacrificed one goat at the altar, then he put his hand on the head of the live goat and confessed Israel's sins. The goat was then taken into the wilderness to carry away the sins of the people. The concept of the goat that escaped into the wilderness gives us our word "scapegoat."

From the fifteenth to the twenty-second day of the seventh month, Israel observed the Feast of Booths, or Tabernacles (Exod. 23:14-17), the final holy days of the year. The Israelites actually lived in booths made of the boughs of trees or palm tree branches during the week, remembering the period of wandering in the wilderness when such temporary abodes served as dwelling places for the people (Lev. 23:43).

In addition to the weekly sabbath, the sabbath principle was applied to years (Exod. 23:10-11). The land was to lie fallow every seventh year (Lev. 25:2-5), after six years of sowing, pruning, and harvesting. Natural growth from the field might be gleaned by the poor, and anything left was for the beasts (Exod. 23:11; Deut. 15:2-18). In the Sabbatical Year any Hebrew who was in bondage to another was to be set free (cf. Jer. 34:14) and creditors were instructed to cancel debts incurred by the poor during the six previous years (Deut. 15:1-11).

After seven sabbatical cycles, the fiftieth year was known as the Jubilee. It was observed like sabbatical years, with the additional provision that property revert to its original owners, debts be remitted, and Hebrews who were enslaved for debt be released. The Jubilee was a time of thanksgiving and genuine rejoicing. The American Liberty Bell which proclaimed the birth of our nation from Independence Hall, Philadelphia, bears the inscription from Leviticus 25:10 describing the significance of the Jubilee: "Proclaim liberty throughout all the land to all the inhabitants thereof."

The concept of justice in Israel is illustrated by provision made for six Cities of Refuge to be designated after the conquest of Canaan (Num. 35:9-28). Three would be located on each side of the Jordan as asylums to which a fugitive man-slayer might flee. The man who had killed another accidentally was allowed to stay in the City of Refuge until the death of the High Priest. There he would be protected from the relatives of the deceased who would otherwise seek revenge. A wilful murderer, however, was not granted asylum, but was sur-rendered to the avenger and put to death.

The provision that the accidental homicide could remain in a City of Refuge until after the death of the High Priest was interpreted in later Jewish writings as a vicarious expiation of life for life. After the death of the High Priest the manslayer was free to leave the City of Refuge and his person was then regarded as safe. The demand for blood revenge was satisfied by the priest's death.

28 | Dates and Figures

In our age of scientific calculations we may grow somewhat impatient at ancient methods of reckoning. Worse yet, we may assume that the Biblical writers used the same rules that we do for historical writing, and judge them harshly when their results do not tally with our expectations. Scholars have long puzzled over the date of the Exodus, and the number of people who left Egypt with Moses—two problems which reflect the use of figures by Biblical writers.

It should be clear to all who read the Book of Exodus, that dates and names which can be compared with known Egyptian history form no part of the Biblical record. The ruler is simply "Pharaoh"—the word used for any Egyptian king. Modern scholars may argue concerning the identity of the Pharaoh of the oppression and the Pharaoh of the Exodus, but the Biblical writer was not interested in supplying that information. To be sure, the identification of these individuals would help us to place Biblical history in its contemporary setting, but we must remember that the Bible itself does not identify them.

It may be argued, however, that the Bible does provide material for an exact chronology. In I Kings 6:1 we read, "In the four hundred and eightieth year after the people of Israel came out of the land of Egypt, in the fourth year of Solomon's reign over Israel ... he began to build the house of the Lord." Since the fourth year of Solomon's reign was about 960 B.C., a simple mathematical solution would suggest that the Exodus took place around 1440 B.C., a date which is defended by some modern scholars. Thutmose III was the Pharaoh at that time. Although he, like the Pharaoh who oppressed the Israelites, was famous for building operations in which slave labor was employed, Thutmose III resided at Thebes in Upper Egypt, while the Pharaoh whose daughter found the infant Moses, and the

A closeup look at one of the statues that stands at the feet of the colossi at the cliff temple built by Ramesses II. These smaller figures represent the royal children.

Pharaoh to whom Moses went with the demand that Israel be released, lived in the eastern Delta, near the land of Goshen. In fact one of the store cities upon which the Israelites labored is named Raamses, evidently the Egyptian Per-Raamses, "the house of Ramesses," named for Ramesses II. Although this may be a modernized form of an older name, other evidence suggests that Ramesses II may have been the Pharaoh who oppressed the Israelites. Nelson Glueck's explorations in Transjordan suggest that Edom and Moab developed into powerful kingdoms defended by border fortifications about 1300 B.C. Had the Israelites sought to pass through these lands prior to 1300 B.C. there would presumably have been no powerful government to impede their progress. The fact that Pharaohs of the Rameside Age had capitals in the eastern Delta at Tanis, which is probably to be identified with Raamses, harmonizes well with the Biblical descriptions of the relations between the Pharaohs and the Israelites in the Book of Exodus.

The four hundred eighty years of I Kings 6:1 has variants, although they do not assist in computing dates. Several of the better Septuagint manuscripts (B and A) read "four hundred and forty years," and Josephus gives "five hundred ninety two years."[1] Josephus probably arrived at his calculations by adding up the figures in the books of Judges, Samuel and Kings. He erred in assuming that such figures were all successive when in reality some are contemporaneous. In all probability Judges overlapped one another in various parts of the country.

Bible students have long been aware that the figure 40 and its multiples appears very frequently in the earlier books of the Bible. Solomon and David each reigned forty years. The judgeships of Eli, Deborah and Barak, Gideon, and Othniel were each forty years, that of Ehud, eighty years. Israel spent forty years in the wilderness until the generation that left Egypt (except for Caleb and Joshua) had died. In this usage forty years appears to be a conventional way of saying a generation, and the four hundred eighty years from the Exodus to Solomon may represent twelve generations.

Such considerations lead us to conclude that we do not have in our Biblical texts for the period before the Israelite monarchy sufficient data to enable us to establish an absolute chronology. If other considerations within the Biblical text suggest the possibility of a date other than 1440 B.C. for the date

---

1. *Antiquities* vii. 3. 1.

of the Exodus, there is no reason for insisting, on the basis of I Kings 6:1, that they should not be carefully considered.

We do know that Israelites were in Canaan by the last quarter of the thirteenth century. A stele of Pharaoh Merneptah, erected about 1200 B.C. mentions Israel by name among the Palestinian peoples defeated by the Egyptians:

> The princes are prostrate, saying, "Mercy!"
>   Not one raises his head among the Nine Bows.
> Desolation is for Tehenu; Hatti is pacified;
>   Plundered is the Canaan with every evil;
> Carried off is Ashkelon; seized upon is Gezer;
>   Yanoam is made as that which does not exist;
> Israel is laid waste, his seed is not;
>   Hurru is become a widow for Egypt!
> All lands together, they are pacified;
>   Everyone who was restless, he has been bound.

Archaeological expeditions at Bethel, Lachish, and Debir in Palestine have produced evidence that these cities fell as a result of violent attack some time between 1250 and 1200 B.C. John Garstang's earlier work at Jericho had convinced him that he had discovered Joshua's wall, and that it fell around 1400 B.C., lending support to the early date of the Exodus. More recent studies at Jericho by Kathleen Kenyon suggest that Garstang was mistaken. The wall which he associated with Joshua was really several centuries older than his 1400 B.C. date, and the Jericho evidence can no longer be cited in favor of an early date for the Exodus.

According to Exodus 12:40, Israel spent four hundred thirty years in Egypt. If this is taken to mean the entire period from Joseph to Moses, the following chronology may be suggested:

Period of Favor in Egypt	1710-1550 B.C. 15th to 17th Dynasties	Hyksos Rule from Avaris in the Delta
Period of Disfavor in Egypt	1550-1308 B.C. 18th Dynasty	Native Egyptian Rulers expel Hyksos and rule from Thebes in Upper Egypt
Period of the Exodus	1308-1290 B.C. 19th Dynasty	Seti I (1308-1290 B.C.) and Ramesses II (1290-1224 B.C.) rule from Tanis (=Avaris) in the Delta.

The above figures presuppose a date for the Exodus around 1290 B.C.[2] The reference in Exodus 12:40 may be interpreted as dealing solely with the years of oppression (cf. Gen. 15:13), yielding a much longer period for the sojourn of Israel in Egypt.

The Merneptah stele includes the first mention of Israel in Egyptian records.

2. Based on the reconstruction suggested by Bernhard W. Anderson, *Understanding the Old Testament* (Englewood Cliffs, N.J.: Prentice Hall, 1960), pp. 26-30.

Conversely, the Greek Septuagint reads that Israel lived in Egypt and Canaan for four hundred thirty years, thus reckoning the whole period from Abraham to Moses as approximately four centuries. Paul, in Galatians 4:13-17, speaks of the Law as given four hundred and thirty years after God's covenant with Abraham. In Stephen's speech, four hundred years is mentioned as the period of oppression (Acts 7:6, based on Gen. 15:13).

If we add the four hundred thirty years of Exodus 12:40 to the 1290 B.C. date for the Exodus we have 1720 B.C. for the entrance of Israel into the land of Egypt. Israel recollected a relationship to the "Era of Tanis" in the note that Hebron was built "seven years before Zoan [=Tanis] in Egypt" (Num. 13:22). The fact that Israel dated events from the era of Tanis suggests relations with the rulers who established Tanis (Avaris) as their delta capital.

Some time during the reign of Horemhab (ca. 1340 — ca. 1303 B.C.), a stele was erected at Tanis commemorating the four hundredth anniversary of the city which evidently was founded around 1700 B.C. By that time the Hyksos were well established in Egypt, and it is probably they who built Zoan-Tanis as their capital in the eastern Delta.

As perplexing as the problem of the date of the Exodus, is the question of the number of participants. In round figures the Biblical text mentions six hundred thousand male Israelites (Exod. 12:37), to which wives, children, and members of the "mixed multitude" of hangers-on must be added. On that basis the total number can hardly have been fewer than two million. Biblical scholars have hesitated to posit so large a figure for a variety of reasons. So large a company could have been enslaved by Pharaoh only with the greatest difficulty, and Pharaoh's attempts to control them would involve staggering expenditures in manpower. The greatest battle during the reign of Rameses II saw but four divisions, 20,000 men, in the field according to Egyptian records.

The logistics of moving two million people across the Reed Sea in one night are themselves staggering. We must not, of course, picture the Israelites marching in columns through the Sinai Peninsula. Alois Musil, a Czech explorer, has noted the movements of modern nomads, which may give some indication of the way the Israelites traveled. As many as five thousand families may migrate at one time, moving in a column three miles deep and twelve miles wide. The wider the line, the greater the amount of available pasture, but also the greater the risk of groups lagging behind and being cut off by an enemy. A deeper line will mean less pasture for the families in the rear, but it provided better protection for the group.

Scholars have resorted to numerous expedients in trying to account for the six hundred thousand men mentioned in the traditional text. One expedient is to suggest a scribal error. If six thousand were meant, we might have a total group of 25,000, a figure more like what we would expect under the circumstances. Those who argue for a smaller number note that but two midwives were able to care for the obstetrical needs of all Israel (Exod. 1:15), and the spies at Kadesh-barnea reported that the Israelites could not hope to conquer the more powerful Canaanites (Num. 13). Although Jericho was a major military engagement we read that "about forty thousand ready armed for war passed over before the Lord for battle to the plains of Jericho" (Josh. 4:13).

George E. Mendenhall has sought to resolve the problems by interpreting the word *Elif*, "thousand" as a tribal subunit or grouping.[3] He argues that the lists are authentic ancient records of the contingents sent to war by each of the tribes, and reckons 5,550 fighting men on the basis of Numbers 1, and 5,750 on the basis of Numbers 26.

Some years ago W. F. Albright suggested that the population figures in the Exodus records were actually figures from the census of David (II Sam. 24). The figures in Exodus and Numbers would thus be misplaced census figures. It might be argued that actually all Israel took part in the Exodus — that later Israelites were represented by the generation which pledged allegiance to Yahweh at Sinai.

No solution to the problem has proved entirely satisfactory. Scripture makes it clear that the number of Israelites in the Sinai Peninsula was so large that supernatural provision had to be made to provide sustenance, but that it was small enough for the Egyptians to oppress and for nomadic Amalekites to threaten. Israel gained victories in Transjordan over Sihon and Og, but these victories were attributed to divine intervention rather than to the might of Israel. Jericho fell as a result of a miracle by which the walls fell to permit the invading Israelites to enter and despoil the city. It is an important motif in the story of the Exodus and Conquest that God brought down the mighty foe in order that His people might be preserved and inhabit the land promised to their fathers.

---

3. "The Census Lists of Numbers 1 and 26," *JBL* (LXXVII) (1958), pp. 52-66.

The death of Moses marked the end of the formative period of the people which later generations were to know as Israel. Moses had been the leader of the Exodus. As God's prophet he had borne with the people the trials of a generation in the Sinai wilderness and the lands of Transjordan. Moses would be honored during subsequent centuries as the lawgiver and prophet of Israel's infancy. He died, however, before he could lead the people into their land. It was his successor, Joshua ben Nun, who brought Israel into Canaan and saw the tribes begin the task of occupation of the land and accommodation to a sedentary life after a generation of nomadic existence.

The Book of Joshua begins with an account of God's commission to Moses' successor. Moses was dead. There was no reason to despair, however, for the God of Moses was the Living God. He would give His people their land, but Joshua must have faith, and show that faith by his actions. He must enter the land and occupy it. The land is specified (Josh. 1:4): It extends from the wilderness to the south and east northward to the Lebanon Mountains and the northern reaches of the Euphrates River. The Jordan River was its eastern border, and it was bounded by the Mediterranean on the west. Two and one-half tribes were later permitted to settle east of the Jordan, but the natural border has always been the Jordan.

Joshua was reminded of his obligations to remain loyal to the "Law of the Lord"—the Torah revealed by God to Moses. The Law would be binding on subsequent generations of Israelites. It should be regarded as a blessing—a revelation from God. Joshua was to delight in it, meditating on its gracious provisions constantly—"day and night." Difficult days were ahead, but God would be with His people in all their trials.

When the tribes of Reuben, Gad, and half the Manasseh tribe suggested that the transjordan lands were suitable for grazing lands, Joshua permitted the wives and children to remain there. He insisted, however, that the men help their brothers in fighting for the land of Canaan. Only after the conquest was complete could they return and occupy their territories east of the Jordan.

PART THREE

Conquest and Settlement

CANAAN AS DIVIDED AMONG THE TWELVE TRIBES

c. 1200-1020 B.C.

Copyright by C. S. Hammond & Co., N. Y.

Scale of Miles

0   10   20   30   40

Sidon

Zarephath

Damascus

Tyre

Kanah

Leontes R.

MOUNT LEBANON

MT. HERMON

DAN
Laish
(Dan)

A S H E R

N A P H T A L I

Kedesh

B a s h a n

Hazor

MANASSEH

Accho

Cabul

Ashtaroth

Sea of
Chinnereth

Aphek

MT. CARMEL

Kishon R.

ZEBULUN

Mt.
Tabor

Hammath

Dor

Megiddo

Shunem

ISSACHAR

Edrei

Yarmuk R.

Ramoth-gilead

Taanach

Jezreel

Beth-
shan

Mahanaim

G i l e a d

The Great Sea

(Mediterranean Sea)

Plain of Sharon

MANASSEH

Mt. Ebal

Mt. Gerizim

Shechem

Jordan

Succoth

Jabbok

Penuel

A M M O N

Jabbok R.

Kanah

Shiloh

EPHRAIM

Jazer

Rabbath-ammon

Joppa
(Japho)

Ajalon

D A N

Beth-
horon

Bethel

Gezer

Gibeon

BENJAMIN

Jericho

Gilgal

River Jordan

Jabneel

Jerusalem
(Jebus)

Heshbon

Mt. Nebo

Ashdod

Libnah

Beth-
shemesh

Bethlehem

Medeba

Ashkelon

R E U B E N

Philistia

J U D A H

Caleb

Salt Sea
(Dead Sea)

Gaza

Lachish

Hebron

Gerar

Ziklag

En-gedi

Arnon R.

Aroer

Raphia

Cherethites

Kenites

Beer-sheba

M O A B

Hormah

River of Egypt

S I M E O N

Rehoboth

Wilderness of
Zin

Zered R.

E D O M

29

Preparation and Crossing

In preparation for the invasion, Joshua sent two spies into the city of Jericho, a strongly fortified city which stood immediately in the path of the Israelites. Excavations at Jericho indicate that it was one of the earliest of fortified cities. It had walls and a tower in pre-pottery neolithic times — as early as 7000 B.C. A perennial spring, known in later times as Elisha's fountain, brings fertility to this area, which otherwise would be desert like the surrounding region. The spring, however, makes Jericho an oasis. It is known as the "City of Palm Trees." From earliest times, nomads who crossed from Transjordan into Canaan first made their way to Jericho, as did the Israelites, in their turn, in the days of Joshua.

The spies made their way to the house of Rahab, the harlot of Jericho. Such a person would be accustomed to the visits of strange men, and the presence of the spies there would not raise the suspicions that it might raise elsewhere. Rahab, however, is considered a heroine of faith (Heb. 11:31). Although a Canaanite with a questionable past, she had heard of the God of Israel, and was convinced that He was about to give victory to Israel over Canaan (Josh. 2:9-11). She risked her own life by hiding the spies and helping them to escape from the men of Jericho who had learned that spies were in the city. On their part, the spies promised to spare Rahab and her household at the time the Israelites took the city.

After the spies made their report, Joshua organized the Israelites for the crossing of the Jordan and the entry into Canaan. The crossing of the Jordan, like that of the Red (or Reed) Sea at the beginning of the wilderness wandering, was the result of God's miraculous provision for His people's needs. The Red Sea had been held back "by a strong east wind" (Exod. 14:21), permitting the Israelites to leave Egypt. Pharaoh's forces were over-

An ancient tower among the excavations at Jericho.

The Jordan River. Israel's crossing the Jordan under Joshua marked the end of the forty years in the wilderness and the beginning of her life in Canaan.

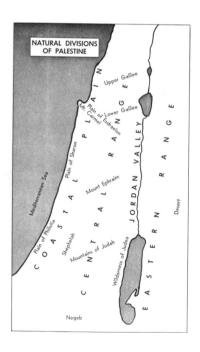

whelmed by the waves of the sea as they sought to follow the Israelites. When the Israelites entered the Jordan, "the waters coming down from above stood and rose up in a heap far off, at Adam, the city that is beside Zarethan, and those flowing down toward the sea of the Arabah, the Salt Sea, were wholly cut off; and the people passed over opposite Jericho (Josh. 3:16). The waters of the Jordan were swollen by the spring floods, but they were held back, perhaps by a landslide. The Jordan Valley is part of the earthquake prone Rift Valley which extends southward through the Arabah and across into Africa. If such an earthquake or landslide occurred, its timing was such as to convince the Israelites that God was indeed making it possible for them to enter the land.

The procession crossing the Jordan was lead by the Levitical priests carrying the ark of the covenant, the sacred cult object which was normally placed in the Most Holy Place, the inner sanctuary of the Tabernacle. The ark represented the presence of Israel's God. On occasion it was taken to the battlefield (I Sam. 4:6-9), but the Biblical writers emphasize the fact that God does not give victory in an automatic or magical way just because the ark is present. The Philistines actually captured the ark in a later moment of Israelite humiliation. Here, however, the ark represented God going before his people, and bringing them to their inheritance.

The significance of the crossing was noted by the Israelites themselves, and by the natives of Canaan. The Israelites built a monument of twelve stones, representing the twelve tribes, with the thought that it would remind later generations of the miracle which God had performed (Josh. 4:19-24). The inhabitants of Canaan, however, were so frightened that they did not know how to react to this threat. Ultimately they would regroup and fight, but for the moment they were completely dissipited (Josh. 5:1).

The Israelites settled at an encampment known as Gilgal, which became their military headquarters. While at Gilgal we read of a transition from the wilderness experience to life in Canaan. The rite of circumcision had been neglected, so the generation born in the wilderness was circumcised at this time. Passover, commemorating the Exodus from Egypt, was observed (Josh. 5:10).

30

The Central Campaign

The Israelite conquest of Canaan is described in the Book of Joshua in terms which seem to indicate a series of lightning battles, beginning with the siege and capture of Jericho. The Book of Judges, however, makes it clear that these victories did not mean the total extinction of Israel's enemies (Judg. 2:21-23). Important areas were not incorporated into Israelite territory, including the strategic valley of Esdraelon and the Philistine Plain. The victory was not complete until the days of David, who finally conquered the Philistines, and Solomon, who received the city of Gezer from the Egyptian Pharaoh at the time of his wedding to an Egyptian princess (I Kings 9:16).

This does not lessen the importance of the campaigns described in Joshua, however. Israelite victories in Transjordan were a prelude to greater victories, and the inhabitants of Canaan were terror-striken at the advance of Joshua and his armies. Rahab was certainly not the only one who sensed that the Israelites would soon occupy the land.

In crossing the Jordan westward from Moab, the walled city of Jericho would pose the first challenge to Israel's armies. Jericho had had a history dating back at least five thousand years prior to Joshua's time. A perennial spring, later to be known as Elisha's Spring (II Kings 2:19-22), provides the water which makes of Jericho a luxuriant oasis. It is surrounded by the Judean wilderness, however, with the traditional site of Jesus' temptation to the west of the site, and Qumran to the south and east. Throughout history, any invader from Transjordan would head first for Jericho.

As a result of Kathleen M. Kenyon's excavations at Tell es-Sultan, ten miles northwest of the mouth of the Jordan at the Dead Sea and one mile northwest of *er-Riha,* modern Jericho, we can now trace the history of Old Testament Jericho from

The oasis of Jericho as seen from the site of Old Testament Jericho.

An air view of Jericho, looking southeastward, with the Dead Sea and the mountains of Moab in the background.

about 8000 B.C. to about 1200 B.C. Important defenses were built for the site during Neolithic times prior to the introduction of pottery. By around 7000 B.C. Jericho was defended by a wall twelve feet high and six feet wide. An adjoining tower was thirty feet high, with twenty-two steps inside. Beyond the wall was a ditch, twenty-seven feet wide and nine feet deep, cut into the rock. Houses of the period were made of brick. They were round in shape, and most had a small porch.

This "pre-pottery Neolithic Jericho" is a puzzle to scholars. We do not know what enemy caused the Jericho people to build such massive fortifications. It would be four thousand years before comparable towns would appear in the valleys of the Tigris-Euphrates and the Nile. Long before the dawn of history, the strategic importance of Jericho was realized.[1]

By the time of Joshua, Jericho was a major Canaanite city devoted, as its name implies, to the Moon god. The Canaanites were heirs to a culture which had been developing for millennia. In material things — walls, buildings, armor and the like — they far excelled the Israelites. The nature of Israel's faith, however, was to prove decisive when the battle began.

Israel's siege of Jericho was unconventional, to say the least. On each of six days, Joshua's army marched around the walls of the city. Some of the priests carried the sacred ark which had been constructed during the wilderness wandering as part of the Tabernacle, which served as Israel's portable shrine. Others blew on trumpets made of the horns of rams. The sound of the "shophar" still heralds holy days among the Jews.

The seventh day marked the climax of the siege. This time the priests marched around Jericho seven times. The priests blew the trumpets, the people shouted, and the Israelites stormed the city. The walls, behind which the Canaanites of Jericho felt secure, fell and Joshua's hosts entered the city without hindrance. The city of Jericho with its inhabitants was utterly destroyed. Only Rahab and her family were spared, as the spies had promised.

As the first city to be taken in Canaan, Jericho was offered totally to the Lord. No Israelite was permitted to take any of the booty of the city. The man who violated this taboo would later pay for his sin with his life (Josh. 6). A curse was further pronounced on any who would attempt to rebuild Jericho.

The victory at Jericho was regarded as proof that God was

1. Cf. Kathleen M. Kenyon, *Digging Up Jericho* (Frederick A. Praeger, Inc., 1957).

indeed fighting on behalf of his people. Canaanites would be terrified and Israelites elated. The next battle, at a place named Ai ("the ruin"), should have resulted in an easy victory. Overly confident, the Israelites sent a small detachment to Ai, east of Bethel, but the men of Ai repelled Joshua's men and thirty-six Israelites were slain, With complete confidence that he was doing God's will, Joshua was utterly perplexed at this defeat.

The cause of the defeat was spiritual. An Israelite had taken some of the spoil of Jericho, and the whole army had suffered. Joshua must now discover the guilty one, and punish him. The method was the casting of lots. The tribes were summoned, and it was determined that the culprit was from the tribe of Judah. The families of Judah were considered, and the family of the Zerahites was found to contain the guilty one. By a similar process among the Zerahites, Zabdi was designated, and finally Achan, son of Carmi, son of Zabdi, was identified as the man who had stolen from Jericho. Achan admitted that he had taken a Babylonian garment, two hundred shekels of silver, and a bar of gold weighing fifty shekels. He hid them in the earth under his tent.

After the booty was found, Achan, his family, and all his possessions were taken to Joshua at a place known as the Valley of Achor ("Trouble"). Achan, the man responsible for Israel's defeat at Ai, was stoned along with his family. Only in this way could Israel be purged of the taint of Achan's sin.

A second battle for Ai brought victory to the Israelites. This time victory came as a result of a ruse. Joshua with a part of his army feigned an attack, then retreated with the men of Ai in pursuit. While the defenders of the city were chasing Joshua's men in an apparent rout, the Israelites who were waiting on the other side of the city entered Ai and burned it. The men of Ai were then caught between the Israelites who had entered the city during their absence, and the army of Joshua which had feigned retreat. The Israelites in this second battle of Ai won a decisive victory.

The name *Ai* means "the ruin." It has been identified with a tell about a mile east of Bethel which is known in Arabic as et-Tell. Archaeological evidence suggests that Bethel was destroyed by fire during the latter half of the thirteenth century B.C. A layer of ash and debris several feet thick is evidence of the destruction. Above the debris were found remains of a poorly built Israelite town, evidence that for several centuries the Israelite material culture did not equal that of the earlier

Ein es Sultan, the spring near Old Testament Jericho.

An ivory bull's head, charred by fire, is among the relics of Jericho dating from the Early Bronze Age.

Canaanites. Some Biblical scholars suggest that Ai may have been a military outpost of nearby Bethel. The fact that there is no record of the conquest of Bethel in the Book of Joshua makes the idea attractive.

The account of the conquest is interrupted by the author of Joshua with the story of a solemn convocation of the Israelite tribes in the mountainous area near Shechem, modern Nablus, about twenty miles north of Ai. Here an altar was erected, and a copy of the Mosaic Law was inscribed on stones. The law code of Hammurabi of Babylon (ca. 1700 B.C.) had been inscribed on stone and set up in a public place for all to read. Evidently the Biblical code was to be set up in a public place for the same purpose.

The topography of the region is such that Mount Gerizim and Mount Ebal make a natural amphitheater. Here the Israelites assembled, half in front of Mount Gerizim and half in front of Mount Ebal, with the ark, attended by the Levitical priests, in the midst. The Law, with its blessings and curses, was read before all the people. Details are given prophetically in Deuteronomy 27. There we are told that the Levites would read a curse, and all the people would respond with, "Amen." The list of curses is very ancient, and it gives an insight into Israelite moral principles. Among the curses we read:

"Cursed be he who misleads a blind man on the road" (Deut. 27:18).
"Cursed be he who perverts the justice due to the sojourner, the fatherless and the widow" (Deut. 27:19).
"Cursed be he who slays his neighbor in secret" (Deut. 28:24),
"Cursed be he who takes a bribe to slay an innocent person" (Deut. 28:25).

Idolatry, removing landmarks (i.e. laying claim to property by removing the marks which indicate true ownership), and incest are among the crimes placed under the curse. Other details of the ceremony, including the blessings, are not recorded. Covenant renewal ceremonies were an important part of Israelite life. At the beginning of the conquest of Canaan, the tribes felt that obedience to the Mosaic law was of paramount importance. Later generations would often forget these solemn commitments, but prophets would arise from time to time to call them back to faith in the Lord and obedience to His Word.

The men of Gibeon, northwest of Jerusalem, learned of the Israelite victories at Jericho and Ai, and determined to save their city from destruction. According to the Mosaic Law (Deut. 25:15-16) the Israelites might make peace with distant cities, but

Mount Gerizim, near Shechem, is now partially reforested.

those nearby were to be conquered and occupied. The Gibeonites determined to take advantage of that provision of the Law.
They came to Joshua with moldy bread, worn out and patched
clothing, and worn sacks and wineskins. Pretending to have
come from a great distance they pursuaded Joshua that he should
make an alliance with them, and Joshua felt bound to honor
the alliance. The word was considered sacred, and when given
it had to be honored at all costs. When Jacob deceived his father
Isaac, pretending to be Esau, Isaac gave the blessing and could
not go back on his word (Gen. 27:1-41). So here, the Gibeonites
had been put under Joshua's protection, and he undertook to
protect them.

As punishment for their deception, however, the Gibeonites
were assigned the position of "hewers of wood and drawers of
water" for the Israelites. This servile status was continued down
through the years, for the author of Joshua states that it continues "to this day." A class of Temple servants, the Gibeonites
continued as one of the non-Israelite peoples who became a part
of the Israelite nation.

The defection of the Gibeonites served as a warning to
Canaanite cities to the south that they were vulnerable. The
reputation which the Israelites gained as effective fighters caused
the native Canaanites to fear for their land. A confederation, including Adonizedek of Jerusalem, Hoham of Hebron, Piram of
Jarmuth, Japhia of Lachish, and Debir of Eglon decided that
they would make an example of Gibeon for making peace with
Israel. They feared that if Gibeon went unpunished, she would
set a precedent which would be followed throughout the land.

The period of Joshua and the Judges was one in which Egyptian power was minimal, and Assyria had not yet become a major power. The result was a situation in which city-states were
free to make such alliances as they wished, with little fear of
outside interference. Canaan was pretty much on its own, and
was determined to solve its own problems.

The federation of kings from southern Canaan turned against
Gibeon, determined to punish the men of Gibeon for their acceptance of Israel. Gibeon, however, sent to Joshua who was
encamped at Gilgal, asking him to hurry to the defense of the
city. Joshua responded at once, marching his army all night and
immediately engaging the enemy. The Israelites pursued the
enemy through the pass controlled by Upper Beth-horon and
Lower Beth-horon. The enemy was chased out of the hill country
to the coastal plain.

In Palestine the commonly recognized
periods are as follows:

Mesolithic (Natufian)	ca. 8000-6000 B.C.
Pre-Pottery Neolithic	ca. 6000-5000 B.C.
Pottery Neolithic	ca. 5000-4000 B.C.
Chalcolithic	ca. 4000-3200 B.C.
Early Bronze (EB)	
EB I	ca. 3200-2800 B.C.
EB II	ca. 2800-2600 B.C.
EB III	ca. 2600-2300 B.C.
EB IV (or III B)	ca. 2300-2100 B.C.
Middle Bronze (MB)	
MB I (or EB-MB Intermediate)	ca. 2100-1900 B.C.
MB IIa	ca. 1900-1700 B.C.
MB IIb	ca. 1700-1600 B.C.
MB IIc	ca. 1600-1550 B.C.
Late Bronze (LB)	
LB I	ca. 1550-1400 B.C.
LB IIa	ca. 1400-1300 B.C.
LB IIb	ca. 1300-1200 B.C.
Iron I	ca. 1200- 900 B.C.
Iron II	ca. 900- 600 B.C.
Iron III	ca. 600- 300 B.C.
Hellenistic	ca. 300- 63 B.C.
Roman	ca. 63 B.C.-A.D. 323
Byzantine	ca. A.D.323-636
Islamic	ca. A.D. 636-present

The Valley of Aijalon, near Lower Beth-horon. In this valley, Joshua gained his victory over the kings "from the south."

The victory came about as a result of Joshua's tactical brilliance, along with a storm which devastated the enemy. A hailstorm which took place during the rout, produced many enemy casualties. The Biblical writer says, "There were more who died because of the hailstones than the men of Israel killed with the sword" (Josh. 10:11).

The Biblical writers frequently describe miracles in terms of the intensification of natural phenomena. The God of Israel is the God of nature, and all natural phenomena are at his disposal. As God of Israel He brought His people from Egypt, protected them and met their needs during the time of wilderness wandering and, in Joshua, brought them into Canaan and gave them victory over their enemies. They were entrusted with His Law and were to be His witnesses among the nations. As God of nature He brought about the plagues on Egypt, hardened Pharaoh's heart, opened the waters of the Red Sea by a strong east wind, opened the Jordan (by an earthquake, it would appear), and now was giving victory to Israel by an opportune hailstorm.

It is at this point that the author of Joshua quotes an ancient book, no longer extant, called the Book of Jashar (Josh. 10:12-14). The Book of Jashar, or "Book of the Upright," seems to have been an ancient poetic account of events in Israel's history. David's lament over Saul and Jonathan (II Sam. 1:19-27) is from the same source. The book was evidently well known to the ancient Israelites, for the author of the prose Book of Joshua quotes Jashar with the assurance that his readers are familiar with it. Most ancient peoples had poetic epics, like the Iliad and Odyssey of Greece, and the Sumerian-Akkadian Gilgamesh Epic, to commemorate the heroes of earlier days. Behind the prose accounts of the Biblical historians we occasionally find evidence of poetic antecedents.

The quotation from Jashar describes what has usually been called "Joshua's Long Day." Joshua, in the process of annihilating his enemies, needed additional time. He addressed the Lord:

> "Sun, stand thou still at Gibeon,
> And thou, Moon, in the valley of Aijalon."

The Lord "hearkened to the voice of a man," granting Joshua's request:

> "And the sun stood still, and the moon stayed,
> Until the nation took vengeance on their enemies."
> Joshua 10:12-14

To the Biblical writer there can be no question that God performed a miracle in answer to Joshua's prayer: "There has been no day like it before or since . . ." (Josh. 10-14). Some Biblical scholars have been content to note the poetic nature of the passage, while others have suggested that a miracle of refraction occurred, causing the sun and moon to appear to be out of their regular place. This would account for the prolonged daylight. A. D. Maunder, in his article in the *International Standard Bible Encyclopedia,* argued that Joshua did not ask for prolonged daylight but rather requested that the sun "be silent," i. e., "keep from shining." The thought is that Joshua's men needed refreshment from the burning sun. The hailstorm both refreshed Joshua's forces and brought destruction on the enemy. Thus Joshua's army was able to do a whole day's march in half a day. God had miraculously intervened.

While the exact nature of the miracle may not be certain, the fact is clear. The hosts arrayed against Joshua were annihilated. The five kings were incarcerated in a cave at Makkedah while the Israelites were pursuing the last of the foe. Then the kings were taken from the cave. The men of Israel placed their feet upon the necks of the kings, killed them and hanged their bodies from trees.

Joshua was able to gain effective control of the south following his victory over the southern confederacy. Horam, king of Gezer, attempted to come to the help of Lachish, but Joshua quickly repulsed him. Before returning to his camp at Gilgal, Joshua was in control of southern Canaan.

A stone serpent discovered at Gezer. The snake was a common object of worship among the Canaanites.

31

The Northern Campaign

With central and southern Canaan in Israelite control, the king of Hazor in northern Canaan was understandably concerned. Hazor was, in the words of the Biblical writer, "head of all those kingdoms" (Josh. 11:10). Yigael Yadin, director of the James A. de Rothschild expedition (1955-58) has traced the archaeological history of the site. The site was first identified by John Garstang during a trial dig in 1926. Hazor (Tell el-Qedah) is one of the most impressive mounds in Palestine. It covers twenty-five acres and reaches a height of one hundred thirty feet.

Yadin discovered remains of a well-built city which was destroyed during the thirteenth century and never again occupied. Floors of the houses were littered with Mycenaean pottery from the late bronze age. Two small Canaanite temples were discovered on different levels, dating to the fourteenth and thirteenth centuries B.C. One contained a sculptured male figure in basalt, seated on a throne in a central niche high above the floor. Another figure found nearby depicts two hands outstretched in prayer. A sun disk within a crescent surmounts the figure. A basalt orthostat bears the sculpture of the head and forelegs of a lion on its narrow side, and a relief of a crouching lion with its tail between its legs on its wide side. These are representative of the religion and art of Hazor before the conquest.

Jabin, the king of Hazor, sent word to the rulers of city states in northern Canaan to join forces for a decisive battle with Israel. The place of the encounter was at a site called in the Biblical text, "The Waters of Merom" (Josh. 11:7). Earlier scholars identified the Waters of Merom with Lake Huleh shown on most maps as a small lake north of the Sea of Galilee in the upper Jordan Valley. Lake Huleh has now been drained as part of Israel's reclamation program. The marshes which were malarial and a threat to human habitation have been transformed

The Huleh Valley in Upper Galilee.

into some of Israel's best agricultural territory. Scholars now tend to place the Waters of Merom at the site of a brook which flows from Merom, modern Meiron, near Safed in upper Galilee. Yohanin Aharoni has made an intensive archaeological survey of Galilee. He has noted that inhabitants of Lower Galilee during the early Iron Age tended to move northward to the more fertile plateau of Upper Galilee. He regards the Battle of Merom as the last attempt of the king of Hazor and his allies from the Plain of Esdraelon and the Plain of Akko to resist penetration.

Joshua marshaled his forces against the Hazor confederacy, using his customary tactic of surprise assault. Hazor was destroyed as Jericho had been destroyed at the beginning of the conquest of Canaan. Other cities were spared to be occupied by the Israelites.

With the fall of Hazor the first phase of the conquest was finished. Three major campaigns — central, southern, and northern — had been fought successfully. Joshua had been an effective leader.

It is possible to exaggerate the victories of Joshua, however. As we learn from the Book of Judges, large areas were bypassed and it was not until the days of David and Solomon that the Israelite tribes were in effective control of their territory. Under Joshua, however, the land was apportioned among the tribes, and the tribes alone, or in concert with neighboring tribes, would have to secure their own territories and fight off potential enemies.

Reuben, Gad, and one-half the tribe of Manasseh settled in the territory east of the Jordan River. This was not properly speaking the Promised Land, but the two and one-half tribes were given permission to settle there after assisting in the conquest of Canaan. The territory extended southward from the Yarmuk River, which enters the Jordan south of the Sea of Galilee, as far as the Arnon, which flows into the Dead Sea about half way down its eastern shore.

The tribe of Judah, later to give David and the Davidic dynasty to Israel, occupied the territory southward from a line extending toward the Mediterranean from the northern end of the Dead Sea. Extending from the western banks of the Dead Sea to the Central Mountain Range was the area frequently described as the wilderness of Judea, a semi-arid area where life was always difficult at best. Along the Mediterranean coast were the Philistine cities of Ashdod, Ashkelon, and Gaza, with Gath and Gaza a bit farther inland. The Philistines were to remain

The site of Hazor before recent excavation. Hazor was the chief city of the north in Palestine at the time of Joshua's conquest.

The Judean Wilderness as seen from the Jericho road, halfway between Jerusalem and Jericho.

The Jordan River, close to its source near Dan (Banias).

as foes of Israel until the time of David. The place where Judah was most successful, and most at home, was the Central Mountain range. Jerusalem, Bethlehem, and Hebron were there. Caleb, who had been a man of faith when the majority of the spies considered it impossible to enter the Promised Land from Kadesh-barnea (Num. 13:30), was given the Hebron region as his allotment (Josh. 15:13). Jerusalem remained a stronghold of the Jebusites until the time of David (cf. Josh. 15:63).

The Joseph tribes, Ephraim and Manasseh, occupied the territory south of the Valley of Esdraelon, including the area later known as Samaria, with the sacred mountains Gerizim and Ebal near Shechem. Between Judah and Ephraim was the smallest tribe, Benjamin, and to the west of Benjamin, extending to the Mediterranean was Dan. Since the Philistines occupied most of Dan, the tribe subsequently migrated to the far north of Canaan, taking the territory of Laish at one of the sources of the Jordan River. A portion of Judah was assigned to Simeon (Josh. 19:9) since Judah was not large enough to occupy all the lands originally assigned to her.

Zebulun, Issachar, Asher, and Naphtali were assigned territories north of the Esdraelon Valley in the area to be known in later times as Galilee, and the coastal area from about fifteen miles south of Mount Carmel northward to the Phoenician cities, modern Lebanon.

Six cities, three on each side of the Jordan, were designated as Cities of Refuge. No part of the land was more than thirty miles from one of these cities. They were needed because of the ancient concept of blood revenge. When a man had been killed, the nearest relative of the deceased was obligated to avenge his death. Israelite law, however, distinguished between murder and accidental homicide. No mercy was shown the murderer: "Whoever sheds the blood of man, by man shall his blood be shed" (Gen. 9:6). Cities of Refuge were instituted for those who had killed "without intent or unwittingly" (Josh. 20:3). They could come to the gate of the City of Refuge and explain their case to the elders of the city. If the elders were satisfied that the death was accidental they would provide lodging for the killer and refuse to turn him over to the avenger of blood. If they were not convinced of the killer's innocence, they could hand the man over to the elders of his own city, and if those elders were convinced of his guilt, they would turn the killer over to the avenger of blood (Deut. 19:12). If granted asylum in the City of Refuge, the one guilty of accidental manslaughter would be expected to stay there. If found elsewhere, the avenger of blood would be free to kill him. Upon the death of the high priest the man was free to leave his place of asylum and return to his own home. Evidently law and custom dictated that he should not be harmed by the avenger of blood after the death of the High Priest.

In the division of the land of Canaan among the Israelite tribes there was one notable omission. The tribe of Levi, the priestly tribe, was not assigned a portion. Instead forty-eight cities were assigned to the Levites from among the cities of the other tribes. In this way the Levites were scattered among the tribes, and readily accessible for all. Since teaching was part of their ministry (Deut. 33:10) it was necessary that they be dispersed in this way. Six of their cities were the Cities of Refuge, in which they would have special functions.

Scholars describe the twelve-tribe league of Israel as an *amphictyony,* a term used for associations of neighboring states or tribes in ancient Greece. Originally they joined together to defend a common religious center. Later legislative and judicial functions developed within the amphictyony. The Israelite tribal league always had twelve members. Levi was given no tribal inheritance but Joseph was divided into two tribes, Ephraim and Manasseh, thus preserving the concept of a twelve-tribe league.

Reuben, Gad, and half the tribe of Manasseh, living east of the Jordan, built a large altar which became a bone of contention with the other tribes. Since Israel had one central sanctuary, the Tabernacle, followed in Solomon's time with the Temple, the building of such an altar could be interpreted as a sign of disloyalty to Israel's God. The other tribes prepared to make war on the tribes east of the Jordan, but the misunderstanding was cleared up when the east Jordan tribes assured their brothers that the altar was not to be used for sacrifices. It was to be a witness or testimony to the fact that the tribes east of the Jordan were one with those in Canaan proper. Phinehas, the son of Eleazar the Priest, heard the explanation and was satisfied that no evil was intended. The altar served as a witness to the oneness of the tribal league and its common loyalty to the Lord.

The final scene in the Book of Joshua is a gathering of the Israelite tribes at Shechem for a covenant renewal ceremony. Joshua, knowing that he is about to die, challenges the people to loyalty to their God. The Lord has graciously brought them from Egyptian bondage to liberty in the land of promise. Now, however, they will be faced with new temptations. If the Law is

The combination of a vat, a platter-stone, and a storage jar was unearthed in a Shechem residential district, which dates from the eighth century B.C. The installation may have been used in making wine or olive oil, or perhaps in some process of dyeing.

forgotten and other gods worshiped, then the Lord's anger will be aroused and he will punish his people for their sins.

The Israelites responded to Joshua's appeal with the pledge, "We will serve the Lord" (Josh. 24:21). Joshua set up a stone at Shechem to serve as a witness to the people's pledge: "Behold, this stone shall be a witness against us; for it has heard all the words of the Lord which he spoke to us; therefore it shall be a witness against you, lest you deal falsely with your God" (Josh. 24:27). G. Ernest Wright in his excavations at Shechem has discovered the "Great Stone" which he thinks may be the very stone described in Joshua 24.

Joshua died at the age of 110. Moses had appointed Joshua as his successor, but Joshua left no designated successor. Charismatic leaders would arise in Israel's times of need, but with the death of Joshua the generation that left Egypt was gone. As a kind of footnote, the author of Joshua reminds us that Joseph's bones had been with the Israelites in Egypt, during the Exodus and wilderness wandering, and during the struggles for the occupation of Canaan. Now, at last, they received permanent burial at Shechem (Josh. 24:32).

32

When the Judges Judged

The Book of Judges provides a transition between Joshua, the designated successor of Moses, and Israel's first king, Saul. The initial battles have been fought. Israel is now in Canaan, although neighboring tribes still hope they can dislodge her and reclaim lost territory. The Book of Judges describes a series of encounters of Israel with her oppressors, who periodically gained the upper hand.

In theological terms, these oppressions are described as the result of Israel's apostasy. Miraculously, the oppressed people of Israel were delivered from slavery in Egypt, sustained by God's hand during a generation of wandering in the wilderness, and given victories of walled cities such as Jericho, strongholds of the Canaanite or Amorite peoples whose material culture was far in advance of the Israelites. Certainly Israel had every reason to be thankful to her God, and to remain loyal to his Covenant.

Still, other factors are evident. A nomadic people, just arrived after a generation in desert surroundings, had much to learn about agriculture. While many of the inhabitants of Canaan had been destroyed during the wars with Joshua, others continued to live as neighbors to the Israelites. Gibeon had made her peace with Joshua, and there is good reason to believe that many others did the same. The religion of the agricultural Canaanites was centered in a fertility cult. While El, "father of gods and men," was the head of the pantheon, his popularity was overshadowed by the more glamorous Baal, "rider of the clouds," who brought fertility to the soil, as well as to animal and human life. Baal had his counterpart in the goddess of fertility, sometimes called Asherah. Anat and Astarte were also fertility goddesses.

Ritual prostitution, in which a priest and a priestess of the

The cult object (top) and the incense stand (bottom), from the Iron Age, were discovered at the temple of Ashtarte in Beth-shan.

fertility cult had sexual relations at a shrine on a "high place" was an important part of the Canaanite agricultural culture. By imitative magic this ritual was thought to insure fertility to fields, as well as to animals and humans.

This means of securing fertility in a land which has very meager rainfall and frequent famine conditions was tempting to the Israelite settlers. With sickening regularity we read, "The people of Israel did what was evil in the sight of the Lord and served the Baals; and they forsook the Lord, the god of their fathers, who had brought them out of the land of Egypt; they went after other Gods, from the gods of the peoples who were round about them, and bowed down to them; and they provoked the Lord to anger. They forsook the Lord, and served the Baals and the Ashtaroth (Judg. 2:11-13).

The nature of Israel's faith during the time of the judges has been the subject of much scholarly discussion. It was long popular to apply concepts of evolution to Israel's religious development, assuming there was a natural progression from animism (the primitive belief whereby rocks, trees, water supplies, and the like were held to possess souls) to polytheism (belief in many gods), then to henotheism (the idea that one god should be worshiped as the god of a tribal unit, although many gods exist and should be worshiped by other peoples), and finally to monotheism (the belief that there is but one God to be honored by all men everywhere). According to this view the Israelites reached monotheism only in the time of the later prophets, men such as Isaiah and Amos, whose faith was in one all-powerful God.

As we have seen, the Canaanite worship was decidedly polytheistic, and Israel lapsed into such polytheistic worship many times. We should note, however, that Israel's prophetic leaders uniformly warn against such apostasy. There is even an inherent suggestion that polytheism is a corruption of earlier monotheism. Canaanite El, father of the seventy *elim* ("gods") is clearly related to the Hebrew *elohim*. The Biblical writer does not hesitate to identify the name Beth-el ("House of God, House of El") with the God of Jacob-Israel (cf. Gen. 28:16-19). Canaanites might claim to worship the descendants of El, but Israelites professed to worship the Creator God Himself. Practically speaking, the Biblical writers refer to the "other gods" (cf. Exodus 20:3), for Israel's neighbors bowed before such creatures. From the Biblical viewpoint, such worship might be regarded as ridiculous. People worshiped gods with eyes that could not see, and ears that could not hear. Such worship was, in a word, stupid.

Yet another more subtle approach toward idolatry developed. The gods represented in the images used in idolatrous worship may have been non-existent, but there was a wicked spirit — satan, or the devil — who deluded people into accepting such a degrading religion that was an insult to the God of Israel Himself. In the name of religion, people practiced ritual prostitution, offered their children as human sacrifices, and reduced religion to the basest of passions. Centuries later, Paul asserted, "They exchanged the truth about God for a lie and worshiped and served the creature rather than the creator . . . (Rom. 1:25).

As the Bible nowhere attempts to prove the existence of God, so it does not provide a philosophical defense of monotheism. It describes God's dealings with His people Israel in a polytheistic environment — and warns them by precept and example that He alone is to be worshiped.

The reader of the Biblical history may be surprised at the lack of philosophical speculation. Ecclesiastes may depict the quest of a wise king for meaning in life, and Job may wrestle with the problem of suffering, but the historical books are concerned with the acts of God. Who is this God of Israel? He is the One who brought His people out of Egypt, sustained them through their period of wandering in the wilderness, and with His mighty hand brought them into the land of Canaan. Israel's God stands in contrast to the nature gods of her neighbors. The fertility god might periodically leave the earth, only to return at the next rainy season. The sun god goes through a daily circuit as he crosses the earth. Israel's God has nothing in common with these gods of her neighbors, save for the fact that the sun, moon, and stars which they worship are the creation of the Lord. The heavens may declare the glory of the Lord, but his revelation concerns his works among his people.

The term "elect" or "chosen" is often used of Israel. The tribes that left Egypt and settled in Canaan were conscious of a special relation to the Lord. Israel did not have the highest culture or the greatest military prowess — Egypt, Babylon, the Hittite lands far outshone her — but she did have a need which the Lord supplied. Election, in other words, was purely of God's grace. The Israelite could testify, "We were Pharaoh's slaves in Egypt; and the Lord brought us out of Egypt with a mighty hand . . . and he brought us out from there, that he might bring us in and give us the land which he swore to give to our fathers" (Deut. 6:21-23). Israel is depicted as persistently unfaithful yet the Lord's grace continued to be shown to her.

Stele of the Hittite storm god, Teshub.

Relief of a structure on wheels, found at the scene of the synogogue at Capernaum, probably represents the Ark of the Covenant.

The relationship between the Lord and Israel is described in terms of a covenant. At Mount Sinai, Israel freely declared, "All that the Lord has spoken, we will do" (Exod. 19:8). In brief, Israel acknowledged God as her sovereign, whose laws she would obey. The Lord agreed to be a God to Israel, who would be uniquely His people, and ultimately His means of bringing blessing to all mankind (Gen. 12:1-3).

During the time of the judges the religious center of Israelite life was at Shiloh, where the Tent of Meeting (or Tabernacle) was located. The Ark of the Covenant, the throne of the invisible God, was located in the Holy of Holies of the Tent of Meeting, symbolic of the fact that God was present in the midst of his people. Sacrifices were offered daily on the altar at the entrance to the Tent of Meeting, and on the great feast days Israelites from all twelve tribes would be found praising God and seeking his forgiveness for their sins. The time of the judges was one of tribal self-consciousness rather than national unity. A man would identify himself as a Danite, rather than an Israelite. Nevertheless the central shrine proved a means of unifying the people in their common loyalty to the Lord.

33

The International Situation

Israel, as a small nation, or a tribal confederacy, was dependent on events among the great powers for her independence and survival. By the time of the judges, Israel was not threatened from major powers because their influence had been effectively neutralized.

Egypt had controlled much of western Asia in the days of Ramesses III. Her energies were expended fighting off invasions of the Sea People beginning with the reign of Merneptah (ca. 1224-1216 B.C.) Ramesses III (ca. 1174-1144 B.C.) spent most of his reign trying to keep the Sea Peoples from overwhelming Egypt, as they did overwhelm the Hittite Empire and bring it to an end. These people have a variety of strange sounding tribal names, a few of which become significant in later history. Among those mentioned by Ramesses III we find the Peleset and the Tjekker, tribes that were repulsed from Egypt but permitted to settle in Palestine. The Peleset became the Philistines, from which our word *Palestine* is derived. The Philistines were the one enemy of Israel that continued to be a threat long after the period of the judges. The Danuna are the Danaoi (Danaeans) of the Iliad.

A firsthand, although boastful, account of the threat of the Sea Peoples was addressed by Ramesses III to his sons:

"The foreign countries made a plot in their islands. Dislodged and scattered were the lands all at one time, and no land could stand before their arms, beginning with Khatti (i.e. the Hittite land), Kode, Carchemish, Arzawa, and Alasiya . . . A camp was set up in one place in Amor (i.e. the land of the Amorites) and they desolated its people and its land as though they had never come into being. They came, the flame prepared before them, onwards to Egypt. Their confederacy consisted of Peleset, Tjekker, Skeklesh, Danu, and Weshesh, united lands, and they laid their hands upon the lands to the entire circuit of the earth, their hearts bent and trustful, 'Our plan is accomplished!' But the heart of this god, the lord of the gods (i.e. Ramesses III), was prepared and ready to ensnare them like birds. . . . I established my boundary in Djahi (i.e. Palestine and Syria), prepared in front of them, the local princes, garrison commanders, and Maryannu (charioteers). I caused to be prepared the river mouth like a strong wall with warships, galleys, and skiffs. They were completely equipped both fore and aft with brave fighters carrying their weapons and infantry of all the pick of Egypt, being like roaring lions upon the mountains: chariotry with able warriors and all goodly officers whose hands were competent. Their horses quivered in all their limbs, prepared to crush the foreign countries under their hoofs. . . . As for those who reached my boundary, their seed is not. Their hearts and their souls are finished unto all eternity. Those who came forward together upon the sea, the full flame was in front of them at the rivermouths, and a stockade of lances surrounded them on the shore."[1]

A naval battle fought by Ramesses III against the Sea People is illustrated on the walls of the king's funerary temple at Medinet Habu. The enemy is in confusion. Egyptian soldiers attack from the deck of their ship, and an enemy vessel is held fast with grappling irons. A shower of arrows from the land falls upon another vessel. The Egyptian fleet is victorious. It returns home with bound captives, closing Ramesses III's most glorious moment.

Actually Ramesses III was so weakened by these encounters that he could do little to strengthen his position. Our only legitimate record of his campaigns in Palestine claims that he "destroyed the Seirites in the tribes of the Shosu." The Shosu were desert bedouin from the south of Palestine. The Seirites got their name from Mount Seir (cf. Deut. 2:1), home of the Biblical Edomites. The defeat of these relatively unimportant bedouin was as much as Ramesses III could boast about during the later part of his long reign.

Egypt never recovered. The reigns of Ramesses IV to XI (ca. 1144-1065 B.C.) were short and, with few exceptions, uneventful. Egypt still claimed Palestine, but she had no power to enforce that claim. The story of Wen-amun, written about 1060 B.C., illustrates Egypt's perilous position. Herihor is the high priest at Karnak, and ruler of Upper Egypt. Nesbanebded ruled Tanis and the delta region. The two were on good terms with one another, but the real Pharaoh, Ramesses XI is mentioned only once in a cryptic utterance. Egypt was clearly divided and her prestige abroad was very low. The story itself tells how Wen-amun went to Palestine to purchase timber for "the great noble bark of Amun-Re, King of the Gods." Egypt did not have good wood, so arrangements were made to import it from Syria and Lebanon (ancient Phoenicia). The money for the purchase was stolen, however, and Wen-amun appealed to the local authorities for help. He was left to his own resources,

Two prisoners from among the Philistines are brought to Ramesses III who celebrated this victory by carving the relief on the walls of the temple at Medinet Habu.

---

1. Quoted in Alan Gardiner, *Egypt of the Pharaohs*, pp. 284-285.

however. In the days of the Egyptian Empire an Egyptian on such an errand would have been given unlimited help. While Wen-amun completed his mission and finally returned home safely, his harrowing experiences illustrate the low prestige Egypt had during the days of the Biblical judges.[2]

There was no other power to fill the power vacuum in western Asia. The Hittite Empire had fallen before the Sea Peoples. Assyria had made a start toward greatness in the days of Tukulti-ninurta I (1234-1197 B.C.) and Tiglath-pileser I (ca. 1116-1078 B.C.), but the days of Assyrian dominance in western Asia were still in the future. Semitic Arameans were a new element in the Fertile Crescent at this time. While never a world power, they established states at Sham'al, Carchemish, Beth-eden, and — most important — Damascus. The Arameans threatened Assyria, so at that moment we find western Asia made up of warring smaller states, with no imperial power to pose a threat.

The ethnic make-up of Canaan had altered also. Israelites under Joshua occupied the central highlands and fanned out toward the coastal regions. The Sea Peoples, particularly the Philistines, occupied the southern coastal regions of the Mediterranean littoral, and challenged Israel's hold on the interior of the country. The centers of Philistine strength were in five major cities: Gaza, Ashkelon, Ashdod, Ekron, and Gath. Each was ruled by a "tyrant" (Heb. *seren*), the very name suggesting Indo-European rather than Semitic origins. To the Israelites, they were "the uncircumcised Philistines." Yet the Philistines had a high material culture, including the use of iron. We read in I Samuel 13:19-21, "No blacksmith was to be found in the whole of Israel, for the Philistines were determined to prevent the Hebrews from making swords and spears. The Israelites had to go down to the Philistines for their ploughshares, mattocks, axes, and sickles to be sharpened. The charge was two-thirds of a shekel for ploughshares and mattocks, and one-third of a shekel for sharpening the axes and setting the goads." The Philistines did not keep their monopoly on the use of iron, but while they had it Israel was at a distinct disadvantage.

Israel's earliest victories were in the central highlands where her foot soldiers could do battle with any forces arrayed against them. The chariotry used by her enemies on the plains formed

2. The story is given in James Pritchard, *Ancient Near Eastern Texts*, pp. 25-29.

The Judean hills as seen from the Jordan Valley just south of Beth-shan.

a challenge which was only overcome in the days of King David. The Israelite tribes thus developed regional differences because they were cut off from one another. Even different dialects are found, as we read in Judges 12:4-6, where the Ephraimites pronounced "shibboleth" as if it were "sibboleth." Loyalty to the Lord was the one factor that brought the tribes together. It is understandable that some were tempted to follow the ways of their idolatrous neighbors.

The Book of Judges begins with the assertion that tribes had to occupy the land that had been assigned to them, and that this meant fighting the earlier inhabitants of the land. Judah, in seeking to secure its tribal inheritance, asked the help of Simeon, a tribe that was later absorbed into Judah. The territory assigned to Judah was occupied, except for the plains. The Biblical writer editorializes: "The Lord was with Judah, and he took possession of the hill country, but he could not drive out the inhabitants of the plain, because they had chariots of iron" (Judg. 1:19).

At first glance the statement appears inconsistent with the omnipotence of Israel's God. Could He not give victory over chariots of iron? The answer is, "Yes, but . . . ." The God of Israel normally worked through historical and natural processes. He could and did perform miracles, but even they were usually natural phenomena with intensity and timing being the miraculous element. The "strong east wind" that held back the waters of the Red Sea, the landslide that held back the waters of the Jordan — such things could happen apart from the miraculous, but providentially God caused them to happen at the moment when His people needed such a miracle. Biblical writers do not discriminate between "nature" and "miracle." God is in all things: the laws of nature are the habits of God. In time, His people will have chariots and occupy the plains. For the moment, God gives victory in the central mountain range, the proper home of Israel, and permits the Canaanites to have their temporary victories.

Even those temporary victories, however, are under the providence of God. It is part of the philosophy of history which underlies the Book of Judges that faithfulness to the Lord brings victory, and apostasy results in defeat. Such defeats may be thought of as both punitive and remedial. God, because He is God, has the right to demand strict obedience to His Law. Blessings for obedience, and curses for non-obedience were enunciated publicly in the great gathering at Shechem. God may be described as kind, merciful, and loving, but He is God, and as God has the right to demand strict obedience. Achan disobeyed God by taking the spoil of Jericho, and as a result Achan died.

The remedial aspect of God's government is evident in the history of the judges, in that punishment leads to repentance. When Israel is defeated on the battlefield and has reached the end of her resources, she looks to God for help. Here the mercy of God is evident. Although defeat was the result of sin, nevertheless God raised up deliverers for His people when they cried to Him in repentance. The term *judge* is used of these deliverers. They occupied a number of functions. They led armies on the battle field; they ruled in the absence of a king; they performed judicial functions as matters were brought to them for adjudication.

In theory, the period of the judges was a theocracy. God was king, and there was no need for an earthly monarch. We suspect that Israel felt proud indeed of her relationship to the Lord — a pride which sometimes produced disastrous results. The period is summarized in the lines: "In those days there was no king in Israel; every man did what was right in his own eyes" (Judg. 21:25). Theoretical theocracy often produced practical anarchy.

The heroes whose exploits are described in the Book of Judges are political heroes. They honor the Lord in an external way, at least, but they are remembered for their feats on the battlefield. Samson, the best known of all, is honored because of the Philistines he slew. The stories reflect the rugged days of Israel's settlement in the land of Canaan.

The judges are charismatic leaders, i.e., they rule because of particular gifts given by God, and qualities of leadership which cause the people to rally to their banners. Priesthood, as presented in the Bible, is dynastic. Priests are of the tribe of Levi and the house of Aaron. Kings were, ideally at least, dynastic. Legitimate rule was from the line of David. Prior to kingship, however, judges were raised up by God without regard to tribal origin or family background. They vary greatly in personal characteristics, but they all have one thing in common: they delivered Israel from an oppressor.

Intermarriage with the Canaanites, Hittites, Amorites, Perizites, Hivites, and Jebusites resulted in idolatry (Judg. 3:5-6). The Israelite partner in a mixed marriage was tempted to adopt idolatrous practices of his mate, with the result that loyalty to the Lord was compromised. The Lord, however, brought punishment in the form of an oppressor.

The first such oppressor is described as "Cushan-rishathaim, king of Mesopotamia" (Judg. 3:8). The name does not appear elsewhere, but scholars have attempted to place Cushan in a historical context. The full name as given is doubtless an editorial comment. It means "Doubly wicked Cushan" or "Cushan of Double Wickedness." A district known as Qusana-ruma is mentioned by Ramesses III as a place in northern Syria, or Aram. The term translated "Mesopotamis" is *aram-naharaim*, Aram of the Two Rivers — northern Mesopotamia, the land of the Arameans. If this view is correct, the first oppressor was a ruler of an Aramean state in northern Syria.[1]

Many scholars suspect that the reading "Aram" is a scribal error for "Edom." There is but one letter difference in Hebrew, and the written "D" and "R" are easily confused. Doubly wicked Cushan, according to this view, may have been originally described as Cushan *rosh hat-temani*, Cushan, chief of the Temanites (so Klosterman) or Cushan *wehat-temani*, Cushan and the Temanites. Edom had copper mines which were worked at this time.[2] It is easy to understand Edomite resentment at the growing power of Judah in southern Canaan, and this may have precipitated Cushan's attack. Israel's deliverer was "Othniel the son of Kenaz" (Judg. 3:9). The Kenazites were a tribe related to the Edomites in that Kenaz was a grandson or descendant of Esau (Gen. 36:9, 11), from whom the Edomites descended. The fact that Kenazites were allying themselves with the Israelites may also explain Edom's desire to intervene.

No details are given concerning the war between Cushan and Othniel. After eight years of subjection, Israel was freed by the valor of Othniel. A generation (forty years) of comparative peace followed (Judg. 3:11).

The next oppressor was Eglon of Moab. It is not necessary to assume that the details presented in the Book of Judges are in chronological order. We are dealing largely with individual tribes or temporary alliances among the tribes to meet threats to their territorial integrity. Some of the oppressions and periods of deliverance and peace may have been contemporary. This fact, plus the consistent use of round numbers (usually

1. Cf. M. F. Unger, *Israel and the Arameans of Damascus*, pp. 40-41.
2. B. Rothenberg, "Ancient Copper Industries in the Western Arabah," *Palestine Exploration Quarterly*, 1962, pp. 5-71.

multiples of forty) for the periods of rest, makes an absolute chronology for the period impossible.

Sihon the Amorite had seized Moabite land north of the Arnon prior to Israel's arrival in transjordan (Num. 21:27-30). Israel took it from Sihon and permitted the tribe of Reuben to settle there (Judg. 11:19-23). Here, Eglon of Moab has not only recaptured the land held by Reuben, but he has crossed the Jordan and occupied territory belonging to Benjamin. For eighteen years the Israelites were subject to Eglon of Moab and his allies, the Ammonites and the Amalekites.

Deliverance came in the person of Ehud, a Benjaminite who, after paying tribute, asked for a private audience with Eglon. When alone with the Moabite, Ehud used his left hand, took his sword from over his right thigh, and murdered Eglon. Escaping, he called to the Israelites to follow him and won a decisive battle with the Moabites. Moab was subdued, forced back across the Jordan and its armies rendered powerless. Israel had two generations ("eighty years") of peace.

Shamgar, the son of Anath (Judg. 3:31) is merely mentioned as one who "killed six hundred of the Philistines with an oxgoad." Since the Philistines were Israel's perennial enemy, this fact caused Shamgar to be listed among the national heroes of the period of the judges. The name Shamgar is Hurrian, an ethnic group known from hieroglyphic inscriptions and cuneiform texts that entered Mesopotamia early in the second millennium B.C. Some Hurrians entered Syria and Palestine, and Egypt used the term Khuru-land for Palestine as attested in texts from Amenhotep II (1450-1425 B.C.). The mention of Shamgar suggests that resident Hurrians joined with Israelites in seeking to repulse the Philistines, a branch of the Sea Peoples which had caused disruption throughout the eastern Mediterranean area.

The description of Shamgar as "son of Anath" may suggest his home area: Shamgar of Beth-Anath. Anat or Anath was a Canaanite goddess of fertility and war. An alternate explanation is that Shamgar son of Anath simply means, "Shamgar the warrior." Aside from this one act of killing Philistines, we know nothing of Shamgar's history.

During Israel's next apostasy she is ruled by "Jabin, king of Canaan who reigned in Hazor." This Jabin was probably a descendant of the Jabin who was slain following Joshua's victory over the confederacy of kings from the North (Josh. 11:1-14). The army of the second Jabin was led by his general Sisera.

Deliverance came to the Israelites during the judgeship of Deborah. Deborah had a variety of gifts. She is called a prophetess. As a wise woman, people came to her as she sat under "the palm of Deborah" between Ramah and Bethel in the hill country of Ephraim. Deborah is a reminder to us that the role of women in ancient Israel was not confined to that of wife and mother. Deborah possessed charismatic qualities that made her an effective leader.

Deborah summoned Barak, a young man from Kadesh in Naphtali to gather the fighting men from the tribes in Naphtali and Zebulun at Mount Tabor in preparation for battle with Jabin's general, Sisera. Barak's reply suggested hesitance, "If you will go with me, I will go; but if you will not go with me, I will not go" (Judg. 4:8). Deborah assured him that she would go along with the fighting men, but she rebuked Barak for his cowardice: "I will surely go with you; nevertheless the road on which you are going will not lead to your glory, for the Lord will sell Sisera into the hand of a woman" (Judg. 4:9). It was not Deborah, but another woman: Jael, the wife of Heber the Kenite, who would kill Sisera.

The account of the battle is given in two recensions: the prose account (Judg. 4) and the poetic account (Judg. 5). The poetry of the Song of Deborah is recognized as natural in its rugged beauty, written very close to the time of the events it commemorates.

The battle was fought along the shores of the Kishon river which waters the plain of Esdraelon. Its northern branch springs from the western slopes of Mount Tabor, and several of its southern branches from the western slopes of Mount Gilboa. The branches meet in the plain northeast of Megiddo, after which the river flows in a northwesterly direction along the northern foot of the Carmel Ridge, entering the Mediterranean at the southeastern corner of the Bay of Acre. The river maintains its year-round flow only for the last seven miles which are watered from the springs at the base of Mount Carmel, and from streams from the northeast that enter the Kishon in the plain of Acre. In the rainy season the entire stream can become swollen and very dangerous. It was this fact that proved disastrous to Sisera's hosts. Deborah wrote:

> From heaven fought the stars,
>   from their courses they fought against Sisera.
> The torrent Kishon swept them away,
>   the onrushing torrent, the torrent Kishon.
> — Judg. 5:20-21

Again God gave a victory, using the elements of nature to accomplish His purposes. The Kishon overflowed its banks. The proud chariots of the Canaanites became a liability instead of an asset. Mired in the mud, the chariots had to be abandoned, "and Sisera alighted from his chariot and fled away on foot" (Judg. 4:15). The Israelites won a decisive victory, but Sisera almost escaped.

The poet pauses to curse the town of Meroz, "because they came not to the help of the Lord" (Judg. 5:23). Evidently the village of Meroz refused to take part in the battle. Blessing, however is pronounced on Jael, the wife of Heber the Kenite. When Sisera escaped he made his way to the tent of Jael, hoping to be hospitably received. Kenites were mine workers and smiths, and many of them were friendly to the Israelites. Moses' father-in-law, Jethro (or Hobab) was a leader of the Kenites, a Midianite clan, and Moses encouraged him to journey with the Israelites and share the blessings God had in store for them (Num. 10: 29-31).

Perhaps the fact that Jael and her husband were not Israelites gave Sisera hope that he might be received hospitably. Jael gave him assurances that he would be safe: "Turn aside, my lord, turn aside to me; have no fear" (Judg. 4:18). Yet Jael had no thought of letting her guest escape safely:

> "He asked water and she gave him milk,
>   she brought him curds in a lordly bowl.
> She put her hand to the tent peg
>   and her right hand to the workmen's mallet;
> she struck Sisera a blow,
>   she crushed his head
>   she shattered and pierced his temple.
> He sank, he fell;
>   he lay still at her feet;
> at her feet he sank, he fell;
>   where he sank, there he fell dead
>
> — Judg. 5:25-27

Jael, of course, risked her life in killing the enemy. With the tent peg and mallet, however, she ended the life of the Canaanite general. With fine artistry, the poet next directs our attention to Sisera's mother. Sisera, like all of us, had a mother, and her reaction was thoroughly human:

"Out of the window she peered,
    the mother of Sisera gazed through the lattice:
'Why is his chariot so long in coming?
    Why tarry the hoofbeats of his chariots?'
Her wisest ladies make answer.
    Nay she gives answer to herself,
'Are they not finding and dividing the spoil? —
    A maiden or two for every man;
        spoil of dyed stuffs for Sisera,
        spoil of dyed stuffs embroidered,
        two pieces of dyed work
        embroidered for my neck as spoil?"
                                    — Judges 5:28-31

The description of Sisera's mother gives us a picture of warfare in antiquity. Following victory the spoils were divided. This included the people taken into slavery. Women were divided among the victorious soldiers. This explains why the Jews at Masada, centuries later, chose mass suicide rather than to fall into the hands of the Romans.

The victory over Sisera's army was a decisive one. Canaanites as such are not seen again as Israel's enemies. Some, doubtless, were incorporated into the emerging Israelite state. Others migrate northward where they become part of the people we call Phoenicians, the people who directed their expansionist goals westward toward the islands and coastlands of the Mediterranean. The Biblical writer notes that Israel enjoyed a forty year period of rest following her victory over Jabin and Sisera.

Following another period of apostasy, we learn that nomadic Midianites along with their allies the Amalekites and the Bene Qedem ("People of the East") are oppressing Israel. Things are in desperate straits. The Midianites come and take everything. Israel feels completely God-forsaken.

It was under these circumstances that God appeared to Gideon with the strange words, "The Lord is with you, you mighty man of valor." (Judg. 6:12). Gideon is thoroughly honest in his reply. The assurance seems meaningless: "Pray, sir, if the Lord is with us, why then has all this befallen us? And where are all his wonderful deeds which our fathers recounted to us, saying, 'Did not the Lord bring us up from Egypt?' But now the Lord has cast us off and given us into the hand of Midian" (Judg. 6:13).

God looked with favor upon Gideon, even in this protestation. Gideon must go to confront the Midianites. God has sent

Gideon, and Gideon will not fail. Gideon makes a final protest. He is from the weakest family of the weakest clan in Manasseh (Judg. 6:15). God, however, rejected the argument with the quiet assertion, "But I will be with thee."

Gideon showed his abhorrence of idolatry by pulling down the Baal altar and destroying the Asherah image which his father had erected, and building an altar to the Lord in its place. Joash, Gideon's father defended his son before the men of the town, insisting that if Baal is a god he should be able to care for his own interests. Gideon was named Jerubbaal — 'Let Baal contend against him" — in token of his antagonism against Baal (Judg. 6:25-32).

Gideon is also remembered because of his desire for a sign from God. He placed a fleece of wool on the threshing floor and asked that God cause dew on the wool alone, and not on the threshing floor, if God would truly deliver Israel. It was so, and on the next night Gideon reversed the sign. He asked that the fleece be dry, and only the ground around it be moist. Again it happened as Gideon had requested, and Gideon felt sure that God would use him to deliver Israel.

At the Spring of Harod, near Mount Gilboa, Gideon assembled his forces to meet the Midianites. The Lord gave directions for reducing the number of the Israelite forces, lest they take pride in their numbers and forget that victory is from the Lord. First Gideon permitted any who wished to do so to return home, which left him with an army of ten thousand out of an original thirty-two thousand. Next he brought the men to the water, and three hundred men lapped the water, the rest kneeling down to drink. The three hundred were the select band that Gideon used in destroying the Midianite forces (Judg. 7:1-8).

The victory came as a result of psychological warfare. He divided the three hundred men into three companies. The men were given trumpets, empty jars, and torches inside the jars. Gideon directed his men to follow his example. All blew their trumpets and broke the jars, holding the torches in their left hands and the trumpets in their right hands, and crying, "A sword for the Lord, and for Gideon" (Judg. 7:19-20). The Midianites, unexpectedly aroused, fled, fighting one another in the confusion. Israelite forces throughout the hill country joined in the attempt to drive the Midianites out of the country completely. Zebah and Zalmunna, Midianite chieftains, were pursued and slain. Thus Gideon fulfilled his destiny in delivering Israel from the Midianite oppression.

The Spring of Harod, where Gideon's men stopped to drink.

Ancient horns and trumpets.

An effort was made to crown Gideon as king, but Gideon insisted that the Lord was Israel's only King (Judg. 8:22-23). Gideon did, however, make a serious mistake in collecting the jewelry of the Israelites (the spoils of war) and making an ephod (probably some kind of image) of it. The ephod was placed in Gideon's city, Ophrah, and it became the object of idolatrous worship.

Unhappily the career of Gideon ends on this negative note. He had been one of Israel's great leaders, and his leadership had resulted in victory over the Midianites and their allies. After Gideon's death, however, we find idolatry rampant in the land, and the makings of further periods of oppression.

Although Gideon had refused the kingship, his son by a concubine from Shechem decided that he wanted the rule for himself. Abimelech sought the cooperation of his relatives at Shechem and secured funds from the shrine there to further his goals. To remove possible rivals to the throne, Abimelech went to Ophrah and slew his half brothers, seventy in all. Only Jotham, Gideon's youngest son was left.

Jotham went to Mount Gerizim and attempted to refute Abimelech's usurpation by means of a parable. In the story that he told, the trees were in need of a king. They went successively to the olive, the fig, and the vine. The olive was too busy producing olives; the fig could not leave its work of making figs; and the vine was needed for the making of wine. Only the bramble, a useless shrub, had any desire to be king, and he threatened with extinction any who challenged him.

The moral was clear. Those who have worthwhile things to do are not interested in bossing others. Only the worthless bramble desires to be king. Jotham was expressing an attitude toward kingship which was common in the period of the Judges. God was king, and men who aspire to kingship are tyrants at heart.

Abimelech played the part of the tyrant for three years. When the men of Shechem resisted him, Abimelech burned the tower of Shechem, killing about a thousand people. He attempted to do the same at Thebez, but a woman of the city threw an upper millstone on Abimelech's head, and put an end to his usurpation.

Tola and Jair are merely mentioned as minor judges between the days of Abimelech and Jephthah. As in previous periods, idolatry grew throughout the land and oppression followed. This time the Ammonites, east of the Jordan, oppressed Israel for eighteen years. The half tribe of Manasseh and the tribe of

Gad occupied Gilead proper — the seventy-mile-long mountain-ous region between the tableland of Moab and the Yarmuk River. Sometimes by extension the whole of Transjordan was called Gilead. This would include the tribe of Reuben. Since the Gileadites had common problems, the tribes located there usually acted in concert.

A young man of Gilead, Jephthah by name, had been forced to leave his home because of rivalries among his half brothers. Jephthah was the child of a harlot, and his half brothers were legitimate children of their father by his wife. Jehpthah fled the taunts and threats of his home and settled in the country of Tob, possibly northeast of Gilead where the land becomes desert. There he consorted with other outlaws, and lived the life of a bandit, preying on caravans that passed through the desert.

As the Israelites were oppressed by the Ammonites they thought of Jephthah as a possible leader. The elders of Gilead sent for Jephthah, but he chided them for only showing friend-ship when they were in need. Jephthah would be their leader only if they would acknowledge his right to rule not only during the fighting, but afterward as well. The elders accepted, and Jephthah went to Mizpah to the sanctuary there, where the agreement was solemnly made binding. (Judg. 11:1-11).

Jephthah tried to negotiate terms of peace with the Ammon-ite king, but he refused to end hostilities (Judg. 11:28). Jeph-thah next prepared for war. His rash vow casts a cloud over the story, and it takes the edge off the victory itself. Jephthah, pre-paring to fight the Ammonites, vowed that he would sacrifice as a burnt offering the one who would first greet him as he re-turned victorious in battle. Human sacrifice was denounced by Israel's prophets and it was never an acceptable part of the faith of Israel. Jephthah, however, had been an outcast from society, and it is not difficult to see how such heathen influences became part of his thinking.

Jephthah was victorious in battle, but his daughter, his only child, was the one who came to meet him (Judg. 11:34). Joy in victory was turned to sorrow. Jephthah's daughter urged her father to perform his vow, only requesting a period of time to "bewail her virginity" in the mountains (Judg. 11:38). After two months she returned, and her father "did with her according to his vows."

Attempts are sometimes ∙made to soften the effect of Jeph-thah's vow by suggesting that her perpetual virginity was the

The Jordan River, a short distance north of its entrance into the Sea of Galilee.

means by which it was filled. The text says, however, that Jephthah did as he had vowed. Jephthah's daughter is a pitiable person from the Biblical perspective for two reasons. She died in in her youth, without having the opportunity to develop into full maturity, and she died childless. Women were expected to marry and raise families. Anything short of that was doubly tragic.

The Ephraimites were angered at the action of Jephthah and the Gileadites in fighting the Ammonites without consultation. Jephthah was angered at this challenge to his integrity. He protested that he had risked his life in the battle, and that Ephraimites had earlier refused assistance. A civil war resulted in which Gileadites were arrayed against the Ephraimites. Jephthah was the victor as the Ephraimites headed for the fords of the Jordan and home. Jephthah, however, controlled the fords and slew Ephraimites as they tried to get across.

The fact that the Ephraimites and the Gileadites spoke different dialects of Hebrew proved fatal to the Ephraimites. When a man claimed to be a Gileadite, the men of Gilead challenged him, "Say Shibboleth." The Ephraimites could not pronounce the "sh" phoneme, so they said, "Sibboleth." This was considered evidence that they were Ephraimites, and Jephthah ordered them slain.

Jephthah judged Israel for six years, during which time he removed the Ammonite threat. Three minor judges are mentioned as his successors: Ibzan, Elon, and Abdon. Then comes the story of Samson, the most colorful of the heroes of the Book of Judges.

We know that Samson differs in many ways from the other judges, for the Bible gives us insights into his personal life. He does not lead armies — large or small — but destroys Philistines as a result of personal anger. He could slay a thousand Philistines with the jawbone of an ass, but he could not resist a pretty female face. Samson was a man of the highest potential, but that potential was largely wasted.

The Samson story takes us to the tribe of Dan where we meet a man named Manoah, whose wife is childless. The angel of the Lord tells her that she will bear a child. She must take care to avoid wine and strong drink, and unclean food, for her child will be a Nazirite, one dedicated to God from birth. He will "begin to deliver Israel from the hand of the Philistines" (Judg. 13:5). It was not until the days of David that the Philistine threat was removed. Samson, however, was to begin acts which would challenge Philistine hegemony over Israel.

In due time Samson was born, and when he grew up he asked his father to arrange a marriage with a Philistine girl from Timnah. Manoah made it clear that he felt Samson should marry an Israelite girl rather than an "uncircumcised Philistine." The Biblical writer tells us: "His father and mother did not know that it was from the Lord; for he was seeking an occasion against the Philistines. God would use the circumstances to destroy Philistines.

As Samson was going to Timnah, a young lion sprang out to attack him. With his bare hands Samson "tore the lion asunder as one tears a kid" (Judg. 14:6) and went on his way. On his return trip he glanced at the carcass of the lion and found honey produced by a swarm of bees. Samson removed the honey and went on his way enjoying the sweetness of the honey.

As preparations were made for Samson's impending marriage to the Philistine girl, Samson and his companions enjoyed a week of festivities. As a means of entertainment, Samson put forth a riddle.

> "Out of the eater came something to eat.
> Out of the strong came something sweet."
> —Judges 14:14

Thirty lengths of linen and thirty changes of clothing would be given to Samson, if the companions could not solve the riddle within the seven days, and, conversely, Samson would give them the garments if they solved the riddle. At first the companions were unable to solve the riddle, but they then threatened to burn the house of Samson's betrothed if she did not give them the answer. She finally got Samson to tell her the answer to the riddle. She gave it to her countrymen, and they provided Samson with the solution:

> "What is sweeter than honey?
> What is stronger than a lion?"
> — Judges 14:18

Samson was angry. "If you had not ploughed with my heifer, you would not have found out my riddle." he chided. Then he went to the Philistine city of Ashkelon, killed thirty men, took their spoil and paid off his debt. In anger he stomped off to his father's house, and the young lady was married to the best man!

Later, when Samson decided to go to claim his bride, he learned that she was already married. The girl's father offered to give Samson her younger sister, but Samson hurried off in a

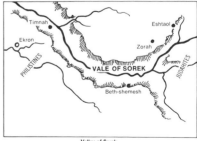

Valley of Sorek

rage. He caught three hundred foxes, tied them tail to tail, put a torch between each pair of tails, and set them loose in the Philistine grain fields. The Philistines determined to punish Samson. They killed the young lady Samson had intended to marry, and her father, but Samson continued to seek revenge on the Philistines.

The second woman in Samson's life was a harlot at Gaza. When the Philistines knew that Samson was with her they planned to kill him in the morning, thinking that he could not escape the city at night when its gates were locked. At midnight he arose, took hold of the doors of the gate of the city, with their posts, pulled them up, and carried them to the top of the hill at Hebron, forty miles away.

Samson's third and last encounter was with Delilah, a woman of the Valley of Sorek. She tried hard to learn the secret of Samson's strength and finally, worn down by her pleadings, he told her, "A razor has never come upon my head; for I have been a Nazirite to God from my mother's womb. If I be shaved, then my strength will leave me, and I shall become weak and be like any other man" (Judg. 16:17). Delilah betrayed Samson to the Philistines, who cut his hair, gouged out his eyes, bound him with fetters, and made him grind at the mill in Gaza. This was the lowest point of his humiliation.

As Samson's hair grew back, his strength was renewed. The Philistines decided to bring Samson to their temple as a trophy of war. A boy brought the once powerful warrior into Dagon's temple, where the blind Samson asked to feel the pillars on which the temple rested. Then, praying to god for vengeance, he leaned on the two middle pillars, knocked the temple down, and died along with the Philistines assembled to make merry. The Biblical writer notes, "So the dead whom he slew at his death were more than those he had slain during his life" (Judg. 16:30). Samson was buried between Zorah and Eshtaol, near his birthplace.

The Sorek Valley.

34

Ruth, the Moabitess

In the midst of the bloodshed and violence which so largely characterized the period of the judges, a quieter life must have been lived by many. The Biblical Book of Ruth describes an episode which had important results for later Israel because it involves the ancestry of King David.

The chain of events described in Ruth began when the Bethlehem area suffered famine. Rainfall in Palestine was marginal at best, and the Bible mentions famine as a recurring problem. It was famine that drove Abraham to Egypt (Gen. 12:10, 11), and somewhat later the sons of Jacob made their way to Egypt where Joseph had become prime minister to save his own brothers as well as his father in a time of famine (Genesis 42-45). The family of Elimelech, including his wife, Naomi, and their sons Mahlon and Chilion, made they way from Bethlehem to Moab, on the east side of the Dead Sea.

Life in Moab must have been quite pleasant at the beginning of their stay there. Food was available, and the two sons married Moabite girls, both of whom seem to have been regarded very highly by Naomi, their mother-in-law. Intermarriage was regarded as a sin by Israelite standards, but the basis was religious, not ethnic. Foreign women proved a snare because they encouraged idolatry among the Israelites (cf. Neh. 13:23-27). The Biblical writer nowhere censures Mahlon and Chilion for marrying Moabite girls. Indeed he seems to be writing to show that God is concerned even about a Moabite, and that Ruth, from the land of Moab became an ancestress of King David.

The happy life of Elimilech's family in Moab soon ended, however. Within ten years all the men of the family were dead: Elimelech, Mahlon, and Chilion. Only Naomi with her two daughters-in-law survived. Naomi learned that the famine had ended at home, and she urged her two daughters-in-law, Orpah and Ruth, to return to the household of their fathers. Naomi assumed that they would wish to remarry, and she saw no future for them with her in Bethlehem. According to the levirate marriage laws (Deut. 25:5-6), surviving sons of Naomi would have been obligated to marry Orpah and Ruth, thus protecting them and raising families, the first sons of which would have been regarded as legal heirs to the deceased first husbands of their mothers. Naomi was a widow with no hope of ever having additional sons, so she urged Orpah and Ruth to return to their homes and begin a new life there.

The genuine affection between mother-in-law and daughters-in-law gives a personal warmth to the story of Ruth. Both girls insisted that they would remain with Naomi, but finally Naomi persuaded Orpah to return home: "Then they lifted up their voices and wept again; and Orpah kissed her mother-in-law, but Ruth clung to her" (Ruth 1:14).

Ruth felt that her life was so entwined with that of Naomi that she must spend the rest of her life with her. Ruth abandoned her family and friends in Moab, and returned to Bethlehem where she would become a worshiper of the God of Israel and become identified with the people of Israel.

The scene of Naomi and Ruth entering Bethlehem must have been a particularly poignant one. Ten years have wrought havoc with Naomi's life. She no longer reflects the meaning of her name, Naomi, meaning "pleasant." "Call me Mara ("bitter") she says, for the Almighty has dealt very bitterly with me" (Ruth 1:20).

Naomi had property and relatives in Bethlehem, although as a widow with no husband to provide for her, she was very poor. The Mosaic law had made provision for such people: "When you reap the harvest of your land, you shall not reap your field to its very border, neither shall you gather the gleanings after your harvest. And you shall not strip your vineyard bare, neither shall you gather the fallen grapes of your vineyard; you shall leave them for the poor and for the sojourner. . ." (Lev. 19:9, 10).

Ruth suggested to Naomi that she would go to gather barley in a field where she would be made to feel welcome. She had no knowledge of where she was going, but she came upon the field of a wealthy Bethlehemite named Boaz, who was a relative of Elimelech. Boaz noticed Ruth and asked where she had come from. When told that she was the Moabite girl who had returned with Naomi, Boaz immediately ordered his men to treat her well. Boaz told Ruth that she should remain in his field and

A section of the town of Bethlehem, across a terraced ravine.

eat and drink with his reapers. He further ordered the reapers to permit her to gather grain wherever she wished, and even to leave some behind purposely so that she would have plenty for herself and for her mother-in-law.

Naomi was delighted to hear Ruth's report of the day's activities. Not only had Ruth been treated well, but she brought home some food for Naomi. When Naomi learned that Ruth had been in the fields of Boaz, she immediately planned to bring them together in marriage. As a close relative, Boaz might be willing to marry Ruth and protect her rights in the property of her deceased husband.

Following Naomi's instructions, Ruth went to the threshing-floor where Boaz was winnowing barley. Since Boaz would spend the night there, Ruth would have opportunity to offer herself to him as a wife, according to levirate marriage customs. Boaz would have been happy to take Ruth immediately, but he felt obliged to consider the prior rights of a kinsman who was more closely related to Elimelech's family than he was. Boaz asked Ruth to remain there for the night, with the understanding that the matter would be decided on the next day.

When Boaz approached the nearer kinsman at the city gate, where business was normally transacted, the nearer kinsman felt that he could not marry Ruth. He was willing to assume responsibility for the property, but he felt that raising a son in the name of Ruth's deceased husband, Mahlon, would impair his own inheritance. The matter of his own rights, and those of his sons, would be confused by such a marriage, so he declined.

Boaz, who wanted to marry Ruth from the beginning, publicly affirmed that he had purchased from Naomi all the inheritance of Elimelech, Mahlon, and Chilion, and that he also took Ruth, Mahlon's widow, as his wife to perpetuate the name and inheritance of Mahlon in Israel.

The people who were at the gate, joined the elders in pronouncing their blessings on this union. A child was born, whom they named Obed. Obed in due time became the father of Jesse, the father of Israel's first king, David.

The story of Ruth illustrates the way in which a foreigner could become a part of the people of Israel. It served as a reminder that, while the history of Israel shows the concern of God for his covenant people, nevertheless that love could encompass others as well. The prophet Jonah would remind a later generation that even the cruel Assyrians were objects of God's love and concern.

The three generations from Saul to Solomon cover about a century, yet they witnessed the growth and decay of a people whose very history is considered sacred by Christians and Jews throughout the world. Egypt was no longer a major power, and the threat of Assyria to the smaller states of western Asia was still future. Smaller states, including Israel, had an opportunity to develop during the time of this power vacuum.

Saul's court at Gibeah was humble by any standards. Solomon's at Jerusalem was known throughout the Near East for its splendor. Materially, Israel made greater progress during these three generations than at any comparable age of her history. Spiritually, however, our appraisals must be qualified. While a splendid Temple with elaborate rites had been built during the reign of Solomon, idolatry was rampant and the king himself was accused of idolatry.

All three of Israel's kings began well, and all three ended tragically. Saul's disobedience, David's sin in the matter of Bath-Sheba and Uriah, and Solomon's idolatry left their mark upon kings and people. The nation was not without a prophetic voice to call for repentance and trust in Israel's God, but Israel's political success had within it the germs of failure. With the death of Solomon the kingdom was shattered, never to be united again.

PART FOUR

The United Kingdom

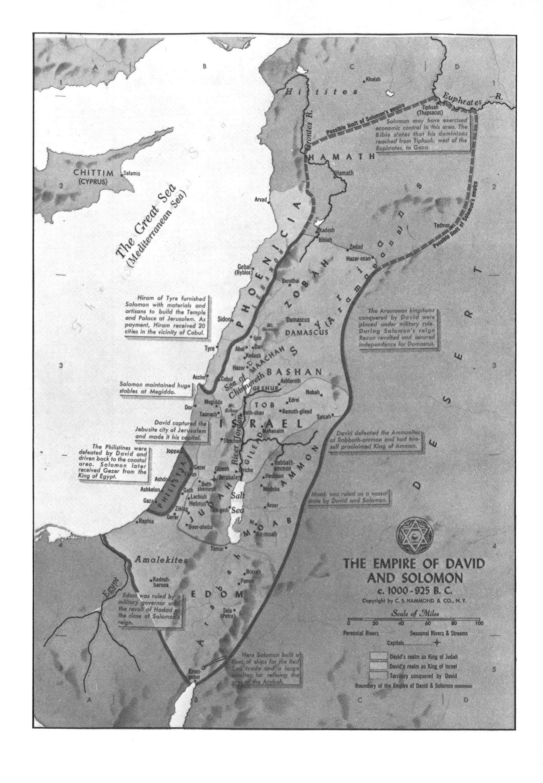

THE EMPIRE OF DAVID
AND SOLOMON
c. 1000-925 B.C.

Copyright by C.S. HAMMOND & CO., N.Y.

35

Samuel, the Kingmaker

The period when charismatic leaders known as Judges exercised civil and military power in Israel came to a close with the career of Samuel, who served as a transition figure. He was the last of the Judges (I Sam. 7:15), a priest (I Sam. 2:18; 7:9), and a prophet (II Chron. 35:18). During his lifetime the more or less independent tribes of Israel, joined together with common traditions and a common loyalty to Yahwah, were forged into a nation under a king, Saul, and subsequently David.

Samuel was born during the judship of a priest, Eli, who ministered at the "house of God" at Shiloh. During the early days of the conquest of Canaan the Tabernacle was set up at Shiloh, a town located on the east side of the highway that leads from Bethel northward to Shechem (Josh. 18:1; Judg. 21:19). During the period of the Judges, Shiloh was the principal sanctuary of the Israelites (Judg. 18:31). As time went on the sanctuary became a permanent structure, so that Eli is described as priest at the "temple of Yahweh" (cf. I Sam. 1:9). Living quarters were maintained for the priest's family, and here young Samuel first came to know the crisis that faced Israel.

Shiloh has been identified with modern Seilun, a place of ruins on a hill nine miles north of Bethel. Danish excavators, working at Seilun during campaigns from 1926 to 1929, and again in 1932, have found evidence that the city was destroyed, presumably by the Philistines, about 1050 B.C. While there are evidences that Shiloh was later occupied by Israelites (I Kings 11:29; 14:2), its destruction by the Philistines was considered by later prophets to be a warning for all time that Yahweh was a holy God. Jeremiah warned the people of Jerusalem, "Go now to my place which was in Shiloh, where I made my name dwell at first, and see what I did to it for the wickedness of my people Israel" (Jer. 7:12).

Eli appears in the Biblical record as a weak man, whose sin was in his failure to discipline his sons more than in overt acts of his own. Hophni and Phineas, Eli's sons, are described as "men of Belial" (I Sam. 2:12), thoroughly unprincipled men whose sole concern was their own lust. So greedy were they that they seized animals as they were being offered as sacrifices to Yahweh, insisting that the priest had the right to take all that he desired (I Sam. 2:13-17). They also indulged in indiscriminate sexual relations at the very shrine of Yahweh (I Sam. 2:22), which the Bible regards as evil in itself, and wicked because of its association with the Canaanite fertility cult which had been the source of a series of tragedies for Israel during the period of the Judges. Canaanite temple prostitutes served the function of insuring fertility to lands, animals, and humans. The God of Israel, Himself, brought fertility, and any compromise with Canaanite religion was regarded as infidelity to Yahweh. The reader of the Bible concludes that the religious life of Israel was at a low ebb at the time of Samuel's birth.

Samuel's parents, Elkanah and Hannah, were pious Ephraim-ites. Elkanah's other wife, Peninnah, had borne children, but Hannah was childless. Feeling that this was a cause of reproach, she went to Shiloh and there vowed that if Yahweh were to grant to her a son, he would be dedicated to God's service. Although Eli first accused Hannah of drunkenness, he later realized that she was praying to Yahweh from the depths of a grieved heart. As she finished her prayer, he said, "Go in peace, and the God of Israel grant your petition which you have made to him" (I Sam. 1:17).

After Samuel, the child born to Hannah, was weaned, his mother took him to Shiloh and left him in the care of Eli. Each year Hannah would make her pilgrimage to Shiloh. There she would see her son and bring to him the garment which she had made for him since the last visit (I Sam. 2:19). The tenderness of the family of Samuel stands out in contrast to the callousness of Eli's sons.

We read of two warnings that Eli's sons would die because of their sins. First a nameless "man of God" told Eli that his descendants would have their priesthood taken from them, and that a faithful priest would take their place. The line of Eli came to an end when Abiathar was replaced by Zadok early in the reign of Solomon (I Kings 2:35). The death of Hophni and Phineas was the more immediate judgment on the house of Eli.

The second warning came through the child Samuel. The Biblical writer artfully describes the voice in the night which aroused young Samuel, causing the lad to hasten to Eli for directions. The third time Samuel appeared, Eli sensed that Yahweh, Himself was speaking to the lad. Eli told Samuel to go back to bed with the counsel that, if the voice call again, the lad should reply, "Speak, Lord, for thy servant hears" (I Sam. 3:9). So it happened, and Yahweh revealed to Samuel the judgment soon to fall on Eli's house. Eli, himself, accepted the message with equanimity, apparently resigned to the prophesied end.

As Samuel grew he became recognized as a leader in Israel. He served as a prophet, with his headquarters at the shrine at Shiloh. At this time the Philistines encamped at Aphek, doubtless planning to take over the entire land from the Israelites. In an initial battle, the Israelites were defeated. The elders of Israel determined to put Yahweh to the test. They took the sacred ark from the shrine at Shiloh and brought it to the battlefield, accompanied by Hophni and Phinehas, the two sons of the priest Eli. The Israelites felt that the presence of their cult object would insure victory, but the fighting was hard, and the result was a resounding victory for the Philistines. The ark was taken as a trophy of war, and Hophni and Phinehas died on the field of battle.

When aged Eli learned what had happened, he too died. Perhaps he suffered a heart attack. The Biblical historian says that he broke his neck as he fell. As a final act in the tragedy, the wife of Phinehas died in giving birth to a child whom she named Ichabod ("no glory"), with the pathetic cry, "The glory has departed from Israel" (I Sam. 4:21).

Israel's fortunes had reached a new low. For the moment it appeared that the Philistine victory was absolute. The old order was gone, yet Samuel lived to breathe fresh hope into his beaten people.

In the meantime the Philistines were to learn that Israel's God was not a commodity to transport from place to place. If Israel was wrong to ascribe magic to the ark, the Philistines were also wrong to assume that they could make the ark into a good luck charm in their temples. They took the ark to the temple of their God Dagon at Ashdod. Dagon was a Canaanite god of grain who was adopted by the Philistines as one of their chief deities. When the ark of Yahweh was placed in Dagon's temple it seemed evidence of a great Philistine victory, but when the

Philistines entered a day later and found the image of Dagon on the ground before the ark, its head and arms severed from its trunk, they were moved with fear. Next they suffered the pains of bubonic plague and their bodies began to swell (I Sam. 5:6). The ark, which first appeared as a symbol of victory, now appeared to be a herald of death.

For seven months the ark remained in the Philistine country. From Ashdod it was sent to Gath, and from Gath to Ekron. Plague and panic continued, however, and the Philistine diviners urged that the ark be sent back to Israelite territory. As an offering to the God of Israel they prepared "golden tumors and golden mice" with the hope that this gift would appease the God of Israel. This would also involve imitative magic. By sending away the replicas of the "mice" (probably rats) and the tumerous growths, they hoped to rid their land of the plague which is usually spread by rats.

The advice of the Philistine diviners was taken. The ark was placed on a cart, drawn by two cows. The Philistines followed the carts as far as the borders of Beth-shemesh, then they turned back, satisfied that the ark had arrived in Israelite territory. The Levites at Beth-shemesh were thankful to have the ark back, and they sacrificed the cows to Yahweh. Some of the men of Beth-shemesh, however, irreverently looked into the ark, and died as a result. The people of Beth-shemesh began to fear for their safety with the ark in their midst. They sent it on to Kiriath-jearim where it remained until the time of David. Abinadab of Kiriath-jearim consecrated his son Eleazar to serve as custodian of the sacred ark.

Samuel appealed to the Israelites to rid themselves of the pagan cults associated with Baal and Astarte. These deities had been objects of worship during the days of the Judges, and they still held an attraction for the Israelites. The people gathered for a solemn religious occasion at Mizpah. They confessed their sins and offered sacrifices to Yahweh. The Philistines, however, learning of the gathering of Israelites at Mizpah, prepared to attack. Samuel rallied the Israelites and put the enemy to flight. In gratitude to God for giving them the victory, the Israelites named the battle sight Eben-ezer ("stone of help"). In the aftermath, Israel was able to regain cities lost to the Philistines and to enjoy peace with the other inhabitants of Canaan, called collectively the Amorites (I Sam. 7:5-14).

Samuel's leadership brought spiritual and material blessing to

At the site of Beth-shemesh.

*Section of the wall at Mizpeh
(Tell en-Nasbeh).*

Israel, but as he grew older his people expressed concern for
the future. The sons of Samuel were not of their father's caliber.
As judges they were willing to accept bribes and pervert justice.
The elders of Israel, conscious of continuing threat from the
Philistines, decided that they must ask Samuel to anoint a king
for them.

In theory Israel had been a theocracy, with Yahweh acknowledged as king. In practice, to be sure, the situation often was one
of anarchy, with every man doing what was right in his own
eyes. When the elders demanded a king of Samuel, he was understandably disturbed. He warned the Israelites of the perils
of kingship — military conscription, high taxes, slavery — but
they insisted that they would not be satisfied without a king.
Slowly Samuel came to see that it was the theocracy that was
being rejected, not his own ministry. Yahweh, Samuel was
convinced, would give a king to Israel.

36

The Philistine Threat

Possible "Philistine" Migrations

Samples of Philistine pottery found at Megiddo.

The crisis which precipitated the desire for kingship in Israel came during the latter part of the eleventh century B.C. Following the death of Joshua, Israelite tribes were content to trust Yahweh as their divine king. In times of crisis, charismatic leaders known as Judges were able to lead the tribes into victory. The Canaanite wars were thus ended, and threats from the Moabites, Ammonites, and other transjordanian peoples were effectively met. Troubles persisted, however, from the Philistines who had entrenched themselves along the coastal plain of southern Canaan.

We first meet the Philistines among the Sea People who invaded Egypt during the eighth year of Ramesses III (ca. 1188 B.C.). During the latter half of the second millennium B.C. there were extensive population movements in southeastern Europe and the eastern Mediterranean. This is the period of the fall of Troy (perhaps around 1200 B.C.) and the end of the Hittite Empire in Asia Minor. Merneptah and Ramesses III were able to turn back the Sea People from Egypt, but the Philistines (Egyptian *prst*) were successful in occupying the coastal regions of southwestern Canaan.

Before their settlement in Canaan, the Philistines had been in Crete (Jer. 47:4; Amos 9:7). Their name appears to have been of Indo-European origin. To the Israelites they were "uncircumcised" strangers who sought to prevent Israel from occupying her land. Their culture was that of the Cretan Minoans and the Greek Mycenaeans. Once in Canaan, however, they very quickly adopted Canaanite customs. We find the Canaanite god Dagon occupying an important place in Philistine religion.

When we first meet the Philistines we find them organized in city-states, each ruled by an overlord who is known as a *seren*. The title is related to the Greek *turannos*, the word for an absolute ruler which ultimately produced the English word "tyrant." The lords of the Philistines met in common council and policies of mutual concern were there determined (I Sam. 29:1-7). The Philistine strongholds were the cities of Ashkelon, Ashdod, Ekron, Gaza, and Gath. They were successful in winning many of the older Canaanite peoples to make common cause with them against the Israelites.

Our knowledge of the material culture of the Philistines comes in large measure from Medinet Habu in Egypt. A palace relief depicts captive Philistine warriors wearing a kilt similar to those used by other Aegean peoples. They are wearing a headdress with plumes and chin straps.

The distinctive Philistine ships depicted at Medinet Habu have straight masts rising from the center. The keel is curved, and there is a high stem and bow. Philistine wagons and chariots are also depicted. From the Bible we know that the Philistines had a monopoly on the use of iron (I Sam. 13:19-22). Until the victories of David, the Israelites were dependent on the Philistines for such metal as they used — a fact which gave the Philistines a distinct military advantage.

Archaeologists are able to trace the patterns of Philistine expansion through the discovery of their pottery at sites in the hill country known as the Shephelah and in the Negev. After about 1150 B.C. the Philistines exerted pressure on the tribes of Dan and Judah which claimed much of their territory. Had they succeeded, the Philistines would have extended their supremacy over all of Canaan, with the resulting destruction of Israelite distinctiveness. Well-trained, well-equipped Philistines might be expected to annihilate the Israelite tribal confederacy in short order. Many in Israel feared this very thing, and it was from them that there arose a clamor for a king.

The fortunes of the Israelites reached their nadir when the Philistines struck at Aphek in the coastal plain near Joppa. After an initial defeat, the Israelites brought their sacred ark from Shiloh in the hope that Yahweh's presence would insure victory. The ark had no magical effect. Israel's army was routed. Eli's sons, Hophni and Phinehas, were killed. The ark was taken as a trophy of victory by the Philistines.

A Danish archaeological expedition worked at Shiloh during the years 1930-32, uncovering evidence that the city was destroyed about 1050 B.C. Centuries later, the prophet Jeremiah warned the people of Jerusalem that Yahweh had permitted

Roman columns at the Ashkelon Antiquities Park.

the shrine city of Shiloh to fall (Jer. 7:12, 14; 26:6, 9) and the city of the later Temple must not expect deliverance. The Bible is reticent concerning the destruction of Shiloh (cf. Ps. 78:60), but there can be no doubt that it was a bitter moment to Israel.

With its central shrine destroyed, its priesthood killed or dispersed, and its armies routed, Israel seemed to have reached the end. Philistine garrisons occupied strategic sites throughout the land. Israel would either end her history ingloriously or rise to meet the crisis.

A Philistine-made, pottery anthropoid coffin with a movable lid, from Beth-shan.

37

Saul:

Israel's First King

Samuel was reluctant to introduce kingship into the life of Israel. Yet the times were such that he could not refuse. A loose confederation of tribes could not stand before the Philistines. Something new was needed, and Samuel was willing to anoint a king.

Saul, the son of Kish of the tribe of Benjamin, would become a charismatic leader in his own way. Benjamin was a small tribe, and a Benjaminite would not be the object of jealousy that a man from Judah or Ephraim might become. Saul possessed a commanding figure, "from his shoulders upward he was taller than any of the people" (I Sam. 9:2). A leader of men was expected to have appropriate physical characteristics, and Saul had them.

The Biblical historian tells us that Saul was anointed secretly by Samuel before he was introduced to the people through a public act of bravery. Kish, Saul's father, was a wealthy man whose asses had strayed away. Saul and his servant searched for them throughout Benjamin with no success. Finally the servant suggested that they consult a "man of God" who might be able to tell them where to find the lost animals.

Saul and his servant entered the city and met Samuel, who had been prepared by Yahweh for this encounter. Samuel assured them that the asses had been found. Then he urged them to join in the sacrifice at the high place, where the best portion had been reserved for Saul. The next morning Samuel anointed Saul as king of Israel and sent him on his way.

Saul emerged as an able leader in a difficult time. He found Israel a loosely-organized group of tribes with a common religious loyalty. Shiloh had been a religious center for the tribes since the days of Joshua, but the city had been destroyed by the Philistines. Happily the tribes rallied to the old shrine at Gilgal,

Philistine Cities and Areas of Expansion

perhaps to be identified with Khirbet el-Mefjer, two miles northeast of ancient Jericho.

As leader of a united Israel, Saul's first challenge was to meet the threat of the Ammonites against Jebesh-gilead (I Sam. 11:1-4). Messengers hurried to Gibeah, a town in Benjamin three miles north of Jerusalem, where Saul lived. While the men of Jabesh lamented the plight of their city, Saul was stirred into activity. He sacrificed a "yoke of oxen" and sent pieces throughout the tribes of Israel. This was a call to arms against the Ammonites, Israel's enemy to the east. The call was answered, and Saul led his people to victory. The men of Jabesh-gilead would never forget what they owed to Saul. All Israel gathered at Gilgal to offer thanks for victory, and there Saul was publicly acclaimed as king (I Sam. 11:14-15).

Having dealt a decisive blow against the Ammonites, Saul turned to the more difficult task of challenging the Philistines who were harrassing Israel from the west. Making Gibeah the seat of his government, Saul prepared to assault the Philistines at Michmash, located nineteen hundred feet above sea level on a hill north of the Wadi es-Suwenit on the east slope of the central mountain range. The enemy had been raiding Israelite territory from the Michmash stronghold, and Israel seemed powerless to do anything about it.

The bravery of Jonathan, Saul's son, changed the tide of the Philistine war. Under cover of darkness, Jonathan and his armorbearer climbed down the rock Seneh, on which Geba was built, stole through the Philistine encampment in the pass, and climbed the rock Bozez on top of which stood Michmash, the Philistine headquarters (I Sam. 14:4-15). Jonathan threw fear into the enemy camp and roused his fellow Israelites to action. The result was more than a local victory for Israel. As the Philistines were defeated, Israelites came out of hiding and joined forces in pursuing the enemy out of the hill country as far as to Aijalon in the Shephelah.

The Philistine threat was not ended, but Israel was able to hold its central strongholds against its enemies throughout Saul's reign. Future battles were fought along the traditional Israelite-Philistine borders, not in the heartland of Israel. Other enemies also threatened — Amalekites from the south, Edomites and Moabites from the southeast, and Arameans from the north. Except for the Phoenician on the northwest, Israel was surrounded by a ring of active foes.

Gibeah of Saul (Tel el-Ful).

Although successful in battle, Saul is remembered more for his failures than for his victories. Samuel had been reluctant to anoint a king for Israel, and we may suspect that he was never really enthusiastic about kingship. No doubt he was grateful for Saul's leadership against Israel's foes, but it was not long before a serious rift developed between the prophet and the king.

During the preparation for battle with the Philistines at Michmash, Saul understandably wanted sacrifices made to insure success. Time was rapidly passing and Samuel did not appear. Finally Saul felt he could wait no longer. He took matters into his own hands and offered the burnt offering. When Samuel appeared he denounced Saul for his rash act: "You have done foolishly; you have not kept the commandment of the Lord your God, which he comanded you; . . . your kingdom shall not continue" (I Sam. 13:13-14). While we may be sympathetic with Saul for acting in an emergency, his act was condemned because he failed to observe the limited nature of monarchy in Israel. Unlike absolute monarchs, the Israelite king was subject to the law of God. The king must not usurp the position of the priest. The circumstances are different from those of our day, but there was a distinct separation between "church" and "state." Priests and kings were anointed to serve the Lord, but their functions were distinct.

The final breech between Samuel and Saul followed the Amalekite war. Samuel, as God's spokesman, ordered Saul to exterminate the Amalekites, who had taken advantage of Israel's pre-occupation with the Philistines to make raids regularly across the southern border. Saul was successful in his campaign, but he spared the Amalekite king, Agag, and spared the best of the sheep and the cattle.

In a dramatic encounter with Samuel, Saul stated that he had obeyed the command given by the prophet. Samuel asked, "What then is this bleating of the sheep in my ears, and the lowing of the oxen which I hear?" (I Sam. 15:14). Piously, Saul protested that he had saved the best of the sheep and the oxen "to sacrifice to the Lord your God." The explanation was not satisfactory. As a simple matter of fact, Saul had not obeyed God, Samuel said:

> "Has the Lord as great delight in burnt offerings and sacrifices, as in obeying the voice of the Lord?
> Behold, to obey is better than sacrifice, and to hearken than the fat of rams.

Michmash, the scene of Jonathan's victory over the Philistines.

> For rebellion is as the sin of divination, and stubbornness is an iniquity and idolatry.
> Because you have rejected the word of the Lord,
> He has also rejected you from being king. (I Sam. 15:22-23).

Saul acknowledged his sin and begged forgiveness, but Samuel would not be appeased. Agag, not knowing of the attitude of Samuel, felt that he was now safe. Samuel asked that he be brought in, whereupon "Samuel hewed Agag in pieces before the Lord at Gilgal" (I Sam. 15:33). The breach was now complete. Samuel did not see Saul again until the day of his death.

The last years of Saul are marked by personal tragedy. Our focus of attention turns to the attractive young son of Jesse, David, who is destined to become Saul's successor. Saul hears the crowds crying, "Saul has slain his thousands, and David his ten thousands" (I Sam. 18:7) and he is understandably jealous. During these years Saul suffered periodically from mental illness, described in Biblical language as "an evil spirit from the Lord" which tormented him. Forsaken by Samuel and eclipsed by David, Saul's condition grew progressively worse. Saul determined to do away with David, and he was prepared to stoop to any depth to do it. He attempted to pin David to the wall with his spear (I Sam. 18:9-16). David succeeded in evading Saul, but the king next exerted every effort to persuade David to marry Michal, his daughter. In this way he would be able to use Michal in getting at David. When a marriage was planned, Saul magnanimously demanded no present "except a hundred foreskins of the Philistines" (I Sam. 18:25). In this way Saul hoped that David would meet death at the hand of the enemy. Saul's purposes were thwarted, however. David was successful in killing two hundred Philistines, and he claimed Michal as his wife. Saul grew increasingly bitter.

Saul next sought to get at David through his son, Jonathan. From Saul's point of view, Jonathan should have been jealous of David. Saul's son should expect to succeed him on the throne, and David would be an obstacle. Yet Jonathan and David became the best of friends, and Jonathan tried to persuade his father to desist from his plan to kill David. Saul probably promised in good faith (I Sam. 19:6), but jealousy soon got the better of him and Saul again tried to pin David to the wall with his spear (I Sam. 19:10). David escaped and Saul sent messengers to David's house to apprehend him. Michal warned him of danger

and let him down through the window. Thus David again
eluded Saul.

Jonathan risked his own life in attempting to reason with his
father. Saul in his disturbed state cast his spear at Jonathan,
but happily he was no more successful in hitting Jonathan than
he had been in aiming at David (I Sam. 20:33). David knew he
could not return to Saul's court, and we follow him from place
to place as he seeks to elude the demented king. The priests at
Nob provided food for David, and gave him the sword of
Goliath which had been kept there (I Sam. 22). When Saul
learned of the help they had given to David he had them
murdered in cold blood.

Only the Philistinees could profit from Saul's senseless pursuit
of David. In a cave at En-gedi, David and his men had the opportunity to kill Saul, but David simply cut off the skirt of
Saul's robe as evidence that the king was in his power. On another occasion, in the Wilderness of Ziph, David and Abishai,
Joab's brother, actually entered the camp of Saul and took the
king's spear and a jug of water while Saul and Abner were sleeping. Saul had many evidences of David's concern for him, and
he did admit, "I have done wrong...I will no more do you
harm" (I Sam. 27:21). Nevertheless David did not feel he could
trust Saul. So he fled to Achish, the Philistine king of Gath.

Saul, however, grew more and more despondent. The Philistines were able to make major gains. God seemed to have forsaken Saul completely, for he could get no communication by
dreams, by Urim, or by prophets. Samuel had died, and Saul
still respected his memory. Although mediums had been out-
lawed Saul made his way to the village of Endor in order to
contact a woman who reputedly had power to communicate with
the dead.

The medium was reluctant to contact the dead, but Saul in
disguise assured her that she would not be harmed. Samuel appeared, frightening the woman and telling Saul that he would
be in the realm of the dead on the next day. The practice of sorcery and necromancy was forbidden in Israel, but the author of
I Samuel indicates that desperate Saul received a message from
the netherworld that pronounced his doom.

At Mount Gilboa the Philistines fought the Israelites, divided
as a result of Saul's pursuit of David. Saul himself was severely
wounded and three of his sons, including Jonathan, were killed.
Saul asked his armorbearer to strike the fatal blow lest the

The village of Nob.

At the base of Mount Gilboa.

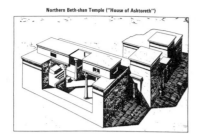

Northern Beth-shan Temple ("House of Ashtoreth")

A reconstruction of the northern Beth-shan temple, the "House of Ashtoreth."

Philistines claim credit for killing him. When the armor-bearer refused, Saul fell on his own sword.

The Philistines found the body of Saul and took it to Beth-shan. Saul's armor was placed in the Ashtoreth temple, and his body hanged on the walls of the city as a warning to others who might rebel against the Philistines. As one crowning act of homage to Saul, the men of Jabesh-gilead risked their lives to take the body from the wall. Then, to prevent it from falling into the hands of the Philistines again, they cremated the body. There is something fitting in this act of valor for Saul began his career by rescuing Jabesh-gilead from humiliation at the hand of the Ammonites.

The mound of Beth-shan.

38

David: The Man
After God's Own Heart

The book of Ruth provides us with an introduction to the career of David, Israel's second king, and the king through whom the messianic line would continue. In seeking to show that Jesus of Nazareth was Israel's Messiah, Matthew asserted that Jesus was the "son of David, son of Abraham" (Matt. 1:1). The Messiah had to be of the seed of Abraham, and he had to trace his lineage through the king with whom Yahweh had made an everlasting covenant (II Sam. 7). Yet Ruth shows that David himself had a Moabitess in his ancestry. This is one of many reminders that the Jew, no more than any other people, can boast of racial purity.[1] Ruth had accepted the God of Israel as her God. Although born an alien, through faith in Israel's God she had become a part of the people of Israel, and an ancestress of Israel's greatest king.

The Biblical historian gives us a threefold introduction to the young David. When we first meet him, the boy is tending the flocks of his father Jesse, a Bethlehemite. When Samuel came to Bethlehem with his horn of oil, prepared to anoint the one whom Yahweh might designate as Saul's successor, he went to the house of Jesse. David's seven older brothers successively passed before Samuel, but none of them proved to be Yahweh's choice. It was only after he made further inquiry that Samuel learned of the youngest son, David, who was tending the sheep. When he was brought in, Yahweh instructed Samuel to anoint

Bethlehem, the street scene at Manger Square. The house of Jesse, David's father, was located near Bethlehem.

---

1. Tamar, Rahab, Ruth, and Bath-sheba are alluded to in Matt. 1:2-6. The writer seems to be self-consciously stating that the Davidic, Messianic line was not characterized by a so-called racial purity.

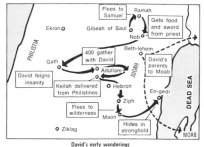

David's early wanderings

him as the king designated to replace Saul on the throne of Israel.[2]

The anointing of David was done in secret. Saul was still on the throne and we can assume that he would have reacted immediately had he known that Samuel had anointed a successor. Since this was unknown to Saul, the historian can tell us of how, in very favorable circumstances, David was introduced to Saul's court (I Sam. 16:14-22).

The latter years of Saul's life were tragic, indeed. The Biblical historian says, "the Spirit of the Lord departed from Saul, and an evil spirit from the Lord tormented him" (I Sam. 16:4). Saul had a mental illness which plagued him from this time until the time of his death. The rift between Samuel and Saul may have helped to unbalance the king. In any event, the king's counsellors learned of the youthful David whose ability to play the lyre might have a wholesome effect upon the disturbed king. David was brought to Saul's court where he served both as court musician and armorbearer to the king (I Sam. 16:14-23).

Following the stories of David's secret anointing, and of his introduction to the court of Saul, we have the account of young David proving his bravery on the battlefield against the hated Philistines (I Sam. 17). Saul and the Israelite army, including Eliab, Abinadab, and Shammah — three of David's brothers — were fighting the Philistines in the Valley of Elah. A Philistine champion, Goliath of Gath, challenged the Israelites to produce a man who would come to fight him in single combat. The outcome of the war would be determined by the contest (I Sam. 17:8-10).

According to the record in I Samuel, Jesse sent his youngest son David to the battlefield with provisions for his older brothers who were fighting the Philistines. Young David was horrified to find the Israelites cringing before the enemy, and volunteered to accept Goliath's challenge. With no weapon but his sling, David met the challenger, felled him, and cut off Goliath's head with his own sword. In II Samuel 21:19 we read that a man

---

2. The law of primogeniture prevailed in Israel. When, however, the first-born does not become the chief heir, this fact must be accounted for, hence the Biblical stories of younger sons surpassing their elder brothers. The stories of Jacob and Esau (Gen. 25; 27), and of Joseph and his brothers (Gen. 37) illustrate the fact that younger brothers often eclipse their elder brothers. When the law of primogeniture is violated, an explanation is given.

named Elhanan slew "Goliath the Gittite," and many scholars have concluded that the deeds of a lesser Israelite hero have been transferred to David. John Bright suggests that "Elhanan and David were the same person, the latter name being perhaps a throne name."[3] David must have performed some conspicuous act of heroism to win the love and loyalty of Israel, and the Goliath episode would provide the basis for the public acclaim he later received.

Following his victory over Goliath, David enjoyed the closest of relations with Saul and his family. Saul looked upon David as a brave and loyal Israelite, and insisted that the young man stay with his court. Soon Saul's attitude would be one of bitter hostility, but for the moment David was highly esteemed by king and people alike.

A particularly close relationship developed between David and Jonathan, Saul's son. Jonathan truly loved David, and his loyalty continued even when he realized that David was to become heir to the throne which he might hope to occupy. Jonathan and David both proved their bravery on the field of battle, and both proved themselves to be above petty jealousy.

Saul, however, soon came to see David as a threat to his throne and dynasty. The mental illness which had afflicted Saul earlier grew worse, and the king seemed to be wholly consumed with his passion to kill David. In the meantime David was growing ever more popular with the people in view of his success against Israel's enemies.

Fearing what might happen if he personally harmed the idol of the crowds, Saul determined to maneuver David into a situation in which he would die at the hand of the Philistines. When Saul learned that his daughter Michal was in love with the young hero, he took it as an opportunity to strike at David. When arrangements were made for a wedding, David protested that he was a poor man and could not hope to give the customary marriage present to the bride's father. Saul, in apparent magnanimity, insisted that he wanted nothing but "a hundred foreskins of the Philistines" (I Sam. 18:25), hoping that David would be killed in the process of killing Philistines. David, however, killed two hundred Philistines and claimed Michal as his wife.

---

3. John Bright, *A History of Israel,* pp. 171-172.

David's continuing victories, and the popularity that attended them, brought Saul to the place where he determined to act decisively. The king dispatched messengers to David's house, but Michal warned him of danger and David was able to flee. Michal fooled her father's messengers by placing an image and pillow on the bed, making it appear that David was sick in his bed (I Sam. 19:13). When Saul learned of the deception, Michal told her father that David had threatened her so that she had to let him escape.

The fleeing David made his way to Samuel at Ramah in the mountain country of Ephraim. Saul learned of the whereabouts of David and sent messengers to take him. Samuel and the prophets with him were engaged in the ecstatic dancing early associated with the prophetic gift (I Sam. 19:20-24), and Saul's messengers were caught up in the enthusiasm. After a second and a third group were affected similarly, Saul personally went to Ramah where he too, joined the prophetic frenzy. In this way David was again protected from Saul's plan to have him killed.

From this time on until the death of Saul, David was a fugitive. At Nob, near Jerusalem, David secured the co-operation of Ahimelech and the priests who gave him bread and a sword. Flight from Saul took him to the Philistines. Achish, king of Gath, recognized David and the fugitive feigned madness in order to save his life (I Sam. 21:10-15). We next find David in Adullam, southwest of Bethlehem. Here he gathered a band of four hundred men, including men of his own family and outlaws who wished to escape from society. David arranged to have his parents stay in Mizpah of Moab while he sought to protect himself from Saul. The unfortunate priests at Nob were slaughtered because of the help they had given David.

When Keilah in the Shephelah, southwest of Bethlehem, was attacked by the Philistines, David and his men moved in to rescue the Israelites there. It is a mark of the impotence of Saul's defense policies at the time that David's outlaw force, rather than Saul's regular army, brought relief to the city. David was not safe in Keilah, however. Abiathar, using his priestly ephod,[4] told David that Saul would pursue him to Keilah and the men of Keilah would surrender David to his enemy.

View from the main entrance to the Cave of Adullam. Possibly, Saul interrogated David from the opposite slope.

---

4. The ephod, here, is the box which contained the sacred lots. These were consulted to give "yes" or "no" answers to questions proposed to the priest who used them.

Again we find David fleeing to the wilderness area east of the central mountain range. The inhabitants of Ziph reported David's presence in their territory, southeast of Hebron, to Saul. David moved farther south to the Wilderness of Maon, where Saul caught up with him. As Saul and his men were closing in on David, a messenger brought word of a Philistine attack (I Sam. 23:24-29). Again David fled from Saul, this time making his way to En-gedi, an oasis near the center of the western shore of the Dead Sea. Here Saul entered the cave where David and his men were hiding. David cut off the skirt of Saul's robe, but he did not take advantage of the opportunity to kill his enemy. In spite of all that Saul did to David, David respected Saul's office and would not lift a hand to harm him (I Sam. 24:1-7).

As David called after Saul, confronting the king with evidence that he was at the mercy of David in the cave, Saul acknowledged in apparent penitence, "You are more righteous than I; for you have repaid me good, where as I have repaid you evil" (I Sam. 24:12). David vowed that he would not exact vengeance from Saul and his descendants. Saul in his madness might rage against David, but the Biblical historian makes it clear that David is God's elect. Nevertheless David treats Saul and his family with respect, and during Saul's lifetime, David did not lift a hand against him. There is no reconciliation, however. David returned to his mountain stronghold, and Saul went home to Gibeah. If chastened, it was a temporary feeling.

While David was in the En-gedi area, the prophet Samuel died. Samuel had been involved in Israel's political history since his youth, and he had become the grand old man of Israelite life. David, in particular, would have looked upon him as a source of strength. In the divided state of the nation, it is noteworthty that "all Israel assembled and mourned for him" (I Sam. 25:1). The prophet was buried in his house at Ramah, traditionally identified with a hill five miles northeast of Jerusalem known as Nebi Samwil ("the prophet Samuel"). The mosque at Nebi Samwil, one of the highest points in Palestine, is supposed to contain the tomb of Samuel. It does bear witness to the fact that Moslem as well as Christian and Jew honor Israel's kingmaker.

Following Samuel's death, David and his followers moved farther south to Maon, south of Hebron. There David and his men continue to live as outlaws, demanding and receiving provisions

Two scenes of the cliffs at En-gedi, near the shore of the Dead Sea.

from those among whom they live. To be sure, they would some-times serve as a police force, protecting their neighborhood from intruders (I Sam. 25:21). Here we meet the churlish Nabal and his discreet wife, Abigail. Nabal was a wealthy sheikh who refused to acknowledge any obligation to David. At the time of sheep-shearing it was usual to give something to needy neighbors, and David sent ten of his young men expecting gifts from Nabal. Wandering groups such as David's retinue represented a real danger in an area, and when they did not resort to plunder they expected some sort of tribute. Nabal treated the request of David's young men contemptuously, with the rhetorical ques-tion, "Who is David? Who is the son of Jesse? There are many servants nowadays who are breaking away from their masters. Shall I take my bread and my water and my meat that I have killed for my shearers, and give it to men who come from I do not know where?" (I Sam. 25:10-11). David was angered at this response, and he prepared to attack and plunder Nabal and his household.

When Abigail learned what had happened she immediately sought to rectify matters. She had appreciated the presence of David and his men, and she feared the consequences of their anger. Sending her young men on ahead, Abigail mounted her ass and approached David with a gift of fig cakes, raisins, bread, wine, sheep, and grain (I Sam. 25:18). As she approached David, Abigail took upon herself the blame for David's young men re-turning empty handed. Nabal had lived up to his name; he was a fool. Abigail should have known of David's demands, but she was ignorant of them. Now she wished to make amends, thereby preventing David from shedding innocent blood (I Sam. 25:23-31). The speech is moving and appropriate. David had spared Saul. His hands were not blood-stained. For him to have re-taliated in anger after Nabal's foolish remarks he would have harmed his own chances for influence throughout Maon. David accepted the gifts and the council of Abigail.

When Abigail returned home she found Nabal drunk; so she delayed telling him what she had done. The next morning Nabal learned what his wife had done in presenting gifts to David. Nabal's "heart died within him" (I Sam. 25:37), perhaps a refer-ence to a heart attack. Ten days later Nabal was dead.

When David heard of Nabal's death, he sent for Abigail and married her. This wise and beautiful widow brought her own loyalty, and there can be no question that the whole of

Maon would look upon David with greater sympathy because of his marriage to Abigail. Saul had given Michal, David's first wife to another, but David had also married Ahinoam of Jezreel. Ahinoam was the mother of David's firstborn, Amnon (II Sam. 3:2), and Abigail bore his second son, Chileab (II Sam. 3:3).

A second time we read that the Ziphites betrayed David's presence to Saul (I Sam. 26). David's spies reported the arrival of Saul, and with his nephew Abishai, David stole into the camp of Saul and stole his spear and a jug of water. Then, from the opposite mountain, David taunted Abner for not remaining awake to protect his master, Saul. Again Saul recognized that David had spared his life, but there was no reconciliation.

Since it was impossible to evade Saul forever in Israel, David decided to move into the Philistine country. There were dangers in such a move, for the Israelites might accuse him of selling out to their perennial foes. Yet the Biblical writer makes it clear that David's loyalty never waivered. Although a vassal of Achish of Gath for a year and four months, David only attacked peoples such as Geshurites, Girzites, and Amalekites. The Philistines thought he was attacking the neighboring Israelites, but David was careful to avoid hostile contacts with his own people (I Sam. 27:8-12). Achish trusted David implicitly, but the other Philistine leaders were suspicious (I Sam. 29:1-4). This proved providential, for the Philistines were preparing for battle with Saul and his forces.

When David returned to Ziklag he found that the Amalekites had burned the city and had taken the women and children captive. David's men were prepared to revolt, but David trusted his God for strength and determined what action had to be taken. He consulted his priest, Abiathar, who counseled him to pursue the enemy with the assurance that he would rescue Ahinoam and Abigail and the others who had been taken captive. Again providence was working for David. His men came upon an Egyptian slave who had been abandoned by the Amalekites after their raid, presuming that the slave was about to die. David's men gave the slave nourishment, and he served as their guide, directing them to the camp of the Amalekites.

David came upon the Amalekites in a surprise attack and liberated the people of Ziklag who had been captured. The four hundred camel riders comprising the Amalekite cavalry escaped, but the rest of the Amalekite army was annihilated. All of the spoil of war was claimed by David (I Sam. 30:20). On the

A view of Hebron across Sultan's Pool.

return trip to Ziklag, David met the two hundred of his men who were too exhausted to join the expedition against the Amalekites. In spite of the counsel of some of his men, David insisted that those who had stayed at home should have their share of the spoil (I Sam. 30:21-25). While not obligated to do so, David sent a share of the spoils to the cities of Judah which had suffered periodically from Amalekite raids. This demonstrated David's loyalty to his own people, in spite of the fact that he had been recently a vassal to the Philistines.

David was not present at the fateful battle on Mt. Gilboa. There Saul and Jonathan met their death and Israel went down in defeat. David expressed his grief in a poetic dirge, quoted by the author of II Samuel from an ancient poetic epic known as the Book of Jasher (II Sam. 1:18). There is irony in the fact that David's bitter enemy — King Saul — and his best friend, Jonathan, died together. Yet David chose to forget the difficult years with Saul, and recall the brave warrior of earlier and happier times. There can be no question that David's grief was genuine. Yet we must note that the death of Saul made it possible for David to become king, even if the initial phase of his kingship was limited to the south.

The men of Judah proclaimed David king in Hebron, while the partisans of the house of Saul acknowledged Saul's son Eshbaal, or Ishbosheth, as king of the north. Saul's commander Abner was loyal to Ishbosheth in the early days of his reign. The forces of Joab, David's general, and Abner tangled at Gibeon. A tournament seems to have been arranged between the opposing forces, the outcome of which would determine whether David or Ishbosheth would be acclaimed king (II Sam. 2:12-17). The result was a bloody draw, for the twelve partisans of David and the twelve partisans of Ishbosheth slaughtered one another. In the battle that followed David's forces prevailed.

David's forces soon gained the upper hand in battle with the forces of Ishbosheth. Asahel, a brother of Joab, David's commander, pursued Abner who was loyal to Saul's son Ishbosheth. When Asahel insisted on taking Abner, Abner smote Asahel with the butt of his spear and killed him. Not only did David lose a loyal warrior, but Asahel's death produced a blood feud between Joab and Abner.

As David was growing stronger, troubles developed between Abner and Ishbosheth. Abner took one of Saul's concubines, and Ishbosheth interpreted the act as treason. A king's concubines were considered royal property, and a man who claimed the wives or concubines of a king could be considered a claimant to the throne. When Ishbosheth took Abner to task for taking the concubine, Abner gave the king a tart reply and promptly prepared to shift his loyalty to David (II Sam. 3:6-11).

When Abner negotiated with David for a covenant. David insisted on the return to him of Michal, Saul's daughter and his first wife (II Sam. 3:14). This would strengthen David's claim to the throne of all Israel, for he would then be son-in-law to Saul. Michal's husband Paltiel was reluctant to part with her, and Michal, herself, had no desire to rejoin David. Abner, however, did as David had requested and brought Michal to him.

Abner then negotiated with the elders of Israel, including Benjamin, Saul's tribe, to persuade them to accept David as king (II Sam. 3:17-19). Having been successful, he journeyed southward to Hebron and told David that the northern tribes were prepared to enter a covenant with him and thus acknowledge him as their king.

Abner did not live to enjoy the position of prominence he doubtless hoped for in the court of David. Joab would naturally be jealous of Abner as a rival commander. Since Abner had killed Joab's brother Asahel, Joab felt justified in murdering Abner (II Sam. 3:26-30). The people of the north would be understandably bitter at the death of Abner, but David made it clear that he had no part in it. David mourned for the fallen Abner, and insisted that Joab alone would bear the curse for the horrible deed. The death of Abner might have alienated the northern tribes, but David was successful in convincing them that he was in no way responsible for the tragedy.

Soon after Abner's death, Ishbosheth himself was murdered. Rechab and Baanah, professional soldiers and captains of guerilla bands, stole into the king's chamber and murdered Ishbosheth. They brought his head to David at Hebron, hoping for a reward. Instead David ordered that Rechab and Baanah be put to death for their crime.

Real and potential enemies of David had been removed one by one, but David was never personally responsible for their death. David mourned for Saul, for Abner, and for Ishbosheth as though they had all been loyal to his cause. There is no reason to see hypocrisy in this. David's conduct at this time of his life won the hearts of friend and foe alike. The hand of God

A girl carrying bread, in Hebron.

might be seen in preparing the way for David to rule over all Israel, but David never forced or hurried the hands of providence.

After David reigned for seven years as king over Judah, the northern tribes assembled at Hebron and entered into covenant to make David king of all Israel. The two parts of the land — north and south — would split permanently after the death of Solomon. At the beginning of David's reign we see that the sections were conscious of distinctive institutions and rights. David was king of the south, and the north acclaimed him as king after the death of Ishbosheth. The union was in the person of David. It persisted through the career of Solomon, but no longer.

Hebron was a satisfactory capital for Judah, but a united monarchy demanded a headquarters farther north. The Jebusite enclave at Jerusalem was a final vestige of Canaanite control of Israel. It was centrally located and had not been incorporated into Judah or Benjamin, the tribes on its borders. It seemed ideally located for a capital. The details of the capture of Jerusalem-Jebus are difficult to follow because of problems in the Biblical text and its interpretation. David's men seem to have stormed the water shaft, overwhelmed the Jebusite guards stationed at its upper end, and conquered the city.[5] Tradition seems to have regarded the capture of the shaft as the decisive event in the capture of the city.

We have no record of David's treatment of the Jebusites, but we may assume that he spared them and permitted them to live in safety in his kingdom. The captured city was not incorporated into the tribal territories but remained a royal city, "the city of David." David was concerned about its defenses. On the long north side of the city hill he built the Millo, perhaps a raised platform or terrace of filled-in masonry. The north was the one direction from which the city was vulnerable, and special precautions had to be made for its defense.

Soon after David united the kingdom under his personal rule, the Philistines began to give him trouble. They had profited from the controversies between partisans of Saul and David and wanted to keep the Israelites weak. David, however, was emerging as a force to be reckoned with, and the Philistines attacked at the valley of Rephaim, southwest of Jerusalem. David was vic-

5. Cf. J. Simons, *Jerusalem in the Old Testament,* Leiden: E. J. Brill, 1957, pp. 165-173.

torious, and he took away the idols of the Philistines as they had once taken the ark of Yahweh, God of Israel (II Sam. 5:21). While we do not have details of David's wars with the Philistines, there is evidence that they ranged over a wide area in central and southern Palestine. On one occasion, while the Philistines were occupying Bethlehem, David expressed his wish to drink water from the Bethlehem well. As a youth he had known that well, and in a moment of nostalgia he craved its water. Three of his warriors actually broke through the enemy line, took water, and brought it to David. Moved by their loyalty and courage, David poured it out as an offering to the Lord (I Chron. 11:17-19). Such acts of understanding generosity endeared David to his warriors.

David planned to make Jerusalem the religious as well as the political capital of his empire, so he ordered that the ark be taken from the house of Abinadab at Kiriath-jearim and brought to Jerusalem. While passing over the threshingfloor of a man named Nacon, Abinadab's son Uzzah reached out to steady the ark which appeared to be moving from the cart on which it was carried. Uzzah died on the spot, for his well-meaning act was considered irreverent because he had dared to touch the sacred ark (II Sam. 6:6-11). David was angry, and probably frightened at the swift retribution meted out to Uzzah. Instead of bringing the ark to Jerusalem, he left it with a man named Obed-edom. During the three months it was with Obed-edom, prosperity came to his house. David then decided to bring the ark to Jerusalem.

The procession to Jerusalem was a noisy and colorful one. David, himself, joined in the procession, dancing and leaping in a frenzied march. Michal, Saul's daughter, was horrified at her husband's lack of dignity, and she told him so. She may have been filled with resentment at being torn from her former husband, Paltiel (II Sam. 3:15-16), and at the decline in her family's fortunes since her father's death. Michal may also have been angered to discover that she was but one of David's many wives. In any event. David resented her criticism. Her's was a difficult burden to bear, for she died childless.

The arrival of the ark in Jerusalem was a happy occasion. Special sacrifices were offered and food was distributed among the crowds (II Sam. 6:18-19). The ark had at last found a home. It moved from place to place during the wilderness wandering, and even in the Promised Land it had no permanent resting place until David brought it to Jerusalem.

The next logical act for David would be to build a magnificent Temple to house the sacred ark. This he purposed to do, and Nathan, the prophet, was enthusiastic in approving the venture. David had built a sumptuous mansion for himself, and it seemed inappropriate to permit the ark to remain in a humble tent.

Yet Yahweh intervened to tell Nathan that he did not wish David to make him an house; conversely Yahweh wished to build David a house (II Sam. 7:11). To be sure, there is a play on the word "house" here. David purposed to build a dwelling-place; Yahweh will build a dynasty. The ideas are interrelated, however, for David's son (Solomon) will build a house for Yahweh. Yet the emphasis is on God's promise to David. David's children will rule after him. On occasion they will sin, and be punished, but the dynasty will not end as Saul's dynasty ended (II Sam. 7:14-15). David, in gratitude, accepted God's promise and covenant.

Following the establishment of the ark in Jerusalem, and Yahweh's covenant with David, we read of yet other victories of David over his foes. Not only must he continually fight the Philistines, but Moabites, Arameans, and Edomites stir up trouble (II Sam. 8). David occupied Damascus in Syria and pushed back the boundaries of his sphere of influence to the Euphrates River. Toi of Hamath, one hundred twenty miles north of Damascus, offered loyalty and tribute to David.

On the personal side we find David remembering his friend Jonathan and showing kindness to his son Mephibosheth. Mephibosheth, as a descendant of Saul, might have aspired to kingship. Yet David would note that he was a cripple, hence hardly one to lead a revolt. There is no reason to doubt that David was really anxious to show kindness to this son of his best friend. The restoration of Saul's lands, and a subvention from the royal treasury for support were the least that David could do for this crippled prince (II Sam. 9:9-13).

David's career, like that of Saul, ended in a series of personal tragedies which affected the fortunes of his people as well. The turning point was the sin which he committed with Bath-sheba (II Samuel 11). The armies of David, under Joab, were fighting the Ammonites east of the Jordan River, but the king himself remained in Jerusalem. This fact suggests that the once mighty warrior was growing careless. Others faced danger while he enjoyed the comforts of home. Worse yet, as he observed the beautiful Bathsheba, wife of one of his soldiers, Uriah the Hittite, he lusted after her and ordered that she be brought to him. They had sexual relations, and in due time David learned that she was pregnant.

Black as David's sin was in the first instance, his efforts to cover it were still blacker. The king invited Uriah to come home for a period of rest. A loyal soldier is entitled to some time away from the battle field. David hoped that Uriah would go to his home, have sexual relations with his wife, and then assume that the child which she would bear was his own. The plot was fiendishly clever, but Uriah failed to cooperate. As a soldier he knew that his companions at the front were dying. It was inappropriate, he felt, to go home to his wife. Perhaps he believed that sexual relations with his wife would weaken him, and incapacitate him for the tasks ahead. Some have suggested that he was suspicious of David's motivation. In any event, by refusing to go home, Uriah signed his death warrant.

Since Uriah would not go home, David resorted to a new strategem. He dispatched a message to his field commander, Joab: "Set Uriah in the forefront of the hardest fighting, and then draw back from him, that he may be struck down and die" (II Sam. 11:15). This was murder just as truly as if David had personally killed Uriah with his own sword.

The order was carried out. Joab placed Uriah in the place of greatest danger, and in the fighting that took place outside Rabbah — modern Amman, the capital of Jordan — Joab was killed. A messenger brought David word that the fighting had gone against his armies. The people of Rabbah had tried to lift the siege, and many Israelites were killed — including Uriah.

David's response was the height of hypocrisy: "Do not let this matter trouble you, for the sword devours now one and now another; strengthen your attack upon the city, and overthrow it" (II Sam. 11:25). Wars involve casualties. Such is life! Try harder next time. All will be well. David's plans were working according to schedule.

There can be no question that David's two-fold sin — murder and adultery — is one of the blackest recorded in or out of the Bible. David was not acting as "the man after God's own heart" but as an absolute tyrant who used his power to cater to his own lusts. He was no better than others of his or later ages who are corrupted with power. We are shocked not at his sin, which was common enough, but at the fact that it was David who committed such sin. We expect better things of our Biblical heroes.

Yet here is where we see the Biblical concept of kingship in action. That a king committed adultery and tried to cover it with a murder was not unique to Israel. That a prophet challenged that king and pronounced the judgments of Yahweh upon him because of his sins — and lived to see another day — was unique. The king was Yahweh's anointed. He was not above law but was subject to the Law of God. Nathan, the prophet, addressed the king in the language of parable. In a certain city there was a rich man who had large flocks and herds. Near him lived a poor man who had only one lamb, which he and his family loved as a pet. A stranger visited the rich man, but he was unwilling to take of his abundant flocks to feed the guest. Instead he took the poor man's lamb and prepared it as a meal. David in anger stated that the rich man, utterly devoid of pity, deserved to die. Nathan quietly replied, "You are the man."

Nathan declared that David would suffer as a result of his sin. The sword would not depart from David's house. Tragedy would stalk his days (II Sam. 12:10-15). The child about to be born to Bath-sheba would die. And so it happened. Although David fasted and prayed, refusing to eat food or to accept consolation, his child died on the seventh day.

After the ordeal of losing their first child, David and Bath-sheba had a child that lived — Solomon, later to become king. Yet the prophecies of Nathan were to come true. One of David's sons, Amnon, raped his half-sister Tamar, the sister of Absalom. When he then rejected her, she told her brother Absalom, who plotted revenge. During festivities at the time of sheep-shearing, Absalom had his servants strike and kill Amnon (II Sam. 13:23-29). Then Absalom fled to the home of his maternal grandfather, remaining at Geshur for three years.

Finally Joab determined to arrange a reconciliation between David and Absalom. He arranged with a woman of Tekoa to come to David with a story about a widow whose sons had quarreled until one son killed the other. She feared to surrender the murderer lest her entire family be obliterated (II Sam. 14:5-7). David immediately became interested in the woman's problem, and promised assistance. As he continued talking with her he realized that Joab had arranged for the interview as a means of asking David to welcome back Absalom. The king accepted the message, and promptly ordered that Absalom be permitted

Two shepherd boys on the open hills near Tekoa.

to return to Jerusalem (II Sam. 14:23-24).

Absalom lived in his own house in Jerusalem for two years before he saw his father, David. During this time he probably conceived the idea of revolt. He was a fine looking young man, and he consciously tried to win the favor of the people. As David was once the young, glamorous warrior in contrast to the older Saul, now David is of the older generation and Absalom captivates the people. He sympathized with people who felt they were wronged, and hinted that he would give them justice if he were only king (II Sam. 15:1-6). After four years he felt strong enough to plot a coup. He found a following at Hebron, which may have resented the fact that David had moved his capital to Jerusalem. David's counselor, Ahithophel, joined the forces of Absalom. The king and his retinue including the palace guard and the priests and Levites left Jerusalem, crossing the Kidron with David. David, however, ordered that the ark be returned to Jerusalem, an act which indicated that he hoped to return. Continuing to flee from Jerusalem, he encountered Shimei of the house of Saul who taunted the king, counting his troubles a just recompense for the blood of the house of Saul (II Sam. 16:5-8). David did not punish Shimei, humbly accepting his abuse.

As David was reaching the Jordan, Absalom was entering Jerusalem in triumph. Following the counsel of Ahithophel, Absalom publicly took his father's concubines, a dramatic way of laying claim to the throne (II Sam. 16:20-23). Then he rejected Ahithophel's advice that he strike at David immediately. Hushai, really on David's side, suggested that Absalom gather an army of men from Dan to Beer-sheba — a policy that would take time and give David an opportunity to prepare his forces (II Sam. 17:11-12). When Hushai's counsel was accepted, Ahithophel hanged himself in disgrace (II Sam. 17:23).

Finally Absalom felt that he was ready to pursue David across the Jordan. Amasa was commander of Absalom's forces, and Joab remained loyal to David. Finally the two armies met in the Forest of Ephraim. David was torn between emotions of love for a son and desire to protect his throne. He wanted victory, but he gave orders that Absalom not be personally harmed (II Sam. 18:5). As it happened, Absalom's mule passed under the branches of an oak tree, and Absalom's head was caught in the oak. The young man who reported the incident to Joab did not

The pool at Gibeon.

know what to do, but Joab did not hesitate. He took three darts in his hand, and thrust them into the heart of Absalom (II Sam. 18:14). Then Joab sounded the trumpet. Absalom was buried under a heap of stones, and a messenger brought word of the victory to David. David, however, was brokenhearted at the message of Absalom's death. In anguish he cried, "O my son Absalom, my son, my son Absalom! Would I had died instead of you, O Absalom, my son, my son!" (II Sam. 18:33).

David and the armies had proved victorious, but the moment of triumph lost much of its joy because of David's attitude. Finally Joab warned David of the seriousness of the situation. Men had risked their lives on David's behalf, and the king was acting as though he would have preferred that they die and his rebellious son live (II Sam. 19:1-8). Joab told David frankly that he should appear before the people or he would lose their loyalty. The king accepted the rebuke.

With the knowledge that Absalom was dead, the tribes of Israel acquiesced in the rule of David. Problems and rivalries between north and south were to flare up periodically, but David's throne had been preserved. He was magnanimous in treating the partisans of Absalom in an effort to recover a degree of normalcy (II Sam. 19).

After the revolt of Absalom we find a Benjaminite named Sheba leading an uprising against David. Sheba was from Saul's tribe, and he was one of the Benjaminites who rejected David's rule. Sheba sounded the cry of independence and war, "We have no portion in David, and we have no inheritance in the son of Jesse; every man to his tents, O Israel!" (II Sam. 20:1). Judah remained true to David, but Sheba found a large following in the north. David called upon Amasa, who had replaced Joab as David's commander, to assemble the men of Judah to put down the revolt. Amasa, however, delayed in collecting the forces of Judah; so David called upon Abishai, Joab's brother, to take to the field against Sheba. Joab, of course, soon took the initiative himself, joined by David's guard of Cherethites and Pelethites. Amasa joined the fighting men at the great stone in Gibeon, but Joab would not tolerate his presence in the camp. Taking Amasa by the beard as though to kiss him, Joab struck Amasa to the ground with one fatal stroke of his sword.

With his rival gone, Joab and Abishai pursued Sheba. Amasa's dead body was left in a field by the side of the road with a garment thrown over it, and the warriors continued northward until they came to Abel of Beth-maacah where Sheba had taken refuge. While Joab and his men were battering the wall of the city in order to take Sheba, a wise woman called down from the city to suggest a way of saving Abel. She offered to throw the head of Sheba to Joab, and he agreed to spare the city under those terms. She lived up to her bargain, and Sheba was murdered and decapitated in Abel.

Abel had been an oracle city in years before the time of David. The wise woman declared, "They were wont to say in old time, 'Let them but ask counsel at Abel'; and so they settled a matter" (II Sam. 20:18). Debir, in the Judean hills, seems to have had a similar reputation, for the name itself means "oracle." Like the Greeks of historical times, the ancient Canaanites evidently had holy places to which they went for an answer to their problems. On occasion at least, the oracle was a wise woman whose knowledge of human nature equipped her to render decisions in perplexing situations. Here the wise woman was instrumental in saving her own city from destruction at the hand of Joab and his forces.

The village of Gibeon (center), looking north.

The next tragedy to face David was a famine which persisted throughout the land for three years. During this time David learned that Saul had not kept the covenant made between Joshua and the Gibeonites (cf. Josh. 9:3-27). Saul had broken the agreement and murdered a number of the Gibeonites. David concluded that the famine was a punishment for this act of Saul, and he set about to make expiation. All of nature would be out of joint until the wrong had been righted; so the Gibeonites demanded that seven members of the family of Saul be executed (II Sam. 21:6). Mephibosheth, the son of Jonathan, was spared but seven other members of the house of Saul were hanged (II Sam. 21:7-10).

The hanging took place at the beginning of the barley harvest, in late April or May. The bodies of Rizpah's two sons and the five others of Saul's family were exposed, unburied for the entire summer until the autumn rains came. In honor to the dead, Rizpah watched over the bodies to preserve them from the birds and animals which would normally devour the dead. Exposure was evidently part of the expiation demanded by the Gibeonites, but David was moved by the loyalty of Rizpah and ordered a proper burial. The bones of those who had been hanged, along with the bones of Saul and Jonathan taken from Jabesh-gilead were buried in the family tomb of Kish, Saul's father (II Sam. 21:10:14).

The wrath of God which resulted from David's census comes at the close of a series of tragedies which plagued David's last days (II Sam. 24:1-17). With the aid of Joab and the army the entire land "from Dan to Beer-sheba" on both sides of the Jordan was covered in nine months and twenty days. Joab reported that there were eight hundred thousand fighting men in Israel, and five hundred thousand in Judah — round figures, of course.

A census was never popular in the East. It had as its purpose the gathering of information for purposes of military conscription and taxation, neither of which were popular with the people. After taking the census, David had an uneasy conscience (II Sam. 24:10) fearing that he had done wrong. The prophet Gad confirmed the fact that he had yielded to temptation and suggested that God's judgment would come upon him in one of three ways. The land might experience three years of famine, or David might flee three months before his enemies, or pestilence might come upon the land for three days (I Sam. 24:12-13). Trusting the mercy of the Lord rather than the wrath of his enemies, David accepted a period of pestilence which filled the land and threatened Jerusalem itself. When the messenger of the Lord was at the threshingfloor of Araunah, his hand was stayed and the plague ended. Then Gad, the prophet, told David to erect an altar of Araunah's threshingfloor. David purchased the threshingfloor and the animals for the sacrifices which he made, and the plague ended.

The site of Araunah's threshingfloor later became the site of Solomon's Temple. David thus prepared the way for the building of the Temple, although it was his son Solomon who would see the sacred structure rise.

The last days of David were marked by senility. Abishag, a young girl from Shumen in the Plain of Esdraelon, was brought to the court to care for the king. Sexually, David proved to be impotent. The fact of David's impotence may have been interpreted as reason for seeking a successor. A king who was sexually dead could not be trusted to rule the people.

39

Solomon in All His Glory

As David reached senility, the factions in his court at Jerusalem were giving serious thought to the question of succession. David's oldest living son, Adonijah, seemed to be the logical choice. Joab, David's general, and the priest Abiathar were among those who were prepared to anoint Adonijah. There were important segments of the court that were not included in these plans. Benaiah, commander of David's personal bodyguard, wielded considerable power. Nathan, David's court prophet and personal counselor, was not ready to support Adonijah, preferring Solomon, the surviving son of Bath-sheba.

While the partisans of Adonijah were offering sacrifices, preliminary to the anointing, Nathan made his way to Bath-sheba to warn her of the impending coup. Although Nathan had denounced David for his affair with Bath-sheba, he now sided with her in her desire to see Solomon on the throne of Israel. In spite of the way in which David's relation with Bath-sheba had begun, the king seems to have developed a close relationship with her, and even Nathan had come to accept her. Bath-sheba reminded David that he had vowed that her son Solomon would succeed to the throne (I Kings 1:17). Adonijah might be expected to purge the land of all possible rivals, with the result that Bath-sheba and Solomon would be killed (1:21).

When Nathan gave further details concerning Adonijah's plans, David determined to act at once. Zadok the priest and Nathan the prophet were instructed to bring Solomon to the Gihon, now called the Virgin's Fountain, a short distance north of En-rogel, "Job's Well," where Adonijah's partisans were assembled. A curve in the valley of the Kidron made it impossible for the two groups to see one another, but they were well within earshot of one another. With the aid of Benaiah and the royal guard, Zadok and Nathan anointed Solomon, and the assembled crowd cried out, "Long live King Solomon" (1:39). The scene was joyful, with singing and the playing of instruments to commemorate the occasion.

Around the bend in the valley, however, the partisans of Adonijah heard the sound and puzzled over its meaning. Finally Jonathan, Abiathar's son, arrived with news that King David had ordered the anointing of Solomon as king. Adonijah realized that he could not hope to stand against the forces of David, so he rushed into the temple and sought sanctuary at the altar. A person touching the projections from the altar ("horns") was not supposed to be slain, and Adonijah determined to stay in the sanctuary until he would get a promise of safety from Solomon. Solomon was cautious, stating that Adonijah would not be harmed as long as he behaved himself (1:52). For the moment Adonijah felt that he was safe.

David died shortly after Solomon took the throne. In his old age a girl from Shunem had been brought to minister to the king. Had he been younger he might have married her, but the Biblical writer tells us "the king knew her not" (1:4), i.e. he had no marital relations with her.

Whatever his motives, Adonijah certainly showed a lack of judgment in approaching Bath-sheba and asking her to intercede with Solomon to permit him to marry Abishag. Such a request could be interpreted as a claim to the kingdom, for a king normally laid claim to his predecessor's harem. Solomon put the worst possible construction on the request, and in anger said to Bath-sheba, "Ask for him the kingdom also . . . !" (2:22). Solomon sent Benaiah, captain of the guard, to kill Adonijah.

Since Abiathar was a priest, Solomon did not order his execution for having taken Adonijah's side. Abiathar had been an honored priest during David's reign, and Solomon was content to banish him to his estate in Anathoth, about three miles north of Jerusalem. Joab, however, did not fare so well. Realizing that Solomon was purging the partisans of Adonijah, Joab fled to the altar and sought sanctuary. Benaiah hesitated to strike him down at a holy place, but Solomon showed no mercy. For justification he could invoke the law of blood revenge. Joab had slain Amasa, one time leader of Absalom's army, and Abner, Saul's commander who had shifted allegiance from Saul's son,

Ishbosheth, to David. At Solomon's command Benaiah killed Joab and succeeded him as commander of the army. Zadok, who had sided with Solomon against Adonijah, became High Priest in place of the deposed Abiathar.

The purge continued as Solomon sought to limit the movements of Shimei, the Benjaminite who had accused David of complicity in the extermination of Saul's house (II Sam. 16:5-8). David, who had not lifted his hand against any of the house of Saul, spared Shimei, but Solomon restricted him to Jerusalem. When Shimei pursued two fugitive slaves to Gath he incurred the wrath of Solomon. Again Benaiah was dispatched to execute an offender. Solomon had purged his realm of real and imaginary foes. Presumably he could now rule without fear.

The personal life of Solomon is full of those contradictions which plague us all. At times he seems a saint, and at other times a scoundrel. History has dealt kindly with Solomon; perhaps too kindly. We choose to remember him as a man of wisdom, forgetting that he was a man of his age and that in many facets of his life he exhibited the worst features of life as it was lived three millennia ago.

Solomon's domestic life is a case in point. Early in his career he married an Egyptian princess (I Kings 3:1), no mean accomplishment in itself. In a day when Egypt was stronger and Israel weaker, a Pharaoh might take an Israelite girl into his harem, but he certainly would not have given one of his daughters to an Israelite king. During the reigns of David and Solomon, Israel reached its highest level of international prestige. At such a time marriage can become a matter of diplomatic convenience: "Solomon made a marriage alliance with Pharaoh" (I Kings 3:1). This was not Solomon's only "marriage alliance." We are told that he had "seven hundred wives, princesses, and three hundred concubines" (I Kings 11:3). A large harem was the result of such alliances, and it also suggests the oriental grandeur which had come to mark Solomon's court. The king of a major state must have a harem worthy of his position. The larger it was, the more prestige would be accounted to the monarch. In simple language, a large harem was a status symbol, and Solomon was interested in status. It is hard to realize that only three generations passed between the days when Saul reigned from his humble court at Gibeah, to the magnificence of Solomon in all his glory. Externally these were years of progress, yet trouble was already on the horizon. Solomon's wives came from many nations, and they worshiped many gods. As a kind husband, Solomon permitted them to build shrines to their deities. Before long we find Solomon, himself, enmeshed in idolatry.

If Solomon puzzles and annoys us with his large harem, he pleases us with his quest for wisdom. As a young king he offered sacrifices to his God at Gibeon. In a dream, Solomon heard the voice of the Lord saying, "Ask what I shall give you" (I Kings 3:5). Solomon is at his best in his reply. He acknowledged the blessings of God upon him, his own inexperience: "I am but a little child," and his lack of knowledge: "I do not know how to go out or come in" (I Kings 3:7). In humility he prayed, "Give thy servant therefore an understanding mind to govern thy people, that I may discern between good and evil" (3:9).

From this time on, Solomon's wisdom became proverbial. The Near East had had a long tradition of Wisdom Literature stretching back to the Egypt and Mesopotamia of the third millennium B.C. Yet, the Biblical historian tells us, Solomon's wisdom "surpassed all the wisdom of all the people of the east, and all the wisdom of Egypt" (4:30). Traditionally the books of Proverbs, Ecclesiastes, and the Song of Solomon have been attributed to him, although the hand of other wise men is occasionally evident in them.[1]

The practical nature of the wisdom Solomon sought is evident in the story of two harlots who had each given birth to a child. One of the infants died, but both women claimed the surviving child as her own. Solomon suggested a solution: "Divide the living child in two and give half to the one and half to the other." One of the women was content to accept the king's solution to the problem, but the living child's mother suggested that the child be given to the other woman, and not slain (3:16-28). The woman who showed concern for the child above her own rights proved to be the mother of the child, and Solomon ordered that the child be given to her.

---

1. Proverbs 25:1 tells us that proverbs attributed to Solomon were gathered into collections as late as the time of Hezekiah. Proverbs 30:1 and 31:1 name Agur and Lemuel (or Lemuel's mother) as authors of collections of proverbs.

That the fame of Solomon spread to distant lands is evident from the story of the visit to Solomon's court of the Queen of Sheba, a land in southern Arabia about twelve hundred miles from Jerusalem. This queen from the area that we know as Yemen was doubtless willing to make the long journey to Jerusalem in order to meet Israel's wise king and to negotiate trade agreements with him. The queen brought a large caravan bearing spices, gold, and precious stones for Solomon. In return, Solomon dealt generously with her, giving her all that she might desire when she returned home. Solomon showed his wisdom in the answers he gave to her hard questions, and the queen observed, "The report was true which I heard in my own land of your affairs and your wisdom, but I did not believe the reports until I came and my own eyes had seen it; and, behold, the half was not told me; your wisdom and prosperity surpass the report which I heard" (9:6-7).

Tradition has added to the story of Solomon and the Queen of Sheba. Ethiopian legend tells of a child of Solomon and the Queen of Sheba who became king and established a Davidic dynasty in Ethiopia. The legend suggests the close connections which existed in antiquity between southern Arabia and eastern Africa. Arabian legends name the Queen of Sheba, Bilqis.

King Solomon was an able organizer, and he gave a form to the political life of Israel such as it never had before. In his court we find the chief priest, royal scribes or secretaries, a recorder, a military commander, a palace governor, the chief of the corvee (forced labor batallions) and other priests and counselors (I Kings 4:1-6).

The country was divided into twelve administrative districts, each of which had a governor who was responsible for providing for the royal household one month a year. The twelve districts did not follow the older tribal lines, a fact which may indicate that Solomon wished to break down old tribal loyalties in the interest of a strong centralized government.

Although best known for the Temple which he built, Solomon built and enlarged many other structures in Jerusalem and elsewhere. He spent thirteen years on his palace and administrative complex (I Kings 7:1-12). Solomon expanded the Jerusalem fortifications and built fortresses in strategic parts of

A restoration of Megiddo of the Iron Age (top) and a reconstruction of the Solomonic gate at Megiddo (below).

the country. Hazor held the key to the far north, and Megiddo protected the Esdraelon Valley. The fortress at Gezer overlooked the Aijalon and the Sorek valleys.

After twenty years of major construction work, Solomon found it difficult to pay his debts. As time went on he found it increasingly difficult to pressure the people into paying higher taxes, and tribute from subject states became increasingly hard to collect. In his extremity Solomon had to cede twenty cities in Galilee to Hiram of Tyre for a cash consideration (I Kings 9:10-14).

Solomon is not remembered as a warrior, but he did give considerable attention to problems of defense. Not only was Jerusalem fortified, but Solomon developed a chain of cities along the perimeter of Israel to provide defense against raids from Israel's neighbors. Hazor in Galilee faced Aramean territory; Meggiddo faced the main pass through the Valley of Esdraelon; Gezer, Beth-horon, and Baalah guarded the western approaches to Israel from the maritime plain, and Tamar, south of the Dead Sea faced Edom (I Kings 9:15-19).

From these strongholds, Solomon could easily maneuver his forces to meet external threats or internal emergencies. In earlier days the mountainous terrain of Israelite territory discouraged the use of chariots. Canaanites found them useful on level ground, but Israelites felt no need for them. With the annexation of Canaanite city-states into Israel, Solomon determined to develop chariot warfare as part of his defense system. We read that he had fourteen hundred chariots and twelve thousand horsemen stationed in Jerusalem and in the chariot cities (I Kings 11:26). Excavations at Megiddo have brought to light stables for four hundred fifty horses, along with city fortifications and the governor's residence. Similar installations have been discovered during excavations at Hazor, Taanach, Eglon, and Gezer. Evidence suggests that Solomon maintained a large standing army as part of his military strategy.

Solomon's age was one in which Israelite trade and commerce flourished by land and sea. Ezion-geber served as the terminal port for trade with southern Arabia (I Kings 9:26-28). This port at the north end of the Gulf of Aqabah, contained a copper and iron smelting refinery, was strongly walled, and located two and one-half miles west of the old city of Elath, modern Aqabah. This site, now known as Tell el-Kheleifeh, stood in the path of winds which howled down the Arabah Valley and provided a natural draft for firing the furnaces. Ores were mined in the Arabah valley which is still rich in copper.

Hiram of Tyre assisted Solomon in building and maintaining a merchant fleet. The Phoenicians of Tyre were old hands at sea trade, for their principal cities were on the Mediterranean coast and Tyrian mariners early built ships and set out for the islands and coastlands bordering the Mediterranean. It was these very mariners who taught their Greek counterparts the use of the alphabet. The best known of their colonies was Carthage, in Africa, which vied with Rome at a later day for control of the Mediterranean.

With Hiram's help, Solomon developed a fleet which brought gold, sandlewood, and precious stones to Jerusalem (I Kings 10:11). Solomon had to import horses for his chariotry. These came from Egypt and from Kue in Cilicia, southeastern Asia Minor. Rulers of the neo-Hittite principalities of northern Syria looked to Solomon for their horses and chariots (I Kings 10:29).

Solomon's merchant fleet went on long journeys, bringing back such exotic items as ivory, apes, and peacocks (or baboons, in an alternate translation). Ships left the port at Ezion-geber and visited the coastal ports of Africa where such items were secured by trade. The Biblical writer tells us that ships returned with these items but once in three years (I Kings 10:22).

More regular was the tribute in silver, gold, garments, myrrh, spices, horses, and mules which tributary kings brought annually to Solomon's court (I Kings 10:23-24). From the standpoint of material grandeur, the era of Solomon was never to be equalled in the history of Israel.

There is, however, a negative side to all of this. Like Saul and David, Solomon was to experience a series of tragedies during the closing years of his reign. His wives and concubines influenced him in the direction of idolatory, so that Solomon, himself, came to worship the gods of the Sidonians, the Ammonites and the Moabites (I Kings 11:5-8). A crowning insult to Yahweh, God of Israel, was the erection of a shrine for the god Molech on the Mount of Olives, east of Jerusalem. The worship of Molech was associated with the sacrifice of children in fire (cf. Lev. 18:21; II Kings 23:10).

During this period of decline we find the beginning of disintegration within Solomon's empire. Hadad, a member of the royal family of Edom, had fled to Egypt when David conquered

A reconstruction of Solomon's stables based on the excavations at Megiddo.

The Araba. Solomon exploited the copper mines in this region. The factory in this scene is used for desalinating sea water.

Edom, but he returned to lead a revolt against Solomon in the interest of Edomite independence (I Kings 11:14-22). Rezon, an Aramean, set up an independent kingdom at Damascus in Syria. He was successful in defying Solomon, outlived the Israelite United Kingdom and established his own dynasty in Damascus.

Even more threatening was Jeroboam the son of Nebat who was in charge of the forced labor units from the Joseph tribes — Ephraim and Manasseh. On day a prophet named Ahijah from Shiloh met Jeroboam on the road. The prophet took his garment, tore it into twelve pieces and gave ten of them to Jeroboam. In explanation he stated that God was about to tear the kingdom from Solomon and give ten of the twelve tribes to Jeroboam (I Kings 11:30). Ahijah, like others who remembered the happier days before Solomon's court had taken on a cosmopolitan air, felt that God was about to judge the king for his idolatry.

When Solomon learned of Jeroboam's ambition he determined to kill him, but Jeroboam fled to Egypt where Shishak was king. At the beginning of Solomon's reign a Pharaoh of Egypt had given his daughter as Solomon's wife. Now a Pharaoh offered refuge to Solomon's enemy. Egypt had seen a change of dynasty, and relations between Israel and Egypt had seriously deteriorated.

The kingdom held together to the end of Solomon's life, but the king who was noted for his wisdom brought the kingdom to the verge of bankruptcy. Within a short time after Solomon's death the prophecy of Ahijah was fulfilled and the Davidic dynasty was limited to the south. Solomon was the last king of the United Kingdom.

40

Solomon's Temple

The crowning achievement of Solomon's reign was the construction of a Temple to the God of Israel. David had made Jerusalem his political and religious capital, and had directed that the sacred ark he brought to the Holy City. During the days of wilderness wandering the Israelites had used a portable shrine, the Tabernacle, as their sanctuary. Now that they were settled in their land, a permanent shrine seemed to be demanded.

Between the fourth and the eleventh years of his reign, Solomon supervised the construction of a small but elegant Temple. Like the Tabernacle which preceded it, the Temple was not designed to accomodate worshipers. Its inner shrine was regarded as God's Throne Room, and it was entered but once a year — on the Day of Atonement — by the High Priest. Priests had access to the outer shrine — the Holy Place — where they would replenish the supplies of oil, incense, and bread.

Since the site of Solomon's Temple has been occupied through the centuries, archaeological studies of the site have not been made. Some light on Syro-Palestinian temples has come from the discovery of an eighth century B.C. temple at Tell Tainat, ancient Hattina, in Syria. The basic ground plan of the Tainat temple is similar to that described in I Kings.

Solomon drew upon his alliance with Hiram of Tyre to procure skilled Phoenician workmen (I Kings 5:6). A contingent came from Gebal (Byblos) to assist in the work. Thirty-thousand Israelites were used in procuring materials (5:13). At the time the Temple was built, Israel enjoyed the prestige and wealth of a nation to which tribute was paid by subject states. No expense was spared in building the Temple. The use of forced labor, however, became very unpopular and it added to Solomon's heartaches during the closing years of his reign.

The Temple was a long, narrow structure, about one hundred feet long and thirty feet wide. At the front was a vestibule, or entrance hall with windows, the number and size of which is not specified. Beyond the vestibule was the Holy Place which was the main room of the Temple. Next, in the form of a perfect cube of twenty cubits in each direction, was the inner shrine, the Most Holy Place.

Around the entire structure, except the vestibule, were side chambers, arranged in three stories. We are not sure how these were divided into rooms, but Temple treasures were assuredly kept in these chambers. The Temple was approached by ten broad steps, with two landings in the flight providing space for ceremonial processions. To the right and the left of the steps were two free standing pillars called Jachin and Boaz. Jachin means "he [God] establishes," and Boaz means, "In Him [God] is strength." The significance of the names for the pillars has been debated, but scholars are not agreed. The pillars were cast in the clay of the Jordan valley, and made of burnished copper. According to the Biblical text they were nearly forty feet high, with a diameter of about six and one-half feet. They appear to have been hollow, with the metal four fingers (about three inches) thick.

The basic material for the Temple was white limestone, finished at the quarries by Hebrew and Phoenician laborers (I Kings 5:18; 6:7). The interior walls were covered with cedar, and the floor with boards of Cyprus so that no stone could be seen from the inside. According to the English translations, much of the cedar wood was overlaid with gold (6:21), but W. F. Stinespring is probably right in suggesting that inlay rather than overlay is intended.[1] Ivory inlay is well known from excavations at Samaria, and it is likely that similar techniques were used with gold. The inside walls were carved with figures of cherubim, palm trees, and flowers (6:29).

There was no door to the vestibule, but large elaborately decorated doors opened into the Holy Place (6:33-35). A smaller double door, with similar decorations, opened into the Holy of Holies (6:31-32). Within the Holy of Holies were two huge cherubim of gold-trimmed olivewood. They were each ten cubits high, with a wingspread of ten cubits. They faced the front so that a wing of each cherub touched the wall, and the other two

Boats transport logs, some carried on board and some towed behind. The logs are from the famed cedars of Lebanon. This relief is from the palace of Sargon at Khorsabad.

1. "Temple, Jerusalem," Interpreter's Dictionary of the Bible, IV, p. 537.

wings touched in the center of the room. Beneath these wings the ark of the covenant was placed (8:6-7).

Within the Holy Place we find a number of articles of gold. Here was the golden Altar of Incense standing before the steps to the Holy of Holies. Five lampstands stood on each side of the entrance to the Holy of Holies, and nearby stood the table for the "Bread of the Presence" or "shewbread." Fresh loaves of bread were brought to the sanctuary each sabbath, and the old loaves were eaten by the priests.

Outside the Temple proper, but within the court we find the great altar for burnt offering, made of bronze, and the huge basin known as the "molten sea" with a capacity of two thousand baths, or approximately ten thousand gallons. The molten sea was ten cubits (about seventeen and one-half feet) in diameter, thirty cubits in circumference, and ten cubits deep. It was a handbreadth thick, and was decorated with two rows of gourds all the way around. The cup-like brim resembled the flower of a lily.

This huge basin rested on twelve bronze bulls, arranged in groups of three, each facing one of the four points of the compass. The author of II Chronicles (4:6) suggests that the molten sea was a place for ceremonial washing by the priests as they prepared to minister in the Temple. Modern scholars see a cosmic symbolism in the molten sea, suggesting that water or the sea is frequently a source of life in Near Eastern mythology. The bulls on which the basin rested may also be likened to representations of the fecundity principle in the Baal cult. In view of the Phoenician artisans and craftsmen who assisted in the building of the Temple, such symbolism may have been intended. The faithful Yahwist in Israel, however, would have rejected pagan symbolism, and would have seen the molten sea as a laver of cleansing for the priest as he would prepare to enter the Sanctuary.

We also find ten highly ornamented bronze wagons, on each of which was mounted one of the ten lavers, or wash basins, in the Temple court. Each of the lavers had a capacity of forty baths (about two hundred gallons). These would serve the priesthood in their ceremonial washings (I Kings 7:27-39).

The splendor and artistry of Solomon's Temple suggests the prestige which Israel enjoyed during the Solomonic age. King Hiram of Tyre sent an architect-artisan, also named Hiram (I Kings 7:13) to the court of Solomon to work on the Temple. He

An interior view of the Dome of the Rock located on the temple site at Jerusalem.

cast the bronze pillars, the molten sea, and other furnishings of the Temple in specially suited clay found in the Jordan Valley between Succoth and Zarethan. Seven years of Solomon's career were spent in the building of the Temple which stood as the center of religious life in Judah until the destruction of Jerusalem by the forces of Nebuchadnezzar in 587 B.C.

41

Israel and the Phoenicians

The northern coastal regions of the Syria-Palestine area, comprising such cities as Tyre, Sidon, and Byblos, were known in ancient times as Phoenicia. The name is the Greek equivalent of the word Canaan, which appears in the form *kinahhu* in the Nuzi texts, with the meaning, "purple." Greek *phoinix* has the same meaning. When used of the Phoenician people it refers to the industry of dyeing fabrics with purple derived from the murex shellfish, which is indigenous to the area which we know as Phoenicia. Since the area was divided into independent city states, our texts are more apt to speak of Tyrians or Sidonians than Phoenicians or Canaanites, yet the culture was sufficiently homogenous to warrant consideration in its own right.

Geography made the life and goals of the Phoenicians differ in a marked degree from that of other Semitic peoples of the Near East, including the Israelites. The distinctive area of the Phoenician cities was bounded by the Lebanon Mountains to the east, and the Mediterranean to the west. The distance between mountains and sea varies from seven to thirty miles. Northern and southern boundaries varied, but Phoenicia was always a narrow strip of land with small valleys bringing water from the mountains, making the land the most fertile of the entire Near East, as visitors to Lebanon observe today.

Rocky promontories stretch into the Mediterranean, and the Phoenicians frequently used them for building cities with harbors that might face both north and south. Roads were difficult to build in this rocky terrain, but sea travel was always at hand, and the Phoenicians excelled as mariners. Instead of building a land empire, thus clashing with Israelite and Philistine goals, the Phoenicians colonized the islands and coastlands of the Mediterranean. Best known of these colonies was Carthage in North

Cedars of Lebanon before a snow-lined slope.

Africa which challenged Roman control of the Mediterranean at a much later time. Vergil in his Aenead has Aeneas forsake Dido of Carthage because destiny has called him to become the ancestor of the Romans in Italy. Dido's curses upon him form a rationale for the subsequent hatred between Carthaginian and Roman. Like other Phoenicians (Canaanites), the Carthaginian pantheon included the god Baal. The great Hannibal had a name comparable to Biblical Hananiah, the former meaning "Baal has been gracious," and the latter, "Yahweh has been gracious."

It was during these journeys of Phoenician mariners that the Semitic alphabet was passed on to the Greeks, another seafaring people. The Greeks modified the Semitic alphabet for their own purposes and, with later modifications, this alphabet is used throughout the West today. Even the Russian alphabet is derived from the Greek, introduced as it was by missionaries in the process of bringing Christianity to the slavic peoples.

Although the extent of arable land was limited, the Phoenicians grew figs, olives, grapes, and wheat. The date palm was abundant in ancient times, as were the cedars which were famous throughout the Near East. Expeditions came from Egypt and Mesopotamia to procure this fine wood for use in temples, palaces, and sacred barges. The cedars are nearly depleted, and the state of Lebanon is preserving the remaining groves as state property.

Phoenician history must be reconstructed from a variety of ancient sources. While we have a corpus of ancient Phoenician inscriptions, they do not enable us to recognize any coherent pattern. They mention individual rulers of Phoenician cities and, on occasion, dynastic successions. Dedicatory inscriptions appear on Phoenician monuments, and the protective deities are frequently invoked. Tenth century Byblos provided many such texts, but on the whole information is scanty.

Although writing in the first century of the Christian era, Josephus quotes valuable matter for understanding Phoenician history from Menander of Ephesus. Menander quoted from a work known as the Annals of Tyre, and his references relate events from the tenth to the eighth centuries, and from the sixth century B.C. Compared with Biblical material and other ancient sources, these quotations appear to be accurate.

Egyptian and Assyrian texts provide a further source of information. The Assyrian annals describe the subjugation of

Phoenician cities during campaigns of the Assyrian kings in western Asia. The Egyptian tale of Wenamun shows that Egyptian prestige had suffered greatly in Phoenician by the middle of the eleventh century B.C.

The invasions of the Sea Peoples, peoples from the Aegean area, about 1200 B.C. had important results throughout the eastern Mediterranean. The Hittite Empire of Asia Minor fell, as did the Phoenician states of Aradus and Sidon. The Egyptian Empire entered a period of weakness from which it never fully recovered, and Assyria was confined within her borders. With the major powers at least temporarily checked, the smaller Hebrew, Aramaean, and Phoenician states emerged as independent units, sometimes co-operating and sometimes fighting one another.

The leading Phoenician cities of the time were Aradus, Byblos (Gebal), Sidon, Tyre, and Akko. The term "Sidonians" is used both in the Old Testament and in Homer for the Phoenicians in general, leading to the conclusion that Sidon was the dominant city of the period. Josephus states that Sidon was defeated by the king of the Ascalonians — Askelon being a Philistine city, and Philistines were among the "Sea Peoples" — at a date which seems to have been shortly after 1200 B.C. According to Josephus, the defeated Sidonians fled to the area of Tyre and founded the city. While Tyre is known to have existed prior to this time, it is possible that the city had been sacked by the Sea Peoples and was rebuilt by the Sidonians. Sidon was the principal Phoenician city until about 1000 B.C., after which Tyre came to dominate the area.

While we might expect that Philistines, Phoenicians, and Israelites would be major rivals in the Syria-Palestine area, the Bible indicates friendly relations between Israel and Phoenicia. It is possible that David included portions of the Phoenician coast in his kingdom.[1] That Tyre remained independent, however, is obvious from the fact that Hiram, its king, provided David with craftsmen and cedar wood for his palace (II Sam. 5:11).

Our knowledge of relations between Hiram and David's successor, Solomon, are more complete. The Annals present Hiram as a builder in his own right. He is said to have enlarged the city

The Phoenician port city of Byblos and the Mediterranean Sea.

---

1. The census account of II Sam. 24:6-7 mentions the regions of Tyre and Sidon.

and to have built new temples to Melqart (Heracles) and Astarte. An impressive golden column was erected in the temple
of Baal Shamem (Zeus Olympus). A war was fought with Kition,
the Phoenician colony of Cyprus, because its inhabitants refused
to pay tribute.[2]

When Solomon determined to build a Temple to Yahweh, he
drew upon the experience of Hiram and requested cedar and
fir trees for use in its construction (I Kings 5:1-11). For his part,
Solomon provided wheat and oil as payment to the Tyrian king.
Evidently Solomon found himself unable to provide adequate
payment for the materials and artisans which Hiram provided,
for he ceded twenty Galilean cities to the Tyrians (I Kings
9:10-14).

The fact that Solomon enlisted the cooperation of Hiram in
sending ships from Ezion-geber into the Red Sea and beyond, is
testimonial both to the wealth of Solomon's kingdom and the
maritime skill of the Phoenicians. Israel was basically a land
state, and it was prudent of Solomon to enlist the aid of the seafaring Phoenicians in his commercial venture to the land of
Ophir (I Kings 9:26-28). The location of Ophir is much disputed, with India, southern Arabia, and Somaliland in Africa
being suggested. While it is unlikely that Solomon's ships traded
directly with India, they brought back exotic products including
gold, silver, ivory, and apes (I Kings 10:22). Such items may
have been secured in Africa or southern Arabia.

The combined Israelite-Tyrian expeditions were evidently
successful, for we are told that the ships went forth once in three
years. We must assume that such cooperative ventures ended
during the last years of Solomon when his kingdom began to
disintegrate. During the period of the Divided Kingdom, Tyre
remained a potent force. The marriage of Jezebel, daughter of
Ittobaal of Tyre, to Ahab, the son of Omri of Israel, precipitated
the religious conflict during which Elijah emerged as the prophet
of Yahweh.

---

2. Josephus, *Contra Apion,* I, 118.

42

Babylonia and Assyria

Shortly after the reign of the famous lawgiver, Hammurabi (*ca.* 1728-1686 B.C.), the Old Babylonian Empire came to an end. The Hittite Empire was extending eastward and southward from its strongholds in central Asia Minor and, under Mursilis I, reached as far as Babylon (1530 B.C.). While Babylon was destroyed, and its first dynasty ended, the Hittites were unable to follow up their victory. Dynastic struggles at home forced Mursilis to return with such booty as he could take with him, only to be assassinated by his brother Hantilis.

Babylon was never incorporated into the Hittite Empire, but Mursilis' raid opened the way for a people from the Zagros Mountain region, the Kassites, to assume power. Kassites had looked upon the fertile Tigris-Euphrates area as ripe for occupation for some time. The Hittites had weakened Babylon to the point that the Kassites found little resistance as they took over. Agum II, a Kassite king, occupied Babylon and extended his power up the Middle Euphrates as far as Hana, and claimed the territory of Gutium in the hills to the east of Assyria.

The culture of the Kassites was inferior to that which had developed in the Tigris-Euphrates valley since the time of the Sumerians. A period of cultural lag followed, but the Kassites soon learned to adopt and adapt the superior culture of the land they had come to occupy. Kassite Babylon adopted the Semitic Akkadian language of the Old Babylonian Empire, and the cuneiform script which had first been introduced into southern Mesopotamia by the Sumerians prior to 3000 B.C.

The Amarna letters, discovered in Egypt in 1887, show that Akkadian cuneiform was the lingua franca of the Middle East during the Amarna Age — the fifteenth and fourteenth centuries B.C. The letters contain correspondence between the Egyptian Pharaohs Amenhotep III (1406-1370 B.C.) and his son

A relief depicting the king of Sumer and his sons.

A game board from Ur (ca. 2500 B.C.).

Amenhotep IV, Akhenaten (1370-1353 B.C.) on the one hand, and the kings of the Hittites, Mitanni, Assyria, and Kassite Babylon, along with princees of the city states of Syria and Palestine on the other. If the Kassites added little to Babylonian culture, at least they preserved what they inherited.

While the Kassites were consolidating control in Babylonia, farther north in Assyria and adjacent lands a people known as Hurrians (Biblical Horites, Gen. 14:6; Deut. 2:12) came to exercise a dominant position. As early as the third millennium B.C. Hurrians had migrated southward from the Caucasus Mountain region into the mountains north of Assyria. By the time of Sargon of Akkad (*ca.* 2360 B.C.) there was a Hurrrian kingdom centered at Urkish, a city in the Habur region west of Assyria. By the time of the Third Dynasty of Ur (*ca.* 2060-1950 B.C.) Hurrian names appear in texts from Dilbat, near Babylon. During the centuries that followed, evidence of Hurrian names appears in documents from Nuzi and Arrapkha in the area east of Assyria near modern Kirkuk, and in the Syrian cities of Qatna, Alalah, and Ugarit. Mari, on the Middle Euphrates, has yielded a number of ritual texts in the Hurrian language.

During his raid on Babylon, the Hittite ruler Mursilis I fought Hurrian princes along the upper Euphrates. After his death, dynastic confusion weakened the Hittite cause with the result that a major Hurrian state known as Mittani developed in the Habur River area of northern Mesopotamia. The Hurrians were the nucleous of the Mittani population, although an Indo-Aryan warrior caste ruled the region. The old Indian gods Mitra, Varuna, Indra, and the Nasitiyas were worshipped at Mitanni. Hurrian and Aryan lived together in peace. There was intermarriage between the two groups, and Hurrians are found among the ruling class.[1]

By the time of the Mitannian ruler Saushsatar (*ca.* 1450 B.C.), a contemporary of Thutmose III of Egypt, Mitanni extended from Nuzi, east of the Tigris, westward to northern Syria, and perhaps as far as the Mediterranean. Assyria was a part of the Mitannian Empire, and the rulers of Mitanni brought booty from the Assyrian cities to their capital city. A letter from Tushratta of Mitanni to Amenhotep III of Egypt states that Ishtar of Nineveh had expressed a desire to visit the Egyptian

---

1. See R. T. O'Callaghan, *Aram Naharaim* (Rome: Pontifical Biblical Institute, 1948), pp. 51-92.

court again, mentioning a former visit in the days of one of Tushratta's predecessors. The goddess Ishtar was a favorite throughout Mesopotamia. The fact that a Mitannian ruler could send her image to Egypt is ample evidence of the power of Mitanni during the Amarna Age.

The Kassites of Babylon appear to have been mild rulers, with the result that the land was not rent with inner dissention. Assyria (a vassal of Mitanni) and Elam continued to threaten Babylon, but internal unity was a help in international relations. A Kassite princess was sent to the court of Amenhotep III to secure an alliance with Egypt. Kurigalzu, king of Kassite Babylon during the Amarna Age, conducted successful campaigns against Elam, over a potential enemy. He also is known for temple restoration at the old cities of Erech, Ur, and Eridu with histories going back to Sumerian times. At Aqarquf, near Baghdad, the visitor may still see the remains of a fortified capital built by Kurigalzu.

By the time of Kurigalzu, Mitanni had passed the zenith of its power. With the accession of the powerful Hittite ruler Shuppululiuma (*ca.* 1390 B.C.), Mittanian power began to decline. Pro-Egyptian and anti-Egyptian factions vied for power. Since Egypt and the Hittites vied for control of Syria and Palestine, Mitanni was in a potentially dangerous position. Tushratta of Mitanni, mentioned in the Amarna letters was pro-Egyptian in his sympathies, but his younger brother, Artatama, became ruler of a break-away section of the kingdom in the old Hurrian homeland south of Lake Van. Artatama was pro-Hittite in his loyalties.

Tushratta looked in vain to Egypt for aid. Shuppululiuma annexed the Hurrian states of north Syria, erstwhile vassals of Egypt or Mitanni. Around 1350 B.C. Tushratta was murdered by a son supporting the party of Artatama and the Hittites. In name the kingdom would continue, but in fact Mitanni had ceased to matter in world politics.

The practical demise of Mitanni brought the possibility of independence and power to Assyria. A measure of freedom came during the days of Tushratta, when Mitanni was threatened with inner dissention. Burnaburiash II, a successor of Kurigalzu on the throne of Babylon, complained when Ashur-uballit I of Assyria had an ambassador accepted at the Egyptian court. With Assyria's independence from Mittani an accepted fact, Babylonia evidently hoped to exercise suzerainty over her neighbor to the north. Babylon's protest was in vain, and an alliance between Assyria and Babylon was established by the marriage of Ashuruballit's daughter to Kara-indash, son and heir of Burnaburiash.

With Assyria's growth in power, Shuppiluliuma evidently saw the wisdom of preserving Mitanni as a buffer zone. The Hittite ruler assisted Matiwaza, heir to Tushratta, to regain the contested throne of Mitanni. With the loss of Assyria to the east, and Carchemish in the west, Mitanni was now relatively small and insignificant in world politics. The name Hanigalbat is usually used of this successor state to the once powerful Mitannian kingdom. Three Hurrian princes of Hanigalbat are known, and all had to defend themselves against the expanding Assyrian state. Adad-nirari I (1307-1275 B.C.) conquered Shatturara I of Hanigalbat and made him his vassal. Shattuara's successor revolted, but he was reconquered. Shalmaneser I (1274-1245 B.C.) conquered Shattuara II, and Hanigalbat became an Assyrian province. About 14,000 prisoners were deported from Hanigalbat, a fact of significance because it illustrates the Assyrian policy of deportation later used against the Israelites in the days of Sargon II.

Tukulti-Ninurta I (1244-1208 B.C.) continued the policies of conquests in the north and west, accompanied by extensive deportations. Most significantly, Tukulti-Ninurta conquered Babylon, bringing it under Assyrian control for the first time. The Assyrian appraisal of the event is given in an Assyrian work known as the *Epic of Tukulti-Ninurta*. It recounts how Enlil — the great god — had chosen Tukulti-Ninurta to overthrow Kashtiliash IV, the Kassite king of Babylon who had broken his oath and, in consequence, was deserted by the gods.

Assyrian administrators found their way to Babylon, and Assyrian control was established with a firm hand. The statue of Marduk, god of Babylon, was taken to Ashur and Babylonian religious customs began to appear in the north. The Babylonian New Year's festival, known as the *akitu*, was introduced to Ashur, and the name of Marduk, along with other gods, appears increasingly in Assyrian personal names.

While Tukulti-Ninurta achieved a military victory over Babylon, it may be argued effectively that Babylon achieved a cultural victory. The religious ideas of the south penetrated Assyria, and the rugged Assyrian peoples began to develop a cosmopolitan attitude toward religion and life.

Important changes were taking place throughout the Near

An Assyrian fishing with a line. He is standing in a pond and is carrying a basket on his back for the fish he caught. The relief is from Nineveh.

East during the closing years of Tukulti-Ninurta's reign. The Sea Peoples were conquering Asia Minor, bringing the Hittite Empire down to defeat. Assyrian sources of metal in the old Hittite lands were cut off. A century of warfare had caused severe economic strain. Troubles were brewing in Assyria, with the result that Tukulti-Ninurta was murdered by a son, Ashur-nadin-apli (1207-1204 B.C.). During this period of Assyrian confusion and weakness, Babylon assumed control of the land. An anti-Babylonian revolt brought Assyrian independence under another son of Tukulti-Ninurta, Enlil-Kudur-usur (1197-1193) B.C.).

Around 1192 B.C., an Assyrian nobleman who had been living in Babylon, backed by the Kassite king of Babylon, seized the throne of Assyria. Ninurta-apal-Ekur (1192-1180 B.C.) maintained independence of Babylon, but Assyria was now reduced geographically to its homeland. Tribesmen were free to loot and pillage the mountainous territory east of Assyria.

Tukulti-Ninurta's attack had wrought havoc on Babylon, and the resulting internal dissension brought about the overthrow of the Kassite dynasty. After a period of confusion, a native Babylonian dynasty known as the Second Dynasty of Isin, came to power. Ashur-Dan I (1179-1134 B.C.) was ruler of a weakened Assyria. After his death the Babylonians were able to secure the Assyrian throne for their protégé Ninurta-tukulti-Ashur who restored the statue of Marduk to Babylon. Tukulti-Ninurta's victory had secured the image for Assyria, but its restoration symbolized the return of Marduk to his own land, Babylon.

The most important king of the Second Dynasty of Isin was Nebuchadrezzar I (1124-1103 B.C.). As a strong ruler, Nebuchadrezzar maintained firm control of his homeland and embarked on an expansionist foreign policy. The Elamites had been perennial foes of Babylon, and in one of their raids they had taken a statue of Marduk. Nebuchadrezzar mounted a campaign against the Elamites. After an initial defeat, Nebuchadrezzar assisted by an Elamite defector, Ritti-Marduk, gained a significant victory. The statue of an Elamite god was captured by the Babylonians, and brought back to Babylon along with the statue of Marduk. A cuneiform inscription notes special privileges granted to Ritti-Marduk in exchange for his aid. Nebuchadrezzar had penetrated deep within Elamite territory, gaining his final victory on the banks of the Ulai River, near Susa.

Another foe of Babylon, the Lullubi, occupied the territory northeast of Babylon. Nebuchadrezzar was able to subdue them, along with Kassite tribes of the mountains. These were related to the Kassites who had earlier established an alien dynasty in Babylon.

The forceful Nebuchadrezzar maintained control over Assyria until the reign of Ashur-resh-ishi (1133-1116 B.C.) who strengthened Assyrian prestige and power throughout the Near East. Both Assyria and Babylonia were facing new threats from the west when Aramaean tribes threatened the trade routes leading to the Syrian coast and Anatolia. Ashur-resh-ishi boasted of victories over an Aramaic tribe known as the Ahlamu. An inscription describes the Assyrian king as "the one who crushes the widespread forces of the Ahlamu." Ashur-resh-ishi also conducted campaigns against tribes in the eastern mountain districts — the Lullubi, the Quti and their allies. Here Assyrian and Babylonian interests clashed. Nebuchadrezzar's heavy siege engines were no match for the chariots of Ashur-resh-ishi. Assyria was the victor and Nebuchadrezzar's successors had to fight to protect their own land against the Assyrians.

Ashur-resh-ishi was succeeded by an able son, Tiglath-pileser I (1115-1077 B.C.). The Assyrian war machine of later centuries drew its inspiration from Tiglath-pileser. Shortly after his accession a people known as Mushku (Biblical Meshech) pushed southward from eastern Asia Minor and invaded the Assyrian province of Kummuh. Tiglath-pileser reacted forcefully, decisively defeating the Mushku and punishing all who had assisted them. Succesive campaigns brought Assyrian power into the areas north, northeast, and northwest of the Assyrian homeland, penetrating deep into Asia Minor.

Tiglath-pileser had more troubles from the west than he did from the north. Population pressures following the invasions of the Philistines and other Sea Peoples made basic changes in the ethnic make-up of western Asia. About this time the kingdom of Saba (Biblical Sheba) emerged as a power in southern Arabia, possibly causing other southern tribes to migrate northward. Assyria would ultimately conquer most of western Asia (the Jerusalem area being a notable exception), but it would take many frustrating campaigns to do so.

The Assyrians never acknowledged defeats, and their annals are not always reliable. Nevertheless the royal scribes give us a good picture of the way in which an Assyrian ruler depicts himself. Here is Tiglath-pileser's boast:

I am Tiglath-pileser, the legitimate king, king of the world, king of Assyria, king of the four parts of the earth, the courageous hero guided by the oracles of Ashur and Ninurta, the great gods his lords; he who has overcome his foes.... At the command of my lord Ashur, my hand conquered from beyond the lower Zab river to the upper sea that lies to the west. Three times did I march against the Nairi countries.... I made bow at my feet thirty kings of the Nairi countries, and took hostages from them. I received as tribute horses broken to the yoke. I imposed upon them tribute and gifts. Then I went to the Lebanon. I cut cedar timber for the temple of Anu and Adad, the great gods my lords, and brought it away. I conquered the entire Amurru country. I received tribute from Byblos, Sidon and Arvad.[2]

Tiglath-pileser claims that he crossed the Euphrates twenty-eight times to attack the Aramean peoples and their allies. His victories made possible a thriving trade along the time-honored trade routes, now in Assyrian hands. The resulting wealth enabled the king to be generous in building and restoring temples, thus assuring a favorable place in history. For recreation he hunted lions, bisons, and elephants, and collected exotic animals in his personal zoo.

After the reign of Tiglath-pileser I, however, Assyrian fortunes sank until the accession of Adad-nirari II. The years from 1077 to 911 B.C. saw Assyria quiescent — and it was precisely at this period that Israel emerged as a potentially powerful state. A power vacuum in the Near East made possible the glories of the court of a Solomon, but three generations after the establishment of the Israelite monarchy.

Babylon's history paralleled that of Assyria. A chronicle dated around 990 B.C. says that, "for nine years successively, Marduk did not go forth, Nabu did not come." The reference is to the annual New Year's feast, when Marduk was taken in solemn procession to a shrine outside the city, and when Nabu of Borsippa visited him on his return. While the sequence of kings is known, the history of this period is obscure. During the days of the Assyrian ruler Ashur-rabi II (1010-970 B.C.) the Arameans were able to occupy Assyrian settlements on the Middle Euphrates (including Pitru, Biblical Pethor). This complicated trade, for even in times of peace customs duties had to be paid to large numbers of small independent states. Assyria, for the moment, was contained.

An Assyrian winged figure, perhaps a priest performing an act of blessing.

---

2. James Pritchard, *Ancient Near Eastern Texts*, pp. 274-275.

43

People on the Move

The thirteenth century B.C. saw mass movements of Indo-European peoples in southeastern Europe, with important results for western Asia, including Palestine. Dorians, Aeolians, and Ionians occupied the Greek mainland, the Aegean islands, and western Asia Minor. The older Mycenaean culture, best known as the Achaeans in Homer's account of the Trojan War, was now past. The Trojan War was fought around 1270 B.C. The historical kernel behind the legendary accretions probably reflects the struggles among the peoples of the thirteenth century. Shortly after 1200 B.C. the Hittite Empire was defeated and the Sea Peoples, as the Egyptians called them, fled eastward along the coast of Asia Minor, and southward through Syria and Palestine to threaten Egypt itself. By sea and by land they challenged the power structure of the lands of the Fertile Crescent and Egypt.

About 1174 B.C. the Egyptian Pharaoh Ramesses III defeated the Sea Peoples in land and sea battles. The threat was a real one for the invaders had come to stay. They brought their women and children in wheeled carts drawn by humped oxen, as we can see depicted on the temple walls at Medinet Habu. Among the tribes of Sea Peoples we find the Tjekker, who later are found at the Palestinian port of Dor, and the Peleset, the Philistinees who settled in southern Palestine and struggled with the Israelites during the days of the Judges and the early period of the monarchy.

Ramesses III in a speech to his sons and courtiers described his response to the attack of the Sea Peoples:

> The foreign countries made a plot in their islands. Dislodged and scattered by battle were the lands all at one time, and no land could stand before their arms, beginning with Khatti (e.g. the Hittites), Kode, Carchemish, Arzawa, and Alasiya (Cyprus)... A camp was set up in one place in Amor, and they desolated its people and its land

as though they had never come into being. They came, the flame prepared before them, onwards to Egypt. Their confederacy consisted of Peleset, Tjekker, Sheklesh, Danu, and Weshesh, united lands, and they laid their hands upon the lands to the entire circuit of the earth, their hearts bent and trustful.... But the heart of this god (Ramesses III, the divine Pharaoh), the lord of the gods, was prepared and ready to ensnare them like birds.... I established my boundary in Djahi (i.e. Palestine and Syria), prepared in front of them the local princes, garrison commanders, and maryannu (chariot warriors). I caused the river mouth to be prepared like a strong wall with warships, galleys, and skiffs. They were completely equipped both fore and aft with brave fighters, carrying their weapons and infantry, of all the pick of Egypt, being like roaring lions upon the mountains; chariotry with able warriors, and all goodly officers whose hands were competent. Their horses quivered in all their limbs, prepared to crush the foreign countries under their hoofs.[1]

Ramesses likened himself to Mont, the god of war, and boasted of his complete victory:

As for those who reached my boundary, their seed is not. Their hearts and their souls are finished unto all eternity. Those who came forward together upon the sea, the full flame was in front of them at the river-mouths, and a stockade of lances surrounded them on the shore.

In gory detail Ramesses glories in the defeat of the foe:

A net was prepared for them to ensnare them, those who entered into the river-mouths being confined and fallen within it, pinioned in their places, butchered and their corpses hacked up.

Following the victory of Ramesses III we find the Pelesct (Philistines) settling in force in southern Palestine, to become the foes of Israel within a short time. The Bible places the home of the Philistines in Caphtor (Deut. 2:23; Jer. 47:4; Amos 9:7), usually identified with Crete, the center of the Minoan culture, one of the most advanced cultures known during the first half of the second millennium B.C.

About the same time that Sea Peoples were storming the gates of Egypt and the Hittite country, other Indo-European peoples were moving southward from the region of the Caspian Sea to become the Madai (Medes) and Parsua (Parthians) of later history. These and kindred tribes were able to gain control of the regions later known as Persia, Afghanistan, and Turkistan.

The Indo-European migrations had little direct affect on Mesopotamia. Kassites from the Zagros Mountain region ruled Babylon for four hundred years with little concern for problems in the west. Farther north, the Semitic Aramaeans took advantage of the confusion to move into the Syrian hinterland

---

1. W. F. Edgerton and J. A. Wilson, *Historical Records of Ramesses III* (Chicago: University of Chicago Press, 1936), p. 42.

and establish a number of petty kingdoms which, collectively, threatened the larger states, particularly Assyria. Israelites at the same time were establishing themselves in the area west of the Jordan which would be the nucleous for the kingdom of Saul, David, and Solomon.

Aside from the Biblical records and Assyrian Royal Inscriptions we have little documentation for the period immediately prior to the establishment of the monarchy. About 1190 B.C. the Hittite archives at Boghazkoy came to an abrupt end. The successors of Ramesses III were impotent rulers, and by the dawn of the eleventh century, Egypt separated into two rival kingdoms.

When our documentation improves, about 900 B.C., we find a new power structure throughout western Asia. Aramaean states are thriving from the Lebanon to the Zagros mountain regions. Damascus is the center of a major Aramaean state with which Israel will have frequent contact. The Philistines are settled on the southern coast of Palestine, while the Phoenicians (as the Canaanites of the area were called by the Greeks), occupied the northern Mediterranean coast with major port cities at Tyre, Sidon, and Arvad.

The contribution of the Phoenicians to subsequent history was both positive and negative. On the positive side is the alphabet, a distinct improvement on earlier hieroglyphic and cuneiform systems of writing. When Greek mariners learned the alphabet from their Phoenician counterparts, the west began its journey into literacy. Similarly the Aramaeans took the alphabet eastward, although cuneiform writing continued to be used in some places until the time of Christ.

The negative influence of the Phoenicians is well documented in the Biblical records. These are the people of Baal, and the Phoenician wife of Ahab, Queen Jezebel, is the one who tried to eliminate Yahwism from Israelite religious life. The fertility cult associated with Baal and his consort reaped the just scorn of Israel's prophets.

The Phoenician cities had excellent harbors, and the abundant timber on the mountains to the east helped make of the Phoenicians a nation of seafarers. With the collapse of the Mycenaean Empire, the eastern Mediterranean was open to mariners of all nations, and the Phoenicians of Tyre, Sidon, and Arvad began to sail the Mediterranean with timber, wine, oil, and the luxury goods of Phoenicia. The purple dye, extracted by the Phoenicians from the murex shellfish, was particularly prized, and royalty in many lands attired itself in the expensive purple of Sidon. Intricate embroidery work was another Phoenician specialty.

Phoenician artisans are not known for their originality, but they learned quickly to imitate the best designs and materials that flowed through their busy ports. They cut jewels and ivory for export and fashioned vessels of translucent glass.

Phoenician influence throughout the eastern Mediterranean was greatest between the ninth and the sixth centuries. David and Solomon used Phoenician artisans and materials in their building operations. The islands of the Mediterranean and the coastlands of northern Africa and southern Europe were dotted with Phoenician colonies. Malta, Sicily, Spain, and — most important of all — Carthage had major Phoenician settlements.

Carthage is remembered because of its battles with Rome in a series of "Punic" (i.e., Phoenician) Wars. Here many heroes had Semitic Phoenician names, such as Hanabal ("The grace of Baal"), comparable to Biblical Hannaniah ("The grace of Yahweh"). Vergil in his *Aeneid* explained the hostility between Carthage and Rome in terms of a love affair between Dido, queen of Carthage, and Aeneas, a Trojan hero who visited Carthage during his journeys following the destruction of Troy. Destiny called Aeneas to leave Dido and move on to Italy where his descendants would become the mighty Romans. As Aeneas prepared to leave, Dido cast herself upon a funeral pyre, calling down curses upon her erstwhile lover and asserting undying enmity between her people and his. Although entirely fictious, Vergil's story underscores the rivalry between the Romans and Tyre's most illustrious daughter city, Carthage.

44

Egypt

The power vacuum which made possible the rise of Israel as an independent state was as obvious in Egypt as it had been in Mesopotamia. Ramesses III had responded vigorously to threats from the Sea Peoples but his successors left no lasting mark on the pages of history. Eight more Egyptian Pharaohs bore the name of Ramesses, but the reigns of all but two (Ramesses IX and Ramesses XI) were very short. The tendency was to live in the Delta, leaving Thebes to the complete control of the Amun priesthood. Egypt conducted no campaigns into Asia during this period, and even Sinai is not mentioned after the reign of Ramesses VI. Egypt retreated into an isolation which Thutmose III or Ramesses II would have had difficulty understanding. Cyril Aldred observes, "She escaped the transfusions of new blood and ideas, such as rejuvenated the peoples of Canaan and created the vigorous Phoenician city-states. Thereafter she lived on, a Bronze Age anachronism in a world that steadily moved away from her."[1]

Egypt, like many nations, thrived on adversity but could not stand success. Egyptians came to desire genteel vocations. The priest and the scribe were honored, yet their work had neither danger nor drudgery associated with it. An Egyptian could seek such a job and fill or create a comfortable bureaucratic office that he might pass on to his son. The army could be left to mercenaries — Nubians, Sudanis, Libyans and others.

As Egypt's Twentieth Dynasty dragged to a close (*ca.* 1075 B.C.) Egypt was virtually two lands with the High Priest at Thebes ruling southern or Upper Egypt, and the Pharaoh ruling in and over the Delta. The Philistines were in control of

---

1. *The Egyptians* (New York: Frederick A. Praeger, 1963) p. 139.

the coast of Palestine, and the Phoenicians had become masters of the sea. Unemployment among the mercenary soldiers increased the lawlessness of the times, and famine caused by a succession of years in which the Nile did not provide adequate water for irrigation, made things worse. Dishonesty was rampant among officials who tried hard to cover their mismanagement of men and material, and the poorer classes resorted to strikes and violence to relieve their hunger.

The tombs of the Pharaohs, once reverenced as manifestations of god on earth, were now pillaged systematically and with the connivance of the officials. Of thirty tombs in the Valley of the Kings, only that of Tut-ankh-amon was preserved, and that probably by accident because the entrance to the tomb was concealed behind debris.

After the death of the last of the Ramesides, the country fell into its natural halves. The fiction of a united Egypt might be observed, but Upper Egypt was clearly a theocracy under the priests at Thebes, and Lower Egypt had a succession of ineffective rulers.

Shortly after 950 B.C. a family of Libyan descent which had settled at Herakleopolis succeeded to the throne. They were in no sense invaders, but probably the descendants of captured prisoners or voluntary settlers who were assigned land on condition that they obligate themselves to perform military service. The founder of the dynasty was Sheshonq (Biblical Shishak, I Kings 11:29-40) who harbored Jeroboam as a fugitive from Solomon. About 925 B.C., after the division of the kingdom, Sheshonq invaded Palestine, subdued Judah, and took Temple treasures as tribute (I Kings 14:25-26). The Libyan dynasty offered the hope of fresh vigor on the throne of Egypt, but Egypt was never to recover the glories of her past when Egypt ruled western Asia from Egypt to the Euphrates. It was in her period of decline that the Israelite kingdom came into being.

45

An Evaluation
of the United Monarchy

Israel developed into an important nation in the ancient Near East during a period when there was no major power that dominated the scene. Following her glorious New Kingdom, when Egypt ruled the East, Egyptian power gradually was lost. Dreams of restoring that power challenged Pharaohs of the first millennium B.C., but with no permanent results. Assyria was developing into an important state in Mesopotamia — a state which would incorporate most of western Asia during the centuries which would follow — but in the days of David and Solomon she was no threat. Political tensions developed among the smaller states of western Asia — Philistines, Phoenicians, Arameans, Moabites, Ammonites, Edomites, and Israelites — but neither the Nile nor the Euphrates gave any real concern.

It was during this time of a power vacuum that Israelite military power reached its zenith. David unified the country and made Jerusalem its capital. Solomon built its Temple during his days of wealth, but seeds of decay were soon evident. With Solomon's death the kingdom was divided, never to be united again.

The period of Israel's political power was not, however, the period of Israel's great contribution to religion and culture. Other nations produced rulers who defeated enemies and ruled in the style of David and Solomon. Israel's uniqueness was in her prophetic spokesmen who dared to challenge erroneous, if popular, views. A Nathan in the court of David was such a person. Nathan made it clear that his royal title and office did not give David license to break the Law of God. In later centuries an Amos, a Hosea, an Isaiah, a Jeremiah and their like, dared to insist that Yahweh demanded more than ritual conformity — that a heart devoted to Yahweh's will and moved with compassion toward all of Yahweh's creatures was essential. Jonah must be concerned even about the wicked city of Nineveh. This was the prophetic message. God would one day vindicate the righteous. The world would experience renewal and regeneration in a day when the earth would be filled with the knowledge of the glory of Yahweh as the waters cover the sea. This was the prophetic hope.

The sin of David and the material splendor of Solomon's court did not give much hope for better things in themselves. The prophetic response, however, gave occasion to the faithful to hope for better things. David's sin would be punished, but David's line would be preserved. The Lord's anointed, the Messiah would come as "the son of David, the son of Abraham" (Matt. 1:1).

Following the death of Solomon the period of Israel's political unity quickly came to an end. An already weakened nation divided into two parts—Israel, the Northern Kingdom, and Judah, the Southern Kingdom. External threats came from Egypt, from the Arameans (A.V. "Syria"), from the land-hungry Assyrian Empire and its successor, the Neo-Babylonian or Chaldean Empire.

Details of the history of the Divided Kingdom are illustrated by archaeological discoveries of the past century. The Egyptian pharaohs of the period, along with the Assyrian and Babylonian kings, left historical monuments and annals which brighten the day of the historian interested in placing Biblical history in its proper international context. Assyrian policy and performance can be learned from the annals of such kings as Tiglath-Pileser III and Ashurbanipal. Sargon writes of the deportation of the Israelites after the fall of Samaria (722 B.C.) and Sennacherib describes his siege of Jerusalem (701 B.C.). Babylonian Chronicles describe the last years of Judah's history. Israel and Judah were in the full light of history during the period of the Divided Kingdom.

King Solomon died about 922 B.C., and Samaria, the capital of Israel fell to the Assyrians in 722 B.C. For approximately two centuries the kingdoms of Israel and Judah existed side by side. For about one hundred thirty-five years after the destruction of Samaria, Judah was able to go it alone. Threats from Assyria did not succeed in humbling Judah, but the armies of Nebuchadnezzar entered Jerusalem in 587 B.C., bringing Judah under Babylonian control.

Although these centuries saw the decline of political power in Israel and Judah, they also saw the emergence of a series of prophets whose faith and messages would do much to shape the thought and activity of successive generations of Jews and Christians alike. These were the days of an Elijah and an Elisha who stood for the purity of Israel's faith in a day when Baal worship posed a threat to the worship of Yahweh, the God of Israel. The writing prophets—Isaiah, Jeremiah, Hosea, Amos, their contemporaries and successors— proclaimed a message of impending doom for faithless Israel. The exiles of Israel and Judah were much in the mind of the prophets. Yet beyond the judgment of exile the prophets declared a ground for optimism. God would not forget His covenant with David. After judgment would come blessing.

PART FIVE

The Divided Kingdom

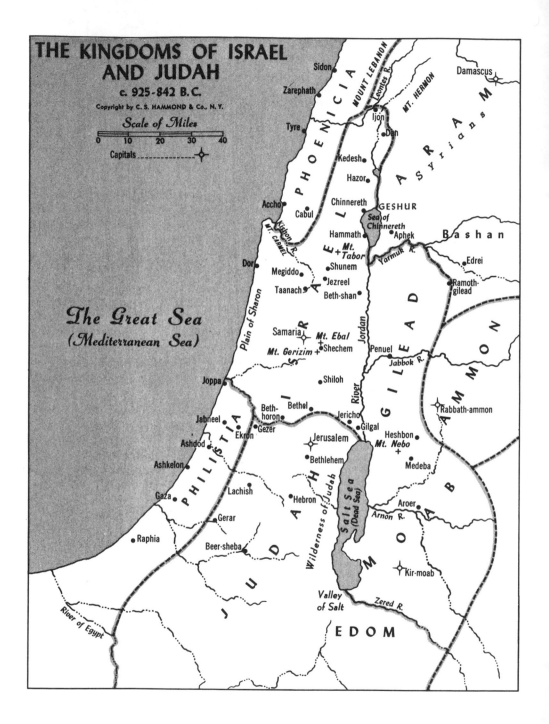

THE KINGDOMS OF ISRAEL AND JUDAH

c. 925-842 B.C.

Copyright by C. S. HAMMOND & Co., N.Y.

Scale of Miles

| 0 | 10 | 20 | 30 | 40 |

Capitals ---------------- ✦

Sidon

Zarephath

Damascus

MOUNT LEBANON

Leontes R.

MT. HERMON

Tyre

Ijon

Dan

PHOENICIA

MT. HERMON

S Y R I A N S

Syrians

Kedesh

Hazor

Accho

Cabul

Chinnereth

GESHUR

Sea of Chinnereth

Aphek

Bashan

MT. CARMEL

Kishon R.

Hammath

Mt. +Tabor

Yarmuk R.

Edrei

Dor

Megiddo

Shunem

Jezreel

Beth-shan

Ramoth-gilead

Taanach

The Great Sea
(Mediterranean Sea)

Plain of Sharon

I S R A E L

G I L E A D

A M M O N

Samaria ✦

Mt. Ebal +

Shechem

Penuel

Mt. Gerizim +

Jabbok R.

Jordan River

Shiloh

Joppa

Beth-horon

Bethel

Jericho

Gilgal

Rabbath-ammon

Jabneel

Gezer

Jerusalem ✦

Heshbon

Mt. Nebo +

Ekron

Ashdod

Bethlehem

Medeba

PHILISTIA

Ashkelon

Salt Sea
(Dead Sea)

J U D A H

Wilderness of Judah

M O A B

Gaza

Lachish

Hebron

Aroer

Gerar

Arnon R.

Raphia

Beer-sheba

Kir-moab

Valley of Salt

Zered R.

River of Egypt

E D O M

46

A House Divided

Solomon brought Israel to the verge of bankruptcy. The United Kingdom survived until his death, but the empire which David had built was already beginning to disintegrate. Hadad, an Edomite prince who had escaped to Egypt after David's victory over Edom, returned to claim his throne (I Kings 11: 14-22) with the result that Israelite forces entrusted with the protection of trade routes to the Red Sea and copper mines in the Arabah had to battle Hadad's forces. In the north an Aramean adventurer who had served under Hadadezer of Zobah seized the city of Damascus and made it the capital of a kingdom extending from Mount Hermon to the Euphrates. Rezin, founder of the Kingdom of Damascus, set a precedent for the later separation of Israel from Judah (I Kings 11:23-25).

So deeply in debt was Solomon to Hiram of Tyre, that the Israelite king ceded twenty cities of Galilee as a means of repayment (I Kings 9:10-14). Forced labor, used on Solomon's building projects, further added to the discontent (I Kings 9:15-22). The orthodox in Jerusalem were scandalized because of Solomon's attachment to his foreign wives and his willingness to worship their gods: "Then Solomon built a high place for Chemosh, the abomination of Moab, and for Molech, the abomination of the Ammonites, on the mountain east of Jerusalem, and so he did for all his foreign wives who burned incense and sacrificed to their gods" (I Kings 11:7-8).

Although Solomon had a thousand wives and concubines in his harem, we read of but one child, Rehoboam, who succeeded his father to the throne. The Israelite monarchy was not so firmly established, however, that an orderly transition could be taken for granted. The monarchy had been in existence for but three generations, and the transition from Saul to David had not been accomplished without bloodshed. David ruled over the southern tribes from Hebron (II Sam. 5:5) for seven years while Ishbosheth (Eshbaal), Saul's son, was acknowledged king in the north. Only after the death of Ishbosheth (II Sam. 4:7) did David rule a united people.

South and north also had differing geographical and commercial orientations. The south was more isolated, hence more conservative. Merchant caravans and military expeditions passing through the Valley of Esdraelon en route from Damascus and the East to Egypt introduced the North to a wider world and tended to make that region more cosmopolitan. Contacts with the Phoenician cities of Tyre, Sidon, and Byblos added a further dimension to life in the north.

Solomon had been able to hold the empire together, but it would have taken an exceptionally wise leader to preserve the union after his death. As a matter of fact Rehoboam proved himself ill-equipped to rule a federation of tribes with diversified interests. When confronted with a request for relief from the taxation which was a carry-over from Solomon's extravagant building program, Rehoboam consulted his counselors. Those of the older generation sensed the difficulty of the situation and suggested that Rehoboam might win over the dissidents by exercising restraint. Rehoboam chose, however, to seek the counsel of his peers — the young men who had grown up with him — and they suggested that he assert his authority in terms that could not be misunderstood (I Kings 12:1-11). An offer of tax relief would have been interpreted as weakness. Rehoboam indignantly told the dissidents that no relief should be expected: "And now, whereas my father laid upon you a heavy yoke, I will add to your yoke. My father chastized you with whips, but I will chastize you with scorpions."

Rehoboam certainly did not realize the seriousness, let alone the justice, of the people's complaint. He had been accepted without question by the southern tribes, and he evidently felt that his journey to Shechem was but a formality, after which his acceptance in the north would promptly follow. The northern tribes were in no mood to accept the king's arrogance.

The northern tribes found a leader for their secession in Jeroboam, an Ephraimite prince of ability who had been appointed foreman of the forced laborers whom Solomon had conscripted from "the house of Joseph," i.e. Ephraim and Manasseh (I Kings 11:28). The forced labor was as unpopular as the excessive taxation, and Jeroboam was able to use his position to stir up dissatisfaction with the government. One day as he was walking outside the city of Jerusalem, a prophet named Ahijah of Shiloh met him. The prophet tore his new mantle into twelve pieces, giving ten to Jeroboam (I Kings 11:29-39). The prophetic act symbolized the division of the kingdom. Ten of the tribes would accept Jeroboam as king. When Solomon learned what happened he tried to kill Jeroboam, but Jeroboam escaped to Egypt and was welcomed by Shishak, the successor to the Pharaoh who had given his daughter to Solomon as a wife (I Kings 11:40).

When Jeroboam learned of Solomon's death he made himself available to the northern tribes. The prophecy of Ahijah was fulfilled. Rehoboam's rejection of the plea of his people was taken as just grounds for revolt from the Davidic line. If Rehoboam had dealt contemptuously with the northern tribes, they answered in the same vein: "What portion have we in David? We have no inheritance in the son of Jesse. To your tents, O Israel? Look now to your own house, David" (I Kings 12:16).

The division of the kingdom marked the end of the empire which David had built and Solomon, in part, had dissipated. Israel (the Northern Kingdom) and Judah (the Southern Kingdom) were no match for the large powers which vied for control of the ancient East. The Aramean state with its capital at Damascus, already lost during Solomon's late years, consolidated its position and became a threat to Israel within a generation. The Philistine cities of the west, except for Gath (II Chron. 11:8), were free, and Ammon, east of the Jordan, gained her independence at this time. Moab was also free, although a later king of Israel, Omri (876-869 B.C.), reconquered her according to an inscribed stele known as the Moabite Stone.

After the division, Judah was reduced to her old tribal lands, with some border territories in the coastal plain and the Negev as far as Ezion-geber. Israel occupied the tribal holdings of the ten northern tribes and, for a time, some of the Aramean lands east of the Sea of Galilee. Trade routes were severely restricted, and the lucrative trade encouraged by Solomon collapsed entirely.

Rehoboam, Judah's first king (922-915 B.C.), wisely made no effort to prevent the secession of the northern tribes. Judah was smaller than Israel, and much of the army was no longer sympathetic with Rehoboam. A prophet, Shemaiah, advised, "You shall not go up or fight against your kinsmen the people of Israel. Return every man to his home, for this thing is from

Bracelet of gold, inlaid with lapis lazuli, made for Nemeretj, a son of Pharaoh Shishak I.

Carved on the temple walls at Karnak is this record of Shishak's campaign in Palestine.

me" (I Kings 12:24). The sentiments were probably characteristic of most of the people of Judah.

Jeroboam was acclaimed king of Israel and ruled from 922 to 901 B.C. While Jerusalem had been centrally located as capital of the United Kingdom, its position on the border between Judah and Benjamin made it precariously near the northern border of the Southern Kingdom after the division. Benjamin, the tribe of Saul, may have been sympathetic with the northern seceders, but Rehoboam could not allow his capital to be exposed. Rehoboam was able to occupy most of Benjamin, and the frontier between the two kingdoms was near the northern limits of Benjamin.

The Egyptian ruler Shishak (Shoshenq) was the energetic founder of the Twenty-second Dynasty who hoped to reassert Egyptian power in Asia. He had overthrown the weak Twenty-first Dynasty, with which Solomon had been allied. The division of the Israelite kingdom played directly into the hands of Shishak, who may have given Jeroboam asylum because he foresaw such an eventuality. In the fifth year of Rehoboam, Shishak invaded Judah (I Kings 14:25-28). The Biblical record can be supplemented by Shishak's own inscription at Karnak on which he lists one hundred fifty places which he claims to have taken. If Jeroboam encouraged Shishak to attack Rehoboam with a view to relieving pressure on his own armies, the Israelite king was to regret this act. Shishak's army passed through Judah and entered Israel, reaching the cities of the Valley of Esdraelon. A triumphal stele of Shishak has been discovered at Megiddo, one of the cities mentioned on the list at Karnak. Shishak's invasion humbled both Israel and Judah. While internal problems prevented Shishak from re-establishing an Egyptian empire in Asia, neither Rehoboam nor Jeroboam was left with any military power. They were in no mood to reconcile their differences, and they had no power to force their will on each other.

Jeroboam, although looked upon as a wicked ruler by Judah's historians because he had rebelled against the House of David and rejected Jerusalem as the site of the national shrine, was a wise and able leader in purely political terms. He chose as his capital the ancient city of Shechem, near the southern border of Manasseh. Schechem was situated in the pass between Mount Ebal and Mount Gerizim which dominated roads to the north and the west. The Biblical statement that Jeroboam "built Shechem" (I Kings 12:25) probably means that he fortified the city to make it a safe capital from which to rule the Northern Kingdom. Jeroboam evidently repaired the older city wall. Excavations at Tell Balatah, the modern name for the mound of Shechem, have brought to light a part of the wall repaired by Jeroboam, which is comparable to the wall Solomon built at Megiddo.[1]

A second city which Jeroboam built was Penuel, east of the Jordan. Probably the king wished Penuel to serve as a military headquarters to secure the loyalty of Gilead. Shishak's conquests list a city called *Per-nu-al,* perhaps the Penuel fortified by Jeroboam.

Jeroboam realized that he needed the religious as well as the political loyalty of his people if he was to be a successful ruler. If his people looked to Jerusalem as their spiritual center, his very throne might be endangered. To prevent this, he chose two cities which had sacred associations to both Canaanites and Israelites: Dan, north of the Sea of Galilee, and Bethel, just ten miles north of Jerusalem. In each of these cities Jeroboam built a shrine in which he placed a golden calf (or bull). Probably the calf was not meant to be worshiped as an idol. The gods of the ancient Near East are frequently represented as standing upon the backs of animals or seated on thrones borne by animals. An eighth century (B.C.) stele from Arslan-Tash, in northern Syria, depicts Baal-hadad, the storm god, standing on the back of a bull. If Jeroboam and his priests thought of the God of Israel as enthroned above the bull, their spiritual concept was not shared by the average Israelite. Worshipers could see the bulls, and the animals themselves became objects of popular worship. While theoretically the people were still worshiping Yahweh at Bethel and Dan, actually they were moving in the direction of Canaanite religion in which El and Baal were frequently likened to bulls.

Jeroboam appointed priests to officiate at his shrines, and he "appointed a feast on the fifteenth day of the eighth month like the feast that was in Judah" (I Kings 12:32). This was to be the Israelite counterpart to the Feast of Tabernacles, observed in Jerusalem during the seventh month (I Kings 8:2).

These acts of Jeroboam were doubtless presented to the people as revivals of ancient tradition rather than as innovations. Ancient shrine cities had been neglected with the centralization of worship in Jerusalem. The calendar reflecting the status of

Near Dan, north of the Sea of Galilee, Jeroboam erected one of the two shrines that provided the northern kingdom with centers of worship to rival Jerusalem.

---

1. G. Ernest Wright, *Biblical Archaeology,* p. 148.

the agricultural year in Judah had been accepted in the north along with other aspects of unified life under the monarchy. Jeroboam emphasized the traditions of the north, and he gave the peasant a calendar of feasts which reflected conditions in Israel rather than Judean agricultural activities.[2]

Rehoboam, meanwhile, took refuge in Jerusalem where he secured the allegiance of the tribes of Judah and Benjamin. When he prepared to send an army northward to subdue the rebellious northern tribes, a prophet, Shemaiah, told him that God willed the separation (I Kings 12:22-24). Not only could Rehoboam anticipate troubles on his northern frontier, but Egypt, to the south, was ready to profit from the dismemberment of Solomon's empire. With that danger in view, Rehoboam fortified cities in Judah: Bethlehem, Tekoa, Beth-zur, Gath, Mareshah, Lachish, Azekah and others (II Chron. 11:5-12).

On the positive side, Rehoboam had the advantage of the Jerusalem shrine within his borders, and the loyalty of those who had attached themselves to the religious practices sanctioned in the Solomonic temple. Priests and Levites who were scandalized by the cult practices at Bethel and Dan made their way southward to Jerusalem (II Chron. 11:13-17) and proved loyal to Rehoboam. In time, however, the reign of Rehoboam was beset by internal difficulties. He added numerous wives and concubines to his harem, after the manner of Solomon (II Chron. 11:18-23). Idolatrous high places with heathen cult objects began to appear in Judah (I Kings 14:22-24). In the light of such practices, the invasion of Shishak was interpreted as evidence of God's displeasure with the idolatry of his people.

Rehoboam's son Abijah[3] ruled but three years in Jerusalem. We read of but one battle during his reign, but Abijah was able to gain a victory over the numerically superior forces of Jeroboam (II Chron. 13). Abijah occupied Bethel and other nearby cities. It is possible that the Arameans of Damascus, honoring a treaty with Abijah (cf. I Kings 15:19) attacked Israel from the north, exposing its weak southern border to invasion from Judah. Israel quickly recovered, however, for in another generation the armies of the Northern Kingdom were pressing hard upon Jerusalem itself.

The Biblical historian asserts that Abijah's heart was "not

An ancient winepress in Jerusalem.

---

2. S. Talmon, "Calendar-Reckoning in Ephraim and Judah," *Vetus Testamentum,* VIII (1958), pp. 48-74.
3. Abijah is also known as Abijam. Abijah means "My father is Yahweh," Abijam, perhaps, "My father is truly (Yahweh)" from *Abuya-mi.*

wholly true to the Lord his God" (I Kings 15:3). After his short reign he was succeeded by his son Asa, the first of Judah's reformers.

Like Rehoboam, Asa had to face an enemy from the south. Zerah "the Ethiopian" (II Chron. 14:9-14) was probably a commander in the service of Osorkon I (*ca.* 914-874 B.C.), Shishak's successor. The Egyptian army which attempted to harass Judah was turned back at Mareshah in the Judean lowlands. Asa ravaged the area around Gerar, evidently a headquarters for Egyptian forces. Egyptian power in Palestine was broken and her armies did not pose a further threat for a century and a half.

Asa showed his zeal for Yahweh by renouncing his mother, Maacah, because of her idolatry. Maacah made "an abominable image for Asherah," a fertility goddess, which Asa destroyed and burned at the brook Kidron (I Kings 15:13). Such idolatry was to be repeated periodically both in the north and south

When Jeroboam died his son Nadab tried to take the throne (I Kings 15:25-31) but he was assassinated by an officer named Baasha (I Kings 16:1-7). Baasha became king of Israel and reigned for twenty-three years (900-877 B.C.). He fortified the city of Ramah, just north of the Judean border, to protect himself against attacks from the south and, perhaps, as a base for launching his own campaigns.

Damascus. The Bride's Minaret at the Great Mosque.

Asa of Judah reacted by mobilizing his own forces and allying himself with the Arameans of Damascus. Damascus threatened Israel's northern and eastern borders (I Kings 15:16-24), thereby relieving Judah of the threat of invasion from Israel.

Baasha died a natural death, but his son Elah was murdered by a commander named Zimri after a reign of but two years (I Kings 16:9). Both Baasha and Zimri had taken the throne after exterminating members of the previous royal house. While Baasha's coup d'e tat was successful, Zimri's lasted but a week (I Kings 16:15). Omri, the commander of the army, beseiged Zimri in his capital at Tirzah. Zimri set fire to his palace and perished in the flames. A period of confusion followed, with some Israelites favoring a man named Tibni, and others preferring Omri. Omri's partisans prevailed and he ruled for six years in Tirzah before choosing Samaria as his capital. The capital had been moved from Shechem to Tirzah, and then to Samaria. It was to remain at Samaria for the remainder of the history of the Northern Kingdom. The southern kingdom had no capital but Jerusalem.

47

The Dynasty of Omri

The Moabite Stone. This black basalt stele contains an inscription commemorating the revolt of Mesha, king of Moab, against Israel. It mentions Omri's conquest of Moab. The revolt probably occurred during the last years of Ahab.

Under Omri (876-869 B.C.) a measure of stability was restored to Israel. Prior to Omri's seizure of power, Ben-hadad I of Damascus (880-842 B.C.), had wrested territory in Galilee and Transjordan from Israel. Damascus had also demanded and received commercial concessions (I Kings 20:34). Farther away, Assyria was experiencing a revival under Ashur-nasir-pal II (883-859 B.C.). Omri's dynasty was to fight both with the Arameans of Damascus and the Assyrians from Nineveh.

The Biblical historians say little of the reign of Omri himself (I Kings 16:23-28). He sought to maintain friendly relations with the Phoenicians — in the tradition of David and Solomon — and arranged a marriage between his son Ahab and Jezebel, daughter of Ittobaal of Tyre. While understandable from a political viewpoint, this marriage proved one of the sorest trials Israel was called upon to endure before the Exile.

The Omri dynasty also sought to maintain friendly relations with Judah. Early in Ahab's reign a marriage was arranged between Ahab's daughter Athaliah, and Jehoram son of Jehoshaphat of Judah. In this way the influence of Jezebel reached into the southern kingdom.

The Moabite Stone, discovered at Dhiban in 1868, tells how "Omri, king of Israel, humbled Moab many days." According to the Moabite recorder the Israelites controlled Moab forty years — "during his (Omri's) time, and half the time of his son (Ahab)."

Assyrian records frequently described the Northern Kingdom as "the house of Omri," an unconscious tribute to the founder of a dynasty who is known to Biblical historians as the rather unimportant father of Ahab. Omri seems to have been an able administrator and a wise diplomat. His dealings with Tyre left problems which were to plague his son, Ahab, all his days.

In bringing a Tyrian bride to Samaria, Ahab did what any ruler of his age would have done. He built a shrine dedicated to the Tyrian Baal, the god whom Jezebel venerated in her home land. On a similar basis Solomon had introduced temples into Jerusalem to care for the religious needs of his foreign wives. In neither Jerusalem nor Samaria could those who sought to maintain pure Yahwistic religion tolerate altars to other gods. We may suppose that prophets such as Elijah denounced Jezebel's shrine, and that she in turn sought to use her royal power to silence them. Ahab was willing to support his wife in this venture and, before long, Baalist religion spread throughout Israel with the blessing of the king and queen. Yahweh's prophets were a persecuted minority, but they clung tenaciously to their task. Elijah dared to challenge Ahab and Jezebel. Drought throughout the land underscored the impotence of Baal, a fertility god. The pendulum swung back following Elijah's contest on Mount Carmel. There the prophet of Yahweh publicly challenged the prophets of Baal to call upon their god to produce fire and consume the sacrifice that was offered to him. Baal proved impotent, but when Elijah calmly offered his prayer to Yahweh, the God of Israel answered by fire and thus proved himself to be the true God, worthy of the worship of His people. In the aftermath many of Baal's prophets were slain, but Jezebel was not ready to yield. The religious problem outlived Ahab.

Ahab was more successful in war and affairs of state than in religious matters. Ben-hadad I of Damascus was greedy for Israelite land, but Ahab was able to defend his territory. So successful was Ahab that he actually captured the enemy king. Ben-hadad offered to restore Israelite land that he and his father had conquered and to give commercial rights in Damascus to Israelite traders (I Kings 20:34). Ahab generously made a treaty with Ben-hadad on terms that permitted the king of Damascus to return home with a light punishment. An unnamed Israelite prophet condemned Ahab for this kindness toward Israel's enemy (I Kings 20:35-43). The prophet's attitude is comparable to that of Samuel at the time Saul spared Agag (I Samuel 15).

Although risking the ire of Yahweh's prophets, Ahab may have had political reasons for sparing Ben-hadad. An enemy more deadly than the Syrian state of Damascus was posing a

This ivory inlay shows a sphinx in a lotus thicket. It was found at Ahab's palace in Samaria.

The Black Obelisk of Shalmanezer III is a four-sided pillar of black limestone, six and one-half feet high, with twenty small panels in bas relief. In the second panel from the top, King Jehu or his representative kneels before Shalmanezer.

threat. When Shalmaneser III (859-824 B.C.), successor to Ashur-nasir-pal, attempted to bring all of western Asia into his empire, the Arameans of Damascus and their neighbors settled their differences and prepared a united defense of their lands. In 853 B.C. the allied states challenged Assyria's expansionism in a battle fought at Qarqar on the Orontes River. The Mono-lith Inscription of Shalmaneser III, now in the British Museum, credits Ben-hadad with providing a contingent of twelve hun-dred chariots, twelve hundred horses, and twenty thousand infantry. "Ahab, the Israelite" is said to have provided two thousand chariots but only ten thousand infantry. The As-syrians gained a victory at Qarqar. Shalmaneser boasted that he made the blood of his enemies flow down the valleys and that he scattered their corpses far and wide. When the Assyrians withdrew, however, life went on much as it had before the battle. Shalmaneser was busy in the east following his victory at Qarqar and several years went by before another Assyrian army appeared in western Asia.

The monarchy in Israel was strictly limited in scope. Not only did a king not have the right to assume priestly functions, but also he was required to respect the rights of each citizen. Ahab recognized this obligation when Naboth of Jezreel re-fused to sell his vineyard to the king. Much as Ahab wanted Naboth's vineyard as an addition to his own holdings, he had no right to force Naboth to sell. Jezebel, however, came from a land where individual rights were not honored as they were in Israel. To her it was unthinkable that a commoner could stand in the way of a king's desire to enlarge his estate. To secure the vineyard for her husband, Jezebel arranged for the judicial murder of Naboth. Hired witnesses affirmed that Naboth had blasphemed the name of God and of the king. Then Naboth was conducted to a spot outside the city and stoned to death. Jezebel had proved herself a woman who could get her way, and Ahab could enjoy the vineyard he had desired. Elijah the prophet, however, pronounced judgment upon Ahab and his house (I Kings 21).

After a period of relative peace, Jehoshaphat of Judah joined forces with Ahab in an attempt to take Ramoth-gilead from the Arameans. The two kings consulted their court prophets, all but one of whom urged the campaign against Ramoth-gilead with promises of success. Micaiah ben Imlah, however, proph-esied that the campaign would end in disaster. A Syrian arrow wounded Ahab, and by nightfall he was dead (I Kings 22).

The unpopular Micaiah had proved right, and the fawning court prophets who told only the things the king wanted to hear were proved to be hirelings.

Jehoshaphat, Ahab's contemporary in Judah, reigned for a quarter century in relative peace (II Chron. 17:10). Tribute was brought to Jerusalem from the Philistine cities and from Arabia. Jehoshaphat's cooperation with Ahab incurred the wrath of the prophet Jehu ben Hanani who reproached his king: "Should you help the wicked and love those who hate the Lord? Because of this, wrath is gone out against you from the Lord. Nevertheless some good is found in you, for you destroyed the Asherahs out of the land, and have set your heart to seek God" (II Chron. 19:2-3).

The Edomites were unsuccessful in throwing off the yoke of Judah during Jehoshaphat's reign. Jehoshaphat decided to make use of the sea port at Ezion-geber (Elath) in sending ships to Ophir for gold. Solomon had earlier used Tyrian sailors in sending commercial fleets through the gulf of Aqabah and thence into the Red Sea and on to the eastern coasts of Africa or eastward to India. Ahaziah of Israel was willing to assist Jehoshaphat in his venture, but again the prophetic leaders of Judah objected. One Eliezer ben Dodavahu of Mareshah prophesied, "Because you have joined with Ahaziah, the Lord will destroy what you have made" (II Cron. 20:37). The ships were wrecked before they could leave port.

On the home front Jehoshaphat was more successful. He sought to abolish idolatrous shrines (II Chron. 17:6) and he ordered priests, Levites, and other officials to go throughout Judah teaching the people in their cities "the Book of the Law of the Lord" (II Chron. 17:9). Religiously Jehoshaphat was a loyal Yahwist, but he allowed political considerations to take precedence over religion when he married his son to Athaliah, the daughter of Ahab and Jezebel.

Jehoshaphat was succeeded by his son Jehoram, whose strong-willed wife, Athaliah, seems to have been the power behind the throne during her husband's lifetime. After a short and uneventful reign Jehoram died, and was succeeded by his (and Athaliah's) son Ahaziah. Within a year Ahaziah[1] died, a victim of Jehu's purge (II Kings 8:28). Thereupon Athaliah, the wife of a king and the mother of a king, seized power in her own name.

---

1. Note that the name Ahaziah, "Yahweh has grasped," was the name of the son and successor of Ahab of Israel, and of the youngest son and successor of Jehoram of Judah.

Ahab's sons did little to redeem the name of the house of Omri. Ahaziah, after ruling but a few months, suffered a fall (II Kings 1) and was incapacitated. In his need he sought the help of Baal-zebub, the god of Ekron, despairing of any help from Yahweh. Ahaziah evidently followed the idolatrous ways of his father Ahab. Elijah pronounced judgment upon him for neglecting the God of Israel. Ahaziah died of his wounds and was succeeded by his brother Jehoram (or Joram).

About the time Jehoram succeeded to the throne, Elisha the Tishbite succeeded Elijah as leader of the prophetic resistance to Baalism in Israel. Jehoram evidently attempted a reform, for we read that "he put away the image of Baal that his father had made" (II Kings 3:2), but the influence of Jezebel was still evident in Samaria and idolatry was still rampant. Elisha looked upon an energetic young Israelite named Jehu as the God-ordained vehicle for cleansing Israel from the sins introduced by the Omri dynasty. Elisha anointed Jehu (II Kings 9:6) even before Jehoram's death. Following a battle with the Syrians at Ramoth-gilead, Jehoram of Israel and Ahaziah of Judah encountered Jehu and his allies at Jezreel. Both kings were killed and, in the language of the prophets the blood of Naboth was avenged in Jezreel (II Kings 9:7).

When Jezebel learned of Jehu's approach she dressed up and looked upon the procession from her upper window. She taunted Jehu with being a murderer like Zimri. In anger Jehu ordered that Jezebel be cast to the street from her window. The procession trampled her corpse and the dogs ate her flesh. For the moment it appeared that the policies of the dynasty of Omri were completely repudiated (II Kings 9:30-37).

48

From Jehu to Jeroboam II

The year 841 B.C. marked the beginning of the reigns of Jehu in Israel and Athaliah in Judah — two people as dissimilar as any in Scripture. Jehu was a Yahwist, determined to obliterate every remembrance of Baalism. Athaliah was equally zealous, but her cause was the establishment of the Baalist cult of Ahab and Jezebel in Judah.

Jehu took the throne of Israel with the blessing of the prophet Elisha and the army quickly pledged their loyalty to the new regime. Determining to eradicate the last elements of Baalism from Israel, Jehu enticed the Baal worshipers into their temple. Eighty armed men were stationed at the exits and, at a word from Jehu, they killed the congregation of Baal worshipers in cold blood. In this way Jehu sought to purge his land of the taint of Baalism. All members of the family of Ahab were also slaughtered (II Kings 10).

Associated with Jehu in his purge of the Baalists was a man named Jehonadab, the son of Rechab (I Kings 10:15). Jehonadab was the first named of a group of Israelites known as Rechabites who sought to maintain the older desert traditions in opposition to the vices of an urbanized society. The Rechabites lived in tents instead of houses and they abstained from the use of intoxicating liquor. As orthodox Yahwists they were sympathetic with Jehu in his efforts to exterminate the last remnants of Baal worship from Israel.

Jehu was not a success as a ruler. By alienating the Phoenicians of Tyre and the rulers of Judah he was forced to stand alone, and Israel was not strong enough for that. Jehu prepared the way for incursions from the north where Hazael of Damascus was building an empire. The Biblical historian cannot give Jehu a clean bill of health. Like other kings of the north, "he did not turn from the sins of Jeroboam" (II Kings 10:31).

Shrines to Yahweh at Bethel and Dan were no substitute for the Jerusalem sanctuary in the eyes of the prophetic writers of Old Testament history.

Jehu's purge had disastrous effects for Israel. While it seemed to be a victory over Baalism, the ruthless manner in which it was carried out antagonized even Yahweh's prophets. Hosea records the Lord's message to his generation, ". . . yet a little while and I will punish the house of Jehu for the blood of Jezreel . . ." (Hosea 1:4). The slaughter of Jezebel turned the Phoenicians of Tyre against Jehu's dynasty. Tyre worshiped Baal, and the anti-Baalist activities of Jehu had political as well as religious overtones. Relations between Israel and Judah were also strained for the Judean king Ahaziah died at Megiddo as a result of wounds inflicted at Jehu's command (II Kings 9:27).

A closeup from the Black Obelisk of Shalmaneser, showing tribute of Jehu.

While Jehu was alienating his neighbors and Israel's erstwhile allies, an energetic Aramean named Hazael was consolidating his postion in the state of Damascus with a view to building an empire of his own. About 841 B.C. Hazael, a servant of Ben-hadad I, murdered his master and seized the throne for himself (II Kings 8:13-15). The prophet Elisha had told Hazael that he would become king in his own right.

Hazael promptly moved southward to challenge Israel's control over Ramoth-gilead. King Jehoram, a son of Ahab, was wounded at Ramoth-gilead and he never saw his home again. An arrow from Jehu's bow pierced Jehoram's heart while he was seeking to recover from his wounds at Jezreel (II Kings 9:20). While Jehu was seeking to exterminate opposition to his reign in Israel, Hazael was able to consolidate his power.

Because Hazael came to power without royal antecedents, the Assyrians contemptuously termed him a "son of a nobody." Shalmaneser III led his Assyrian armies to Damascus and beseiged Hazael's capital (841 B.C.). The environs of the city were mercilessly destroyed but Shalmaneser could not make Hazael capitulate. The Assyrians pressed southward, leaving Hazael to his own devices. Tyre, Sidon, and Israel were among the states that brought tribute to Shalmaneser. Among the subject peoples bringing tribute, as depicted on the Black Obelisk of Shalmaneser, is Jehu of Israel. Without allies, Jehu could only accept the terms of survival decreed by the Assyrian ruler.

The Assyrians did not leave permanent garrisons in the conquered lands, however. They were content to extract tribute, and demanded continued loyalty in the form of annual tribute.

When this was withheld, Assyrian armies reappeared to punish the defector. When Shalmaneser withdrew from Syria and Palestine, Hazael and his Syrian armies pressed southward. For the moment Assyria was occupied with problems closer home, and Hazael was able to expand his Aramean state with no serious challenge. The whole of Transjordan as far south as the Arnon (II Kings 10:32-33) was wrested from Jehu of Israel. Jehoahaz, Jehu's son, lost additional territory and was reduced to the status of a vassal (II Kings 13:7). Hazael allowed Jehoahaz but ten chariots, fifty horsemen and ten thousand infantry.

Hazael threatened the southern kingdom also, but Joash (Jehoash) of Judah was unwilling to risk battle. Instead the Judean king stripped the palace and the temple of their treasures (II Kings 12:17-18) and used them as a bribe to keep Hazael out of Jerusalem. The tribute was evidently sufficient, for Hazael did not bother Jerusalem again.

About 804 B.C. the Assyrian king Adad-nirari III marched against Syria and received the tribute of a king of Damascus named *mari* in the Assyrian annals. *Mari is* an Aramaic word meaning "lord," and it is probably a title rather than a personal name. Roland de Vaux is among the scholars who identify Hazael with *mari*.[1] A label has been found at Arslan Tash, the site of the ancient Assyrian provincial capital, Hadatu, marking the couch, among the remains of which it was found, as "belonging to our lord Hazael." Perhaps this very "ivory couch" was among the precious objects which Adad-nirari III took from Hazael (Mari). Some scholars, however, identify Mari with Hazael's son, Ben-hadad II.

Hazael was probably the most successful of the kings of Damascus. He is remembered as a successful warrior who also gave attention to the building and beautification of Damascus, his capital. He was succeeded by Ben-hadad II, a son who was unable to maintain the empire built by his aggressive father.

Jehoahaz, the son of Jehu, came to the throne of Israel with a depleted army and the threat of recurring trouble with the rulers of Damascus (II Kings 13:1-9). Philistines and Ammonites took advantage of Israel's weakness to stage raids into her territory.

Things took a turn for the better, however, under Joash

---

1. R. de Vaux, *"La chronologie de Hazael et de Benhadad III, Rois de Damas,"* R. B., XLIII (1934), pp. 512-518.

(Jehoash) of Israel, the son of Jehoahaz. By this time the Assyrians had crippled Damascus and Israel was able to regain her lost territories (II Kings 13:25). Between the defeat of Damascus and the assertion of Assyrian power in western Asia, Israel had an opportunity to develop without outside interference.

While Jehu was attempting to eradicate Baalism from Israel, Athaliah was introducing it into Judah. Jehoram (Joram), the son of Jehoshaphat, had married Athaliah of the house of Omri (II Kings 8:16-24). To secure an uncontested throne, Jehoram, probably at Athaliah's suggestion, killed all his brothers and their partisans when he took the throne. After a short reign Jehoram died and was succeeded by Ahaziah, a son of Jehoram and Athaliah. Ahaziah was killed in battle by Jehu — a fact that made Jehu utterly repulsive to Athaliah. Under the circumstances we may understand Athaliah's seizure of power and her attempts to suppress Yahwism in favor of the Baal cult of her parents. Athaliah seized the throne and proceeded to murder all the surviving members of the Davidic line. Had she been successful there could have been no Messiah of the line of David. Happily an infant son of Ahaziah named Joash (Jehoash) was rescued by his aunt, the wife of the priest Jehoiada (II Chron. 22:11).

Athaliah's rule was doubtless resented by the masses of the people of Judah. She was looked upon as a usurper, and her god was clearly not the god of Abraham, Isaac, and Jacob. When the child Joash was seven years of age the priest Jehoiada arranged for him to be presented in the temple. With the support of the officers of the royal guard the child was crowned king. When she heard the commotion, Athaliah rushed into the temple crying, "Treason!" It was too late, however. At Jehoiada's word Athaliah was led out and executed. The Baal temple was demolished; its priest was slain. The boy king Joash reigned with the priest Jehoiada holding the real power of government (II Kings 11).

While under the tutelage of Jehoiada, Joash ordered a collection to be made in order to restore and repair the temple which had fallen into disrepair during Athaliah's usurpation (II Kings 12). Money was collected and the laborers paid for their work on the temple. Although Joash favored the Jerusalem temple, popular worship continued at the high places, a fact which the Biblical historian notes as a criticism of Joash's religious policy (II Kings 12:3). Politically Joash was not successful, for he found it necessary to take the treasures of the temple and the palace to offer as tribute to Hazael of Damascus (II Kings 12:17-18).[2] No doubt Joash was criticized for this policy. Dissatisfaction led to his assassination at the hand of one of his servants (II Kings 12:21).

Amaziah, the son of Joash came to the throne of Judah about the year 800 B.C. When he had secured the throne for himself he slew the murderers of his father but, contrary to custom, he spared their children (II Kings 14:5-6). Amaziah planned an expedition against Edom and hired mercenary soldiers from Israel. A prophet, called "a man of God" in the Biblical text, warned Amaziah that God could not bless such a venture that made use of idolatrous Israelites. With some reluctance Amaziah released his mercenaries who plundered the land of Judah on their way home.

The power of Damascus was checked when Adad-nirari III (811-783 B.C.) came to the throne of Assyria. Neither Israel nor Judah knew that the yoke of Assyria would be much heavier than the yoke of Damascus. Indeed the Assyrian pressure on the Aramean states to the north must have seemed a mercy to the harassed Israelites.

Adad-nirari crushed Damascus. Israel and Judah paid their tribute to Assyria for a time, but the yoke of Damascus was lifted and Israel enjoyed a brief respite. The successors of Adad-nirari were largely inefficient, with the result that Palestine was able to enjoy half a century without fear of invasion. Under Jehu's grandson Jehoash, Israel was able to recover territory lost to Hazael during the heydey of Aramean power. Amaziah of Judah was able to reconquer Edom (II Kings 14:7) but he foolishly picked a fight with Jehoash of Israel. The two kings fought at Beth-shemesh (II Kings 14:11-14) with disastrous results for Judah. Jehoash captured Amaziah at Beth-shemesh, then he moved on to Jerusalem, broke down a part of its wall, seized silver, gold, and hostages from the palace and temple, and returned to Samaria.

Jehoash could have annexed all of Judah had he desired to do so. He chose rather to return to Samaria with his plunder. Amaziah kept his throne but his popularity was certainly diminished. He discovered a plot to kill him in Jerusalem and fled to Lachish where the conspirators were successful. He died

A scene along the "Street called Straight" in Damascus.

2. See p. 28.

in Lachish and his body was returned for burial in Jerusalem (II Kings 14:17-20).

Something of the prosperity of the times can be seen in the remains of ancient Samaria, modern Sebastiyeh. The palace which dates from the time of Jeroboam II was approached through a main gateway with a columned entrance court. Archaeologists discovered more than two hundred ivory plaques and fragments in a store room of the palace. The art form shares characteristics of both Phoenicians and Egyptians. The plaques may have served as inlays for palace furniture. A reservoir or pool thirty-three and one-half by seventeen feet adds to the feeling of grandeur associated with the palace.

Uzziah (Azariah) succeeded Amaziah to the throne of Judah a few years after Jeroboam (II) succeeded Jehoash (Joash) as king of Israel. The reigns of Uzziah and Jeroboam were both long and prosperous, with a degree of success at home and abroad that had not been enjoyed since the division of the kingdom. Jeroboam II (786-746 B.C.) "restored the border of Israel from the entrance of Hamath as far as the Sea of the Arabah" (II Kings 14:25). Territorial expansion might be interpreted as a sign of national vigor, but a succession of prophets underscored the moral corruption that was destroying the spiritual vitality of Israel. Amos and Hosea were the vanguard of a company of prophets who insisted that sacrifice and ritual was of no value to the man or nation devoid of righteousness: "I hate, I loathe your pilgrimages, nor will I inhale the odors of your convocations. Though you make sacrifices to me I shall not accept your offerings, nor shall I regard the peace offerings of your fatlings. Take away from me the noise of your songs for I will not listen to the music of your harps. But let justice roll on like the waters, even righteousness like a mighty stream" (Amos 5:21-24). The nation was prospering. The rich were growing richer, the poor, poorer. Moabites and Ammonites were again subject to Israel, but Israel had forgotten her God. The prophets pronounced oracles of impending doom, and the Assyrian was beginning to stir on the horizon to fulfill those prophecies.

The prosperity of the north was paralleled in Judah. Uzziah (783-742 B.C.) repaired the walls and defenses of Jerusalem and reorganized the army (II Chron. 26:9, 11-15). He controlled Edom and opened the industries and port facilities of Eziongeber (Elath, II Kings 14:22). The Negev and the north and east parts of the Philistine Plain were incorporated into Judah.

A Roman road in the Wadi Raman near the Arabah. It followed along one of the ancient trade routes that connected Palestine with northern Arabia.

By the middle of the eighth century B.C. Israel and Judah were at peace, enjoying the fruits of trade and commerce. Merchants secured luxury goods at the Phoenician ports and transported them into Israel and Judah. Overland trade routes passed through Transjordan into northern Arabia. Copper was mined in the Arabah and the Red Sea trade was probably revived through the port of Ezion-geber.

49

Prophets to Israel

Israel's prophets were primarily messengers of God, divinely commissioned to present God's Word to men. The popular concept of the prophet as one who predicts the future is alien to the spirit of Biblical prophecy because it does not describe his true function. The prophet is a spokesman, and it was in this sense that Aaron was termed a "prophet" or spokesman for his brother Moses (Exod. 7:1-2), as Moses was a spokesman for Israel's God.

Since prophetism became an institutionalized human movement, we should not conclude that all who came to Israel professing to present a message from Yahweh were completely pure in their motivation. Amos found it necessary to deny any connection with the professional prophetic guilds of his day (Amos 7:10-17). Among the foes of Jeremiah were false prophets who assured the people of Judah that God would break the yoke of Nebuchadnezzar within a short time (Jer. 28). Such prophets may have fancied themselves patriotic in predicting good things, but history proved them wrong. Nebuchadnezzar's armies destroyed Jerusalem.

The prophet who gave a favorable oracle would often be richly rewarded, for many believed that the prophecy itself had power to effect its accomplishment. Jeremiah's unfavorable prophecies would be interpreted as curses, and efforts should be taken to silence him. It was considered appropriate to reward prophets for giving favorable messages. When Saul was persuaded to ask Samuel to help him find his lost asses, Saul protested, "But behold, if we go, what shall we bring the man?" (I Sam. 9:7-8). Naaman the Syrian wanted to present a suitable gift for Elisha in thanks for the healing of his leprosy. Elisha, however, refused the reward, although his servant Gehazi sought the gift for himself (II Kings 5:15-27). When Amos was declaring the impending judgments of God at Bethel, its priest assumed that the prophet was making a living from his oracles (Amos 7:12). Amos insisted that he was a herdsman and dresser of sycamore trees by profession, and that Yahweh called and commissioned him to bring a message to Israel with no thought of reward.

While the prophetic movement in Israel goes back at least to Moses, prophets were particularly active during the period of Israel's divided kingdom. Before the division, Ahijah of Shiloh approached Jeroboam and acted out a prophecy. The prophet stripped off a new coat, tore it into twelve pieces, and handed ten of them to Jeroboam, saying, "Behold, I will rend the kingdom out of the hand of Solomon and will give ten tribes unto you" (I Kings 11:29-32). Solomon's policies which had brought Israel to the verge of bankruptcy and encouraged idolatry had disillusioned Ahijah, who hoped that Jeroboam would prove more faithful to Yahweh than Solomon had been. Rehoboam, Solomon's son, was following his father's footsteps so that a new regime seemed to offer the only hope. The idolatry introduced by Jeroboam proved offensive to Ahijah (I Kings 14: 6-16) and Jeroboam's name became associate with the shrines at Bethel and Dan which were set up as rivals to the Jerusalem Temple. Still there is every reason to believe that Ahijah was acting from the highest motives when he prophesied the rule of Jeroboam over ten of the tribes.

During the reign of Baasha of Israel we meet a prophet named Jehu ben Hanani (I Kings 16:1-7) who pronounced judgment on Baasha's house because of its idolatry. The Davidic dynasty continued throughout the history of the southern kingdom, but Israel suffered a succession of dynasties, not one of which is considered blameless by the prophetic writers of the books of Kings and Chronicles. There is reason to believe that each founder of a dynasty hoped that his descendants would reign after him in an unbroken succession. Ahijah and Jehu ben Hanani successively warned Israel's first two kings that their dynasties would not remain in power. Baasha began the series of attacks on Judah which caused Asa of Judah to request aid from Ben-hadad, the king of the Syrian state of Damascus.

Prophets were particularly active in Israel during the reign of Ahab and Jezebel. The worship of Baal, fostered by Jezebel, proved a challenge to Israel's prophets who insisted that Yahweh alone was the God of Israel. While the worship of Yahweh at the shrines at Bethel and Dan was considered unorthodox by the prophets with an orientation toward the Jerusalem shrine, the introduction of Baal worship was considered to be infinitely worse. Although in many ways apostate, the Northern Kingdom was still considered a part of God's people and, in moments of political crisis Yahweh is still found fighting on behalf of Israel.

In the battles between Israel and the Arameans of Damascus, Yahweh gave victory to Israel. An unnamed prophet denounced Ahab for sparing Ben-hadad when the Syrian king was in Ahab's power (I Kings 20:35-43). During plans for the campaign against Ramoth-gilead, four hundred prophets encouraged Ahab to enter the battle — but one, Micaiah ben Imlah, predicted Ahab's death in the battle (I Kings 22:17, 18, 28). Micaiah insisted that the four hundred had been inspired by Yahweh to tell the king a lie (I Kings 22:20-23). In the theology of ancient Israel even false prophets serve a function in furthering God's purposes. False prophets will lull the king into a false sense of security, after which he will be an easy prey to his enemy.

Micaiah, in speaking to Ahab's messenger, insisted that he could but declare the word of God (I Kings 22:14). The messenger shared the common view that a prophet could bring about events by uttering a potent word. Micaiah insisted that he could but declare God's word. He had no control over the future.

Elijah the Tishbite, and his successor Elisha, are the best known of Israel's prophets who were active during the dynasties of Omri and Jehu. Elijah was concerned about Baalism, which was encouraged by Ahab's wife Jezebel and was a direct result of the internationalism which Omri fostered and sealed by the marriage of his son Ahab to the Phoenician princess Jezebel. When Jezebel came to the palace at Samaria she was permitted to continue the worship of Baal. Being a strong personality she promptly secured official status for the Baal cult at the expense of the worship of Yahweh, Israel's God. Elijah saw this as a direct threat to Israel's ancestral faith. His challenge to the Baalist, and the subsequent encounter on Mt. Carmel (I Kings 18) gives us an excellent picture of the religion of Baal on one hand, and of the calm faith of an Elijah on the other. The prophet "repaired the altar of Yahweh that had been thrown down" (I Kings 18:30), prepared his sacrifice, and quietly prayed. The fire of Yahweh consumed the sacrifice, and all the people acknowledged, "Yahweh, he is God; Yahweh, he is God" (I Kings 18:39). Baalism was not permanently eradicated, as we know from subsequent Biblical history, but the courage of an Elijah did much to reassert the claims of Yahweh during the difficult days of Ahab and Jezebel.

On the ethical side, the matter of Naboth's vineyard demonstrated that the claims of Israel's God could not be divorced from the daily concerns of life. Ahab wanted to add to his properties the vineyard of an Israelite named Naboth which adjoined the royal domains in Jezreel (I Kings 21). Naboth did not wish to part with his vineyard, and Israelite law assured him of his rights. When Jezebel saw that Ahab was disappointed because he could not acquire the land for a vegetable garden, she determined to acquire it for him. Unwilling to see any restraint on the power of a king, the autocratic Jezebel had Naboth judicially murdered. False witnesses were hired, and they accused Naboth of cursing God and the king. Naboth was stoned outside the city and Ahab was able to take his vineyard.

When Elijah learned what had happened he appeared before Ahab and accused him of murder and larceny. Elijah prophesied that Ahab's house would be cut off "like the house of Jeroboam the son of Nebat, and like the house of Baasha the son of Ahijah" (I Kings 21:22). The judgments pronounced on Ahab and Jezebel are evidence that Israel's God was concerned about justice at all levels of society. Even kings were subject to Yahweh's law, and they did not have the right to trespass on the rights of others. Like Nathan declaring God's anger with David for taking Bath-sheba and judicially murdering Uriah (II Sam. 11-12), Elijah reminds Ahab that even a king must account for his deeds.

Elisha continued the work of Elijah and served the nation as a patriot-prophet. He encouraged Jehu, a loyal Yahwist, to stage a coup which would forever end the Omri-Ahab dynasty with its Baalist tendencies. Ahab's widow Jezebel was thrown from a window and trampled to death (II Kings 9:30-37), and Jehu began a campaign to wipe out all traces of Baalism with all the enthusiasm Jezebel had shown in her antagonism to Yahweh.

During the eighth century B.C. a herdsman named Amos became the first of a series of prophets whose utterances have been preserved for us in Biblical books bearing their names. Earlier prophets had performed much the same function as these "writing prophets," as they are sometimes called, but it was not until the eighth century that books were ascribed to Israel's prophets.

The first half of the eighth century B.C. was a period of pros-

Baal, a storm god, is represented holding a club in his right hand and a lance in his left hand. The lance extends upward in the form of a tree or stylized lightning. From Ras Shamra.

perity for both Israel and Judah. Adad-nirari III of Assyria crushed Damascus, Israel's rival to the north, in 805 B.C. This left both Israel and Judah free to regain lost territory and to expand northward (cf. II Kings 13:25). With the death of Adad-nirari (782 B.C.), Assyria entered a period of weakness with no strong ruler until 745 B.C. when Tiglath-pileser III began a new and vigorous policy.

During this period when neither Damascus nor Assyria posed a threat to Israel, Uzziah of Judah and Jeroboam II of Israel enjoyed reigns of prosperity unequalled since the days of Solomon. A rich merchant class developed and merchants and nobles alike built elaborate houses and revelled in the comforts which wealth made possible. The poor, however, did not share in the prosperity. Small farmers were put out of business to make room for the estates of the wealthy. Society was divided between the dissolute rich and the embittered poor. The rich thronged the religious shrines and offered expensive gifts and sacrifices as a means of securing greater material blessings. Prosperity was interpreted as proof of God's blessing. Priests and prophets were delighted to be honored by the wealthy.

Under such circumstances a prophet of doom is not wanted. Yet some time after 760 B.C., a man who would not associate himself with the professional prophets of his day, but who clearly showed evidence of prophetic calling, dared to pronounce divine judgment upon the people of Israel. Amos, a Judean from Tekoa, was regarded as a treasonous outsider when he dared to prophesy the fall of the dynasty of Jeroboam II (Amos 7:9). While contemporaries of Amos looked forward to a "day of Yahweh" when God would show his favor to Israel and annihilate her enemies, Amos warned Israel that she must face a "day of Yahweh" during which God's judgment would fall on his disobedient people (Amos 5:18-20). A proud and self-righteous people would go into exile (Amos 6:7), yet beyond the exile God would bring restoration to his people (Amos 9:11-12), remembering His covenant with David.

Although primarily a prophet to Israel, there is an international flavor to Amos' message. Israel's God is concerned about all peoples, and the moral code knows no boundaries. Aram, Philistia, Phoenicia, Edom, Ammon, Moab, and Judah are judged by Yahweh when they indulge in cruel acts and fail to show the compassion which one human being owes to another (Amos 1:3-2:16). The God who brought Israel out of Egypt at the time of the Exodus also brought the Philistines

In the Judean wilderness near Tekoa.

from Caphtor and the Syrians from Kir (Amos 9:7). The God of Amos was a God of all men. Although particularly blessed by Him, Israel had sinned. Judgment was impending, but beyond the judgment Amos envisioned the day of restoration and future blessing (Amos 6:14; 9:13-15).

Hosea, a younger contemporary of Amos, was the only one of the writing prophets to come from Israel. The period during which Assyria's preoccupation with problems in the East was ending, and the energetic Tiglath-pileser III was marching his armies westward with the goal of making Assyria master of the world. Menahem of Israel paid tribute to Tiglath-pileser ("Pul" in II Kings 15:19-20).

The domestic life of Hosea provided a background against which the prophet proclaimed his message to Israel. Hosea's wife, Gomer, was a prostitute — perhaps a temple prostitute associated with the degenerate fertility cult. Hosea had loved her and married her, yet she did not remain loyal to him. Gomer abandoned herself to her lovers, but Hosea refused to give her up. He wooed her and ultimately won her back to himself. The prophet used these experiences as an allegory to show Israel her own black history. God had loved Israel and entered into a covenant (comparable to a marriage contract) with her at Sinai. God had agreed to be Israel's God, and she, His people. God had protected her and provided for her miraculously during the wilderness wanderings. He gave her victories over her enemies, Sihon and Og, east of the Jordan, and Jericho and the other fortified cities of Canaan fell to Joshua's armies as a result of divine power. Israel was not grateful to God, however. No sooner had she entered the land than she found the local deities — Baal and the Asherim — fatally attractive. As Hosea's wife had forsaken him, so Israel had forsaken her God.

But Hosea loved his wife even in her time of estrangement, and Yahweh continued to love idolatrous Israel. Hosea, no less than Amos, underscores the righteousness of God and the judgment that must fall on the transgressor (cf. Hosea 10:10). He is particularly conscious of the compassion of God, however: "How can I give you up, O Ephraim! [Israel], How can I hand you over, O Israel! How can I make you like Admah! How can I treat you like Zeboiim![1] My heart recoils within me, my compassion grows warm and tender" (Hosea 11:8).

---

1. Admah and Zeboiim were cities of the plain, destroyed along with Sodom and Gomorrah (cf. Deut. 29:23).

Hosea did not picture Yahweh as given over to sentiment, however. In Canaan, Israel had turned her back on Yahweh and chosen licentious lovers. Yahweh had tried to regain her love, but His voice was not heard. The remedy was to take Israel away from Canaan, back to the wilderness (Hosea 2:14-20). There, away from the distractions of the lovers (Baal and the other gods), God could declare his love anew. The valley of Achor ("trouble") would become a door of hope. There was no hope for idolatrous Israel in Canaan. There she was given over wholly to idolatry. The troubles of exile, however, might restore Israel to a sense of her privilege as God's beloved. There she might renounce the Baals and renew her covenant with Yahweh. Hosea envisioned exile as both punishment for sin and the means of a fresh start for a renewed relationship of love between Yahweh and his people Israel.

A stone idol of Baal discovered in the ruins at Baalbek, Lebanon.

50

The Assyrian Threat

According to Genesis 10:11-12, immigrants from Babylon journeyed northward and settled such Assyrian sites as Ashur, Nineveh, and Calah. The historical Assyrians are a mixture of people from Sumer, from the western desert regions, and from the hills to the north. After a period of greatness during the second millennium B.C., the growing power of the Aramean tribes challenged Assyrian expansionism to the west. The rise of the kingdom of David and Solomon took place during a period when western Asia was experiencing a power vacuum. No major power was present to keep the Israelites in a dependent status.

When Tukulti-Ninurta II (890-885 B.C.) took the Assyrian throne he began a determined campaign to crush the tribes which challenged Assyria's bid for power. His son Ashur-nasir-pal II (883-859 B.C.) marched his armies westward until he reached the Lebanon Mountains and the coastal cities of the Philistines. He was also successful in northern Babylonia and in the mountainous regions east of Assyria. Ashur-nasir-pal's annals boast of the magnitude of his building operations at Calah. He used fifty thousand prisoners to enlarge the city. Slave labor built a new citadel, a palace, and numerous temples. Artists engraved sculptures in Ashur-nasir-pal's audience chambers. Botanical and zoological gardens and a park added to the comfort of the Assyrian capital.

Shalmaneser III (859-824 B.C.) continued the policies of his father Ashur-nasir-pal. Under Shalmaneser's efficient rule Assyrian power reached from Urartu (Armenia) southward to the Persian Gulf, and from the mountains of Media westward to the Phoenician coast and into Cilicia in eastern Asia Minor. In 853 B.C. Shalmaneser fought a coalition of twelve kings at Qarqar on the Orontes River in Syria. The battle is described on Shalmaneser's "Monolith Inscription" now in the British Museum. Among Shalmaneser's foes were Hadadezer of Damascus, Irhuleni of Hamath, and "Ahab, the Israelite." The inscription describes the fighting force engaged in battle, and we learn that Ahab commanded two thousand chariots and ten thousand soldiers. Damascus provided but twelve hundred chariots, but double the number of soldiers available to Ahab — 20,000 in all. The battle of Qarqar is not mentioned in the Bible, but the Monolith Inscription provides evidence that Israel was a leader among the smaller states of western Asia in the ninth century B.C. Shalmaneser boasted of a decisive victory over his enemies, claiming to have caused their blood to flow down the valleys and to have scattered their corpses far and wide. Actually he avoided campaigning in Syria for several years after the Battle of Qarqar, and his victory was but a temporary one. Once the Assyrian army left, the states of Syria and Palestine continued a policy of business as usual.

During a later campaign into western Asia, Shalmaneser extracted heavy tribute from a number of the city states which he conquered. The "Black Obelisk of Shalmaneser," discovered by Austin Henry Layard in his excavation of Shalmaneser's palace at Nimrud in 1846, portrays emissaries from five different regions bringing tribute. In the second row of reliefs on the front of the obelisk is a representation of Jehu of Israel kneeling before Shalmaneser. Jehu is clothed in a sleeveless jacket and a long fringed skirt with girdle. He has a short beard and wears a soft cap. Israelites in long robes follow the king. They carry tribute for Shalmaneser. A cuneiform inscription reads, "The tribute of Jehu, the son of Omri.[1] I received from him silver, gold, a golden bowl, a golden vase with pointed bottom, golden tumblers, golden buckets, tin, a staff for a king, and wooden [word unknown]." An inscription dated during the eighteenth year of Shalmaneser's reign also mentions tribute taken from Jehu, the son of Omri.

Shalmaneser III described himself as "the mighty king, king of the universe, the king without rival, the autocrat, the powerful one of the four regions of the world, who shatters the might of the princes of the whole world, who has smashed all of his foes like pots." The close of his reign was marred by revolts, however, and the short reign of his son Shamshi-Adad V

---

1. The expression "son of Omri" does not imply that Shalmaneser was ignorant of the family relations of Israel's kings. Son, in this sense, simply means "succesor."

(824-811 B.C.) was spent largely in putting down revolts in Armenia, Elam, and Babylonia. Shamshi-Adad's widow, Sammuramat (Semiramis), acted as regent until her son Adad-nirari III (805-783 B.C.) was old enough to rule in his own right.

Adad-nirari attacked Damascus in 804 B.C., intervening in a dispute between Hamath and Damascus. Hazael, the son of Ben hadad II, king of Damascus is called *Mari,* his Aramaic title, in Adad-nirari's account of the conflict. The attack on Damascus indirectly helped Judah which had been suffering as a result of attacks by the Aramean rulers of Damascus (cf. II Kings 12:17; II Chron. 24:23-24). Adad-nirari claimed to have received tribute from "Hatti [northern Syria], Amurru [eastern Syria], Tyre, Sidon, the Land of Omri [Israel], Edom, and Philistia as far as the Mediterranean." Joash of Judah recovered towns on his northern border which had been lost to Hazael of Damascus before the Assyrian advance (II Kings 13:25). Adad-nirari built a new palace for himself outside the citadel walls at Calah.

Following the death of Adad-nirari III, Assyrian power was on the wane. His successor, Shalmaneser IV (782-773 B.C.), continued to exert pressure on Damascus, with the result that Jeroboam II of Israel was able to extend his northern frontier northward to the "entrance of Hamath" (II Kings 14:25), the opening from the south into the Beqaʿ, the valley between the Lebanon and the ante-Lebanon ranges. Assyria, however, was feeling pressure on its northern border from Armenia (Urartu), and its internal politics were in a state of flux. Adad-nirari had died young and childless, with the result that the succession was uncertain. No advances were made during the rules of Ashur-dan III (772-755 B.C.) or Ashur-nirari V (754-745 B.C.). An eclipse of the sun in 763 B.C. was considered a sign of ill omen as it marked a defeat of Assyrian arms in the north. The states in western Asia seemed free to regroup and to challenge Assyrian claims on their territory.

After a generation of uncertainty an Assyrian warrior and statesman who took the name Tiglath-pileser (III) usurped the throne in 745 B.C. Tiglath-pileser sought to restore the lost glories of Assyria. Under the name Pulu, or Pul (II Kings 15:9; I Chron. 5:26) he was proclaimed king of Babylon. He achieved victory on his northern borders over the Armenians and turned his attention to the west where the local princes had thrown off the Assyrian yoke. From 743 to 740 B.C. Tiglath-

This relief from Nimrud shows Shamshi-Adad V standing under symbols of his gods.

In one of the campaigns of Tiglathpileser III, Assyrian archers and siege engines are storming an enemy stronghold. Prisoners are being beheaded and impaled.

pileser besieged Arpad. Rezin of Damascus and other rulers in the area paid their tribute. In 738 B.C. Tiglath-pileser was faced by a coalition of rulers including the king of Hamath and *Azriau* of *Yaudi*. This has been interpreted as a reference to Azariah (Uzziah) of Judah,[2] although some scholars suggest that *Azriau* was the name of the ruler of a state in northern Syria named *Yaudi*.[3]

In II Kings 15:19-20 we read, "Pul, the king of Assyria, came against the land, and Menahem gave Pul a thousand talents of silver that he might help him to confirm his hold of the royal power. Menahem exacted the money from Israel, that is from all the wealthy men, fifty shekels of silver from every man, to give to the king of Assyria. So the king of Assyria turned back and did not stay there in the land." From Assyrian contracts we learn that fifty shekels was the value of a slave.[4] Each man was required to pay the price of a slave to avoid deportation. In one of his inscriptions, Tiglath-pileser mentions the tribute he received from "Menahem of Samaria" and Hiram of Tyre. The date of this inscription is not known.

A few years later Pekah of Israel joined Rezin of Damascus in an alliance against Assyria. They moved against Ahaz of Judah in an attempt to force Judah into an anti-Assyrian alliance (II Kings 16:5-9). Ahaz turned to Tiglath-pileser for help, with disastrous results for the whole of western Asia. Tiglath-pileser marched westward and then down the coast of Palestine. The king of Gaza, Hanunu, fled across the River of Egypt (Wadi el 'Arish) to find sanctuary in Egypt. Ammon, Moab, Edom, Ashkelon, and Judah paid their tribute to the Assyrians. Rebellious Israel was attacked.

Damascus fared even worse than Israel. In 732 B.C. Tiglath-pileser entered Damascus, executed Rezin its king, ravaged the city, and deported a large portion of its population. Then Tiglath-pileser organized the territory of the former state of Damascus into four Assyrian provinces. While his predecessors had been content to take tribute from conquered peoples,

---

2. So John Bright, *A History of Israel* (Westminster Press, 1959, pp. 252-253. The text is found in Pritchard, *ANET*, p. 282.
3. Pritchard, *ANET*, p. 283.
   > Bit Humria ["The House of Omri," Israel] ... all its inhabitants and their possessions I led to Assyria. They overthrew their king Paqaha [Pekah] and I placed Ausi' [Hoshea] as king over them. I received from them ten talents of gold, 1000 talents of silver as their tribute, and brought them to Assyria."
4. Pritchard, *ANET*, p. 283.

Tiglath-pileser adopted the policy of incorporating them into his empire. Among those who hastened to Damascus to pay tribute to Tiglath-pileser we meet the name *Iauhazi* of Judah, i.e. Jehoahaz, the fuller form of the Biblical name Ahaz.[5] While in Damascus, Ahaz was impressed with an altar which he saw there, and he made a model to be used in the building of a similar altar in Jerusalem (II Kings 16:10-17).

Judah was a vassal of Assyria as a result of the policy of King Ahaz, but Israel still hoped to be able to resist Assyrian power. When Tiglath-pileser III died in 727 B.C. he was succeeded by his son Shalmaneser V (727-722 B.C.). Hoshea of Israel listened to his pro-Egyptian counselors and refused to pay tribute to Shalmaneser. Egypt promised help (II Kings 17:4), but help never arrived. Shalmaneser besieged the Israelite capital at Samaria, and after three years the city fell, bringing the northern kingdom to an end (722 B.C.).

Sargon II (722-705 B.C.) actually claims credit for the destruction of Samaria. In his so-called Display Inscriptions at Khorsabad, Sargon boasted, "I besieged and conquered Samaria, led away as booty 27,290 inhabitants of it. I formed from among them a contingent of 50 chariots and made the remaining inhabitants assume their social positions. I installed over them an officer of mine and imposed upon them the tribute of the former king."[6]

In his Annals, Sargon also states, "The town I rebuilt better than it was before, and settled herein people from countries which I myself had conquered."[7] This policy of transportation caused the Israelites to be scattered throughout the Assyrian Empire, and brought into their former territory the ancestors of the people who came to be known as Samaritans (II Kings 17:24-41).

Other campaigns in Syria and Palestine took Sargon to Raphia where he defeated an Egyptian army. This was the first clash between the Egyptians and the Assyrians, the two nations that would vie for control of western Asia. In 717 B.C. Sargon conquered Carchemish and campaigned farther north in Cilicia. In 715 he sacked the Philistine cities of Ashdod and Gath, and claimed to have subjugated Judah. In 714 he was in the Lake Van area attempting to pacify the Mannai and other tribes. In the south he gained effective control of Elam and sacked the

Horses' heads in relief, from Sargon's palace in Khorsabad.

---

5. Pritchard, *ANET*, p. 282.
6. Pritchard, *ANET*, pp. 284-285.
7. Pritchard, *ANET*, p. 284.

Facade of the inner temple of Nabu at Khorsabad (ca. 722-705 B.C.).

city of Susa. Merodach-baladan (Marduk-apla-iddina), the Chaldean prince who sought to establish an independent Babylon was driven into the marshlands at the head of the Persian Gulf in 710 B.C.

While Sargon's career appears to have been eminently successful, he actually spent much of his time putting down revolts throughout his empire. He had made his capital successively at Ashur, Calah, and Nineveh. East of Nineveh he built a new capital, Dur-Sharruken ("Sargonsburg") which later historians called Khorsabad after the Sasanid hero Khosroes. The large palace built during the last years of Sargon's rule was discovered in 1843 by Paul Emile Botta, the French consul at Mosul. Sargon's palace was among the first structures carefully studied by scientific archaeologists. Sargon, himself, died in battle before he could move into his new palace.

Sennacherib (705-681 B.C.) spent the early years of his reign putting down the revolts which broke out following the death of his father. Marduk-apal-iddina seized the throne of Babylon and attempted to set up a state there free of Assyrian control. It was probably at this time that he sent an emissary to Jerusalem to show friendship to Hezekiah and enlist his support (II Kings 20:12-19). Late in 702 B.C. Sennacherib defeated Marduk-apla-iddina and his Elamite and Arab allies at Cutha and Kish. Thereupon Sennacherib entered Babylon, installed a vassal on the throne, and took prisoners to Nineveh. Marduk-apla-iddina, however, escaped to Elam.

The northern frontier of Assyria was quickly pacified, after which Sennacherib was free to turn his attenion to the west, where Egypt was stirring up trouble among the smaller states. Hezekiah of Judah was a leader in the opposition to Sennacherib. Hezekiah had seized Padi, the pro-Assyrian king of Ekron (II Kings 18:8) and had strengthened his fortifications in Jerusalem. Anticipating trouble from Assyria, Hezekiah called upon Egypt for help (Isa. 30:1-4).

The annals of Sennacherib describe his third campaign which took him into Syria and Palestine. The Assyrian army marched down the Phoenician coast and received the submission of Sidon, Arvad, Byblos, Beth-Ammon, Moab, and Edom. Ashkelon resisted and was destroyed. Sennacherib states that he defeated the Egyptians at Eltekeh. Their promise of help proved futile, and the smaller states had to stand up against Sennacherib alone.

The Bible records victories of Sennacherib in the land of Judah: "In the fourteenth year of King Hezekiah, Sennacherib king of Assyria came up against all the fortified cities of Judah and took them" (II Kings 18:13). Hezekiah sent messengers to Lachish to negotiate the payment of tribute (II Kings 18:14-15). Sennacherib later ornamented his palace at Nineveh with bas reliefs depicting his siege of Lachish and the tribute which he received. The inscription on the reliefs, now in the British Museum, states, "Sennacherib, King of Assyria, sitting on his throne while the spoil from the city of Lachish passed before him."

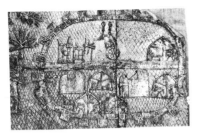

The bas-relief above depicts the Judean city of Lachish besieged by the army of Sennacherib. Below, soldiers of Sennacherib are beheading captives.

Scholars differ in their efforts to date Sennacherib's siege of Jerusalem. It may have been later in the same campaign that the siege described in II Kings 18 and 19 took place. Since II Kings 19:37 describes Sennacherib's death, some scholars have dated the siege during which "the angel of the Lord went forth and slew a hundred and eighty-five thousand in the camp of the Assyrians" (II Kings 19:35) in a later campaign, perhaps that of 686 B.C. against the Arabs. There is no necessity to assume that the death in Nineveh immediately followed the campaign in Judah, however, and it seems proper to regard the Biblical and Assyrian accounts of the Siege of Jerusalem as two versions of one event.

In Sennacherib's annals he states, "As to Hezekiah, the Jew, he did not submit to my yoke, I laid siege to forty-six of his strong cities, walled forts, and to the countless small villages in their vicinity, and conquered them. . . . I drove out of them 200,150 people, young and old, male and female, horses, mules, donkeys, camels, big and small cattle beyond counting, and considered [them] booty. Himself I made a prisoner in Jerusalem, his royal residence, like a bird in a cage. I put watch-posts closely round the city, and turned back to his fate anyone who came out of the city gate."[8]

Sennacherib's account does not mention the lifting of the siege or of a plague visited upon his army. It is clear, however, that Hezekiah was not taken captive and that the siege was lifted. The Assyrians boasted of their victories but were silent concerning defeats, and the silence may be accounted for on that basis. Herodotus, in describing Sennacherib's attack upon Egypt dur-

8. Pritchard, *ANET,* p. 288.

ing his third campaign, states that "one night a multitude of fieldmice swarmed over the Assyrian camp and devoured their quivers and their bows and the handles of their shields, likewise, insomuch that they fled the next day unarmed and many fell."[9] Since mice are associated with the plague, it is possible that Herodotus is giving a version of the Biblical account of the destruction of the Assyrian army by the Angel of the Lord."[10]

Many of Sennacherib's energies were expended on constructive enterprises. He largely rebuilt Nineveh, his capital. The Jerwan Aqueduct built to convey water into Nineveh, is one of history's first aqueducts. Its waters irrigated the large parks which served to beautify Nineveh and its environs.

According to II Kings 19:35, Sennacherib met his death at the hands of his sons Adrammelech and Sharezer who slew their father and then escaped into Ararat (Armenia).[11] Esarhaddon, Sennacherib's younger son and successor states that he pursued his rebel brothers into Armenia. These brothers may be the two mentioned in II Kings.

Sennacherib's son, Esarhaddon (681-669 B.C.), had served as viceroy in Babylon before his father's death. Shortly after taking the throne of Assyria, Esarhaddon was confronted with revolt in southern Babylonia and in the province of Elam. With little difficulty Babylonia was pacified, but it required a number of campaigns to put down the revolt in Elam. Difficulties were experienced in maintaining Assyrian power in the north where Cimmerian and Scythian tribes were not willing to accept Assyrian domination unless forced to do so.

In the meantime Egypt was continually stirring up trouble for Assyria throughout Syria and Palestine. Both Tyre and

Captive lyre players, possibly Jews from Lachish, march under the watchful eye of an Assyrian guard. The relief is from a wall of Sennacherib's palace at Nineveh and dates from the seventh century B.C.

9. Herodotus, *Histories* ii. 141.
10. A. D. Godley in the Loeb Classical Library edition of Herodotus (I) writes, "This is Hdt.'s version of the Jewish story of the pestilence which destroyed the Assyrian army before Jerusalem. Mice are a Greek symbol of pestilence; it is Apollo Smintheus (the mouse god) who sends and then stays the plague in Homer, *Il. i.* It has long been known that rats are carriers of the plague."
11. The Babylonian Chronicle states that Sennacherib was murdered by "his son." The death of Sennacherib is mentioned in the annals of Ashurbanipal: "I tore out the tongues of those whose slanderous mouths had uttered blasphemies against me, his god-fearing prince; I defeated them completely. The others I smashed alive with the very same statutes of protective deities with which they had smashed my own grandfather Sennacherib—now (finally) as a belated burial sacrifice for his soul." See Pritchard, *ANET*, p. 288.

Sidon rebelled against Assyria with the encouragement of Egypt. Esarhaddon moved to punish both the states that refused tribute and the Egyptians who encouraged them. Heavy tribute was demanded of the subject peoples, and with it Esarhaddon built a new palace at Calah and reconstructed much of Babylon. Among the kings who paid tribute, Esarhaddon lists "Manasseh of Judah."[12] The Biblical Chronicler states that the Assyrians "took Manasseh with hooks and bound him with fetters of bronze and brought him to Babylon (II Chron. 33:11).

In 672 B.C. Esarhaddon launched a major expedition with the determination to conquer Egypt, the source of Assyria's troubles in Syria and Palestine. Esarhaddon's victory stele, set up at Zinjirli in northern Syria, depicts the Assyrian king with a mace in his left hand and a libation bowl in his right hand. From the left hand extends ropes which pass through the lips of two figures crouched before him. One of these is Taharqu (Tirhakah) of Egypt (685-664 B.C.). The monument bears an inscription which boasts: "I fought daily, without interruption, very bloody battles against Tirhakah, king of Egypt and Ethiopia, the one accursed by all the great gods. Five times I hit him with the point of my arrows inflicting wounds from which he should not recover, and then I laid siege to Memphis, his royal residence, and conquered it in half a day by means of mines, breaches and assault ladders; I destroyed it, tore down its walls, and burnt it down."[13]

Esarhaddon took the title "King of the kings of Egypt," and installed Assyrian governors in Thebes and Memphis. With the usual exaggeration of Assyrian annals, he boasts, "Everywhere in Egypt I appointed new kings, governors, officers, harbor overseers, officials, and administrative personnel." Actually Assyrian power was ineffective in Egypt, and as soon as Esarhaddon left, his power was challenged. Tirhakah incited the Egyptians to rebel against Assyria, and it was while Esarhaddon was en route to crush this revolt that he died at Haran, leaving the throne to his son Ashurbanipal.

Ashurbanipal had been declared Crown Prince of Assyria by his father in 672 B.C., his brother Shamash-shum-ukin becoming Crown Prince of Babylonia. In this way Esarhaddon provided for an orderly change in government at the time of his death. Ashurbanipal (669-633 B.C.) continued the Assyrian

Stele of Esarhaddon showing a seed plow and other implements.

12. Pritchard, *ANET,* p. 291.
13. Pritchard, *ANET,* p. 293.

campaign against Egypt and marched southward to confront the rebellious Tirhakah. In his annals, Ashurbanipal wrote: "In my first campaign I marched against Egypt and Ethiopia. . . . Tirhakah, king of Egypt and Nubia, heard in Memphis of the coming of my expedition and he called up his warriors for a decisive battle against me. . . . I defeated the battle-experienced soldiers of his army in a great open battle. . . . He left Memphis, and fled, to save his life, into the town of Thebes. This town too, I seized and led my army into it to repose there. . . . The terror of the sacred weapon of Ashur, my lord, overcame Tirhakah where he had taken refuge, and he was never heard from again."

A second campaign was necessary, however, for Tirhakah's successor, Tanutamun, whom Ashurbanipal calls Urdamane, continued the revolt. In a second campaign Ashurbanipal personally conquered Thebes from which he took everything movable to Assyria. His annals boast: "From Thebes I carried away booty, heavy and beyond counting: silver, gold, precious stones, his [Tanutamun's] personal possessions, linen garments with multicolored trimmings, fine horses, certain inhabitants, male and female. I pulled out of their bases two high obelisks, cast of shining bronze, the weight of which was 2,500 talents, standing at the door of the temple, and took them to Assyria. . . . With full hands and safely, I returned to Nineveh, the city where I exercise my rule."[14]

The Biblical prophet Nahum (3:8-10), refers to Ashurbanipal's campaign against Thebes, called in the Hebrew, No-amon ("the city of Amun"). Nahum, pronouncing judgments upon Assyrian Nineveh, asks, "Are you better than Thebes that sat by the Nile, with water around her, her rampart a sea, and water her wall? Ethiopia was her strength, Egypt, too, and that without limit; Put and the Libyans were her helpers. Yet she was carried away, she went into captivity; her little ones were dashed in pieces at the head of every street; for her honored men lots were cast, and all her great men were bound in chains." The sack of Thebes was in 663 B.C., and in 612 B.C. Nineveh fell.

During the reign of Ashurbanipal, however, the Assyrian empire reached its greatest territorial extent. The empire was to have only a brief respite, however. The Medes in the east were gaining power, and Shamash-shum-ukin, Ashurbanipal's

---

14. Pritchard, *ANET,* p. 294-295.

brother who was ruler of Babylon formed an anti-Assyrian alliance in 652 B.C. Ashurbanipal put down the revolt after six years of fighting. In 648 B.C. he sacked the city of Babylon, and then marched in Elam to punish Shamash-shum-ukin's allies there. Susa fell in 639 B.C.

While Ashurbanipal was busy putting down the revolt in the east, the states of western Asia were free to go their own ways. Josiah of Judah (640-609 B.C.) was successful in bringing about religious reforms which resulted in a revived worship of Yahwism accompanied by the rejection of foreign (including Assyrian) gods. Egypt, too, was free to follow her own policies free of interference from Nineveh.

While the annals depict Ashurbanipal as one of Assyria's cruelest rulers, he is also remembered as a lover of books whose library has enriched our knowledge of the lands of the Fertile Crescent. Ashurbanipal's scribes traveled throughout Assyria and Babylonia copying and translating the historical, scientific, and religious texts that they found. Business documents and letters were collected along with the official archives of Ashurbanipal's predecessors. In 1853, during excavation of Ashurbanipal's palace at Nineveh, his library containing thousands of clay tablets was discovered. Here the stories of creation and the flood which were current among the Sumerians and their Assyrian and Babylonian successors were discovered.

The banquet scene (above) shows Ashurbanipal feasting with his queen and the relief (below) depicts the Assyrian king hunting lions both on horseback and on foot.

Ashurbanipal took pride in his education. He wrote:

> "I, Ashurbanipal, learned the wisdom of Nabu [god of writing], the entire art of writing on clay tablets .... I received the revelation of the wise Adapa, the hidden treasure of the art of writing .... I read the beautiful clay tablets from Sumer, and the obscure Akkadian writing which is hard to master. I had my joy in the reading of inscriptions on stone from the time before the flood...."[15]

The late years of Ashurbanipal's life and the circumstances of his death are somewhat of a mystery. Scythian hordes were pressing down upon the Middle Euphrates area, and Kyaxeres, the Mede was developing into a major threat from the east. About 633 B.C. Ashurbanipal may have turned the kingdom over to his son Ashur-etil-ilani who then reigned until about 629 B.C. He, in turn, was succeeded by his brother Sin-shar-ish-kun who held the throne until 612 B.C.

In 625 B.C. the Assyrians were driven out of Babylonia by the Chaldean prince Nabopolassar, founder of the Neo-Babylonian or Chaldean empire. Nabopolassar capitalized on the

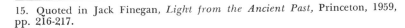

15. Quoted in Jack Finegan, *Light from the Ancient Past,* Princeton, 1959, pp. 216-217.

anti-Assyrian feeling throughout western Asia. In 614 **B.C.** Nabopolassar joined forces with the Medes, under Kyaxeres to attack the city of Ashur. Two years later, in 612 B.C., Nabopolassar and Kyaxeres again united to bring about the destruction of Nineveh, the Assyrian capital. With the fall of Nineveh, Assyria was reduced to chaos. Pursued by the Babylonians, the Assyrians retreated westward and set up a government at Haran under Ashur-uballit II (612-609 B.C.). Assyria awaited help from Egypt — her one time enemy — against the new danger from Babylon, but help did not come. Josiah of Judah marched his armies to Megiddo to prevent Necho II of Egypt from passing through the valley of Esdraelon en route to Haran. Josiah was killed at Megiddo (II Kings 23:29-30), but he may have succeeded in delaying Necho long enough to permit Nabopolassar to strike the death blow to the Assyrian Empire. With the fall of Haran, Assyria was no more. Power passed to the now aged Nabopolassar, who entrusted his armies to the crown prince Nebuchadnezzar. Claiming to be successor to the Assyrian Empire, Nebuchadnezzar claimed Syria and Palestine on behalf of Babylon. Egypt was ready to dispute that claim, but in 605 B.C. Nebuchadnezzar made a surprise attack on Carchemish on the Orontes River in Syria. The Egyptian army was almost annihilated and Nebuchadnezzar might have moved down the Palestinian coast to Egypt itself but for the fact that he received word of the death of his father, Nabopolassar. Nebuchadnezzar was now crowned king in his own right, and in a short time, he was back campaigning in Syria and Palestine. The king of Judah wavered between paying tribute to Nebuchadnezzar and trusting Egypt for aid against the Babylonians. Ashkelon had refused tribute and was sacked by Nebuchadnezzar's army. Jehoiakim of Judah was probably among those who paid tribute in 604 B.C., but he subsequently changed loyalties. In 601 B.C. the Babylonians fought the Egyptians with heavy losses on both sides. The next year the Babylonian armies did not appear in Syria and it looked as though Egypt might be the victor after all. Jehoiakim transferred his loyalty to Necho II of Egypt. Babylon, however, had no intention of abandoning her western provinces. With his army re-equipped, Nebuchadnezzar appeared before Jerusalem in December, 598 B.C. By March of the next year (597 B.C.) Jerusalem was at Nebuchadnezzar's mercy. According to the Babylonian Chronicle, "He captured its king, appointed a ruler of his own choice and, having taken much spoil from the city, sent it back to Babylon." Jehoiachin of

Mountains of Gilboa as viewed across the Plain of Esdraelon.

Judah went into exile, succeeded by his uncle Mattaniah who was given the name Zedekiah (II Kings 24:10-17).

During the next decade, however, troubles continued. Zedekiah rejected the counsel of Jeremiah and entrusted his foreign policy to the pro-Egyptian party at court. When Zedekiah rebelled, Nebuchadnezzar again appeared at its gates. This time the siege ended with the destruction of Jerusalem (587 B.C.) and the end of the kingdom of Judah (II Kings 25:1-17).

51

Religion in
Assyria and Babylonia

The challenge to Israel, first from Assyria and later from Babylonia, was cultural as well as military. It was in the name of the god Ashur that a Sennacherib or an Ashurbanipal marched his armies into Asia. Marduk of Babylon was the patron of Nebuchadnezzar. Since these were gods of powerful nations, they had an appeal to many in western Asia. Vassals of the kings of Assyria and Babylonia had to pay homage to their gods.

A. Leo Oppenheim warns us that materials are not at hand to write a "Mesopotamian Religion."[1] Archaeologists have studied the ruins of temple towers ("ziggurats") but they still know little of the cultic activities which they served. Texts from Sumerian, Assyrian, and Babylonian times mention the gods of ancient Mesopotamia, but their study leads us into an apparent maze of inconsistencies and contradictions. This is doubtless due to the many elements which at one time or another contributed to the religious ideas of the peoples of Mesopotamia. The peoples of Mesopotamia were polytheistic, and they were willing to incorporate into their religious concepts the new gods that appeared from time to time.

When the priests attempted to classify the gods they worshiped, they named a triad — Anu, Enlil, and Ea — as supreme in the regions, respectively, of air, earth, and water. During Sumerian times Anu was the supreme god, with his abode in heaven. Along with his daughter, Ishtar, he was worshiped in Uruk at the temple E-anna ("the house of Anu"). Until Marduk of Babylon attained the primacy at the beginning of the Old Babylonian period, Anu was acknowledged as the greatest of the gods. In actual worship, however, his daughter Ishtar became more popular than her father.

---

1. A. Leo Oppenheim, *Ancient Mesopotamia*, p. 172.

The lord of earth was Enlil, known to the Semites as Bel, whose shrine during Sumerian times was at Nippur. When Marduk became the supreme god he took Bel's name, becoming known as Bel-Marduk. The story of Bel and the Dragon, an apocryphal addition to the book of Daniel, seeks to prove the folly of worshiping Bel-Marduk.

Ea, Sumerian Enki, was lord of the abyss of waters upon which, according to the mythology of the time, the terrestrial world floated. Wisdom and knowledge were thought to dwell in this abyss, and, as a result, Ea was the god noted for his wisdom. According to the Gilgamesh Epic it was the wise and kindly Ea who warned Utnapishtim to build an ark and thus save himself and his family from impending disaster during the flood.

A second triad, popular in Mesopotamian mythology, was composed of the moon, the sun, and the planet Venus. Sin, the moon god, was deemed the father of the other two — Shamash, and Ishtar. Sin, like Ea of the first triad, was a god of wisdom. He governed the passing of the months and was associated with the thirty day lunar cycle. His worshipers envisioned him as a man in the prime of life with a long beard of lapis lazuli. The crescent moon was thought to be the boat in which Sin sailed through the heavens. The city of Ur, Abraham's birthplace, was dedicated to the moon god, as was Haran, the place where the patriarchs sojourned before moving on to Canaan.

Shamash, the sun god (Sumerian Utu), was not always regarded as the friend of mankind. While the morning sun was welcomed, as the sun reached its zenith it parched the earth and seemed a relentless foe from which man must flee. The sun brought light and heat — sometimes unbearable heat — to the world of men. Another aspect of Shamash is the justice which he represents. He is the all-seeing eye who ends the night and brings to light all the evil doers who lurk in the darkness. The lawgiver Hammurabi is depicted on the stele of his famous law code standing in the presence of Shamash. Hammurabi associated himself and his reign with justice and wished that fact commemorated on the stele bearing his laws.

The concepts of love and warfare are both represented in Ishtar (Sumerian Inanna). At one time or another Ishtar was linked with the "great god" of almost every Mesopotamian city. Her presence was thought to guarantee fertility, and in her absence the land, humans, and animals could not reproduce. Ishtar served the same function in Mesopotamia that Venus

The figure of a Sumerian priest, recovered from Tell Asmar.

A gateway stone figure in the form of a colossal winged human-headed lion, from the palace of Ashurnasirpal II, king of Assyria.

served in Greece. Anat, the sister of Baal, was the Canaanite goddess of warfare and fertility.

The Mesopotamian pantheon had scores of other gods who occupied specialized functions subsidiary to the great gods. In the Sumerian period Ninurta, or Enurta, was the lord of Girsu (Nin-girsu), the sacred quarter of Lagash. He was a fertility god, responsible for the annual flooding of the rivers which made vegetation possible in the otherwise arid regions of southern Mesopotamia. His earliest symbol was a plough, but by Assyrian times the plough was replaced by weapons and Ninurta was a god of warfare. Baba, Ninkarrak, and Gula appear in various texts as wives of Ninurta. Sometimes they are kindly desposed toward mankind, watching over man in his infirmities and healing his sicknesses. Occasionally, however, they are responsible for his death.

Fire was deified in the Sumerian god Gibil, known to the Semites as Nusku. As the flame it was he who consumed burnt offerings. The nether regions were ruled by Nergal, originally a sun god. The sun in his unfriendly aspect was a destroyer of life. He went to seek a kingdom for himself, and forced his way into the nether world, the domain of Ereshkigal, sister of Shamash and Ishtar. Ereshkigal made him her consort, whereupon the world of the dead became his domain.

The storm god of Mesopotamia was named Adad or Hadad, the form known to the Arameans of Damascus, several of whose kings bore the name Hadad-ezer or Ben-Hadad. Among the Canaanites he was known simply as Baal, "lord," the god responsible for fertility among men, animals, and vegetation. Baal was the rider of the clouds, whose absence produced famine.

In addition to the gods, the demons — good and bad — were very much a part of the religious picture in ancient Mesopotamia. Evil demons were thought to be descended from the evil gods whom Marduk had vanquished in order to deliver his fellow gods from their power. Good demons — or genies, as they are often called — might be the descendants of great and good gods who continued to be worshiped by the people of Assyria and Babylonia.

The winged bulls which decorated the gates to Assyrian palaces were representations of the good genies. They served to protect the palace from evil powers — human or demonic. Bad genies, however, far outnumbered the good. They appeared as deformed monsters, and it seems to have been their lot to make life miserable for mankind. They forced their way into houses to harm their inhabitants, and into stables where they might injure or kill the animals. The evil genies could take possession of a man, particularly if they found him in sin, hence away from the protection of his god. This concept is comparable to the demon possession mentioned in the New Testament.

Evil genies were blamed for all human woes. They caused families to quarrel and set man against man. They prevented childbirth at the proper time and killed new-born babies. They kept rain from falling and produced sterility on earth. Throughout life the demons were a potent influence for good or evil, but the evil more than balanced the good.

The ghosts of people who had been deprived of a satisfactory life formed another group of evil spirits. Those who had died virgins, those who had died in childbirth, those who had not been given proper burial, and multitudes more whose hopes had been frustrated were living as evil spirits who took delight in tormenting the living.

Each of the Mesopotamian gods had a city particularly dedicated to his worship. Marduk was the god of Babylon, Shamash of Sippar, and Sin, the moon god, had his abode in Ur. A temple to the god was built in his city, and it was surrounded by a complex of buildings housing the priests and priestesses who functioned in the cultic observances and administered the estates which belonged to the temple. Although temples varied in plan, each had a central court and a cella, or chamber in which there was a niche and a pedestal for a statue of the god. Large temples had side chapels for the lesser gods, rooms for the priests to robe in, libraries, schoolrooms, slaughtering-houses, and kitchens.

On a feast day, worshipers would enter the main gate of a temple, pass through the forecourt and vestibule into a central court. After entering the antechamber they would bring the gifts to the god or goddess in the cella, then leave through an exit so as not to interfere with the procession of other worshipers.

The largest temple in Babylon was dedicated to Marduk, the principal god of the city. The temple was known as E-sag-ila, "the house that lifts up its head." It was a quadrangular enclosure in the northern part of Babylon with the temple tower, or ziggurat in the northern part of the court. Ziggurats were rectangular towers, rising by diminishing stages to a summit on which a chapel was located. External ramps or stairways

This clay model of the liver, inscribed with cuneiform writing, was used by Babylonian diviners about 1600 B.C. The liver, because it is a bloody organ, was believed by these ancients to be the source of life itself and therefore to be a reliable instrument for determining the will of the gods.

connected the different levels. Ziggurats were introduced into southern Mesopotamia by the Sumerians. They may have worshiped mountain deities in their earlier home, creating the zuggurats as man-made mountains for their gods when they settled in the flat area north of the Persian gulf.

In Sumerian days the king and priest were the same individual — the *ensi* of a city who ruled the people on behalf of his god. The land belonged to the god, and the people were his tenants. The *ensis* administered the estates of the gods and collected the rents which came to the temple as the "great house" (Sumerian E-GAL) of the god. Our earliest cuneiform tablets were written by the priests of Uruk (Biblical Erach) to record the receipt of payments made in kind to the temple.

With the passing of time the work in a great city temple became quite complicated, with the result that various classes of priests developed with highly specialized functions. The king continued as chief priest, but most of his religious functions were assigned to others.

A class of priests known as *kalu* was responsible for temple music. Such priests chanted hymns and liturgies in order "to appease the heart of the great gods." The *lilissu*-drum and other musical instruments were used by the *kalu*-priests. They had a significant part in the annual New Year festivals.

The *baru*-priests were seers who accompanied kings on their military campaigns. It was their responsibility to interpret dreams and observe omens. They observed new moons and the movements of the planets and had oversight of the calendar. Certain days were interpreted as lucky, others as unlucky, and this information was given to the king so that he would know when it was safe to begin a new enterprise.

A class of priests named *mashmashu* or *ashipu* sought to protect people from the evil genies who formed a constant threat to human welfare. Through magical incantations such priests would bring protection to a woman who was pregnant. Other spells might drive out the demon associated with some disease. One text describes a ritual in which a sick person is told to have a kid placed in bed with him. A wooden dagger is used to strike a man's throat and a copper dagger to cut the kid's throat. The kid is then clothed with the sick man's clothes and lamentations are made for him as if he were a dead man. Funerary offerings are made to Ereshkigal, queen of the underworld and the priest recites appropriate incantations. After this ritual, in which the kid is substituted for the man, it is

This stone tablet records the refoundation of the temple of the Sun-God at Sippar, Babylonia, by Nabu-apal-iddina in the ninth century B.C.

presumed that the sick man will recover.

Women as well as men served in the priesthood and several kings are said to have dedicated their daughters as priestesses. Among the functions of the priestess was that of service at the great seasonal festivals in the capacity of ritual prostitutes. Their ministrations in this capacity were designed to insure fertility to the land.

The Mesopotamian gods were thought of in strictly human terms and the priests and priestesses served as servants in the divine households. Each day the image of the god was washed, dressed, and fed. Flowers and food for the god were placed on a table in the temple. Incense was burned and pure water sprinkled by the priest attending the god in order to insure that the shrine was made pure. The food consisted of bread and cakes, the flesh of bulls, sheep, goats, or seed, fish and poultry.

In the spring of each year a great New Year's festival was observed at Babylon, and its observance became general throughout southern Mesopotamia. The Creation Epic, known as Enuma Elish, was repeated twice during the New Year's Festival, and scholars think that a series of ritual acts performed at this time was designed to re-enact the main features of the creation myth. A fight took place between Marduk, god of Babylon, and the monster Tiamat, associated with chaos. At one point in the ritual Marduk is slain, but he is magically restored to life and enabled to vanquish his foe.

On the fifth day of the feast the king was brought into the temple and placed before the statue of Marduk. The high priest then removed the king's royal insignia, and struck the king on the cheek, pulled his ears, and made him kneel before the image of Marduk. The king then uttered a prayer in which he declared his innocence of any acts which might injure Babylon. The priest then blessed him, and promised him success and prosperity. The king then arose and received his royal insignia from the hands of the priest. Again the priest struck the king in order to secure an omen. If the blow brought tears the god was considered propitious. Otherwise disasters might be anticipated. This rite may reflect a magical means of promoting the growth of vegetation in the spring. Some scholars suggest that it reflects an earlier custom when each year the old king was killed and a younger and stronger king was anointed to take his place.

At the New Year's festival the destiny of the nation was fixed for the year ahead. The ritual was thought to determine

Statue of a guardian deity, from the palace of Sargon II, king of Assyria.

the prosperity of the year, hence the great care with which all its details were carried out. In a chapel at the top of the ziggurat the king, representing the god, and a priestess, representing the goddess, engaged in ritual prostitution to insure the fertility of the land.

The climax of the occasion was a procession along the Sacred Way from the temple of Marduk to the *Bit-akitu,* or festival house outside the city. The king took the hand of Marduk to lead the god at the head of the procession. Visiting gods, priests, and the populace joined in the march. Although in Assyria the national god Ashur was the central figure of the ritual, instead of Marduk, even Assyrian kings went to Babylon to take the hand of Marduk at the New Year's Festival.

52

The Fall of Samaria

After the death of Jeroboam II, the Northern Kingdom entered a period of decline from which she could not save herself. Instability in Israel combined with the growing strength in Assyria spelled chaos and disaster for the people of the Northern Kingdom. Zechariah, the son of Jeroboam II, reigned but six months before he was assassinated by Shallum. After a reign of but one month, Shallum was murdered by Menahem (*ca.* 742 B.C.). Menahem reigned for ten years in Samaria, and is remembered for his atrocities (cf. II Kings 15:16).

During the reign of Menahem, a new threat came from the east in the person of Tiglath-pileser III (745-727 B.C.) who adopted a new policy in dealing with conquered peoples. Earlier conquerors would strike, carry off slaves and booty, and return home, leaving the conquered territory to care for itself as long as the tribute was paid faithfully. Tiglath-pileser began the policy of incorporating conquered territory into his empire. Syria, Babylonia, and Anatolia were divided into provinces directly responsible to Nineveh.

Tiglath-pileser also inaugurated the policy of transporting rebellious peoples to parts of his empire where they would be powerless to unite against him. Peoples were exiled from their homelands and other exiles were brought in to the evacuated territory. In this way continuity between old and new settlers would be broken, and there would be no possibility of the older population returning to their homeland. As a result of this policy Israel, which was taken into exile by the Assyrians, lost its identity, whereas Judah, which survived until Babylonian times, could and did return to Jerusalem and thereby maintain its identity. The shifting of populations hastened the spread of Aramaic as a lingua franca, replacing the local tongues of the various peoples of the empire.

When Tiglath-pileser came to the throne he faced challenges to his power from Babylonia to the south, and Urartu (Armenia) to the north. He put down revolts in these areas, enforced Assyrian control, and even extended his rule as far as the region of Mt. Demavend, south of the Caspian Sea. Beginning in 743 B.C. Tiglath-pileser conducted campaigns in Syria where he was opposed by a coalition of states headed by "Azriau of Yaudi," a name which may be translated "Azariah of Judah." Scholars have debated whether this Azriau of Yaudi could be the Biblical Azariah, or Uzziah who ruled Judah from 783 to 742 B.C. If so, we would assume that Azariah/Uzziah was the outstanding leader of the Syria-Palestine area following the death of Jeroboam II of Israel (*ca.* 746 B.C.). Azariah/Uzziah spent his last years as a leper, with his son Jotham functioning as king. If Azriau of Yaudi was Azariah/Uzziah, then he remained the power behind the throne during the period of his leprosy, and he became the center of opposition to the Assyrians in their campaign of 743-742 B.C. Presumably Azariah/Uzziah died soon after the campaign. No further mention is made of him in the Assyrian annals.

Cyrus Gordon argues that Azriau was not the Judean king, but a native north Syrian who ruled a city state in the area named Yaudi, or Samal.[1] Eduard Meyer suggested that Azriau was an Israelite adventurer who had journeyed northward and established himself among the Aramean states of that region.

By Tiglath-pileser's time the Assyrians had developed siege warfare into an effective weapon. Battering rams and other devices for breaching strong city walls struck terror into the peoples of western Asia. By 738 B.C. Tiglath-pileser was collecting tribute from Asia Minor, Syria, the Phoenician cities, an Arab queen named Zabibe, Rezin of Damascus, and Menahem of Israel. Menahem gave Tiglath-pileser (Biblical Pul) "a thousand talents of silver that he might help him to confirm his royal power" (II Kings 15:19). While Menahem had little choice, the Biblical text implies that he felt that prompt payment of tribute might cause the Assyrian king to look favorably on his kingship over Israel.

Menahem's willingness to court Assyrian favor to strengthen his hold upon the throne was bitterly resented in Israel. When his son Pekahiah took the throne (738/737 B.C.), opposition flared into the open. One of his officers, Pekah ben Remaliah,

---

1. Cyrus H. Gordon, *The World of the Old Testament,* p. 219, 228.

assassinated Pekahiah and seized the throne. Pekah had the
help of a company of Gileadites (II Kings 15:25) who shared
his anti-Assyrian sympathies. He may also have had the tacit
support of Rezin, king of Damascus, and certain of the Philistine leaders who resented the pro-Assyrian policies of Menahem
and Pekahiah. In the event of trouble with Assyria, they doubtless hoped for Egyptian help.

As soon as Pekah was on the throne of Israel he revealed his
anti-Assyrian bias. Judah, now ruled by Jotham, the son of
Azariah/Uzziah, chose to follow an independent policy and
refused to join Pekah and Rezin in their opposition to Assyria.
A showdown came under Jotham's son, Ahaz, when Rezin and
Pekah attacked Jerusalem, determined to remove Ahaz from
his throne and install a ruler of their choice, Ben Tabeel
(Isa. 7:1-9). At the height of the crisis, Isaiah tried to encour-
age Ahaz with the assurance that God would not allow the
Davidic line to be obliterated, and that the kingdoms ruled by
Rezin and Pekah would quickly fall to Assyria (Isa. 7:10-17).
Indeed, Assyria was the rod of God's anger (Isa. 10:5) to punish
Israel because of her idolatry.

*The bas-relief shows
Tiglath-pileser III at the city of
Ashtaroth.*

While Pekah and Rezin were beseiging Jerusalem, other parts
of Judah were exposed to the enemy. Uzziah had fortified the
port of Elath (Ezion-geber) on the Gulf of Aqabah, but now the
Edomites drove out the Israelites and occupied the port city.
The traditional (Massoretic) text of II Kings 16:6 states that
the Arameans (A.V. "Syria") took Elath, but many scholars,
including the translators of the R.S.V., think that "Aram"
was misread for "Edom" by copyists of ancient manuscripts.
The two words are almost identical in Hebrew. It is clear, from
II Chronicles 28:17, that Edomites invaded Judah during the
reign of Ahaz. Philistines also took advantage of Judean weakness by invading Judah from the west (II Chron. 28:18). Thus
Ahaz was confronted with invasions of Arameans and Israelites
from the north, Philistines from the west, and Edomites from
the south.

Although Isaiah had counseled faith in God, Ahaz chose
a more mundane way of resolving his problems. He sent tribute
to the Assyrian king, and asked Tiglath-pileser to come to his
aid (II Kings 16:7, 8). While this appeared to be the solution
to an immediate problem, it had disastrous results. Tiglath-
pileser probably would have come without Ahaz' appeal, but
the appeal gave the invasion a type of legitimacy it did not
deserve.

A pottery incense stand from Megiddo.

Both the Bible and Tiglath-pileser's inscriptions report the events that followed. The Assyrian Annals state:

> [As for Menahem I] overwhelmed him [like a snowstorm] and he ... fled like a bird, alone, [and bowed to my feet (?)]. I returned him to his place [and imposed tribute upon him, to wit:] gold, silver, linen garments with multicolor trimmings, great ... I received from him. Israel (lit. "Omri-land") ... all its inhabitants [and] their possessions I led to Assyria. They overthrew their king, Pekah and I placed Hoshea as king over them. I received from them ten talents of gold, one thousand talents of silver as their tribute and brought them to Assyria.[2]

Tiglath-pileser first moved down the seacoast (734 B.C.). He passed through Israelite territory and punished the Philistine cities, particularly Gaza, for their part in resisting Assyrian encroachments. Tiglath-pileser then moved southward and established a base at Wadi el- 'Arish ("The River of Egypt") the natural boundary between Egypt and Palestine. This was his means of isolating Egypt and keeping Egyptian arms out of the conflict in Palestine.

The next year (733 B.C.) the Assyrians were again in Israel. Galilee and Transjordan were overrun and large segments of their populations were deported (II Kings 15:29). Megiddo was destroyed and rebuilt as a provincial capital. G. Ernest Wright has described the palace-fort which served as the headquarters of the Assyrian commandant:

> It was some 220 feet long and at least 157½ feet wide, though part of its eastern side may long since have tumbled down the side of the hill. The stone walls of the fort were very thick, varying from 6½ to 8¼ feet wide. The plan suggests a large interior courtyard, surrounded on at least three sides by rooms.[3]

The Assyrians divided the occupied territory of Israel into three provinces. Transjordan comprised the province of Gilead. The province of Megiddo included Galilee, and Dor served as headquarters for Assyrian control of the coastal plain.

Doubtless at the instigation of the pro-Assyrian members of the court of Israel, or even of Tiglath-pileser himself, an Israelite named Hoshea ben Elah (II Kings 15:30) murdered Pekah. Hoshea became a vassal state of Tiglath-pileser.

In 732 B.C. Tiglath-pileser took Damascus and summoned Ahaz and other vassal princes to pay homage to him. It was on this occasion that an altar in Damascus so impressed Ahaz that he had a large model of it made and sent to Uriah, the High Priest in Jerusalem, with instructions to have a replica of it made and placed in the Temple court (II Kings 16:10-16).

Tiglath-pileser ravaged the city of Damascus. He executed

2. Prichard, *ANET*, pp. 283-284.
3. G. Ernest Wright, *Biblical Archaeology*, pp. 164, 165.

Rezin and deported much of its population. The territory of the Aramaic kingdom of Damascus was divided into four Assyrian provinces.

Shortly after Shalmaneser V succeeded his father Tiglath-pileser as king of Assyria, Hoshea of Israel withheld tribute and sought an alliance with Egypt. Hoshea made an alliance with So (II Kings 17:14), Egyptians Sib'e, known from Assyrian texts as a *turtan* or commander-in-chief serving one of the rival rulers of Egypt. This was a fatal mistake for Hoshea, for Egypt was in no position to offer effective aid against Assyria. In 724 B.C. Hoshea appeared before Shalmaneser, still hoping to come to terms. The Assyrians were convinced that they could not trust Hoshea, so they took him prisoner and occupied the land of Israel except for the city of Samaria which withstood siege for two more years.

While the siege of Samaria was in progress, Shalmaneser died. His successor, Sargon II (722-705 B.C.) has left records of the fall of Samaria.[4] Many of the Israelites were deported to Upper Mesopotamia and Media and lost their identity there. It is this fact that has given rise to the idea that there are "lost tribes" which either have turned up in the past or will turn up at some future day. As a matter of fact many of the people of Israel lost their national identity through assimilation during the centuries following their deportation. Others made their way southward to Judah, and remnants of them appear among the later Jews. Paul, before Agrippa, spoke of the promises of God "to which our twelve tribes hope to attain" (Acts 26:7). He did not believe that some of the tribes were "lost."

Samaria was organized into an Assyrian province under an Assyrian governor. Sargon's inscriptions tell us of revolts that broke out in Hamath, Gaza, and other provinces, including Damascus and Samaria, but the Assyrians were in firm control and insurrection was quickly put down. In succeeding years Samaria was repopulated in accord with Assyrian policy of transplanting peoples: "And the king of Assyria brought people from Babylon, Cuthah, Avva, Hamath and Sepharvaim, and placed them in the cities of Samaria instead of the people of Israel; and they took possession of Samaria and dwelt in its cities" (II Kings 17:24).

From the standpoint of orthodox Jewish thought these people had an eclectic faith: "So they feared the Lord but also served

---

4. See p. 81.

Samaritans, in the midst of their Passover celebration, are heating water for the ceremonies.

their own gods, after the manner of the nations from among whom they had been carried away" (II Kings 17:33). They brought their local cults with them to Samaria, but when settled there they sought to learn "the law of the god of the land" (II Kings 17:27). The Assyrians permitted a priest to teach the Yahwistic faith of Israel, although Israel disowned them (II Kings 17:34-41). Jesus, however, dared to speak of "The Good Samaritan," and to identify himself as the Messiah to a Samaritan woman. A few hundred Samaritans survive to this day.

53

Prophets to Judah

Kings of Judah traced their ancestry to David. While the Northern Kingdom had a succession of dynasties, God's covenant with David (II Sam. 7) settled the question of legitimate rule for the South. Individual kings (e.g. Ahaz, Manasseh, Amon) might prove unworthy of the Davidic name and a usurper, Athaliah, actually ruled for a time, but the ideal of a righteous king of the Davidic line was never wholly forgotten. The pious in Israel, and sometimes the impious as well, were assured that God would never forsake his promises to David.

At Sinai, Israel had accepted the covenant with Yahweh. Israel agreed to be Yahweh's people and to obey his law (Exod. 24:7). Disobedience would bring the righteous judgments of God. The covenant with David had no conditions, however. If a son of David would sin, he would be punished (II Sam. 7:14), but God said categorically to David, "your throne shall be established forever" (II Sam. 7:16). Many interpreted this to mean that under no circumstances would God allow his people to fall before their enemies. Jerusalem and the Davidic line were regarded as inviolable. Samaria might go, and other cities of Judah might fall, but never Jerusalem — and certainly never God's House, the Temple.

The prophets had to contend with this popular doctrine, and contend they did. As preachers of righteousness they insisted that God would punish the evildoer in Judah. Those who sat at ease in Zion, those who cried, "Peace, peace," when there was no peace, were challenged by a succession of prophets who were largely despised and rejected by the official religious functionaries and the political leadership.

In the death year of Uzziah (Azariah), a young man named Isaiah began a prophetic ministry that was to last about forty years. Isaiah had witnessed the rapid development of Judah into a strong commercial and military state. Under Uzziah, Judah had attained a degree of strength and prosperity which she had not enjoyed since the days of Solomon. While Jeroboam II was ruling a prosperous and apostate Israel in the north, Uzziah was extending the power of a self-satisfied Judah in the south. During a fifty-two year reign Uzziah had developed a large standing army and built the walls, towers, and fortifications necessary for defense. He dismantled the Philistine strongholds at Gath, Jabneh, and Ashdod, and built cities for himself among the Philistines. Ammonites and Edomites became vassals. Commerce through the port at Ezion-geber brought the products of Africa and India into the markets of Jerusalem and Judea.

Isaiah did not rejoice in these evidences of prosperity. As Amos and Hosea had denounced the idolatry and hypocrisy of Israel, so Isaiah underscored God's anger with a proud and arrogant Judah. Prophets in both the north and the south spoke of imminent judgment. Isaiah lived to see the siege of Samaria and the end of political independence for Israel. He did not live to see Jerusalem fall, but he did see it edging closer and closer to the precipice.

Temple revenues were at an all time high during the lifetime of Isaiah, but the prophet was convinced that the people were paying lip service to their God. Protesting undue emphasis on religious externals, Isaiah cried out, "To what purpose is the multitude of your sacrifices? . . . I do not delight in the blood of bulls. . . . incense is an abomination to me. . . . your new moons and your appointed feasts my soul hates. . . . when you spread forth your hands, I will hide my eyes from you. . . . your hands are full of blood" (Isa. 1:11-15).

When vacillating Ahaz sent for Assyrian aid to help him defeat the Syro-Ephraimitish coalition, Isaiah appeared to challenge the king and urge trust in God (Isa. 7). Ahaz spurned the prophet's advice and probably hastened the fall of western Asia to the forces of Assyria. Isaiah also opposed a plan to join Egypt and the Philistines in an anti-Assyrian coalition (cf. Isa. 18; 14:28-32). Isaiah insisted on trust in Yahweh, and feared alliance either with or against Assyria.

In 701 B.C. the armies of Sennacherib were at the gates of Jerusalem but Isaiah's message was still the same: "Trust God." The prophet assured Hezekiah, his king, that God would save Jerusalem for the sake of his own name, and for the sake of David (Isa. 37:35). God had not forgotten his covenant with

David. The proud Assyrian was turned back, although the people of Judah had proved faithless again and again.

Micah, a contemporary of Isaiah, was from the village of Moresheth-gath in southwestern Judah (Micah 1:1). To Micah, the sins of Samaria and Jerusalem were comparable (1:5-9). If God had allowed Samaria to fall, Jerusalem should not be esteemed a privileged sanctuary.

The wealthy aristocrats of Micah's day were oppressing the poor (2:1-2), while quietly assuming that God would allow no harm to befall them. Micah dared to proclaim that God would judge faithless Judah and make of Jerusalem a heap of ruins (3:12). Micah felt assured that calamity was ahead, but he also saw a day of blessing beyond the immediate catastrophies. Yahweh would bring blessing to His people. A Davidic king from Bethlehem would rule in peace and righteousness (5:2).

Zephaniah, who prophesied during the reign of king Josiah, is described in the first verse of his prophecy as a great grandson of Hezekiah. The fact that his genealogy is given in this unusual form suggests that the Hezekiah here named may actually be the king of that name. Zephaniah may have been born during the idolatrous reigns of Manasseh and Amon but his ministry is dated from the time of Josiah. Perhaps Zephaniah's prophecies encouraged Josiah in his policies of reform.

With prophetic fervor, Zephaniah denounced the sins of his generation and insisted that the day of Yahweh's wrath was imminent (Zeph. 1:2-3). The only remedy was to be found in a heart-felt repentance (2:1-3). Beyond the day of doom, however, Zephaniah saw a faithful remnant purified by God and restored to favor (3:9-13).

Nahum of Elkosh, probably in Judah, prophesied some time between the destruction of Thebes ("No-Amon") at the hand of the Assyrian ruler Ashurbanipal (664-663 B.C.) and the destruction of Nineveh in 612 B.C. The three chapters of his book describe in eloquent poetry God's controversy with Nineveh. The city which had repented at the preaching of Jonah was now ripe for judgment. Egypt had been powerful, too, but her capital fell. Now Nineveh will suffer siege and disgrace. The Medes and the Babylonians joined forces against Nineveh and the prophecies of Nahum proved true.

We are not sure when Habakkuk lived, but his reference to the Chaldeans (Hab. 1:6) suggests that he may have uttered his oracles some time after the battle of Carchemish (605 B.C.) when the armies of Nebuchadnezzar routed the forces of

Pharaoh Necho. Habakkuk was troubled at the thought that the wicked Chaldeans would be used of God to chastize Judah. The prophet saw that the arrogance of the Chaldeans brought with it its own destruction. The just man could trust God, knowing that the proud would ultimately be humbled and the righteous, vindicated.

The prophet Jeremiah was destined to live from the time of Josiah's revival to the destruction of Jerusalem in the days of Zedekiah. Jeremiah doubtless approved of Josiah's reforms, but he lived to see how superficial they were. Yahweh was worshiped and the externals of religious life were maintained. Prophets and priests were assuring the people of Jerusalem that no harm would befall the city at the very time when Jeremiah was calling for repentance to avert impending destruction. To those who felt that there was some magic in a shrine to Yahweh, Jeremiah held out Shiloh as a horrible example (Jer. 26:6). God's ark had fallen to the Philistines and Shiloh, its home during the days of Eli, had been destroyed. Jerusalem was not immune to divine wrath.

Jeremiah's ministry was a difficult one. The fact that he counseled submission to Babylon made him appear disloyal to his own people. Prophets, priests, and people were arrayed against him, but history proved him right. In spite of Jeremiah's pleas, Zedekiah rebelled against Nebuchadnezzar. Jeremiah remained in Judah for a time after the destruction of Jerusalem but, following the murder of Gedaliah, Jeremiah was taken to Egypt where he prophesied during his last days.

While Jeremiah was in Jerusalem warning Zedekiah of Judah's impending destruction, a prophet named Ezekiel was telling the exiles in Babylon that Jerusalem would soon fall and additional exiles would be taken to Babylon. Ezekiel probably went to Babylon along with Jehoiachin and other exiles in 597 B.C., a decade before Jerusalem fell. While we do not know that Ezekiel ever met Jeremiah, we know that their messages were similar. Ezekial agreed that Yahweh could not allow his house to fall to the heathen, but he refused to identify the physical structure on Zion with God's house. In vision, Ezekiel described Yahweh leaving his Temple. The divine glory cloud hovered for a time over the Temple, as though reluctant to depart. Then it moved eastward and hovered over the Mount of Olives, as though still giving the people of Judah an opportunity to turn to their God. Finally the glory departed, the

Air view of Anathoth, hometown of Jeremiah. The village is located two and one-half miles northeast of Jerusalem.

Jerusalem, including the temple area, as seen from Dominus Flevit on the Mount of Olives.

Temple was no longer the abode of Israel's God, and the armies of Nebuchadnezzar could destroy it with impunity (Ezek. 9:3; 10:15-19; 11:22-23). The very destruction of the Temple would vindicate God's righteousness. The heathen might blaspheme, thinking God powerless to defend his people, city, and temple. God was more concerned, however, that his people know him as the holy God who could not allow the faithlessness and idolatry of his people to go unchallenged.

For fifteen years after the destruction of the Temple, Ezekiel continued to prophesy among the exiles in Babylon. Following the fall of Jerusalem, however, Ezekiel became a prophet of hope. The God who had destroyed would restore. The exiles would return amid scenes of victory and rebuild their cities and their Temple, and Jerusalem would bear a new name, "The Lord is there" (Ezek. 48:35).

54

The Days of Isaiah

One of the major Biblical prophets, Isaiah the son of Amoz, was born about 760 B.C., probably in Jerusalem. He dated his call to the prophetic ministry from the year that King Uzziah died, about 742 B.C. (cf. Isa. 6:1). Isaiah's career is important in itself, and it is doubly important because of the fast moving international scene which ultimately touched even Judah and Jerusalem. Isaiah's career extended to Sennacherib's siege of Jerusalem (701 B.C.)

Like the prophets before him, Isaiah condemned the religious hypocrisy of a people that was content with the observance of religious externals (cf. Isa. 1:12-15). The political leaders did not hesitate to accept bribes (1:23), even at the expense of exploiting widows and orphans. Isaiah was sure that a righteous God would judge such transgressions of the moral law, but he was also sure that at some future day God would vindicate the righteous and restore Jerusalem to the status of a faithful city (1:26). God's law would go forth from Zion, bringing peace and blessing to all the nations (2:2-4).

Isaiah first appeared as a public figure at the time of the Syro-Ephraimitish invasion of Judah in 734 B.C. Rezin of Damascus allied himself with Pekah of Israel in a confederation of states designed to check the growing power of Assyria in the west. Jotham of Judah, and his son Ahaz, refused to join the anti-Assyrian coalition, with the result that Judah was invaded from the north. Rezin and Pekah determined to replace Ahaz with a king who would join their anti-Assyrian alliance. They had already chosen a puppet, Ben Tabeel (Isa. 7:7), who would replace Ahaz and follow the dictates of Rezin and Pekah. To add to Ahaz' troubles, the Edomites who had been subject to Judah, rebelled and secured their independence, possibly with the aid of the Arameans of Damascus (II Chron. 28:17; II Kings 16:6).

Faced with invasion and fearing defeat, Ahaz determined to ask Tiglath-pileser of Assyria to rescue him (II Kings 16:7). From the long range viewpoint this was folly, for Assyria was the greatest threat to the freedom of western Asia. For the moment, however, Ahaz was convinced that his salvation could only come from Assyria. As he was preparing for the siege, repairing the fortifications, and securing the city's water supply, Ahaz met the prophet Isaiah. From the prophet's viewpoint, Ahaz was guilty of unbelief in Israel's God in seeking help from Assyria. God could take care of those two "smoldering stumps of firebrands" (Isa. 7:4), Rezin and Pekah. Rezin's capital, Damascus, and Pekah's capital, Samaria would soon fall. Ahaz must trust Yahweh.

Ahaz, however, looked to Assyria for aid. Tiglath-pileser destroyed the coalition which had threatened Judah, and began to subdue the territory of Israel and the coastal cities of the Philistines. Assyrian power reached the River of Egypt (Wadi el-Arish) thereby cutting off the possibility of Egyptian aid for Israel. Israelite lands in Galilee and Transjordan were seized and portions of the population were deported (II Kings 15:29). Hoshea ben Elah murdered Pekah of Israel (II Kings 15:30) and promptly paid tribute to Assyria, thereby preserving Samaria from immediate destruction. In 732 B.C. Tiglath-pileser took Damascus, executed Rezin, and took large portions of the population into exile. The area formerly ruled from Damascus was organized into four Assyrian provinces.

The kingdom of Israel lasted but a decade longer than Damascus. When Tiglath-pileser was succeeded by his son Shalmaneser V, Hoshea felt bold enough to ally himself with Egypt and withhold tribute. This was the end. Shalmaneser promptly marched westward and confronted Hoshea. For two years the city of Samaria held out, but in 722 B.C. the Assyrians entered Israel's capital. Sargon II, successor to Shalmaneser, deported its most influential citizens into northern Mesopotamia and organized the territory of Samaria into an Assyrian province.

Isaiah was not directly affected by these events, for Judah was still in the good graces of the Assyrians. Nevertheless the fall successively of Damascus and Samaria served as a warning that the Assyrians would not be content until they had gained control of the whole of western Asia. Ahaz' willingness to trust Assyria for aid was foolhardy from a political viewpoint. Assyria gladly came, but she was less willing to go. The most charitable thing we can say of Ahaz is that he was weak. Happily he was succeeded by a son whose faith and courage exceeded that of his father.

Hezekiah, the son of Ahaz, reversed his father's policy and tried to free Judah of Assyrian domination. In part this was motivated by religious convictions, for Isaiah was given ready access to Hezekiah's court. The fall of Samaria must have had important repercussions in the south. If the sins of the Northern Kingdom had hastened her downfall, could Judah consider herself blameless? Must she not purge herself of heathen practices, including those enforced by Assyrian overlords? Had not God promised a righteous king, a Messiah who would deliver Israel from her foes and rule in righteousness? Such questions demanded an answer and a response. If the prophets were to be heeded, a spiritual revival would be experienced throughout Judah.

While Hezekiah and his counselors were seeking a spiritual renewal, the international situation favored a challenge to Assyrian hegemony. Shortly after Samaria fell to Sargon II, the Assyrians faced a major defection in Babylonia. Marduk-apal-iddina, the Merodach-baladan of Scripture (II Kings 20:12; Isa. 39:1), aided by the king of Elam, rebelled against Assyria and maintained an independent Babylon for about twelve years. Troubles also arose in Asia Minor where Mita, the classical King Midas, challenged Assyrian rule and stirred up a rebellion in the Syrian state of Carchemish (717 B.C.). Sargon destroyed Carchemish and deported its population, after which he conducted a series of campaigns in Asia Minor. Sargon's time was also taken in conquering the Urartu people of Armenia and the Median princes of northwestern Iran. There was no weakening of Assyrian power as a result of these campaigns, but vassals in Palestine might have assumed that they could go their own way with impunity.

Important changes were also taking place in Egypt. After a period of instability during which Pharaohs of rival dynasties vied for power, the Ethiopian king Piankhi appeared in Upper Egypt (ca. 716 B.C.) and soon overran the entire country. He founded the Twenty-fifth (Ethiopian) Dynasty and inaugurated a new period of Egyptian unity and power. Although Egypt was not destined to develop a mighty empire, the vigor of her new rulers gave occasion for hope in the hearts of vassal states that were restive under Assyrian rule. For her part, Egypt wished to undermine Assyrian power in Palestine as a means of guarding her own borders against the presence of Assyrian overlords.

About 713 B.C. the Philistine principality of Ashdod rebelled. Its king refused to pay tribute to Assyria. The Assyrians removed him and placed his brother on the throne, but the populace ousted the Assyrian puppet. Other Philistine towns joined the revolt and Judah, Edom and Moab were invited to join. Isaiah warned against an alliance with Egypt, and his influence may have kept Judah from becoming a party to the revolt. In 711 B.C. the Assyrian army seized Ashdod and reorganized it as an Assyrian province. Egypt provided no help for the rebels.

Keeping free of difficulties with Sargon, Hezekiah was able to devote his energies to internal reform. The Bible states: "He removed the high places, and broke the pillars, and cut down the Asherah, and he broke in pieces the bronze serpent that Moses had made, for until those days the people of Israel had burned incense to it; it was called Nehushtan" (II Kings 18:4).

It took courage for Hezekiah to destroy the bronze image of a snake which had been regarded as sacred by generations of Israelites, but the king was determined to allow no compromise with heathen practices. The "high places" had become tainted with Canaanite rites, and Hezekiah sought to abolish them.

Hezekiah sought to encourage the people of the north to join with Judah in observing the Passover at Jerusalem (II Chron. 30:1). For both religious and political purposes he sent couriers "from Beer-sheba to Dan" (II Chron. 30:5) with his invitation, but only a few came to Jerusalem. The Assyrians had allowed a former Israelite priest to minister at Bethel to the Samaritans (II Kings 17:28), and they certainly would not have looked with favor on Hezekiah's attempt to centralize worship in Jerusalem.

No open break took place between Hezekiah and the Assyrians as long as Sargon reigned. When his son Sennacherib (705-681 B.C.) came to the throne, however, Hezekiah refused tribute and declared his independence (II Kings 18:7). Sennacherib faced a series of such challenges as he attempted to take the throne of Sargon. Marduk-apal-iddina (Merodach-baladan) again rebelled and, with Elamite help, seized control of Babylon. He evidently hoped for a general challenge to Assyria, for he sent emissaries to enlist the help of kings throughout the east. Such an envoy reached Hezekiah during his sickness, and the

Pool of Siloam in Jerusalem.

Judean king showed the royal treasury to the Babylonians (II Kings 20:12-15). Egypt, too, might be counted upon to lend support in the revolt against Assyria.

Soon the various states of western Asia took sides. The king of Tyre was leader of the Phoenician cities that prepared to rebel. The people of Ashkelon and Ekron were anti-Assyrian, and Hezekiah himself, in spite of Isaiah's warnings, became a ringleader of the revolt. Padi, king of Ekron, remained loyal to Assyria, but his subjects handed him over to Hezekiah who held him prisoner in Jerusalem.

Hezekiah was aware of the dangers of his position. He ordered repairs made on the walls of Jerusalem and provided weapons and shields for his people (II Chron. 32:2-5). To provide a water supply for Jerusalem, Hezekiah "closed the upper outlet of the waters of Gihon and directed them down to the west side of the city of David" (II Chron. 32:30). This was one of the great engineering feats of antiquity. He first built a reservoir, enclosing it within fortifications located in the southwest quarter of Jerusalem (cf. Isa. 22:9, 11). Then he diverted the Gihon waters from the "old" or "lower" pool into the new reservoir through a tunnel known as the Siloam tunnel which extends one-third of a mile. A Hebrew inscription on the roof of the tunnel gives an eye witness account of its construction:

> ... the breakthrough. Now this is the manner of the breakthrough: While still ... the axe, each toward his fellow, and while three cubits still remained to be tunnelled, the voice of a man was heard calling to his fellow, for there was a fissure (?) in the rock on the right ... Now when the tunnel was cut through each of the excavators hewed through to meet his fellow, axe against axe, and the waters began flowing from the source toward the reservoir for 1200 cubits, 100 cubits being the height of the rock above the heads of the excavators.[1]

In 701 B.C., after having pacified Babylon, Sennacherib was free to conduct a campaign in the west to punish those who had rebelled against Assyrian authority. The account of this campaign is given both in II Kings 18:13-16 and in Sennacherib's own annals. Sennacherib moved down the Mediterranean coast. The rebellious king of Tyre fled to Cyprus, and Sennacherib appointed a ruler of his own choice. The victory over Tyre caused many erstwhile rebels to hasten to Sennacherib with tribute. Byblos, Arvad, Ashdod, Moab, Edom, and Ammon were ready to make peace.

The Philistine states of Ashkelon and Ekron, along with Hezekiah of Judah continued their opposition. Sennacherib

1. Cf. D. Winton Thomas. ed. *Documents from Old Testament Times,* p. 210.

marched south taking everything he passed. Egypt sent an army to help defend Ekron, but Sennacherib defeated it at nearby Eltekeh. Ekron and other Philistine cities were taken and Sennacherib's foes were either slaughtered or deported.

Next the Assyrian king moved against Judah. In his annals Sennacherib boasts that he took forty-six fortified cities and deported their people. Only Jerusalem was left, and the Assyrian armies surrounded the Holy City. Sennacherib tells us that he shut up Hezekiah "like a bird in a cage." Hezekiah, however, was willing to pay tribute to Sennacherib (II Kings 18:13-16). The Assyrian army was encamped at Lachish, and there Sennacherib received his tribute. Back at Nineveh, Sennacherib commemorated his capture of Lachish with a series of stone reliefs depicting the siege of the city. The relief shows the siege in progress. One section depicts Sennacherib on his throne receiving the submission of the elders of Lachish.

From Lachish the Assyrian king sent officials, including the Rabshekeh (a title rather than a name), to Jerusalem to urge the people of Judah to submit. A crowd was gathered on top of the city wall when the Rabsaris uttered his challenge, an excellent example of psychological warfare (II Kings 18:19-35). Fearing for the morale of the Jerusalemites, several of Hezekiah's officers asked the Rabshakeh to speak to them in Aramaic instead of Hebrew (the language of Judah). The people all knew Hebrew, but the ruling class was conversant in Aramaic, the diplomatic language of the day. Later, during the time of exile in Babylon, Aramaic was to become the common language of the Jews, Hebrew being reserved for religious use. The Rabshakeh refused to use the language of diplomacy, insisting that his message was for all the people of Jerusalem (II Kings 18:27).

The address indicates a high degree of efficiency on the part of Assyrian officials fighting in western Asia. The Rabshakeh not only knew Hebrew, but he was also familiar with recent events in Judah. The gods of other peoples had not delivered them from Sennacherib (II Kings 18:33-35). Hezekiah had removed the high places of Yahweh so he could not be counted on to help Judah in its hour of need (II Kings 18:22). Egypt is a "broken reed of a staff, which will pierce the hand of any man who leans on it" (II Kings 18:22). The only solution was to submit to Sennacherib, who would deal kindly with those who would accept his terms. In time they would be transported to another land, but it would be a pleasant land in which they

Inside the Siloam tunnel.

could live in peace (II Kings 18:28-32). In this way the Rabshakeh attempted to reason with the people of Jerusalem. Had Sennacherib succeeded, however, the history of Judah would have paralleled that of the Northern Kingdom, and its continuity would have been lost through assimilation among the nations of the ancient Assyrian Empire.

The Biblical historian states that 185,000 men in the Assyrian camp perished as a result of God's intervention on behalf of His people (II Kings 19:35). This record finds an interesting parallel in the writings of the Greek Historian Herodotus.

The assertion that Hezekiah paid tribute to Sennacherib, recorded both in the Bible (II Kings 18:13-16) and in Sennacherib's annals, followed by the record of the Rabshakeh's taunt and the subsequent destruction of the Assyrian army has posed problems for Old Testament scholars. If Hezekiah paid tribute why would Sennacherib besiege Jerusalem? Did the Assyrians insist on unconditional surrender because of the part Hezekiah played in leading the anti-Assyrian revolt?

Some scholars, facing the difficulty of harmonizing the two aspects of the battle, suggest that the author of II Kings has telescoped the accounts of two campaigns, one in 701 B.C., also documented in the Annals of Sennacherib, and a second sometime later, perhaps about 688 B.C.[2] It is admitted that there are no Assyrian records of a later campaign, but details are lacking concerning the closing years of Sennacherib's life.

While clarification of details must await further discoveries, the Biblical and the Assyrian accounts of Sennacherib's campaign in Palestine are in general agreement. Both agree that Sennacherib posed a serious threat to the continuity of Judean independence. Both state Hezekiah paid tribute to Sennacherib. The fact that the Assyrian texts as well as the Bible make it clear that Sennacherib did not occupy Jerusalem is particularly significant. Hezekiah had defied Sennacherib by leading opposition to Assyria, but Sennacherib lifted the siege of Jerusalem and returned home without taking the city and punishing its ruler. Quite properly the Biblical writer interpreted this as a miracle of divine intervention.

The men of Judah did not respond to the Rabshakeh (II Kings 18:36). They trusted in Yahweh and looked to Hezekiah to provide leadership in the crisis. The prophet Isaiah gave

Entrance to the "Tomb of Kings," near Jerusalem.

2. This view is presented in Excursus I, "The Problem of Sennacherib's Campaigns in Palestine," in John Bright, *A History of Israel*, pp. 282-287.

an encouraging message, assuring Hezekiah that Sennacherib would be forced to lift the siege (II Kings 19:7). Isaiah prophecied, ". . . thus says the Lord concerning the king of Assyria, He shall not come to this city nor shoot an arrow there, or come before it with a shield or cast a mound against it. By the way that he came, by the same shall he return, and he shall not come into this city, says the Lord, for I will defend this city to save it, for my own sake and for the sake of my servant David" (II Kings 19:32-34).

Hezekiah and his people were tacitly reminded that God will not save Jerusalem because of their faithfulness. While Hezekiah had brought about a spiritual revival, such revivals proved highly unstable and impermanent in the history of Judah. Deliverance would come for God's own sake, i.e., because God's name and reputation were at stake in the destruction of the Holy City and its Temple. God would bear testimony to His power before the Assyrian. A second reason for deliverance is the covenant which God entered with David (II Sam. 7.8-16). Hezekiah was a king of the Davidic line, and as such God would preserve him from destruction at the hand of the Assyrian. God's deliverance of Hezekiah would be remembered later when the Babylonians besieged Jerusalem, and finally destroyed it in the reign of Zedekiah (587 B.C.). At that time, however, exile would be looked upon as a means of purifying the Jews before permitting them to return to their land and re-establish their social and religious life in Jerusalem. The Babylonian policy toward captured people made that possible.

The Biblical historian closes his account of Hezekiah's life with a reference to a sickness from which he was miraculously cured. The sickness evidently took place about the time of Sennacherib's invasion (II Kings 20:1). Isaiah brought a message from God to the effect that Hezekiah would live fifteen more years (20:6). Evidently the last years of his life were peaceful (20:20) but we have no details.

Hezekiah's son Manasseh took the throne at the age of twelve and ruled for fifty-five years. Hezekiah had showed his loyalty to Yahweh and had taken a stand against the ever present idolatry. Manasseh, however, reversed his father's policy, and built altars to Baal and the other gods of Canaan whose worship had been encouraged by Ahab (II Kings 21:3). Idolatrous altars were built in the temple courts (II Kings 21:5) and human sacrifice was practiced in the valley of Hinnom (II

Kings 21:6). Many who attempted to remain loyal to Yahweh were killed (II Kings 21:16).

The political overtones of Manasseh's reign may be gleaned from Assyrian sources. The prism of Esarhaddon mentions "Manasseh king of Judah," and the Ashurbanipal prism mentions Manasseh among twenty-two princes that paid tribute to Assyria. The religious syncretism which Manasseh encouraged may have been due in part to the fact that he was a vassal of Assyria and was forced to do homage to the gods of Assyria.

The Chronicler states that the Assyrian king "took Manasseh with hooks and bound him with fetters of bronze and brought him to Babylon" (II Chron. 33:11). It is possible that Manasseh sided with Shamash-shum-ukin, viceroy of Babylon in his rebellion against Assyrian rule. When the Assyrians put down the revolt, Manasseh was taken to Babylon for punishment. Assyrian captives were sometimes literally led along the road with hooks piercing their lips. This was the punishment for refusing to honor Assyria with suitable tribute.

Manasseh was permitted to return to Judah, presumably after appropriate tribute was offered to the Assyrians. Although the Chronicler states that Manasseh repented of his earlier idolatry, his reformation seems to have been superficial (II Chron. 33:10-13). When his son Amon took the throne he pursued the policies of Manasseh's earlier years (II Chron. 33:21-25).

55

Josiah's Reformation

The career of Josiah (640-609 B.C.) was one of genuine devotion to Yahweh, along with a realistic approach to the politics of the day. When Josiah came to the throne of Judah, the Assyrian Empire was in trouble. Ashurbanipal, whose annals depict him as a cruel conqueror, had to put down a rebellion in Babylon led by his own brother, Shamash-shum-ukin (652 B.C.). The Chaldeans of Babylon were joined by Elamites and other peoples of the Iranian highlands in a bid for independence. The attempt failed when, after a two year siege, Babylon fell to Ashurbanipal in 648 B.C. Shamash-shum-ukin committed suicide, and Ashurbanipal marched his armies into Elam and took Susa (640 B.C.). Peoples deported from Babylon and Elam were settled in Samaria and in other western provinces where Ashurbanipal had effective control (Ezra 4:9-10).

Egypt had proved more successful than Babylon in challenging Ashurbanipal's rule. Around 655 B.C., Psammeticus, founder of the Twenty-Sixth (Saite) Dynasty, refused to pay tribute to Assyria and extended Egyptian power eastward into Palestine. Gyges, king of Lydia in Asia Minor supported Psammeticus in his revolt against Ashurbanipal.

Happily Ashurbanipal is remembered more for his contribution to culture than for his prowess in battle. In Nineveh he gathered together a collection of cuneiform tablets containing the myths, legends, and annals of his predecessors— the Sumerians, Babylonians, and Assyrians. Ashurbanipal's library, probably the richest archaeological discovery of the nineteenth century, contained copies of the epic of Creation ("Enuma Elish") and the flood story (in the Gilgamesh Epic) which helped western man to understand the Biblical records in the light of their Near Eastern setting.

Ashurbanipal died around 633 B.C. After the short reign of his son Ashur-etil-ilani (*ca.* 633-629 B.C.), a second son Sin-shar-ishkun came to the throne (*ca.* 629-612 B.C.). The sons inherited the problems of their father, and they were less successful than he in solving them. Babylon revolted under the Chaldean prince Nabopolassar (626-605 B.C.). Outside the city of Babylon, Nabopolassar defeated the Assyrians in 626 B.C. The Medes, under Cyaxeres (*ca.* 625-585 B.C.) joined in the attack on Assyria.

The combined might of the Medes and the Babylonians hastened the end of the Assyrian Empire. Egypt, evidently fearing the consequences of a takeover by the Medes and Babylonians, decided to aid her former enemy Assyria. By 616 B.C. Egyptian armies were in Mesopotamia, but it was too late to bring effective aid. Cyaxeres took Ashur, the old Assyrian capital, in 614 B.C. Two years later, Nabopolassar and Cyaxeres joined forces in besieging Nineveh. The siege lasted three months. When the city fell, the Medes and the Babylonians utterly destroyed it. Sin-shar-ishkun was killed, but the Assyrians attempted to regroup under Ashur-uballit II at Haran, the ancient city of upper Mesopotamia at which Abraham and Terah had sojourned centuries before. In 610 B.C. the Babylonians and their allies took Haran, and Assyrian history was for all practical purposes over. An attempt to retake Haran in 609 B.C. failed, and we hear no more of the might of Assyria. The Biblical prophet Nahum expresses the feelings of the peoples who suffered the results of Assyrian tyrany: "Your shepherds are asleep, O king of Assyria; your nobles slumber. Your people are scattered on the mountains with none to gather them. There is no assuaging your hurt, your wound is grievous. All who hear the news of you clap their hands over you. For upon whom has not come your unceasing evil?" (Nahum 3:18-19).

Josiah's two predecessors — Manasseh and Amon — were vassals to the Assyrian kings Esarhaddon and Ashurbanipal. Manasseh evidently took part in a revolt against Assyria led by Babylon (II Chron. 33:11-13), but he learned his lesson and, after a period of captivity, was permitted to return.

In the eighth year of Josiah's reign, the young king "began to seek the God of David his father" (II Chron. 34:3), a fact which would place him in opposition to his Assyrian overlords whose gods he had self-consciously rejected. The Assyrians were not in a position to oppose this reform which Josiah instituted nor, evidently, were they able to hinder his program of territorial acquisition. Not only did Josiah honor the God of David, but he also sought to incorporate into the kingdom of Judah the lands which David had ruled. The reforms instituted in Josiah's twelfth year (628 B.C.) were not confined to Judah, but reached to "Manasseh, Ephraim, and Simeon, and as far as Naphtali" (II Chron. 34:6). Josiah's control extended as far as the northernmost tribe of the old kingdom of Israel.

The reforms of Josiah's twelfth year placed the king in opposition to the old Canaanite practices of worship — the worship of Baal and the Asherim, the male and female fertility gods. Since Yahwism was the distinctly Israelite faith, this rejection of Canaanite religion in favor of Yahwism could be interpreted as a revival of Israelite nationalism.

The eighteenth year of Josiah's reign (622 B.C.) marks one of the important episodes of Old Testament history. Having purged the land of idolatry, Josiah determined to cleanse, renovate, and repair the Jerusalem temple. The Levites collected money throughout the land — from "the remnant of Israel" as well as "all Judah and Benjamin" (II Chron. 34:9). Stone and timber was purchased and carpenters and builders began the repair work. While the work was going on, Hilkiah the priest found "the book of the law of the Lord given through Moses" (II Chron. 34:15).

When Josiah heard the reading of the Law, he was concerned because both he and his people had not been obeying its precepts. Hilkiah and a company of others went to a prophetess named Huldah for word concerning the curses which the Law had enunciated. The prophetess assured her visitors that the curses of the law would come upon the land because of the sin of its people. Josiah, however, because of his integrity, would not live to see the coming judgments: "Behold, I will gather you to your fathers, and you shall be gathered to your grave in peace, and your eyes shall not see all the evil which I will bring upon this place and its inhabitants" (II Chron. 34:28).

When the king received this message he assembled the elders and people of Judah and Jerusalem and read "all the words of the book of the covenant which had been found in the house of the Lord" (II Kings 23:2). After renewing the covenant, Josiah sought to remove every trace of idolatry from his kingdom. High places were broken down, and idolatrous priests deposed. The altar which Jeroboam I had built at Bethel was pulled down (II Kings 23:15), along with later altars at Samaria.

After his efforts to purify the land of its idolatry, Josiah ordered the observance of a great passover observance (II Kings 23:21-23; II Chron. 35). He hoped that this would remind the people in a positive way of Yahweh's past deliverances, and of the obligation of the people to be faithful to Him. Josiah's reforms did not, however, have any lasting effect upon the people. The prophet Jeremiah's ministry began in the thirteenth year of Josiah and extended to the fall of Jerusalem in 587 B.C. It is evident that idolatry continued to tempt the people of Judah down to the very moment of the fall of Jerusalem.

Josiah died honorably, defending his country, on the battlefield of Megiddo. Pharaoh Necho was marching his armies northward to join forces with the Assyrians at Haran. He wanted to control Syria and Palestine for Egypt. Babylonia was developing into a powerful empire, and it would have been to Necho's advantage to keep a weak Assyria as a buffer state between Egyptian territory and Babylonia. Josiah was anti-Assyrian. Had Necho's plan been successful, the state of Israel could not have survived. To thwart the Egyptians, Josiah marched his armies north to Megiddo. Necho was forced to lose valuable time in besieging the city. Josiah died in the battle, but he had succeeded in delaying Necho. Haran fell to the Babylonians.

56

The Rise of the Chaldeans

The Chaldeans were a Semitic people who first appeared in Southern Mesopotamia about 1000 B.C. Beginning about the ninth century we read of Chaldeans struggling with Assyrians for the control of Babylonia. Assyrian records from the time of Ashur-nasir-pal II (883-859 B.C.) show that the Chaldeans posed a threat to Assyrian expansionist plans. In 731 B.C. a Chaldean prince, Ukin-zer, attacked Babylon and seized the throne. Three years later Tiglath-pileser III of Assyria, supported by the priesthood, launched a counter attack and deposed Ukin-zer. By keeping the Assyrians busy defending their Babylonian dependencies, the Chaldeans provided some relief for Israel and Judah from interference in their affairs.

During the reign of Shalmaneser V (727-722 B.C.) the Chaldeans were restive. Under his successor Sargon II (722-705 B.C.) a Chaldean named Marduk-apal-iddina (Biblical Merodach-baladan, II Kings 20:12-15), who had ruled a small principality named Bit Jakin, dominated Babylon (720-710 B.C.). Shalmaneser had begun the siege of Samaria, and Sargon took the city and deported its population during the period when the Chaldeans were asserting control over Babylon. During the reign of Hezekiah of Judah, Merodach-baladan sent an envoy to Jerusalem to congratulate the king on his recovery from sickness and, at the same time, to urge him to ally himself with the Chaldeans against Assyria. Hezekiah proudly showed his treasures to the visiting Chaldeans, an action which the prophet Isaiah denounced. The very Chaldeans who were showing friendship to Hezekiah would one day conquer Judah (Isa. 39:1-8).

Sennacherib was able to conquer Marduk-apal-iddina (703 B.C.) and restore Babylonia to the Assyrian Empire. The Assyrians maintained a tight grip on their Babylonian province,

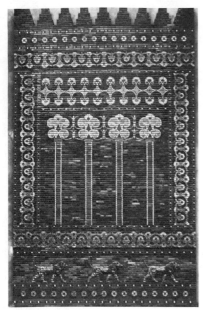

Facade from the throne room of Nebuchadnezzar.

but the Chaldeans remained the dominant ethnic group in southern Mesopotamia. They were marking time until the moment was right for a fresh declaration of independence.

It was not until 626 B.C. that Chaldean power was able to challenge successfully the Assyrian rule over Babylon. In that year Nabopolassar (626-605 B.C.) rebelled against his Assyrian overlord and established what was to become the Neo-Babylonian, or Chaldean Empire. Nabopolassar found an ally in Cyaxeres the Mede (625-585 B.C.) and the combined Chaldean and Median forces attacked Nineveh, the Assyrian capital. Nineveh fell in 612 B.C. Although the Assyrians attempted to salvage parts of their empire during the years that followed, for all practical purposes the fall of Nineveh meant the end of the Assyrian Empire. Nabopolassar rebuilt the city of Babylon and made it the capital of his empire. The empire of the lawgiver Hammurabi, who flourished in the sixteenth century B.C., is known as the Old Babylonian Empire. That of Nabopolassar and his better-known son, Nebuchadnezzar, is the New or Neo-Babylonian Empire, sometimes called the Chaldean Empire.

The Chaldeans laid claim to the vast empire that once had been Assyria. Egypt, however, remembered the days when her Pharaohs ruled the east and dreamed again of empire. Challenging the rising Chaldean power, Egyptian armies moved into Palestine. At the decisive Battle of Carchemish (605 B.C.) on the upper Euphrates River, Nebuchadnezzar, the son of Nabopolassar inflicted a crushing blow on the Egyptians.

In the showdown between Egypt and Babylon, Josiah of Judah proved a staunch ally of the Babylonians. Josiah lost his life in seeking to prevent an Egyptian army from passing the fortress of Megiddo. We do not know if Josiah had a formal treaty with Babylon, or if he was simply acting in what he considered to be in the best interests of Judah. The Egyptians had hoped to join forces with the remaining Assyrian forces to challenge the rising power of Babylon. Although Josiah did not succeed in preventing the Egyptians from passing Megiddo, he was successful in delaying the Egyptians. That delay may have been sufficient to allow Nebuchadnezzar to disable completely the last contingent of the Assyrian army at Haran.

Following Carchemish, Nebuchadnezzar might have marched his armies down the Palestine coast as far as to Egypt but for the fact that he received word of the death of his father. Thereupon he hastened home to Babylon to assume kingship in his own name. After securing his succession he returned to the battlefield and by the end of 604 B.C. Chaldean armies were on the Philistine plain. Ashkelon was taken (cf. Jer. 47:5-7) and Jehoiakim of Judah (609-598 B.C.) became a vassal (II Kings 24:1). During the years that followed the kings of Judah wavered between a pro-Egyptian and a pro-Babylonian policy. Egypt was not to become a dominant force in western Asia, and the pro-Egyptian policy of Judah's last king ultimately brought on the destruction of Jerusalem at the hand of Nebuchadnezzar.

While Nebuchadnezzar was best known for his military achievements, the cuneiform documents from ancient Babylon also depict him as a great builder. During his reign, Babylon became the most beautiful city of the ancient world (cf. Dan. 4:30). Nebuchadnezzar's son and successor, Awil-Marduk (Evil-Merodach of II Kings 25:27-30), released Jehoiachin from prison and dealt kindly with the Jews. After a reign of but two years he was murdered by his brother-in-law, Neriglissar (560-558 B.C.). He, in turn, was succeeded by Labashi-Marduk who reigned but three months before being succeeded by another usurper, Nabonidus. It was Belshazzar, the son of Nabonidus, who acted in his father's behalf as co-regent until the fall of the Babylonian empire to Cyrus the Persian (538 B.C.; cf. Dan. 5). The successors to Nebuchadnezzar were not strong characters. The priests of Marduk, the god of Babylon, were so disillusioned with their rulers that they welcomed Cyrus as a liberator when his armies reached Babylon.

A brick from Babylon that bears the name and titles of Nebuchadnezzar and of his father, Nabopolassar.

57

The Last Days of Judah

Pharaoh Necho dreamed of an Asiatic empire such as the New Kingdom Pharaohs had ruled. Babylon, however, under the energetic prince Nebuchadnezzar was not content to destroy the power of Assyria. The Assyrian provinces in western Asia were regarded as the spoil of war, and Nebuchadnezzar was not prepared to see Necho build an empire.

Necho intervened directly in the affairs of Judah in his attempt to consolidate power. After Josiah's death, his son Jehoahaz was acclaimed king (609 B.C.) Within three months, Necho summoned Jehoahaz to his headquarters at Riblah, in central Syria (II Kings 23:31-35; cf. Jer. 22:10-12). The king was deposed and deported to Egypt. His brother Eliakim had his name changed to Jehoiakim and was seated on the throne of Judah as an Egyptian vassal (609-598 B.C.). Heavy tribute was laid upon the land (II Kings 23:31-35).

For a brief time after Pharaoh Necho's defeat of the Israelite forces at Megiddo (609 B.C.) it looked as though Egypt might gain control over Syria and Palestine. Israelite territories were diminished, yet tribute was demanded by the victorious Egyptians. Jehoiakim was a most ineffectual king. Josiah's reforms were largely forgotten and pagan practices were introduced throughout Judah (cf. Jer. 7:16-18; 11:9-13). Jehoiakim insisted on building an expensive new palace for himself using forced labor battalions to accomplish the work (Jer. 22:13-19).

Nebuchadnezzar of Babylon defeated Necho at the battle of Carchemish, in northern Syria in 605 B.C. (cf. Jer. 46:2-24). This was but the prelude of the utter rout of Egyptian armies which Nebuchadnezzer was to inflict as he laid claim to all of western Asia. A second defeat of the Egyptians at Hamath opened the way to all of southern Syria and Palestine for Nebuchadnezzar. That advance was delayed, however, for in

August, 605 B.C., Nebuchadnezzar received word of the death of his father Nabopolassar. Nebuchadnezzar hastened home to claim his throne.

The following year (604 B.C.) we find Nebuchadnezzar's armies in the Philistine plain. Ashkelon fell to the Babylonians and Jehoiakim found it expedient to transfer his allegiance to Nebuchadnezzar (II Kings 24:1). The court had a pro-Egyptian faction, however, and many felt that an alliance with Egypt would be good protection against the Chaldeans. Late in 601 B.C. Nebuchadnezzar met Necho in a pitched battle near the Egyptian frontier. Both sides had heavy casualties. Nebuchadnezzar returned home and it was two years before his armies appeared next in Palestine. During this time Jehoiakim rebelled (II Kings 24:1), trusting Egypt to come to his aid if necessary. Nebuchadnezzar immediately dispatched such contingents of Babylonian troops as were available along with guerilla bands of Arameans, Moabites, and Ammonites (II Kings 24:2; Jer. 35:11) to harass the land. The Babylonian army marched toward Judah in December, 598 B.C., and at about the same time Jehoiakim died (II Kings 24:6). It seems likely that some courtier murdered Jehoiakim in hope of gaining favorable terms from Nebuchadnezzar. Jehoiachin, the eighteen year old son of Jehoiakim took the throne (II Kings 24:8). Three months later Jerusalem surrendered to Nebuchadnezzar. Jehoiachin, the queen mother, leading citizens and heavy booty were taken to Babylon (II Kings 24:10-17). Egypt had proved a broken reed.

Zedekiah, the last king of Judah (597-587 B.C.) was a weak ruler occupying an ambiguous position. Many of the Judeans still regarded his nephew Jehoiachin as the legitimate, though exiled, ruler. The Babylonians, too, regarded Jehoiachin as a true king, held in hostage in Babylon to guarantee the good behavior of the Judeans.

A collection of cuneiform tablets, published in 1939 by Ernst F. Weidner of Berlin, contains lists of payments of rations in oil and grain to captives and skilled workmen living in Babylon between 595 and 570 B.C. Among the princes is one named Yaukin (Jehoiachin) of Judah. The fact that Yaukin is considered king of Judah by the Babylonians suggests that Zedekiah was actually a regent. Ezekiel, too, regarded Jehoiachin as king even while in exile. In dating his vision (Ezek. 1:2) he observes, "It was the fifth year of the exile of king Jehoiachin."

Three inscribed jar handles found in Palestine bear the

inscription, "Belonging to Eliakim, steward of Jehoiachin." Two of these were found at Debir, in southern Judah, and the third at Beth-shemesh, fifteen miles west of Jerusalem. All were made from the original stamp seal. On the basis of this inscription we may conclude that a man named Eliakim was the steward of Jehoiachin's crown property while the king was in captivity.[1] Zedekiah did not appropriate Jehoiachin's property.

Although Jeremiah urged Zedekiah to exercise restraint and reject the advice of his pro-Egyptian counselors, the weak king allowed himself to be led on the path that brought destruction to Jerusalem, and exile to Judah. False prophets assured the exiles in Babylon that they would soon be back in Judah. Jeremiah, on the other hand, urged the exiles to make the best of their position in Babylon:

> Build houses and live in them; plant gardens and eat their produce. Take wives and have sons and daughters; take wives for your sons and give your daughters in marriage, that they may bear sons and daughters, multiply there and do not decrease. But seek the welfare of the city where I have sent you into exile, and pray to the Lord on its behalf, for in its welfare you will find your welfare.
>
> (Jer. 29:4-7).

Jeremiah had a firm faith that God would bring his people back from exile (Jer. 29:10), but he insisted that it would be a long time — seventy years — before Judah would return. Those prophets who said that the exiles would soon come home and Jerusalem would be spared were false, crying "Peace, peace" when there was no peace. Those who insisted that Yahweh would assuredly protect his Temple, and that the Babylonian would never be able to enter its sacred precincts (Jer. 7:4) were reminded of the fate of Shiloh (Jer. 7:12) where the ark had once rested before it fell before the Philistines.

By 589 B.C. the pro-Egyptian party had its way in Zedekiah's court. Pharaohs Psammeticus II (593-599 B.C.) and his son Hophra (Apries, 588-569 B.C.) were intent on expansion into Asia at the expense of Babylon. Much of western Asia was willing to let well enough alone, but Tyre was determined to throw off the yoke of Nebuchadnezzar and Zedekiah was reluctantly brought to an anti-Babylonian position. Ammon also committed itself to the revolt (cf. Ezek. 21:18-32).

The Babyloniain army was entrenched outside the walls of Jerusalem by January, 588 B.C. One by one the Judean strongholds fell before Nebuchadnezzar's armies until only Azekah,

This seal impression, on a jar handle, identifies the steward of King Jehoiachin (ca. 597 B.C.).

---

1. W. F. Albright, "The Seal of Eliakim and the Latest Pre-Exilic History of Judah," *Journal of Biblical Literature*, LI (1932), pp. 77-106.

Lachish, and Jerusalem remained. Events of these times may be documented from the Lachish Letters a collection of eighteen broken pieces of pottery containing hastily written letters and lists discovered in 1935 in the burned debris of the guardroom in the city gate of Lachish. Three more were discovered in 1938. Only about one-third of the letters are legible.

Most of the Lachish Letters are notes addressed by a man named Hoshaiah to Yaosh, commander of the Judean forces at Lachish. Hoshaiah was evidently in charge of an outpost north of Lachish in a position where he could see the smoke signals from Azekah. The fourth letter says, "And let (my lord) know that we are watching for the signals of Lachish, according to all the indications which my lord hath given, for we cannot see Azekah." According to Jeremiah 34:7, Lachish and Azekah were the last cities to fall to Nebuchadnezzar before the capture of Jerusalem itself. Hoshaiah seems to be writing shortly after the fall of Azekah. He has not sighted the smoke (or fire) signals of Azekah and is concerned for the fate of Lachish. As a matter of history, Azekah fell, then Lachish, and finally Jerusalem itself.

Two scenes of the site of Lachish: ruins of the wall and gate (above) and the cistern (below).

In the summer of 588 B.C. the siege of Jerusalem was temporarily lifted when news reached the Babylonians that an Egyptian army was approaching. Jerusalem rejoiced; only Jeremiah insisted that disaster was ahead (Jer. 37:6-10; 34:21-22). Jeremiah was proved right, for the Babylonians quickly drove the Egyptians back and continued the siege.

Jerusalem continued to resist, but her food supply was dwindling. July 587 B.C. saw the Babylonians breaching the walls and entering the city. Zedekiah tried to escape by night, but he was captured near Jericho and taken to Nebuchadnezzar's camp at Riblah in Syria. He was forced to watch the execution of his sons, then he was blinded and taken in chains to Babylon where he died (II Kings 25:6, 7; Jer. 52:9-11). A month later Nebuzaradan, captain of Nebuchadnezzar's bodyguard, burned the Temple, the palace, and the private houses of Jerusalem and broke down its walls (II Kings 25:8-10). Some of the leaders of Jerusalem were taken to Riblah, judged before Nebuchadnezzar, and executed (II Kings 25:18-21). Others were deported to Babylon where they joined those who had been exiled earlier. Israel's prophets insisted that the exile was Yahweh's punishment upon His people because of their sin. Yahweh had permitted Nebuchadnezzar to gain a temporary victory in order to chastize idolatrous Israel. Israel was

assured, however, that God would bring His people back to their own land. While some settled permanently and profitably in Babylon, others longed for the day of deliverance.

After the fall of Jerusalem, Judah was a ruined land. Its principal citizens were either killed or deported. The population consisted largely of poor peasants who were regarded as too weak to make trouble (II Kings 25:12). The Babylonians appointed a man named Gedaliah to serve as governor of the province of Judah, with headquarters at Mizpah because Jerusalem was in ruins. Gadaliah was a noble whose father Ahikam had once saved Jeremiah's life (Jer. 26:24). His grandfather Shaphan was probably the Shaphan who was an official in Josiah's court at the time of the great reform (II Kings 22:3). A seal found at Lachish bears the inscription, "To Gedaliah, who is over the house." The document which it sealed has long since been destroyed by the weather, but the presence of the seal at Lachish suggests that Gedaliah served as one of the last prime ministers of Judah. The title "who is over the house" was used of the highest official of the land next to the king.

The appointment of Gedaliah as governor of Judah may be regarded as a conciliating gesture toward the remaining Judeans. Gedaliah sought to lead the people to a return to normalcy (Jer. 40:7-10), but his efforts were thwarted. A group of extremists looked upon Gedaliah as a collaborator with the hated Babylonians. Ishmael, a member of the royal house of Judah who had fled to Ammon, gained the cooperation of the king of Ammon in a plot to slay Gedaliah. Gedaliah refused to believe friends who warned him of the plot, but they proved correct. Ishmael and his band of conspirators killed Gedaliah, along with the Jews who were with him and the Babylonian garrison at Mizpah (Jer. 41:1-3). Ishmael escaped to Ammon, and the Judeans who remained feared the vengeance of Nebuchadnezzar after this act of defiance in killing the appointed governor. Contrary to the advice of Jeremiah (Jer. 42) they determined to flee to Egypt, and the prophet was forced to accompany them. The province of Judah was probably abolished and its territory incorporated into the province of Samaria, although records have not been preserved.

Mount Hermon across Baaka Valley. Nebuchadnezzar and his army traversed this valley, which lay between Palestine and his headquarters in Riblah.

Between 600 and 400 B.C.—the era covered in Part Six—the world received much of its present religious and philosophical inheritance. During the time of Judah's Exile, the Persian religious leader Zoroaster was developing his dualistic concepts which were to become the state religion of Persia until the Mohammedan conquest. At about the same time, Confucius, the Chinese sage, was born in what is now Shantung Province; and Buddha Gautama, born into an environment of luxury in India, determined to lead the ascetic life and, as a result, developed the principles of Buddhism.

Both the Neo-Babylonian and the Persian empires, successively, reached the zenith of their power during these centuries. Before they were over, Greece had proved her ability to resist encroachments from the East at Marathon (490 B.C.); Persian power was checked; and the tide of empire began to move westward. The noblest achievements of Athenian culture found expression during the Age of Pericles (461-429 B.C.). Socrates (469-399 B.C.) and Plato (427-347 B.C.) were developing their philosophies before the close of our period and before the end of the next century Hellenism was to dominate the East.

Important changes were also taking place among the Israelites. Judah, the Southern Kingdom, had maintained a precarious existence for almost a century and a half after the fall of her northern neighbor, Israel, to Assyria in 722 B.C. When the armies of Nebuchadnezzar finally breached the walls of Jerusalem (587 B.C.), Judah, as a political entity, was absorbed into the Neo-Babylonian Empire, and most of her people were taken into exile.

The Exile was the watershed between ancient Israel as a political unit and the religion known as Judaism. The Jews of the Post-exilic period had their spiritual roots in the institutions and prophetic utterances of their earlier history. Political Israel, however, had been anchored to a geographical area and a civil ruler in a way which differed markedly from Post-exilic Judaism. Although Jews of the dispersion (i.e., those away from Palestine) loved Zion and sent their gifts to the paternal homeland, the institution of the synagogue, which developed after the destruction of the first Temple (587 B.C.), made corporate Jewish life possible in any land.

PART SIX

Exile and Return

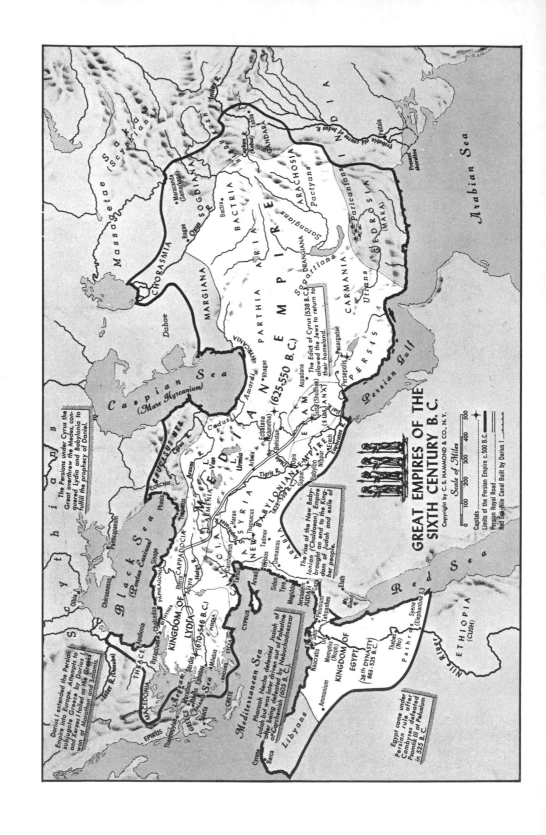

GREAT EMPIRES OF THE SIXTH CENTURY B.C.

Copyright by C. S. Hammond & Co., N.Y.

Scale of Miles
0 100 200 300 400 500

Capitals
Limits of the Persian Empire c.500 B.C.
Persian Royal Road
Red Sea-Nile Canal Built by Darius I

The Persians under Cyrus the Great overthrew the Medes, conquered Lydia and Babylonia to fulfill the prophecy of Daniel.

The Edict of Cyrus (538 B.C.) allowed the Jews to return to their homeland.

The rise of the New Babylonian (Chaldaean) Empire brought an end to the Kingdom of Judah and exile of her people.

Pharaoh Necho defeated Josiah of Judah but was later driven out of Palestine after being defeated at Carchemish (605 B.C.).

Egypt came under Persian rule after Cambyses defeated Psamtik III at Pelusium in 525 B.C.

Darius I extended the Persian Empire into Europe. Attempt to subjugate Greece by Darius I and Xerxes I foiled as the Greeks won at Marathon and Salamis.

Arabian Sea

INDIA

Probable old course of Indus

Present shoreline

Pattala

Cophen R. (Kabul)
GANDARA
Taxila
Indus R.
ARACHOSIA
Paricanians
Pactyans
Sarangians
GEDROSIA (MAKA)
Hindu Kush
BACTRIA
Bactra
Sogdiana
Oraus R.
Maracanda (Samarkand)
Bagae
CHORASMIA
Massagetae (Scythians)
DRANGIANA
Sagartians
ARIA
PARTHIA
CARMANIA
Utians
PERSIS
Pasargadae
Persepolis
Persian Gulf
Aspadana
P E R S I A N   E M P I R E (625-550 B.C.)
HYRCANIA
Rhagae
MEDIA (625-550 B.C.)
Caspian Sea (Mare Hyrcanium)
Amardi
Cadusii
Dahae
MARGIANA
ELAM (SUSIANA)
Susa (Shushan)
Behistun
Ecbatana (Achmetha)
Ecbatana
MEDIA
Urmia
Van
ARMENIA
Araxes R.
Cyrus R.
CAUCASUS MTS.
COLCHIS
Phasis
Panticapaeum
Chersonesus
Black Sea (Pontus Euxinus)
Sinope
Olbia
Apollonia
Byzantium
Chalcedon
THRACE
MACEDONIA
EPIRUS
Thermopylae
GREECE
Marathon
Athens
Sparta
Aegean Sea
Ephesus
Miletus
Sardis
KINGDOM OF LYDIA (670-546 B.C.)
PISIDIA
CAPPADOCIA
PAPHLAGONIA
BITHYNIA
Halys R.
Ancyra
Pteria
Thapsacus
Trapezus
Scythians
Ister R. (Danube)
CRETE
RHODES
CYPRUS
Tarsus
CILICIA
Arvad
Byblos
Sidon
Tyre
Damascus
Tadmor
Haran
Carchemish
ASSYRIA
Arbela
Tigris R.
Nineveh
Opis
Sippar
Babylon
Nippur
Erech
Ur
Euphrates R.
NEW BABYLONIAN EMPIRE (625-538 B.C.)
ARABIA
Megiddo
JUDAH
Jerusalem
Gaza
Pelusium
Tahpanhes
Mt. Sinai
Elath
Red Sea
Mediterranean Sea
Libyans
Cyrene
Barca
KINGDOM OF EGYPT (26th DYNASTY 663-525 B.C.)
Naucratis
Sais
Memphis (Noph)
Thebes (No)
Pathros
Syene (Elephantine)
Ammonium
Nile River
ETHIOPIA (CUSH)

58

The Campaigns
of Nebuchadnezzar

The center of power in the Tigris-Euphrates Valley periodically shifted. The Amorite lawgiver, Hammurabi, ruled from
ancient Babylon during the eighteenth century B.C. With the
decline of the Old Babylonian Empire, the political center
moved northward and the Assyrians came to control not only
Babylon but most of Western Asia. Sargon II (721-705 B.C.) established his capital at Nineveh, and his successors marched eastward to the Mediterranean in quest of tribute and booty.

The Assyrians were humbled by the Chaldeans, a Semitic people who had been in Babylon since about 1000 B.C. Nabopolassar (626-605 B.C.) threw off the Assyrian yoke and founded an
independent Chaldean, or Neo-Babylonian Empire. Not only
were the Assyrians unsuccessful in putting down his revolt, but
they lost their own capital, Nineveh, when Nabopolassar joined
forces with Cyaxeres the Mede in 612 B.C. The Assyrians retreated westward to the ancient city of Haran, but it too fell to
the Babylonians and their allies (610 B.C.). The following year
Pharaoh Necho of Egypt (609-593 B.C.) marched northward to
Carchemish on the Euphrates to assist the Assyrian king, Ashur-
uballit, in an effort to retake Haran from the Babylonians. Josiah
of Judah sought to prevent Necho from marching his troops
through the Valley of Jezreel, but Josiah was killed in a battle
fought at the fortress of Megiddo. The effort to regain Haran for
the Assyrians failed, and Assyrian power was never felt again.
Babylon took its place as a world power. Egypt, however, saw an
opportunity to gain control of Syria and Palestine. Necho deposed Jehoahaz, the son of Josiah, after a short reign of but three
months. Eliakim, a brother of Jehoahaz was appointed king of Judah by Necho, who renamed him Jehoiakim.

Nabopolassar died in 605 B.C. shortly after his son Nebuchadnezzar[1] had defeated the Egyptians at Carchemish and, again, at Hamath. Nebuchadnezzar returned to Babylon to claim his throne. It may be that he sent his armies to secure the allegiance of the peoples of Syria and Palestine at that time. This would explain the reference in Daniel 1 to exiles taken to Babylon during Jehoiakim's reign.

We possess records of the campaigns of Nabopolassar and Nebuchadnezzar for the twenty-three year period between 616 B.C. and 594 B.C. in the Chaldean Chronicle.[2] It contains a report of the Battle of Carchemish (605 B.C.):

> In the twenty-first year the king of Akkad stayed in his own land. Nebuchadrezzar his eldest son, the crown prince, mustered the Babylonian army and took command of his troops; he marched to Carchemish which is on the bank of the Euphrates, and crossed the river to go against the Egyptian army which lay at Carchemish .... He accomplished their defeat and to non-existence beat them. As for the rest of the Egyptian army which had escaped from the defeat so quickly that no weapon had reached them, in the district of Hamath the Babylonian troops overtook and defeated them so that not a single man escaped to his own country. At that time Nebuchadnezzar conquered the whole area of the Hatti-country. For twenty-one years Nabopolassar had been king of Babylon. On the 8th of the month of Abu he died; in the month Ululu, Nebuchadrezzar returned to Babylon and on the first day of the month Ululu he sat on the royal throne in Babylon.[3]

The Chronicle speaks of a series of campaigns in "the Hatti-country" or Syria. In his first year as ruler of Babylon we read, "All the kings of the Hatti-land came before him and he received their heavy tribute."[4]

Another cuneiform inscription boasts of the accomplishments of the king:

> In exalted trust in him (i.e., Marduk, god of Babylon), distant countries, remote mountains from the upper sea (Mediterranean) to the lower sea (Persian Gulf), steep paths, blockaded roads, where the step is impeded, where was no footing, difficult roads, desert path, I traversed, and the disobedient I destroyed; I captured the enemies; established justice

---

1. The Babylonian form of the name is Nabu-kudurru-usur, which approximates the Biblical Nebuchadrezzar, the form of the name frequently used in Jeremiah and Ezekiel. The Old Testament historical books, and Daniel, use the form Nebuchadnezzar.

2. D. J. Wiseman, *Chronicles of Chaldaean Kings: (626-566 B.C.) in the British Museum*. See also David Noel Freedman, "The Babylonian Chronicle," *The Biblical Archaeologist*, XIX, 3, pp. 50-60. Dr. Freedman's article appears as Chapter 10, *The Biblical Archaeologist Reader* (edited by G. Ernest Wright and David Noel Freedman).

3. Wiseman, *op cit.*, pp. 67-69.

4. Wiseman, *op. cit.*, p. 25.

in the lands; the people I exalted; the bad and evil I separated from the people.[5]

Nebuchadnezzar subdued the Lebanon mountain region and established his sovereignty there. The trail which he took in ascending the Wadi Brissa can still be followed. As we go up the gorge from the Riblah plain we reach a place where the rock is smooth. On one side we see a relief of Nebuchadnezzar standing before a cedar, and on the other he is depicted warding off a lion. His accomplishments are described in a nearby inscription:

> Trusting in the power of my lords, Nebo and Marduk, I organized my army for an expedition to the Lebanon. I made that country happy by eradicating its enemy everywhere. All its scattered inhabitants I led back to their settlements. What no former king had done, I achieved: I cut through steep mountains, I split rocks, I opened passages, and thus I constructed a straight road for the (transport of the) cedars. I made the Arahtu float down and carry to Marduk, my king, mighty cedars high and strong, of precious beauty and of excellent dark quality, the abundant yield of the Lebanon, as (if they be) reed stalks (carried by) the river. Within Babylon (I stored) mulberry wood. I made the inhabitants of the Lebanon live in safety together and let nobody disturb them . . .[6]

Nebuchadnezzar continued southward to the Dog River which enters the Mediterranean north of Byblos. Near the mouth of the river three Egyptian and four Assyrian inscriptions already commemorated the prowess of Nebuchadnezzar's predecessors. On its north bank Nebuchadnezzar inscribed a copy of the Wadi-Brissa Inscription.

The smaller states of Syria and Palestine were easy prey for Nebuchadnezzar. His real foe and potential rival was Egypt. During Nebuchadnezzar's fourth year, the Chronicle tells us, he marched against Egypt. The battle seems to have been indecisive, for each side inflicted heavy casualties upon the other. Nebuchadnezzar was sufficiently weakened that he found it necessary to return to Babylon.[7] Since he had been the aggressor, it could be considered a defeat for Babylon.

During the period of Nebuchadnezzar's advance in Syria and Palestine, Jehoiakim of Judah paid tribute to the Babylonians (II Kings 24:1). When Nebuchadnezzar was forced to return home after his unsuccessful attempt to subdue Necho of Egypt,

Assyrian campaign inscriptions at Dog River, which record military victories.

---

5. Translated from G. A. Rawlinson, *Cuneiform Inscriptions of Western Asia*, I 33, col. 11, line 12 ff. in G. A. Barton, *Archaeology and the Bible*, p. 478.
6. From the so-called Wadi-Brissa Inscription. Translation adapted from A. Leo Oppenheim, "Babylonian and Assyrian Historical Texts," James Pritchard, ed. *Ancient Near Eastern Texts*, p. 307.
7. Wiseman, *op. cit.*, p. 71.

Jehoiakim rebelled, trusting Egypt to come to his aid if necessary. The year following the Egyptian fiasco, Nebuchadnezzar "stayed in his own land and gathered together his chariots and horses in great numbers."[8] His absence from western Asia doubtless strengthened the hands of the pro-Egyptian groups.

Judah's respite was short, however. In December, 598 B.C. the Babylonian army was on the march again. The same month, Jehoiakim died. It is likely that he was assassinated (cf. Jer. 22:18-19; 36:30) by Judaeans who hoped to placate Nebuchadnezzar. The Chronicle reads:

> In the seventh year, the month of Kislimu, the king of Akkad mustered his troops, marched to the Hatti-land, and encamped against (i.e., besieged) the city of Judah (i.e., Jerusalem), and on the second day of the month of Addaru he seized the city and captured the king. He appointed there a king of his own choice, received its heavy tribute and sent them to Babylon.[9]

Jehoiachin, the eighteen-year-old son of Jehoiakim, who had succeeded to the throne at the death of his father, reigned but three months before Jerusalem surrendered to Nebuchadnezzar and he was taken to Babylon (II Kings 24:12). The "king of his own choice" whom Nebuchadnezzar placed on the throne of Judah was Mattaniah (II Kings 24:17), an uncle of Jehoiachin. Nebuchadnezzar gave him the name, Zedekiah. The exiles looked upon Jehoiachin as their legitimate king, however. Dates were reckoned "from the exile of King Jehoiachin" (Ezek. 1:2). Babylonian administrative documents list provisions assigned to individuals who were prisoners of war or, for other reasons, dependent upon the king. Among those who receive provisions is *Ya'u-kinu* king of *Yahudu*.[10]

The Chaldean Chronicle closes with the eleventh year of Nebuchadnezzar (594-593 B.C.). From other sources, however, we are able to piece together the trouble-filled years preceding the fall of Jerusalem. When Pharaoh Necho died (593 B.C.) the Palestinian states of Edom, Moab, Ammon, Tyre, and Sidon met at Jerusalem (Jer. 27:3), hopeful that the new Egyptian ruler, Psammetichus II, would aid them in a fresh challenge to the power of Babylon. Psammetichus pursued a policy of non-interference, however, and the plot against Babylon proved an embarrassment to Zedekiah, who was evidently its leader. The Judaean king journeyed to Babylon (Jer. 51:59) and swore allegiance to Nebuchadnezzar.

---

8. *Ibid.*
9. Wiseman, *op. cit.*, p. 73.
10. See pp. 395-396.

Zedekiah is not an attractive character. Although at times he seems to have been "more sinned against than sinning," Zedekiah was guilty of vacillation. Jeremiah urged him to remain loyal to Nebuchadnezzar, but the pro-Egyptian party in court called for rebellion. Loyal Judaeans thought of Nebuchadnezzar as an oppressor, and many false prophets joined in the plea for Judah to assert its independence. At the death of Psammetichus II (588 B.C.), his successor, Apries (Biblical Hophra) decided upon a more energetic participation in Asiatic affairs. He gained control over the Phoenician cities and encouraged a league of Palestinian states to resist Babylon. Zedekiah succumbed to the pro-Egyptian party in his court and became a participant.

Nebuchadnezzar reacted swiftly. By January, 588 B.C. (II Kings 25:1; Jer. 52:4), Jerusalem was under siege (Jer. 21:3-7). From his headquarters at Riblah, on the Orontes River, Nebuchadnezzar was able to take the Judaean strongholds, one by one, until only Lachish, Azekah, and Jerusalem were left (Jer. 34:6-7). A glimpse of life during these difficult times is given in the Lachish Letters, a collection of pieces of broken pottery inscribed with ink, discovered by the late J. L. Starkey at Tell ed-Duweir, southwest of Jerusalem. Tell ed-Duweir is now identified with Biblical Lachish.

The letters reflect conditions outside the capital in a way comparable to Jeremiah's description of things in Jerusalem itself. A tragic note appears in the fourth letter which concludes:

> And let (my lord) know that we are watching for the signals of Lachish, according to all the indications which my lord hath given, for we cannot see Azekah. (See illustration on page 16.)

The writer of the letter was probably with the Judaean fighters in the field.[11] The signal of which he speaks was probably a fire signal, as the Mishna suggests. The writer gave the sad news that the signal from Azekah had failed. Evidently the city had fallen to Nebuchadnezzar's army.

There was one glimmer of hope left for Judah. Egypt might yet come to her rescue and challenge Nebuchadnezzar. As a matter of fact Egypt did march northward: "The army of Pharaoh had come out of Egypt; and when the Chaldeans who were besieging Jerusalem heard news of them, they withdrew from Jerusalem" (Jer. 37:5).

When Pharaoh Apries' forces advanced into Judah, the pro-

---

11. See Chapter 62.

Egyptian nobles felt that their policies were vindicated. Only Jeremiah injected a sour note, prophesying defeat for Judah (Jer. 37:6-10; 34:21). Jeremiah, however, was right. Nebuchadnezzar turned back the Egyptian force and resumed the siege of Jerusalem.

During the summer of 587 B.C. the end came. The army of Nebuchadnezzar breached the walls of the city which was facing starvation in any event. The Babylonian king's patience was exhausted. He determined to raze and burn the city and appointed Nebuzaradan, the captain of the guard, to oversee the destruction of Jerusalem. The Temple treasure was pillaged and the city walls were reduced to rubble. The Temple, palace, and other buildings were completely destroyed. Zedekiah attempted to escape toward Ammon (II Kings 25:3-4; Jer. 52:7-8), but he was taken near Jericho and brought to Nebuchadnezzar's headquarters at Riblah. There Zedekiah witnessed the execution of his sons before he was blinded and taken in chains to Babylon (II Kings 25:6-7) where he died.

Nebuchadnezzar determined that Judah should never again challenge his authority. He sent a commander, Nebuzaradan, to Jerusalem with orders to destroy the city. Jerusalem was burned and its walls leveled. Military, civil, and religious leaders were executed at Riblah (II Kings 25:18-21) and less dangerous elements in the population were exiled to Babylon.

The poor peasants of Judah were permitted to remain in the land which, as a matter of fact, was completely desolate (II Kings 25:12). To keep some semblance of order among them, Nebuchadnezzar appointed a Judaean noble named Gedaliah to govern the remnants of Judah from Mizpah, north of the ruins of Jerusalem. A seal discovered at Lachish identifies Gedaliah as chief minister in Zedekiah's cabinet. His father, Ahikam, had once saved Jeremiah's life (Jer. 26:24), a fact which may show his sympathy with Jeremiah's desire to co-operate with Nebuchadnezzar.

Gedaliah's reign was short-lived, however. He was regarded as a collaborationist because he attempted to "do business" with Nebuchadnezzar. A member of the Judaean royal house named Ishmael gained the backing of the king of Ammon and plotted to kill Gedaliah. Although warned of danger, Gedaliah refused to believe the reports he heard about Ishmael.

Ishmael, however, went through with his plans. Joined by his fellow conspirators he attacked Gedaliah, killed him along with members of a Babylonian garrison stationed at Mizpah, and a number of the Jews who were nearby. Although pursued by Gedaliah's men, Ishmael made good his escape to Ammon. The surviving Judaeans, fearing reprisals from Nebuchadnezzar because of this treachery, determined to flee to Egypt. Jeremiah urged them not to do so, but they could not be dissuaded, and Jeremiah, himself, was forced to accompany them there.

Mention is made of a further deportation of Judaeans in 582 B.C. (Jer. 52:30). This may have been brought on by the disorders which followed the murder of Gedaliah. Neither the Scriptures nor Babylonian records give any hint concerning the length of Gedaliah's governorship, although it appears to have been of short duration. With the death of Gedaliah and the dispersion of the surviving Judaeans, corporate Israelite life in Palestine came to an end. The bulk of the territory once belonging to kings of the Davidic dynasty was probably incorporated into the territory of Samaria, one of the provinces of the Babylonian Empire.

At Tyre, this Roman road, lined with ruined columns, endures. The Hellenistic ruins testify to Tyre's importance extending past Old Testament times.

Nebuchadnezzar had begun the siege of Tyre the year before the fall of Jerusalem. Ittobaal III, however, was able to withstand Nebuchadnezzar and his generals for thirteen years. As the great commercial city of the eastern Mediterranean, Tyre was supplied by sea and was not crippled by Nebuchadnezzar's land blockade. Tyre could boast "I am a god. I sit in the seat of the gods in the sea's midst" (Ezek. 28:2). Tyre occupied both a site on the Phoenician mainland and an island one-half mile from the shore. In time of siege, the Tyrians moved to their island and, protected by a large and efficient navy, they felt themselves impregnable.

In 574 B.C., Tyre was forced to come to terms with Nebuchadnezzar. Ittobaal abdicated his throne in favor of Baal II (574-564 B.C.) and a nominal Babylonian suzerainty was recognized. Tyrian business documents after that time were dated in the year of Nebuchadnezzar.

Nebuchadnezzar also subdued the Ammonites and destroyed their capital city, Rabbah. Jeremiah had prophetically described its desolation:

> Therefore, behold, the days are coming, says the Lord,
> When I will cause the battle cry to be heard
> against Rabbah of the Ammonites;
> it shall become a desolate mound,
> and its villages shall be burned with fire;
> then Israel shall dispossess those who dispossessed him,
> says the Lord (Jer. 49:2).

The Ammonite king was taken as a captive to Babylon. A few years after the capitulation of Tyre, Nebuchadnezzar undertook a campaign against Egypt (568 B.C.) and defeated Amasis but made no attempt to penetrate into Egypt.

59

Judah's Last Kings

The death of good King Josiah brought to a close an era in Israelite history. His reign had been marked by revival. During the latter days of his rule the Assyrian Empire was destroyed and Nahum could glory in the destruction of the enemy of God's people — and of all western Asia. Neither the spiritual revival nor the defeat of Assyria had permanent effects on the future of Judah, however. Idolatrous kings were to nullify Josiah's spiritual impact, and the Chaldean or Neo-Babylonian Empire would become heir to Assyria as the threat to the East.

1. Jehoahaz

The people of Judah did not realize the changes which were in store for them following Josiah's death. His younger son, Jehoahaz (or Shallum), was anointed by "the people of the land" (II Kings 23:30) who expected him to continue a policy of friendship with Babylon and political independence for Judah. Jehoahaz, however, reigned but three months (609 B.C.). Pharaoh Necho, whose armies had been responsible for the death of Josiah at Megiddo, deposed Jehoahaz and imprisoned him in the Egyptian camp at Riblah (II Kings 23:33). Leaving an army of occupation in Syria and Palestine, Necho took Jehoahaz to Egypt where he subsequently died. Eliakim, his older brother, renamed Jehoiakim, was appointed by Necho to rule Judah. Jehoiakim evidently was pro-Egyptian in his sympathies, and was ready to become a vassal to Necho. This may be the reason that he had been passed over in favor of his younger brother at the time of Josiah's death.

2. Jehoiakim

Jehoiakim's loyalty to Egypt proved costly to his subjects in

Judah. The heavy tribute he was forced to pay certainly became a drain on the national economy:

> And Jehoiakim gave the silver and the gold to Pharoah, but he taxed the land to give the money according to the command of Pharoah. He exacted the silver and the gold of the people of the land, from every one according to his assessment to give it to Pharaoh Necho (II Kings 23:35).

Judah, as a vassal state, doubtless faced serious economic problems. The equivalent of over two million dollars had to be paid to Egypt. Tribute is never easy to pay, and the irresponsibility of Jehoiakim did not help matters. Early in his reign he built a new palace, using forced labor (Jer. 22:13-14 R.S.V.). Expensive cedar paneling and costly paint added to its magnificence. Jeremiah looked upon this as symptomatic of a heart that was not right with God. He warned:

> O inhabitant of Lebanon,
> nested among the cedars,
> how you will groan when pangs come upon you,
> pain as of a woman in travail! (Jer. 22:23).

The reformation associated with Josiah had never been popular, and subsequent events seemed to discredit it. The death of Josiah would be regarded by those who had no sympathy with his reformation as a divine judgment upon one who had effected religious change. Man constantly asks, "If he was right, why was he taken?" Then, too, times were hard. Some looked back to days before the revival and felt that they were better off then. They said to Jeremiah:

> As for the word which you have spoken to us in the name of the Lord, we will not listen to you. But we will do everything that we have vowed, burn incense to the queen of heaven and pour out libations to her, as we did, both we and our fathers, our kings and our princes, in the cities of Judah and in the streets of Jerusalem; for then we had plenty of food and prospered and saw no evil (Jer. 44:16-17).

Along with the lapse into idolatry there arose a false confidence in the inviolability of Jerusalem and its Temple. Had not God entered into covenant with David saying, "Your house and your kingdom shall be made sure for ever before me; your throne shall be established for ever" (II Sam. 7:16)? False prophets were saying to the people of Jerusalem, "He will do nothing; no evil will come upon us, nor shall we see sword or famine" (Jer. 5:12).

In 605 B.C. Nebuchadnezzar defeated the Egyptian army at Carchemish, on the Euphrates River. He followed them southward to Hamath on the Orontes where they suffered a second defeat. The following year Nebuchadnezzar was back in Syria and, by the end of 604 B.C. his armies were in control of the Philistine Plain. Jehoiakim, seeing Nebuchadnezzar so close, broke his ties with Egypt and offered to become a vassal to Babylon (II Kings 24:1). He was a vassal through expediency, not loyalty. As soon as Nebuchadnezzar suffered a reversal, urged on by the pro-Egyptian party at court, Jehoiakim rebelled. The act was a foolish one, for Nebuchadnezzar promptly dispatched against Jehoiakim "bands of the Chaldeans, and bands of the Syrians, and bands of the Moabites, and bands of the children of Ammon" (II Kings 24:2). Then, in December, 598 B.C. the Babylonian armies were ready to march against Judah. While Jerusalem was under siege, Jehoiakim died. Jeremiah had prophesied, "With the burial of an ass he shall be buried, dragged and cast forth beyond the gates of Jerusalem" (Jer. 22:19). Probably Jehoiakim was murdered by his own courtiers who hoped thereby to gain some favor from Nebuchadnezzar.

3. Jehoiachin

Jehoiachin, the eighteen-year-old son of Jehoiakim was ill prepared to lead his people when he took the reins of government. Within three months after Jehoiachin became king, Jerusalem surrendered to the Babylonians (II Kings 24:12). The young king was taken to Babylon along with his queen mother, palace officials, artisans, and other leaders in the community. Ezekiel, later to become known as the great prophet of the Exile, was taken captive at this time.

Young Jehoiachin seems to have been looked upon as the legitimate king of Judah even though he was succeeded in Jerusalem by his uncle, Zedekiah. Jehoiachin remained in Babylon as a political prisoner for thirty-seven years. We are told that Evil-Merodach, Nebuchadnezzar's successor, "graciously freed Jehoiachin king of Judah from prison and he spoke kindly to him, and gave him a seat above the seats of the kings that were with him in Babylon" (II Kings 25:27-28).

The fact that Jehoiachin was given a food allowance by the Babylonian king (II Kings 25:29-30) is mentioned in Babylonian cuneiform records. Three hundred dated tablets found years ago in the ruins of a vaulted building near the famed Ishtar Gate were published in 1939 by Ernst F. Weidner, then of Berlin. They list payments of rations from the government to captives and skilled workmen who were in Babylon from 595 to 570 B.C. Included are people from Egypt, Iran, Media, Asia Minor, Phoenicia, the Philistine cities, Syria, and Judah. Among the latter we read of *Ya'u-kinu* of the land of *Yahudu,* i.e., Jehoiachin of Judah, together with his five sons.[1]

Discoveries in Palestine also illustrate the position of Jehoiachin. Three stamped jar handles have been discovered (two at Debir and one at Beth-shemesh) bearing the Hebrew inscription, "Belonging to Eliakim, steward of Yaukin." These discoveries lead us to believe that a man named Eliakim was custodian of the property of Jehoiachin while he was in Babylon. The exiled king's possessions seem to have been kept intact, and there were doubtless many who hoped that he would soon return and replace Zedekiah.

4. Zedekiah

When Jehoiachin was taken to Babylon, he was succeeded in Jerusalem by his uncle Mattaniah whom Nebuchadnezzar renamed Zedekiah. Zedekiah was expected to be a puppet of Nebuchadnezzar. He ruled a land whose cities had been severely damaged, whose population had been in part deported, and whose economy was certainly crippled.

An abler man might have used his energies in rebuilding his nation, leaving strictly political matters for later consideration. Zedekiah's position was, to be sure, difficult. He seems to have been well-intentioned, but he could not resist the counsel of his nobles and the clamor of the populace. Egypt was constantly offering aid to encourage Judah to rebel against Babylon.

The nobles who surrounded Zedekiah were inexperienced. Those wise in the way of government had gone to Babylon with Jehoiachin. The very fact that Jehoiachin was in Babylon added indirectly to the troubles of Zedekiah. If, as the false prophets declared, the exiles would soon return, then Zedekiah must be prepared to meet Jehoiachin's challenge to his throne.

The exiles did not return. Instead Zedekiah's problems arose from his own princes who, in the words of Ezekiel, were "like wolves tearing the prey, shedding blood, destroying lives to get dishonest gain" (Ezek. 22:27). The nationalistic, pro-Egyptian, anti-Babylonian party soon gained royal support. By the fourth year of Zedekiah's reign we find him in consultation with ambassadors from Tyre, Sidon, Edom, Ammon and Moab — all of whom were bitterly anti-Babylonian. At about this time Zede-

---

1. W. J. Martin, "The Jehoiachin Tablets," in D. Winston Thomas, *Documents from Old Testament Times,* p. 86.

kiah journeyed to Babylon (Jer. 51:59). Perhaps Nebuchadnezzar heard rumors of defection and wanted to discuss matters with Zedekiah. Evidently Zedekiah was able to satisfy Nebuchadnezzar of his loyalty.

Open rebellion was not long in coming, however, Zedekiah made an alliance with Egypt, the hereditary enemy of Babylon. A new Pharaoh, Apries (Biblical Hophra) had come to the throne of Egypt in 588 B.C. He determined to invade Palestine and establish Egyptian suzerainty there. Ezekiel describes these events: "But he [Zedekiah] rebelled against him [Nebuchadnezzar] by sending ambassadors to Egypt that they might give him horses and a large army" (Ezek. 17:15). Nebuchadnezzar took note of Zedekiah's treachery, and sent an army into Judah. Soon the whole countryside except the cities of Azekah, Lachish, and Jerusalem, was in Babylonian control (Jer. 34:7).

Egypt made a feeble attempt to come to the aid of her ally. The Babylonians who, by this time had laid siege to Jerusalem itself, were forced to turn their forces toward the Egyptian border. For a moment it appeared that Jeremiah, who had urged loyalty to Babylon, was wrong and deliverance would come from Egypt. The hope was ill-founded. The Egyptian force was driven back by the might of Nebuchadnezzar, and the siege of Jerusalem was resumed.

From this moment on, the situation of Jerusalem was hopeless. Zedekiah realized that Jeremiah was right, but the king feared it was too late to surrender (Jer. 38:14-23). Famine and pestilence devastated the city before it was finally taken by the enemy. In July, 587 B.C., Nebuchadnezzar's armies breached the walls of Jerusalem. Zedekiah fled toward the Jordan, doubtless hopeful of a place of sanctuary in Ammon. He was captured near Jericho and taken to Nebuchadnezzar who was encamped at Riblah in central Syria. There, after witnessing the execution of his sons, Zedekiah was blinded and taken to Babylon in chains.

60

Egypt and the Exile

When Necho II became Pharaoh of Egypt (609 B.C.) he dreamed of restoring his land to the glories which it had enjoyed during its great Empire Period. Psammetichus I, his father, had taken the throne of Egypt with the blessings of Ashurbanipal of Assyria. Ashurbanipal, however, was plagued with troubles in Babylon, Arabia, and Asia Minor, and could not prevent Psammetichus from ridding himself of his Assyrian counselors and adopting an independent course of action. Psammetichus built an army of mercenaries, including Greeks who began to enter Egypt in large numbers during his reign. Greeks came to Egypt as merchants and in the western Delta they established communities which became manufacturing centers. Memphis and other large cities had Greek quarters. Strabo states that the first settlements of Greek traders from Miletus took place during the reign of Psammetichus. On the eastern edge of the Delta the Greeks were encouraged to establish the trading post which they named Daphne (Biblical Tahpanhes, Jer. 44:1). It served as a frontier fortress defending Egypt from attack from the east.

Other foreign merchants were permitted to settle in Egypt under Psammetichus. The sea-going Phoenicians sent their galleys to the mouths of the Nile Delta. Aramaeans from Syria were welcomed as permanent settlers, as were Carians, Lydians, and other peoples of Asia Minor. The Jewish mercenaries who are known to have been in Elephantine, at the first cataract of the Nile, during the fifth century B.C., may have come to Egypt during the reign of Psammetichus I, although some scholars date their arrival in Egypt at the time of Psammetichus II (593-588 B.C.). Egypt became a prosperous land, and Psammetichus dreamed of empire. By 640 B.C. Psammetichus I was ready to dispute Assyria's claim to Syria and Palestine. He invaded the Philistine territory and took Ashkelon with little difficulty. Ashdod was secured after a twenty-nine year siege. Although faced with opposition from the Scythian invaders, Psammetichus was able to restore Egypt to a position of strength which it had not enjoyed since the days of Ramesses III (1175-1144 B.C.).

With the fall of Nineveh (612 B.C.), Egyptian interests demanded a change in policy. No longer was Assyria the villain in the plot to keep Egypt weak. Babylon was the new rival, and the Egyptians determined to check Babylonian power at all costs. One of the first acts of Necho, as Pharaoh, was to march his army toward Carchemish in a vain effort to help the Assyrian, Ashur-uballit, to retake Haran from the Babylonians. It was during this march that Necho passed the Israelite stronghold at Megiddo and killed Josiah of Judah who was seeking to prevent the Egyptians from joining forces with Assyria against Babylon.

On his way north from Megiddo, Necho, aided by his Greek mercenaries, took the Syrian city of Kadesh-on-the-Orontes. He showed his appreciation for the help of the mercenaries by dedicating the garments worn during the victorious battle in the Temple of Apollo at Branchidae in Miletus.

Although unable to prevent the Babylonians from taking over the eastern portions of the Assyrian Empire, Necho was able to control for himself much of Syria and Palestine. Josiah's son, Jehoahaz was sent to Egypt in chains after a three month rule over Judah. Eliakim, another of Josiah's sons, was installed as Necho's puppet, and renamed Jehoiakim. Judah was forced to pay one hundred talents of silver, and one of gold, as tribute to Necho.

Necho's purposes were soon to be thwarted, however, by the young Chaldean prince, Nebuchadnezzar, who was heir to the throne of Babylon. When Necho attempted to defend his Syrian dominions at Carchemish (605 B.C.), Nebuchadnezzar's armies gained a decisive victory. The Egyptians would certainly have been pursued into their own country had not Nebuchadnezzar been called home by the death of his father. Necho agreed to relinquish his claims to Syria and Palestine. The Biblical historian simply states the result: "And the king of Egypt did not come again out of his land, for the king of Babylon had taken all that belonged to the king of Egypt from the Brook of Egypt to the river Euphrates" (II Kings 24:7). Even when Jehoiakim, who had been placed on the throne of Judah by Necho, rebelled against Nebuchadnezzar (597 B.C.), Necho did not come to his aid. Although Jerusalem was despoiled and part of its popula-

Remnants of Roman times are preserved in the Ashkelon Antiquities Park. This panel shows Nike — the winged goddess of victory — standing on the world supported by the shoulders of Atlas.

tion taken into exile, Necho reconciled himself to the situation.

Necho turned his attention instead to the development of commerce and the defenses of Egypt. About 600 B.C., he began the construction of a canal which was to connect the eastern arm of the Nile River with the Red Sea. Herodotus states that one hundred and twenty thousand men perished during the construction of the canal, and that Necho stopped the work when warned by an oracle that his canal would benefit the barbarian (i.e., foreigner) rather than the Egyptian.[1] Diodorus, on the other hand, tells us that Necho abandoned his project because he was told by his engineers that the Red Sea was higher than the Delta, and the canal would flood the entire Delta region.[2]

The canal left the Pelusiac branch of the Nile a short distance north of Bubastis. It circled eastward to Lake Timsah, and then turned southward parallel to the present Suez Canal along the west side of the Great Bitter Lake to the head of the Gulf of Suez. Its completion would have been of both commercial and military significance to Necho.

Necho dreamed of making Egypt a great sea power. He built an impressive fleet which sailed both the Red Sea and the Mediterranean. Necho also is remembered in the annals of exploration as the one who dispatched a crew of Phoenician mariners with instructions to sail around the African continent, known to the ancients as Libya. It took the Phoenicians three years to complete their mission.

In 593 B.C., Psammetichus II succeeded his father Necho as Pharaoh and continued his policies. Accompanied by a retinue of priests, he visited Phoenicia in 591 B.C. The trip was purely religious in motivation, however, for we are told that he brought along a votive wreath which was probably placed at the ancient Egyptian shrine at Byblos. No attempt was made to challenge the Babylonians in Syria. Instead he headed southward into lower Nubia and sent a body of troops as far as Abu Simbel, where they left a Greek inscription on one of the colossi of Ramesses II in front of his great temple there. The results of this campaign were not lasting, for we know that lower Nubia was not incorporated into Egypt.

Psammetichus was dependent on his Greek mercenaries, and seems to have been a great admirer of Greek culture. We are even told that the Eleans sent a deputation to ask his judgment

These columns and other ruins of Byblos are reminders of the past greatness of this Phoenician city.

1. Herodotus, *Histories,* II, 158.
2. Diodorus, I, 33.9

as to the fairness of their administration of the Olympic Games. The native Egyptians tended to resent the preference which their ruler gave to the foreigners.

When Pharaoh Apries (Biblical Hophra) came to the throne in 588 B.C. he determined to challenge Nebuchadnezzar's control over Syria and Palestine. H. R. Hall calls him, "a headstrong and unwise person with neither the political wisdom of the elder Psammetichus nor the ordered energy of a Necho." He was, Hall continues, "The typical young king of the ancient world, full of energy, without the sagacity or cunning of his seniors and liable to be supported in foolish courses by an ignorant public opinion . . . largely of priestly inspiration."[3]

He found willing allies in Moab and Ammon. Zedekiah of Judah, although vacillating at times, decided to back the pro-Egyptian party in his court, and a major revolt against Nebuchadnezzar appeared imminent.

Apries, however, made the mistake of attacking his potential allies, the Phoenician cities of Tyre and Sidon. After a victorious naval engagement against the Tyrians, they yielded, and soon the Phoenician cities were all subject to him. Nebuchadnezzar, however, encamped at Riblah, on the Orontes River, taking no immediate steps against the Egyptians. Instead he turned his attention southward and besieged Jerusalem. The pro-Egyptian party there had expected Egyptian aid in such an emergency, but Egypt proved to be a broken reed.

In the summer of 588 B.C. an Egyptian army did march to challenge Nebuchadnezzar, and the siege of Jerusalem was temporarily lifted. Egypt, however, was no match for the Babylonian forces. The Egyptians under Apries were driven back, and the siege of Jerusalem continued until the city fell to Nebuchadnezzar (587 B.C.).

Things were not all easy for Nebuchadnezzar, however. Tyre was able to hold out against him until 574 B.C.

It was during the reign of Apries that the Jews were taken into Exile. Many Jews were able to escape southward into Egypt where they were permitted to settle in colonies of their own. Some journeyed as far as to Elephantine Island, at the first cataract of the Nile. The reign of Apries was a prosperous one, although he did have troubles keeping his troops content. On one occasion the Libyans, Greeks, and Syrians of his army

---

3. *The Cambridge Ancient History*, III, p. 502.

attempted to migrate to Nubia. They were dissuaded, however, by the governor of Aswan, and punished by Apries.

More serious difficulties developed when Greek settlers at Cyrene began to encroach on the territory of Libya, which lay between Cyrene and Egypt. The Libyans appealed to Apries who sent a force of Egyptians to aid them. He could not use Greek mercenaries against the Greeks of Cyrene. The Egyptian forces were almost annihilated by the Greeks of Cyrene and they became bitter against Apries. The Pharaoh tried to conciliate them by sending a member of the royal household, Ahmose, or Amasis as Herodotus designates him, to bring the rebels into submission. Amasis betrayed Apries by so manipulating the situation that the disaffected Egyptian soldiers proclaimed him king. A period of indecision and warfare ensued. After a brief co-regency, during which Apries took a subordinate position to Amasis, warfare broke out. The Greek mercenaries supported Apries but Amasis was supported by the native Egyptians. Apries died as a fugitive while resting in one of his few remaining boats. Amasis gave him an honorable burial, and secured for himself the throne of Egypt which he occupied until 525 B.C.

The forty-four year reign of Amasis saw no violent changes in Egyptian life, but the drift toward a Greek-oriented society continued. Nebuchadnezzar's armies approached the Egyptian Delta in 568 B.C., but details of his invasion are not known. A Babylonian text reads: ". . . in the 37th year, Nebuchadnezzar king of Babylon marched against Egypt (Mi-sir) to deliver a battle. (Ama)-sis of Egypt called up his army from the town of *Putu-Yaman.. . .*"[4] *Putu-Yaman* or *Putu-Javan* was probably the name of the Ionian city from which Amasis was able to summon mercenaries. Nebuchadnezzar did not conquer Egypt, but the campaign did force Amasis to renounce any plans for the conquest of Syria and Palestine.

Under Amasis, the Greek merchants were permitted to trade in only one city in the western Delta. Naucratis, on the Canopic Branch of the Nile, became both the home and market place of the Greeks and the most important commercial city of Egypt. Foreigners were forced to leave Daphne (Tahpanhes) and Migdol in 564 B.C. The Jews probably joined other of their people in upper Egypt, although some may have returned to Palestine.

---

4. A. Leo Oppenheim, "Babylonian and Assyrian Historical Texts," in James Pritchard, *Ancient Near Eastern Texts,* p. 308.

Amasis kept on very friendly terms with the Greeks, even marrying a Cyrenaean Greek, Ladice. Greek mercenaries served as a palace guard at Memphis where they could be depended upon to guarantee Amasis' personal safety in the event of revolt. He contributed toward the erection of Greek temples and had warm friendships with such Greek rulers as Polycrates of Samos.

As a wise statesman, Amasis did not neglect his own people. Additions were made to the temples at Sais and Memphis. Herodotus speaks of him in glowing terms:

> It is said that in the reign of Amasis, Egypt attained to its greatest prosperity, in respect of what the river did for the land and the land for its people: and that the whole sum of inhabited cities in the country was twenty thousand. It was Amasis also who made the law that every Egyptian should yearly declare his means of livelihood to the ruler of his province, and, failing so to do or to prove that he had a just way of life, be punished with death. Solon the Athenian got this law from Egypt and established it among his people; may they ever keep it! for it is a perfect law.[5]

Amasis did not, of course, rule an empire which could be compared with that of the ancient Pharaohs. His was an Egypt which was soon to lose its distinctive culture and its very independence. Although Nebuchadnezzar did not conquer Egypt, and Babylon itself fell to the Persians in 539 B.C., Egypt would not stand long before the powerful forces which were developing in the East. Cambyses, the son and heir of Cyrus the Persian, was to conquer Egypt in 525 B.C. — just months after the death of Amasis.

---

5. Herodotus, *Histories,* II, 177.

61

Jeremiah of Jerusalem

Much of our knowledge of the events preceding the capture of Jerusalem comes from the Book of Jeremiah. The prophecies of Jeremiah were largely unheeded by the generation which heard them but, faithfully preserved by the scribe Baruch, they became a source of hope and challenge to subsequent generations.

Jeremiah was a native of Anathoth, a city in Benjamin near the northern boundary of Jerusalem. Anathoth had been allotted to the priests of the line of Ithamar, the youngest son of Aaron. Eli, a descendant of Ithamar, had served as priest at Shiloh. A later descendant, Abiathar, supported David's son Adonijah in his bid for the throne. When Solomon succeeded in thwarting the plans of Adonijah, Abiathar was expelled and Zadok, a priest of the family of Eleazar, Aaron's oldest son, replaced him. In expelling Abiathar, Solomon said, "Go to Anathoth, to your estate" (I Kings 2:26).

The opening words of the Book of Jeremiah identify the prophet as "of the priests who were in Anathoth." There is no hint, however, that he ever functioned as a priest. While quite young (Jer. 1:6) he was called to the prophetic office. Anathoth was but three miles northeast of Jerusalem and it is probable that Jeremiah continued to live in his home town during the early years of his ministry. Later his townsmen expressed active hostility (Jer. 11:21; 12:6) and the prophet moved into Jerusalem.

Jeremiah's call to a prophetic ministry came during the reign of Josiah. This was the last great period of spiritual revival in the history of Judah. Josiah called his people back to God and obedience to the Law which had long been forgotten. It is probable that Jeremiah himself joined in this ministry, perhaps carrying the reform message to Anathoth. With the death of Josiah on the battlefield of Megiddo, the old idolatry became more firmly entrenched than ever and Jeremiah was to spend years of loneliness as he attempted to hold forth God's message to a restless and rebellious people.

The terms of Jeremiah's call were a foreshadowing of the nature of his ministry:

> Behold, I have put my words in your mouth.
> See, I have set you this day over nations and over kingdoms,
> to pluck up and to break down,
> to destroy and to overthrow,
> to build and to plant (Jer. 1:9-10).

There was a strong negative side to Jeremiah's work. He was to stand against prophets, priests, kings, and people in championing the cause of the Lord. He would be considered a traitor for predicting defeat at the hand of Judah's enemy, Babylon. Yet there was a building and planting which his ministry accomplished. After the death of Jeremiah, his word found a response in the hearts of a people chastened through exile, yet conscious that their God had not utterly forsaken them.

Jehoiakim came to the throne of Judah as a vassal of Egypt. Jeremiah insisted that the only hope for Judah was in the recognition of the Babylonian power. Thus the policy of the prophet was diametrically opposed to that of the king. Most of the religious leaders of Judah were sympathetic with Jehoiakim. They assured their fellow-countrymen that Nebuchadnezzar would do them no harm. Had not God delivered Jerusalem from Sennacherib during the days of Hezekiah and Isaiah? The Holy City was inviolable. God would never allow the heathen to desecrate Jerusalem!

A closeup view of Anathoth, the hometown of Jeremiah.

These sentiments stirred Jeremiah to the point where he went to the gate of the Sanctuary and delivered his famous Temple Address. He called upon the people to turn from their evil ways and warned them against false prophets who cried out, "This is the Temple of the Lord, the Temple of the Lord, the Temple of the Lord" (Jer. 7:4). Their attitude reduced the God of Israel to the level of the gods of the heathen who were unconcerned with morality. God could save His people from their enemies, but He also could deliver His people into the hands of their enemies for chastisement. Jeremiah drew upon history: "Go now to my place which was in Shiloh, where I made my name dwell at first, and see what I did to it for the wickedness of my people Israel" (Jer. 7:12). Shiloh had been a sanctuary in the days of Eli and Samuel, but it was destroyed in the wars with the "uncircumcised Philistine." The Northern

Kingdom, the "offspring of Ephraim" (Jer. 7:15) had gone into captivity a little more than a century before Jeremiah's ministry. They had resisted the ministries of Hosea, Amos, and others who called them back to God. Jeremiah insisted that there was no room for complacency on the part of idolatrous Judah. False prophets cry "Peace, peace," but there is no peace (Jer. 8:11). Judgment is at hand!

Jeremiah's Temple Address produced an immediate and hostile response from his audience. The priests and prophets said to the princes and people, "This man deserves the sentence of death, because he has prophesied against this city, as you have heard with your own ears" (Jer. 26:11). Prophets were expected to predict good things and build up the morale of the people. Jeremiah dared to do the opposite.

The prophet was spared, however, when certain of the elders reminded the people of the words of Micah who had prophesied in the days of Hezekiah saying: "Zion shall be plowed as a field; Jerusalem shall become a heap of ruins, and the mountain of the house a wooded height" (Jer. 26:18; cf. Micah 3:12). The words proved timely. Jeremiah was not put to death. Another prophet, Uriah the son of Shemaiah, had prophesied against Jerusalem and was killed for his insolence. He had found temporary asylum in Egypt, but Jehoiakim sent for him and killed him (Jer. 26:20-24).

During the fourth year of Jehoiakim, Jeremiah was directed by God to gather together the prophecies which he had delivered during a ministry which had lasted about twenty-three years. Jeremiah dictated the messages to his scribe Baruch, who recorded them on a scroll. Subsequently, when the people were gathered at the Temple to observe a fast decreed by Jehoiakim, Baruch took his book and read it "at the entry of the New Gate of the Lord's house" (Jer. 36:10). Some of the princes wanted the king to hear these prophecies. They questioned Baruch concerning them, and then had the scroll read before Jehoiakim. The king showed his contempt for Jeremiah and his message by burning the scroll in the fire of his brazier (Jer. 36:1-22).

Jeremiah and Baruch would certainly have been killed had they not been protected by friendly princes who urged them to find a secret hiding-place (Jer. 36:19). When word reached them of the destruction of the first scroll, Jeremiah dictated another to which "Many similar words" were added (Jer. 36:32). This may be considered the earliest edition of what became our Book of Jeremiah.

Within three months after Jehoiachin succeeded his father Jehoiakim to the throne of Judah, Nebuchadnezzar was besieging the city of Jerusalem (cf. Jer. 22:18-30). The Egyptians were powerless to interfere, and the young king was taken into exile by the Babylonians. Jerusalem was not destroyed, but tribute was imposed upon its rulers and ten thousand of its inhabitants went into exile (II Kings 24:14).

When Zedekiah was confirmed on the throne of Judah by Nebuchadnezzar, the prophecies of Jeremiah and the policy which he endorsed should have gained a respectful hearing. Indeed we do read of Zedekiah seeking counsel of the prophet (Jer. 37:16-21). The king was a confused man, however. The pro-Egyptian party was not dead, and its prophets declared that Jehoiachin and the exiles would be back from Babylon within two years (Jer. 28:1-5).

Jeremiah sought to show the error of the false prophets, and insisted that the exiles would remain in Babylon for seventy years (Jer. 29:10). He went so far as to address a letter to them, urging them to build homes, marry, and raise families in their new surroundings (Jer. 29:1-7). He assured them that God would ultimately bring them back, but urged them to seek the welfare of the city in which they would dwell until that distant day should arrive (Jer. 29:7).

During the eleven year reign of Zedekiah, Jeremiah continued to announce the impending judgment which would fall upon Israel. His gloomy predictions were relieved only by the message that God would not cast off His people forever. There were no violent persecutions of the prophet during the early years of Zedekiah's reign. As things reached a climax, however, Jeremiah could not escape the antagonism of his people. Determined to rebel against Nebuchadnezzar, the rulers of Jerusalem could not permit Jeremiah to prophesy Babylonian victory. The prophet was arrested while journeying to Benjamin, charged with being a deserter, and cast into the common prison. There he remained "many days" (Jer. 37:16). Zedekiah, who both respected and feared Jeremiah, later ordered the prophet removed to the court of the guard (Jer. 37:21), evidently a much more pleasant place of confinement. The king actually sought the advice of Jeremiah from time to time, but the message he received was unvarying: "You shall be delivered into the hand of the king of Babylon" (Jer. 37:17).

The prophet's dark forebodings and the approach of Nebuchadnezzar's armies, threw all Jerusalem into turmoil. The

The upper Tyropoeon Valley in Jerusalem.

princes could delay no longer. They approached Zedekiah with the demand: "Let this man be put to death, for he is weakening the hands of the soldiers who are left in this city, and the hands of all the people, by speaking such words to them. For this man is not seeking the welfare of this people, but their harm" (Jer. 38:4).

The nobles, armed with the royal mandate, entered the court of the prison and took Jeremiah, casting him into a cistern which was so deep that he had to be let down by ropes (Jer. 37:6). There he sank into the mire and would have died but for an Ethiopian eunuch, Ebed-melech, who pleaded with the king on Jeremiah's behalf, and secured an order for his release. Ebed-melech and three companions, armed with ropes and old rags, went to the cistern and drew out the prophet. Jeremiah remained in the court of the guard until released by Nebuchadnezzar after the fall of Jerusalem.

The imprisonment of Jeremiah must have continued for more than a year. During this time the prophet continued to declare the word of God and depict events in the immediate and the more remote future. We hear his triumphant assurance:

> In this place of which you say, "It is a waste without man or beast," in the cities of Judah and the streets of Jerusalem that are desolate, without man or inhabitant or beast, there shall be heard again the voice of mirth and the voice of gladness, the voice of the bridegroom and the voice of the bride.... For I will restore the fortunes of the land as at the first, says the Lord (Jer. 33:10-11).

Jeremiah demonstrated his faith in deed as well as word. Hanameel, his uncle's son, offered to sell the prophet a plot of ground in Anathoth. Jeremiah knew that Jerusalem would soon be in Babylonian control, and Nebuchadnezzar's armies may already have reached Anathoth. Yet Jeremiah had implicit faith in God's promises, and knew that the land would one day return to Israelite control. After proper legal formalities were concluded, Jeremiah weighed out the seventeen shekels of silver which he agreed to pay for the property and took possession. He then turned the deed over to Baruch with the injunction, "Take these deeds, both this sealed deed of purchase and this open deed, and put them in an earthen vessel that they may last for a long time" (Jer. 32:14).

The fall of Jerusalem vindicated the ministry of Jeremiah, but it certainly brought him no joy. The beautiful palace was in ruins. The Temple, built by Solomon in an era during which the glories of Jerusalem were known throughout the East, was but rubble. The wavering Zedekiah, who from time to time had sought counsel of Jeremiah, was blinded, chained, and taken as a trophy of war to Babylon. The king's sons and the nobles had been slain.

Jeremiah was not deported, however. He, with the remnants of the Judaeans, remained in Palestine where a loyal Israelite, Gedaliah, was appointed by Nebuchadnezzar to serve as governor at Mizpah. A pretender, Ishmael, with Ammonite support, murdered Gedaliah and attempted to set up an independent government. In spite of the warnings of Jeremiah, the remnant of the Judaeans determined to flee to Egypt to escape the wrath of Nebuchadnezzar which would surely be felt after the murder of the governor he had appointed. Jeremiah and his scribe, Baruch, were forced to journey to Egypt along with the men of Judah who hoped to find a place of refuge there. In the Egyptian city of Tahpanhes, Jeremiah uttered his last recorded prophecies (Jer. 43:7).

Jeremiah has been called "the weeping prophet." Whether or not he wrote the Book of Lamentations, the description is a fitting one. Few men have been as lonely as he. From the purely human viewpoint, Jeremiah's life was a failure. His people continued in the sins which he denounced. They could not see the will of God in submission to the power of Babylon as he demanded, and the pro-Egyptian party gained the ear of both Jehoiakim and Zedekiah. A fictionalized ending of the story of Jeremiah tells us that he was released from Egypt and spent his last years in Babylon. The wish seems to be father to the thought, however. Ironically the Scripture leaves him in Egypt — the source of promised help which never came to Judah, and the nation whose promises were never taken seriously by Jeremiah.

The life span of Jeremiah encompassed the years from the last great revival under Josiah, to the defeat of his country and the desecration of its Temple. Jeremiah did more than weep, however. He saw through his tears the promise of a bright future when God would restore Zion and write a new covenant upon the hearts of His people. Plagued by weak and idolatrous kings, Jeremiah looked to the day when God would "raise up for David a righteous Branch" who would "execute justice and righteousness in the land" (Jer. 23:5).

62

The Lachish Letters

The prophecies of Jeremiah give us a vivid picture of life in Jerusalem during the difficult years before the city fell to Nebuchadnezzar. Thanks to the work of J. L. Starkey, the British archaeologist who excavated Tell ed-Duweir, Biblical Lachish, we now have a description of life outside Jerusalem during the time of the Babylonian invasion.

In 1935 Starkey, while directing the Wellcome-Marston Research Expedition, came upon a small guardroom adjoining the outer gate of Lachish. There, buried in a layer of charcoal and ashes, he found sixteen broken pieces of pottery which contained writing in the Old Hebrew, or Phoenician script. Two other pieces were found nearby and three additional pieces were discovered in 1938, one on the roadway and two in a room near the palace.

These inscribed potsherds, technically known as ostraca, were for the most part letters written by the scribes of Hoshaiah, evidently an Israelite soldier stationed at a military outpost. The messages were addressed to Yaosh, the commanding officer at Lachish. They are written in a terse, telegraphic style, and the modern reader has difficulty reconstructing the exact circumstances during which they were written. Mr. Starkey noted that the ostraca which were arbitrarily numbered II, VI, VII, VIII, and XVIII are all pieces of the same pot, indicating that they were written at about the same time. Professor Harry Torcyner, who edited the texts for publication, noted similarities in handwriting between these letters and other potsherds from a different source. The numbers assigned to the ostraca provide a convenient means of reference, but they have no significance. Some of the ostraca are merely lists of names which were meaningful to the original writer and recipient, but serve only to illustrate Israelite names of the time for the modern student. Although they are not to be identified with the Biblical characters who bore the same names, it is of interest that the first Lachish letter mentions a Yirmiyahu, or Jeremiah, and a Mattanyahu (Mattaniah), the name of Zedekiah before Nebuchadnezzar appointed him king.

The letters make use of conventional expressions. A flowery salutation may open the letter, and the writer often speaks of himself in abject humility as a dog (cf. II Sam. 9:8). Similar expressions are used in the Amarna Letters (14th century B.C.) in which a vassal deprecates himself in addressing his overlord.

The second of the Lachish Ostraca illustrates these conventions. It reads:

> To my lord, Yaosh: May Yahweh cause my lord to hear tidings of peace this very day, this very day! Who is thy servant (but) a dog that my lord hath remembered his servant? May Yahweh afflict those who report an ⟨evil⟩ rumor about which thou art not informed!

Evidently things were not going well for the Judaeans. The writer of the letter feared that an evil report had reached Yaosh. He expresses a desire that the commander will hear tidings of peace, but we know that this did not take place.

The longest of the ostraca is the third. It is a letter from Hoshaiah to Yaosh:

> Thy servant Hoshaiah hath sent to inform my lord Yaosh: May Yahweh cause my lord to hear tidings of peace! And now thou hast sent a letter, but my lord did not enlighten thy servant concerning the letter which thou didst send to thy servant yesterday evening, though the heart of thy servant hath been sick since thou didst write to thy servant. And as for what my lord said, "Dost thou not understand? — call a scribe!" as Yahweh liveth no one hath ever undertaken to call a scribe for me; and as for any scribe who might have come to me, truly I did not call him nor would I give anything at all for him!
>
> And it hath been reported to thy servant, saying, "The commander of the host, Coniah son of Elnathan, hath come down in order to go into Egypt; and unto Hodaviah son of Ahijah and his men that he sent to obtain . . . from him."
>
> And as for the letter of Tobiah, servant of the king, which came to Shallum son of Jaddua through the prophet, saying "Beware!" thy servant hath sent it to my lord.

Evidently Hoshaiah had been scolded for disregarding orders contained in an earlier letter. Some think that he disclosed the contents of a secret communication. He insisted that he had not wilfully disobeyed. The letter speaks of a trip to Egypt made by a man named Coniah, son of Elnathan. The Judaean kings looked to Egypt for help during the time of their war with Babylon. Egypt, fearful of the growing power of Babylon, and anxious to build an empire for herself, gladly supported any movement in Judah that sought to resist Nebuchadnezzar. Pharaoh Psammeti-

Lachish Letter IV. The Lachish Letters indicate the military situation in Judea in the months prior to the fall of Jerusalem to the Babylonians. In this letter, a field commander reported that the signals from Azekah were no longer visible. Evidently, Azekah had capitulated. Soon afterward, both Lachish and Jerusalem were occupied by Nebuchadnezzar's armies.

chus II sent a force to relieve besieged Jerusalem (Jer. 37:15), but the Babylonians soon dispersed them and resumed their siege.

Mention is also made of a prophet who had delivered a letter of warning to a man named Shallum. We cannot identify this prophet, but we know that there were many men who bore the title "prophet" during the years before the fall of Jerusalem. Letter 16 also speaks of a prophet and his name is known to have ended with the familiar *-iah* suffix. Some have suggested that he was the Uriah of Jeremiah 26:20-23, or even Jeremiah himself, but we have no real basis for such identifications. False prophets plagued Jeremiah and soothed the people with words of peace when Jeremiah assured them, "There is no peace."

Ostracon Four appears to have been written shortly before the fall of Lachish itself. It reads:

> May Yahweh cause my lord to hear this very day tidings of good! And now according to everything that my lord hath written, so hath thy servant done; I have written on the door according to all that my lord hath written to me. And with respect to what my lord hath written about the matter of *Beth-haraphid,* there is no one there.
>
> And as for Semachiah, Shemaiah hath taken him and brought him to the city. And as for thy servant, I am not sending *anyone* thither. (today(?), but I will send) tomorrow morning.
>
> And let (my lord) know that we are watching for the signals of Lachish, according to all the indications which my lord hath given, for we cannot see Azekah.

Writing "on the door" was tantamount to posting on the bulletin board for all to see. It will be remembered that Luther's famous theses were posted on the door of the Castle church at Wittenburg over two thousand years after the Lachish letters!

The last paragraph of the letter contained the sad news that the fire signals from Azekah could no longer be seen. This could mean but one thing. Azekah had fallen to the enemy. By 588 B.C. only three cities remained to the Judaeans — Azekah, Lachish, and Jerusalem (Jer. 34:6-7). Our letter must have been written that year. Azekah had fallen, but Lachish was still in Judaean hands. This situation did not last for long, however, for soon Lachish fell, then Jerusalem, and Judah as an independent political state lost its identity.

The Lachish correspondence tells us something of the military organization of the day. A system of signals had been devised and reports could normally be made from a distance. We read of these signals in Jeremiah 6:1 where the prophet cries out: "Blow the trumpet in Tekoa, and raise a signal on Beth-haccherem; for evil looms out of the north, and great destruction." Written reports were regularly sent to headquarters, and orders from head-

Reconstruction of Lachish. Excavations indicate that Lachish was one of the largest occupied sites in ancient Palestine.

The mound of Lachish, located thirty miles southwest of Jerusalem. Lachish was strategically situated on the main road between central Palestine and Egypt.

quarters were sent to the field commanders at military outposts.

Morale was a problem during Judah's last days. Jeremiah was threatened with death for discouraging the people with his prophecies of doom (Jer. 38:4). The sixth ostracon reflects a lowering of morale:

> To my lord Yaosh: may Yahweh cause my lord to see this season in good health! Who is thy servant (but) a dog that my lord hath sent the letter of the king and the letters of the princes saying, "Pray, read them!" And behold the words of the princes are not good, (but) to weaken our hands (and to sla)cken the hands of the m *(en who are informed about them* (...And now) my lord, wilt thou not write to them saying, "Why do ye thus *(even)* in Jerusalem? Behold unto the king and unto *(his house)* are ye doing this thing!" (And,) as Yahweh thy God liveth, truly since thy servant read the letters there hath been no *(peace)* for (thy ser)vant...

Only one of the texts, Ostracon Number 20, is dated. It begins "In the ninth year." That was the year during which Nebuchadnezzar invaded Judah to put down Zedekiah's revolt (II Kings 25:1). Two years later (July, 587 B.C.) during the eleventh year of Zedekiah, the walls of Jerusalem were breached and the city fell. The inscribed potsherds from Lachish give us a picture of life during those difficult years. Jeremiah was prophesying within Jerusalem. His prophecies, and the cryptic notes of Judaean field commanders found by Starkey at Lachish, give us a first hand account of life both within and outside Jerusalem during the months before the last stronghold of Judah fell to Babylon.

Dr. W. F. Albright, writing about the Lachish ostraca, observes,

> In these letters we find ourselves in exactly the age of Jeremiah, with social and political connotations agreeing perfectly with the picture drawn in the book that bears his name.[1]

---

1. "The Oldest Hebrew Letters," *Bulletin of the American Schools of Oriental Research*, Number 7 (April 1938), p. 17.

63

Judah During
the Exilic Period

With the destruction of Jerusalem, Judah ceased to exist as a sovereign state. Zedekiah died shortly after being taken to Babylon. Jehoiachin, although looked upon as the legitimate king, had no reasonable hope of returning to his land.

The Babylonians established a military government for Judah with headquarters at Mizpah, about eight miles north of Jerusalem. A Judaean, Gedaliah, was named governor. Gedaliah was the son of Shaphan who had protected Jeremiah from the wrath of Jehoiakim and his nobles (Jer. 26:24). He would have been considered pro-Babylonian and thus suitable for an appointment which must be sympathetic to Babylonian rule. After Jerusalem fell to Nebuchadnezzar, the Babylonian military officers asked Gedaliah to look after the safety of Jeremiah (Jer. 39:11-14).

Gedaliah formed a center around which the Judaeans who had not been taken into exile might gather. Those who had fled to Edom, Moab, and Ammon trickled back. Gedaliah counseled loyalty to Nebuchadnezzar: "Dwell in the land, and serve the king of Babylon, and it shall be well with you" (Jer. 40:9). Evidently a degree of prosperity ensued for "they gathered wine and summer fruits in great abundance" (Jer. 40:12).

In the ruins of Mizpah (Tell en-Nasbeh) a seal was found bearing the identifying inscription "To Jaazaniah, servant of the king." Jaazaniah was one of the officials associated with Gedaliah (II Kings 25:23; Jer. 40:8). A seal impression found among the ruins of Lachish bears the inscription, "To Gedaliah who is over the house."

George Ernest Wright suggests that Gedaliah had served as one of the last prime ministers of Judah. He notes that the seal found at Lachish must antedate the destruction of the city by Nebuchadnezzar's armies. The words "who is over the house" suggest the office of prime minister. Not only was Gedaliah's

father a high official in his own right (Jer. 26:24), but his grandfather, Shaphan, had served Josiah as Scribe, or Secretary of State
(II Kings 22:3, 8-12).[1]

The wise rule of Gedaliah at Mizpah came to a violent end.
Ishmael, a man whose royal blood encouraged him to seek the
throne for himself (Jer. 41:1; II Kings 25:25), had fled to Ammon
during the siege of Jerusalem. He found a ready ally in Baalis,
the king of Ammon. Learning that Gedaliah was governor of the
remnant of the Judaeans at Mizpah, Ishmael went there with a
band of ten men and treacherously killed Gedaliah. Gedaliah
had been warned about the plot, but he refused to believe the
evil report concerning Ishmael (Jer. 40:16).

In addition to Gedaliah, Ishmael killed eighty men who had
come to worship at the shrine at Mizpah (Jer. 41:4-7), and took
captive the others who had settled there, intending to bring them
to Ammon (Jer. 41:10). At Gibeon, Ishmael was challenged by
the forces of the loyal Judaean, Johanan the son of Kareah. Although Ishmael escaped and presumably reached Ammon, his
captives were freed and then, contrary to the counsel of Jeremiah, fled southward to Egypt.

The history of Judah between the destruction of Jerusalem
(587 B.C.) and the return of the first group of exiles following the decree of Cyrus (536 B.C.) is largely a blank. The
province of Judah, which Gedaliah had ruled, was abolished,
and its territory incorporated into the neighboring province
of Samaria. Some of the older Biblical scholars held that
there was no drastic break in the continuity of life in Judah
following Nebuchadnezzar's destruction of Jerusalem. It was assumed that natives returned to their homes and life continued
without serious interruption. According to these scholars, the
exile involved only a few nobles, and the accounts in Kings,
Ezekiel, and Ezra-Nehemiah are grossly exaggerated.

Archaeology, however, has shown a decisive break in Palestinian life during the years following 587 B.C. No town in Judah
was continually occupied throughout the exilic period. While
there was a complete break in the history of Judah, this was not
true of the area north or south of the Judaean border. Bethel
and the Samaritan cities were not destroyed and the towns of the
Negeb were left undisturbed. Discussing the excavation of towns
and fortresses in Judah, Albright says,

---

1. *Biblical Archaeology,* p. 178.

The site of Beth-shemesh.

The results are uniform and conclusive: many towns were destroyed at the beginning of the sixth century B.C. and never again occupied; others were destroyed at that time and partly occupied at some later date; still others were destroyed and reoccupied after a long period of abandonment, marked by a sharp change of stratum and by intervening indications of use for non-urban purposes. There is not a single known case where a town of Judah proper was continuously occupied through the exilic period. Just to point the contrast, Bethel, which lay just outside the northern boundary of Judah in pre-exilic times, was not destroyed at that time, but was continuously occupied down into the latter part of the sixth century.[2]

Among the towns of Judaea which were destroyed and never rebuilt were Beth-shemesh and Tell Beit Mirsim (Kirjath-sepher). Excavators found that there were some periods when sites were not in use as they studied layers which date earlier than the sixth century B.C. It was only during the period of the Babylonian conquest of Judah that large numbers of sites permanently ceased to be occupied.

Unlike the Assyrians, who repopulated the Northern Kingdom after its fall in 722 B.C. (II Kings 17:24), the Babylonians did not make it a policy to repopulate areas from which captives had been taken. Instead the land was gradually occupied by neighboring tribes — Edomites and Arabians pressing in from the south and Ammonites and other tribes from east of the Jordan crossing the river to occupy such territory as they could claim. Before the return of exiles from Babylonia, Judah was dominated by alien peoples with those descendants of the former Jewish population that had not been deported. The area occupied by the Jews who returned following the decree of Cyrus was not much more than Jerusalem and its suburbs.

The Jews who were left in Palestine during the period of the Exile had much in common with their Samaritan neighbors to the north. Both groups worshiped the same God, Yahweh, and both accepted the Mosaic Law as Holy Writ. The syncretism which marked the earliest Samaritans (II Kings 17:33) seems to have disappeared in later Samaritan thinking. Their distinctive faith was in the sanctity of Mount Gerizim as the Temple site (John 4:20). This, however, was not implemented until the Sanctuary was built on Mount Gerizim in post-exilic times.

Judging by the problems faced by reformers of a later day the Jews and Samaritans of Palestine must have gotten along quite well together. Intermarriage became quite common, for it was a serious problem in the days of Ezra and Nehemiah (cf. Ezra

---

2. *The Archaeology of Palestine*, pp. 141-142.

Samaritan camp for the Passover celebration on the top of Mount Gerizim.

10:18-44; Neh. 13:23-28). Sanballat, the governor of Samaria, gave his daughter in marriage to a grandson of the High Priest Eliashib, much to the dismay of Nehemiah (Neh. 13:28). It was the Jews who returned from exile who insisted on strict separation from the Samaritans and other non-Jewish peoples of Palestine.

For fifty years after the destruction of Jerusalem, Judah was left to its own devices. While exiles in Babylon dreamed of returning to their Palestinian homes, the inhabitants of Judah — Jews, and non-Jews — had adjusted to a new mode of life. It is understandable that Samaritans should resent the return of exiles from Babylon and that some Jews would desire to keep ties of friendship with them.

64

The Crises of Exile

Of the many crises which Israel had experienced, none was more fraught with danger than the Babylonian Exile. The persecutions in Egypt had welded the tribes into a unified people during the time of Moses. The Philistine threat brought about the demand for a king and national solidarity in the days of the later Judges. The disruption of the kingdom following the death of Solomon was followed by a period of political weakness and civil war, but the Davidic throne was preserved in Judah even during periods of apostasy.

The Exile, however, was an event to challenge the faith of the most orthodox Jew. The Lord of hosts who had delivered Jericho into Joshua's hand had gone down in defeat — or so it seemed. Ancient peoples thought of battles among the nations as reflecting a parallel warfare among the gods. The nation with the strongest god would be expected to win. When Jerusalem was destroyed it would have been natural to conclude that Marduk, the god of Babylon, had proved himself stronger than the God of Israel. The very vessels from the Lord's house in Jerusalem became trophies of victory in Marduk's shrine in Babylon.

Gods were usually associated with the territory of the people who worshiped them. Yahweh, the God of Israel, would be reckoned as the God of a land which had been stripped of its population. Years before the Exile, Ben-hadad of Damascus had shown that he thought of Israel's god in geographical terms when he concluded, "Their gods are gods of the hills, and so they were stronger than we; but let us fight against them in the plain, and surely we shall be stronger than they" (I Kings 20:23).

Naaman, the Aramaean captain, showed the same feeling toward Israel's God, although he wished to become a worshiper of Yahweh when he returned to his Aramaean home. Through the instrumentality of Elisha, Naaman had been cured of leprosy.

Faced with the problem that Rimmon was the god who was worshiped in his native Damascus, Naaman devised a rather unorthodox solution. He made a simple request: ". . . let there be given to your servant two mules' burden of earth; for henceforth your servant will not offer burnt offering or sacrifices to any god but Yahweh" (II Kings 5:5). He could bring to Damascus some of the land where Yahweh was worshiped!

One of the great burdens of the prophetic writers of the exilic period was the proneness of the people to entertain localized views of Israel's god. Yahweh was the God of all the earth! He was the creator, not of Israel alone, but of all mankind. Although banished from the land which He had given to the fathers and, later, to Joshua, Israel must see that her God was not a weakling, but One whose purposes were carried out even in the moment of the defeat of His people. The second verse of the Book of Daniel contains the startling assertion: "The Lord gave Jehoiakim, king of Judah, into his [Nebuchadnezzar's] hand, with some of the vessels of the house of God." Only as the faithful of Israel could discern the significance of such words could the nation survive the Exile.

Power and holiness were important attributes of Israel's God. In the crisis of the Babylonian threat, these attributes might seem to involve an impasse. If the armies of Nebuchadnezzar should actually destroy Jerusalem and its Temple, Israel's God would appear to be weak in not protecting His people. God's name, or reputation, seemed to be at stake. The Psalmist cried out, "For thy name's sake, O Lord, preserve my life!" (Psalm 143:11). God is concerned about His name. He desired that his Name be reverenced not alone in Israel but also among the nations.

Yet God revealed Himself both in His Word and in His works as a holy God. What could be gained in delivering Israel from the pagan Babylonian if pagan elements were permitted to continue in Israel? Jeremiah accused his countrymen of worshiping as many gods as Judah had cities (Jer. 11:13). Even Babylon was no more idolatrous than that. God had given solemn warning in His Law:

> You shall remember Yahweh your God, for it is he who gives you power to get wealth; that he may confirm his covenant which he swore to your fathers, as at this day. And if you forget Yahweh your god and go after other gods and serve them and worship them, I solemnly warn you this day that you shall surely perish. Like the nations that Yahweh makes to perish before you, so shall you perish, because you would not obey the voice of Yahweh your God (Deut. 8:18-20).

Six captive Elamite musicians, followed by clapping women and children. The relief is from Ashurbanipal's palace at Nineveh.

This solemn warning might well raise the question of Israel's divine election, and the covenants which God had made with David. Through Nathan, the prophet, God said, "I will appoint a place for my people Israel, and will plant them, that they may dwell in their own place, and be disturbed no more; and violent men shall afflict them no more . . . and I will give you rest from all your enemies . . ." (II Sam. 7:10-11). Addressing David, Nathan continued: "And your house and your kingdom shall be made sure forever before me; your throne shall be established for ever" (II Sam. 7:16).

With the disruption of the kingdom following Solomon's death and the checkered history of Israel and Judah, the significance of these words must often have been missed. Yet they were never forgotten. When the armies of the Assyrian king, Sennacherib, were at the gates of Jerusalem, Hezekiah was understandably worried. The prophet Isaiah assured him that the city was inviolable, quoting an oracle from the Lord: "I will defend this city to save it for my own sake and for the sake of my servant David" (II Kings 19:34). Sennacherib was forced to lift his siege. The power of Israel's God was demonstrated. Hezekiah, David's "son" (i.e., descendant) was left secure on the throne. God had not forgotten His covenant with David.

Hezekiah's godly reign was followed by apostasy, however. Except for the significant revival during the reign of Josiah, Judah's subsequent history was marked by idolatry and religious formality devoid of spiritual meaning. The populace took their spiritual blessings for granted and assumed that they were safe because of their favored position as a "chosen people."

In Jeremiah's day false prophets were confidently proclaiming, "This is the Temple of the Lord, the Temple of the Lord, the Temple of the Lord" (Jer. 7:4). They assumed that the Babylonian could not touch it because of its sacred associations, but Jeremiah warned, "This house shall be like Shiloh, and this city shall be desolate, without inhabitant" (Jer. 25:9).

While insisting that Jerusalem would be destroyed and its people taken into exile, Jeremiah was not unmindful of the covenant between God and His people. In holiness, God would deliver His people to their enemies, but in power He would bring them back to their own land. Through the affliction of captivity, Israel would be prepared for a brighter future: "There is hope for your future, says the Lord, and your children shall come back to their own country" (Jer. 31:17).

Ashurbanipal's soldiers lead away prisoners of war. Four women captives are seated in a cart with spoked wheels.

Hope, however, was conditioned on a change of heart. Idolatry is an offense to God, and His people can expect no blessing as long as they continue in rebellion against Him. Jeremiah assured the exiles, in an oracle of God, "You will seek me and find me; when you seek me with all your heart, I will be found by you, says the Lord, and I will restore your fortunes and gather you from all the nations and all the places where I have driven you, says the Lord, and I will bring you back to the place from which I sent you into exile" (Jer. 29:14).

In his letter to the exiles in Babylon, Jeremiah urged them to build houses, plant gardens, raise families, and seek to live normal lives in the land of their captivity. They were urged to seek the welfare of Babylon, for their own welfare would be contingent on the welfare of the land in which they lived. They were not to assume that the captivity would be permanent, however, for they were assured. "When seventy years are completed for Babylon, I will visit you, and I will fulfill to you my promise and bring you back to this place" (Jer. 29:10).

The words of Jeremiah were not appreciated by the generation in which he lived. It was easier to believe the prophets who cried out "Peace, Peace," and assured the people that all was well. These false prophets said that the people who had gone into captivity with Jehoiachin would be back within two years (cf. Jer. 28:1-4). Jeremiah was considered a defeatist if not an actual enemy of the people because he dared to assert that Israel's armies would go down in defeat before Nebuchadnezzar.

Yet Jeremiah prepared Israel for the crisis of the Exile. Events proved that his words were true. Trusting the words of false prophets, Israel went down in defeat. Jerusalem was destroyed and her people deported. Could God watch over his people in a strange land and bring them back? Those who had a lesser concept of Israel's God were destined to be absorbed among the gentiles and never heard from again. The remnant which believed in the power and the purposes of God, even in Babylon, formed the nucleus which one day was to return and rebuild the desolate cities of Judah.

65

Life Among the Exiles

The Jews in Exile were permitted to form colonies in which their communal life could continue. The pious Jew wept when he remembered Zion. He felt that he could not sing the Lord's song in a strange land. In time, however, most of the Jews made adjustment to their Babylonian environment. They took to heart the counsel of Jeremiah and prepared for an exile of seventy years. The prophet had urged them to marry, build houses, plant vineyards, and in other ways adapt themselves to Babylonian life. Few who had left Jerusalem could expect to return. Most would spend their remaining days in the land of their exile, and it was incumbent on them to find a satisfactory life there.

We do not know anything about Tel-abib, the settlement in which Ezekiel ministered, except for the fact that it was on the river Chebar, an important canal located southeast of the city of Babylon. As a smaller community, Tel-abib would not possess the splendors of Babylon but life there would have its compensations. Country houses away from the larger cities were often set in gardens which were irrigated by the canals which controlled the flood waters of the Tigris and Euphrates rivers. These canals greatly increased the area of arable land in Babylonia.

Monument of Merodach-baladin.

Gardens were rectangular in shape, situated alongside irrigation ditches. A detailed description of such a garden belonging to Merodach-baladan has been preserved. It included date palms and trees bearing apricots, plums, peaches, figs, and pomegranates. The sesame plant was cultivated for oil. Gourds and melons are also mentioned. Since this was a royal garden we must not take it as typical, but it does indicate the possibilities of life during exilic times. Among the other products of Merodach-baladan's garden we read of garlic, onion, leeks, mint, saffron, coriander, rue, thyme, pistacio, lettuce, fennel, lentils, beets, and kohl-rabi. The royal table did not lack variety!

Such houses with gardens were usually located at the outskirts of the towns. Within the towns, houses tended to be huddled together toward the center. Houses were successively rebuilt on the roughly leveled debris of earlier ones. The household rubbish would be thrown into the streets to be eaten by dogs and scavenger animals. What was not devoured would be left to burn dry by the sun and be trodden under foot.

The early houses of Babylon had been made of intertwined branches which were covered with thatch and cemented with mud which, when hardened, held the framework together. In very early times these buildings were round and had a central post like a tent. Later such structures were used as stables or sheepfolds.

Babylonian homes of the exilic period were built with bricks of clay mixed with finely chopped straw. The bricks were formed in molds and dried in the sun. Fired bricks were only used for special buildings because of the high expense of fuel. Sun-dried bricks were used when they were three-quarters dry. These were bonded together with mortar made of diluted clay. Houses were built around a central courtyard which provided light for the rooms which led off from it. One room was provided with a narrow door which led to the street.

Floors were normally made of beaten earth. The well-to-do might use flagstone or baked brick, sloped slightly to the center so the rain water and waste could be drained away. Drainage was provided by terra-cotta conduits which carried the water into underground cesspools. We even find toilets made of flagstones with a hole in the center.

Along the courtyard wall we frequently find the kitchen range. A hole was cut in the wall to allow the smoke to leave the room, or it found its way out through the door. Water was kept in earthen jars half sunk in the courtyard. Jars containing grain would hang from the walls out of reach of the rats and mice. An ingenious method of air vents was devised to keep out the rodents. Channels were cut through the walls, but they were then blocked with terra-cotta tiles pierced with holes which let the air in but kept out the rats and mice.

In a middle class home we would find mats, rugs, or mattresses used as beds. The more wealthy people had high beds with one end built up to form a bolster. The poorer folk sat on stools of palm wood and ate from raised trays which served as tables. The wealthy enjoyed the luxury of chairs, with deeply curved reed backs. They ate from high tables. On such tables there were numerous bowls and dippers made of terra-cotta. Early lamps were in the form of a shallow saucer with a pointed spout for the wick. By exilic times, lamps in the shape of a pointed shoe were in use, with wicks placed in a hole at the point. Unrefined crude oil was used in these lamps.

The roof of a Babylonian house was made of planks of palm wood arranged so as to span its rooms. The wood was then covered with reeds and palm leaves, on top of which a layer of earth was leveled and packed tight by a stone roller. From time to time, particularly after storms, the roof needed repair. The roller was again used and the roof was firm until the next storm.

An outside stairway usually led from the courtyard to the roof which served as a comfortable family room where the cool evening breezes could be enjoyed. In the summer the roof provided a comfortable place for sleeping. Houses of the poorer folk were undecorated except for a whitewash which concealed the drab, clay wall. Those who could afford to do so frequently painted their rooms halfway from the floor to the ceiling. This would often be in a black color derived from diluted bitumen. Above this area they would paint a decorative band in some other color. Door frames were often red, a color thought to keep away demons and guard against the evil influences which might attack a house.

Along the rivers and canals of ancient Babylonia the Israelites would have seen numerous boats conveying both people and merchandise. Small boats were frequently propelled by poles in the calm water. Sails were sometimes made of matting, and an oar at the stern would serve as a rudder. These boats could be hired by those who had temporary need of them.

Some boats still seen on the Tigris and Euphrates rivers are similar in design to those used since Sumerian times. A basket-type boat known as the coracle is made of plaited rushes. Its flat bottom is covered with skins and caulked. One or two men propel the coracle with oars.

Cargo was frequently shipped on a *kelek,* the name given to a raft made of strong reeds or wood. The under surface of the *kelek* was given support by inflated goatskins which were attached to add buoyancy and enable the raft to carry a heavy load.

Individuals frequently crossed the rivers of Babylon on inflated goatskins which served as a kind of life preserver. The head and the hoofs of the animal were cut off and the skin inflated. This was then placed beneath the chest of the man who would then use it to cross a stream. Whole armies crossed rivers on these inflated goatskins. Waterways were also crossed on floats made of reeds. A quantity of reeds would be bound at each end and flattened in the center to form such a float. The rivers and canals had a good supply of fish which formed an important part of the diet of the people of Babylon. Fish were usually caught on the line, but nets were also used.

While in Babylon, the Jews adopted a calendar which, with refinements dating from the fourth century A.D., is still the basis for the reckoning of the Jewish year. The Babylonians had a year of twelve lunar months, each consisting of thirty days. They early learned that this differed considerably from the solar year of approximately 365¼ days. To make the lunar and solar years coincide it was necessary to add an intercalary month (Second Adar) every sixth year. The twelve months, with Babylonian and Jewish names are:

The two parts of the city of Babylon were linked by a bridge set on boat-shaped piers. From a painting by Maurice Bardin.

Hebrew Name	Babylonian Name	Corresponding Months
Nisan	Nisannu	March-April
Iyyar	Ayaru	April-May
Sivan	Simanu	May-June
Tammuz	Du'uzu	June-July
Av	Abu	July-August
Elul	Ululu	August-September
Tishri	Tashretu	September-October
Marsheshvan	Arakshamna	October-November
Kislev	Kislimu	November-December
Tevet	Tabetu	December-January
Shevat	Shabatu	January-February
Adar	Addaru	February-March

The Babylonians reckoned their days from sunset to sunset, as did the Hebrews (cf. Gen. 1:5). The names of Hebrew months based upon the Babylonian calendar only appear in post-exilic writings: Nisan in Nehemiah 2:1; Esther 3:7; and Adar in Ezra 6:15. Years were designated according to the year of the monarch's rule both in Neo-Babylonian and in Persian times. This was normal Biblical usage both before and after the Exile (cf. II Kings 22:3; Jer. 25:1; Ezra 1:1; 6:15).

During the Exile a change took place in the speech habits of the Jews. Their language in pre-exilic days was Hebrew. At the time of Sennacherib's siege of Jerusalem, Aramaic was the language of diplomatic communication between Assyria and the provinces of western Asia. The Rab-shakeh addressed his challenge to the people of Jerusalem in the Hebrew language, much to the distress of Hezekiah's officials who informed him that they could speak the official Aramaic. The Rab-shakeh, however, wanted the populace to understand his message, so he spoke in the vernacular of the time (II Kings 18:17-37).

Aramaic became the language of diplomacy in the Persian Empire. It is possible that the Aramaic letters to and from Artaxerxes and Darius in the Book of Ezra (Ezra 4:11-22; 5:7-17; 6:6-12; 7:11-26) are actually copies of original texts kept in the Persian archives.

During the Exile, the Jews doubtless learned Aramaic as a means of communication with their non-Jewish neighbors. When they returned to Jerusalem they carried their newly learned language with them. It remained the vernacular language of Syria and Palestine until the Arab conquest of the seventh century A.D. It was the daily language of Palestine during New Testament times.

Hebrew, however, continued to be a living language after the return. The writings of Haggai, Zechariah, and Malachi were written in Hebrew, as were the writings of the Qumran community. Most of the people, however, spoke only Aramaic. When Ezra read the Law to the men of Jerusalem it was necessary to give an interpretation, probably in the Aramaic tongue (Neh. 8:8). Although most of the Old Testament was written in Hebrew, Aramaic was the language used in Daniel 2:4b-7:28 and Ezra 4:8 — 6:18; 7:12-26.

Life during the exile was highly diversified. Although most Jews doubtless practiced agriculture as a means of livelihood, some ultimately entered business. During the Persian period the Murashu family of Nippur operated an important mercantile house.[1] Other Jews became trusted men in government. The Zoroastrian Persians looked with favor on the monotheistic Jews whose lives were lived on a plane much higher than that of most Persian subjects.

---

1. See p. 495.

66

Nebuchadnezzar's Babylon

A clay tablet which dates back to Persian times contains a map of the world. Various towns are marked, along with the canals and waterways which made them possible. Around the whole span of the earth's surface is an ocean which has the appearance of a tire on a wheel. Beyond are yet other regions, indicated by triangles which touch the outer rim of the ocean. The geographical center of this universe, however, was the city of Babylon.

Babylon was an ancient city. We are told that Nimrod began his ancient empire there (Gen. 10:10). About 1830 B.C. a dynasty of kings from Babylon began to annex surrounding city-states and the First Dynasty of Babylon began its quest for power. The famed Hammurabi codified Babylonian law (*ca.* 1700 B.C.) and ruled all of southern Mesopotamia, extending his conquests as far as Mari on the middle Euphrates.

The glory of Babylon declined and southern Mesopotamia was ruled for centuries by governors appointed by the Assyrians who ruled from Asshur and Nineveh. When, under Nabopolassar, the Babylonians rebelled against Assyria and, in 612 B.C., helped destroy Nineveh, the center of empire, if not the center of the universe, could be identified with the ancient Babylon.

Our knowledge of ancient Babylon comes from a variety of sources. It is described in the Bible as the capital city of the nation which took Judah into captivity. Daniel and his companions were trained as courtiers in the schools of Babylon. The Greek historian Herodotus, who wrote a century and a half after Nebuchadnezzar, described the city as a vast square, 480 stades (55¼ miles) in circumference, surrounded by a huge moat of running water, beyond which were ramparts two hundred cubits high and fifty cubits broad! Herodotus tells us that the streets were arranged at right angles, a fact later verified by Koldewey, the excavator of Babylon. The Euphrates was walled on both

This painting of Babylon by Maurice Bardin shows a procession moving along Marduk's Way and entering the precincts of Nebuchadnezzar's palace through the Ishtar Gate.

sides as it made its course through the city, a series of gates providing the inhabitants of Babylon access to the river.[1] Diodorus Siculus and other Greeks spoke in admiration of Babylon, unquestionably the largest and most magnificent city of the ancient world.

The Book of Daniel records the boast of Nebuchadnezzar, "Is not this great Babylon that I have built?" (Dan. 4:30). The words are not without meaning. In addition to the walls which surrounded Babylon, Nebuchadnezzar was personally responsible for much that was within the city. He laid out and paved with bricks the great Procession Way which led to the temple of Marduk. The palace of his father Nabopolassar was completely rebuilt. Beams of cedar were imported from distant Lebanon for the project.

Nabopolassar had already begun the rebuilding of Babylon, but it was left to Nebuchadnezzar to pursue the work in earnest. Before the death of Nabopolassar about two-thirds of the work he had planned for the protection of Babylon had been completed. The inner wall of the city, known as Imgur-Bel, was finished. He also had built an outer wall, the Nimitti-Bel, and reconstructed the city gates with cedar wood covered with strips of bronze. Symbolic guardians of the city were the half-human, half-animal bronze colossi which stood at the threshold.

Nebuchadnezzar took up where his father left off. A third massive wall was built on the east side of the city at a distance of four thousand cubits from the outer wall. Before this was a moat, walled around with bricks. Similar defenses were built on the west, but they were not as strong because the desert formed a natural barrier.

To the north, the direction from which trouble might be expected, Nebuchadnezzar pursued a different plan. Between the two walls, and between the river and the Ishtar Gate he constructed an artificial platform of brick laid in bitumen. Upon this elevated platform he built a citadel which was connected with his royal palace. In this way he made the north wall so solid that it could be neither broken down nor breached. The citadel could be used as a watch-tower and, if need be, destructive missiles could be shot or thrown from it upon any enemy who might have reached the outside of the walls. Apart from the possibility of treachery within, Babylon appeared impregnable.

---

1. Herodotus, *Histories*, I, 178-187.

The Neo-Babylonian period is well documented, and Nebuchadnezzar has left us accounts of his building operation. In describing his work on the walls he declares:

> Nebuchadrezzar, king of Babylon, the restorer of Esagila and Ezida, son of Nabopolassar am I. As a protection to Esagila, that no powerful enemy and destroyer might take Babylon, that the line of battle might not approach Imgur-Bel, the wall of Babylon, that which no former king had done, I did; at the enclosure of Babylon I made an enclosure of a strong wall on the east side. I dug a moat, I reached the level of the water. I then saw that the wall which my father had prepared was too small in its construction. I built with bitumen and brick a mighty wall which, like a mountain, could not be moved, and connected it with the wall of my father; I laid its foundations on the breast of the underworld; its top I raised up like a mountain. Along this wall to strengthen it I constructed a third, and as the base of a protecting wall I laid a foundation of bricks, and built it on the breast of the under-world, and laid its foundation. The fortifications of Esagila and Babylon I strengthened, and established the name of my reign forever.[2]

Archaeology has provided us with the tools to evaluate the boasts of Nebuchadnezzar and the reports of Herodotus. In 1898 Robert Koldewey began the excavation of Babylon under the auspices of the *Deutsche Orientgesellschaft*. Work continued for more than eighteen years. Full reports of Koldewey's work appeared in his book, *Das wieder erstehende Babylon*, which contained photographs and plans of the city and its principal structures. The foreword to the first edition was dated, "Babylon, May 16, 1912." A fourth edition appeared in 1925.

Koldewey came upon the walls of Babylon during the early days of his dig. It took considerable time to excavate them, but the results were indeed impressive. Around the ruins of the city was a brick wall 22-1/3 feet thick. Outside this wall was a space 38-1/3 feet wide, then another brick wall, 25 feet thick. If the outer wall were breached the invader would find himself trapped between two walls. Lining the inner side of the citadel moat was still another wall, 12 feet thick. In times of danger the moat could be flooded.

The walls were surmounted every 160 feet by watchtowers. Koldewey suggests that there were 360 such towers on the inner wall (an estimate based upon the pattern of the ruins). Excavations indicate that the towers were 27 feet wide, and they probably were 90 feet high (much less than the 300 feet mentioned by Herodotus). Ancient historians tell us that two chariots could be driven abreast on the road which ran on top of the wall and

Ruins of the Ishtar Gate of Babylon.

---

2. Translation by G. A. Barton, *Archaeology and the Bible,* pp. 478-479, from *Zeitschrift fur Assyriologie,* I, 337 f.

completely surrounded the city. The walls were constantly patrolled by guards.

There were numerous gates in the walls, although Herodotus' reference to one hundred gates must be dismissed as hyperbole. The most famous entrance into the city was the Ishtar gate which led from the north of the city into the Procession Way. The gate was fifteen feet wide and its vaulted passageway was thirty-five feet above the street level. The bricks were so molded that they form bas-relief figures of bulls and dragons. Their surfaces were overlaid with thickly colored enamels. Nebuchadnezzar used properly fired bricks, and they have remained through the ages. The sun baked bricks used by his predecessors have disintegrated long ago.

The Procession Way was primarily used for the great annual occasion when king and people went to the temple of Marduk at the New Year's Festival. During the forty-three years of his reign, Nebuchadnezzar continued to beautify the Procession Way. He wrote:

> Aibur-shabu, the street of Babylon, I filled with a high fill for the procession of the great lord Marduk, and with Turminabanda stones and Shadu stones I made this Aibur-shabu fill for the procession of his godliness, and linked it with those parts which my father had built, and made the way a shining one.[3]

The pavement of the Procession Way was built over a base of bricks covered with bitumen. It consisted of blocks of limestone with sides more than a yard wide, pointed with asphalt. Inscribed on the underside of each of the slabs were the words:

> Nebuchadnezzar, King of Babylon, son of Nabopolassar, King of Babylon, am I. Of the streets of Babylon for the procession of the great lord Marduk, with slabs of limestone, I built the causeway. Oh, Marduk my lord, grant eternal life.[4]

Along the walls of the Procession Way was a series of 120 lions in enameled relief. They were spaced at 64 foot intervals and gave a sense of awe to the street. The lions had hides of white or yellow, with manes of yellow or red. They were posed against a background of light or dark blue. The Procession Way was 73½ feet wide.

At the annual New Year's Festival, statues of the principal deities were assembled from all the provinces of the kingdom and solemnly carried through the Ishtar Gate out to the northern outskirts of the city. There they were transferred to boats and taken to the Garden Temple up the river. This was followed

The Ishtar Gate of Babylon reconstructed. The structure is housed at the State Museum at Berlin.

3. Hugo Winckler, *Keilinschrift. Bibl.*, III, part 2, pp. 60-61.
4. From R. Campbell Thompson, "The New Babylonian Empire," in *The Cambridge Ancient History*, III, p. 217.

by the consummation of the sacred marriage of the principal god and goddess, which was presumed to guarantee the fertility and prosperity of the whole land. On the eleventh day of the month Nisan the procession joyously returned through the Ishtar Gate from the north. Marduk led the procession in his chariot-boat. Behind the chief god of Babylon rode the king in his chariot. Behind the king were carriage-boats containing the images of the other gods worshiped in Babylon.

Dragon from Ishtar Gate.

Along the Procession Way was the famous staged-tower or ziggurat of Babylon known as E-temen-anki — "The House of the Foundation of Heaven and Earth" — which rose 300 feet into the air and could be seen from a distance by travelers approaching the city. Fifty-eight million bricks are said to have been used in its construction. Like Babylon itself, the ziggurat goes back to remote antiquity. On its top was a Temple to Marduk, the god of Babylon. Enemies of the state — such as Tukulti-Ninurta, Sargon, Sennacherib, and Ashurbanipal — devastated the city and destroyed the Marduk shrine. The tower was rebuilt by the Neo-Babylonian rulers Nabopolassar and Nebuchadnezzar. In a sense it pictured both the glories of Marduk, and of Marduk's city, Babylon. Nabopolassar declared:

> The lord Marduk commanded me concerning E-temen-anki, the staged tower of Babylon, which before my time had become dilapidated and ruinous, that I should make its foundations secure in the bosom of the nether world, and make its summit like the heavens.[5]

The ziggurat consisted of seven terraces, on the top of which was a temple made of bricks enameled bright blue to represent the heavens. The temple was approached by a triple staircase, at the middle of which there was a place where the visitor might rest. Within the temple was a couch and a golden table. This was regarded as the abode of Marduk. No one except a priestess, who served as the consort of the god, was to enter this shrine. The prosperity of the land was thought to depend upon this sacred marriage ritual.

Across the street from the ziggurat was the temple area known as E-sag-ila ("The house which lifts up the head"). Herodotus visited the E-sag-ila and was much impressed by its golden figure of "Zeus" (Babylonian Bel-Marduk) seated in the shrine beside a golden table. According to the statistics which Herodotus gives (which may be exaggerated) the gold of these objects weighed about 800 talents, or 4800 pounds with a current value of $24,000,000. "Zeus" appeared as a half-animal, half-human creature.

---

5. André Parrot, *The Tower of Babel*, p. 18.

Outside the sanctuary were a number of other altars and statues including a standing figure of Marduk, twelve cubits (twenty feet) high, of solid gold. The complex of buildings occupied sixty acres, bounded on the west by the Euphrates and on the east by the Procession Way. Towering 470 feet above the ground was the shrine known as the E-kur ("Temple mountain") built on a terrace of asphalted bricks like the nearby ziggurat.

The total number of shrines in ancient Babylon, as recorded in contemporary inscriptions, appears incredible. We read that,

> There are altogether in Babylon fifty-three temples of the great gods, fifty-five shrines dedicated to Marduk, three hundred shrines belonging to earth divinities, six hundred shrines for celestial divinities, one hundred and eighty altars to the goddess Ishtar, one hundred and eighty to the gods Nergal and Adad, and twelve other altars to various deities.[6]

North of the ziggurat was a mound called Kasr on which Nebuchadnezzar built the most imposing of his palaces. The palace walls were of finely made yellow brick, and floors were of white and mottled sandstone. The palace was adorned with reliefs in blue glaze. Its gates were guarded by gigantic basalt lions.

Near the palace were the famed Hanging Gardens, considered to be one of the Seven Wonders of the Ancient World. Nebuchadnezzar built the gardens for his wife who missed the hills of her Median homeland. The gardens appear to have been terraced and set on a small hill beside the palace, flanked by the Procession Way and the Ishtar Gate.

Josephus quotes from Berossus, *History of Chaldea,* an account of the building of Nebuchadnezzar's palace and the hanging gardens,

> In this palace he erected retaining walls of stone to which he gave an appearance very like that of mountains and, by planting on them trees of all kinds, he achieved this effect and built the so-called hanging garden because his wife, who had been brought up in the region of Media, had a desire for her native environment.[7]

The gardens were irrigated by means of an endless chain of buckets which raised water to the highest point of the terrace. The gardens were impressive when viewed from a distance from the city. The visitor to Babylon could see the tops of the trees towering above the city walls.

Nebuchadnezzar's Babylon was an excellent example of early city planning. The city was divided into a number of rectangles by wide roads which were named after the gods of the Babylonian pantheon. On the left bank of the Euphrates we find the streets of Marduk and Zababa intersecting at right angles with

---

6. Quoted in M. Rutten, *Babylone,* p. 47.
7. Josephus, *Antiquities,* X, 226.

the streets of Sin and Enlil. On the right bank we find an intersection of the streets of Adad and Shamash. Except for the famed Procession Way, Babylon's streets were not paved.

A bridge connecting the eastern or New City with the western city of Babylon had stone piers and a timber foot path which could be withdrawn in times of emergency. Permanent bridges were rare in the ancient East, and the one across the Euphrates was a source of wonder to travelers.

The business life of the city centered in the wharves which flanked the Euphrates. Business offices were located along the river bank. The market sector of ancient Babylon has not been identified, but it was probably located in the *Merkes* quarter.

The houses of the city were frequently three or four stories high, being built according to a pattern which has been familiar in the East from ancient times to the present. Each home would be built around a central courtyard. There would be no windows facing the street, but all light would come through the courtyard. Access to the rooms of the second story was by a wooden balcony which extended around the entire inner courtyard. A narrow door in one of the first floor rooms opened into the street.

Ancient Babylon required a system of canals if the best use was to be made of the waters of the Tigris and the Euphrates. Hammurabi, the famed king of the Old Babylonian Empire had been a canal builder, and his successors needed to be careful to insure proper irrigation of the fields. When Nebuchadnezzar came to the throne of Babylon, its eastern canal had so deteriorated that there were places where its channel could not be traced. Nebuchadnezzar had it redug, and then walled up from the bottom. Because the canal passed through Babylon, it was necessary to build a bridge across it.

Although most of his energy was spent on Babylon itself, Nebuchadnezzar did not completely neglect the other cities of Mesopotamia. He rebuilt the walls of Borsippa and restored the temples of the city to a good state of repair.

Nebuchadnezzar was an able and an energetic sovereign. He was in all respects the most able as well as the most ambitious ruler of his day. In him the Neo-Babylonian Empire reached its zenith. Great as were his accomplishments both on the field of battle and in building the cities of his kingdom, Nebuchadnezzar left an empire that had no political stability. His own personality held it together, and when that was gone it was not long before his dynasty came to an end.

This one-mina weight dates back to the time of Nebuchadnezzar. Sixty shekels made a maneh (mina) and sixty manehs equaled a talent (biltu).

67

The Wisdom
of the Babylonians

Daniel was expected to become proficient in the "letters and language of the Chaldeans" (Dan. 1:4). He was enrolled in a school and given the ancient equivalent of a liberal education. The Babylonia of Daniel's day preserved its records on clay or stone. A scribe would use a stylus to cut cuneiform (i.e., "wedge-shaped") characters on a soft piece of clay. When baked in the sun, this would become a permanent record.

The cuneiform method of writing was adopted by the Semitic peoples of the Fertile Crescent as a result of contacts with the Sumerians who first used it as a means of communication shortly before 3000 B.C. The Sumerians, like the Egyptians, began with a system of picture writing. It was the nature of the writing material of Sumer that produced cuneiform. The stylus used for writing on clay tablets could be used most efficiently in forming wedges on the soft clay. Pictures early became conventionalized into groups of wedges, and the pictorial character of the language was lost.

In the earliest stage of the language, signs stood for the objects which they represented. In time, however, the signs came to represent syllables with no necessary relationship to their origin. With this development, any word in the language could be written. If we were to adopt such a system, a conventionalized picture of a cat would represent our noun "cat." As a syllable, the symbol could represent the first part of the word catalogue, or catacomb, or any word beginning with "cat." If we worshiped the cat, its symbol, prefixed by a sign representing deity, could also represent the cat-god. If our culture conceived of the cat as a sly creature, we might even use the cat symbol to represent the verb "to be sly." In such a usage the syllable "cat-" would not have to appear in the verb. The reader would know that the verb "to be sly" was meant in a given context.

The Sumerian writing system was indeed cumbersome, but it did make possible written communication in all its forms — religious epics, historical annals, law codes, personal letters, contracts, receipts, and all that makes possible civilization as we know it. The alphabet, a much more efficient system of written communication, did not completely replace cuneiform until shortly before the time of Christ. Cuneiform writing was used for the thousands of ancient records which archaeologists use in reconstructing the history of the ancient Near East. The fact that they were written on clay renders them almost indestructible as compared with papyrus and leather which quickly deteriorate in moist climates.

Our finest collection of cuneiform literature comes from the library of Ashurbanipal, the Assyrian ruler known as Osnapper in the Old Testament (Ezra 4:10). Ashurbanipal was characterized both by ruthlessness and culture. A relief shows him in the royal garden enjoying a banquet with Ashur-sharrat, his wife. The scene is almost idyllic until we note, hanging from a coniferous tree, the head of an Elamite chieftain whom he had conquered.

On the other hand, Ashurbanipal boasts of his education and culture. He writes:

> I, Ashurbanipal, learned the wisdom of Nabu, the entire art of writing on clay tablets . . . . I learned to shoot the bow, to ride, to drive and to seize the reins.
>
> I received the revelation of the wise Adapa, the hidden treasure of the art of writing....I considered the heavens with the learned masters....I read the beautiful clay tablets from Sumer and the obscure Akkadian writing which is hard to master. I had my joy in the reading of inscriptions on stone from the time before the flood . . . . The following were my daily activities: I mounted my horse, I rode joyfully...I held the bow...I go around . . . . At the same time I learned royal decorum and walked in kingly ways.[1]

Ashurbanipal's library was discovered in 1853 by Hormuzd Rassam, the brother of the British vice-consul at Mosul, who was continuing the work of Austin Henry Layard. We gain some idea of the literary resources of the seventh century before Christ when we realize that the library contained over 22,000 clay tablets containing religious, literary, and scientific works. Among these were the Babylonian creation and flood epics.

Tablets in Ashurbanipal's collection came from a variety of sources. Many were copied from originals by his own scribes. He dispatched officials to the cities of his Empire with orders to gather all texts of importance. One of his extant directives ends

A clay tablet with an outline map of the regions of the world. The cuneiform text below the map relates the conquests of Sargon of Agade, who reigned about 2300 B.C.

---

1. Quoted in Jack Finegan, *Light from the Ancient Past*, pp. 216-217.

with the words, "If you hear of any tablet or ritualistic text that is suitable for the palace, seek it out, secure it, and send it here."

A writing system as complex as cuneiform required a class of professional scribes to read and write the numerous documents required by an advanced culture. Scribal schools were the centers of learning in the ancient Near East. A number of cuneiform "textbooks" were discovered at the site of ancient Shuruppak, the home town of the Sumerian Noah, in 1902-03. A scribal school is known to have been conducted at Shuruppak around 2500 B.C. Archaeologists have discovered hundreds of practice tablets from a later period. We can read on them the actual exercises prepared by pupils as a part of their school work.

Since the scribe represented a learned profession, it might be expected that recruits would come from the upper level of society. A German cuneiformist, Nikolaus Schneider, studied thousands of published economic and administrative documents from about 2000 B.C. and found the names of about five hundred individuals who listed themselves as scribes. Many of them listed the name and occupation of their fathers. These include temple administrators, priests, military officers, ambassadors, sea captains, accountants, high tax officials, other scribes, and the like. All appear to have been wealthy citizens of urban communities.[2]

Although a youth might be able to enter a scribal school because of the wealth or influence of his father, nevertheless he would have to prove himself by careful attention to his studies. The scribe was honored as a member of a learned profession, but he gained competence only through years of hard work.

I. Literature

Among the great religious writings of the time when Daniel would have gone to school in Babylon was the *Enuma Elish,* the Babylonian account of creation. The Babylonians believed that the world originated in Chaos — a waste of waters with Apsu (sweet water) and Tiamat (salt water) constituting the primordial elements. From these deities other gods were formed. The theogony was patterned after human life, with the gods arranged according to sex and generation. For some reason the great gods Anu, Enlil, and Ea aroused the wrath of Apsu and Tiamat, and the older gods determined to rid themselves of their offspring.

---

2. See Samuel N. Kramer, *From the Tablets of Sumer,* p. 5.

Ea, however, was able to destroy Apsu, a fact which enraged Tiamat, who gave birth to eleven horrible monsters, their leader being named Kingu. She expected them to avenge the death of Apsu and subdue the rebellious gods. In the meantime, the kindly Ea gave birth to a son, Marduk, who was destined to save the gods from Tiamat's murderous plan.

Terrorized by Tiamat and her monsters, the gods looked for some way to destroy her. Marduk accepted the suggestion that he be their champion on condition that he be given absolute authority over all the gods, and that his decisions be accepted as final. The gods, helpless against the wrath of Tiamat, agreed to his conditions.

After suitable preparation, Marduk was ready for his encounter with Tiamat. As she prepared to devour him, Marduk cast one of the four winds of heaven into her open mouth, and thrust his sword into her distended body. In this way Tiamat was killed and her body cut in two. From one half of her corpse Marduk made the sky, and with the other half he formed the earth. Subsequently he created man, and Kingu — who had been taken captive — provided the necessary blood.

Although at first glance fantastic, the *Enuma Elish* was designed to teach some important lessons. One of them was political. Marduk was the god of Babylon, and the story tells how his place of supremacy was recognized by all the other gods. If the god of Babylon is the greatest of gods, then Babylon itself must be the greatest of cities and have a divine right to rule all others. There are other forms of the creation story, but the one promulgated in Babylon sought to justify the supremacy of Babylon. This is not to suggest that the story was maliciously invented to serve utilitarian ends. On the contrary, when Babylon became a world power, her success was considered an evidence of the power of her god. Since Babylon's armies had destroyed other nations, her god must have been supreme!

The fact that human blood finds its origin in the evil Kingu is not an accident, either. Although not possessing the moral consciousness of the Hebrew prophets, nevertheless the Babylonians knew that man tended to be perverse in his ways. Why is man such a rebellious fellow? The *Enuma Elish* gives the answer — Man has the blood of Kingu.

The famous Gilgamesh Epic probably dates back to the third millennium before Christ. Fragments of it have been discovered in the Hittite and Hurrian languages, and it probably was translated into many others as well. The theme of the Gilgamesh Epic

This cuneiform tablet contains a part of the Babylonian Creation story.

is man, with his struggles and hopes. This may be the reason for its popularity.

Gilgamesh, the tyrant of Erech, was part human and part divine. He acted in such a highhanded way that the people cried to their gods for deliverance. The gods thereupon formed Enkidu, who was a bull from the waist down and human from the waist up. Enkidu was destined to oppose and vanquish Gilgamesh.

We first meet Enkidu in the fields where he was a friend of the wild animals. He released them from traps and helped them to thwart hunters. One day, however, a hunter saw Enkidu and told his father about this unusual being. The father sent his son to find a girl who would bring about a change in Enkidu's character. The girl, Shamhat, was brought to Enkidu. She had carnal relations with him, whereupon he became a changed creature. He accompanied her to Erech, ate bread instead of grass, drank from vessels, anointed himself with oil, and put on clothes. Enkidu had been introduced to human culture, and would never again be at home in the world of the wild animals.

Eventually Enkidu and Gilgamesh met. Instead of fighting one another they decided to join forces to slay dragons and help the cause of righteousness to triumph. After his victory over the dragon Humbaba in the Cedar Forest, the goddess Ishtar proposed marriage to Gilgamesh. The ruler of Erech spurned the goddess, however. He reminded her of her long and shameful record. She had loved a horse, then beat him. A shepherd whom she loved was later turned into a wolf. Gilgamesh could not permit himself to become entangled with such a woman! She, however, was a goddess, and determined to punish him for his impertinence. Ishtar asked the Bull of Heaven (a human-headed bull) to kill Gilgamesh, but Gilgamesh and Enkidu managed to kill the Bull of Heaven, instead. Enkidu cut off a leg from the Bull of Heaven and threw it at Ishtar. She could not let this insult go unpunished, so she plotted his death.

The death of Enkidu brought Gilgamesh face to face with life's starkest reality. Gilgamesh, mourning his friend, determined to find immortality for himself. A man named Utnapishtim was the one mortal who had achieved immortality, and Gilgamesh set out to find him in order that he might learn his secret. Along the way Gilgamesh met a barmaid who tried to dissuade him from his quest, urging him to enjoy the present life and forget about the uncertain future. Gilgamesh continued his quest, however, until he found Utnapishtim.

The story which Utnapishtim told to Gilgamesh is familiar to Bible students, because it contains the Akkadian parallel to the Biblical flood story. In the Babylonian version, the gods determined to rid themselves of mankind by means of a flood. The kindly Ea warned Utnapishtim of the impending flood and urged him to build an ark in which he might save the lives of his family and of representative members of the animal creation. Utnapishtim obeyed the word of Ea, built the ark, and not only saved his life but procured immortality for himself as well.

Gilgamesh, however, did not achieve immortality. Utnapishtim challenged him to remain awake for a week, but he was unable to do so. As a substitute for immortality Utnapishtim gave Gilgamesh a magic plant which had the power to rejuvenate him. The possession of this plant guaranteed that its owner would become young again — an early form of the "fountain of youth" motif. Tragedy struck, however, for when Gilgamesh paused for a drink of water, the plant slipped from him and was swallowed by a snake. As a result, the serpent can shed its old skin and become rejuvenated, but man must face the certainty of old age and death! Gilgamesh continued his journey to Erech. If he had not gained immortality, he at least could admire his earthly abode.

The gods of the Gilgamesh Epic possess thoroughly human characteristics. They not only strive with one another, but they are so famished at the end of the flood that, as Utnapishtim prepares sacrifices for them, "The gods smelt the sweet savour: like flies they gathered together over him that sacrificed."[3]

The Gilgamesh Epic probably contains the memory of real floods which covered much of the Tigris-Euphrates area. Such floods took place at the end of the last ice age (*ca.* 8000 B.C.) and may be reflected in both the Biblical and the Babylonian accounts.

2. Mathematics

The Babylonians inherited the sexagesimal system from the ancient Sumerians. This system of numbering by sixties is still in use. We reckon sixty seconds to the minute, and sixty minutes to the hour. The system is also used in the division of the circle into three hundred and sixty degrees.

---

3. *The Gilgamesh Epic*, XI, lines 160-161.

The cuneiform syllabary was adapted to the writing of mathematical texts. An upright stroke would mean either "one" or "sixty" depending on its position and context. An angular stroke stood for the number ten. The system was such that any number could be written, although the concept of zero, and its usefulness as a mathematical symbol were not known.

Mathematical problems which have been preserved for us on cuneiform tablets show that by 2000 B.C. the Babylonians could measure the area of rectangles and of right and isoceles triangles. Subsequently we know that they could calculate the exact volume of a pyramid and of a truncated cone. The mathematical value of pi was defined as three, an approximation of our more accurate 3.1416.

An amazing knowledge of algebra is also shown in the Babylonian literature. From the Old Babylonian period we have tablets of squares, square roots, cubes, and cube roots. We even find tables of the sums of squares and cubes needed for the numerical solution of special types of cubic equations. Babylonian mathematical texts prove that the Pythagorean theorem was known more than a thousand years before Pythagoras.[4]

3. Astronomy

Closely related to Babylonian mathematics, and using it as an important tool, was the science of astronomy. By 800 B.C. Babylonian astronomers had attained sufficient accuracy to assign positions to the stars and note their heliacal settings. An attempt was made to determine cause and effect relationships between the motions of the heavenly bodies and purely human events. If an eclipse was once followed by a war with Elam, a second eclipse might be considered the portent of another such war. Astronomers of this period reported regularly to the court concerning their observations. In taunting the proud Babylonians, Isaiah said, "You are wearied with your many counsels; let them stand forth and save you, those who divide the heavens, who gaze at the stars, who at the new moons predict what shall befall you" (Isa. 47:13).

During this period no distinction was made between astronomical and meteorological phenomena. Clouds were reported in the same way as eclipses. Through observation, however, astronomers noted that solar eclipses could take place only at the end of the month, and lunar eclipses only at the middle.

---

4. O. Neugebauer, *The Exact Sciences in Antiquity,* p. 36.

A cuneiform tablet from about 700 B.C. classifies the fixed stars. They were arranged on three "roads," the middle of which was an equatorial belt of 30° width. The Road of Enlil contained thirty-three stars, that of Anu, twenty-three, and that of Ea only fifteen. A companion tablet discusses the planets, the moon, the seasons, the lengths of the shadow, and related problems. A distinction is made between planets, termed "wild goats" because they wandered in the heavens, and fixed stars, or "tame goats" because they did not roam! The concepts discussed in these tablets are elementary indeed, but they are significant in that they describe astronomical phenomena with no reference to mythological concepts.

By 500 B.C. we find, as the reference system for solar and planetary motion, a zodiac of twelve sections, each thirty degrees in length. The main sequences of planetary and lunar phenomena had been observed. Arithmetical progressions were in use to describe periodically variable quantities. Lengths of daylight and darkness at a given time could be predicted.

The planets were named for the gods of Babylon and, in their Graeco-Roman form, we still so designate them. Ishtar, the Babylonian goddess of love became Venus in the classical world. Similarly Marduk became Jupiter; Nabu, the announcer, became Mercury; Nergal, God of war, became Mars; and Ninib, patron of agriculture, became Saturn. The days of the week were, in Babylonian thought, ruled by the heavenly bodies, and ultimately each of the seven days was devoted to a specific deity. Thus we have the day of the sun, the moon, Nergal (Mars), Marduk (Jupiter), Ishtar (Venus), and Ninib (Saturn). With little variation this is still the order of our week, with first, second, and last days preserving the Roman form of the names. Since our calendar came through a northern route it reflects Norse mythology in such names as Woden's day (Wednesday) and Thor's day (Thursday). All, however, ultimately go back to the gods of ancient Babylon.

The tribal name Chaldean came to be used as a specialized term for astrologer or magician in the Greek and Roman writers.[5] The pseudo-science of astrology came into its own in Seleucid times, and proved attractive to many throughout the classical world.

---

5. Cf. also Dan. 2:2 ff.

4. Medicine

Babylonian medicine was largely associated with concepts of demons and evil spirits and the means of counteracting their harmful spells. The physician-priest was a man noted for his ability to use potent spells to exorcise evil spirits. In the field of surgery, however, real advances were made among the Babylonians. The attempt to learn the will of the gods by an examination of animal entrails furnished, by way of analogy, some idea of human anatomy. As early as the Code of Hammurabi (*ca.* 1700 B.C.) physicians performed delicate operations on the human eye. A surgeon who opened an abscess in a man's eye and blinded him was punished by having his own fingers removed.

5. The Natural Sciences

Babylonian science was the result of observation, and it consistently served practical purposes. Plants and animals were named, and we possess plant lists with Sumerian and Akkadian names listed in parallel columns. Stones are listed and classified. An ancient legend tells us that the great god Ninurta was confronted by an alliance of his enemies. His friends, who came to his aid, and his foes, who sought to overthrow him, were the various types of stones. After his victory, the stones which helped him were assigned beautiful names and became the precious stones which adorn temples and are fashioned into exquisite jewelry. The hostile, defeated stones were assigned menial tasks — they became paving stones, door sills or pebbles on the road.

Chemistry, likewise, served a practical function. Minerals were refined by burning, and unusual alloys were compounded. A type of glass known as "copper-lead" had as its ingredients 60 parts of ordinary glass, 10 of lead, 15 of copper, $\frac{1}{2}$ of saltpeter and $\frac{1}{2}$ of lime. The purity of gold was a constant source of contention. Burra-buriash of Babylon (14th Century B.C.) complained to Amenhotep IV of Egypt that the twenty minas of gold which had been sent to him became five minas of pure gold after the refining process. Tests made on the gold articles discovered in ancient Sumer and Babylon show a wide variety in the purity of the gold of which they were made.

68

Babylonian Religion

The religion which the Jews of the Exile found in Babylon had roots which went back over two thousand years. The ancient Sumerian city-states were theoretically under the protection of patron deities. Semitic invaders brought a new set of gods into southern Mesopotamia. Sumerians, Semites, and other settlers were polytheistic and did not object to incorporating new gods and goddesses into their religious scheme. When alliances were made, or conquests achieved, the gods of the city-states were subject to new classifications. The god of a victorious state was considered to be the most powerful deity, for warfare was always waged on two levels. The earthly states were championed by their celestial deities, and the battles in the sky were accounted as real as the battles on earth. Assyrian kings did battle in the might of Asshur, and Babylonian rulers looked to Marduk as their guide and protector.

A modern logician has a difficult time with the religion of ancient Babylon and Assyria. When the Semites entered the Tigris-Euphrates Valley they found the Sumerians worshiping the mother goddess Inanna. This posed no problem, for they simply gave her the Semitic name Ishtar and worshiped her as devoutly as did their Sumerian neighbors. In practice, however, Inanna and Ishtar became two goddesses, for each had her devotees. The deities were classified according to sex and marital status and genealogies, or, more strictly, theogonies were arranged. Since Inanna or Ishtar was the chief goddess we would expect her to be the consort of the chief god. Who was this supreme deity? The people of Asshur, the Assyrians would insist that their god was supreme, and the Babylonians would hail the power of Marduk. Thus Ishtar would be regarded as the wife of different gods, depending upon the city in which the claim was made.

There is, of course, a logic in this very illogical approach to religion. Each people thought its god supreme, and imputed to it those powers and attributes which are usually associated with a great god. To the Assyrians, Asshur was the god responsible for the creation of the universe; to the Babylonians it was Marduk who made all things. In each nation, however, there were numerous other gods who were worshiped. It is the fact of a common religious tradition, coupled with the concept of local patron deities, that produces the illogical pantheons of the eastern Fertile Crescent peoples. Heaven itself was divided into three parts, each assigned to one of the great deities.

During Sumerian times, the chief god was known as An, or Anu, the sky god who was regarded as father of the great gods. In "the heaven of Anu" the other deities gathered in times of festivity or sorrow. It was there that the gods whose earthly shrines were destroyed by the flood found a place of refuge. Anu is represented in the cuneiform characters by a star, symbolic of both the god and his heavenly abode. Cult centers of Anu were located at Der in Akkad and at Uruk in Sumer where the temple known as E-anna ("the house of Anu") was located. An important temple to Anu was located in the *girsu* or holy quarter of Lagash.

Anu was remote from the world of men, and does not seem to have been a popular god. His worship was complemented, however, by that accorded to his daughter Ishtar, who made up for any lack in her father's popularity. Ishtar, the goddess of love, was worshiped along with Anu both at the E-anna of Uruk and the *girsu* of Lagash.

Until the rise of the Marduk cult in Babylon, Anu was reputed to be the supreme deity in the Tigris-Euphrates valley. He possessed the symbols of kingship — scepter and diadem, staff and crown. All subordinate rule was responsible to him.

The second great god, honored alike by Sumerians and Semites, was Enlil or Bel. Bel is another form of the Semitic Baal, a word which means "Lord." Enlil-Bel was the lord, or ruler of earth. His abode was the "Great Mountain" in the heaven of Bel which united heaven and earth. As storm god he was, "Lord of the winds." During Sumerian times his worship was centered at Nippur. Since his domain was the earth, Enlil was closer to the affairs of men than was Anu, his father in the theogony. Enlil is described as "the wise" and "the prudent" but he can, on occasion, bring suffering to the world of men. He defied the wishes of Ea and Ishtar and ordered the onset of the flood which destroyed man and beast. He was also deemed responsible for the destruction of Ur by the Elamites. Through Enlil-Bel, divine power was executed on earth.

Important changes took place in the Enlil cult when Marduk was recognized as supreme god in Babylon. Marduk assumed the name of Bel, and became known as Bel-Marduk. Enlil was then designated, "Bel the ancient." His wife was Belit, the feminine form of the name Bel.

The third of the great Sumerian gods was known as Enki, Semitic Ea. Enki ruled the waters upon which, according to the Babylonian cosmology, the terrestrial world floated. He bore the epithet, "Lord of the watery deep." Some traditions made Enki-Ea the creator of the world. In extravagant language he is called, "King of the abyss, Creator of everything, Lord of all." Like Anu he is even designated as "father of the gods."

Enki-Ea was considered to be both wise and kindly disposed toward mankind. It was he who taught men the art of writing and geometry. From him man learned how to build temples and cities and to cultivate the soil. Magic, medicine, and divination were subject to his control. His kindness toward mankind was exhibited when he warned the Sumero-Babylonian Noah to build an ark as a place of safety in the impending flood. Enki's ancient cult center was at Eridu, at the head of the Persian Gulf.

Anu, Enlil and Ea formed a triad of great gods exercising power over air, earth, and water. There were however, many other gods who demanded the worship and offerings of the people. Some of these had specific functions or were the embodiment of forces of nature. A second generation triad — Sin, the moon-god; Shamash, the sun-god; and Adad, the storm god, largely supplanted the older deities in the popular affection.

The Mesopotamian world ascribed great importance to Sin, the moon god, whose waxing and waning governed the passing of the months. Divination and astrology were largely dependent on the moon, and were closely related to his worship. As with Enki-Ea, wisdom was associated with Sin. In Sumerian times, Sin bore the name Nanna. Both Ur and Haran were devoted to his worship.

Corresponding to Sin, the moon god, we find Shamash, the sun, known to the Sumerians as Utu. Shamash was considered to be the son of Sin. Although westerners might expect the relationship to be reversed, we must remember that the Semite begins his day with sunset. This is the order used in describing the creative days of Genesis: "And it was evening, and it was morning, day one" (Gen. 1:5b). Although welcomed at dawn when the

The text of this impression of a Babylonian cylinder seal reads: "Manum, the Diviner and servant of the God Enki (Ea)." It dates from about the nineteenth or eighteenth century B.C.

light of day drives away the evil spirits thought to dwell in the darkness, as the day advances Shamash is looked upon as a foe. The heat of the sun parches the land. Activities must cease at midday lest sunstroke and death result from his activities in the hot regions of the Near East.

Shamash, as bringer of light, was also associated in the mind of the ancient Babylonian with justice. He is termed, "the light of things above and things below" and "the supreme judge of heaven and earth who guides aright living creatures." The evil that can lurk under cover of darkness is forced into the open by the appearance of Shamash. As god of justice, it is Shamash who is depicted on the top of the stele containing the law code of King Hammurabi. He was worshiped at shrines in Larsa, in southern Babylonia, and at Sippar, farther north.

Adad, the storm god, was worshiped throughout the Near East. The Aramaeans knew him as Hadad, and his name appears in the Biblical Ben-hadad, the king of Damascus. As a god of fertility, Adad was called, "Lord of abundance, Irrigator of heaven and earth." His home was in the mountain heights from which he could thunder forth with lightning and rain. In the Babylonian flood story it was Adad who let loose the deluge which turned mankind into clay. Since man's life depended, in large measure, on the fertility which Adad could bring, he was a god whose worship was seldom neglected. In Syria and Palestine, Hadad was identified with Baal, who was "rider of the clouds" and through whom fertility was provided for man and beast as well as for the parched fields. Adad's consort was Shala, "lady of the ear of grain."

Fertility and reproduction in the Tigris-Euphrates valley were associated with Ishtar, the popular daughter of Anu. She was also the goddess of war. The Sumerian form of her name, Innana, means "Lady of heaven," and Innana-Ishtar was identified with the planet Venus. She was the great mother goddess of the ancient Near East and, throughout all the changes which the religion of Babylon and Assyria underwent, Ishtar always maintained her independent position. At one time or another she was considered to be the wife of the "great god" of almost every city in Mesopotamia. Her most famous shrine was in Uruk, Biblical Erech.

The priestly theologians of ancient Babylon attempted to breathe order into the confused picture of their historic pantheon which grew more complex with the passing of the years. They classified the status, rank, and function of each of the gods,

The Kudurra boundary stone dates from the time of Nebuchadnezzar I (twelfth century B.C.). Symbols of major deities were inscribed on such stones to discourage their removal.

and developed a hierarchy patterned after human affairs. Gods were grouped into families, and their servants and slaves are indicated. There were four thousand gods in all, many of whom had highly specialized functions. A few, however, will suffice to show the development of the religious life in ancient Babylonia.

During the earliest Sumerian period the lord of the *girsu* of Lagash was known as Ninurta, or Enurta. At that time he was a fertility god who was responsible for the annual flooding of the rivers. Early texts symbolize him by the plough, indicating his function of making agriculture possible. In time, however, another side of his character was emphasized. By the late Assyrian period he was symbolized by weapons and he became known as the god of battles.

Semitic Nusku, Sumerian Gibil, was the god of fire. He was invoked by magicians in their tasks of exorcism. They called upon Nusku to burn to death evil spirits and sorcerers. Nusku was also associated with worship, for he made burnt offerings possible.

Nergal had originally been a sun god, but as the destroyer of life (one attribute of the sun god), he went to the nether regions to found a kingdom for himself. There he became the god of pestilence and death. His domain was known as "the land of no return." His wife was Ereshkigal, the sister of Shamash and Ishtar. She had ruled the nether regions before the arrival of Nergal. On his arrival they became husband and wife. The nether regions were also populated by monsters with both human and animal forms.

The scribe of the gods was Nabu (Nebo), the patron of Borsippa, who was reputed to have great wisdom. The Table of Fate was in his keeping, and he had power to prolong or shorten life. Nebuchadnezzar's name, meaning, "Nebo has established the boundary," expresses faith in Nebo, identified as a son of Marduk, the great god of Babylon.

During the period of the First Dynasty of Babylon an important revolution took place in the religion of the country. A minor deity named Marduk was chosen as the principal god of the whole of Babylonia. Although the older deities were accorded their accustomed worship, Marduk, a son of Ea, was placed at the head of the pantheon. The *Enuma Elish,* which dates from this time, relates the way in which the gods and goddesses, terrified by the primordial monster, Tiamat (Chaos), appealed for help. The youthful Marduk, on condition that all acknowledge his supremacy, accepted the challenge, slew the monster, and from her corpse created the heaven and the earth. Thus the supremacy of the god of Babylon became acknowledged by the entire pantheon. Since Marduk was the god of Babylon, this myth sought to convince the world that Babylon was the supreme nation, as it worshiped the supreme god. A similar development took place in Assyria where Asshur was acknowledged as the supreme god. The worship of Marduk or Asshur did not lessen the importance of the other deities, however. It seems illogical to us, but the temples and shrines of the pantheon were as busy as ever. The only change was in the new honors due to Marduk. Polytheism can be very tolerant, and the Babylonians did not strive after logic in their religion.

A faithful son of Ishtar, the mother goddess, bore the name Tammuz, Sumerian *Dumu-zi,* "faithful son." Tammuz was a god of vegetation who disappeared each year in the late summer and returned (i.e., was resurrected) the following spring. Tammuz was the suffering god whose career paralleled the natural seasons. With the deadly summer heat he left the earth, but the life-giving springtime saw his triumphant return. In the Greco-Roman world he was worshiped as Adonis, a name which is a variant of the Semitic *Adon,* lord, or master.

In addition to the great gods of the Babylonian pantheon, each individual of latter-day Babylon looked to a personal god who was thought to be his protector and provider — a kind of "guardian angel" who never left his charge except when the person was guilty of grievous sin. In the early stages of Assyrian and Babylonian thought, the king alone was the favorite of a special deity, but by the beginnings of the Old Babylonian Empire this distinction was enjoyed by commoners as well. The faith of the Babylonian in his personal gods is exemplified by names which individuals bore. We meet people who bear names meaning: "My god hath hearkened unto me," "My god is my father," "My god is my refuge."

The colossal winged bulls which guarded the approaches to Assyrian and Babylonian palaces were not solely decorative. They exemplified the good genies, or spirits, and served as guards for the protection of palaces or city gates. They had their counterpart, however, in the evil genies who sought to bring harm to mankind.

The evil genies were thought to be responsible for the strife which enters human relations. They entered houses even when the door was bolted and barred. They set family members at

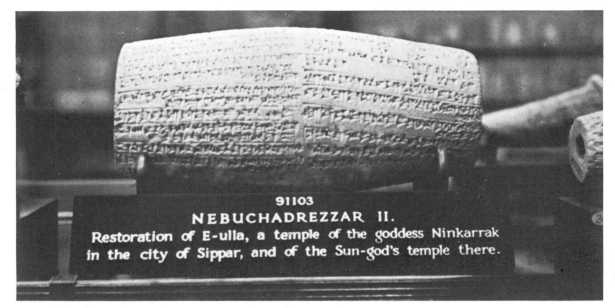

91103
NEBUCHADREZZAR II.
Restoration of E-ulla, a temple of the goddess Ninkarrak
in the city of Sippar, and of the Sun-god's temple there.

Cylinder of Nebuchadnezzar II.

strife with one another. They might turn everything in the house upside down, enter the stable and injure or kill the animals. If they found a man in sin without the protection of his personal god, they might enter that man and "possess" him. The man could not escape this evil genie, for the records assure us, "The man who hath not god as he walketh in the street, the demon covers him as a garment."

The origin of the genies is somewhat obscure. The good ones, fewer in number, were descended from the great gods who continued to be worshiped in Babylon. The evil genies, however, were traced back to the evil gods whom Marduk destroyed in order to free the other gods from the evil which they purposed. At times the evil genies were described as children of Bel or Anu, although their mother was thought to be a goddess of the nether regions. On occasion, however, even the offspring of good gods such as Ea and his wife Damkina might become evil genies.

In addition to the offspring of the gods, whom we have called genies, the Babylonian felt himself surrounded by ghosts, or spirits of men whose lives had proved unhappy on earth. The ghosts had been cheated out of happiness in this life. Some of them had died violent deaths. All experienced what we term frustration. Nursing their grief, they were determined to torment the living.

69

The Babylonian Priesthood

In ancient Babylon the king served as both High Priest and civil ruler. He performed sacrifices and determined the religious life of his subjects. Since the king could not personally officiate in each of the temples in his realm, he appointed substitute priests to perform the routine priestly labors. Each temple would have a high priest, appointed by the king, and a number of lesser priests, known as *shangu,* who were also responsible to the king. The temple affairs were administered by these men who were chosen because of their fitness for the work.

There were other priestly functions of a specialized nature which presupposed specific training. The task of divination, the interpreting of dreams, and otherwise determining the will of the gods, was entrusted to the *buru* priests. The interpretation of oracles and dreams was on the basis of a long tradition of divination which the *buru* priest was expected to master. Hepatoscopy, or divination by the liver, was an ancient method of divination used by Hittites and Etruscans as well as by the Babylonians. The liver was regarded as the seat of the mental life. At the time of sacrifice, a god was thought to take hold of the victim, and the god's thoughts were presumed to enter the animal's liver. After a kid or sheep was slaughtered sacrificially, the victim's body was opened and preliminary conclusions drawn. Then the liver was removed and subjected to careful examination. Actual livers were compared with terra-cotta models and abnormalities were noted. We do not know how various configurations were interpreted but we know that ancient kings and their officers had a high regard for divination by the liver.[1]

Hittites and Etruscans, in common with Babylonians, also studied the flight patterns of birds as a means of divination. We

---

1. Divination by liver was one means used by Nebuchadnezzar in determining whether to attack Jerusalem or Rabbath Ammon (Ezek. 21:18-23).

do not know exactly what they looked for, but diviners skilled in this type of divination regularly accompanied the armies of Babylon.

Babylon was noted for its astrology, but this differed in important particulars from the astrology which developed in medieval times, based on Greek antecedents. Babylonian astrologers noted the direction of the winds, the color of the stars, and the occultation of planets and eclipses. The information provided by Babylonian astrologers was used in agriculture as well as in matters of national policy.[2]

The Babylonian priests were constantly on the lookout for the abnormal. Any unusual circumstance attending a birth, human or animal, would be considered a sign which needed interpretation. If an exorcist were called to the home of an invalid, everything which he encountered along the way would be considered significant. If water were spilled on the road, its pattern might contain a message. The shape of oil which had formed on the surface of water would be duly noted. If an animal or plant were encountered, its significance would require interpretation.

To the Babylonian with his world of gods and demons it was particularly important to have means of frustrating the forces of evil. A class of priests known as *ashipu* specialized in counteracting the work of demons. A formula used in one of their spells runs:

> Thou art not to come near to my body,
> Thou art not to go before me,
> Thou art not to follow after me,
> Where I stop thou art not to stop,
> Where I am thou art not to sit,
> My house thou art not to enter,
> My roof thou art not to haunt,
> Thou art not to put thy foot in my foot's imprint,
> Where I go thou art not to go,
> Where I enter thou art not to enter.[3]

The purpose of the *ashipu* was always benevolent. He sought to help the sufferer who was physically ill, and in this sense his work anticipates the physician. All sickness was associated with sin in Babylonian thought, so the *ashipu* sought to discover what sin had been committed by his "patient." A list of possible sins would be read with the thought that one of them might have been committed unconsciously. Only when the proper sin had been identified could the *ashipu* overcome the demon that had controlled the individual.

---

2. See p. 69.
3. G. Contenau, *La magie chez les Assyriens et les Babyloniens*, p. 147.

Sometimes demons were induced to leave their victims on the basis of a promise that the *ashipu* would give. A substitute habitation (such as a pig) was sometimes offered. At other times the demon might be bribed with a list of gifts that would be his as a reward for leaving his victim.

Another technique was to drive the demon from his victim. This might be done by preparing medicines of nauseous and putrid substances which the victim was required to eat. Presumably, if they were vile enough, the demon himself would not wish to remain. Eventually, by the process of trial and error, some substances were employed which had genuine medicinal value. Thus medicine, although mixed with magic, became a genuine science.

Sometimes demons could be fooled. One recognized means of doing this was by placing an animal on top of a sick man. By following a prescribed ritual, the demon might be persuaded to enter the animal instead of the human. One such prescription reads:

> Take a sucking-pig and set it level with the head of the sick man. Take out its heart and put it over the sick man's heart. Sprinkle the sides of the bed with its blood. Dismember the sucking-pig and lay the parts on the sick man's members. Then purify this man with pure water... Offer the sucking-pig in his place. Let its flesh be as the flesh of the sick man, his blood as the blood of the sick man.[4]

The *ashipu* priest was clothed in red when performing his functions. Red was deemed particularly potent in warding off evil spirits. He might also be dressed in a fish-like skin to emphasize his relationship to the wise god, Ea. Traditional formulae were uttered verbatim. The priest would call upon the demon by name, demanding that he cease tormenting his victim and depart. Calling upon the good gods to aid the sufferer, the *ashipu* priest would exorcise the demon.

Another specialized functionary was the chanter who, by his songs, was supposed to "soften the heart of the gods." Prayers were intoned by the chanters, who were accompanied by large drums or lyres. The lyre was usually decorated with a bull's head, and the tone itself was likened to the bellowing of a bull. Of the ancient Babylonian chants which we possess, fifty-seven require the accompaniment of a drum, forty require a flute, and forty-seven involve the "lifting of hands" in the attitude of prayer.

The Book of Daniel gives us a Biblical picture of the Babylonian priests and wise men at work. Diviners claimed to have existed as a separate order from remote antiquity, and it was required that they be physically sound. Daniel and his companions are

---

4. G. Contenau, *op. cit.*, p. 225.

described as "children in whom was no blemish" (Dan. 1:4). The Babylonian texts insist: "the diviner whose father is impure and who himself has any imperfection of limb or countenance, whose eyes are not sound, who has any teeth missing, who has lost a finger, whose countenance has a sickly look or who is pimpled, cannot be the keeper of the decrees of Shamash and Adad."[5]

Those who purposed to be Babylonian diviners were required to take a long course of study before they could serve at the Babylonian court. The Hebrew captives were subjected to a three year training program in "the learning and the tongue of the Chaldeans" (Dan. 1:4-5) after which they were given court appointments. It is evident that Babylonians were receiving the same schooling, for we are told that Daniel and his friends were "ten times better than all the magicians and astrologers" (Dan. 1:20). When the wise men of Babylon were unable to interpret the dream of Nebuchadnezzar we are told that Daniel did so, after which the king placed him "over all the wise men of Babylon" (Dan. 2:48).

The Book of Daniel makes it clear that diviners were expected to be able to interpret anything, and that they formed an important element in the king's court. The godly Daniel, however, humbly trusting his God, showed Nebuchadnezzar that the magic and sorcery of Babylon could not be trusted to meet the basic problems of men or nations.

---

5. G. Contenau, *Everyday Life in Babylon and Assyria*, p. 281.

70

Babylon's Last Kings

The Babylonian Empire reached its zenith under Nebuchadnezzar and, twenty-three years after his death, its capital city fell before Cyrus of Anshan, the founder of the Persian Empire. Three rather unpretentious and largely ineffective rulers governed Babylon during that scant quarter century.

1. Amel Marduk (562-560 B.C.)

At the death of Nebuchadnezzar his throne was taken at once by Amel Marduk, the Evil-merodach ("man of Marduk") of Scripture. He is known to Bible students as the kindly Babylonian ruler who released Jehoiachin from prison during the thirty-seventh year after his captivity and provided him with suitable garments and meals — appropriate for his royal station (II Kings 25:27-30). Berossus, however, describes Amel Marduk as a tyrannical ruler who despised the laws of his people.[1] It may be that his attitude toward Jehoiachin and other captives proved offensive to Babylonian rulers who felt that he had set aside the policies of Nebuchadnezzar in favor of an independent course of action. In any event, he was assassinated during the second year of his reign by his sister's husband, Neriglissar, who usurped the throne.

The French archaeologist, De Morgan, while excavating Susa, in Persia, discovered a vase which had been taken from Babylon to Persia in ancient times. It bore an inscription which read, "Palace of Amel-Marduk, King of Babylon, son of Nebuchadnezzar, King of Babylon."[2]

---

1. Berossus, Frag. 14, in C. Müller, *Fragmenta Historicorum Graecorum*, II p. 507.
2. George A. Barton, *Archaeology and the Bible*, p. 479.

2. Neriglissar (Nergal-shar-usur) (560-556 B.C.)

It is probable that Neriglissar was a leading prince in the Babylonian court long before he seized the throne. A man of that name entered Jerusalem with the armies of Nebuchadnezzar and held the post of Rab-mag with the occupying armies (Jer. 39:3). The meaning of Rab-mag (Akkadian *rab-mugi*) is uncertain but it designates a high political office. Nergal-shar-usur was one of "the princes of the king of Babylon" and he sat "in the middle gate" of Jerusalem, which evidently served as the center of government for the Babylonians before they destroyed the city. Nergal-shar-usur as Rab-mag was a member of the delegation assigned to release Jeremiah from prison and entrust him into the friendly hands of Gedaliah (Jer. 39:11-14). He had married a daughter of Nebuchadnezzar and, for that reason, considered himself a legitimate successor to his throne.

Neriglissar took pride in the adornment of Babylon and the beautifying of its temples. As a practical consideration he regulated the course of the canal upon which the city of Babylon was built. This was a channel of the Euphrates, but it was altered to permit it to pass by the E-sag-ila temple. The eastern arm of the canal was walled up so that its current might flow with sweet water, unmixed with sand.

Neriglissar also repaired his palace, which had earlier been the residence of Nebuchadnezzar. Its foundations were strengthened and a lofty summit was added to the structure, made of brick, the usual building material of Mesopotamia, and expensive cedar beams imported from Lebanon.

We know of no wars during the reign of Neriglissar. The Empire was preserved intact and the four years of his reign appear to have been prosperous ones. He died a natural death, albeit in the very prime of life. His son, Labashi-Marduk was named his successor, but after a reign of but nine months he was murdered and a successor, satisfactory to the priestly party, was chosen to serve as king.

3. Nabonidus (Nabu-na'id) (556-539 B.C.)

After the murder of Labashi-Marduk, the priestly party in Babylon chose as king Nabonidus, the son of Nabu-balatsu-iqbi, a man who had distinguished himself both in the affairs of state and church. His chief energies seem to have been extended in building and restoring temples.

Nabonidus was thorough in his work. In rebuilding a temple he was not content merely to level off the ground and make a fresh beginning. Nabonidus searched diligently until he found the original foundation stone. Then he could read the name of the king who first ordered the construction of the temple. In this way both a religious and an antiquarian interest were served, for Nabonidus could have his royal scribes determine the number of years which had passed since the temple foundations were first laid. Such lists are invaluable to students of ancient Near Eastern history. A daughter of Nabonidus is said to have maintained a small museum of archaeological finds. Another, Bel-shalti-nannar, served as a priestess in the famed temple to the moon god at Ur which her father had restored.

In building inscriptions left by Nabonidus he designates himself as "Preserver of E-sag-ila and E-zida" the great shrines of the city of Babylon. Actually the chief interest of Nabonidus was not in these shrines and he incurred the anger of his priests for neglecting the annual visit to the E-sag-ila shrine which every Babylonian king was expected to make on the New Year's Day.

Year after year he remained at Tema, according to the Nabunaid Chronicle. The records bear the disquieting note, "The king did not come to Babylon for the ceremonies of the month Nisanu, Nabu did not come to Babylon, Bel did not go out from E-sag-ila in procession, the festival of the New Year was omitted." The Babylonian priests considered Nabonidus guilty of sacrilege in failing to take the hand of Marduk at the New Year's festival. This rite was thought to convey ceremonially the right to rule for the ensuing year.

While neglecting the shrines of Babylon, Nabonidus found satisfaction in such activities as the rebuilding of the temple to the sun god at ancient Sippar. Nebuchadnezzar had rebuilt this structure forty-five years earlier, but it had already fallen into disrepair. After providing temporary quarters for Shamash, the sun god, Nabonidus ordered the temple razed. Then he searched for the original foundation which was far below the surface of the ground. It had been laid by Naram-Sin, a king of the Akkad Dynasty (ca. 2360-2180 B.C.), who had ruled seventeen hundred years before Nabonidus!

Nabonidus was delighted with the find, asserting that Shamash himself had shown the foundation stone to him. On the exact site of the old sanctuary, Nabonidus built the new temple, E-babbara. He spared no expense. Five thousand cedar beams were imported for its roof, and more of the wood was required for its great doors. When completed, Nabonidus conducted the god Shamash into his new temple with prayers that the god might honor and protect the king who had provided this new temple for him.

Another shrine at Sippar, E-ulmash, the temple of Anunitum, was rebuilt by Nabonidus at about the same time as the E-babbara. Even more ambitious was his concern for E-khulkhul, the shrine of Sin, the moon god, at the ancient city of Haran in northern Mesopotamia. Haran had been devoted to the same god as the city of Ur, in southern Mesopotamia, and the patriarchal family sojourned there en route to Canaan.

During the first year of his reign, Nabonidus dreamed a dream in which he received a command: "Nabonidus, king of Babylon, on thy cart-horses bring bricks, build E-khulkhul, and let Sin, the great lord, take up his residence within it."[3] Nabonidus objected that the temple was surrounded by the Manda, a generic term for the northern barbarians. It may refer here either to Medes or Scythians. The oracle assured Nabonidus that the Manda were no longer in the vicinity of Haran, and that it would therefore be safe for Nabonidus to enter the city. This episode tells a great deal about the character of Nabonidus. One of the Assyrian rulers would have marched his armies against the Manda and stormed their city. Nabonidus, however, was strictly a man of peaceful pursuits.

Men and materials were gathered from the entire Babylonian Empire. Great new walls, which Nabonidus assures us were stronger than the earlier ones, soon arose. Again, as for the temple for Shamash, cedar was used for the roof and the doors. Sin and his companions (the lesser gods) were escorted into the new temple amidst pomp and splendor.

The religious and antiquarian interests of Nabonidus might have appeared innocent enough had he given due attention to the affairs of state, but this was his prime weakness. He chose to live at Tema, an oasis in the Hejaz region of Arabia. Recognizing the need of someone to care for the more prosaic affairs of state, he appointed his son Belshazzar (Bel-shar-usur) as co-regent.

The Verse Account of Nabonidus tells of his expedition to Tema:

> He entrusted the "Camp" to his oldest son, the first-born
> The troops everywhere in the country he ordered under his
>   command.

---

3. T. Fish, "Texts Relating to Nabonidus," in D. Winston Thomas, *Documents from Old Testament Times*, p. 89.

He let everything go, entrusted the kingship to him
And, himself, he started out for a long journey,
The military forces of Akkad marching with him;
He turned toward Tema, deep in the west.
He started out the expedition on a path leading to a
    distant region. When he arrived there,
He killed in battle the prince of Tema,
Slaughtered the flocks of those who dwell in the city
    as well as in the countryside
And he, himself, took his residence in Tema, the forces
    of Akkad were also stationed there.
He made the town beautiful, built there his palace
Like the palace in Babylon, he also built walls
For the fortifications of the town and...
He surrounded the town with sentinels 4

Among the Qumran discoveries is a document known as the Prayer of Nabonidus which was published in 1956 by J. T. Milik.[5] The document begins: "The words of the prayer which Nabonidus, king of Assyria and Babylon, the great king, prayed . . . ." It tells how Nabonidus came down with a "dread disease by the decree of the Most High God." Therefore he was "set apart from men" for seven years in the Arabian Oasis of Tema. An unnamed Jewish diviner appeared to remind the king of his idolatry in worshiping "gods of gold, bronze, iron, wood, stone, silver . . . ."

This episode is reminiscent of the account of the humbling of Nebuchadnezzar in Daniel 4. Nebuchadnezzar, while boasting about his accomplishments as king in Babylon, was stricken by a divine judgment and became insane. He lived like an animal until seven "times" (probably years) had passed, after which he acknowledged the sovereignty of the Most High and was restored to his throne. It is the view of some scholars that the events described in Daniel 4 actually took place during the lifetime of Nabonidus and that a scribal error associated them with the more familiar name of Nebuchadnezzar.[6]

4. Belshazzar

Belshazzar was co-regent with Nabonidus from the third year

---

4. A. Leo Oppenheim, "Babylonian and Assyrian Historical Texts," in James Pritchard, *Ancient Near Eastern Texts*, pp. 313-314.
5. "Priere de Nabonide' et autres ecrits d'un cycle de Daniel," *Revue Biblique* 63 (1956), pp. 407-15.
6. The suggestion of a copyist's error is given in the *Catholic Biblical Encyclopedia* (Edited by John E. Steinmueller and Kathryn Sullivan), p. 145. Others suggest that the tradition associated with the name of Nabonidus was erroneously ascribed to Nebuchadnezzar. See: David Noel Freedman, "The Prayer of Nabonidus," *Bulletin of the American Schools of Oriental Research*, No. 145 (1957), pp. 31-32.

The ruins of Babylon were covered for centuries by soil and debris. The spade of the archaeologist now makes it possible for us to trace the buildings and thoroughfares which once were the pride of Nebuchadnezzar.

of his reign. Nabonidus never abdicated his throne, but for all practical purposes Belshazzar served as king. In the cuneiform documents Belshazzar is consistently called "the son of the king." Texts from the fifth to the thirteenth years of the reign of Nabonidus speak of offerings of silver, gold, and sacrificial animals which Belshazzar made to Babylonian temples.

Belshazzar did not make a strong ruler. He is best known for his impious feast, described in the fifth chapter of the Book of Daniel, which was going on while the Persian armies were approaching Babylon. Belshazzar was in Babylon when it fell to the armies of Cyrus. Although the city fell without a battle, Belshazzar himself was slain.

71

Daniel of Babylon

Daniel was a young man of noble descent and high physical and intellectual endowments when Jehoiakim came to the throne of Judah. He was probably born during the reign of Josiah, and his home appears to have been one in which the Law of the Lord was honored. During the years when idolatry ran rampant, following Josiah's death, Daniel was to form the attitudes of faithfulness to his God which would help him to meet the later temptations of idolatrous Babylon. In Daniel's youth he learned of the fall of Nineveh, a fact which changed the course of history and made the Babylonians the new masters of western Asia.

The Book of Daniel tells us that Nebuchadnezzar of Babylon besieged Jerusalem during the third year of Jehoiakim's reign. The siege was successful, and Jehoiakim gave the Babylonian king temple treasures which were taken to Babylon. More important, however, was the fact that Nebuchadnezzar ordered that a number of young men of good families who were physically strong and intellectually of high calibre, be transported to Babylon where they might serve him in an official capacity. This was an act of wisdom on Nebuchadnezzar's part. Taking the best youths of Jerusalem would weaken the state of Judah, and thus reduce its potential for rebellion. If he could win the loyalty of these young men, Babylon itself would be the stronger for their presence.

The treatment accorded Daniel and his companions who were taken to Babylon at Nebuchadnezzar's command, is comparable to modern techniques of "brain washing." These lads were not subjected to torture. They were, instead, given every encouragement to forget past loyalties and become well integrated Babylonians.

The names which the Judaean lads bore were indicative of their Jewish origin. Daniel means, "God is my judge." His three companions bore names meaning, "Yahweh is gracious," (Hananiah) ; "Who is what God is?" (Mishael), and "Yahweh has helped" (Azariah). In each instance the Babylonian substitute name removed the reference to Israel's God —El (Elohim), or Yahweh (Dan. 1:7).

Daniel became Belteshazzar, a name which appears in Babylonian documents as Balatsu-usur ("Protect his life!"). Hananiah became Shadrach (perhaps Shadur-Aku, "the command of Aku" a name for the Babylonian moon god). Shadrach may be an intentional corruption of the name of Marduk, the chief god of Babylon. Mishael's Babylonian name, Meshach, seems to correspond to his Hebrew name. Babylonian Meshach may mean "Who is what Aku is?" although scholars are not certain of its derivation. Azariah's Babylonian name, Abed-nego, however, follows a common pattern in Semitic languages. A man is considered to be a servant of his god, hence the term "servant" is common in Semitic names. Abed-nego means "servant of Nego," a corruption of "servant of Nebo," the popular Babylonian god whose name appears in that of the king Nebuchadnezzar (Babylonian, Nabu-kudurru-usur, "Nabu, establish the boundary!"). The Scriptures contain several names which are compounds of *abed*: Obadiah "Servant of Yahweh," and Ebed-melech, "Servant of (the god) Melech." The term "servant" or "slave" speaks of one who is a worshiper of his deity. The common Moslem name Abdullah ("slave [or worshiper] of Allah") is based on the same pattern.

The assigning of new names to people who enter new cultural (and, particularly, political) situations was relatively common in the ancient world. Joseph, in Egypt, was assigned the name Zaphnath-paaneah (Gen. 41:45). Other Jews in Babylon bore such distinctly pagan names as Zer-Babili (Zerubbabel), "the seed of Babylon," and Marduka (Mordecai), the name of the god of Babylon. It is significant that the Hebrew youths did not make an issue of the change in name imposed upon them. Usually, however, the Book of Daniel refers to them by their Jewish names.

An important element in the preparation of the youths for service to Babylon was the training program in which they were enrolled. At the time of choosing suitable youths for Nebuchadnezzar's purposes it was determined that they must be "skilful in all wisdom, endowed with knowledge, understanding, learning." It was the king's purpose "to teach them the letters and language of the Chaldeans" (Dan. 1:4).

Preliminary to studying the religion, science, and cultural traditions of the Babylonian people, Daniel and his companions had to learn to read and write the language which we now term Akkadian. This was written in cuneiform characters impressed on clay tablets. These hundreds of signs, in part pictographs and in part syllables, had been in use since Sumerian times.[1]

A third part of the acculturation of the Hebrew youths was in the matter of diet, for: "the king assigned them a daily portion of the rich food which the king ate, and of the wine which he drank" (Dan. 1:5). From the Babylonian viewpoint this was a gracious act. Captive youths had come from many places, and the living standards of most would be far inferior to that of Babylon. They should be grateful for such treatment as the king now provided. They would enjoy meals truly "fit for a king."

Yet, strange as it may seem to us, it is precisely here that Daniel and his companions drew the line. The names and the schooling were accepted in good grace, but "Daniel resolved that he would not defile himself" (Dan. 1:8) in the matter of eating the king's food. The Law of Moses contained explicit commands concerning clean and unclean foods, and Daniel knew that the Babylonian kitchens cared nothing for the Levitical regulations. The gods of Babylon would be invoked at these Babylonian festivities, and Daniel could not conscientiously take part in them.

The manner in which Daniel sought release from the obligation to eat the royal meals explains in part his effectiveness in a heathen court. Daniel quietly approached the steward who was responsible for the care of the lads. He suggested a ten day testing period during which a vegetable diet might be eaten and water drunk (Dan. 1:11-13). The four youths would then be examined by the steward who could determine for himself if they were physically weaker than those who ate the royal dainties. When the time came, Daniel and his friends were found to be "better in appearance and fatter in flesh" than those who had eaten the meals provided by the king (Dan. 1:15).) The steward being convinced that it was safe to permit the Hebrew lads to continue their vegetable diet, the pressure to conform was relieved. During the three year training period the young men were not molested again.

When Nebuchadnezzar dreamed, and forgot his dream, none of the wise men of Babylon could help him (Dan. 2:1-11). It was Daniel who, under God, was able to tell Nebuchadnezzar

1. See Chapter 67.

both the dream and its interpretation (Dan. 2:12-45). Nebuchadnezzar had seen a large image, the parts of which were made of different metals: "The head of this image was of fine gold, its breast and arms of silver, its belly and thighs of bronze, its legs of iron, its feet partly of iron and partly of clay" (Dan. 2:32-33). A stone struck the top-heavy image, totally destroying it. The stone, however, grew until it filled the whole earth.

In interpreting the dream, Daniel told the king that the image represented a series of world powers. The head of gold represented Nebuchadnezzar and his Babylonian kingdom. Babylon would be succeeded by three kings, becoming successively inferior. At the close of this period of world empire, "the God of heaven will set up a kingdom which shall never be destroyed, nor shall its sovereignty be left to another people" (Dan. 2:44). Daniel clearly asserts that God is to have the last word on the human scene, and that Nebuchadnezzar and all that should follow him indulged in a transient glory.

The king recognized his dream, and honored Daniel for his ability in interpreting it. Daniel was made governor of the province of Babylon and chief prefect over the wise men of the land. He occupied a place at the royal court (Dan. 2:48-49). The king also honored Daniel's God, recognizing that He had enabled Daniel to become the interpreter of the dream (Dan. 2:46-47).

Nebuchadnezzar saw in a second dream a great tree which reached to heaven. The tree was then cut down with only its stump remaining. This was bound with a band of iron and left with the grass of the field. A second time Daniel was able to interpret the king's dream. The great tree was Nebuchadnezzar himself. As the tree was cut down, so Daniel assured the king that he would be humbled. Daniel predicted that Nebuchadnezzar would become insane and live like the beasts of the field until he would give due glory to God (Dan. 4:1-27). A year later, as Nebuchadnezzar was boasting about his accomplishments,[2] Daniel's interpretation of the dream proved correct. Nebuchadnezzar "ate grass like an ox, and his body was wet with the dew of heaven till his hair grew as long as eagles' feathers, and his nails were like birds' claws" (Dan. 4:33). His insanity continued until he ascribed glory to the Most High (Dan. 4:34-35). Then his reason returned and he honored the God of Daniel as King of Heaven (Dan. 4:37).

2. See Chapter 64; Daniel 4:30.

We read no more of Daniel until the reign of Belshazzar.[3] As the Persians were marching upon Babylon, Belshazzar prepared a great feast for his loyal courtiers. In his impiety, the king drank wine from the very vessels which had once been used in the Temple at Jerusalem (Dan. 5:3). Suddenly God spoke in judgment. The fingers of a hand were visible at the wall of the chamber. They wrote an inscription on the plaster and Belshazzar was terrified. As in the days of Nebuchadnezzar, the wise men of the realm were called in but they were unable to decipher the strange writing. Remembering that Daniel had shown supernatural wisdom in the days of Nebuchadnezzar, the queen suggested that he be asked to read and interpret the mysterious writing. Daniel, spurning any idea of reward, reminded Belshazzar of the way in which Nebuchadnezzar had been humbled by God (Dan. 5:17-21). Belshazzar had not profited by his knowledge of God's dealings with Nebuchadnezzar, but instead had defied the Lord (Dan. 5:22-23).

Daniel read the words on the palace wall: Mene, Mene, Tekel, and Parsin. These words could represent Babylonian weights — "a mana, a mana, a shekel, and a half-shekel." They also could be interpreted as verbs — "numbered, numbered, weighed, and divided." It was in the latter sense that Daniel interpreted the words. The days of Belshazzar's kingdom were *numbered*. He was *weighed* in the balances and found wanting. His kingdom was *divided* and given to the Medes and Persians (Dan. 5:25-28). The word "Peres" (singular of *parsin*) would also bring to mind the Persians whose kingdom would supplant that of the Babylonians.

On that very night the Persian armies entered the city of Babylon. Belshazzar was slain and the Neo-Babylonian Empire was at an end. The city of Babylon was not destroyed, however. Cyrus was soon to enter the city and be proclaimed as its deliverer from the misrule of Nabonidus and Belshazzar.[4]

Daniel was not a minister to the people, as was Ezekiel, but he did represent the claims of Israel's God before the Babylonian court. His efficient service and his pious example proved an effective testimony. The Persian conquerers preserved much of the governmental structure of their predecessors, and Daniel appears to have continued his official tasks (Dan. 6:1-4). The other officials grew jealous of the power vested in Daniel and determined

---

3. See pp. 458-459.
4. See p. 473.

to get rid of him. They knew that he was faithful in his official functions, so they contrived a plot to have him killed on religious grounds. They appealed to the Persian ruler, Darius[5] suggesting that he issue an edict forbidding prayers to any but the king for a thirty day period (Dan. 6:6-9). Any who would presume to disobey would be cast into a den of lions.

As they expected, Daniel paid no attention to the edict. Regularly, three times a day, he turned toward Jerusalem in prayer (Dan. 6:10). Darius was unhappy at the thought of casting his faithful courtier to the lions, but the edict could not be changed (Dan. 6:14). Daniel did not flinch. He was cast to the lions, but Darius seems to have spent more of a restless night than he (Dan. 6:18). God protected his faithful servant and, the next morning, his accusers were cast to the lions (Dan. 6:19-24). Darius, like Nebuchadnezzar, honored the God of Daniel (Dan. 6:25-28).

We know nothing about the close of Daniel's life. He lived through the entire period of the Exile and, while he did not return to Jerusalem, it was uppermost in his thoughts. He studied the prophecies of Jeremiah (Dan. 9:2) and prayed that God might restore the people to their city: "O my God, incline thy ear and hear; open thy eyes and behold our desolations, and the city which is called by thy name; for we do not present our supplications before thee on the ground of our righteousness, but on the ground of thy great mercy. O Lord, hear; O Lord, forgive, give heed and act; delay not, for thy own sake, O my God, because thy city and thy people are called by thy name" (Dan. 9:18-19).

---

5. The identity of "Darius the Mede" is a vexing historical problem. See John C. Whitcomb, *Darius the Mede,* for a proposed solution.

72

Ezekiel and the Exiles

The great prophetic figure in Babylon during the Exile was Ezekiel, the son of Buzi, a priest who had been deported at the time of Jehoiachin's captivity, eleven years before the destruction of Jerusalem (II Kings 24:12-15). Ezekiel prophesied in Babylon during the years when Jeremiah was uttering God's message to Judah in Jerusalem. The two prophets declared essentially the same truths, but their backgrounds as well as their environment give each a peculiar cast.

As a young man, Ezekiel may have actually ministered in the Jerusalem Temple. He certainly mastered both the ritual and moral law of Israel, and was thoroughly familiar with all of the priestly duties of his office. As a student of Torah, the "Law" or "instruction" in the widest sense, Ezekiel also came to know the history of his people. He studied about the call of the patriarchs, the deliverance from Egypt, the giving of the Law through Moses and the establishment of Israel in Canaan as evidence of the mighty power of God on behalf of His people. Ezekiel was certainly conscious of the many apostasies of Israel, and of the great prophets — men such as Elijah — raised up of God to call His people back from their evil ways. Ezekiel probably had a first-hand knowledge of the teaching of Jeremiah, his older contemporary. He was sympathetic with the great revival under King Josiah, with its implications for his priestly ministry. Ezekiel, like Jeremiah, mourned because of the idolatry of Israel as it was ripe for exile.

Ezekiel's training and priestly service came to an end in 597 B.C. when he was taken to Babylon along with many other talented youths from Judah. Scripture gives us no hint of his age at the time of the exile, Josephus[1] says that he was a boy, but this

---

1. Josephus, *Antiquities,* X, vii, 3.

is probably a guess. He may have been thirty years of age at the time, or even older. Neither the record in II Kings 24:10-16 nor the Book of Ezekiel mentions priests among those deported with Jehoiachin. Ezekiel was probably taken because of his high reputation among the priests. He must have impressed his contemporaries as a man of uncommon ability, and it was that type of individual that Nebuchadnezzar took into exile.

In Babylon, Ezekiel settled with his fellow countrymen in a community named Tel-abib along the River Chebar, a short distance southeast of Babylon. From an incidental allusion (Ezek. 8:1) we learn that he was married and had a house of his own. His wife was suddenly taken from him (Ezek. 24:18). Since she is termed the delight of his eyes (Ezek. 24:16) we may assume that his marriage was a happy one and that the death of his wife brought genuine grief to the prophet. He used the occasion to warn his countrymen that God was about to bring judgment upon their Temple and their loved ones.

Five years after his deportation, Ezekiel saw a remarkable vision of the glory of the Lord (Ezek. 1), after which he received a commission to bring God's Word to the rebellious house of Israel (Ezek. 2). He ate the scroll which was offered to him, and found it sweet (Ezek. 3:1-3). Led by the Spirit, he went to Tel-abib where he remained in silence for seven days (Ezek. 3:12-15). Reminded that he was responsible to God as a watchman of His people (Ezek. 3:16-21), he there began his active ministry.

Ezekiel was directed to draw the city plan of Jerusalem on a brick[2] and make an iron plate to serve as its wall. This mock city was to be besieged in a realistic way. Ezekiel was told to build a tower, throw up a mound, establish camps, and set battering rams around it (Ezek. 4:1-3). Then the prophet was instructed to lie on his left side for three hundred and ninety days to symbolically bear the punishment of the house of Israel, and forty days to bear Judah's punishment (Ezek. 4:4-8). Each day was to represent a year of punishment for Israel and Judah because of their sin. Food and water were to be measured as a reminder that siege conditions would prevail in Jerusalem (Ezek. 4:9-17).

The prophet was next instructed to shave his head and beard and weigh the hair in a balance. A third he burned in the city; a third he struck with the sword outside the city walls; and a third he scattered to the winds. A remnant he bound in his garment,

---

2. This would be a clay tablet such as was used for writing. A map of the world as known to the ancient Babylonians appears on such a tablet.

Interior view of the Golden Gate at Jerusalem.

only to throw part into the fire. This symbolic act portrayed the future of Jerusalem: "A third part of you shall die of pestilence and be consumed with famine in the midst of you; a third part shall fall by the sword round about you; and a third part I will scatter to all the winds and will unsheathe the sword after them" (Ezek. 5:12).

The following year Ezekiel was taken in spirit to Jerusalem where, at the north gate of the inner Temple court, he was shown the "image of jealousy" which provoked the wrath of God (Ezek. 8:1-6). It derived its name from the fact that it served as a challenge to the rights of the Lord over his people. In the Law, Israel's God declared Himself to be "a jealous God" (Exod. 20:5), and insisted that no image of any kind should receive worship. God said to Ezekiel, " 'Son of man, lift up your eyes now in the direction of the north'. So I lifted up my eyes toward the north, and behold, north of this altar gate, in the entrance, was this image of jealousy. And he said to me, 'Son of man, do you see what they are doing, the great abominations that the house of Israel are committing here to drive me far from my sanctuary?' " (Ezek. 8:5-6). God did not wish to leave His people. He was being driven away!

Ezekiel was next taken to the Temple wall and ordered to dig. He found a hidden door which opened into a secret room, the walls of which were decorated with serpents and wild beasts (Ezek. 8:7-10). The description is reminiscent of the walls along the famed Procession Way in the city of Babylon, adorned with lions, bulls, and dragons.[3] Seventy elders were inside the room burning incense in an idolatrous ritual (Ezek 8:11-13).

At the north gate of the Temple, Ezekiel saw more evidence of idolatry. The women were weeping for Tammuz,[4] the Babylonian vegetation deity whose death was mourned each year by his worshipers (Ezek. 8:14-15). The worst scandal of all was at the Temple entrance. There Ezekiel saw about twenty-five Jerusalemites with their backs to the Temple, facing eastward as they adored the sun god[5] (Ezek. 8:16).

In Ezekiel's vision he saw swift judgment fall on the idolatrous city. God said, " . . . I will deal in wrath; my eye will not spare nor will I have pity; and though they cry in my ears with a loud voice, I will not hear them" (Ezek. 8:18). Six executioners were

3. See p. 430.
4. See p. 448.
5. See p. 446.

dispatched into the city. Those who shared Ezekiel's sorrow over the abominations of Jerusalem were given a special mark (Ezek. 9:4). All the others were slain (Ezek. 9:5-6). Finally, burning coals were scattered over the doomed city (Ezek. 10:1-2).

Prophets and psalmists had long encouraged Israel to trust in the God who is an ever present help. Ezekiel dared to say that God would forsake Zion. In graphic language he told how God would leave the Holy City. He described the departure of the Shekinah glory cloud from the Holy of Holies in the Temple: "And the glory of the Lord went up from the cherubim to the threshold of the house; and the house was filled with the cloud, and the court was full of the brightness of the glory of the Lord" (Ezek. 10:4). God seemed to be reluctant to leave. He tarried over the threshold as if to give the people an opportunity to turn from their idols and live. Yet they did nothing to keep the "glory" with them. From the threshold, cherubim lifted the glory cloud to "the door of the east gate of the house of the Lord" (Ezek. 10:18-19). Finally, "the glory of the Lord went up from the midst of the city, and stood upon the mountain which is on the east side of the city" (Ezek. 11:23). The glory had left the Holy City! It was hovering over the Mount of Olives as though still reluctant to depart.

The departure of the divine glory symbolized the departure of God. The false prophets were right in insisting that the heathen could never take Jerusalem because God dwelt in the Temple there. They were wrong in assuming that God would continue to make His abode in the midst of a rebellious and idolatrous people. When, six centuries later, another generation was to reject the glory of God in the Person of Jesus Christ, He uttered the fateful words, "Your house is left unto you, desolate" (Matt. 23:38). The Temple, without its God, is simply a house, and God was in no way constrained to preserve its barren walls from the enemy's ax.

By another symbol, Ezekiel translated the message of the departing glory to his people. The prophet dug through the mud brick wall of his house and brought out his personal property, covering his head as he went so he could not see the ground. So, Ezekiel intimated, the king of Judah would come as a captive to Babylon, but he would not be able to see the land (Ezek. 12:1-13).

Such predictions would hardly make Ezekiel a popular man. Although not subjected to the persecution which Jeremiah endured, Ezekiel, like his counterpart in Jerusalem, found his message opposed by the leaders of the community. Some may have admired Ezekiel's oratory, but few paid serious attention to his utterances. Like Jeremiah, Ezekiel was frequently opposed by false prophets who made optimistic predictions of a quick return from exile and the re-establishment of the Davidic throne in the person of Jehoiachin (Ezek. 13:1-10). From time to time the "elders of Judah" consulted Ezekiel, and his selfless identification with the people must have won him the respect of the spiritually discerning members of the community.

Following the destruction of Jerusalem (587 B.C.) we note a marked difference in Ezekiel's ministry. Before Jerusalem fell he could be characterized as the prophet of doom, categorically stating that the Holy City would be forsaken by God and destroyed by Nebuchadnezzar. Afterward, however, he emphasized the hope of a restored Jerusalem, with a restored Temple in which sacrifices would again be offered. It is in the closing chapters of his book that we note Ezekiel's priestly interest in the minutia of Temple worship.

During the latter period of his ministry, Ezekiel was probably given a more sympathetic hearing. His dire predictions had proved correct, and those who had entertained false hopes were now humbled. The fresh influx of exiles brought to Babylon following the destruction of Jerusalem probably included some who had been sympathetic with Jeremiah. They would be expected to rally around Ezekiel as a prophet in the same tradition as their former leader.

Ezekiel has been termed the architect of the restoration. The last eight chapters of his book describe the New Jerusalem of the restoration, the city which shall bear the name "The Lord is There" (Ezek. 48:35). From below the threshold of the Temple, Ezekiel sees waters gushing forth to bring refreshment to the entire land (Ezek. 47:1). Along the banks of the rivers he sees trees bearing fruit for food and leaves for healing (Ezek. 47:12).

The book of Ezekiel is difficult to fathom because of its rich imagery, some of which escapes us because of our removal in time and space from the world in which Ezekiel lived. Like Jeremiah, Ezekiel saw Babylon as the rod in God's hand to chasten rebellious Israel. He used all that he observed in drawing lessons for his people. The winged creatures of Babylonian art (Ezek. 1:8) formed the basis of his vision of the great chariot. Perhaps his knowledge of Babylonian temples as well as his recollection of the Jerusalem Sanctuary and the Scriptures which describe it formed the basis for his description of the Temple in the re-

Tradition suggests that Ezekiel died in Babylon during the reign of Nebuchadnezzar and that he was buried at Kefil (the scene above), near Babylon, between the Chebar and the Euphrates rivers.

stored Jerusalem. His long and accurate list of the natural resources and industrial products of different countries (Ezek. 27) shows him to have been a man of broad experience.

Although interested in the restoration of national Israel, Ezekiel stresses the importance of the individual. He insisted that "the son shall not suffer for the iniquity of the father, nor the father suffer for the iniquity of the son" (Ezek. 18:20; 33:12). He predicted judgment on sinful Israel, but also held forth the possibility of a heart of flesh which might replace the heart of stone. He envisioned a new relationship for those who would be indeed the people of God (Ezek. 11:19-20).

73

Return From Exile

Nabonidus had not proved popular, and the expediency of appointing Belshazzar as co-regent had not helped matters. The Neo-Babylonian Empire might have struggled along for decades, or even centuries, were it not for the fact that an energetic young ruler from the Persian province of Anshan had dreams of conquest. Cyrus had incorporated Media into his own Persian domains and marched northward into Asia Minor. The Lydian Empire, ruled by the fabulously rich Croesus, was subdued, and it was obvious that Cyrus would soon turn back toward Babylon in his quest for even wider territorial expansion.

The Babylonian governor of Elam (Gutium) had deserted to Cyrus. The loss to Nabonidus was great. Elam was a large and influential province, and its governor, Gobryas, was an able general. Gobryas was soon leading sorties against Babylonia.

The religious innovations of Nabonidus had alienated him from many of his own people. Concern for foreign shrines, coupled with the neglect of the religious demands of his office, caused many of his own people to wish to be rid of him. He seems to have reinstituted the New Year Festival in April, 539 B.C., but it was too late by that time to reverse the trend which led to the downfall of his dynasty.[1]

By the summer of 539 B.C. the Persian armies were ready to attack Babylon. Nabonidus, sensing the situation, brought the gods of the outlying regions into his capital, trusting that they would aid him in his time of need! This only antagonized those whose gods were taken away and brought further resentment to the priests of Babylon.

The decisive battle was fought at Opis, on the Tigris River. The Babylonian forces were crushed and rendered incapable —

---

1. Cf. the *Nabonidus Chronicle*, iii, reverse. Translated by A. Leo Oppenheim in *Ancient Near Eastern Texts* (J. Prichard, ed.), p. 306.

psychologically as well as militarily — for further resistance. Babylon itself fell in October, 539. Belshazzar was killed and Nabonidus, who had fled, was subsequently imprisoned.

The impregnable walls of Babylon were of no help to Nabonidus, for his capital city surrendered without a fight. Gobryas, the governor of Gutium, is probably to be identified with the Biblical "Darius the Mede" who led the Persian troops into Babylon (Dan. 5:30).

When Cyrus personally entered Babylon he was welcomed by the populace. He proclaimed peace to everyone in the city. The temples functioned as usual and care was taken to make the transition to Persian rule as painless as possible. Gobryas was made satrap of the new province of Babirush (i.e., Babylon) and many of the former officials of government were kept at their posts. A citizen of Babylon would have been unaware of the fact that a new era of history had begun.

One aspect of the new policy of Cyrus had important bearings on subsequent Biblical history. Nabonidus had antagonized the Babylonian priesthood by bringing into the city the gods of other regions. Cyrus made it a point to return these captive gods, with due reverence, to their former shrines. This directly affected the Jews for, although there were no images of their God in Babylon, vessels from His Temple in Jerusalem had been taken by Nebuchadnezzar.

During the first year of his reign in Babylon, Cyrus issued a decree authorizing the rebuilding of the Jerusalem Temple and the restoration of the gold and silver vessels which were in Babylon. The expense of the project was to be met from the royal treasury (Ezra 6:3-5). To accomplish this it was necessary to permit such Jews as wished to do so, to return to their ancestral homeland and rebuild the city of Jerusalem. There was no thought that Jews would be required to leave Babylon, or other parts of the Persian Empire. As a matter of fact only a small remnant had any desire to return. It was that remnant, however, which made possible subsequent Palestinian Jewish history.

The return of the sacred vessels and the leadership of the band of Jews who chose to return to Jerusalem was entrusted to a Jewish noble, or "prince of Judah" named Shesh-bazzar. The name appears as Sanabassar in I Esdras and Josephus and probably was the Babylonian name Sin-ab-usur. It is possible that Shenazzar (I Chron. 3:18), a son of Jehoiachin, is the same person as Shesh-bazzar, the "prince of Judah" (Ezra 1:8).

A panoramic view of Jerusalem that includes the southeast corner of the wall and the temple area.

The relationship between Shesh-bazzar and Zerubbabel is enigmatic. Many scholars suggest that they are different names for the same individual. In Ezra 5:14, however, Shesh-bazzar is mentioned as though he were dead ("one whose name was Shesh-bazzar") although Zerubbabel was clearly alive at the time. It may be that Shesh-bazzar died soon after the return to Jerusalem and Zerubbabel became his successor. Zerubbabel, a name meaning "seed of Babylon," i.e., "begotten in Babylon," was the son of Shealtiel (Ezra 3:2), hence the grandson of Jehoiachin (I Chron. 3:17). If Shesh-bazzar was a son of Jehoiachin, then he was uncle to Zerubbabel.

The first group of Jews to trek back to their homeland numbered close to 50,000. There were 42,360 free citizens, 7,337 slaves, and 200 Temple singers (Ezra 2:64-65). It was doubtless an enthusiastic group that journeyed back to Jerusalem a half century after its destruction by Nebuchadnezzar's army. These pilgrims would eagerly anticipate the fulfillment of prophecies of Jeremiah and Ezekiel, and see, in the return to Judah, a new beginning for their people.

The first responsibility of the returnees was the erection of a sanctuary and the renewal of the Levitical worship which had been held in abeyance since the destruction of the first Temple. An altar was first erected, and daily burnt offerings were made under the direction of Jeshua (or Joshua), the High Priest. Jeshua was the grandson of Seraiah who had served as the last High Priest before the destruction of the Temple in 587 B.C.

However enthusiastic the first group of pilgrims returning to Zion may have been, there is no question that they soon found reason for discouragement. The country was desolate, and squatters from among the Edomites, Moabites, Ammonites, Philistines, and Samaritans had profited by the absence of the Jews by occupying the Judaean countryside. The Samaritans, in particular, were openly hostile.

Shortly after the commencement of corporate life around the rebuilt altar, the Jews had an important decision to make. A group of Samaritans approached Zerubbabel with the suggestion, "Let us build with you; for we worship your God as you do, and we have been sacrificing to him ever since the days of Esarhaddon king of Syria who brought us here" (Ezra 4:2). The leaders of Israel were unwilling to form such a co-operative venture. Samaritan worship was syncretistic in the eyes of the Jews. The Samaritans had merely added the worship of Yahweh, the God of Israel, to the gods they had brought with them when they entered the land (II Kings 17:29-34). The Jewish leaders declined the Samaritan offer of assistance, noting that Cyrus had given to *them* the responsibility for rebuilding the Temple (Ezra 4:3). The Exile had been a bitter experience, and pious Jews were persuaded that the idolatry of their fathers had brought it about. They were determined that the post-exilic nation would be uncorrupted by heathen practices.

As might be expected, the Samaritans were hostile following this rebuff. They used every means at their command to frustrate the Jews in their efforts to build the Temple, and were successful in delaying the completion of the work until the reign of Darius (Ezra 4:5).

Shortly after Cyrus conquered Babylon he installed his son, Cambyses, as governor of Babirush (Babylonia), thus preparing him for the day when he would succeed his father to the throne of the Empire. Cyrus was killed during a military campaign in 528 B.C. and Cambyses took the throne. Under Cambyses, Egypt was incorporated into the Persian Empire and Egyptian autonomy came to an end. The Jews would look with favor on such a move for the Persians had treated them well. Cyrus may have seen the wisdom of having a friendly state on the border of Egypt at the time he issued his decree permitting Jews to return to their homeland. The Nabataean Arabs supplied the troops of Cambyses with water in the desert regions which separate Judah from Egypt.

In 522 B.C. Cambyses died. He was on his way home from Egypt when he received word that a usurper had seized the throne and was recognized as king by the eastern provinces of the Empire. It is thought that Cambyses took his own life, but the circumstances are obscure. An officer of Cambyses, himself of royal blood, claimed the throne as Cambyses' successor, marched against Gaumata, the usurper, and executed him. A period of rebellion ensued, and all parts of the Empire were affected. For two years Darius had to quell opposition in Babylon, Asia Minor, Egypt, and his eastern provinces — Media, Elam, Parsa, and Iran.

Where was Judah at this time? Its Temple had not been completed, but it is certain that the international upheavals spurred the people on to renewed activity. Could the Messianic Age, long hoped for, be at hand? Judah was but a part of the friendly Persian Empire, but she did have hopes of a day when a Davidic king would rule from a rebuilt Jerusalem.

Such hopes were particularly stressed by the prophets Haggai and Zechariah. Through their exhortations the leaders determined to take up the task of building the Temple which had been neglected because the people felt the time inopportune (Hag. 1:2; Ezra 5:1-2). The prophets pleaded for a purified Israel, separate from all heathen associations (cf. Hag. 2:10-14). To a purified nation, the "Branch" of David's line would appear (Zech. 3:8).

To what extent could such hopes be considered treason in the Persian court? The Samaritans would surely twist them to imply a plot on the part of the Jews to start an insurrection. Tattenai, the satrap of Abar-nahara, the satrapy which included Palestine and Syria, felt called upon to investigate the building operations of the Jews (Ezra 5:3-5). The Jews told him of the decree of Cyrus, and Tattenai sent to the Persian court to check their claims. In the state archives at Ecbatana, Darius found the decree of Cyrus, whereupon he ordered Tattenai to expedite the work of the Jews and meet the cost of their work from the royal treasury (Ezra 6:6-12).

The work went forward until March, 515 B.C., when the Second Temple was dedicated amid scenes of great rejoicing (Ezra 6:13-18). The new Temple was small in comparison with that built by Solomon. Israel was no longer a prosperous, sovereign state with kings who received tribute from distant lands. Instead it was a part of the Persian Empire, paying tribute to gentile kings. Nevertheless the Second Temple was to become a rallying point for post-exilic Israel.

Zerubbabel quietly, if not mysteriously, passes from the scene. Some think the Persians feared his political goals and removed him as a potential rebel. We do know that the Persians chose to rule the Jews through their High Priests — Jeshua and his successors. Perhaps they heard of the Messianic hopes of the Jews and felt that it would be safer to work through the priests than through secular princes who traced their lineage to David.

74

Ezra the Scribe

Among the Biblical characters of the post-exilic period none assumes a greater historical importance than Ezra. There has been considerable disagreement concerning the date of Ezra, for some very able scholars feel that our texts have been dislocated and that Nehemiah should be placed before Ezra.[1] The traditional order, maintained in the Massoretic Text of Scripture, fits in well with our knowledge of the post-exilic age and may be adhered to until convincing evidence to the contrary is produced.

Over fifty years pass in silence between the dedication of the Second Temple (515 B.C.) and the arrival of Ezra in Palestine in the seventh year of Artaxerxes (457 B.C.). Although successful in building the Temple, the Palestinian Jews were certainly not a prosperous group during this period. Their city had no walls and it was open to attack from their numerous enemies. The people had become dispirited. Earlier resolves to live lives of separation from their neighbors had been quietly forgotten and mixed marriage was common.

Back in Babylon and in other parts of the Persian Empire there were numerous Jews who still looked with fond associations to Jerusalem as the center of their religious life and their spiritual hopes. Such a man was Ezra, a pious Levite who had devoted his life to the study of God's Law. As a lover of Zion, Ezra appealed to Artaxerxes for help in making it possible for a fresh company of exiles to return to the land of their fathers. The king granted his request (Ezra 7:11-26) and authorized Ezra to assemble such Jews as would volunteer to join him on the journey to Palestine. Ezra was authorized to take with him offerings for the Jerusalem Temple sent both by Artaxerxes and

---

1. H. H. Rowley, "The Chronological Order of Ezra and Nehemiah," in *The Servant of the Lord and other Essays on the Old Testament*, pp. 131-159.

by the Jewish community. Ezra was instructed to use it to purchase sacrificial animals. The remainder could be spent as Ezra and his brethren saw fit (Ezra 7:17-18). Authority was also given to draw upon the royal treasury of the province of Syria if necessary (Ezra 7:20). Ezra was further authorized to appoint magistrates and judges and to teach the Law of God and the king to any who might not be familiar with it. The Law was to be rigorously enforced by imprisonment, confiscation of property, banishment, or even death (Ezra 7:26). Empowered in this way, Ezra was not merely a pious pilgrim but a representative of the Persian government with power to act. The provincial rulers were told, "Whatever Ezra the priest, the scribe of the Law of the God of heaven, requires of you, be it done with all diligence" (Ezra 7:21).

In all, about eighteen hundred men and their families responded to Ezra's appeal (Ezra 8:1-14). As the group gathered at Ahava, Ezra noted that there were no priests in the company. A special appeal was made and thirty-eight priests and two hundred and twenty Temple servants joined the party (Ezra 8:15-20). Artaxerxes in his decree had exempted priests and Temple servants from the Persian tax. Their reluctance to come may indicate that they were comfortably settled in Persia and felt no emotional ties with Jerusalem.

Having assured Artaxerxes of his confidence in divine protection, Ezra did not feel justified in requesting the usual military escort (Ezra 8:22). The group fasted and prayed (Ezra 8:23) before starting out on a journey of four months. No details are given concerning the journey itself, but we know that Ezra entrusted the silver, the gold, and the vessels which were to be brought to the Jerusalem Temple into the hands of the priests and Levites (Ezra 8:24-30).

As a delegated representative of the Persian Crown in Jerusalem Ezra bore the title, "Scribe of the law of the God of heaven" (Ezra 7:12). In modern language we might designate him, "Minister of State for Jewish Affairs."[2] The Persians were tolerant of the many religions in their Empire, but they did wish them to be regularized under responsible authority. Ezra, armed with his official rescript, was responsible for Jewish affairs in the province of Abar-nahara, i.e., Syria and Palestine (Ezra 7:25).

Shortly after their arrival in Jerusalem, Ezra and his company brought their treasures to the Temple and offered special sac-

---

2. Cf. John Bright, *A History of Israel*, p. 370.

rifices on the altar in the Temple court. They could testify that, "... the hand of our God was upon us, and he delivered us from the hand of the enemy and from ambushes by the way" (Ezra 8:31).

Ezra did not find the populace enthusiastic about the measures which were close to his heart. Some of the people had grown prosperous (Hag. 1:4), but spirituality was largely missing. Many of the Jews, including priests and Levites, had taken foreign wives (Ezra 9:1). Marriage, to Ezra, was not simply a matter of social arrangement, but one which involved obedience to the Law of God. Of the Gentile nations God had said, "You shall not make marriages with them, giving your daughters to their sons or taking their daughters for your sons" (Deut. 7:3). Intermarriage, as in the case of Solomon (I Kings 11:1-8), was a prelude to idolatry — the sin which had brought on the Babylonian Exile. Moved to contrition as he associated himself with his sinning compatriots, Ezra poured out his soul to God in confession and penitence (Ezra 9:6-15).

As the people gathered around Ezra, one of their number, Shecaniah, suggested that they all put away their foreign wives and their children (Ezra 10:2-3). Ezra then proposed that all Israel, led by the priests and Levites, vow to do as Shecaniah had suggested (Ezra 10:5). A decree was issued that all the people should assemble at Jerusalem within three days under penalty of confiscation of goods and excommunication (Ezra 10:7-8). When the people assembled they found that the task was too great to accomplish in the open square during a rain storm (Ezra 10:9-15). A divorce court was established (Ezra 10:16-17) and arrangements were made for the Jewish men to put away their foreign wives and children (Ezra 10:44).

Ezra's attitude in the matter of the foreign women was governed by his zeal for purity of Jewish life and faith. He was willing to sacrifice anything (and any one) that endangered that purity. His edict was certainly resented by many Jews and there can be no doubt that it stirred up the non-Jewish population in hostility against their Jewish neighbors.

Ezra had brought with him from Babylon "the Book of the Law of Moses" (Neh. 8:1) which he publicly read from a wooden pulpit (Neh. 8:4). Along with the reading there was an explanation (Neh. 8:8), probably in the Aramaic language which had become the popular language of the Jews during the time of their exile. When the people learned that it was the time of the Feast of Tabernacles which, through ignorance, they were not observing, they built booths for themselves and observed the ancient feast (Neh. 8:14-18).

The feast was followed by a solemn fast during which the Jews separated themselves from all foreigners and confessed their sin (Neh. 9:2). Again the Law was read (Ezra 9:4) and Ezra uttered a remarkable prayer in which he traced the mercies of God to Israel and deplored his people's unfaithfulness (Ezra 9:6-37). The princes, Levites, and priests solemnly covenanted before all the people to be faithful to God's Law (Neh. 9:38).

What was this Law that Ezra brought to Jerusalem? It was certainly not a new law, for it professed to go back to the days of Joshua (Neh. 8:17). It is termed "the Law of Moses" and was studied by the Jews of Babylon as the revelation of God's will which had been given to Moses at Mount Sinai. Whether Ezra had the completed Pentateuch, or some portion of it, we cannot say. We do know that the Babylonian Jews became diligent students of the Law during the period of the Exile.

This Law was received by the Palestinian Jewish community in solemn covenant before their God (Neh. 10). Although they lacked political independence, they became a religious community, subject to a religious Law. This was to mark the future of Judaism. Jews might exist under a variety of governments, but all could cherish the Law. They might be removed geographically from the Temple, or the Temple might be destroyed (as it was by the armies of Titus, A.D. 70), but the Law would still be theirs to cherish and obey. Legends were to develop around the person of Ezra, but his relationship to Israel as a second lawgiver, makes them unnecessary. His place in Jewish history is secure. Later generations said, "When the Law had been forgotten in Israel, Ezra came up from Babylon and established it."[3] A second century Jewish scholar, Rabbi Jose of Palestine gave him the highest compliment: "Ezra was worthy of having the Law given through him to Israel, had not Moses preceded him."[4]

---

3. Quoted in G. F. Moore, *Judaism*, I, p. 7
4. Quoted in Harry M. Orlinsky, *Ancient Israel*, p. 136.

75

Nehemiah the Builder

A Persian Jew named Nehemiah had risen to the post of cup-bearer[1] to Artaxerxes Longimanus (465-424 B.C.). This was a position of honor[2] for it involved an intimate relationship with the king. One of the responsibilities of the cupbearer was to taste the wine to see that it was not poisoned. He thus became the king's confidant.

When his brother Hanani and others from Judah came to visit Nehemiah at the Persian court, they told him of the difficulties of the Jews in Palestine (Neh. 1:1-3). Jerusalem had no walls to protect it from its many enemies. Although reckoned as the Holy City because the Temple of the Lord had been built there, few people dared live among its ruins.

Nehemiah was filled with grief at the report of the suffering of his brethren in Palestine. He prayed for guidance and sought an opportunity to present his burden to the king. Four months went by before Nehemiah could present his request. Then Artaxerxes, noticing the sadness of his cupbearer, asked Nehemiah to explain his problem (Neh. 2:1-3).

When Nehemiah told the king of his burden for Jerusalem, Artaxerxes readily granted him a leave of absence to visit the city and do the work that was on his heart. The length of the leave was agreed upon (Neh. 2:6) and Artaxerxes issued a royal re-script authorizing the building of the walls of Jerusalem. Letters were sent to the governors of the provinces west of the Euphrates and to Asaph, the keeper of the royal forest directing that Nehe-miah be provided with the materials he would need for the gates of the citadel, for the wall of the city, and for the Temple itself

---

1. For the office of cupbearer, cf. Xenophon, *Cyropaedia*, i. 3, 4. Nehemiah was probably an eunuch. This would account for the fact that he had access to the king when the queen also was present (cf. Neh. 2:6).
2. Cf. Herodotus, *Histories*, iii, 34.

(Neh. 2:7-8). Nehemiah was appointed governor of Judah (Neh. 5:14), thus making it a province separate from Samaria. This was to be one factor in the rivalry that developed between Sanballat, governor of Samaria, and Nehemiah.

The generosity of Artaxerxes was not without political implications and possible benefit to Persia. Egypt had been perennially restive, and Persia wanted her Palestinian provinces which bordered Egypt to be in friendly, loyal hands. The Jews, moreover, had smarted under Samaritan officialdom and were generally demoralized. If successful in his mission, Nehemiah could help both his own people and the king whom he served.

After making necessary preparations, Nehemiah and a group of companions made the long journey from Susa to Jerusalem. His first concern was for the building of the walls of the city. In the company of a few associates he inspected the ruined walls by night (Neh. 2:12-15). Again his heart was heavy. A city without walls was not really a city at all. The ruined walls were a reproach both to Judah and to Judah's God (Neh. 2:17).

After inspecting the ruins, Nehemiah sought out the leaders of the Jerusalem community — the priests and nobles (Neh. 2:16-17) — and explained his mission. He told them of the way in which God had prospered his efforts and the co-operation which had been promised by Artaxerxes (Neh. 2:18). The response of the leaders of Jerusalem was gratifying. They caught something of Nehemiah's enthusiasm and said "Let us rise up and build" (Neh. 2:18).

Initial plans had no sooner been made when serious opposition developed. It found its focal point in three non-Jews, although important elements in Jerusalem were sympathetic with their plans. Sanballat, governor of Samaria, is identified as "the Horonite" (Neh. 2:19). He was probably a native of Beth-horon in Samaria. His companions are identified as Tobiah, an Ammonite slave, and Geshem, probably the chief of a tribe in northwestern Arabia. These men mocked the Jews for their efforts to rebuild the walls of Jerusalem and insinuated that this was an act of rebellion against Persia (Neh. 2:19-20).

Nehemiah pressed on with his plans. The people responded to his appeal for help and soon labor battalions were assigned to the various sections into which the wall had been divided. Workers came from outside villages — Jericho, Gibeon, Mizpah, Beth-haccherem, Zanoah, Beth-zur, Keilah, and Tekoa. Priests, Levites, goldsmiths, and merchants all labored together (Neh. 3).

Excavations by Kathleen Kenyon near the Gihon Spring near Jerusalem.

Sanballat and his allies, seeing that mockery did not deter Nehemiah from his building program, determined to take more positive action. The wall had reached half its desired height (Neh. 4:6) and Sanballat determined to send guerilla bands against Jerusalem. Arabians, Ammonites, and Ashdodites (Neh. 4:7) began to harass the Jews who were working on the wall. They planned a sneak attack, but Nehemiah was ready for them (Neh. 4:11). He stationed armed men to guard the unprotected places in the wall (Neh. 4:13). When the enemy learned that the Jews were armed, they abandoned their plan to make a frontal attack (Neh. 4:15), but sought other means to hinder Nehemiah from accomplishing his goals.

From this time on the workmen were armed: "Each of the builders had his sword girded at his side while he built" (Neh. 4:18). A trumpeter stood beside Nehemiah ready to give warning in the event of attack. The people whose homes were outside the city were not permitted to leave Jerusalem. The enemy was in the outlying territory and the city could not be left without defenders. Neither Nehemiah nor his people removed their clothes at night. They slept with weapons at their side, ready to respond at the sound of the trumpet (Neh. 4:22-23). There is no record of an actual battle. The Samaritans and their allies did not make an open attack, but they posed a constant threat and worked serious hardships on the Jews.

Although able to stand up under pressures from without, Nehemiah faced the collapse of his cause as a result of internal problems. The people working on the walls had no source of income. Many had left homes and farms, only to have them looted and plundered by the enemy. People had to mortgage fields, vineyards, and houses to provide food and to pay their taxes (Neh. 5:3-4). Some had pledged their children for debt, and they were sold into slavery (Neh. 5:5). Isaac Mendelsohn notes, "Nehemiah 5:1-5 proves that in Palestine loans were obtained, as in Assyria, on security. Houses, fields, vineyards, olive groves, and children were pledged, and if the debts were not repaid, the creditors would retain the land as their property and the children as slaves."[3]

Nehemiah was angered at this report of the way in which the wealthy class had taken advantage of the poor during a time of national crisis (Neh. 5:6). He summoned the offenders to a public meeting, during which he reviewed his own financial rec-

---

3. *Legal Aspects of Slavery in Babylonia, Assyria and Palestine,* p. 19.

The pitched tents of Bedouins rest at the base of the east wall of Jerusalem.

ord (Neh. 5:14-19). Nehemiah had refused to accept the allowances to which he was entitled as governor and had actually supported one hundred and fifty Jews at his own expense. The nobles and officials who had exploited the poor responded to Nehemiah's plea and vowed to restore that which they had taken (Neh. 5:12).

Having failed in other ways, Nehemiah's enemies attempted to defeat him by intrigue. Four times they invited him to confer with them in the valley of Ono in Benjamin, but he insisted that he could not leave the great work in which he was engaged (Neh. 6:1-4). A fifth messenger came with an open letter from Sanballat accusing Nehemiah of a conspiracy to rebel against Persia and establish himself as king in Judah (Neh. 6:5-7). Nehemiah refused so much as to discuss the charge, bluntly stating that they were the fabrication of Sanballat's evil mind (Neh. 6:8). Sanballat and Tobiah went so far as to hire prophets to induce Nehemiah to lock himself in the Temple to avoid assassination. Nehemiah saw through this plot and refused to go (Neh. 6:10-13). It is a sad commentary on the religious life of the times that men who considered themselves prophets could sell their services to Judah's enemies.

Undisturbed by the many devices fashioned to deflect him from his goal, Nehemiah pressed on toward the completion of his work. In less than two months (Neh. 6:15) the wall was completed. Josephus tells us that it was further strengthened with battlements and gates over an additional two years and four months.[4] Nehemiah appointed his brother Hanani and a man named Hananiah, the governor of the castle, to assume responsibility for the welfare of Jerusalem. He charged them to keep the city gates closed until the sun was well up in the heavens, and to keep a guard posted (Neh. 7:2-3).

The inhabitants of Jerusalem were few, for houses were still in ruins. It was necessary to encourage people to settle within the city, because life was more pleasant in other parts of Judah. Those who volunteered to live in Jerusalem were highly regarded. They had to be augmented by a forced draft which brought one-tenth of the country people into the Holy City (Neh. 11:1).

The completion of the walls was an occasion of celebration and spiritual dedication. After ceremonies of purification (Neh. 12:30), two processions were formed to move around the walls in opposite directions. Ezra was at the head of one company, and

---

4. *Antiquities,* XI, v, 8.

Nehemiah of the other. They met near the Temple area where the people gave expression to their joy and offered appropriate sacrifices (Neh. 12:31-43).

With the rebuilding of the walls and adequate provision made for the observance of the sacrifices and holy days prescribed in the Mosaic Law (Neh. 12:27-30), Nehemiah was free to end his leave of absence and return to the Persian court (Neh. 13:6). We can imagine the enthusiasm and the gratitude with which he greeted Artaxerxes at Susa. The problems in Judah were not over, however. Within a short time — perhaps from one to three years — Nehemiah was granted a second leave of absence to return to Jerusalem.

During Nehemiah's absence at the Persian court, the situation in Jerusalem had deteriorated. Although freed from the threat of enemies from without, the Jews themselves grew careless and internal dissention and infidelity brought on a new crisis. The wine presses were in operation on the sabbath day, and Tyrian merchants brought their fish and other merchandise into Jerusalem contrary to the Sabbath law (Neh. 13:15-16). The perennial problem of intermarriage came to the fore again during the absence of Nehemiah (Neh. 13:23). Israelite men had married women from Ashdod, Ammon, and Moab. The effect was evident even in the speech of the people, for the language of these wives was spoken by their children in the very streets of Jerusalem (Neh. 13:24). A grandson of Eliashib, the high priest, married a daughter of Nehemiah's inveterate enemy, Sanballat (Neh. 13:28).

The religious life of the people had also fallen into decay. Eliashib befriended Nehemiah's enemy Tobiah, the Ammonite, and housed him in one of the Temple chambers (Neh. 13:4-5). The Levites were not given their allowances with the result that they had to find other work to do (Neh. 13:10). Many returned to their fields and earned their living as farmers.

When Nehemiah heard of these things he was understandably disturbed. He returned to Jerusalem and, with characteristic vigor, determined to set things right. Tobiah's belongings were cast out of the Temple and it was restored to its sacred use (Neh. 13:8-9). The fiscal policy of the Temple was reorganized and tithes of corn, wine, and oil were collected so that provision could be made for the Levites to give their time to their Temple ministrations (Neh. 13:11-13). Nehemiah appealed to the leaders of Jerusalem to close the city gates on the Sabbath Day (Neh. 13:17-18). The command for strict Sabbath observance was given and, when some merchants attempted to circumvent the law by selling their wares outside the city wall, Nehemiah threatened to forcibly remove them (Neh. 13:20-21).

The problem of intermarriage was a vexing one. Nehemiah asked the Jews to swear that they would not permit their children to marry into the families of neighboring peoples. He reminded them that even godly Solomon was led astray by his foreign wives (Neh. 13:25-27). Eliashib's grandson, who had married the daughter of Sanballet, was a notorious offender and Nehemiah banished him from Jerusalem (Neh. 13:28).

An important sequel to this episode is recorded by Josephus,[5] who states that Manasseh (the grandson of Eliashib) married Sanballat's daughter, Nicaso. When Nehemiah gave him the choice between abdicating his priestly office or divorcing his wife, Manasseh took the problem to his father-in-law. Sanballat, we are told, offered to make Manasseh the High Priest in Samaria and promised to build for him a temple on Mount Gerizim as soon as the permission of the Persian king (Darius, in Josephus' account) could be secured. He further promised to make Manasseh his successor as governor of Samaria.

Josephus was evidently following Samaritan sources in his account of the building of the temple on Mount Gerizim. He states that Sanballat offered his troops to Alexander (!) upon his entrance into Palestine following the battle at Issus, and gained as a boon the permission to build the temple on Mount Gerizim. Josephus tells us that many priests and Levites went to Samaria with Manasseh and that they were given lands in Samaria by Sanballat.

The chief objection to the record as given by Josephus is the chronological discrepancy of placing Sanballat in the era of Alexander the Great — a century later than the time of Nehemiah. This misplacement of the episode need not argue against its essential historicity, however. James A. Montgomery notes:

> The age of the Conqueror is the one bright point in the reminiscences of the ancient world, and was a shining mark for the art of legend-manufacture. Just as the Jews had their legend concerning Alexander's favor to Jerusalem, so the Samaritans told their fables concerning his connection with their sect and temple; probably in this point Josephus was depending upon some Samaritan tradition, which he, or rather the legend-cycle which he followed, brought into connection with the history of Sanballat.[6]

It is clear from the Biblical picture of Nehemiah that his leadership was not unchallenged. An important party in Jerusalem was sympathetic with Sanballat. During the absence of Nehemiah

5. *Antiquities*, XI, vii. 2; viii. 2.
6. *The Samaritans*, p. 69.

The southeast corner of the old city wall of Jerusalem.

they came to positions of prominence, but with his return they were put on the defensive. With the expulsion of Manasseh, their power was broken, the schism became permanent, and Jew and Samaritan went their separate ways.

Nehemiah is best remembered for his work on the rebuilding of the walls of Jerusalem. Sirach says of him, " . . . he raised for us the walls that had fallen, and set up the gates and bars and rebuilt our ruined houses" (Sir. 49:13) . Josephus echoes, "He was a man of good and righteous character, and very ambitious to make his own nation happy; and he hath left the walls of Jerusalem as an eternal monument of himself."[7]

---

7. *Antiquities*, XI, v. 8.

76

Esther
and the Persian Court

The focus of attention in the books of Ezra and Nehemiah is upon the faithful remnant of Jews who returned to Palestine in the years following the decree of Cyrus. Jewish life continued in the East, since many who thought of themselves as loyal Jews, preferred to live in their adopted country.

The incidents described in the Biblical book of Esther indicate some of the trials and victories experienced by Jews who chose to remain in Babylon and Persia. We find ourselves in the court of Xerxes (486-465 B.C.), son and successor of Darius the Great. The king provided lavish entertainment for his nobles and, at the height of his party, sent for his queen, Vashti, and ordered her to make a lewd display of herself. When Vashti refused, the nobles suggested that Vashti be deposed lest her refusal to obey the king become an example to other wives who might not respect the word of their husbands.

It was in the third year of Xerxes (Biblical Ahasuerus) that Vashti was deposed, and four years were to pass before another queen would be chosen. These were difficult years for the Persian king who had determined to conquer Greece. In 480 B.C. Greece defeated the Persians in a naval encounter at Salamis, and the next year was one of further reverses for Persia at Plataea. Xerxes was far from achieving his goals on the field of battle.

When the king decided to find a wife to take the place of Vashti he sent to the many provinces of his Empire to secure young ladies from whom the choice might be made. We might term this an ancient beauty contest. The plan was suggested by the courtiers of Xerxes and approved by the king himself.

Among the young ladies brought to Susa (Biblical Shushan), the capital of Susiana and winter palace of the Persian kings, was a Jewess named Hadassah, or Esther, the cousin of a Jew of Susa named Mordecai. Mordecai was a faithful Jew who could trace his ancestry back to Benjamin (Esther 2:5). The name of Mordecai appears in the Persian and Neo-Babylonian cuneiform literature. We know that a man named Mordecai (Marduka) was a high officer in the court of Susa during the early days of Xerxes' reign.[1] The German cuneiform scholar, Arthur Ungnad, asserts that this text which was discovered at Borsippa is our first and only extra-Biblical reference to the Mordecai of the Esther story. Mordecai bore a name which honored Marduk, the god of Babylon. The name was a common one, and Ungnad's identification need not be insisted on. We do know that a faithful Jew with that name was in Susa at the time.

The ancestors of Esther and Mordecai had been deported from Jerusalem with Jehoiachin in 597 B.C. (Esther 2:6). When Esther's parents died, her cousin, Mordecai, assumed responsibility for her. Conscious of her great beauty, Mordecai brought Esther to the court where she immediately captivated Xerxes. She may have been conscious of anti-Semitic feelings at court, for she did not reveal the fact that she was a Jewess. In the seventh year of his reign, amidst scenes of rejoicing, Xerxes married Esther (Esther 2:17-18).

Trouble came to a head for the Jews when Haman, termed "the Agagite" (after the Amalekite king defeated by Saul) was chosen as grand vizier to Xerxes (Esther 3:1). Mordecai, proud of his Jewish blood and conscious of ancient rivalries between Jews and Amalekites, refused to bow before Haman. Incensed by this lack of respect, Haman determined to have all of the Jews in Persia executed.

By casting a lot ("pur," from which the Jewish holiday Purim is named), Haman determined that the thirteenth day of Adar (February-March) was the most auspicious day for his pogram. He then told Xerxes of "a certain people" scattered throughout the Empire who refused to obey the king's laws. Haman was so anxious to destroy these "people" that he offered to pay to the royal treasury ten thousand silver talents (about eighteen million dollars), if the king would back his project. Xerxes placed his signet ring on Haman's hand and authorized him to proceed with his plans. Orders were dispatched to the provincial governors to destroy all of the Jews on the thirteenth of Adar, eleven months from the date of the edict.

---

1. Cf. A. Ungnad, "Keilschriftliche Beitrage zum Buch Esra und Ester," *Zeitschrift für die Alttestamentliche Wissenschaft*, LVIII (1940-41) pp. 240-244.

Mordecai and the Jews mourned when they learned of the decree which had been devised to exterminate them. Esther, unaware of what had happened, sent for Mordecai, providing him with a suitable robe so that he might visit the palace. Mordecai refused to come, but sent Esther a copy of the decree, and urged her to intervene on behalf of her people. She, in turn, replied that she could not appear before the king unannounced. Such an act might anger the king and cause him to kill her. Mordecai warned Esther that the enforcement of the decree would bring about her death in any event (Esther 4:13) and suggested that she had "come to the kingdom for such a time as this" (Esther 4:14). With the heroic words, "If I perish, I perish" (Esther 4:16), Esther determined to go to the king.

When she entered the forbidden inner court, Esther was graciously received by the king. Instead of stating her request she invited Xerxes and his vizier, Haman to dinner (Esther 5:1-4). When the wine was served at the end of the meal she invited them to a second banquet the next day. Haman, overjoyed at the deference paid him by the queen, was later annoyed as he passed Mordecai (Esther 5:9). Determining to rid himself of this hated Jew he erected a gallows over 83 feet high on which to hang his imagined foe (Esther 5:14).

That night when Xerxes had difficulty sleeping he ordered the royal chronicles read to him (Esther 6:1-3). When the account of Mordecai's act in saving the king from a conspiracy on his life (Esther 2:21-23) was reached, Xerxes insisted that some suitable reward should be provided for his faithful courtier. Haman came early to ask permission to hang Mordecai, but before he could make known his request, the king asked him to suggest a means of honoring a particularly faithful subject. Haman, thinking that he was the one to be honored, suggested that the man be led through the streets on horseback, attired in royal garments and preceded by a herald proclaiming the meaning of the honor. Crestfallen when he learned that Mordecai was the man to be honored, Haman nevertheless carried out his own recommendation (Esther 6:4-11). Returning home he found his wife and friends pessimistic about his contest with Mordecai. While they were talking, the king's chamberlain came to take Haman to the queen's banquet (Esther 6:12-14).

At the end of the meal, Esther, at the king's request, presented her petition (Esther 7:3-4). She asked that she and her people be spared from the destruction which had been determined. Wondering who had plotted such evil, Xerxes was told that it was none other than his grand vizier, Haman. While the king, in great agitation, walked in the garden, Haman approached Esther to plead for his life. Returning, however, the king saw Haman with the queen and suspected him of assaulting her. Xerxes ordered that Haman be executed on the gallows that had been built for Mordecai (Esther 7:5-10).

Unable to revoke the edict of Haman, the king authorized Mordecai, his new grand vizier, to issue a decree permitting the Jews to massacre and despoil all who would attack them on the fateful thirteenth of Adar (Esther 8:8-14). The Jews rejoiced at this new decree and many of their neighbors professed to become Jews to avoid the retribution which they feared the Jews would take upon their enemies (Esther 8:16-17).[2]

On the thirteenth of Adar the two decrees went into effect. Because of the influence of Mordecai, the provincial rulers sided with the Jews in their conflict with their enemies. In Susa the Jews slew five hundred men in addition to the ten sons of Haman (Esther 9:1-11). The king acceded to Esther's request that the Jews be granted a second day to take vengeance on their enemies, and on the fourteenth of Adar they slew three hundred more (Esther 9:13-16). In the provinces the Jews had slain 75,000 of their enemies on the thirteenth of Adar, and celebrated a joyous festival on the fourteenth (Esther 9:16-17). The Septuagint gives the number killed as 15,000. In Susa the Jews celebrated their victory on the fifteenth of Adar. Mordecai and Esther wrote letters instructing the Jews to celebrate Purim both on the fourteenth and fifteenth of Adar by "feasting and gladness, sending portions (of food) one to another, and gifts to the poor."

Among the unusual characteristics of the Book of Esther is the total absence of the word "God." Although we do read of fasting, there is no mention of prayer. Mordecai and Esther both appear as godly Jews, however. In the dire need which faced them following Haman's decree, Mordecai suggested that if Esther did not go to the king deliverance might come "from another place" (Esther 4:14), an expression which implies the intervention of God. Although far from the land of Palestine, the Persian Jews knew that their God ever stood "within the shadows keeping watch above His own."

---

2. Cyrus Gordon interprets this as an example of the doctrine of *kitman* or dissimulation which permits one to deny his religion and pose as a member of another religion to avoid danger. He points out that Esther hid her Jewish affiliation (Esther 2:10) before the Iranian gentiles pretended to be Jews (Esther 8:17). Cf. Cyrus H. Gordon, *The World of the Old Testament,* pp. 283-284.

77

The Emergence of Judaism

During the years of exile Israel became a religious community which was not related to any political entity or cultic center. This fact made changes in her thinking and her political institutions which have continued to the present. Although some Jews would later return to Jerusalem, the majority would continue to live at a distance from the Holy Land. Their ties would be cultural and religious, but not political.

The term "Israel" is frequently used to describe the earlier period of Jewish life, when the tribes dwelt in proximity to one another and religious life was conveniently centered in one central sanctuary. As a political unit, Israel was a world power in the days of David and Solomon, and even after the division of the kingdom she remained a political force to be reckoned with. After the Exile, Judah remained a subject state which, except for the Maccabean interlude, was dependent upon the great powers among whom she lived — Persia, Macedonia, the Ptolemies of Egypt, the Syrian Seleucids, and Rome. Her people lived not only in Palestine, but also in Egypt, Persia, Babylon, Syria, Asia Minor, Greece, and Rome. These Jews might visit Jerusalem at the great religious festivals (cf. Acts 2:8-11), but they had found their livelihood in a wider world and made some adaptations to a wider culture.

Exilic and post-exilic Judaism was the heir to the Law and the prophetic writings of pre-exilic Israel. The Exile itself had underscored the need of faithfulness to Israel's God. Idolatry had been the besetting sin of the pre-exilic period, and those who had suffered the loss of home and Temple could be expected to turn in horror from the sins which brought on the Exile.

The Israeli scholar, Yehezkel Kaufmann, has summarized the effect of the Exile upon the Jewish tendency toward idolatry:

Vestiges of an ancient fetishistic idolatry reinforced by foreign influences, continued to exist among the people down to the fall of Judah. It was the catastrophe of the Fall that aroused in the people a spirit of remorse. The pious viewed the sin of idolatry as the crucial national sin. The prophets had predicted doom for the worship of gods of wood and stone. God-fearing kings such as Asa, Jehoshaphat, Hezekiah, and Josiah had destroyed idolatrous cults, but had been unable to root out idolatry entirely. The Fall worked a revolution. The nation accepted the verdict that God's wrath had poured down upon them for the sin of idolatry, and they drew the ultimate conclusion from their monotheistic faith: all traces of idol-worship must be extirpated. It was thus in the realm of the cult that the final victory of monotheism in Israel took place. Henceforth Israel was a nation jealous for its Jealous God.[1]

The rejection of idolatry had, as its positive side, a deepening appreciation of Israel's historic monotheistic faith as enunciated in the body of sacred writings known as the Torah, or Law. Torah must not be thought of as law in the restricted sense of rules for conduct. The Torah contains such, of course, but it includes a great deal more. The Hebrew Torah is our Pentateuch — the first five books of the Bible. Parts of Exodus, Leviticus, and Deuteronomy give us codified law, but much of the Torah instructs us by example. Biographies of godly men — Abraham, Joseph, Noah, Moses — and a host of others, provide instruction. The evil deeds of men so realistically described, provide instruction also. Bad examples as well as good examples are necessary if we are to understand life in its totality. The evil must be shunned, and the good imitated, but both are illustrated and described in the Torah of Israel.

Kaufmann observes the need for Torah in exilic Judaism: "With land, temple, and king gone, only one contact with the holy was left, the divine word."[2] There were no Jewish altars in Babylon. The Jews shrank even from singing the songs of Zion in the land of exile (Psalm 137:4). The Scriptures — the Bible of ancient Israel — filled the vacuum produced by the crisis of Exile.

Not only the Law, but pre-exilic prophetic writings were studied by faithful Jews in Babylon. Daniel tells us that it was his study of the prophecies of Jeremiah that caused him to humble himself before God in anticipation of the day when the enforced exile would come to an end (Dan. 9:1-19). In contemplating the time when a new Temple would be built in Jerusalem, the priests and their descendants concerned themselves with the minutia of the Levitical laws. Those whose hearts were still in Zion occupied themselves with the Scriptures. There

1. "The Biblical Age," in *Great Ages and Ideas of the Jewish People,* p. 79.
2. *The Religion of Israel,* p. 448.

This stone relief of the seven-branched lampstand was recovered from a synagogue of New Testament times, at Kefr Birim.

they learned both the reason for the Exile and the manner of life which the people of God should live both in the land of their captivity and, at a later time, in a restored Zion.

The synagogue, the characteristic institution of post-exilic Judaism, had its roots in the religious needs of those who could not attend the Temple worship to which they were accustomed. Orthodox Judaism permitted but one Sanctuary, that which had first been built by Solomon in Jerusalem. The Temple was the successor to the older Tabernacle, a movable structure which had been built during the period of the wilderness wandering before Israel, under Joshua, entered Canaan. The sacred ark, the most important element in the Tabernacle, had later been located at Shiloh where "the temple of Yahweh" (I Sam. 1:9) was located in the days of Samuel. Shiloh was destroyed during the battles between Israelites and Philistines, and the ark had no permanent abode until David brought it to Jerusalem (II Sam. 6:1-19). From that time to the present, Jerusalem has been considered the religious center of Jewish life and the only appropriate place for the Holy Temple.

No Temple was built in the Jewish settlements of Babylon. The exiles did need to have occasions of fellowship in prayer and Bible study to augment their personal devotional times. Out of this very real need the institution known as the synagogue gradually developed. The synagogue became the community center for Jewish life.

During the Exile there arose a change in the linguistic habits of the Jews. Aramaic, the language of diplomacy in the Persian Empire, became the vernacular of the Jews — both those who returned to Palestine and those who remained in the eastern provinces of the Empire.[3]

Jews who spoke only Aramaic would not be able to understand the Hebrew Scriptures without an interpreter. The custom arose of reading the Hebrew Bible in the synagogue service, after which an explanation would be given in the vernacular Aramaic. This oral explanation in time became a discourse, interpreting and applying the Biblical message. Generations later these explanations, or "targums" were themselves written down, but in their early history they were simple explanations of the Biblical text, ranging from word-by-word translations to quite free paraphrases. More liberties were permitted with the prophetic litera-

3. See pp. 425-426.

ture than with the Torah which was accorded the highest degree of inspiration in Jewish thought.

The reading of the Scripture was probably preceded by a prayer. In later Jewish practice the reading from the Torah was preceded by the recitation of the *Shema'* — Deuteronomy 6:4-9; 11:13-21; and Numbers 15:37-41. The *Shema'* gets its name from the Hebrew word "hear," the first word of Deuteronomy 6:4-9 which begins, "Hear, O Israel!"

The institution of the Sabbath, frequently neglected by the pre-exilic communities, became the hall-mark of Judaism during the exilic period. From sundown on Friday to sundown on Saturday the Jew refrained from all work. The Sabbath became a day of rest and worship. In addition to the sacred festivals of the Levitical calendar, the Jews of the exile observed fasts in memory of the national calamities attending the fall of Jerusalem (Zech. 7:3, 5; 8:19). Later the feast of Purim was observed to commemorate the victory of the Jews over their foes in Persian times (Esther 9:27-32).

Corporate worship did not take the place of personal devotion for the godly Jew. Daniel made it a practice to pray three times daily with his face turned toward Jerusalem (Dan. 6:11). Confession of sin and prayers for divine compassion were certainly stimulated by the Exile. Those who, in a spirit of haughtiness, presumed upon God's goodness in pre-exilic times would now see their plight in the light of His holiness. The author of Lamentations cried out, "Turn thou us unto thee, O Lord, and we shall be turned; renew our days as of old" (Lam. 5:21).

It would be dangerous to generalize on the attitude of Babylonian Jews toward their idolatrous associates. Some, probably, had little contact with their non-Jewish neighbors. We do know, however, of many Jews who rose to important positions in the political and business world of the time. Daniel in the courts of Babylon and Persia; Nehemiah the cupbearer to Artaxerxes Longimanus; and Esther the queen serve as notable examples of Jews who were in no sense isolated. We also know that some Jews made a name and fortune for themselves in the world of commerce. The business archives of the Murashu family of Nippur provide an early example of Jews who became successful men of business.[4]

---

4. Cf. H. V. Hilprecht and A. T. Clay, *Business Documents of Murashu Sons of Nippur Dated in the Reign of Artaxerxes I* and Albert T. Clay, *Business Documents of Murashu Sons of Nippur Dated in the Reign of Darius II.*

One result of this new chapter in Jewish life was the impact which Jews had on their non-Jewish associates. Prior to the Exile conversion was largely a matter of living in the land of Israel and assimilating Israelite culture. Ruth the Moabitess determined to serve Naomi's God when she returned with her to Bethlehem, whereas Orpah, Ruth's sister-in-law, returned to Moab and served the gods of Moab (Ruth 1:14-16). During and after the Exile, however, Judaism became a missionary religion. The Jews looked with scorn on the idolatry which once had been so great a temptation to their fathers. They saw idolatry as something evil not only for themselves as Jews, but for all men. A significant and growing number of converts or "God-fearers" looked upon Judaism as the true religion and turned their backs upon paganism. The early church found a ready audience that had been providentially prepared by post-exilic Judaism for the preaching of the Christian gospel.

The time between the close of Old Testment history and
the beginning of the New Testament period has often been
called "the four hundred silent years." To the historian,
however, these centuries were anything but silent, and they
seem to become more vocal with each passing decade.

To the student of ancient history, names like Cyrus, Darius,
and Alexander the Great make this period one of
paramount importance. The Jew notes during these centuries
the development of synagogue worship, the successful
Maccabean revolt, and the emergence of those parties within
Judaism which have set the pattern for Jewish life
and thought during the past two millennia.

The Christian looks upon the Old Testament as preparatory,
looking toward the fulfillment of its hopes and promises
in the Person of Jesus Christ. He is interested in the history
of the centuries preceding the coming of Christ, for he sees
in them a preparation for the advent, and a progress toward
that period of history termed "the fulness of time" (Gal. 4:4).

PART
SEVEN

Between
the Testaments –
The Persian Period

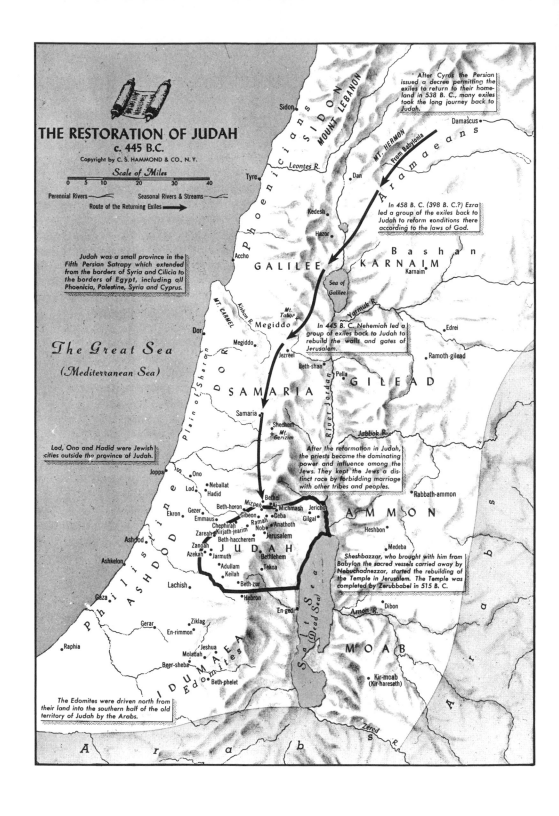

THE RESTORATION OF JUDAH
c. 445 B.C.

Copyright by C. S. HAMMOND & CO., N. Y.

Scale of Miles

0 5 10   20   30   40

Perennial Rivers ⌇⌇⌇   Seasonal Rivers & Streams ⌇⌇⌇

Route of the Returning Exiles ➤

After Cyrus the Persian issued a decree permitting the exiles to return to their homeland in 538 B. C., many exiles took the long journey back to Judah.

In 458 B. C. (398 B. C.?) Ezra led a group of the exiles back to Judah to reform conditions there according to the laws of God.

Judah was a small province in the Fifth Persian Satrapy which extended from the borders of Syria and Cilicia to the borders of Egypt, including all Phoenicia, Palestine, Syria and Cyprus.

In 445 B. C. Nehemiah led a group of exiles back to Judah to rebuild the walls and gates of Jerusalem.

The Great Sea
(Mediterranean Sea)

Lod, Ono and Hadid were Jewish cities outside the province of Judah.

After the reformation in Judah, the priests became the dominating power and influence among the Jews. They kept the Jews a distinct race by forbidding marriage with other tribes and peoples.

Sheshbazzar, who brought with him from Babylon the sacred vessels carried away by Nebuchadnezzar, started the rebuilding of the Temple in Jerusalem. The Temple was completed by Zerubbabel in 515 B. C.

The Edomites were driven north from their land into the southern half of the old territory of Judah by the Arabs.

Sidon · PHOENICIANS · MOUNT LEBANON · MT. HERMON · Damascus · From Babylonia · Aramaeans

Tyre · Leontes R. · Dan

Kedesh

Hazor

Accho · GALILEE · KARNAIM · Bashan · Karnaim

Dor · MT. CARMEL · Kishon R. · Mt. Tabor · Sea of Galilee · Yarmuk R.

Megiddo · Megiddo · Edrei

DOR · Jezreel · Ramoth-gilead

Beth-shan · Pella · GILEAD

SAMARIA · River Jordan

Plain of Sharon · Samaria · Shechem · Mt. Gerizim · Jabbok R.

Joppa · Ono · Neballat · Hadid · Bethel · Ai · Michmash · Jericho · AMMON · Rabbath-ammon

Lod · Mizpeh · Geba · Gilgal · Heshbon

Ekron · Gezer · Beth-horon · Gibeon · Ramah · Anathoth · Medeba

Emmaus · Chephirah · Nob

Zareah · Kirjath-jearim · Jerusalem

Ashdod · Zanoah · Beth-haccherem · JUDAH · Bethlehem · Dibon

Ashkelon · Azekah · Jarmuth · Adullam · Tekoa · Armon R.

Gaza · Keilah

Lachish · Beth-zur · Salt Sea (Dead Sea) · MOAB

Hebron · En-gedi

Gerar · Ziklag

En-rimmon · Kir-moab (Kir-haraseth)

Raphia · Jeshua · Molada · IDUMAEA · Edomites

Beer-sheba · Beth-phelet

PHILISTINES · ASHDOD · Zered

A r a b i a

78

Cyrus and the
Rise of the Empire

I. The Beginnings

The Persian Empire came into being as the result of the efforts of one man — Cyrus. Of his background we know nothing. His father was named Cambyses, and the ancestry of his mother is unknown. Tradition makes her the daughter of a Median king. The story was probably invented to make Cyrus appear as a legitimate monarch of royal Median ancestry.

Cyrus first appears in history when, in 559 B.C., at the age of forty, he inherited the small kingdom of Anshan. This territory was tributary to the Median Empire, one of the eastern rivals of Babylon.

The Medes and the Babylonians were former allies. In 612 B.C. their combined forces destroyed Nineveh, the capital of the Assyrian Empire. Kyaxeres the Mede seems to have taken the lead in the assault on Nineveh. Nabopolassar of Babylon, however, fought the Assyrians alone after the destruction of their capital city. Perhaps the Medes were called home by problems that required immediate attention. Median and Babylonian leaders may have become estranged as a result of a conflict of interests. In any event, the Medo-Babylonian alliance was short-lived. The fall of Nineveh and the subsequent end of Assyria brought about a realignment of the states of the ancient Near East.

Babylon quickly capitalized on Assyria's disaster. Nebuchadnezzar, son of Nabopolassar and commander of the Babylonian armies, marched westward and annexed the territories which had once belonged to Assyria. Egypt tried to make trouble for Nebuchadnezzar, with a view to the annexation of additional territory, but the tide of Babylonian victory could not be stopped.

At the Apadana in Persepolis, the relief on the stairway shows Babylonians and Syrians bringing tribute.

All this also affected the Jews. The last kings of Judah were torn between the claims of Egypt and Babylon. Jeremiah had insisted that resistance to Nebuchadnezzar was futile, and the pro-Egyptian party succeeded in bringing about a series of rebellions. The result was tragic. By 587 B.C. Nebuchadnezzar had destroyed Jerusalem, with its Temple. Most of the Judeans were taken to Babylon.

Exile in Babylon brought the Jews to a fresh realization of the nature of their God. Idolatry had been rampant during the years before the fall of Jerusalem. The exile was seen as punishment for this unfaithfulness to Yahweh, the God of Israel. With the destruction of the Temple, animal sacrifices ceased. In place of the Temple, synagogues became the accepted houses of worship. There the sacred *Torah* was read and explained. It comprised the first five books of the Bible, the pentateuch. The word "Torah" is usually translated "law," but might better be rendered "instruction." The *Torah* gave instruction by example as well as by precept. Ultimately other sacred books were accepted as inspired Scripture. Jeremiah was lightly dismissed during the years of his ministry in Jerusalem, but in Babylonian exile his countrymen came to see that his prophecies were true. A collection of the "Prophets" — including some of our historical books — came into being. The Synagogue also recognized a third section of the Old Testament, the "Writings," beginning with the Book of Psalms and including books of poetry as well as history and prophecy. The New Testament bears testimony to the Law, the Prophets, and the Psalms as the three sections of Scripture. This threefold division is still used in printed editions of the Hebrew Bible.

When Cyrus came to the throne of Anshan, Nabonidus (Nabu-naid) was the unpopular king in Babylon. A philosopher and mystic, he felt called by Marduk to restore the temple of the moon-god Sin at Harran. When Nabu-naid protested that the proximity of the Medes would prevent the enterprise, Marduk, through his priests, replied:

> "The Mede of whom you are speaking, he himself, his land, and the kings who march at his side are not! When the third year comes, the gods will cause Cyrus, king of Anshan, his little slave, to advance against him with his small army. He will overthrow the wide extending Medes; he will capture Astyages, king of the Medes, and take him captive to his land."[1]

Had Marduk been a true prophet he might have added that Babylon would soon fall into the hands of Cyrus also.

1. Abu Habba Cylinder, col. 1, ll. 8-32. Quoted in A. T. Olmstead, *History of the Persian Empire*, p. 36.

In 550-549 B.C. Cyrus revolted against Astyages, his Median overlord. Meanwhile Nabonidus turned the kingship of Babylon over to his eldest son Bel-shar-usur (Belshazzar of the Book of Daniel) and headed for Harran, confident that the Medes had trouble enough with Cyrus to keep them busy. Such proved to be the case. Astyages sent an army under Harpagus against Cyrus, but Harpagus, remembering how Astyages had cruelly slain his son, deserted with most of his soldiers to Cyrus. Then Astyages determined personally to lead a second army against Cyrus. Reaching Parsa, the capital of Anshan, this second army mutinied against Astyages and handed him over to Cyrus.

Cyrus proved to be a generous conqueror. Although he did not hesitate to plunder the wealth of Ecbatana, the Median capital, the city itself was spared and became one of the capitals of the Medo-Persian Empire. Many of the Median officials were kept at their posts. This policy of clemency was new in the politics of the Near East, but it was to characterize the reign of Cyrus.

With the conquest of Media, Cyrus fell heir to Median claims in Assyria, Mesopotamia, Syria, Armenia, and Cappadocia. Some of these claims conflicted with those of Babylon, and we read no more of an alliance between Babylon and Cyrus. Beside the Medo-Persian Empire there were now three great powers — Lydia, Babylonia, and Egypt. The first two of these were subdued by Cyrus himself. His son Cambyses was to conquer the third.

2. Cyrus and Lydia

The Kingdom of Lydia first enters history when, in 660 B.C., Ashurbanipal demanded tribute of a Lydian king "Gyges of Luddi." The kingdom of Lydia was the country lying west of the Halys River in Asia Minor. It was blessed with fertile land and natural resources, not the least of which was gold. Gyges had conquered an area known as the Troad, giving his people an outlet to the sea. Under the fifty-seven year reign of Alyattes, grandson of Gyges, Lydia became a major power. Alyattes took Smyrna, the greatest port on the Asia Minor coast and, one by one, added the Greek coastal towns to his domain. Benevolent in his rule, Alyattes permitted the Greek cities to retain their own customs, institutions, and local government. Their taxes, however, helped the Lydian monarch to become the richest ruler of his age.

Croesus, the son and heir of Alyattes, completed the capture

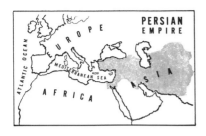

of the Greek settlements on or near the Aegean Sea by adding Ephesus and Miletus to his empire. His fabulous wealth is responsible for the simile, "as rich as Croesus." Herodotus repeats a legend to the effect that Solon visited Croesus and instructed him in the meaning of life by a series of illustrations summarized in the phrase, "Call no man happy until he is dead."

After the conquest of the Medes, the outer fringes of Cyrus' empire reached the eastern bank of the Halys River. Sooner or later a showdown must come with Lydia.

Cilicia offered no resistance when Cyrus laid claim to his provinces in Asia Minor. Realizing the imminence of attack, Croesus, however, hastily made alliances with Amasis, king of Egypt, and Nabu-naid of Babylon. Sparta offered him her fleet. Cyrus determined to strike immediately when he learned of Croesus' action through Eurybatos, a trusted friend of Croesus who betrayed his country. Eurybatos had been entrusted with large sums of money to be used in raising mercenaries in the Peloponnesus. Instead he fled to Cyrus and informed him of the plans of Croesus.

Leaving Sardis, Croesus crossed the Halys River for his first encounter with Cyrus. He consulted the oracles. They told him that, if he should send an army against the Persians, he would destroy a great empire. They had failed to tell him which empire! Croesus' initial victories over the Cappadocians filled him with confidence. When Cyrus offered Croesus his throne and kingdom in exchange for recognizing Persian sovereignty, Croesus was in no mood to accept. He indignantly retorted that he had never been subject to another power, whereas the Persians had been slaves to the Medes and would be the future slaves of the Lydians. Cyrus attacked at once.

After two indecisive battles, Croesus was driven from the field in a hopeless rout. He felt sure that Cyrus would not pursue him to Sardis because of the cold, snowy season which was approaching. Cyrus determined, however, not to wait until the allies of Croesus could come to his aid. Herodotus tells of the decisive battle in which camels were placed in the Persian front line to face the famed cavalry of Croesus. The horses, which had never seen camels before, stampeded. The infantry was unable to rally, and the battle became a rout, with the broken forces of Croesus seeking refuge in Sardis.

Although Croesus sent pleas for aid to Egypt, Greece, and Babylon, it was too late to save the day. The Spartans hastened to prepare their fleet, but before it could be launched, word arrived that Sardis had fallen and Croesus was a prisoner of the Persians.

The Nabu-naid Chronicle gives this official report of Cyrus: "In the month Aiaru (May) he marched against the country Lydia . . . killed its king, took his possessions, put (there) a garrison of his own."[2] Legends suggest that Cyrus dealt kindly with Croesus, allowing him to live in comfort near the ancient capital of Media. Actually it appears that Croesus followed the oriental custom of immolating himself to escape the usual indignities heaped upon a captured monarch before he was put to death. An Attic vase painter, Myson, within a half century of the death of Croesus, depicted him enthroned upon a pyre which a servant was about to light.

The once wealthy Lydian Empire now became the Persian satrapy of Saparda, or Sardis. A native Lydian, Pactyas, was placed in charge of the captured treasure of Croesus.

3. Cyrus and the Greeks

The conquest of Lydia brought Cyrus into contact with the Greek cities of Asia Minor which had made their peace with Croesus. Cyrus demanded that the coastal cities recognize his sovereignty, but they refused, only to be conquered one by one by the might of Persian arms or the diplomacy of Persian gold. There were Greeks, however, who welcomed Cyrus. The city of Miletus was shrewd enough to realize that Cyrus held the future, and submitted to him.

For some reason, the priests of Apollo, the Greek god of oracles, were thoroughly sympathetic with Cyrus. It was Apollo of Delphi who had uttered the ambiguous oracle that lured Croesus to his death. Apollo of Miletus, through his priests, was also clearly sympathetic with the Persians. When the city of Cyme asked counsel of the Apollo oracle concerning the disposal of a Greek who had rebelled against the Persians, Apollo ordered the surrender of the Greek rebel.

With the conquest of Greek Asia Minor, two Persian satrapys were formed. The Ionian satrapy was joined to Sardis, and the area south of the Hellespont was organized into a satrapy named "Those of the Sea."

Sooner or later Persia would have to fight the mainland Greeks. The Persians learned much from their dealings with the Greek cities of Asia Minor. Other important conquests in the

The Grand Temple of Apollo, at Delphi, Greece.

2. Translation of A. Leo Oppenheim in James B. Pritchard, ed., *Ancient Near Eastern Texts*, p. 306.

East must precede a final showdown with the Greeks, however.

4. Cyrus Heads Eastward

While Cyrus was conquering Lydia and Greek Asia Minor, Nabonidus was having his own troubles in Babylon. Under Nebuchadnezzar, Babylon had developed into a progressive and efficient state. Graft and mismanagement which developed under Nabonidus and his son Belshazzar brought on conditions of near starvation. Gobryas, or Gubaru as the Babylonians called him, had been one of Nebuchadnezzar's ablest generals. To him was entrusted the governorship of the Babylonian province of Elam, or Gutium. To add to the woes of Nabonidus, Gobryas deserted to Cyrus and began to attack Babylonian territory. His first blows were directed against the ancient city of Uruk, the Erech of Genesis 10.

Meanwhile Cyrus was giving his attention to the less civilized but strategically important lands to the east. While the wealth of his empire came from the west, for security reasons Cyrus had to control the east. The lands of Hyrcania and Parthia had been united before Cyrus had turned eastward. Their *kavi*, or local kinglet, was Hystaspes, famous as the father of Darius the Great. Hystaspes acknowledged the sovereignty of Cyrus and continued his rule as a Persian satrap.

The details of Cyrus' eastern campaign were not chronicled, as were those of his conquests of Lydia and Babylon. We know, however, that Cyrus continued his eastward march, incorporating Dragiana, Arachosia, Margiana, and Bactria into his empire. He crossed the Oxus River and reached the Jaxartus, where he built fortified towns to defend his northeastern frontier against the attacks of central Asian nomads.

5. The Fall of Babylon

Cyrus next turned his attention to Babylon. In this expedition he considered himself the deliverer rather than the conqueror of Babylon, and this feeling was shared by many Babylonians. The priests of Marduk, the god of Babylon, were happy to welcome Cyrus.

There was good reason for dissatisfaction with Nabonidus. He was an archaeologist and a mystic at heart. Like the famous Pharaoh Akhnaton of Egypt, Nabonidus was wholly unsuited by temperament for the office of ruler. An incompetent may succeed for a time if his challengers are equally incompetent, but Nabonidus was faced with the genius of a Cyrus. There was a time when Cyrus might have been stopped. Croesus might have succeeded in checking him had Babylon acted swiftly to aid her northern ally. But Nabonidus was spending his time in Teima watching the excavation of temple sites and admiring the handiwork of his predecessors. No aid reached Croesus, and Cyrus marched on.

Nabonidus was a very religious man. He chose to let the gods act as his guardians. When Babylon was threatened, he imported images of the gods from the surrounding cities, but this only added to dissatisfaction. The custodians of these local shrines were unhappy to have their temples plundered. The priests of Marduk in Babylon felt neglected, because Nabonidus seemed preoccupied with a host of "foreign" deities. Nabonidus alone lived in a fools' paradise.

In early October, 539 B.C., Cyrus was ready to invade lower Mesopotamia. Since the defenses of Babylon were reputedly impregnable, Cyrus had wisely bypassed Babylon until he had secured the territory to the east and to the west of the fabulous city. When Cyrus arrived, however, he was able to advance unchecked.

After an initial encounter at Opis, Sippar was taken without battle on October 11th. Nabonidus fled from Babylon, leaving his son Belshazzar in charge. Two days later, Gobryas, the governor of Elam (Darius of Daniel 6), captured Babylon without battle. Belshazzar was slain. Gobryas was named satrap of the new province of Babirush by Cyrus, who personally entered Babylon later in the month and proclaimed peace to everyone in the city.

The Cyrus Cylinder.

The Cyrus Cylinder gives Cyrus' own account of the capture of Babylon:

> "Marduk, the Great Lord, a protector of his people / worshipers, beheld with pleasure his [i.e. Cyrus'] good deeds and his upright mind [lit.: heart] [and therefore] ordered him to march against his city Babylon. He made him set out on the road to Babylon going at his side like a real friend. His widespread troops — their number, like that of the water of a river, could not be established, could not be established — strolled along, their weapons packed away. Without any battle, he made him enter his town Babylon, sparing Babylon any calamity."[3]

Cyrus realized the value and the need of a "return to normalcy" in Babylonian affairs. The reign of Nabonidus had been abnormal, but Marduk himself had provided a righteous ruler in the person of Cyrus. This is the way Cyrus himself describes it: "Marduk . . . scanned and looked [through] all the countries, searching for a righteous ruler . . . he pronounced the name of

3. Cyrus Cylinder, Pritchard, *op. cit.*, p. 315.

Cyrus, king of Anshan, declared him to be [come] the ruler of all the world."[4]

The disapproval of the priests of Marduk had been a major factor in the downfall of Nabonidus. Cyrus showed his co-operation with the Babylonian priests by going through the prescribed ritual at the great New Year Festival. By taking the hand of the god of Babylon he legalized the new line of Babylonian kings. Cyrus became "king of Babylon, king of the land."

Cyrus also determined to restore to their own shrines the gods which had been taken to Babylon by Nabonidus. The Cyrus Cylinder declares this as a matter of policy: "Furthermore, I re-settled upon the command of Marduk, the great lord, all the gods of Sumer and Akkad whom Nabonidus has brought into Babylon to the anger of the lord of the gods, unharmed, in their [former] chapels, the places which make them happy."[5]

The Babylonians had made it a practice to remove peoples from their homeland and settle them under the watchful eyes of the Babylonian kings. Such a policy had been used by Assyria. Assyria not only moved populations from their former homes, but moved others in to occupy the vacated areas. The ancestors of the Biblical Samaritans had such a history (II Kings 17:23-24, see also Chapter VII).

The Assyrian policy of permanent transportation meant the end of any hope for return to its former territory by the members of the exiled northern tribes. The Babylonians had not re-settled the Jerusalem area, however, and the exiles beside the waters of Babylon continued to weep as they remembered Zion. They longed for return to the land of their fathers.

Such restorations were part of the "back to normalcy" policy of Cyrus. Of the captive peoples he writes: "I [also] gathered all their [former] inhabitants and returned [to them] their habitations."[6]

The motives of Cyrus may not have been entirely humanitarian. Egypt was on the agenda, and thoroughly loyal settlers in the buffer area of Syria-Palestine would be of great help when Persia undertook the conquest of Egypt. Cyrus was wise as well as humane, and his policy with respect to captive peoples exhibited both aspects of his character.

6.   Cyrus and the Jews

When Cyrus became lord of Babylonia, the dependencies of

---

4. *Ibid.*
5. *Ibid.* p. 316.
6. *Ibid.*

Babylon likewise came under his control. He adopted a benevolent policy toward those former Babylonian provinces on the principle that the happier their lot, the more likely they would be to co-operate with Persian aims and goals. Phoenicia pledged its loyalty and its fleet, which was the match of any the united Greeks could raise.

The policy of the restoration of captive deities and captive peoples had special application to the Jews, whose religious ideals were respected by Cyrus and his successors as superior to those of the other nations with whom they dealt. To be sure, the Jews had no image that must be restored to its shrine, but Nebuchadnezzar had taken utensils from the Temple at Jerusalem. They had been used in Belshazzar's feast. If the gods of the other nations were restored, certainly the vessels used in the worship of the God of Israel must receive similar treatment.

Many Jews had prospered in Babylon and had no desire to leave. Not only were they permitted to remain, but many of them prospered in business and government during the Persian period. Daniel was among those that remained. The Book of Esther records both the influence and the trials of Jews in the Persian Empire. Nehemiah was cupbearer to a Persian king.

Yet the prophetic predictions of a return to a glorious Zion were not wholly unheeded. The permission to return for the purpose of rebuilding the Temple was made the subject of an official decree:

> "As for the house of God which is at Jerusalem, Let the house be built, the place where they offer fire continually; its height shall be ninety feet and its breadth ninety feet, with three courses of great stones and one of timber. And let its cost be given from the king's house. Also, let the gold and silver utensils of the house of God, which Nebuchadnezzar took from the house of God and brought to Babylon, be restored and brought again to the Temple which is in Jerusalem, each to its place. And you shall put them in the house of God" (Ezra 6:3-5).

The utensils were taken from Esagila, the temple of Babylon, and entrusted to a Jewish prince who had been appointed governor of Judah, Sheshbazzar (perhaps Shamash-apal-usur) by name. About 50,000 Jews availed themselves of the opportunity to return to their fatherland with the blessing and help of Cyrus. Aside from the assertion in Ezra 5:16 that he "laid the foundation of the house of God which is in Jerusalem" in 537 B.C., we read no more of the activity of Sheshbazzar.

The leadership of the band of returned exiles passed to Zerubbabel *(Zer-babili,* "seed of Babylon") and Jeshua (or Joshua) the priest. Consonant with the edict of Cyrus, they built the

Altar of Burnt Offerings and began the offering of daily morning and evening sacrifices (Ezra 3:3). In the second year of their return the foundations of the Temple were laid amid scenes of great rejoicing (Ezra 3:12). Nothing more was accomplished in the work of rebuilding the Temple during the lifetime of Cyrus (Ezra 4:5).

The joyful enthusiasm of the early days of the return gave way to the gloomy frustration which resulted from the activities of "the adversaries of Judah and Benjamin" (Ezra 4:1). Northern Palestine was populated with the deported captives from the Assyrian conquests to whom the name Samaritan was given (see Chapter VII). In the Judean highlands, the Negev, and in southern Judah as far north as Hebron, the Edomites, or Idumeans, had settled. The Nabatean Arabs had pressed from the Arabian desert into the area that had been occupied by the Edomites from Patriarchal times. North of the Edomites, people known as the Calebites occupied the territory up to Bethlehem (I Chron. 2:50 ff.) These nations had profited from the expulsion of Judah in the days of Nebuchadnezzar. They could not be expected to hail the returning pilgrims with any enthusiasm.

To be sure, some of those, called "the adversaries of Judah and Benjamin," offered to co-operate in the task of rebuilding, alleging that they had been worshipers of the God of Israel, since they had been introduced to the land of Israel as a result of one of Esarhaddon's deportations (Ezra 4:2). They seem to have shared the common concept that each land has its own god and that, as settlers in Israel, they must worship the God of that land. The leaders in Israel were not convinced of the purity of their faith and replied bluntly: "You have no part with us in building an house unto our God. We ourselves, together, will build unto Yahweh, God of Israel, as King Cyrus, the king of Persia, has commanded us" (Ezra 4:3).

The "people of the land" used every conceivable tactic to hinder the Jews from their work of rebuilding the Temple. However, the power of the Persian Empire seems to have restrained the "adversaries of Judah and Benjamin" from a policy of open war. Ezra tells us that the adversaries "troubled them in building" and tried to persuade the Persian court that the rebuilding of Jerusalem would prove detrimental to Persian interests (Ezra 4:5, 11-16). The adversaries were temporarily successful. For a period of about eighteen years little or no progress was made in the rebuilding process. In the meantime Cyrus died and Cambyses and Darius succeeded to the throne of the Empire.

7.   The Last Days of Cyrus

After the conquest of Babylon, Egypt alone remained of the allies of Croesus who had challenged Cyrus in his bid for world power. Plans for a campaign against Egypt were entrusted to Cyrus' son, Cambyses, while Cyrus personally set out to deal with a revolt of the nomads on the eastern frontiers of the empire. There, in what should have been a mere skirmish, Cyrus was wounded. In the steppe country east of the Caspian Sea he died. His body was carried back to Pasargadae, one of his capital cities.[7] There his body was covered with wax, according to Persian custom, and placed in a stately, dignified tomb which was guarded by faithful priests for two centuries. The tomb is still standing, but its contents have long since been removed.

Few world conquerors have been regarded as highly as Cyrus. The Persians called him father. The Greeks regarded him as a master and lawgiver. When Alexander the Great found that Cyrus' tomb had been rifled, he ordered that the body be replaced and the contents of the tomb be restored as far as possible. To the Jews he was the Lord's anointed who ended the Babylonian exile and opened a new era in the history of Israel. Cyrus did not force Persian ideas on his subjects, but rather formed a synthesis of the ancient cultures of Mesopotamia, Syria, Asia Minor, the Greek cities, and parts of India.

---

7. The others: Ecbatana, Babylon, and Susa.

79

Cambyses and the
Conquest of Egypt

For eight years before the death of Cyrus, his eldest son Cambyses had lived in Babylon and acted as his father's representative at the annual New Year's festival. A document dated February 20, 535 B.C., gives us a clue concerning the nature of his administration. Reference is made to the house of Nabu-mar-sharri-usur, steward of the King's Son. The name means "May Nabu protect the King's Son," and refers to Belshazzar, son of Nabonidus. The name suggests that its possessor was a palace dignitary, responsible for the welfare of members of the royal family. It is significant that Cambyses not only retained the civil officers of the Nabonidus regime, but kept the palace dignitaries as well.[1]

Persian custom decreed that the king should not leave his empire unprotected when he left for a foreign war. Before leaving to defend his eastern borders, Cyrus recognized Cambyses as regent with authority to use the title "King of Babylon." When news of his father's death reached Cambyses, he assumed his father's full title, "King of Babylon, King of Lands."

A second son, Bardiya, or Smerdis as the Greeks call him, was entrusted with the eastern provinces of the Empire. When the news of Cyrus' death reached the Empire, disorders broke out on all sides. These have commonly been attributed to an attempt of Bardiya to challenge Cambyses' right to the throne. The period is obscure, and the facts that have reached us have been interpreted differently. Cambyses is reported to have murdered his brother, concealing his death. Later, however, on his return from Egypt, Cambyses was to learn of the revolt of one who called himself Bardiya (known as Pseudo-Smerdis by the Greeks). The Behistun inscription (see Chapter III, sec. 2) of

---

1. A. T. Olmstead, *The History of the Persian Empire*, p. 87.

Darius agrees with the tradition that Cambyses actually murdered Bardiya:

The Tholos at Delphi.

> "He who was named Cambyses, the son of Cyrus, one of our race was king before me. That Cambyses had a brother, Bardiya by name, of the same mother and father as Cambyses. Afterwards Cambyses slew this Bardiya. When Cambyses slew Bardiya it was not known unto the people that Bardiya was slain."[2]

With the question of succession settled, Cambyses was free to proceed with the long-planned expedition against Egypt. The era of Egypt's greatness was long past, but her Pharaohs still had illusions of grandeur. Pharaoh Hophra had contested Nebuchadnezzar's claim to Palestine and encouraged Zedekiah to revolt. Trusting in Egyptian aid, Zedekiah defied Nebuchadnezzar. When Jerusalem fell in 587 B.C., the prestige of Egypt reached a new low.

Repercussions at home were hardly favorable to Hophra. A revolt among the warrior class was quelled by the skill of Amasis, a man who had come up through the ranks and held their confidence. Amasis was actually hailed as king, but a compromise was effected and a co-regency established in which Amasis had full power. Differences between Amasis and Hophra led to war and the death of Hophra. He was accorded a royal burial, but Amasis was free to go on with his own plans.

Seeing the rise of Cyrus and the Persian army, Amasis realized that he needed powerful friends. When the temple of Delphi was destroyed by fire in 548 B.C., he made a substantial contribution toward its rebuilding. He made an alliance with Polycrates, tyrant of Samos. The Greek world was the one hope of Amasis in his determination to challenge the Persian Empire. This alliance, however, was as much a disappointment to Egypt as Egypt had been to Judah in the contest with Nebuchadnezzar.

In about four years after his accession, having settled his domestic problems, Cambyses was ready to turn toward Egypt. While he halted at Gaza to survey the problems of marching his troops through the deserts and marshes which separated him from Egypt, unexpected help came. Polycrates of Samos decided to desert Amasis. In this way one of the best Greek generals in the service of the Pharaoh came to Cambyses to reveal the secrets of the Egyptian defense. This general, Phanes of Halicarnassus, put Cambyses in touch with the Sheikh of the Bedouin who arranged to station relays of camels with water

2. The Behistun Inscription, col. 1, line 10. Olmstead considers this account a fiction devised by the usurper Darius to legitimize his own rule. *Op. cit.*, p. 107 f.

along the route of march! The fifty-five miles of desert were quickly traversed, and Cambyses approached the walls of Pelusium where the Greek mercenaries were commanded by a son of Amasis, Psammeticus III. Amasis did not live to meet the attack of Cambyses. He died after a short illness. This seemed to be another ill omen to the already pressed Egyptians. A few days after the accession of Psammeticus III, rain fell at Thebes — a rare event which added to the nervous fear of the Egyptians.

After a fierce battle at Pelusium, Psammeticus and his armies fled to Memphis. Eighty years after the battle of Pelusium, Herodotus was shown the bones of the dead strewn over the battlefield.[3] He was told that Egyptian skulls were harder than those of the Persians!

By fleeing to Memphis, Psammeticus put himself into the position where one more battle would decide the destiny of Egypt. When Cambyses demanded that the capital surrender, his messengers were murdered. Then Cambyses attacked in strength. Firm Egyptian resistance delayed the fall of Memphis for a time, but in the end the city fell to Cambyses, and the land of Egypt entered a new period of history. Psammeticus III was deported to Susa, and Cambyses behaved as a true successor to the Pharaohs. He paid homage to the gods of Egypt and entrusted a high Egyptian official with the administration of the country. Reforms were ordered in the interest of the Egyptian people.

Cambyses determined to become a good Egyptian. As Cyrus had determined to legitimize his claim to the throne of Babylon, so Cambyses determined to ascend the throne of the Pharaohs as a legitimate sovereign. He adopted the royal costume and laid official claim to be the son of the sun-god Re. A firsthand account of Cambyses as he looked in Egyptian eyes was given by Udjahorresne, admiral of the royal fleet under Amasis and Psammeticus, and priest of the goddess Neith at Sais. Udjahorresne was appointed by Cambyses as head physician and served as a companion of the king and major domo of the palace. He prepared the official cartouch which designates Cambyses as "king of Upper and Lower Egypt" and descendant of Re. At the suggestion of Udjahorresne, Cambyses ordered the temple to be cleared of foreigners who had taken residence there.[4] Revenues which had been diverted from the temple at Sais to pay for Greek mercenaries were restored.

---

3. Herodotus, *Histories* III, 11,12
4. J. Couyat and P. Montet, *Les Inscriptions du Ouadi Hammamat*, No. 164.

Thus religious policy inaugurated by Cyrus seems to have been carried on by Cambyses. In some cases, however, gifts to the temples diminished and the activities of the priests were restricted. Later writers imputed to Cambyses an attitude of cruelty and ruthlessness which does not do justice to his character.

With Egypt firmly under control, Cambyses determined to press on to other African areas and add them to his domains. Carthage was then the dominant power in the western Mediterranean. Carthage had been colonized by Phoenicians, and the Phoenicians of Tyre refused to dispatch their ships against their own flesh and blood. Canaanite influence on the culture of Carthage is mentioned as late as the time of Augustine.

A land expedition of 50,000 men was sent against the Oasis of Ammon, west of Egypt. The expedition passed successfully the oases of el-Khargeh and ed-Dakhlah and continued their march through the desert. The Greek sources which relate this expedition tell us that it was overwhelmed by a sandstorm. The troops were never heard from again. Their utter annihilation is still a mystery. That the efforts of Cambyses to conquer African areas west of Egypt did not end in total failure, however, is evident from the fact that the Greeks of Libya, Cyrene, and Barka submitted.

Greek sources also tell of an expedition into Ethiopia, led personally by Cambyses. Before one-quarter of the distance had been covered, the army ran short of provisions and it was necessary to give orders to retreat. During this campaign Cambyses received news of troubles at home. The throne had been usurped by one who claimed to be his brother Bardiya.

Cambyses remained at Memphis for a short time after his return from the Ethiopian campaign. According to Greek sources, he abandoned his earlier kindly attitude toward Egyptian religion, ridiculed the god Ptah, ordered the statues to be burned, and stabbed to death the Apis-bull at Memphis. Olmstead discounts these tales. He states that the Apis-bull died while Cambyses was on his Ethiopian campaign, and the next Apis-bull, born in the fifth year of Cambyses, survived to the fourth year of Darius.[5]

As the news from Iran became more alarming, Cambyses determined to return home. Egypt was left with garrisons at Daphnae, east of the delta, at Memphis the capital, and at Elephantine at the first cataract of the Nile. The Elephantine

5. A. T. Olmstead, *op. cit.*, p. 90 f.

garrison is of particular interest because it was garrisoned by Jewish mercenaries who had a temple of their own and had correspondence with their Palestinian co-religionists (see Chapter VIII).

On the course of his journey homeward, probably in northern Palestine, Cambyses received confirmation of the report of the usurpation of the throne by the pretender Gaumata who had assumed the name of Bardiya, or Smerdes. The new ruler was accepted by nearly all the provinces of the Empire. He attempted to win the favor of the people by remitting taxes for three years, and he attempted a religious reform.

Cambyses never reached home. Herodotus says his death resulted from a wound accidentally self-inflicted when mounting his horse. The Persian record suggests suicide. We know that Cambyses suffered from epileptic fits, and there are evidences of insanity in his latter days, particularly if the reputed atrocities committed in Egypt after his return from the Ethiopian campaign are to be believed.

After Cambyses died, the army remained loyal to the government which he represented. Two months later the pretender Gaumata was taken prisoner and executed. Darius, son of Hystaspes was to become the next Persian monarch.

80

Darius and the
Reorganization of the Empire

Darius claimed to be the legitimate successor of Cambyses. In the eyes of many of his contemporaries he was a usurper. Olmstead entitles his chapter on Darius, "Usurper Darius." The Behistun inscription shows the pains which Darius took to prove that he was the scion of the house of Achemenes. He gives his pedigree thus:

> "My father is Hystaspis; the father of Hystaspis was Arsames; the father of Arsames was Ariyarmenes; the father of Ariyarmenes was Teispes; the father of Teispes was Achaemenes...on that account are we called Achaemenians; from antiquity are we descended; from antiquity hath our race been kings...eight of my race were kings before me, I am the ninth."[1]

Legend states that, after the death of Cambyses, seven Persian nobles, under the leadership of Darius, conspired against the false Bardiya. They agreed to choose as king the one whose horse neighed first after sunrise. Through the ruse of his groom, the throne was won for Darius.

I. Revolt in the Empire

Whatever may be said of Darius' claim to the throne, it was established with the greatest of difficulty. With the assassination of Bardiya, the empire began to split apart. Darius, however, was not one to sit idly by and see the empire dismembered. When but twenty years of age, he had accompanied Cyrus in his campaign against the northwestern mountaineers. He had been in Egypt with Cambyses. Revolts began in Elam and Babylon and spread through most of the empire. Within two years, however, Darius was firmly established as the Persian monarch. To accomplish this, he adopted a policy of firmness reminiscent of the cruelty of Assyrians such as Ashurbanipal. More than once we read of the treatment of a rebel in which

---

1. The Behistun Inscription, col. 1, lines 2-4.

Darius boasts that he "cut off his nose and his ears and his tongue and put out his eyes,"[2] and cast him in fetters at the royal court to be gazed at by the people as a warning that rebellion does not pay.

2.   The Behistun (Bisitun) Inscription

Darius wanted his victories to be remembered by posterity. He likewise wished to have his contemporaries respect his power. It was the policy of many Pharaohs and kings of the Near East to prepare monuments to commemorate their victories. The stela of the Egyptian Merneptah commemorates a victory in Palestine and is the first Egyptian mention of Israel. The black obelisk of Shalmaneser shows subject peoples, including Jehu of Israel, paying tribute to the Assyrian. The annals of Sennacherib boast of the victories of the Assyrian who besieged Jerusalem and shut up Hezekiah "like a bird in a cage." Cyrus had recorded his choice by Marduk and his benevolent policy toward captive peoples and gods. None of these ever attempted a monument on so grand a scale as the Behistun inscription of Darius. He chose a mountainside on which to record his deeds on imperishable stone. On the main caravan route between Bagdad and Tehran, sixty-five miles from Hamadan, at an altitude of five hundred feet, a series of inscriptions fifty-eight feet, six inches long can still be seen. By the side of the road is a spring where the ancient traveler had to stop. Darius used the techniques of the modern billboard advertiser!

Beneath the symbolic figure of his god, Ahuramazda, stands Darius, with his foot resting on the prostrate form of Gaumata, the false Bardiya. The uplifted hand of Darius demands the attention of the passer-by, insisting that he stop and read. Behind Gaumata are nine men, their hands bound behind their backs and cords about their necks. These are the pretenders and rebels whom Darius has defeated. Behind Darius are two armsbearers.

The inscription itself was written in Old Persian, Babylonian, and Elamite. As a tri-lingual inscription it may be compared with the Egyptian Rosetta Stone. As the Rosetta Stone provided the key to the decipherment of Egyptian hieroglyphics to Champollion and his successors, so the Behistun inscription provided the key to the decipherment of Babylonian (or Akkadian) cuneiform to Rawlinson and later cuneiformists. It would be

---

2. The Behistun Inscription, col. 2, line 13.

hard to exaggerate the value of such studies in helping us to reconstruct the history of the ancient Near East.

3. Darius and the Jews

The work of rebuilding the Jerusalem Temple, begun as a result of the edict of Cyrus, had come to a halt. The last days of Cyrus and the reign of Cambyses were times of disillusionment and adjustment for the returned exiles. Harassed by unfriendly neighbors, they found they had all they could do to provide for the necessities of this life. The people were agreed on one thing: "The time is not come, the time that the Lord's house should be built" (Hag. 1:2).

This spirit of defeatism was not shared by Haggai and Zechariah, two prophets who began to prophecy to Judah in the second year of Darius. They were aware of the problems which the Jews faced, but theirs was the heroism of faith:

> "Yet now be strong, O Zerubbabel, saith the Lord; and be strong, O Joshua, son of Josedech, the High Priest; and be strong, all ye people of the land, saith the Lord, and work: for I am with you, saith the Lord of hosts: according to the word that I covenanted with you when ye came out of Egypt, so my spirit remaineth among you: fear ye not" (Hag. 2:4-5).

The threats and the promises of Haggai and Zechariah stirred discouraged Judah to renewed activity. The work of rebuilding began in earnest. Perhaps at the instigation of "the adversaries of Judah and Benjamin," the Persian governor "beyond the river," Tattenai (perhaps "Thithinaia" in Persian) made a visit to investigate the activities of the Jews. Anything that savored of rebellion against Darius would be dealt with promptly. Tattenai's question was a pointed one: "Who gave you a decree to build this house and to finish this wall?" (Ezra 5:3). The Jews appealed to the decree of Cyrus, and suggested that a search be made of the royal archives for the royal decree.

In the royal archives at Ecbatana the decree was found. Darius determined that it must be honored. His royal order said: "Let the work of this house of God alone; let the governor of the Jews and the elders of the Jews build this house of God in his place" (Ezra 6:7). He further decreed that funds be given the Jews from the royal treasury to assist in the rebuilding project (Ezra 6:8).

The difficulties of the Jews were not over. The adversaries continued to stir up trouble, but it is to the credit of Darius that he honored the decree of Cyrus and encouraged the Jews in their labors.

A stone slab with a figure of a sphinx, from the palace of Darius at Persepolis.

In the sixth year of Darius (516 B.C.) the Temple was completed. Special dedicatory sacrifices were offered, and the priests and Levites were assigned their respective tasks (Ezra 6:15-18).

4.   Civil Government under Darius

The policy of ruling through native princes, which Cyrus followed, had certain political weaknesses. The opening days of Darius' reign were proof that instability was fostered when the central government was not independently strong. The death of a king was a signal to the native princes to revolt in the hope that the new king would not be able to assert imperial authority.

The institution of the satrapy existed before Darius. The word, in its Persian form *Khshatrapava,* occurs in the Behistun inscription. Darius developed the institution and extended it over all his empire.

In government as organized by Darius, the king was supreme and absolute. Yet there were certain restrictions upon his liberty. The other six of the seven Persian nobles who had conspired against the false Bardiya had extensive land grants. They also had the right to provide the king's wives. Unless the king married within the royal Achemenian line as did Darius, he was permitted to marry only the daughters of the Persian nobles. These men must be consulted on important occasions. Seven counselors might be consulted in matters of lesser importance.[3] On points of law, seven judges, appointed for life, must be consulted. The king was bound by his own decisions, as is reflected in the proverbial expression, "the law of the Medes and Persians which altereth not" (Daniel 6:8, 14, 15; cf. Esther 1:19, 8:8).

This Greek drawing in graffito appears on a fragment of a shod foot from a Persian relief of Darius in Persepolis. The fragment dates from the sixth century B.C.

Under the king were the satraps, each restricted to his own satrapy. The satrap was a civil governor only. The military chief in the satrapy was independent of the governor, and responsible directly to the king. The chief satrapies were filled by members of the royal house. Where such were not available, the king's daughters might be married to a satrap. Rogers observes, "So complete was the process of appointing in the first instance and of hedging about with surveillance within and without that we hear astonishingly little of malfeasance in office among the satraps."[4]

The disappearance of Zerubbabel from his position as governor of Judah may be a result of the civil reorganization effected

3. Cf. Herodotus, *Histories* VII. 8: Ezra 7:14.
4. Robert William Rogers, *A History of Ancient Persia,* p. 112.

by Darius. There is no hint in the Biblical records that he was removed for sedition, as some have suggested. The fact that his name simply drops out of the Biblical record may suggest that the change of policy which Darius inaugurated resulted in his removal.[5]

A gold daric of Darius I.

The development of roads and the postal system was another of the projects which Darius designed to facilitate the government of his far-flung empire. Several great roads were inherited from the old Assyrian Empire. One of these extended from Babylon to Carchemish, with a connecting spur to Nineveh, and was prolonged westward and southward to Egypt. Another bound Babylon to the heart of Media. Darius rebuilt the road which connected Nineveh to Ecbatana, passing over the Zagros Mountains, and the road from Ecbatana to Sardis passing through Harran with a spur going down to Susa.

The Persian postal system far surpassed all of its predecessors. The network of roads was divided into post routes with horsemen stationed at regular intervals. Any message from king to satrap, or satrap to king, was carried from one stage to the next until it reached its destination. Herodotus' famous description of the Persian Post can be seen engraved across the front of the New York post office: "These neither snow nor rain nor heat nor darkness of night prevent from accomplishing each one his appointed task, with the very utmost speed."[6]

One hundred and eleven post-stations were located along the one thousand six hundred and seventy-seven mile road from Susa to Sardis and Ephesus. The caravans took ninety days to travel this road from end to end. The royal couriers, availing themselves of the fresh relays of horses at the post-stations, covered it in a week.

5.   Military Tactics of Darius

The standing army maintained by Darius was surprisingly small. His personal bodyguard consisted of 2,000 cavalry and 2,000 infantrymen of noble birth and 10,000 "immortals" recruited from the Medes and Persians. Further recruits from the Median or Persian nobility might be summoned as needed.

At the most important fortresses, such as Sardis, Memphis, Elephantinae, Daphnae, and Babylon, forces of the standing army were kept. In the event of minor rebellions, the satraps, either alone or in concert with neighboring satraps, were ex-

5. N. H. Snaith, *The Jews from Cyrus to Herod*, p. 17.
6. Herodotus, *Histories* VIII, 98.

The Taurus mountain range in Asia Minor (present-day Turkey).

pected to find means to restore order. The king himself was responsible for meeting a major threat. The guard was mobilized and a levy was made to secure recruits. Their lack of adequate training would be a weakness in the event of a major attack. The empire suffered only minor skirmishes for a long period, and the military program was adequate for such.

Darius had been most successful in administering his government. Like many another ruler, he could not stand inactivity. Herodotus reports a conversation in which Atossa, Darius' wife, challenged him with the words, "Sire, you are a mighty ruler; why sit you idle, winning neither new dominions nor new power for your Persians?"[7]

In 512 B.C. Darius decided to attack the Scythians. These nomadic people had come southward and westward from the steppes of Russia and had settled north of the Black Sea, and west and south as far as the Danube.

Tales of the Scythians had spread throughout the Persian Empire. They were ready to occupy Thrace, and Asia Minor would be next! Gold mines were abundant in their country, guarded by griffins and worked by harmless ants as large as foxes! The satrap of Cappadocia had crossed the Black Sea and taken several prisoners from among the Scythians. Darius determined to teach the Scythians respect for Persian arms, and add some Scythian gold to the royal treasury at the same time.

Although Darius knew little about the Scythians, he had had dealings with the Greeks, and probably hoped to take the Balkans from the rear, and at the same time, deprive Greece of timber for its fleet. Control of the entire Black Sea region would also cut off much of the wheat supply from Greece.

Greek sources suggest that the army raised by Darius for his Scythian campaign numbered about 700,000. This was the first military encounter between Asia and Europe.

Darius' Greek physician, Democedes, was sent with a fleet to reconnoitre the Greek coast and is thought to have reached Tarentum. A force of thirty more ships explored the western waters of the Black Sea. Byzantium accepted Persian rule. The beginnings of the campaign appeared auspicious.

The army passed over the Straits on a bridge of boats and conquered eastern Thrace with little resistance. They followed the contour of the Black Sea to the mouth of the Danube, then followed the Danube west to the head of the Danube Delta where a bridge was built by the Ionians of Darius' army. It was

7. Herodotus, *Histories* III, 134.

Darius' hope to carry out his land operations in conjunction with the fleet which was to follow along the coast, but the navy and the army soon lost contact and Darius had to plunge into the interior of the country. The Scythians would not stand to give battle, but withdrew before the Persians, forcing the Persians to enter an unknown country. The "scorched earth" policy of the Scythians soon produced real suffering in an army which expected to find its support from the land. Darius was compelled to give up the pursuit of fleeing nomads and retreated toward the Danube bridge and civilization.

The Scythian campaign was not a complete failure. Before recrossing the Bosphorus, a force of 80,000 men was dispatched to complete the conquest of Thrace, and this was successfully carried out. The Persian boundaries were now in contact with the northern Greeks. Macedonia recognized the suzerainty of Darius.

Marble Street of ancient Ephesus.

Back in Asia Minor the Greek coastal cities successively fell into the hands of Darius. The centers of the Black Sea wheat trade were all in his hands. Except for Greece itself, Darius was sovereign of the Greek world.

About the time of the Scythian campaign in the west, the Persians decided to descend from the Iranian plateau upon the plain of the Punjab region of India. The project was easily accomplished, and a new satrapy was formed which yielded immense revenues for the Persian crown.

Resisting the temptation to push east to the Ganges, Darius turned his attention to the southeast. He ordered the building of a fleet which was put under the command of Scylax, a Greek admiral in the employ of Darius. For thirty months Scylax explored the Indus River, the Indian Ocean, and the Red Sea.[8]

Darius was interested in exploration because of his desire to connect Egypt with the rest of his empire. Scylax discovered the relation between the Red Sea, the Persian Gulf, and the Indian Ocean.

In the days of Pharaoh Necho an unsuccessful attempt had been made to build a canal between the Nile River and the Gulf of Suez. In 518, while in Egypt, Darius evidently noticed traces of this earlier enterprise. His desire for a cheaper and

8. Aristotle refers to an account of his experiences written by Scylax (*Politics* VII. 14. 2). In modern times it has been questioned by many competent scholars and the episode simply ignored by others. Meyer, *Geschichte des Altertums*, III, p. 99 ff, and Rogers, *op. cit.* p. 119, accept it as true.

more direct route to India caused him to give orders for the digging of a new canal. Five red-granite stelae were erected along the banks of the canal. On them Darius declares:

> "I am a Persian. From Parsa I seized Egypt. I commanded this canal to be dug from the river, Nile by name, which flows in Egypt, to the sea which goes from Parsa. Afterward this canal was dug as I commanded, and ships passed from Egypt through this canal to Parsa as was my will."[9]

A Median guard, from the relief on the Apadana at Persepolis.

6. Greek Rebellion

Darius was never able to incorporate the mainland Greeks into his empire. His successes in Thrace and Macedonia served to put the democratically minded Greek city states on guard. Darius tried to interfere in the internal affairs of Athens, which had a pro-Persian party, but the presence of Persian gold in Athens had a negative effect. Athens threw in her lot with the opposition.

The courage of the European Greeks in daring to defy Darius sparked a revolt of the Ionians who had been Persian subjects. The Ionian league was re-established, and the aid promised by European Greece was proclaimed. The Greeks seized Sardis but had to retreat before Persian reinforcements. Meanwhile the European Greeks withdrew because of war between Athens and Aegina. The area suffered at the hands of the Persians to such an extent that the consequences were felt for two centuries.

Since the revolt of the Ionians had been encouraged by the European Greeks, Persia decided it must take action against the continent. A fleet of 600 ships left Asia Minor with the avowed purpose of strengthening the pro-Persian elements in Greece by a show of force. Half the ships and about 20,000 men were lost in a severe storm off Mt. Athos. A second attempt was more successful. Datis, the Median admiral, besieged the Greek city of Eretria. When it was betrayed into his hands, Datis made the mistake of burning the temples, destroying the town, and selling its inhabitants as slaves to Susa. This served to unite the various factions of Greeks against Persia. They saw clearly that the Persians would show no mercy toward the conquered Greeks.

When Darius landed at Marathon, he was met by the Athenian army. Before reinforcements could arrive from Sparta, the Athenians met the Persians and won a resounding victory. Seven Persian ships were captured by the Greeks, and the re-

9. Diodorus, i. 33.9, claims that the canal was not completed because the king was told that the level of the Red Sea was higher than that of the Nile, and therefore Egypt would be flooded if the canal were actually opened.

The stairway to Darius's palace at Persepolis.

mainder withdrew. Troubles in Egypt demanded the attention of Darius, and he gave up his plans for resuming his operations against Greece.

Shortly after Marathon, Egypt was in open revolt against Darius. The heavily garrisoned troops living off the land, and the heavy tribute and taxes demanded by Darius, proved too much for the Egyptians. The Greeks had probably encouraged revolt in Egypt and other trouble spots in the Persian Empire.

7. The End of Darius

Before the Egyptian revolt was ended, Darius had died. As an organizer of the civil government he has seldom been equaled. The royal palace which he built at Persepolis was one of the great structures of antiquity. Darius could be cruel. He ruled as an absolute monarch. Organizationally, the Persian Empire reached its peak of efficiency under Darius, but decay had already begun to set in.

81

Xerxes and the

Attempted Conquest of Greece

Xerxes had been carefully groomed as successor to Darius. If some question exists concerning the right of Darius to the throne, the line of Xerxes cannot be challenged. He was the son of Darius by Atossa, a daughter of Cyrus. For twelve years he served under his father as viceroy of Babylon before succeeding to the throne at the death of Darius. The Persian form of the name Xerxes is Khshayarsha, which, in Hebrew, is rendered Ahasuerus (Ezra 4:6 and the Book of Esther).

I. Revolts in the Empire

When, at the age of thirty-five, Xerxes succeeded his father as king, the land of Egypt was in rebellion and the Greek problem had not been resolved. Xerxes acted promptly. Egypt was made submissive to the Persian crown, and Achemenes, a younger brother of Xerxes, was placed in charge.

Babylon next rebelled, with several claimants assuming the royal title "King of Babylon and of the Lands," but Xerxes decided to act. Zopyros was appointed Satrap by Xerxes, only to be slain by the rebellious Babylonians. Megabysos, the son of the slain satrap, was appointed in his stead, and Xerxes determined to thoroughly humble the Babylonians.

The walls of the city were razed by the Persians, and the ornate temples of Babylon were destroyed. The famous temple, Esagila, was demolished, and the golden statue of Bel-Marduk was melted down. Every king who claimed to be the legitimate ruler of Babylon was required to take the hands of this statue of the god of Babylon every New Year's day. In destroying the statue, Xerxes attempted to end the very concept of a continuing Babylonian empire. The title "King of Babylon," which had been part of the royal title of the Persian kings since

Cyrus, was dropped. Xerxes simply called himself "King of Persia and Media," with Babylon continuing as a part of the Persian Empire.

2. Xerxes and Greece

After successfully resolving the problems within the empire, Xerxes turned his attention westward. Careful preparation was made for a simultaneous land and sea attack on Greece, a project attempted but not successfully executed by Darius.

For three years Xerxes planned for the impending invasion. A canal was built to avoid the tempestuous cape of Athos, where Darius had lost a large portion of his fleet. Bridges were erected and provisions were assembled at strategic places in preparation for the attack.

Xerxes recruited his army from forty-six nations. Twenty-nine Persian generals commanded the army, with Xerxes as commander-in-chief. The straits which separate Asia Minor from Europe were spanned by a bridge of boats built by the Phoenicians. Xerxes made a libation to his gods, and cast a cup, a sword, and a bow into the waters to insure success.

Our information comes from the Greek historians, and we suspect that some of their figures are exaggerated. The importance of the invasion, and the subsequent withdrawal of Xerxes, can hardly be exaggerated, however.

The fleet of Xerxes numbered, we are told, 1,207 fighting vessels with additional large ships driven by as many as fifty oars. The number of transports — 3,000 — is almost certainly an exaggeration. The ships were manned by the Phoenicians, but among the navigators were also Cypriots, Ionians, Cilicians, and Hellespontese. Four hundred and seven Greek ships are said to have been enlisted in Xerxes' navy.

After spending the winter in Sardis, the armies of Xerxes crossed the bridge from Asia to Europe in May or June, 480 B.C. The fleet then sailed to Sarpedon. In the meantime Xerxes sent heralds to the Greek cities to give them an opportunity to submit voluntarily. They were asked to send back earth and water in token of their submission.

While Xerxes was temporarily encamped at Therma, the heralds made their reports. A few brought earth and water, but most of Greece was determined to fight for its independence. Early in August, Xerxes began to move forward.

Athens and Sparta resolved their own differences and formed a coalition to fight the Persians. They appealed to all the Greeks to join them in fighting for their liberty. They met

This statue of a Spartan hoplite warrior was found in Arabia. It dates from the sixth century B.C.

The front of the Parthenon at Athens.

with considerable, but not universal, success. Argos and Crete adopted a policy of neutrality.

The early battles were disastrous for the Greeks. Thessaly was lost in spite of the valiant fighting of ten thousand heavily armed infantry who had been sent to guard the vale of Tempe. The middle of Greece was next under attack and the Greeks determined to hold Mt. Oeta, which was flanked on the right by the Euboean Straits and the Gulf of Malis. Ten thousand men under the Spartan, Leonidas, determined to defend the only road through the pass at Thermopylae. A Greek fleet was sent to meet the Persian navy at Artemisium.

A storm destroyed three of the Greek ships sent to Artemisium, but the Persians lost, according to Greek figures, four hundred ships of war, and a larger number of transports off the Artemisium promontory. Fifteen Persian ships seeking refuge from the storm were captured by the Greeks.

The Spartans, under Leonidas, were prepared to check the advance of the Persians into central Greece, but Greece was betrayed by a Malian named Ephialtes. The Persians were shown a path over the mountain to the rear of the Greeks. The Spartans fought to the end, and Leonidas became a hero by dying at his post. The Persians, however, won an important objective, for mid-Greece had opened before them. By August Xerxes was in Athens. He burned the temples on the acropolis, allegedly in revenge for the burning of Sardis.

The goals of Xerxes appeared about to be realized. Xerxes hoped to complete the conquest of Greece by engaging the Greek fleet which was concentrated at Salamis. The Greeks had about 380 ships, only half the number the Persians could place in battle. Yet the Battle of Salamis, September 27th or 28th, 480 B.C., became one of the decisive battles of history. The destruction of Athens had shown the Greeks that their culture and civilization would not be respected by a conqueror like Xerxes. Fighting for their homes and their lives, the Greeks so thoroughly defeated the Persians at Salamis that the Persian fleet, with Xerxes, was forced to flee.

The Persians still had a large land army, and Xerxes entrusted the Greek campaign to Mardonius, one of his generals. First seeking success through diplomacy, Mardonius was unable to make any headway with the Greeks.

Mardonius next fought a series of battles designed to bring Greece finally to her knees before Persia. Much of Attica was despoiled and Mardonius moved on to Boeotia. The Greeks of the Peloponnesus took the offensive, however. Mardonius was defeated at Meggara. A defensive position was taken by Mardonius between Plataea and the river Asopus. With 50,000 Asiatic troops and 10,000 Greek allies he awaited attack. Twelve thousand Spartans, heavily armed, joined other Greeks to make a comparable army of 50,000 poised against the Persians. In cavalry, Mardonius had an advantage, but otherwise the armies were of comparable strength.

After ten days of waiting for favorable omens, Mardonius used his cavalry to attack the Greeks. The Persians were decisively defeated. The Greeks, who had been warned of the impending attack, were able to make the best use of their forces. Mardonius was slain and his army fled, leaving immense stores of provisions and booty in the field. Herodotus says that not 3,000 Persians remained alive, although this is considered to be an exaggeration.

At the same time the Athenians succeeded in conquering Persia's Greek allies. Before autumn the entire Hellespont area was in Greek hands. The following spring Byzantium, the last Persian stronghold in the Greek world, fell, and the bitter struggle between the Persians and the Greeks was ended.

3. The Close of Xerxes' Reign

After the Greek debacle, Xerxes was not to distinguish himself again on the field of battle. He lived fourteen years after the loss of Greece, but little is known about them. He was murdered by a usurper, Artabanus, who is said to have reigned seven months before being killed by Artaxerxes, the third son and legitimate heir of Xerxes. The first son born after the king's accession to the throne was regarded as legitimate successor.

4. Xerxes and the Bible

There is only one brief reference to Xerxes in the annals of Palestinian Judaism. Ezra 4:6 is the one Biblical reference which bridges the fifty-eight year period between the dedication of the Temple and the arrival of Ezra in the seventh year of Artaxerxes. The only information we have states that "the people of the land," that is, the Samaritans, Edomites, and other enemies of Judah, in the beginning of the reign of Ahasuerus (Xerxes) wrote an accusation against the inhabitants of Judah and Jerusalem.

Xerxes seems to have been too busy elsewhere to trouble himself with the problems of Judah. The period was one of

The black-figure ware (top) from Athens shows Theseus cutting off the head of the Minotaur. The red-figure ware (below) from Athens portrays Leto, Apollo, and Artemis. The ware dates from the fifth century B.C.

The Gate of Xerxes in Persepolis was guarded by man-headed bulls at the eastern doorway.

frustration and disappointment for the Jews who were looking for deliverance from their foes.

The lot of the Jews who had chosen not to return to Judah is described in the Book of Esther. The virtuous Vashti was deposed by Xerxes who searched the realm for a suitable substitute. Esther, who was not known to be a Jewess, was chosen as the fairest maiden in the empire and brought to be a wife to Xerxes. When the royal favorite, Haman, determined to rid himself of the hated Mordecai, cousin and guardian of Esther, along with all the Jews of the realm, Mordecai urged Esther to intercede with Xerxes on behalf of her people. He was convinced that she had "come to the kingdom for such a time as this." She risked her life by seeking an audience with the king. Xerxes received her kindly, however. He determined to save the Jews from the persecution that had been decreed. Haman was hanged on the gallows which he had prepared for Mordecai. The Jewish feast of Purim commemorates this deliverance of the Jews in the days of Esther.

Xerxes was reputed to act habitually like a spoilt child. The Esther episode agrees well with this description. He was given to ostentation and loved display, and appears to have been susceptible to the flattery and intrigue of fawning courtiers. Religiously he was a Zoroastrian, which may account, in part, for his willingness to destroy the Bel-Marduk temple in Babylon. He was assassinated by the captain of his bodyguard, Artabanus, in the twentieth year of his reign.

82

Artaxerxes I and the
Loss of Persian Prestige

The age of Artaxerxes is one of the best documented periods of classical antiquities. Herodotus, the "father of history," was traveling throughout the world and writing his famous histories. Pericles was in power in Athens. The famous monuments of the Parthenon were built during the Periclean age, and Athens reached the zenith of its culture and influence.

Artaxerxes Longimanus (i.e., "the long handed" because his right hand was reputedly longer than his left hand) had the usual problem of putting down rebellions in various parts of the realm when he became king of the Persian Empire. The efficient governmental system of Darius had been weakened during the reign of Xerxes, with the result that rebellion was more likely to succeed. Hystaspes, a brother of Artaxerxes, attempted to assert independent rule in Bactria, but Artaxerxes acted quickly and forcefully to re-establish his own royal authority.

Disturbances in Egypt gave Artaxerxes more cause for concern. Familiar with Greek defiance of Persia, many in Egypt hoped for a similar position of independence. Inaros, a son of the Pharaoh Psammeticus, was recognized as king by a group of the nomes of the eastern Delta. Achemenes, son of Darius and brother of Xerxes, represented the Persian interests in Egypt. While Artaxerxes was putting down the Bactrian revolt, Achemenes appeared in Persia to seek help in bringing Egypt into submission. An army was raised, and Achemenes returned to Egypt.

Achemenes defeated Inaros in the initial battle. A Greek fleet of two hundred vessels subsequently came to the aid of the rebellious Egyptians, and most of the city of Memphis was lost to the Persians. Artaxerxes raised a new army under the leader-

A tribute bearer from Greece portrayed at Persepolis. The style of hair in tight spiral curls was a convention of archaic Greek art.

ship of Megabyzos and enlisted the aid of a Phoenician navy under Artabazos. A decisive battle was fought in the Delta, and Inaros was wounded. The Egyptians and their Greek allies barricaded themselves in Prosopitis for eighteen months. Unable to dislodge them by military attack, the Persians diverted the branch of the Nile in which the Greek fleet was anchored. The desperate crew burned the ships before surrendering to the Persians. The Phoenicians sank a fleet of fifty Greek triremes which had been sent to reinforce the rebels. Thus the rebellion in Egypt was put down, but Persia had had to pay a large price to retain control over Egypt.

At this time Ezra "the scribe" requested permission of Artaxerxes to lead a fresh group of Jews back to Judea. Ezra was called "the scribe of the law of the God of heaven." Olmstead suggests that this would be equivalent to "Secretary of State for Jewish Affairs." Ezra would thus be responsible to the king for the Jewish community.

Jews had prospered in Babylonia during the Persian rule. Great business houses like that of the Murashu family of Nippur have left us cuneiform texts which describe the details of their extensive business enterprise.[1] While the more worldly minded would have little concern for the settlement which had been established in Jerusalem in the days of Cyrus, the spiritually minded knew that God was working out His purposes through that remnant that had returned.

Ezra gathered together 1,500 such Babylonian Jews as a group of colonists who would reinforce and assist the earlier settlers, and help accomplish the necessary rebuilding and defense operations. In the seventh year of Artaxerxes I the group organized at Ahava, a district in Babylonia. Bearing gold, silver, and Temple utensils, they started out on a journey which would take them over five months to complete.

Arriving safely on the twelfth day of the seventh month, Ezra lost no time in beginning his ministry. The reading and interpretation of the Law, and its enforcement, particularly in the matter of mixed marriages, occupied much of his time and energies. It should be remembered that he was acting on the authority of the Persian government, and that his decrees were binding in a political as well as in a religious sense.

Men who had returned from Babylon were frequently guilty of divorcing their lawful Jewish wives and marrying the women

---

1. H. V. Hilprecht and A. T. Clay, *Business Documents of Murashu Sons of Nippur.*

of the land. In pre-exilic days mixed marriages had been a temptation. Solomon was led astray by his foreign wives. The restored community must, according to Ezra's interpretation of Scripture, rid itself of the "daughters of the peoples of the lands." The people were ordered to assemble in Jerusalem, under penalty of the "devotion" (i.e., destruction) of their property and exclusion from the congregation. At the appointed assembly the divorce of alien wives was accepted in principle, with provision for detailed examination of individual cases.

Enemies of Judah sought to find some excuse to prevent the Jews from fortifying and protecting the city of Jerusalem. Ever since the first return the adversaries had been at work. In the days of Artaxerxes a letter of accusation was addressed to the Persian king in which the Jews were accused of plotting rebellion against the crown. Artaxerxes, nervous at the thought of rebellion, ordered the Jews to stop their rebuilding operations until he should make a further decree (Ezra 4:1-21). The enemies of Judah used force (Ezra 4:23) to prevent the Jews from completing their work of rebuilding the city walls. It is this state of affairs that challenged Nehemiah.

In the court of Artaxerxes in Susa (or Shushan), Nehemiah was functioning as royal cupbearer. The exact nature of his work is not known, but his was a position of importance which brought him into close terms with the king. When the king learned of the distress of heart which plagued Nehemiah, he gave him a leave of absence to return to Jerusalem to assist in repairing the broken walls.

With an armed escort, Nehemiah reached Jerusalem and surveyed the needs of the city. He summoned the leaders of the city and assured them that God's hand was upon him. Unitedly they began to build. The old enemies of the Jews were as active as ever. A cry of rebellion was made. They attempted to lure Nehemiah to a conference in the valley of Ono. They charged Nehemiah with assuming royalty. Nehemiah disregarded the charges of the enemy and patiently continued his work.

In spite of opposition from without and from within, the walls went up, the gates were set in place, and the city was able to function once more. A city without walls was no city at all, according to ancient standards.

The completion of the work was enthusiastically celebrated. Ezra and Nehemiah headed processions which moved around the walls in opposite directions, meeting near the site of the

The mound of Susa (top) from the air. The scene below is part of a bronze model from Susa that represents the worship of the dawn.

Temple. Sacrifices were offered, and the sound of rejoicing was heard afar off.

With pomp and ceremony the populace gathered in the Temple courts to hear the reading of God's Word and to pledge their obedience to its precepts. It was probably the Pentateuch that Ezra had in his hands as he read the Law of the Lord. The Feast of Tabernacles was observed as the people rejoiced in the goodness of God.

After an absence of twelve years, Nehemiah returned to Susa to report to the king. He had no sooner left Jerusalem than the old problems began to reappear. The enemies came back on the scene to make trouble, the Levites did not receive the dues to which they were entitled, the laws of the sabbath were forgotten, and foreign marriages became common again. The children were heard speaking the languages of their non-Jewish mothers (Neh. 13:23, 24).

Nehemiah made a second trip to Jerusalem. Dependent on God to help him enforce the divine Law, Nehemiah accomplished a second reformation of the religious and civil life of Jerusalem. With this, both the Book of Nehemiah and the history of the Old Testament comes to a close.

Artaxerxes was not in the position to strengthen his holdings in the west, and the decline of the Persian Empire is usually dated from his reign. Egypt and Cyprus were still subject to Persia, but most of the rest of the west was gone. The Athenian fleet dominated the eastern Mediterranean. Thrace was self-governing. The conquests of Cyrus in Ionia were in Greek hands.

83

The Latter Achemenians,
Approaching the End

The reign of Darius II was one of intrigue and corruption. Although no battles were fought with the Greeks, Persian gold was used to incite Athens against Sparta in the Peloponnesian War. Persian influence over the Greek cities of Asia Minor was thus strengthened.

Minor successes did not change the pattern of history, however. Revolts continued throughout the Persian Empire. The Medes rebelled. Egypt was restive. The Jewish temple at Elephantine was destroyed, but Persia was unable to punish the insurgents.

Artaxerxes II barely missed being killed by his brother Cyrus during his coronation ceremony at Persepolis. At the intreaty of his mother, Artaxerxes pardoned Cyrus. Returning to his satrapy, Cyrus again plotted rebellion. He raised an army and came close to winning a decisive battle near Babylon. Cyrus was a man of courage. He might have arrested the decline of the dynasty had he occupied the throne. But he was killed in battle, and the dreams of his followers were dissipated.

The story of the Greek contingent in Cyrus' army was immortalized by Xenophon. After the disastrous battle of Cunaxa (401 B.C.), the Ten Thousand, as the Greeks were called, fought their way back home, passing through hostile territory and harried by the Persians under Tissaphernes. After the Greek generals had been killed by the Persians, Xenophon was chosen as one of the leaders of the retreat. He led the Ten Thousand up the Tigris, past the ruins of Nineveh (now a forgotten city), to the Black Sea and Byzantium. Xenophon's account of this famous retreat in *The Anabasis* became one of the great books of military science in the ancient world.

Although Persian arms were weak, Artaxerxes was able to

maintain some prestige at home and abroad by the use of Persian gold. In Greece, Athens and Sparta were played off against one another to the benefit of Persia. The Greek cities of Asia Minor were subject to Artaxerxes, and opposition found a quick response. Persian forces on land and sea maintained control over the Ionian Greeks, although the glory of Persia was a thing of the past.

Within Persia new problems arose. A number of the satrapies had become powerful, hereditary offices. High taxes were imposed on the native population, with the result that revolt was fomented. Egypt had declared its independence at the accession of Artaxerxes and had never been reconquered. Cyprus, Phoenicia, and Syria took advantage of Persian weakness to follow suit. Revolts of peasants and artisans were savagely repressed, but the disintegration of the empire continued. One after another the western satrapies all fell away from the empire. They formed a coalition and issued their own coinage.

When Egypt, allied with Sparta and the rebel satraps, marched against Artaxerxes, the empire seemed doomed. A reprieve came, however, when a revolt against Pharaoh Takhos made it necessary for Egypt to abandon its plans and surrender. The threat against Persia was relieved for the time being, but disturbances continued until the death of Artaxerxes II.

Before its downfall, the Achemenian Persian Empire was to enjoy one more period of power. Artaxerxes III determined to rule with the strength of a Darius the Great. He began his reign by murdering all his brothers and sisters — several dozen in all. Sidon, which had sympathized with rebellious Egypt, was burnt and left in ruins. Egypt was reconquered, its cities taken, and their walls razed. Persia was again in a position to menace the Greeks.

Hellenism existed as a cultural if not a political force. Patriotic Greeks urged all who shared Greek culture to unite against the Persians. The mainland Greeks lacked the unity which could accomplish such a mission. To the north, however, Macedon was ruled by an energetic leader who became the dominant personality among the Greeks.

Prodded by the oratory of Demosthenes, Athens concluded an alliance with Persia. Philip of Macedon interpreted this as an unfriendly gesture. In 338 B.C. Philip and his son Alexander won a decisive victory over Athens. The Persian threat was removed, but Greek independence was also destroyed. Philip of Macedon and his son Alexander (later "the Great") now held

These ruins of a Crusader castle are situated on a small island in the Sidon harbor. The island is connected to the mainland by an arched bridge.

the destiny of Greece. In the same year Artaxerxes was poisoned.

The murderer of Artaxerxes was Bagoas, a eunuch who had political ambitions of his own. Bagoas spared the life of Arses, the youngest son of Artaxerxes, expecting to use him as a puppet ruler. When Arses showed evidence of having a mind of his own, Bagoas poisoned him also.

In looking for someone whom he might trust, Bagoas chose a cousin of Artaxerxes III who had distinguished himself in battle and had become satrap of Armenia. Bagoas had chosen unwisely again, however. The new monarch took the name of Darius III. Fearing the power and treachery of Bagoas, Darius had him poisoned.

The gold medallion shows a winged lion with horns. Iranian in origin, it dates from the sixth or fifth century B.C.

Darius III became king of Persia in 336 B.C. The same year twenty-year-old Alexander ascended the throne in faraway Macedonia with a commission from his father to make war upon Persia. The tide of empire moved toward Alexander and away from Darius. In 333 B.C. Darius was defeated in the battle of Issus. Two years later the center of the empire was pierced by Alexander's victory at Gaugemela, or Arbela. Darius fled to Ecbatana, and then on to Bactria, where he was murdered by his cousin Bessus who took command of the unsuccessful opposition to Alexandria in Bactria.

It is probable that Darius III is the "Darius the Persian" mentioned in Nehemiah 12:22. According to Josephus[1], Jaddua, who is listed as a contemporary of "Darius the Persian," was also a contemporary of Alexander the Great.

With the death of Darius III the empire founded by Cyrus the Great came to an end. The dynasty is named after Achemenes, a minor ruler of a mountainous district in southwestern Iran. The period of ancient Persia's greatness extended from about 550 B.C. to 330 B.C.

---

1. *Antiquities* xi. 8. 4.

84

The Problems and
Progress of the Jews

The Samaritan countryside, near Jacob's well.

I. The Samaritans

The name Samaria first appears in the Bible as the name of the capital of the northern kingdom. Omri and Ahab built luxurious palaces there, and on occasion the name of the capital is used for the whole kingdom. Samaria was the last city of Israel to fall to the Assyrians. In 722/721 a large number of influential citizens were deported to various cities of the Assyrian Empire. Conversely, colonies of non-Jews from Babylonia, Syria, and Elam were settled in Samaria (II Kings 17:24-29). The result was a mixed population and a disposition to worship Yahweh as the god of the land, along with a reverence for the other gods which the new settlers had formerly worshiped.

The latter kings of Judah, particularly Hezekiah (during whose reign Samaria fell) and Josiah seem to have attempted to expand their borders northward to include some of the territory formerly ruled from Samaria. Faithful Yahwists made their way down to the Jerusalem Temple and relations between Samaria and Judah were quite cordial.

The destruction of Jerusalem and the Babylonian exile, taking place about a century and a half after the fall of Samaria, seem to have changed the picture somewhat. During the time that there was no effective government in Jerusalem, the Samaritans and other neighbors of the Jews were able to occupy former Judean territory and develop a new economy in which the Jews-in-exile had no part. Such Jews as remained in Palestine doubtless made their peace with their neighbors, and a new mode of life was developed.

When the first settlers returned to Jerusalem, following the decree of Cyrus (536 B.C.), the Samaritans and their neighbors faced a crisis. If the Jews were to become independently strong, the possessions of the Samaritans might be threatened. From the earliest days of their settlement, the returned exiles met with difficulty from the Samaritans and their other neighbors.

The Samaritans offered to help in the rebuilding operations, but they were rebuffed. The Jews had learned that co-operation with the idolater would bring the judgment of God. They chose to labor on alone.

When Sanballat, the governor of Samaria under the Persians, was unable to get at the Jewish problem by co-operation, he chose the path of attempted coercion. Neither threats nor armed intervention succeeded, however. The Jews were able to rebuild Temple and walls without outside help and in spite of outside interference.

A Samaritan priest stands in solitude on Mount Gerizim.

One of the burdens of Ezra and Nehemiah was that of the mixed marriages of many of the colonists who had returned from Babylon. One of the sons of Joiada, the High Priest, married a daughter of Sanballat, governor of Samaria. This was not only a mixed marriage, but a marriage with an avowed enemy. When the son of the priest, Manasseh by name, refused to give up his Samaritan bride, Nehemiah expelled him.

We know that the Samaritans had a temple on Mt. Gerizim which was destroyed by the Jews in the days of John Hyrcanus. Josephus says that this temple was built by Sanballat for Manasseh so that he could both function as priest and be married to Sanballat's daughter. Other priests who refused to divorce their non-Jewish brides are said to have joined Manasseh (*Antiquities* XI. vii, viii). The Josephus account is repudiated by some scholars, including Montgomery, who regards it simply as a midrash on Nehemiah.

In succeeding years the Jews and the Samaritans became bitter enemies. The statement in John 4, "The Jews have no dealings with the Samaritans," had behind it years of bitterness between the two peoples. It is noteworthy that Jesus saw fit to go through Samaria and thus show that His disciples were not to allow any restrictions to be placed on the preaching of the gospel. The Parable of the Good Samaritan and the miracle in which the Samaritan is commended as the one who returned to thank God for cleansing from leprosy further illustrate the attitude which Jesus commended toward those who would be looked upon as aliens from the commonwealth of Israel.

2. The Jews of Elephantine

During the years 1907 and 1908 excavations were carried on

at the island of Elephantine, ancient Yeb, opposite Assuan (Syene, Ezekiel 29:10; 30:6) at the first cataract of the Nile. Many ancient papyri written in Aramaic were discovered. They were written by Jews between the years 494 and 400 B.C. Most of them were business documents, involving contracts for loans, conveyance of property, and similar activities. The names used are familiar to all readers of the Bible. They include Hosea, Azariah, Zephaniah, Jonathan, Zechariah, Nathan, and Azariah.

The most interesting document is a letter written in 407 B.C. and addressed to Bigvai, the governor of Judea. It tells how Egyptian priests, with the connivance of the local governor and the active assistance of the governor's son, destroyed the temple which the Jews had built at Elephantine:

> "They entered that temple and razed it to the ground. The stone pillars that were there they smashed. Five 'great' gateways built with hewn blocks of stone which were in that temple, they demolished... and their roof of cedar wood, all of it... and whatever else was there, everything they burnt with fire. As for the basins of gold and silver and other articles that were in that temple, they carried all of them off and made them their own."[1]

The Egyptian priests resented the sanctuary of an alien deity in their midst, and determined to cleanse their land of its defilement. They doubtless found enough anti-Jewish sentiment among the people to implement their purposes.

The Elephantine Jews asked help in rebuilding their temple.[2]

> "Now your servants Yedoniah and his colleagues and the Jews, the citizens of Elephantine, all say thus: If it please our lord, take thought of this temple to rebuild it, since they do not let us rebuild it. Look to your well-wishers and friends here in Egypt. Let a letter be sent from you to them concerning the temple of the God Yaho, to build it in the fortress of Elephantine as it was built before; and the meal-offering, incense, and burnt offering will be offered in your name and we shall pray for you at all times, we, and our wives, and our children, and the Jews who are here, all of them if you do thus, so that that temple is rebuilt. And you shall have a merit before Yaho the God of Heaven more than a man who offers to him burnt offering and sacrifices worth a thousand talents of silver and (because of) gold. Because of this we have written to inform you. We have also set the whole matter forth in a letter in our name to Delaiah and Shelemiah, the sons of Sanballat the governor of Samaria. Also, Arsames[3] knew nothing of all that was done to us. On the twentieth of Marheshwan, year 17 of King Darius."[4]

The Elephantine Jews, while much concerned about the temple and worship of the God of Israel, whom they called Yahu or Yaho, did not maintain the purity of worship insisted

---

1. Pap. 1. 9-13; H. L. Ginsberg's Translation.
2. Pap. 1, 22-30, *op. cit.*
3. Arsames was the satrap of Egypt. According to an earlier passage in the papyrus (4,5) he was in the Persian court during the time of the outrage.
4. Darius II, 424-405 B.C.

on by the prophets of Israel. Among the other gods whom they worshiped were Ishumbethel, Herembethel, 'Anathbethel and 'Anathyahu. Anath was the Canaanite goddess of fertility and war, sister and consort of Baal. The name at Elephantine seems to imply that she was there regarded as the consort of Yahu.

The very existence of a temple and fully developed sacrificial system indicates that the Elephantine Jews rejected the concept of a single central sanctuary as the place to which sacrifices to Yahu (Yahweh) must be brought. Through much of the history of the divided kingdom a conflict existed between those who advocated a central sanctuary and those who preferred the multitudinous "high places." The unity of the God of Israel was inherent in the concept of a central sanctuary, and reformers like Josiah (621 B.C.) insisted on destroying the "high places" as centers of idolatry. The pagan elements in the religion of the Elephantine Jews would underscore the necessity for insisting on the Jerusalem Temple as the one place where sacrifice might be offered.

The Elephantine Jews doubtless considered themselves to be wholly orthodox. Their letters mention the observance of the Jewish Passover and the Feast of Unleavened Bread. A priesthood and sacrificial system patterned after that of the Jerusalem Temple functioned at Elephantine. The fact that appeals are made to Samaria as well as to Jerusalem indicates that the Elephantine Jews did not deem it necessary to take sides in the conflicts between Jerusalem and Samaria.

The origin of the Elephantine community has puzzled scholars, and no theory that has been propounded is without its problems. Contacts, favorable and unfavorable, had been maintained between Israelites and Egypt from Patriarchal times. When Jeroboam found it necessary to flee from King Solomon, he found sanctuary in Egypt. A party friendly to Egypt had existed in both Samaria and Jerusalem before the destruction of these capital cities by the Assyrians and Babylonians. Jeremiah had urged Zedekiah not to heed the pro-Egyptian party, but the promise of aid from Egypt was a deciding factor in Zedekiah's defiance of Nebuchadnezzar. Jeremiah was taken to Egypt where he presumably spent his last days.

One of the Elephantine papyri clearly indicates that the Jewish colony there antedates the invasion of Egypt by Cambyses, the son and successor of Cyrus: "Now our forefathers built this temple in the fortress of Elephantine back in the days of the Kingdom of Egypt, and when Cambyses came to Egypt he found it built. They knocked down all the temples of

A sealed contract from Elephantine.

the gods of Egypt, but no one did any damage to this temple."[5]

The apocryphal *Letter of Aristeas* states that Jews entered Egypt with "the Persian" (Cambyses), and that others had earlier come to Egypt to fight as mercenaries in the army of Pharaoh Psammeticus. Herodotus tells us that Psammeticus II (593-588 B.C.) waged war with the Ethiopians. This leads to the supposition that the Jewish mercenaries were used by Psammeticus in this war, after which they were garrisoned at Elephantine, near the Egyptian-Ethiopian border.

If this reconstruction of the history is correct, the settlement which produced the Elephantine papyri was comprised of the descendants of these earlier settlers, possibly augmented by fresh recruits from Palestine, all of whom were now serving in the Persian army.

While this view appears plausible, and cannot be ruled out as a possibility, there are several problems. The language of the papyri is Aramaic, rather than Hebrew. It would be supposed that Jews coming to Egypt before the exile would have brought their mother tongue with them. A further problem is one of chronology. Psammeticus II was on the throne of Egypt during the years immediately preceding the fall of Jerusalem to Nebuchadnezzar. Are we to picture Jewish soldiers forsaking their own land to fight in the army of Psammeticus against the Ethiopians? Psammeticus seems to have had access to Greek mercenaries, so that there would have been no real need for Jewish recruits.

Another theory, suggested by W. O. E. Oesterley, maintains that the Elephantine Colony was comprised of northern Israelites from Assyria. It is suggested that the second generation of the captives who were removed from Israel after the fall of Samaria were enrolled, either voluntarily or by compulsion, in the army of Ashurbanipal. After Ashurbanipal's conquest of Egypt, Assyrian garrisons were stationed in various parts of the country. The Assyrian hold on Egypt was short-lived, however. Ashurbanipal's victories dated from 667 B.C., but by 663 B.C. Psammeticus I had cleared out the Assyrian garrisons. Oesterley assumes that Psammeticus recognized the Elephantine garrison as Israelite, and permitted the Israelites to enlist in his own army. He suggests that these Israelites would be glad to remain away from Assyria. The language of that part of the Assyrian Empire from which they came was Aramaic, hence the Aramaic of the Elephantine papyri.

---

5 Pap. 1, 14-15, *op. cit.*

Oesterley's view also helps explain the reason for addressing a request for aid to the Samaritans. Presumably the larger part of the community owed its ancestral origins to Samaria. The elements of paganism at Elephantine have something in common with the Scriptural description of the Samaritans who "feared Yahweh" but also served other gods.

While a final word concerning the origin of the Elephantine community cannot yet be given, and no view is without objections, the existence of the community shows us something of the development of Jewish religion during the Persian period. If a reformer like Nehemiah appears Puritanical in his attitude toward his Samaritan neighbors, Elephantine shows the danger which beset a community which left its moorings and allowed a religious syncretism in which Yahweh could be associated with a pantheon of deities.

3. The Synagogue

Origin of the Synagogue

During the time between the Old Testament and the New Testament period, there arose the institution which was to become the focal point of Jewish life through the centuries. No record has been left of the origin of synagogue worship. Jewish tradition suggests that the first synagogues were established during the time of Babylonian exile.

Pre-exilic Judaism looked to the Jerusalem Temple as the focal point of its spiritual life. Worship at local shrines, or "high places," continued through much of Israelite history, but the prophets, and the kings who supported them, abolished such worship and insisted on the primacy of the Temple. In this way the unity of the God of Israel was emphasized, in contrast to the concept of local gods which was prevalent in the ancient world. Jeremiah complained of his generation, "...according to the number of thy cities are thy gods, O Judah" (2:28).

When the armies of Nebuchadnezzar destroyed Jerusalem with its Temple, a new orientation was demanded in the worship of the Israelite. According to popular views, a god was expected to protect his people, and the victory of an enemy meant that the gods of the enemy were the strongest of the contending divine beings. Wars were fought on two levels — human and divine. The strongest god would win.

Many in Israel doubtless shared these viewpoints, for the temptation to idolatry and conformity with the current religious practices and ideals was an ever present one. This was not true, however, of those religious leaders of the Jews whom we call the prophets. Defeat in battle did not mean that the God of Israel was weaker than the gods of the Babylonians. It meant that Israel's God was chastening His rebelling people. The prophets saw a divine purpose in Israel's calamities. Daniel writes, "The Lord gave Jehoiakim king of Judah into his (Nebuchadnezzar's) hand" (1:2). The destruction of the Temple was not an evidence of the weakness of Israel's God, but an evidence of His holiness.

Psalm 137 describes the attitude of exiles in Babylon. They are in a strange land, weeping at the remembrance of Zion. Their captors ask them to sing one of the songs of Zion, but Israel protests, "How shall we sing the Lord's song in a strange land?" They remember Jerusalem, and long for the day of restoration.

All evidence, including the prophetic word of Jeremiah, indicated that the exile would be a long one. Before Jerusalem fell, Jeremiah had written to the exiles who had been deported earlier, "Build ye houses, and dwell in them; and plant gardens and eat the fruit of them; take ye wives and beget sons and daughters; and take wives for your sons, and give your daughters to husbands . . . and seek the peace of the city whither I have caused you to be carried away captives, and pray unto the Lord for it, for in the peace thereof shall ye have peace" (29:5-7).

With the destruction of the Temple, sacrifices ceased. Prayer, and the study of the sacred Scriptures, however, knew no geographical limitations. The Book of Ezekiel describes the elders of Israel gathering in the prophet's house (8:1; 20:1-3). Such gatherings became more regular and more organized in nature, resulting in the weekly synagogue services, after which the weekly services in the Christian church were patterned.

The word "synagogue" is of Greek origin, meaning a gathering of people, or a congregation. The Hebrew word for such a gathering is *keneseth,* the name used for the parliament in the modern state of Israel. The word *synagogue* is used for the local congregation of Jews and also for the building in which the community meets for its assemblies and services. In Hebrew the building may be referred to as the *beth hakkeneseth,* "the house of assembly."

With the return from exile following the decree of Cyrus, a second Temple was built in Jerusalem. This again became the focal point of Jewish religious life until its destruction in A.D. 70. Large numbers of Jews did not return to Palestine, however, and the institution of the synagogue continued to fill the spiritual needs of Jews who remained in "the dispersion," whether in Babylon, other cities of the Persian Empire, Egypt, or — later — the cities of Asia Minor, Greece, and Rome. In New Testament times we read: "For from early generations Moses has had in every city those who preach him, for he is read every sabbath in the synagogues" (Acts 15:21).

For the Jews who returned to Palestine, the synagogue became the place of prayer and Bible study, as the Temple served as the place of sacrifice and the center of the great annual convocations. In Nehemiah 8 we read of a great gathering for the public reading of the "Book of the Law of Moses." Ezra made use of a pulpit, or platform, from which he read and explained the Scriptures to the assembled throngs. The fact that the Scriptures were written in Hebrew, and that Aramaic was the spoken language of post-exilic Judaism, provided a further reason for gatherings to translate and interpret the ancient Scripture. In Palestine, as in the dispersion, a quorum of ten heads of families could organize a synagogue.

In the larger towns a body of twenty-three elders formed the sanhedrin, or governing body of the synagogue community. In smaller communities the number of elders was seven. These elders *(presbuteroi)* are sometimes called rulers, *(archontes)*. From this group one was designated "chief ruler" *(gerousiarches)*. The sanhedrin served as a court, and in Judea it represented the civil as well as the religious government. Punishment of scourging, excommunication, and death could be decreed. Scourging was inflicted in the synagogue building. It consisted of "forty stripes save one" (cf II Cor. 11:24; Josephus *Antiquities* iv. 8:21). Excommunication was regarded as a more serious sentence. In its earliest form it meant absolute and final exclusion from the Jewish community. The Hebrew term descriptive of this is *herem.* This is the equivalent of the Greek *anathema,* descriptive of one who is under the curse of God. A temporary excommunication (Hebrew *nidduy*) later developed as a severe rebuke to those whose transgression was not so outrageous as to evoke the *anathema.*

Although the sanhedrin could impose the death penalty in extreme cases, under the Roman rule capital punishment required the confirmation of the Roman procurator (cf. John 18:31).

Each community had its local sanhedrin, but that of Jerusalem attained the eminence of the highest Jewish judicatory. This became known as the Great Sanhedrin. It was presided over by the High Priest and met in a hall associated with the Temple structure. Scribes and the most eminent members of the high-priestly families were associated with the Great Sanhedrin. Its mandates were recognized wherever Jews dwelt (cf. Acts 9:2) .

Synagogue Worship

The worship services of the synagogue enjoyed great freedom. Any competent Israelite could officiate. The liberty which was accorded the apostle Paul illustrates this fact.

The leaders of the worship at the synagogue were not the same as those who cared for the legal side of the life of the community, although the same persons could serve in both capacities. The "ruler of the synagogue" *(archisunagogos)* super-vised the service and assumed responsibility for the care and or-der of the synagogue building. The *hazzan*, or "minister" (A.V.) , of the synagogue brought the Scriptures to the reader and replaced them in their receptacle after the lesson had been read. He served as the agent of the sanhedrin in scourging of-fenders, and is thought by some to have been responsible for the teaching of children.

Synagogue worship was doubtless very simple in its early his-tory. The elements of prayer and the reading and explanation of a portion of Scripture were doubtless parts of the service from the earliest days. By the time of the Mishna (2nd and 3rd cen-turies after Christ) five principal parts of the service are enu-merated: The Shema, prayer, the reading of the Law, the reading of the prophets with the benediction, and the translation and explanation of the Scripture lesson.

The Shema receives its name from the Hebrew word meaning "hear." It consists of Deuteronomy 6:4-9; 11:13-21; and Num-bers 15:37-41. A benediction is uttered before and after the reading of the *Shema*. The reciting of the *Shema* doubtless stems from the desire of the pious in Israel to teach the sacredness and importance of the Law. Outward, symbolic signs known as frontlets (N.T. "phylacteries") are enjoined as reminders of God's Law. The opening words of the *Shema* were quoted by Jesus (Mark 12:29) in answer to the question, "Which com-mandment is the first of all?" The use of phylacteries and fringes is well known in the New Testament (cf. Matt. 23:5), giving evidence of the use of the *Shema* in the synagogue service during pre-Christian times. The conception of the *Shema* as a confes-sion of faith and a substitute for animal sacrifices is a later development.

At the beginning of the second century the chief prayer of the synagogue was the *Shemoneh 'esreh,* "eighteen (benedictions)." These prayers traditionally are ascribed to the time of Ezra, with a final redaction around A.D. 110 by Rabbi Simeon ha-Pakkoli. In point of fact the New Testament does not give evidence of a fixed form of prayer. Great leaders and learned rabbis seem to have suggested suitable prayers which were adopted by their disciples. We are told that John the Baptist taught his disciples a form of prayer (Luke 11:1). The disciples asked Jesus to do likewise, and the Savior responded with the Lord's Prayer.

The present form of the *Shemoneh 'esreh* comes from the period subsequent to the fall of Jerusalem (A.D. 70). It exists in two different recensions, one from Palestine and the other from Babylon.

The reading of a lesson from the Law was the most prominent part of the synagogue service. Tradition says, "Moses instituted the reading of the Law on the sabbaths, feast-days, new moons, and half feast days; and Ezra appointed the reading of the Law for Mondays and Thursdays and the sabbath afternoons" (Jer. *Meg.* 75a). Actually the development of the reading of the Law went through a varied history. There were annual cycles for completing the reading of the Law, two-year cycles, three-, and three-and-a-half-year cycles in use at different times. These cycles were based on the consecutive reading of the Law, with portions assigned for both weekdays and sabbaths. Special readings were chosen for the four Sabbaths before passover, festivals, half-festivals, new moons, and fast days.

Every Israelite, even minors, could partake in the public reading of the Law. On the Sabbath day at least seven readers were chosen. If priests were present, they were called on first, followed by Levites, and then by lay members of the congregation. Special benedictions were pronounced by the first reader before the reading, and by the last reader at the end. After each verse an Aramaic rendering *(targum)* was given by an interpreter *(methurgeman).* In Palestine the interpreters were not permitted to use written translations. They were required to adhere to the traditional rendering and to refrain from allegorizing.

The selection of a portion from the Prophets forms a further step in the development of the synagogue ritual. The readings from the Prophets seem to have been chosen with a view to the explanation or illustration of the Law. It is thought that the reading of prophetic portions had not yet been systematized by New Testament times, and that the selection read by Jesus in the synagogue of Nazareth (Luke 4:16) was his own choice. As in the case of the Law, an interpreter translated the lesson from the Prophets into Aramaic. He was permitted to translate three verses at a time from the prophetic portions.

Although the sermon was not an essential part of the synagogue service, the translation and explanation of the Scripture lesson was a step in the direction of a preaching service. There is evidence that an exposition of the lesson formed a part of the Sabbath afternoon service. In earliest times the sermon seems to have been connected with the reading from the Prophets. Anyone able to instruct might be asked to preach (Acts 13:15). The preacher spoke from a sitting position on an elevated place (Luke 4:20).

At the close of the service a blessing was pronounced by a priestly member of the congregation. All present responded with an Amen. If no priest or Levite was present, the blessing was made into a prayer.

The Building

Our knowledge of the synagogue buildings is derived from descriptions in ancient literature and the discovery of the ruins of ancient synagogues by archaeologists. The chief article of furniture in the synagogue was the "ark," containing the scrolls of the Law and other sacred writings. The ark stood by the wall farthest from the entrance. In the center of the synagogue was a raised platform *(bemah)*, on which was placed a lectern. The rest of the room contained wooden seats. The chief seats were those nearest to the ark, facing the people. Since the Middle Ages, women have been assigned to the balconies of orthodox synagogues, but it is not at all certain that this was true in antiquity. There is evidence, on the contrary, that women could sit in the chief seats of the synagogue and bear titles of honor in the synagogue.

Probably the most spectacular synagogue discovery is that of Dura-Europus in Syria, excavated by M. I. Rostovtzeff of Yale from 1932-1935. Elaborate murals show such scenes as the resurrection of the dry bones described by Ezekiel, and the anointing of David.

As a rule the front of a synagogue faced Jerusalem, and contained three entrances. There was a desire to place the synagogue on the highest spot in the city. Proximity to water was desirable because of the necessity for ceremonial ablutions.

Most of our information on ancient synagogues comes from the period after the ministry of Jesus. It does exhibit, however,

Ruins of the synogogue at Capernaum. This building, which dates to the second century A.D., was probably constructed on the same site as the synogogue that existed in Jesus' day.

a variety which was hardly expected. Elaborate murals, mosaics with designs of lions, horses, goats, and different varieties of birds, elaborate Doric and Corinthian type pillars show a feeling for art which was earlier thought incompatible with Jewish loyalty to the Law which forbade "graven images." It may be unwise to generalize as the result of a limited number of synagogue discoveries, but it seems safe to say that varying attitudes existed among the Jews with reference to art in the synagogue. In some ages, and in some places, a very tolerant attitude prevailed. In other times, a rigorous attitude toward the Law resulted in iconoclastic movements.

Renan called the synagogue "the most original and fruitful creation of the Jewish people." As an institution it has been the rallying point of Judaism from the Babylonian exile to the present day. In Jewish synagagues Jesus spoke and Paul preached. The earliest Christian church adapted the synagogue type of service as the vehicle of Christian growth and evangelism. Without the development of the synagogue, neither Judaism nor Christianity could exist as we know them today.

Alexander the Great was an apostle of Hellenism. His teacher, Aristotle, helped Alexander appreciate the literature and cultural institutions of Greece. A conqueror and empire-builder often has little time for the "finer" things. But this was not so with Alexander. Convinced of the superiority of Greek institutions, Alexander spread Hellenism so effectively that it continued to be the dominant pattern of life long after his death and the disintegration of his kingdom.

The Dead Sea Scrolls have done much to quicken an interest in the literature of the Jews during the inter-Testament period. It is the purpose of Part Eight of this volume to outline the broader background necessary for the appraisal of those movements which immediately precede the advent of the Savior.

PART EIGHT

Between the Testaments – The Hellenistic Period

CHRONOLOGY

Persian Period

Date B.C.

612	Nineveh destroyed by Medes and Babylonians.
587	Jerusalem destroyed by Nebuchadnezzar.
559	Cyrus inherits kingdom of Anshan, tributary to the Medes.
549	Cyrus of Anshan conquers Astyages, the Mede.
539	Babylon falls to Cyrus. End of Neo-Babylonian Empire.
530-522	Cambyses succeeds Cyrus. Conquest of Egypt.
522-486	Darius I ruler of the Persian Empire.
515	Completion of Second Temple in Jerusalem.
486-465	Xerxes I attempts the conquest of Greece. Time of Esther.
480	Greek naval victory at Salamis. Xerxes flees.
464-424	Artaxerxes I rules Persia. Age of Nehemiah.

The Hellenistic Period

334-323	Alexander the Great conquers the East.
330	Macedonian conquest of Palestine.
311	Seleucus conquers Babylon. Beginning of the Seleucid dynasty.
223-187	Antiochus (III) the Great, Seleucid ruler of Syria.
202	Rome defeats Carthage at Zama.
198	Antiochus III defeats Egypt, gains control of Palestine.
175-163	Antiochus (IV) Epiphanes rules Syria-Palestine. Proscribes Judaism. Persecution of the orthodox Jews.
168	Battle of Pydna. Romans defeat the Macedonians.
167	Mattathias and his sons rebel against the Syrians. Beginning of the Maccabean Revolt.
166-160	Leadership of Judas Maccabaeus.
160-142	Jonathan, High Priest.
146	Scipio Africanus destroys Carthage. Rome controls western Mediterranean.
142-135	Simon, High Priest.
134-104	John Hyrcanus, son of Simon, High Priest and King.
103	Aristobulus.
102-76	Alexander Jannaeus.
75-67	Salome Alexandra ruler; Hyrcanus II High Priest.
66-63	Aristobulus II. Dynastic battle with Hyrcanus II.
63	Pompey invades Palestine. Roman rule begins.
63-40	Hyrcanus II rules, subject to Rome. Antipater exercises increasing power.
40-37	Parthians conquer Jerusalem. Establish Aristobulus II as High Priest and King.
37-4	Herod the Great, son of Antipater, rules as king, subject to Rome.
31	Battle of Actium. Octavian emerges as ruler of the Roman world.

85

Alexander, the Apostle
of Hellenism

Since the days of Xerxes, Greek power had been on the increase and Persia had trouble in keeping its wide empire in submission. The city states of Greece, however, never formed a united government, and the wily Persian kings were able to play off one state against another.

When a real union of Greek states was achieved, it was the genius of Philip of Macedon — not, strictly speaking, a Greek at all — that brought it about. The Hellenic League, comprising all the Greek states except Sparta, became the instrument which gave the Persian Empire its death blow.

Philip was unable to bring his plans to fruition. He was murdered in 336 B.C., and his mantle fell on his young son Alexander. Like most great leaders, Alexander represented a mass of conflicting strands. He was a Macedonian by nationality, and he dreamed of national glory as the heir of Philip. Culturally he was a Greek, educated by Aristotle himself. He carried the *Iliad* and the *Odyssey* with him on his campaigns. Alexander was thoroughly sold on the excellences of the Greek "way of life," although the Greeks gave him little support. When the people of Thebes assassinated the Macedonian garrison, Alexander burned the city and sold its inhabitants into slavery. This was to serve as a warning that the "alliance" between the Greeks and Macedon must be respected.

The apostle of Hellenism made a very humble beginning. With a small army, largely of Macedonians, and a staff of historians, geographers, and botanists, Alexander crossed the Dardanelles by boat at the very spot where Xerxes had taken his army across on a carefully prepared bridge. Alexander captured Troy and sacrificed to the *manes* of the Greek heroes, thereby proclaiming the fact that a new war had begun.

The Persian sovereign, Darius III, did not take this expedition seriously. He ordered that Alexander be seized and brought to Susa. An army of Persian cavalry, Greek mercenaries, and native troops was sent by Darius to stop Alexander. Expecting an easy victory, the Persians clashed with Alexander at the river Granicus. It was a close fight, and Alexander nearly lost his life, but the Persians were defeated. Alexander did not pursue the retreating Persian cavalry, but he ordered the Greek mercenaries massacred as traitors to the Greek cause. With the victory at the Granicus, the way into Asia Minor lay open before Alexander.

The Greek cities of Asia Minor were taken and "liberated," in many instances against their will. Halicarnasus remained loyal to Persia, and was burned during a siege. Alexander was able to move eastward, conquering and organizing the districts that fell before him, with no serious challenge until he came to the Cilician Gates at Issus. Here Darius advanced with his Persian army to stop the Macedonian. Instead the Persians fell back before Alexander. Damascus was taken by surprise. The family of Darius, immense stores of booty, and ambassadors from Sparta, Athens, and Thebes were captured.

Alexander decided not to pursue Darius. Military tactics demanded that Alexander secure his rear. The Phoenician cities, except Tyre, surrendered and were occupied. On two occasions Darius offered to negotiate with Alexander, offering him territory, a large sum of money, and the hand of his daughter in marriage in return for the return of his family. By this time, however, Alexander had decided upon a policy of world conquest, and Darius' offer went unheeded.

The resistance of Tyre occupied Alexander for seven months. The persistence of Alexander is seen in the causeway which he built from the mainland city to the island city of Tyre, in order to bring the Tyrians into submission. The very map of Phoenicia was changed during this siege of Tyre. The city finally fell, and with the fall of Tyre the maritime and commercial predominance of the Phoenicians came to an end.

After a two month siege of Gaza, during which Alexander was wounded, the victorious Macedonians pressed on to Egypt. The Egyptians hated the Persians, and welcomed Alexander as a deliverer. Alexander entered the temple of Ammon where the oracle announced that Alexander was the son of Ammon and that he would conquer the world. The Hellenism of Alexander must have worn thin when he accepted the role of a

This silver drachma of Alexander the Great was found at the Treasury at Persepolis.

son of Ammon, but he gladly did so, being recognized as a legitimate Pharaoh with a chapel in the temple at Karnak. The administration of Egypt was reorganized. Egyptians were given a large share of the control of their country, but Macedonians were placed in charge of the army. The new city of Alexandria was the enduring monument to the Macedonian conquest of Egypt. It replaced Tyre as the commercial metropolis of the eastern Mediterranean. Jewish colonists were encouraged to settle in Alexandria, and their presence there had an important bearing on the subsequent history of Judaism and Christianity.

Jewish traditions show Alexander in a friendly light, although Hellenism was to become the great enemy of orthodox Judaism. Josephus tells a story of Alexander's coming to Jerusalem and offering sacrifice in the Temple "according to the High-priest's direction." Although regarded as unhistorical, it shows the friendly attitude of the Jews to Alexander.

In 331 B.C., Alexander retraced his steps northward through Palestine and Syria. He now felt ready to meet the Persian army in its home territory. At the battle of Gaugamela, in the Mesopotamian plain, Alexander outmaneuvered and defeated the "Grand Army" of Darius. The Persian monarch escaped, however. With no army to impede his progress, Alexander marched on until he had taken the entire territory of Persia. The capitals of the Persian Empire — Babylon, Susa, Persepolis, and Ecbatana — were successively occupied.

The conquest of Babylon was reminiscent of the days of Cyrus. Alexander was welcomed as a liberator. The priests of Marduk and the nobles of the city brought gifts and promised to surrender the treasures of Babylon to Alexander. The garrison commander ordered flowers for the streets and crowns to honor the new Great King. Costly perfumes were burned on the altars. Magi chanted hymns. Alexander responded by ordering the rebuilding of temples which had lain waste since the days of Xerxes. The temple of Bel Marduk was to become the glory of Babylon again.

Twenty days after he left Babylon, Alexander entered Susa where the treasure of the palace of Darius I was his for the taking. Having plundered Susa, Alexander went on to Persepolis which was reported to be the richest city in the world. Historians are puzzled by the cruelty of Alexander at Persepolis. The men were all slain, and the women enslaved. The Macedonians fought one another over the plunder. By 330 B.C., Darius was dead, and Alexander assumed the title *Basileus*

(Great King). The sack of Persepolis was probably designed to mark the end of the Persian monarchy.

With the conquest of Persia behind him, Alexander continued his eastern conquests. Bactria and Sogdiana (Russian Turkestan) cost him three years of bitter fighting. As a gesture of reconciliation, Alexander married Roxana, a Bactrian princess. The Punjab region of India was the limit of Alexander's conquests. His army refused to travel further.

Alexander began his career as an apostle of Hellenism. Completely convinced that the Greek way of life was superior to any other, he began his crusade with a missionary zeal. When he was recognized in Egypt as a son of Ammon he took a major step away from Greek ideology. In Persia, Alexander decided to adopt Persian dress, and he began to rule as an oriental despot. A conspiracy against Alexander was said to implicate the son of one of his most able generals, Parmenion. Father and son were both put to death.

Tragedy crowned the last years of Alexander. Half of his army took the return trip from India in a navy of newly built ships. From the Indus Delta the fleet successfully made the voyage to the Persian gulf. The rest of the army traveled by land. In 324 Alexander arrived in Susa to find misrule on the part of the officials left in charge of the city. He also found that resentment to his own rule was growing. In Greece many were scandalized when they heard that Alexander had executed his own nephew, the historian Callisthenes. The Greeks were angered at the report that Alexander wished to be treated as a god. Alexander's Macedonian officers resented his commands to mingle with the Persians and take Persian wives. The orientalizing ways of Alexander resulted in a mutiny, which was put down.

In 323 B.C. Alexander planned a sea voyage around Arabia, but he died of a fever before the voyage was accomplished. He was only thirty-three years of age. His only son was born to Roxana after Alexander's death. In so short a life, Alexander conquered more territory than any of his predecessors. Although he had not had time to mold the government of his empire into a cohesive whole, the eleven years from the time that Alexander crossed the Dardanelles until his death in Babylon changed the course of history. Hellenism was to outlive its militant apostle.

86

The Jews
Under the Ptolemies

When Alexander died in 323 B.C., he left no heir. A son was posthumously born to Roxana, Alexander's Bactrian wife, but the *diadochoi,* or "successors" of Alexander, seized power before he could reach maturity. One of the *diadochoi,* Cassander, murdered Roxana and her son.

Alexander had had many able generals, but there was not one that arose as his logical successor. By 315 B.C., after seven years of struggle, four outstanding leaders appeared: Antigonus, who occupied the country from the Mediterranean to central Asia; Cassander, who ruled Macedonia; Ptolemy Lagi, who ruled Egypt and Southern Syria; and Lysimachus, ruler of Thrace. Ptolemy's foremost general was Seleucus who occupied an important role in the subsequent history of Palestine.

In 315 B.C., Ptolemy, Cassander, and Lysimachus formed an alliance to check Antigonus, who aspired in his own right to be a second Alexander. Ptolemy demanded that Antigonus yield part of the Asiatic territory which he had conquered. Seleucus was to receive Babylon, from which he had previously been driven out. When Antigonus failed to heed Ptolemy's demands, fighting broke out. Ptolemy and Seleucus defeated an army led by Demetrius, Antigonus' son, at Gaza in 312 B.C. They pressed on, taking the important Syrian cities, including Zidon.

Josephus quotes Agatharchides' account of Ptolemy's capture of Jerusalem:

> "The people known as Jews, who inhabit the most strongly fortified of cities, called by the natives Jerusalem, have a custom of abstaining from work every seventh day; on those occasions they neither bear arms nor take any agricultural operations in hand, nor engage in any other forms of public service, but pray with outstretched hands in the temples until the evening. Consequently, because the inhabitants, instead of protecting their city, persevered in their folly, Ptolemy, son of Lagus, was allowed to enter with his army; the country was thus given over to a cruel master, and the defect of a practice enjoined by law was ex-

posed. That experience has taught the whole world, except that nation, the lesson not to resort to dreams and traditional fancies about the law, until its difficulties are such as to baffle human reason."[1]

The *Letter of Aristeas* says of Ptolemy:

"He had overrun the whole of Coele-Syria and Phoenicia, exploiting his good fortune and prowess, and had transplanted some and made others captive, reducing all to subjection by terror; it was on this occasion that he transported a hundred thousand persons from the country of the Jews to Egypt. Of these he armed some thirty thousand chosen men and settled them in garrisons in the country."[2]

Egyptian inscriptions and papyri indicate the presence of large numbers of Jews in Ptolemaic Egypt. Some of these had come earlier, but there is no reason to doubt that large numbers were brought to Egypt by Ptolemy Lagi.

Our sources of information concerning life in Palestine during the century of Ptolemaic rule are very scanty. For the most part the Jews were permitted to live in peace and in accord with their religious and cultural traditions. There are no records of tyranny such as characterized the Seleucid rule of Antiochus Epiphanes. Tribute was paid to the Egyptian government, but local affairs were administered by the High Priests who had been entrusted with responsibility for the government of the Jews since Persian times.

The one great figure among the Jews of the Ptolemaic period is Simon the Just, the High Priest who is the subject of the highest praise in the post-Biblical writings. Ecclesiasticus calls him "great among his brethren and the glory of his people." He is credited with rebuilding the walls of Jerusalem which had been demolished by Ptolemy I. He is said to have repaired the Temple and directed the excavation of a great reservoir which would provide fresh water for Jerusalem even in times of drought or siege.

In addition to his office as High Priest and head of the community, Simon was reputed to be the chief teacher of the people. His favorite maxim was, "The world rests on three things, on the Law, on Divine Service, and on Charity."[3]

The identity of Simon the Just is a historical problem. Simon I lived during the middle of the third century, and Simon II lived around 200 B.C. One of these is doubtless the Simon the Just of Jewish tradition and legend.

Nothing is known about the High Priest Onias I, but the house of Onias and the house of Tobias were to become bitter

---

1. Josephus *Contra Apion* i. 209, 210.
2. *Aristeas to Philocrates*, 12-13. Translation of Moses Hadas.
3. *Pirke Aboth* i. 2.

rivals. The house of Tobias was pro-Egyptian and represented the wealthy class of Jerusalem society. The Tobiads may have been related to "Tobiah the Ammonite" who gave so much trouble to Nehemiah (Neh. 2:10, 4:3,7; 6:1-19). A papyrus from the time of Ptolemy II speaks of a Jew named Tobias who was a cavalry commander in the Ptolemaic army stationed in Ammanitis, east of the Jordan.[4] A third century B.C. mausoleum with Aramaic letters "Tobiah" was discovered at 'Araq el-Emir in central Jordan.

The Tobiads are thought to have been tax collectors, occupying the same function as the "publicans" of New Testament times.

Josephus states that Onias II refused to pay Ptolemy IV twenty talents of silver, which seems to have been a kind of tribute demanded of the High Priests. By refusing payment, Onias appeared to be renouncing allegiance to Ptolemy. Joseph, a member of the house of Tobias, thereupon succeeded in having himself appointed tax farmer for the whole of Palestine. The "tax farmer" had to go to Alexandria each year and bid for the renewal of the license to gather taxes. Joseph held this influential post for twenty years, under the Ptolemies and, after the victory of Antiochus III, under the Seleucids.

Ptolemy's triumph in Palestine was short-lived, for Antigonus promptly drove him out of Syria and held it firmly. Seleucus also gained strength as an independent conqueror, no longer subject to Ptolemy. Antigonus tried to check Seleucus, but was unable to do so. In 311 B.C. Seleucus conquered Babylonia, marking the beginning of the Seleucid dynasty. Antigonus, however, continued to hold Syria, which served as a wedge between the holdings of Ptolemy and Seleucus.

In 301 B.C. Lysimachus, Seleucus, and Cassander with their combined forces met and overcame the forces of the empire-conscious Antigonus at Ipsus, in Phrygia. Antigonus died on the battlefield, and his Asiatic empire came to an end, although his son Demetrius Poliorketes managed to retain Macedonia and the Phoenician coast of Syria.

Ptolemy had remained on the sidelines during the fighting at Ipsus. It had been agreed that Coele-Syria, or Palestine, would be assigned to Ptolemy in the event of victory over Antigonus. Since Ptolemy had not taken an active part in the fighting, the other three allies decided that the territory should be assigned

---

4. Zenon Papyri, No. 13 publication by C. C. Edgar, in *Annales Serv.*, Vol. xviii (1919).

The Rosetta Stone is the trilingual inscription that provided the key for deciphering hieroglyphics. This stele was a decree issued by the priest of Memphis in honor of Ptolemy V, Epiphanes (ca. 203-181 B.C.).

to Seleucus. In the meantime, however, Ptolemy had taken possession of the land. Diodorus describes the problems involved:

> "When Seleucus, after the partition of the kingdom of Antigonus, arrived with his army in Phoenicia, and tried, according to the arrangements concluded, to take over Coele-Syria, he found Ptolemy already in possession of its cities. Ptolemy complained that Seleucus, in violation of their old friendship, should have agreed to an arrangement which put territory governed by Ptolemy into his own share. Although he (Ptolemy) had taken part in the war against Antigonus, the kings had not, he protested, assigned him any portion of the conquered territory. To these reproaches Seleucus replied that it was quite fair that those who fought the battle should dispose the territory. With regard to Coele-Syria, he would not, for the present, for the sake of friendship, take any action; later on he would consider the best way of treating friends who tried to grasp more than was their right."[5]

Syria was nominally a part of three domains after the battle of Ipsus. Demetrius Poliorketes, son of Antigonus, occupied the Phoenician coast. Seleucus possessed northern Syria where he built Antioch as his capital. Syria south of Aradus (Arvad) was retained by Ptolemy, who was able to encroach on the claims of his northern neighbors. While Demetrius was busy elsewhere, Ptolemy quietly occupied Phoenicia. Seleucus made no attempt to occupy Coele-Syria, so that Ptolemy remained its *de facto* ruler.

Ptolemy Lagi was succeeded by his son Ptolemy Philadelphus in 283 B.C. Seleucus was murdered in 281 B.C. and succeeded by his son Antiochus I. In the years that follow, three great powers shared the empire of Alexander. The Ptolemies of Egypt, the Seleucids of Syria, and the house of Antigonus in Macedonia were rival powers. The Seleucids and the Antigonids were either singly, or unitedly, at war with the Ptolemies during most of the third century B.C.

In 275 B.C. Ptolemy invaded Syria and was repulsed by the Seleucid forces. Ptolemy's naval power, however, enabled him to prolong the war. Hostilities ceased in 272 or 271 B.C. without a decisive victory for either side.

When Antiochus II succeeded his father to the Syrian throne in 261 B.C., war broke out again. The results were indecisive, and peace was concluded in 252 B.C. Ptolemy's daughter, Berenice, was betrothed to Antiochus II, thus uniting the two rival houses by marriage.

In 246 B.C. Antiochus died, being succeeded by his son Seleucus II. The following year Ptolemy II died and was succeeded by Ptolemy III, Euergetes, who had been joint-ruler since 247 B.C.

---

5. Diodorus, *Histories*, xxi, 5.

This pottery jug, filled with thirty-five silver tetradrachmas, probably was the private bank of a Shechem resident in the second century B.C. The coins cover a minimum of ninety years, from at least 285-193 B.C.

War broke out between the Seleucids and the Ptolemies when it was learned that Berenice had been murdered, with her infant son, through the intrigue of Laodice, half sister and wife of Antiochus II. Laodice wanted to insure that her own son, rather than the son of Berenice, would succeed to the Syrian throne. The murder of the daughter and grandson of Ptolemy II, however, was an outrage to the honor of the Ptolemies and resulted in the "Laodicean War."

After a series of brilliant victories in which northern Syria was completely subjugated, Ptolemy III was called back to Egypt to care for a local problem. Seleucus was able to regain lost territories as far south as Damascus, but attempts to take Southern Palestine were futile. Peace was concluded in 240 B.C., and no further attacks were made on Syria during Ptolemy III's reign. He died in 221 B.C. and was succeeded by Ptolemy IV Philopater, one of the worst of the Ptolemaic house. Seleucus II was succeeded, in 226, by Seleucus III who died by poison, according to Appian. He was succeeded by his younger brother who is known as Antiochus III, the Great.

87

The Jews
Under the Seleucids

1. Antiochus III and the Conquest of Palestine

Antiochus III was only eighteen years of age when he came to the throne of Syria in 223 B.C. He had had experience in government, however, having served as ruler of Babylonia under his brother Seleucus III.

After crushing a revolt in the eastern part of his empire, Antiochus attempted to invade Coele-Syria in the summer of 221 B.C. He got as far as the fortresses of the Marsyas valley in Lebanon, but was forced to withdraw by Theodotus, the commander-in-chief of the Egyptian forces in Syria.

A second invasion was attempted in 219 B.C. with greater success. Seleucia in Pieria fell before Antiochus, and Theodotus transferred his loyalty from Ptolemy Philopater to Antiochus and delivered the cities of Ptolemais (Acre) and Tyre to the Syrians. Nicolaus, an Egyptian general, delayed Antiochus at the fortress of Dora, south of Mt. Carmel. When a rumor reached him that a strong Egyptian army was awaiting him at Pelusium, Antiochus accepted a truce and withdrew to Seleucia, leaving Theodotus in charge of the conquered territory. Sosibius, the Egyptian commander-in-chief, reorganized his army for a showdown.

Early in 218 B.C. Nicolaus marched with an Egyptian army to the Lebanons to meet the Syrians. Polybius describes the encounter:

> "When Theodotus had forced back the enemy at the foot of the mountain, and then charged from the higher ground, all those who were with Nicolaus turned and fled precipitately. About two thousand of them fell during the flight, and a not less number were captured; all the rest retreated on Zidon."[1]

Antiochus pursued the retreating army of Nicolaus down the Phoenician coast. Leaving Nicolaus in Zidon, Antiochus took

1. Polybius, *Histories*, v, 69.

Tyre and Ptolemais, then turned inland and came to Philoteria (Tiberias) on the Sea of Galilee. He crossed the Jordan taking the strong trans-Jordanian cities, including Gadara, and Philadelphia (Rabbath-Ammon). He returned to winter at Ptolemais.

In the spring of 217 B.C. Antiochus continued his conquests, conquering Philistia, including Gaza, before reaching the frontier town of Raphia. An Egyptian army under the personal command of Ptolemy Philopater met the Syrians south of Raphia. Here the armies of Antiochus met a disastrous defeat. Polybius says that Ptolemy "remained three months in Syria and Phoenicia setting things in order in the cities."[2]

The third book of Maccabees tells how Ptolemy visited the cities of Syria after his victory at Raphia. The Jews are alleged to have sent a group of elders to congratulate him on his victory. Ptolemy is reputed to have insisted on entering the Holy of Holies, only to flee in confusion and terror when he had gotten as far as the Holy Place (III Maccabees 1:9-11, 24). The story cannot be regarded as historical. It is significant that nothing is said of the incident in Daniel 11, which describes the incident at Raphia in considerable detail.

For a number of years Antiochus was busy in the East, but he never gave up his plans for annexing Coele-Syria to his domains. At the death of Ptolemy IV, Philopater, in 203 B.C., Egypt was rent with turmoil and rebellion. In the spring of 202 B.C. Antiochus launched an attack which accomplished little or nothing. The following spring another attack was launched, with bitter fighting in the Palestinian cities, including Gaza. Scopas, the Egyptian general, pushed the Syrians back to the sources of the Jordan during the winter of 201-200 B.C.

The decisive Syrian victory came at the Battle of Panion, near the sources of the Jordan. Scopas fled to Zidon where he was besieged by land and sea. In the spring of 198 B.C. Scopas was forced to surrender, leaving the whole of Syria in the hands of Antiochus. In passing through his newly acquired territories, Antiochus came to Jerusalem where, according to Josephus, the inhabitants gave him a cordial welcome.

When the Carthaginian, Hannibal, was defeated by the Romans at Zama (202 B.C.), bringing to an end the Second Punic War, he fled eastward and took refuge in the court of Antiochus. Still interested in stirring up trouble for Rome, he encouraged Antiochus to invade Greece. Rome thereupon declared war on Antiochus.

Ruins of a Roman theatre in Amman, Jordan. In Old Testament times Amman was the chief town of the Ammonites and known as Rabbath-Ammon. Later it was rebuilt and renamed Philadelphia by Ptolemy Philadelphus (245-246 B.C.).

---

2. Polybius, *Histories*, v, 86, 87.

The Roman forces moved into Greece, defeated Antiochus, and forced him to retreat to Asia Minor. There at Magnesia, between Sardis and Smyrna, the Romans under Cornelius Scipio defeated Antiochus (190 B.C.). He had to pay an enormous indemnity, surrender his war elephants and his navy. The younger son of Antiochus the Great, later to rule as Antiochus Epiphanes, was taken to Rome as a hostage for the payment of the indemnity. His twelve years in Rome gave him a healthy respect for Roman power and Roman ways of doing things.

2.   Antiochus Epiphanes and the Persecution of the Jews

The fall of Palestine into Syrian hands, following the victory of Antiochus the Great at Panion (198 B.C.), ushered in a new era of Jewish history. The rule of the Ptolemies had been tolerant. The Seleucids determined to force the Jews to accept Hellenism.

Antiochus IV bore the surname Epiphanes ("the illustrious," almost a title of deity). The Jews, masters of innuendo, gave him the nickname, Epimanes ("the madman"). He was born in Athens, and had served as chief magistrate of the city whose culture was the epitome of everything Greek. Antiochus spent twelve years as a hostage in Rome, where he learned to respect the new power which was about to conquer the world. With a sense of mission coupled with political astuteness, Antiochus determined "to civilize," which meant "to Hellenize," the domain over which he ruled.

It is possible to misrepresent Antiochus. He was not a foreigner intent on enslaving a persecuted minority group. On the contrary, a sizable number of Jews were impressed with the possibilities of greater conformity to the Hellenistic manners and customs. Antiochus used this inner dissension among the Jews, coupled with his own need of funds, to interfere in the internal affairs of Judea.

In the early days of the reign of Antiochus IV, Jerusalem was ruled by the High Priest, Onias III, a descendant of Simon the Just, and a strictly orthodox Jew. The Jews who looked favorably on Greek culture opposed Onias and espoused the cause of his brother, Jason. By promising larger tribute to Antiochus, Jason succeeded in having himself appointed High Priest.

To Antiochus, the high priesthood was a political office. As Syrian king, he would have the right to appoint whomever he chose. To the pious Jews, however, the priesthood was of divine origin, and its sale to the highest bidder was looked upon as a

Mount Hermon, as seen from the Syrian wheat fields. The photo, taken in July, shows snow on the summit.

sin against God. Since the priesthood involved both civil and religious functions, both viewpoints would appear valid to their respective adherents.

Jason encouraged the Hellenists who had sought his election. A gymnasium was built in Jerusalem. There Jewish lads exercised in the nude in accord with Greek custom. Greek names were adopted in place of the more pious-sounding Jewish names. Hebrew orthodoxy was looked upon as obscurantist and obsolete. Antiochus visited Jerusalem in 170 B.C. He showed his approval of the new order of things by authorizing the citizens to call themselves "Antiochites" after their sovereign.

With the developing tide of Hellenism, however, there developed a resistance movement. The Hasidim (the "pious") followed the paths of their fathers and attempted a defense of orthodox Jewish institutions.

Antiochus, who was having trouble elsewhere in his empire, looked upon Jewish orthodoxy as a divisive force. Aiming at a united Hellenistic empire, he awaited an opportunity to implement his program.

Such an opportunity came when a dispute arose between Jason and one of his closest associates. Menelaus was of the tribe of Benjamin. As such, he had no right to the priestly office. Nevertheless, by offering higher tribute to Antiochus than that paid by Jason, he was nominated to the office of High Priest. A Syrian garrison was stationed in the citadel in Jerusalem to insure order and respect for the new High Priest.

If the Hasidim were scandalized when Jason replaced his brother Onias, they were infuriated when a Benjamite, who was a thoroughgoing Hellenist, was installed by force of Syrian arms.

The deposed Jason did not quietly acquiesce in the change. Unable, for the time being, to resist the forces of Antiochus, he awaited an opportunity to reassert himself.

Several years after Menelaus became High Priest, while Antiochus was busy fighting in Egypt, Jason raised an army in Transjordan and raided Jerusalem. Menelaus beat off the attack, but it became obvious to Antiochus that large segments of Judaism were still opposed to Hellenism and Syrian control in Palestine.

On the return of Antiochus from Egypt, Menelaus welcomed him to Jerusalem. What was left of the Temple treasure was placed at his disposal. Since Menelaus was unpopular with many of the Jews, he found it all the more necessary to court the favor of Antiochus.

During a second campaign in Egypt, Antiochus came as close

as he ever came to subduing the empire of the Ptolemies. He was deterred by the rise of a new power which was soon to transform the Mediterranean into a Roman lake.

At the Battle of Pydna (168 B.C.) the Romans defeated the Macedonians in one of history's decisive battles. On the ruins of the Macedonian empire, Rome was to make a name for herself. In his younger days Antiochus had come to know and respect the Romans. Rome was not ready to annex Syria and Egypt, but Rome was determined that Antiochus should not strengthen himself by annexing Egypt. In a famous scene outside the city of Alexandria, the Roman envoy demanded that Antiochus, before he stirred from a circle drawn around him in the ground, promise to evacuate Egypt. With dreams of grandeur suddenly dissipated, Antiochus turned back in bitterness.

If Egypt was to remain a rival power, Antiochus found it more necessary than ever to retain his hold on Palestine. He sent Appolonius, his general, to occupy the city of Jerusalem. In a Sabbath attack, when he knew that the orthodox Jews would not fight, he slaughtered large numbers of the opponents of Menelaus. The city walls were destroyed, and a new fortress, the Akra, was built on the site of the citadel. The Akra was garrisoned by a large force which was expected to keep the Jews in submission to the policies of Antiochus.

One of Israel's darkest periods began. A systematic attempt was made to Hellenize the country by force. An edict demanded the fusion of all the nationalities of the Seleucid empire into one people. Greek deities were to be worshiped by all.

An elderly Athenian philosopher was sent to Jerusalem to supervise the enforcement of the order. He identified the God of Israel with Jupiter, and ordered a bearded image of the pagan deity, perhaps in the likeness of Antiochus, set up upon the Temple altar. The Jews popularly spoke of this as "the Abomination of Desolation."

Greek soldiers and their paramours performed licentious heathen rites in the very Temple courts. Swine were sacrificed on the altar. The drunken orgy associated with the worship of Bacchus was made compulsory. Conversely, Jews were forbidden, under penalty of death, to practice circumcision, Sabbath observance, or the observance of the feasts of the Jewish year. Copies of the Hebrew Scriptures were ordered destroyed.

These laws promulgating Hellenism and proscribing Judaism were enforced with the utmost cruelty. An aged Scribe, Eleazar, was flogged to death because he refused to eat swine's flesh. A mother and her seven children were successively butchered, in the presence of the governor, for refusing to pay homage to an image. Two mothers who had circumcised their new-born sons were driven through the city and cast headlong from the wall. Later ages may have exaggerated the atrocities of Antiochus, but there is no possibility of seeing him as anything but an oppressor who merited the name Epimanes — the Madman.

By force of arms the Hellenizing party had gained a victory. Menelaus continued as High Priest. Where once his worship was directed to Yahweh, the God of Israel, now he served Jupiter. Yet the Hellenizers had gone too far. Their very zeal for a quick defeat of the "old order" evoked a reaction which drove the Hellenizers out of power and brought into being an independent Jewish state.

88

The Impact of Hellenism

on the Jews

Alexander the Great had been a missionary as well as a conqueror. From his teacher Aristotle he had been taught the virtues of Greek philosophy and the Greek "way of life." Although his journeys toward the east caused him to adopt non-Greek practices, and a Greek purist would be shocked at his assumption of the role of a deity, Alexander continued to think of himself as one who was bringing the blessings of Hellenism, as the Greek way of life is called, to more benighted parts of the world. Alexander had attempted to establish a model Hellenistic community in each of the lands he had conquered. Alexandria in Egypt is the best known and most successful of these planned communities. Alexander was sure that the excellences which these communities represented would have the effect of making Hellenism attractive to the countries in which they were located.

Although the empire of Alexander was short lived, being divided shortly after his death, his cultural accomplishments were of much longer duration. In the years following Alexander's death, Palestine was subject successively to the Egyptian Ptolemies and the Syrian Seleucids, but in each case the culture was Hellenistic. Although military rivals, culturally the states which emerged from the empire of Alexander were one. The city-states of mainland Greece became stagnant during the three pre-Christian centuries, but Hellenistic centers such as Alexandria, Pergamum, and Dura became centers of cultural activity.

The Hellenistic city could readily be identified. Fine public buildings were erected. A gymnasium was built for that culture of the body which the Greeks always stressed. An open air theater was built to entertain the populace. Greek dress was observed in the city, with people speaking the Greek language and subscribing to one of the schools of Greek philosophy. The city government was modeled along the lines of the Greek city-states.

Hellenism was not all bad, or all good. It did, however, present a challenge to Judaism both in the "dispersion" and in Palestine proper. Norman Bentwich observes, "The interaction of Judaism and Hellenistic culture is...one of the fundamental struggles in the march of civilization..."[1] If the great temptation to pre-exilic Israel was the idolatry of its Canaanite neighbors, the great temptation of post-exilic Judaism was Hellenistic attitudes toward life.

1. Hellenism in the Dispersion

General Influence

At no time after the Babylonian exile did the majority of Jews live in Palestine. Many remained in their settlements in Babylon, or settled in other parts of the Tigris-Euphrates valley. Others went to Syria where there were large Jewish settlements, particularly in Antioch and Damascus. Asia Minor had large Jewish communities. Lydia, Phrygia, Ephesus, Pergamum, and Sardis all had numerous Jews in their population. The account of the visitors to Jerusalem on the day of Pentecost (Acts 2) and the journeys of the apostle Paul give us a significant picture of the settlements of the Jews of the dispersion. These Jews remained loyal to the Jerusalem Temple. Every male Israelite over the age of twenty was expected to pay his Temple dues, and pilgrimages were made whenever possible. Each settlement, however, took on something of the characteristics of its neighbors, so that the Jews of Babylon would not have the same attitudes as those of Egypt. Those of Palestine would be apt to consider themselves alone the truly orthodox.

The most significant group of Jews of the dispersion, historically speaking, was that of Alexandria. From the initial settlement of Alexandria the Jews had formed one of the most important and largest segments of the city. Here was the temptation to assimilate to the prevailing Hellenistic pattern, and here also was the determination to remain true to the faith. A third century B.C. writer, Hecataeus of Abdera, wrote, "In recent times under the foreign rule of the Persians, and then of the Macedonians by whom the Persian Empire was overthrown, intercourse with other races has led to many of the traditional Jewish ordinances losing their hold."[2]

1. Norman Bentwich, *Hellenism*, p. 11.
2. E. R. Bevan, *Jerusalem Under the High Priests*, p. 43.

The nature of the temptation which beset the Jews in the midst of Hellenism may be noted from the writings of the ancient historian Posidonius:

> "The people of these cities are relieved by the fertility of their soil from a laborious struggle for existence. Life is a continuous series of social festivities. Their gymnasiums they use as baths where they anoint themselves with costly oils and myrrhs. In the *grammateia* (such is the name they give to the public eating-halls) they practically live, filling themselves there for the better part of the day with rich foods and wine; much that they cannot eat they carry away home. They feast to the prevailing music of strings. The cities are filled from end to end with the noise of harp-playing."[3]

Even for those who might not be tempted by such a prospect of a life of ease, there were other aspects of Hellenism that seemed to offer a fuller life than the older ways. The merchant class was able to amass great wealth which could purchase better housing and food than the pre-Hellenistic world could have imagined. Great libraries in Alexandria and other Hellenistic centers, together with schools emphasizing a Greek education, would appeal to many of the nobler youths of Israel. Sculpture and the fine arts offered an aesthetic outlook which would be frowned upon by the orthodox, but which would make an impact on the young in particular. In Alexandria a synthesis developed between Judaism and Hellenism.

The Septuagint

The greatest monument of Alexandrian Judaism was, without question, the translation of the Hebrew Old Testament into the Greek vernacular. While the origin of this version is unknown, legend places the beginning of this translation in the reign of the first of the Ptolemies (Philadelphus). While the legends suggest that the work was done in order to provide a copy of the Hebrew Scriptures for the Alexandrian library, it is more likely that the translation was made at the impulse of Alexandrian Jews who wanted their Greek-speaking children to be able to read the Scriptures. As the mother tongue (Hebrew) was forgotten by the younger generation, some provision had to be made for the preservation of the Hebrew sacred literature in the popularly spoken Greek. The Torah, or Pentateuch, was translated sometime around 250 B.C. The remainder of the canonical books of the Old Testament were subsequently translated, as were the apocryphal books. By the time of Origen (third century A.D.) this entire collection was called "the Septuagint," although the term originally referred

3. *Ibid.* p. 43 f.

only to the Greek translation of the Pentateuch. That a copy found its way into the library need not be doubted.

Around 100 B.C. a letter known as the *Letter of Aristeas* was written to describe the way in which the Septuagint was produced. This letter purports to have been written by an official in the court of Ptolemy Philadelphus of Egypt (285-246 B.C.). Philadelphus was an enlightened ruler who distinguished himself as a patron of the arts. Under him the great Library of Alexandria, one of the cultural wonders of the world for almost a millennium, was inaugurated. It was for Ptolemy Philadelphus that Manetho compiled his great history of Egypt which divided the history of Egypt into thirty dynasties. Although inaccurate in many places, Manetho's divisions are still used today.

According to the *Letter of Aristeas,* Demetrius of Phalerum, said to have been Ptolemy's librarian, aroused the king's interest in the Jewish Law. At his suggestion, Ptolemy sent a delegation to the High Priest, Eleazar, in Jerusalem, who chose six elders from each of the twelve tribes to translate the Law into Greek. These seventy-two elders, with a specially accurate and beautiful copy of the Law, were sent to Alexandria where they proved their fitness for their important task. They were sent to the island of Pharos, famed for its lighthouse, where, according to the Letter of Aristeas, in seventy-two days they completed their translation work and presented a version which they all agreed upon. The story was later embellished with the idea that the seventy-two were sent into individual cells, each translating the whole Law, all versions agreeing exactly when compared with one another after seventy-two days!

There can be no doubt that the legends which have been advanced concerning the origin of the Septuagint were designed to prove that it was an inspired and authoritative translation. When Jerome went behind the Septuagint to the Hebrew Old Testament, he was censured by many of his contemporaries who looked upon the Septuagint as the official Bible of the church in the fourth century.

Although the legends contained in the *Letter of Aristeas* cannot be believed, they do reflect a belief that the Law was translated into Greek during the time of Philadelphus. There is evidence that this is correct. Quotations from the Septuagint text of Genesis and Exodus appear in Greek literature before 200 B.C. The language of the Septuagint, however, suggests that it was made by Egyptian Jews rather than Jerusalemite elders. The story contained in the *Letter of Aristeas* evidently had a specific propaganda purpose. As numerous translations appeared, there was a desire to make one superior version definitive. If it could be proved that the Septuagint had been inspired in the same sense as the Hebrew originals, then the Greek-speaking Jew would have an infallible authority comparable to that of his Palestinian brother.

Although without question translated by Alexandrian Jews for their own use, the Septuagint did serve as a means of acquainting the non-Jew with the principles of Jewish faith and practice. No doubt a copy was placed in the famous Alexandrian library. When we come to New Testament times, we read of many "God-fearers" among the gentiles. In a real sense the Septuagint helped to pave the way for the ministry of the apostle Paul and others who took the message of Christ to non-Jew as well as to Jew. The Biblical preaching in the Greek-speaking world was based on the Septuagint text. Many of the New Testament quotations from the Old are taken from the Septuagint, although others are translated from the Hebrew and others do not accord perfectly with either the Hebrew or Greek texts which we know. In most, if not all, of these cases the writers are apparently paraphrasing the Scripture which they assume to be known to their readers.

Alexandrian Allegorism

With no intention to abandon their ancestral faith, Alexandrian Jews followed their gentile neighbors in subscribing to a school of Greek philosophy. This resulted in that attempt to harmonize Scripture with Greek thinking which produced the allegorical method of interpreting Scripture. Aristobulus and Philo were the great allegorizers. To them the literal meaning of the Bible was vulgar, misleading, and insufficient. A hidden, deeper meaning must be sought. By reading into the Bible their pagan philosophy, they were able to consider themselves enlightened Hellenists and orthodox Hebrews at one and the same time. Some of them adopted Greek names to help in the process of assimilation.

The allegorist regards the literal sense of Scripture as the vehicle for a secondary sense which is regarded as more spiritual and profound. The method is associated with the name of Origen, one of the early Church Fathers. As a method of Biblical interpretation it is rejected by careful scholars, but vestiges of it do appear in the extreme typology which is still prevalent in some circles.

Allegorism is of Greek origin. With the development of a philosophical and historical tradition which appealed to the thinking man, a serious problem was raised. Homer's *Iliad* and *Odyssey,* and Hesiod's *Theogany* contained ideas which the sophisticated Greek could no longer seriously accept. Yet these writings were cultural and religious classics. Was there no way in which they might be preserved?

The Stoics produced a solution. The stories of the gods, their lust and jealousy, their drunkenness and revelry, should not be accepted as historical truth. These stories really illustrated the struggle among the virtues. Zeus became the Logos ("Word" or "Idea"). Hermes represented Reason. Once such a "key" was developed to explain the "real" meaning of the classical epics, the Greek felt secure both in his ancient epic-religious heritage and his modern philosophical-historical attitude. Through allegorical interpretation the Alexandrian Greeks preserved their religious literature from oblivion by making it mean what it certainly was never intended to mean.

The Alexandrian Jew took a lesson from his Greek neighbor. As a loyal Jew he looked upon his Bible as the Word of God. He loved his Jewish faith with its religious observances and emphasis on the faithfulness of God and His call to Abraham and his descendants. Yet the Alexandrian Jew was more than a son of Abraham. He was also an heir to the culture of Greece as that culture had been spread abroad by Alexander. There was much in Hellenism that he esteemed. The Alexandrian Jew wanted to be a child of his times as much as the Alexandrian Greek did, and he used similar means.

Convinced that he could be a faithful Jew and a consistent Hellenist, the Alexandrian decided to accept a Greek philosophy and apply the allegorical method to bring harmony between the two. About 160 B.C. an Alexandrian Jew named Aristobulus taught that the Greek philosophers had actually borrowed much of their thought from the Mosaic Law. To Aristobulus, Moses and the prophets presented the same truths as those enunciated by the great Greek philosophers.

The most famous name in Jewish allegorical thought is Philo, the son of a wealthy Alexandrian merchant, who lived from about 20 B.C. to about A.D. 50. A man of great erudition, Philo mentions sixty-four Greek writers, including Homer, Hesiod, Pindar, Solon, the tragedians, and Plato. To Philo, these Greeks were not heathen. They were men of God, on a par with Israel's prophets. From Pythagoras, Plato, Aristotle, and the Stoics, Philo was able to weave for himself a philosophical system. Moses was looked upon as the greatest thinker of all. The lesser sages had all learned from him, and all truth could be found in the Law of Moses. Philo recognized that this was not always apparent in the letter. Under the letter of the Law, however, it could be found by using allegorical interpretation.

Philo regarded himself as a thoroughly orthodox Jew. He may not have known the Hebrew language at all, but he accepted the Greek Septuagint Version as a mechanically inspired volume. In his Septuagint he determined to find the "true" or allegorical sense. The literal sense might be tame, or even absurd, but the "true" sense could be learned by applying certain basic principles.

Allegorical interpretation is thoroughly subjective. If the literal sense of Scripture suggested something which the interpreter deemed unworthy of God, he considered this sufficient warrant to seek a "hidden" allegorical meaning. Anything deemed impossible or contrary to reason was allegorized. Anthropomorphism was offensive to the Greek mentality, so all references to God which imply human characteristics were eliminated by means of the allegorical concept. Abraham's journey to Palestine is made to be the story of a Stoic philosopher who leaves Chaldea (sensual understanding) and stops for a time at Haran ("holes" or "the senses"). Abraham's marriage to Sarah is the marriage of the philosopher to "abstract wisdom."

Considerable attention was paid to the form of Scripture. Any repetition in Scripture was interpreted as pointing to something new. If one of several possible synonymous words was chosen in a passage of Scripture, this pointed to some special meaning. A word in the Septuagint might be interpreted according to every shade of meaning it bore in Greek. By slightly altering the letters, still other meanings might be derived.

From the Jewish allegorists, the Christian church adopted a method of Biblical interpretation which has persisted in some places to the present. From the time of Origen it dominated the thinking of the Roman church. In antiquity there were notable exceptions, however. The Syrian school of Antioch, including such writers as Theodore of Mopsuestia, insisted on a literal interpretation of Scripture. Syria was removed from the influence of Alexandria, and showed a feeling for the true nature of Scripture, as over against allegorizing tendencies.

The reformation brought a renewed emphasis on the literal, historical interpretation of Scripture.

Summary

From the Christian point of view the Judaism of the dispersion served an important function. The translation of the Bible into Greek provided the church with a mighty weapon in its first contacts with the Greek-speaking gentile world. The Jewish communities were centers from which the gospel could be preached, during the lifetime of the apostle Paul, throughout the empire. The attempt to interpret Scripture allegorically and to form a synthesis between Biblical revelation and Greek speculative thought proved a snare to the early church. Under Origen, allegorical interpretation became the norm of Biblical study and remained such, with notable exceptions, until the Reformation in the sixteenth century.

2.   Hellenism in Palestine

Palestine itself was not so far removed from the centers of Hellenism as to be untouched. Especially the educated classes were enamored with the Greek way of doing things. The amphitheater and the gymnasium were attractive to the young, and a strong Hellenistic party emerged.

In Judea, however, the lines were more closely drawn than they were in the dispersion. An anti-Hellenistic party arose which considered the Greek manner of life a threat to Judaism. The emphasis on things material, the nude appearance of athletes in the gymnasium, the neglect of Jewish rites, were regarded as evidence of defection from the law of God. The Hasidim, or "the pious," were ready to defend their ancestral faith to the death if need be, and in the days of Antiochus Epiphanes many of them did die for that faith. Future history shows us how necessary the Hasidim were in maintaining the place of the Law of the Lord in a day of moral and spiritual decay. A generation that was tempted to accept the worst aspects of Hellenistic life needed the corrective of a vibrant Hasidism.

89

The Maccabees
and the Struggle Against Hellenism

The oppressions of the Jews by Antiochus Epiphanes produced a reaction which stunned Antiochus and surprised many of the Jews themselves. The Hasidim needed but a leader. From the obscure village of Modin one emerged.

1. Mattathias

The emissaries of Antiochus erected a pagan altar at Modin. In order to show their loyalty to the government, the Jews were asked to come forward and sacrifice at the altar. The aged priest of the village, Mattathias, was asked to come forward first to set a good example for the others. Mattathias refused to sacrifice at the pagan altar. Fearing the wrath of Antiochus, a timid Jew made his way to the altar. Mattathias was enraged. He approached the altar, slew the apostate Jew and the emissary of Antiochus. With his five sons, Mattathias destroyed the heathen altar and fled to the hills to avoid the certain reprisals which might be expected from Antiochus. Others joined the family of Mattathias.

The early days of the Maccabean revolt, as the struggle against Antiochus and Hellenism came to be called, were days of guerrilla warfare. From their mountain strongholds, the sons of Mattathias and their allies raided the towns and villages, killing the royal officers and the Hellenistic Jews who supported them. A religious factor, however, favored the Syrians. Religious scruples kept the Maccabees from fighting on the Sabbath. On one Sabbath, a band of Maccabees was surrounded and slaughtered. They would not defend themselves. Sensing the gravity of the situation, Mattathias adopted the principle that fighting in self-defense was permissible even on the Sabbath day.

2. Judas the Maccabee

Soon after the beginning of the revolt, Mattathias died. He

urged his followers to choose as military leader his third son Judas (Hebrew, *Judah*), known as "the Maccabee" (usually interpreted as "the hammer"). Continuing victories in guerrilla warfare proved the choice a good one. More and more Jews rallied to the banner of Judas.

In the early days of the revolt the Syrians underestimated the strength of the Maccabees. Thinking the revolt only a minor skirmish, they sent inferior generals and small detachments of soldiers into the field. The Maccabees, however, were able to hold their own. They defeated one after another of the Syrian armies thrown against them.

Before long Antiochus realized that he had a full-sized rebellion on his hands. Because of its proximity to Egypt, Judea was particularly important. Yet Antiochus could not throw his full strength into Judea because he was faced with another revolt in Parthia at the same time. Antiochus moved eastward to Parthia, leaving his general Lysias to take care of the revolt in Judah.

Lysias sent an army of Syrians, Hellenistically minded Jews, and volunteers from the neighboring countries to defeat the Maccabean rebels. Nicanor and Gorgias, subordinates of Lysias, were in charge of the engagement. Judas, however, by a surprise night attack, annihilated the Syrian army and seized enormous stores of booty. This victory at the town of Emmaus opened the road to Jerusalem to the Maccabees.

Judas and his army moved on toward Jerusalem. Menelaus and his sympathizers fled. The Maccabees entered the city and were able to take everything except the fort known as the Akra. They entered the Temple and removed all of the signs of paganism which had been installed there. The altar dedicated to Jupiter was taken down and a new altar was erected to the God of Israel. The statue of Zeus-Antiochus was ground to dust. Beginning with the twenty-fifth of Kislev (December) they observed an eight-day Feast of Dedication, known as Hanukkah, or the Festival of Lights. In this way they celebrated the end of the three-year period during which the Temple had been desecrated.

Peace was short-lived, however. The neighboring lands had been sympathetic with the Syrians and had constantly harassed the Jews. Lysias, himself, marched against the Maccabees and defeated them in a battle near Jerusalem. He next besieged Jerusalem, hoping to starve the Maccabees into submission. During his siege, however, he learned that a rival was marching against Antioch, the capital of Syria. Anxious to head north, Lysias made an offer of peace to the Jews.

In the name of Syria, Lysias offered to refrain from interference in the internal affairs of Judea. Laws against the observance of Judaism would be repealed. Menelaus was to be removed from office, and the high priesthood given to a certain Jakim or Eliakim, better known by his Greek name of Alcimus. In this way a mild Hellenizer was to be recognized as High Priest. Lysias promised that Judas and his followers would not be punished. The walls of Jerusalem were to be razed, however.

These terms of peace were considered by the council at Jerusalem, a kind of provisional government. This council included the Maccabean army officers and the respected scribes and elders associated with the Hasidim, the party of orthodox Jews which had supported Judas.

The goal of the Hasidim had been religious liberty. This goal seemed to be in sight. Judas was not satisfied with anything short of full political as well as religious liberty. However, the appeal of a combination of peace and religious freedom won the day. The Hasidim had achieved their goal, and they were able to outvote the followers of Judas. The peace terms were accepted. Alcimus was installed as High Priest. Menelaus was executed. Judas and a few of his followers left the city.

The fears of Judas proved to be correct. Alcimus had a number of the Hasidim seized and executed. Many loyal Jews turned to Judas again and the civil war was renewed. This time, however, Judas was faced with more formidable opposition. Alcimus appealed to Syria for aid, and a sizable army was sent. The Hellenizing Jews adopted a more moderate attitude and won over large segments of the followers of Judas. Left with an ill-equipped army of eight hundred men, Judas bravely met the large Syrian army. He died in battle, ending the first phase of the Maccabean struggle.

3. Jonathan

Simon, Jonathan, and Johanan, brothers of Judas, with several hundred Maccabean soldiers, fled across the Jordan. From the standpoint of Syria they were a band of outlaws. To many of the Jews, however — even those who had made their peace with Alcimus — they were the true patriots. Jonathan became the leader of the band, and young Jews were constantly being attracted to their ranks. Syrian attempts to destroy this band of patriots were uniformly unsuccessful.

Victory finally came to Jonathan by diplomacy rather than

by war. When a pretender, Alexander Balas, claimed the Syrian throne of Demetrius II, both parties sought help from the Jews. They turned to Jonathan as the man best able to raise and lead a Jewish army, bypassing the Hellenistic Jews. Jonathan had no interest in either the pretender or Demetrius, who had tried to destroy him several times. He played a delaying action which proved successful. He supported Balas and made treaties with Sparta and Rome. Before the war was over, Jonathan was High Priest, governor of Judea, and a member of the Syrian nobility. Jonathan's brother Simon was governor of the Philistine coastal area.

Since both Judah and Rome were hostile to Syria, an alliance seemed desirable. The Roman senate declared itself the "Friend" of Judah, but no efforts were made to implement the declaration. In time, of course, Rome was to prove as much of an enemy as Syria.

Jonathan's foreign policy promoted the internal prosperity of Judah. The coastal cities, ruled by Simon, were practically annexed. When Judah died at the hand of a Syrian general, his brother Simon succeeded him as ruling High Priest.

4. Simon

Simon was advanced in years when he assumed office. Syria was again rent between two factions, one looking to Demetrius II as king, and the other recognizing the legitimacy of Antiochus VI, a boy under the guardianship of Tryphon. This Tryphon deposed Antiochus "and reigned in his stead, and put on him the diadem of Asia" (I Maccabees 13:31-32). Tryphon was the first Syrian king who was not of the Seleucid line. Simon ignored him, recognizing Demetrius as rightful king in Syria. Demetrius, in return, granted the Jews full immunity from taxes. This was interpreted as an acknowledgement of independence, and occasioned great rejoicing among the Jews. Simon was also able to starve out the Syrian garrison at the Akra and to occupy the cities of Joppa and Bethsura.

During the period of peace which marked the high priesthood of Simon, the question of the legitimacy of the Maccabean priests was settled. The Hasidic party recognized the line of Onias as the legitimate heirs to the Aaronic priesthood. The family of Onias had gone to Egypt during the Maccabean conflict, however, and any claims they had to the priesthood were thereby forfeited. In recognition of his wise rule, a convocation of the leaders in Israel named Simon "leader and High Priest for ever, until there should arise a faithful prophet" (I Maccabees 14:25-49).

This act legitimized a new dynasty which is known in history as the Hasmoneans. The name is thought to be derived from an ancestor of the Maccabeans named Asmonaeus, or (in Hebrew) Hashmon. Simon was the last of the sons of Mattathias. Under him, however, the concept of a hereditary high priesthood in the Hasmonean family was legitimized.

In 134 B.C., Simon and two of his sons were murdered by an ambitious son-in-law. A third son, John Hyrcanus, managed to escape. He succeeded his father as hereditary head of the Jewish state.

90

The Hasmonean Dynasty, Growth and Decay

I. John Hyrcanus

With the death of the last of the sons of Mattathias, in 135 B.C., the heroic age of the Maccabean struggle came to an end. The generation which had fought for religious liberty was dying out. The new generation was proud of the Maccabean victories and hopeful of even greater successes at home and abroad.

Syria had to respect the leadership of her neighbor to the south. Although powerful enough to conquer Jerusalem, she offered recognition to Hyrcanus on condition that Hyrcanus consider himself subject to Syria and promise help in Syrian military campaigns. Hyrcanus was also asked to give up the coastal cities which had been annexed by his father and Jonathan. He was permitted to keep Jaffa which served as the port of Judah. The Syrian king left Palestine, and the Hellenizing party disappeared from the Jewish political scene.

This change in political alignments is an important factor in the reign of Hyrcanus. Previously the lines were closely drawn. The Hasidim represented the conservative elements who wished to retain their religious liberty and resist Hellenism. The Hellenizers were willing to sacrifice their religious heritage in order to achieve the real or imaginary gains included in the concept of "the Greek way of life." The Maccabean struggle resulted in victory for the Hasidim, although the Hasidim did not wholly align themselves with the Maccabees. They were willing to stop short of political independence in their dealings with the Syrians.

With the recognition of the government of Hyrcanus by the Syrians, the older Hellenists were completely discredited. Their conflict with the Hasmoneans was ended, and they became loyal members of the Jewish community.

The adage, "If you can't lick them, join them," is illustrated in the subsequent history of this Hellenistic party. Its ideals were perpetuated in the party of the Sadducees, as the ideals of the Hasidim were perpetuated in the party of the Pharisees. These parties are first mentioned during the lifetime of Hyrcanus. Before his death he repudiated the Pharisees and declared himself a Sadducee.

The reign of John Hyrcanus began a policy of territorial expansion including the re-conquest of the coastal cities ceded to Syria during the first years of his reign and the subsequent conquest of Edom, or Idumea.

The coastal cities were the commercial highways of Palestine. From time immemorial the roads of commerce and warfare passed up the Palestinian coastland from Egypt to Syria and Mesopotamia. Without the control of these commercial highways, Hyrcanus knew that Judea would sink into insignificance. As soon as Syrian internal affairs made interference from the north unlikely, Hyrcanus captured the cities and promoted the development of Jewish commerce.

Another ancient trade route passed south of Judea, through Idumea, to Egypt. Hyrcanus conquered this territory and compelled the Idumeans to be circumcised and accept Judaism. This action has been condemned by later Judaism. It even met opposition in his own lifetime. There is something ironical in the thought of a grandson of Mattathias forcing religious conformity on a people conquered by Jewish arms! Many historical parallels may be drawn. The oppressed frequently become the oppressors. That human nature frequently descends to such depths does not lessen the tragedy, however.

Hyrcanus' policy of conquest was supported by the men of wealth and the aristocrats who hoped to grow in power and prestige as a result of new commercial opportunities and larger territories to govern. Some support probably came from extreme nationalists who dreamed of glory and conquest.

The mass of the population, however, could not hope to profit from the policy of territorial expansion. On the contrary, they were alarmed at the growing secularism of the age. The high priesthood had little semblance to a sacred office.

There were practical considerations, too. Wars are expensive — in lives as well as money. The Jew might applaud the conquest of Samaria, whose rival temple on Mt. Gerizim always annoyed him. Perhaps he would even deem the coastal cities a rightful part of his Judean homeland. The annexation of Idumea, however, was something different.

Although there was difference of opinion, and the emergence of rival parties during the reign of Hyrcanus, the unity of the Hasmonean state was not threatened. The borders had been extended on all sides before Hyrcanus died in 104 B.C. Although devout Jews frequently differed with his policies, his personal life was free from suspicion. His devout, Hasidic background bore fruit in a life which could not offend the most meticulous scribe. His children, however, had grown up in a palace and numbered themselves among the aristocrats. Their training was more in Greek than in Hebrew thought, and they looked upon the Pharisees with disdain.

2. Aristobulus

The death of John Hyrcanus precipitated a dynastic struggle among his children. His eldest son, who preferred his Greek name, Aristobulus, to his Hebrew name, Judah, emerged as the victor. As a typical tyrant, he cast three of his brothers into prison, where two are thought to have starved to death. Another brother was murdered in the palace.

Aristobulus continued the policy of territorial expansion begun by Hyrcanus. In his short reign he pushed his borders north to the territory around Mt. Lebanon, and took to himself the title "King." Drink, disease, and the haunting fear of rebellion brought death after only a one-year reign. There was little mourning among the masses of the Jews.

3. Alexander Jannaeus

At the time of Aristobulus' death he had but one brother alive in prison. His Hebrew name was Jonathan, and his Greek name, Alexander. History knows him as Alexander Jannaeus.

Any who hoped for a change in policy when Alexander Jannaeus assumed office were bitterly disappointed. The policy of territorial expansion continued. Although not always successful on the battlefield, Jannaeus extended his frontiers along the Philistine coast, toward the frontiers of Egypt and in the Trans-Jordan area. The size of the Jewish state was comparable to that of the glorious days of David and Solomon. It incorporated the whole of Palestine proper, with adjacent areas, from the borders of Egypt to Lake Hulah. Perea in Trans-Jordan was included, as were the Philistine cities of the coastal plain, except Ascalon. The Hasmoneans aspired to become a maritime power. Ships were sculptured on the family tomb near Modein and were depicted on the coins minted by successive Hasmonean rulers.

The territories incorporated into the Hasmonean kingdom were, with some exceptions, quickly Judaized. The Idumeans came to exercise an important place in Jewish national life. Galilee became one of the principal centers of Judaism. The Samaritans, however, resisted assimilation. Cities like Apollonia and Sythopolis, with only a small Jewish element in their population, likewise retained their non-Jewish character.

The rift between the Pharisees and the Hasmonean rulers, first noted in the reign of John Hyrcanus, reached its climax during the days of Alexander Jannaeus. Jannaeus kept the Pharisees in subjection by the use of foreign mercenaries.

Open rebellion broke out at a memorable Feast of Tabernacles when Jannaeus was officiating in the Temple as King-Priest. Showing his contempt for the Pharisees, Jannaeus poured out a water libation at his feet instead of on the altar, as prescribed by Pharisaic ritual. The people in the Temple, enraged at this impious act, pelted Jannaeus with the citrons which they were carrying in honor of the feast. Jannaeus called upon his soldiers to restore order. Hundreds of defenseless people were killed in the process.

The result was open civil war. The Pharisees invited the king of Syria to aid them. War brings strange allies! The descendants of the Hasidim asked the descendants of Antiochus Epiphanes to aid them against the descendants of the Maccabees.

The Syrians came and, aided by the Pharisees, forced Jannaeus into hiding in the Judean hills. The Pharisees did some serious thinking. Fearing that the Syrians would claim Judea as the fruit of victory, and thinking that Alexander Jannaeus and his Sadducean sympathizers were sufficiently punished, thousands of the Pharisees deserted the Syrian army and went over to Jannaeus. The Syrians were defeated by this realignment of forces.

Jannaeus was not content to learn from his near-defeat, however. He instituted a hunt for the leaders of the rebellion, and made a horrible example of those he caught. He gave a banquet to the Sadducean leaders to celebrate his victory. Eight hundred Pharisees were crucified in the presence of his celebrating guests. Alexander Jannaeus thus goes down in history as a tyrant. Compromise between the Pharisees and the Sadducees was rendered impossible. Many students of the Dead Sea Scrolls identify Jannaeus as the Wicked Priest who persecuted the pious leader known as the Teacher of Righteousness.

Tradition suggests that Jannaeus repented on his deathbed. It relates how he instructed his wife, Salome Alexandra, to dismiss his Sadducean advisers and reign with the aid of the Pharisees.

4. Alexandra

Salome Alexandra had been married successively to Aristobulus and Alexander Jannaeus. The widow of two Hasmonean rulers, she succeeded to the throne as queen in her own right. Alexandra was nearly seventy years of age when she began her reign. Being a woman, she could not officiate as High Priest. Her elder son, Hyrcanus, assumed the priesthood, and his brother Aristobulus received the military command. Alexandra's brother, Simeon ben Shetah, was a leader of the Pharisees, a fact which may have disposed Salome Alexandra to seek peace between the opposing factions.

Under Alexandra, the Pharisees had their opportunity to make a constructive contribution to Jewish life. In many areas, particularly that of education, they were eminently successful. Under the presidency of Simeon ben Shetah, the Sanhedrin (the Jewish Council of State) decreed that every young man should be educated. This education was, of course, primarily in the Hebrew Scriptures. The importance of training the young was emphasized in the Old Testament, and the successors of Ezra had stressed the necessity of becoming acquainted with the Sacred Scriptures. Under the leadership of Simeon ben Shetah, a comprehensive system of elementary education was inaugurated, so that the larger villages, towns, and cities of Judea would produce a literate, informed people.

The reign of Alexandra was peaceful in comparison with the years which preceded it. Her son Aristobulus led an expedition against Damascus, which proved futile. A threatened invasion from Armenia was averted by bribes and diplomacy.

Alexandra's reign did not answer her country's problems, however. It did not even heal its wounds. If the Pharisees were happy in their new-found recognition, the Sadducees were resentful of the fact that they were deprived of power. To make matters worse, the Pharisees used their power to seek revenge for the massacre of their leaders by Alexander Jannaeus. Sadducean blood was spilt, and the makings of another civil war were in the air.

The Sadducees found in Aristobulus, the younger son of Jannaeus and Alexandra, the man they would support as Alexandra's successor. He was a soldier, and appealed to that party which dreamed of imperial expansion and worldly power. Hyrcanus, the elder brother and rightful heir, was congenial to the Pharisees. With the death of Alexandra, the partisans of the two sons were ready for a showdown.

5.   Hyrcanus II

At the death of Alexandra, her older son Hyrcanus, who had been serving as High Priest, succeeded to the throne as Hyrcanus II. Immediately Aristobulus led an army of Sadducees against Jerusalem. Hyrcanus and the Pharisees had neither enthusiasm for, nor ability in war. Declaring that he never really desired the throne, Hyrcanus surrendered all his honors to Aristobulus who became king and High Priest under the name Aristobulus II.

6.   Aristobulus II

By right of conquest, the Judean throne was safely in the hands of Aristobulus II, backed by the Sadducees. Hyrcanus and Aristobulus vowed eternal friendship. Aristobulus' eldest son, Alexander, married Hyrcanus' only daughter, Alexandra. Peace between the brothers was short-lived, however. Hyrcanus found it advisable, or necessary, to flee to Aretas, king of the Nabatean Arabs.

The city of Petra was located in a fertile basin at an elevation of 2700 feet, about fifty miles south of the Dead Sea. The urn tomb, in this scene, is situated in the southern part of the city.

7.   Antipater

Antipater, an Idumean by birth, saw in the position of Hyrcanus an opportunity to fulfill his own dream of being a political power in Judea. It was not difficult to persuade Hyrcanus that he had been unjustly deprived of his hereditary rights by his younger brother. The Nabatean Arabs would come to Jerusalem, drive out the usurper, and restore Hyrcanus to his rightful position. Such was the suggestion of Antipater. Hyrcanus agreed. Aretas and his Nabatean Arabs invaded Palestine and besieged Jerusalem. Aristobulus was caught by surprise. He shut himself up in Jerusalem and both sides prepared for a long siege.

8.   Enter the Romans

Learning about the quarrel between the brothers, Pompey, who was in the East in the interest of building up the Roman Empire there, took an immediate interest in Jewish politics. Under the guise of a willingness to arbitrate the difficulties, Rome became the force which was to determine the future of Palestine.

91

The Romans Take Over

I. Roman Beginnings

About three decades before Samaria fell to the Assyrians, legend states that Romulus and Remus founded the city of Rome (753 B.C.). Among the nations of antiquity, Rome was a newcomer. The glories of the Sumerians, the Hittites, Mittani, the old Babylonian empire of Hammurabi, and the best periods of Egyptian history had faded centuries before Rome appeared as a city state on the Tiber. During the early years of her existence the mighty Assyrian Empire was defeated by Cyaxeres the Mede and Nabopolassar, the founder of the Neo-Babylonian Empire. Before Rome became a power to be reckoned with, Nabonidus, the last of the Neo-Babylonian kings, was defeated by the armies of Cyrus the Great, and Persia became mistress of the entire East, including Egypt. The son of Philip of Macedon, Alexander the Great, reversed the process of history by invading the East as a missionary for Hellenism and a military conqueror. Alexander's death precipitated the division of the Hellenistic world, which was united again by the diplomacy and the military might of Rome.

Although we are dependent on legend for our accounts of the founding of Rome, its later history is well documented. In the fifth century B.C. the city state of Rome was a thriving republic. By the middle of the third century a series of wars with the Etruscans and other tribes made the whole Italian peninsula subject to Rome. After three wars with the Carthaginians, Rome gained control of the western Mediterranean in 146 B.C. The Carthaginians traced their roots back to the Phoenician city of Tyre, and the wars between Rome and Carthage are known in history as the Punic wars. In 146 B.C. Carthage was completely destroyed by the Roman general,

Scipio Africanus, who put an end to a power which had threatened Rome itself when Hannibal invaded Italy.

Turning toward the east, Rome was able to add to her territories with little opposition. Shortly after the destruction of Carthage, Roman rule was extended over Macedonia, Corinth, and all Achaia. In 133 B.C., Attalus, king of Pergamum, bequeathed his territory to the Romans. The Roman province of Asia was then organized.

2.   Pompey Enters Palestine

In Palestine the strength — both moral and physical — of the Maccabees was fast waning. Following the death of Alexandra, her sons Aristobulus II and Hyrcanus II were fighting for the right of succession. The news of the chaos in Palestine reached Rome. Pompey, the Roman general who had been so successful in bringing Roman power to the East, determined to intervene. Scaurus, one of Pompey's subordinates, decided to support Aristobulus, on the theory that he would be best able to pay the bribe for Roman support which had been offered by each of the contestants.

Pompey personally intervened to get at the root of the quarrel between Aristobulus and Hyrcanus. He observed evidences of the plan of Aristobulus to revolt against Rome. A Roman army besieged Jerusalem. Hyrcanus supported Pompey against his brother. Jerusalem was besieged for three months. Finally the fortifications were breached. Twelve thousand Jews are said to have been slaughtered in the battle which followed. Pompey, with his officers, entered the Holy of Holies in the Temple. This act scandalized the Jews, for none but the High Priest ever had access to the inner court of the Temple. Pompey did not plunder the Temple, however. He left its costly furnishings untouched and permitted the Temple worship to continue. Jerusalem was, in the words of Josephus, "made tributary to the Romans," and the last vestige of Jewish national independence was removed.

With the defeat of Aristobulus, Judea was made a part of the Roman province of Syria. The coastal cities, the district of Samaria, and the non-Jewish cities east of the Jordan were removed from Judea. Hyrcanus was rewarded for his loyalty to Pompey by being named Ethnarch of Judea, including the districts of Galilee, Idumea, and Perea. He was also confirmed in the office of High Priest. A yearly tribute was paid to Rome.

Aristobulus and a number of other captives were taken as prisoners to grace Pompey's triumph in Rome. Enroute to

Rome, Aristobulus' son, Alexander, escaped and attempted to organize a revolt against Hyrcanus. With the aid of the Romans, Hyrcanus was able to meet this challenge to his authority. Alexander was forced to surrender, but his life was spared.

3.   The Power of Antipater

During the years of strife between Aristobulus II and Hyrcanus II the Idumean governor Antipater, or Antipas, took a lively interest in the politics of Judea. Antipater was bitterly opposed to Aristobulus, partly through fear and partly because of his friendship for Hyrcanus. It appears that Hyrcanus relied much on Antipater, who became the virtual power behind the throne.

The Jews resented the presence of Antipater almost as much as they resented the fact that they were subject to Rome. Antipater was an Idumean, or Edomite according to Old Testament nomenclature. The Edomites had been the hereditary enemies of the Jews. From the territory south of the Dead Sea they had been pushed northward to the area around Hebron by the Nabatean Arabs. Under John Hyrcanus the Idumeans had been forcibly incorporated into the Jewish nation, and the antipathy continued. Antipater did not let this hinder him from seeking an ever increasing amount of power under Hyrcanus II and his Roman overlords, and from seeking positions of influence for his sons Phasael and Herod.

4.   Herod the Great

In the crisis which followed the murder of Julius Caesar, Antipater and his sons showed their loyalty to the new regime of Cassius by zealously collecting tribute. Herod was given the title "Procurator of Judea," with the promise that he would one day be named king. When Anthony defeated Brutus and Cassius at Philippi, Asia fell into the hands of a new Roman regime. Herod, ever an opportunist, quickly changed his loyalties and bribed his way to favor with Anthony.

The Parthians, who occupied a part of the eastern territory of the once mighty Persian Empire, had not been subdued by Rome. In 41 B.C. they attacked and took Jerusalem and made Antigonus, son of Aristobulus II, king and High Priest. Herod, the son of Antipater, who had inherited the throne of Judea at the death of Hyrcanus, was forced to flee to Rome. There he won the favor of Anthony who bestowed upon him the title "King of the Jews," which was to have meaning only after the

El-Khazneh, the treasury, near the entrance of the Siq to the basin of Petra.

Parthians were driven out. The Roman forces helped Herod in this military operation.

Herod's rule spanned the eventful years of 37 B.C. to 4 B.C. He is best known as the king who feared the birth of a rival "King of the Jews," and caused the murder of the infants of Bethlehem at the time of the birth of Jesus. While that act of Herod has not been preserved in secular records, his other atrocities are well documented.

Shortly after capturing Jerusalem from the Parthians, Herod appointed Hananiel of Babylon as High Priest. Herod had married Mariamne, a descendant of the Hasmoneans, thus strengthening his claim to the throne. Her mother, Alexandra, resented the fact that a non-Hasmonean priest occupied the highest office. She determined to have Aristobulus, grandson of Hyrcanus II, as High Priest, and used all of her wiles to accomplish her purpose. Alexandra communicated with Cleopatra of Egypt to influence Anthony to bring pressure on Herod! Her plan was successful. Contrary to Jewish law, Hananiel was removed from office and Aristobulus was named High Priest.

For a time it looked as though Herod and Alexandra were on friendly terms. Herod, however, learned of Alexandra's communications with Cleopatra and realized that she could not be trusted. He insisted that she remain in the palace, and ordered guards to keep constant watch over her movements. On one occasion she tried to escape to Egypt with her son Aristobulus in two specially prepared coffins, but one of Herod's servants discovered the plot and prevented the escape.

Aristobulus was a real threat to Herod. As a Jew of priestly line, he had an advantage which the Idumean, Herod, could not attain. When the news that Aristobulus had drowned while bathing reached Herod, he feigned great sorrow. Alexandra was sure that Aristobulus had been murdered at Herod's instigation. There is a flaw in Josephus' account of the incident. He records that Aristobulus "was sent by night to Jericho, and was there plunged into a pool till he was drowned, by the Gauls, at Herod's command." The Gauls were not in Herod's service until five years after Aristobulus' murder.[1] Nevertheless it seems that Josephus is correct in ascribing to Herod the murder of Aristobulus.

Alexandra again requested Cleopatra to intervene on her behalf, and was again successful. Anthony commanded Herod to appear before him to answer for his crime. Herod could not defy

A reconstruction of the Antonia, Herod's fortress in New Testament Jerusalem.

---

1. *Antiquities* xv. 217; *Bell, Jud.* I, 397.

Anthony, so he planned to go to Egypt. First, however, he asked his uncle, Joseph, to look after his affairs during his absence. In the event that Anthony pronounced the death sentence upon Herod, Mariamne, his wife, was to be immediately killed. Herod could not bear the thought of her belonging to anyone else, and he suspected that Anthony had been attracted by her beauty.

When a report reached Jerusalem that Herod had been slain, Alexandra made plans to secure the kingdom for her family. Joseph told Mariamne of the order which Herod had made before leaving for Egypt. Alexandra's plans to secure the kingdom from Anthony, with Mariamne's aid, were frustrated when Herod returned home. The report of his death was untrue. He had explained things to Anthony and had returned with full power.

When Mariamne revealed her knowledge of the order which Herod had given to Joseph, Herod concluded that there had been criminal relations between Joseph and Mariamne. Joseph was put to death with no opportunity to defend himself. Alexandra was "bound" and "kept in custody" because of her part in the affair. For the moment, Mariamne escaped censure. Herod seems to have truly loved her, unwise though he was in his expressions of love.

The next crisis in Herod's life was related to the struggle for power within the Roman Empire. The conflict between Anthony and Octavian for supreme control began in 32 B.C. Herod was the protégé of Anthony and desired to actively support him in his bid for control. Anthony, however, realized his need for a buffer state in the East against the Parthians. Herod did not remain idle, for he had to fight the Nabatean Arabs who were taking advantage of the general unrest. After some hard fighting, Herod overcame the Arab resistance.

Anthony did not fare so well, however. The battle of Actium (September 2, 31 B.C.) ended in defeat for Anthony, and Octavian emerged as the ruler of the Roman world. Herod managed to emerge on the winning side after a meeting with Octavian on the Isle of Rhodes. Josephus tells how Herod boasted of his friendship for Anthony and the help he had given in the fight against Octavian, concluding with the observation that Octavian could observe the kind of person Herod is and the loyalty he would show his benefactors, pledging equal loyalty to Octavian.[2] Octavian confirmed Herod in the kingship of Judea.

After the defeat at Actium, Anthony fled with Cleopatra to

The west slope of Masada. Its sheer cliffs (top), provided an ideal site for Herod's rock fortress. The middle terrace (below) has been excavated to reveal Herod's northern palace.

2. *Antiquities* xv. 187-93.

This wall shows the huge blocks typical of Herodian construction. The pavement at the bottom also is Herod's. This excavation is south of the temple area.

The family tomb of the Herods, in Jerusalem. Note the stone that rolls to form the door.

Egypt where the last act of their tragedy was played. The Roman armies reached the environs of Alexandria, and Cleopatra determined to rid herself of Anthony. She barricaded herself in a monument with two of her women and made Anthony think she had committed suicide. Anthony, according to plan, thrust his sword into his body but did not succeed in taking his own life. Cleopatra and her women drew the badly wounded Anthony into the monument. His corpse was found there by the Romans when they broke into the monument. It is suspected that Cleopatra realized that her chances of making terms with the Romans would be enhanced if she could rid herself of Anthony.

Octavian personally entered Alexandria, August 1, 30 B.C. Legend says that Cleopatra tried to charm Octavian with her feminine wiles, only to be repulsed by him. Cleopatra's death remains a mystery. One day she was found dead in her royal robes. The story was circulated that she had had an asp (or two asps) brought to her secretly. Small marks, reportedly discovered on her body, were considered proof that she had committed suicide by allowing herself to be bitten by the snakes.

The death of Cleopatra and the conquest of Egypt by the forces of Octavian strengthened Herod's hand in Palestine. Cleopatra's possessions in Palestine, given to her by Ptolemy, were added to Herod's domain. With other cities deeded to Herod by Octavian, Herod ruled a country equal in size to that which Alexander Jannaeus had ruled.

Successful in politics, Herod's domestic problems were to plague him again. Mariamne, who had been entrusted to a servant, Sohemus, when Herod went to meet Octavian at Rhodes, again learned of a plot to kill her in the event of her husband's death. When she greeted Herod angrily on his return, he ordered Sohemus put to death without trial. Mariamne was tried and condemned to death on the charge of adultery and attempt to poison. Remorse and its aftermath, illness, plagued Herod more effectively than his enemies. Alexandra soon afterward was put to death for a new plot against Herod.

Herod did have the confidence of Octavian, who assumed the name Augustus, but he had to make the best of difficult circumstances in his kingdom. He attempted to gain the good will of the Judeans by remitting a third part of their taxes, but antipathy to him continued. The oath of allegiance to Herod and Caesar was resented by the more religious elements among the

Jews. Herod thought highly of the Essenes, and excused them from taking the oath.

Although Herod's reign was one of trouble, much of it brought on by his own jealousy, there are accomplishments for which he should be given credit. Foremost among these are his buildings. Whole cities were built or rebuilt by Herod: Samaria became Sebaste in honor of Augustus; Straton's Tower became Caesarea, with a harbor protected by a mole and a wall with ten towers; Antipatris, northeast of Joppa; Phasaelis in the Jordan Valley, north of Jericho; and Anthedon, thoroughly renovated, became Agrippeion. Fortresses were built: Herodeion, Alexandreion, Hyrkania, Machaerus, and Masada. The gymnasiums, baths, parks, marketplaces, streets, and other luxuries of a Hellenistic culture were part of his building programs.

In the eighteenth year of his reign (20/19 B.C.), Herod began the work of building, or, more correctly, rebuilding the Temple in Jerusalem. The Temple proper, on which priests and Levites were employed, was finished in a year and a half with no interruption in the daily sacrifices. It took eight more years to complete the courts. The entire structure was arranged in terrace form, with one court higher than the other, and the Temple highest of all. The outer court was open to the gentiles and Jews who were unable to approach closer to the Temple because of ceremonial impurities. A "court of the women" and an inner "court of the Israelites" provided, respectively, for the women and men to approach more closely to the sacred Temple precincts which, of course, were entered only by the officiating priesthood.

Work on the surrounding buildings of the Temple was still going on during the ministry of Jesus (cf. John 2:20). The work was completed during the time of the procurator Albinus (A.D. 62-64), only a few years before the armies of Titus destroyed the city of Jerusalem with its Temple (cf. Matt. 24:2, 15-22, 32-35).

Herod's interest in the Temple was doubtless inspired by his love of grandeur, and his desire to be well received by his Jewish subjects. His personal life was such, however, that his gift of the Temple could not clear his name before the Israelites of his own, or subsequent generations.

The last years of Herod were marked by intrigue and conspiracy. Alexander and Aristobulus, his sons by Mariamne, were educated in Rome. They openly boasted of what they would do to those who had been the enemies of their mother when

Caesarea was the center of Roman provincial government. This scene shows the vaulted Crusader street.

A model of Herodian Jerusalem. In the background is the temple area on its elevated site.

once they came to power. Antipater, Herod's son by his first wife, Doris, determined to eliminate Alexander and Aristobulus as rival claimants to the throne. Charging that they were plotting against Herod's life, Antipater produced documents which incriminated Alexander and Aristobulus. They were tried, convicted, and strangled to death. Antipater himself was later found guilty of attempting to poison Herod, and given the death sentence. Augustus is reported to have commented, "I'd rather be Herod's hog *(hus)* than his son *(huios)*." Out of deference to Jewish dietary laws, Herod did not kill his hogs.

When it was known that Herod was sick and nearing death, several zealous Pharisees pulled down the golden eagle which Herod had unwisely erected over the great gate of the Temple. Regarding this as a "graven image," the Jews resented its presence. Herod ordered the death of these Jewish leaders, a final act of tyranny which caused his memory to be hated by the Jews.

Herod's death came April 1st, 4 B.C. Cancer of the intestines and dropsy are suggested as its causes. It is said that Herod knew that there would be no mourning when he died, so he ordered the imprisonment and death of a number of the leaders of the Jews that there might be mourning throughout the land. Although this story is probably untrue, Herod left behind him a reputation of infamy. True, he was manipulated by evil people, and was often "more sinned against than sinning," yet he allowed his passions to master him and he must go down in history as one of the world's great failures. That he was jealous even of the infant Jesus shows the extent to which the desire for worldly sovereignty may lead a man astray.

92

The Origin
of the Jewish Sects

The rise of the Jewish sects is traceable to the impact of Hellenism on the life and culture of the Near East. When the new clashes with the old, violent reactions frequently result. This is particularly true when the new ideology has religious and moral overtones.

Many of the Jews were willing to attempt a synthesis of Greek civilization and Hebrew religion. Jews in Palestine as well as Jews throughout the Hellenistic world, adopted Greek names, subscribed to Greek philosophies, and looked to Greek institutions as the harbingers of cultural progress. The Jews in Palestine were generally more conservative than their Greek-speaking cousins in Alexandria and the other great Hellenistic centers, but they were not unaffected. We may assume that these Jews felt that their loyalty to the faith of their fathers was in no way impaired by making peace with the new attitudes which Alexander and his successors had advocated.

Other Jews reacted violently against the Hellenizers. They saw Hellenism as a way of life which was opposed to that prescribed in their Torah. The immodesty of the Greek gymnasium and the neglect of Jewish religious rites by the Hellenistically minded younger generation seemed to indicate trouble. As idolatry had been the besetting sin of Israel before the exile, so Hellenism was regarded as the new temptation to unfaithfulness.

The Jews who reacted against Hellenism are known as the Hasidim (Chasidim) or Assidians. They were, by definition, the party of "the pious." As the Sadducees of New Testament times continued the basic ideology of the earlier Hellenizers, so the Pharisees and the Essenes sought to preserve the basic tenets of the Hasidim. The law of God was basic in Hasidic thought. They were willing to suffer martyrdom rather than transgress its precepts. They supported the sons of Mattathias in the early days of the Maccabean revolt, but they left the Hasmoneans as soon as their religious liberties had been won from the Seleucids. Freedom to obey the law was to them an adequate goal, and political independence was quite unnecessary.

I. The Pharisees

The party of the Pharisees is first mentioned by name during the reign of John Hyrcanus (134-104 B.C.). According to Josephus, Hyrcanus expressed his friendship to his fellow Pharisees by inviting them to a feast, during which he urged any who observed anything unbecoming in his conduct to correct him. A Pharisee replied that, if Hyrcanus really wanted to be righteous, he should surrender the office of High Priest and be content with his position as civil ruler. The Pharisee suggested that Hyrcanus' mother had been a captive in the days of Antiochus which, it would be presumed, would have involved her in immorality.

Hyrcanus was enraged at this suggestion, and the other Pharisees seemed to resent the charge made by one of their number. Josephus tells us that a Sadducee took advantage of the embarrassment of the situation by suggesting that Hyrcanus ask the Pharisees to suggest a suitable punishment for their offending member. In this way the attitude of the Pharisees as a sect would become apparent. When the Pharisees suggested "a moderate punishment of stripes" rather than the death penalty, Hyrcanus felt that the Pharisees were really opposed to him, and he espoused the cause of the Sadducees.

To what extent the story is to be regarded as sober history would be difficult to determine, but it suggests the antagonism between the Pharisees and Sadducees as early as the reign of Hyrcanus. It is clear that the Pharisees resented the combination of high priesthood and civil authority in the successors of the Maccabees. It has been suggested that the outspoken Pharisee who incurred the wrath of Hyrcanus may have left the more moderate Pharisees to become the founder of the Essenes. This is, of course, only a conjecture.

The word "Pharisee" means "separated ones." Although some have suggested that the separation was from the common people, it is more probable that the Pharisees were so named because of their zeal for the law which involved separation from the influences of Hellenism. In this sense they were the heirs of the Hasidim. Josephus says that the Pharisees "appear more religious than others, and seem to interpret the laws more accurately."

The laws regarding ceremonial purity were punctiliously observed by members of the Pharisaic brotherhood. No items of food or drink were to be purchased from a "sinner," for fear of ceremonial defilement. For the same reason, a Pharisee might not eat in the house of a "sinner," although he might entertain the "sinner" in his own house. When this was done, however, the Pharisee was required to provide the "sinner" with clothes to wear, for the "sinner's" own clothes might be ceremonially impure.

The particular domain of the Pharisees in pre-Christian Judaism was the synagogue. The synagogue seems to have had its origin in the Babylonian captivity when the Jews were prevented from participating in the sacrificial offerings which could be offered only in the Jerusalem Temple. Prayer and the reading of Scripture, however, were not subject to limitations of geography. Wherever ten Jewish families settled, a synagogue could be formed, according to later usage. After the return from exile, the synagogue was retained as the place of non-sacrificial worship in Israel, as it is to this day. The Sadducees gained control of the Temple ritual during the period that the Hasmoneans ruled, and down to New Testament times, but the scribes and Pharisees maintained the synagogue as the center of worship and instruction.

In a sincere desire to make the law workable within the changing culture of the Greco-Roman world, the Pharisaic scribes developed the system of oral tradition which proved such a burden to Judaism during the time of Christ.

Beginning with Scripture itself, the Pharisees quoted the "case decisions" of famous rabbis who had been consulted concerning the application of Scripture to individual problems. If the revered exegetes of Scripture (the *hakamim*, or sages) had expressed an opinion concerning the application or meaning of Scripture, this was given due consideration. Thus the observant Jew was frequently faced with conflicting viewpoints on the nature of correct Sabbath observance, the application of dietary rules to new articles of food, and the multitude of problems with which the legalistic mind was burdened.

During the first century before Christ, two influential Pharisaic teachers gave their names to the two historic schools of legal thought among the Pharisees. Hillel was the more moderate of the two in his legal interpretations. He was known for his regard for the poor and was willing to accept Roman rule as compatible with Jewish orthodoxy. Shammai, on the other hand, was more strict in his interpretation, and was bitterly opposed to the Romans. This viewpoint ultimately found expression in the Zealots, whose resistance to the Romans brought on the destruction of Jerusalem in A.D. 70. The Talmud preserves the record of 316 controversies between the schools of Hillel and Shammai.

The attempts at applying the Law to new situations were rejected by the Sadducees who restricted their concept of authority to the Torah, or Mosiac Law. The medieval Jewish sect of Karaites similarly rejected the rabbinical interpretations of Scripture and appealed for a return to the Bible itself as alone valid as the standard of faith. To the Pharisees, however, tradition was not simply a commentary upon the Law, but was ultimately raised to the level of Scripture itself. To justify this attitude it was stated that the "oral law" was given by God to Moses at Mt. Sinai, along with the "written Law" or the Torah (*Pirke Aboth.* 1:1). The ultimate in this development is reached when the Mishna states that the oral law must be observed with greater stringency than the written Law, because statutory law (i.e., oral tradition) affects the life of the ordinary man more intimately than the more remote constitutional Law (the written Torah) (M. Sanhedrin 10:3).

In addition to the charge that traditions had largely made void the intent of the Law, the New Testament makes it clear that the mentality of Pharisaism involved little more than a concern for the minutia of the Law during the time of Christ. Like many worthy movements, the early piety of those who had separated themselves from impurity at great cost was exchanged for an attitude of pride in the observance of legal precepts. The Pharisee scrupulously tithed even his wild herbs (Matt. 23:23; Luke 11:42), but he did not hesitate to oppress the weak and needy at the same time. (cf. Matt. 23:14). Fasting, ceremonial ablutions, Sabbath observance were all proper in their place, according to Jesus, but they were not enough. They must be accompanied by evidence of a heart that truly loved the Lord. Conspicuous tassels and phylacteries (Matt. 23:5) and long public prayers (Mark 12:40, Luke 20:47) gave a degree of sanctity to the Pharisees in the eyes of the people, but this must not be confused with true piety before God. If the Pharisees desire to be seen of men, "they have their reward." This must not be confused with a life lived to the glory of God, however.

In men like Nicodemus, Joseph of Arimathea, Gamaliel, and Saul of Tarsus we meet some of the nobler souls of the Pharisaic tradition in the New Testament. To Saul of Tarsus who became Paul the apostle, the Pharisee represented the epitome of orthodoxy, "the most straitest sect of our religion" (Acts 26:5). The degeneracy of Pharisaism serves as a warning to those who take a stand for separation from evil. Self-complacency and spiritual pride are temptations to which the pious are particularly susceptible.

2. The Sadducees

Although the Pharisees and Sadducees are frequently denounced together in the New Testament, they had little in common save their antagonism to Jesus.

The Sadducees were the party of the Jerusalem aristocracy and the high priesthood. They had made their peace with the political rulers and had attained positions of wealth and influence. Temple administration and ritual was their specific responsibility. In the later Hasmonean period and the Roman period which followed it, the high priesthood had become a political football so that the religious interests of the office tended to be pushed into the background. The Sadducees held themselves aloof from the masses and were unpopular with them.

Theologically the Sadducees must be described with a series of negatives. They did not accept the oral law which developed under the Pharisees, and seem to have limited their canon to the Torah, or Pentateuch. They did not believe in resurrection, spirits, or angels (cf. Mark 12:18; Luke 20:27; Acts 23:8). They left no positive religious or theological system.

The Pharisees welcomed and sought proselytes (cf. Matt. 23:15), but the Sadducean party was closed. None but the members of the High Priestly and aristocratic families of Jerusalem could be Sadducees. With the destruction of the Jerusalem Temple in A.D. 70, the Sadducees came to an end. Modern Judaism traces its roots to the party of the Pharisees.

3. The Essenes

The Essenes and the Pharisees both continued the testimony of Hasidim. The Pharisees maintained their strict orthodoxy within the framework of historical Judaism. Their separation was from defilement, but not from institutional Judaism as such. Even though the Temple worship was conducted by the

The scene above shows the Qumran site as it overlooks the Dead Sea. Below is a closeup of the potter's kiln at Qumran.

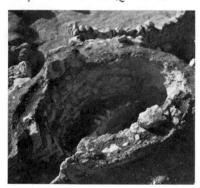

Sadducees, the Pharisees esteemed it a basic part of their religious inheritance. The Pharisee might hold himself aloof from "sinners," but he lived among them and coveted their esteem.

A more extreme reaction against the influences which tend to corrupt Jewish life was taken by the sect which the ancient writers Philo, Josephus, and Pliny call the Essenes. They seem to have lived for the most part in monastic communities, such as that with headquarters at Qumran, from which the Dead Sea scrolls have come.

In seeking to explain Judaism to the Greek-speaking world, Josephus spoke of three "philosophies" — Pharisees, Sadducees, and Essenes. The term "Essene" seems to have had quite an elastic usage, however, including various groups of monastically minded Jews who differed among themselves in certain of their practices. Pliny says that the Essenes avoided women and did not marry, but Josephus speaks of an order of marrying Essenes. The excavations of the cemetery at Qumran similarly reveal that women were a part of the Qumran community.

The ancient writers deal in a sympathetic way with the Essenes. The life of the Essene was one of rigor and simplicity. Devotion and religious study occupied an important place in the community. Scripture and other religious books were studied and copied by members of the Essene community. Each Essene was required to perform manual labor to make the community self-supporting. Community of goods was practiced in the Essene communities, and strict discipline was enforced by an overseer. Those groups which renounced marriage adopted boys at an early age in order to inculcate and perpetuate the ideals of Essenism. Slavery and war were repudiated.

The Essenes accepted proselytes, but the novice was required to go through a period of strict probation before he could become a full-fledged member. Numerically the Essenes were never large. Philo says that there were four thousand of them. Pliny says that they were settled north of En Gedi, an apparent reference to Qumran, northwest of the Dead Sea. That there were other settlements is clear, for we are told that all members of the sect were welcome in any of the Essene colonies.

Although it has been suggested that the Essenes are an off-shoot of Pharisaism, dating back to the time of John Hyrcanus, nothing certain is known of their early history. Considering themselves the true Israel, they trace their history back to the beginnings. Philo states that Moses instituted the order, and Josephus says that they existed "ever since the ancient time of the fathers." Pliny agrees that their history covers "thousands of ages." It is certain that Essenes existed for two centuries before the Christian era and that they lived at first among the Jewish communities. When they ultimately withdrew, many seem to have settled at Qumran, others living in scattered communities throughout Syria and Palestine.

The question of foreign influences on Essene thinking has been the subject of much scholarly debate. While some maintain that the Essenes are a purely indigenous growth within Judaism, others suggest that they were influenced from without — either from western Greek ideas, or from eastern Syrian or Persian concepts.

Josephus tells us that the Essenes believed in immortality but rejected the doctrine of bodily resurrection. This seems to be related to the philosophical concept of the evil of matter. The body is material, and if matter is evil, then salvation comes by escaping the body, and a bodily resurrection would be undesirable. Enforced celibacy fits into the same concept, which is contrary to the teaching of both Old Testament and New Testament Scripture. Early Christian theology was confronted with a similar heresy when the Docetists claimed that Jesus did not really have a body. Since they believed that matter is evil, they could not conceive of the Son of God as having a real body.

Although the Essenes either discouraged or forbade marriage, the Pharisees expected every man to take a wife at the age of eighteen. In this respect they were closer to the ideals of Biblical religion than were the Essenes.

While the Pharisees took part in the Temple services, even though they were unhappy at the position of the unorthodox Sadducees, the Essenes regarded themselves as the only true, or pure, Israel and refused to co-operate with what they believed to be the corrupt religious observances at the Jerusalem Temple. The carefully regulated life at the Essene center seems to have served as a substitute for the Temple in the eyes of the Essenes.

The strictness of Essene discipline and the rigidity with which the law was enforced are stressed by all who write about them. Josephus says that they were stricter than all Jews in abstaining from work on the Sabbath day (*Wars*. II. vii. 9). A passage in the Damascus Document, related to the Dead Sea Scrolls, says that it is unlawful to lift an animal out of a pit on the Sabbath day. Such a view was considered extreme even by the legalistic Pharisees (cf. Matt. 12:11).

The absence of references to the Essenes in the New Testa-

Ruins of the domestic section of the Qumran community. A mill for grinding grain is in the foreground.

Writing tables and bench from the Qumran scriptorium.

ment has led many writers to conclude that Jesus and the early church were Essene in sympathies, if not in origin. Renan called Christianity "an Essenism which succeeded on a broad scale," and E. Schure held that Jesus had been initiated into the secret doctrines of the Essenes.

Although the Essenes are not mentioned in the New Testament, they are also absent from the Jewish Talmud. The Pharisees and the Sadducees were the groups with which Jesus had immediate contact, and it is to be expected that they would be the ones who were the subjects of His discourses.

The teaching and practice of Jesus is diametrically opposed to the legalism and asceticism of the Essenes. Although the Essenes considered that contact with a member of their own group of a lower order than themselves was ceremonially defiling, Jesus did not hesitate to eat and drink with "publicans and sinners" (Matt. 11:9, Luke 7:34). Although obedient to the Mosaic Law, Jesus had no sympathy with those who made of the Law a burden instead of a blessing. The Sabbath was made for man, and Jesus insisted that it was lawful to do good on the Sabbath day (Matt. 12:1-12; Mark 2:23-36; Luke 6:6-11; 14:1-6).

Contrary to the Essene idea that matter is evil, Jesus insisted that it is from within, out of the heart of man, that evil comes. His first miracle was performed at a wedding (John 2:1).

Jesus denounced abuses in the Temple, and prophesied its destruction, but he did not repudiate the Temple services. He came to Jerusalem for the great feasts of His people, and after His resurrection we find Peter and John going to the Temple at the hour of prayer (Acts 3:1).

Asceticism and monasticism early gained entrance to the Christian church. Christianity in its earliest period, however, cannot be called an ascetic movement. The ministry of Jesus was largely to the "common people" who "heard Him gladly" (Mark 12:37), when the self-righteous despised both Him and them. He was called "a winebibber" and "a friend of publicans and sinners"—names which would scandalize Pharisee, Sadducee, and Essene alike (Luke 7:34).

4. The Zadokites

Since the publication in 1910 by Solomon Schechter of *Fragments of a Zadokite Work*—discovered in 1896 in the genizeh, or storage room for worn out manuscripts, of a Cairo synagogue—the term "zadokite" has entered the discussion of sectarian Judaism. The term "zadokite" appears to be related to the word

"Sadducee," but the two groups had different historical developments. Some have suggested that a group of spiritually minded priests, alarmed at the drift toward worldliness of early second century B.C. Sadduceeism, separated from it and formed the nucleus for the new group of "sons of Zadok." Whether this movement found spiritual affinity with a group like the Essenes, or whether a new beginning is to be posited for the group at this time is not clear.

The Zadokite Work speaks of a group which was compelled to migrate to Damascus where, under the leadership of a man called "the star" (cf. Num. 24:17), they entered into a New Covenant (cf. Jer. 31:31). A prominent leader of the sect, who may have been the founder, is the Teacher of Righteousness mentioned in the Zadokite work and the Qumran scrolls.

Scholars are agreed that the Zadokite work is related to the Qumran manuscripts. Style, vocabulary, and historical allusions first suggested a relationship. The discovery of copies of the Zadokite work in Cave 6, Qumran, removed any doubts. The history of the Qumran community and its relationship to known groups of pre-Christian Jews is still obscure.

The Zadokite work speaks of a migration to Damascus by the group of which the document speaks. The circumstances of this migration are not given in sufficient detail to warrant a positive statement of date. It has been thought that the removal of Onias III from his office as High Priest in the days of Antiochus Epiphanes was the occasion for the flight of the Zadokites to Damascus. Charles Fritsch in *The Qumran Community* suggests that the sojourn took place during the reign of Herod the Great (37 B.C. to 4 B.C.). Archaeological evidence indicates that the Qumran community center was unoccupied at that time, and Fritsch considered this the key to the date of the sojourn in Damascus. This gives rise to several questions: "Did the Zadokites leave Jerusalem around 175 B.C., sojourn for a time in Damascus, and then settle at Qumran? Did they go from Jerusalem to Qumran, then to Damascus during the reign of Herod, and then return to Qumran? Did the Damascus Covenanters, as the Zadokites are called, join forces with another group such as the Essenes?"

A Jewish scholar, Rabinowitz, has suggested that the withdrawal from Judea to Damascus is but another way of describing the Babylonian captivity. The faithful in Israel are thus thought of as learning lessons of loyalty to the Lord "beyond Damascus." Although this view would eliminate certain histor-

The area of the Qumran caves lies in the Judean wilderness, about two miles from the Dead Sea. Cave 4, marked by a circle in the photo, contained what seems to have been the bulk of the library of the Qumran community.

ical problems, the Zadokite Work does appear to discuss a historical migration to Damascus in days following the return from Babylonian exile.

Present knowledge seems to indicate that a group of priests, "sons of Zaddok," started a movement to which lay members were attracted. In Qumran the priestly prerogatives are jealously guarded. The name Zadokite was applied to the movement because of its stress on its own priestly legitimacy *vis-a-vis* the Jerusalem priesthood. The latter was corrupt in the eyes of the Zadokites. If this reconstruction is correct it would seem that the Qumran community included those who are called the Zadokites. Since the term Essene seems to have been a rather general term assigned to various ascetic groups within pre-Christian Judaism, it seems probable that this group of Zadokites was identified as Essene by Philo, Pliny, and Josephus. Since the historical origins of both Zadokite and Essene groups are still matters of conjecture, we cannot state which group existed first. That there were affinities, however, seems clear.

5. Zealots

Roman rule was not popular with the majority of Jews. To the Pharisees, Roman overlordship was a punishment visited upon Israel because of its sins. It was to be accepted with humility, in prayerful anticipation of the day when God would remove the horrible Roman yoke.

A more extreme attitude was taken by the party known from the writings of Josephus as the Zealots. They first appeared in Galilee under the leadership of Judas the son of Ezekias during the early years of Roman rule. They refused to pay taxes and considered it a sin to acknowledge loyalty to Caesar. God alone was to be reckoned as king of Israel!

The Pharisee, Gamaliel, mistakenly regarded Peter and the apostles as Zealot leaders. He urged that no action be taken against them, believing that if the movement they represented were not of God it would come to naught, as in the case of Theudas and Judas of Galilee. (Acts 5:35-39). The Galilean origin of most of the disciples and the fact that one of them was named Simon Zelotes (Simon, the Zealot) would make such a misunderstanding possible.

Ultimately the Zealots succeeded in winning the bulk of the people to their side. Their continual defiance of Rome brought on the destruction of Jerusalem in A.D. 70.

93

Rise of Apocalyptic Literature

During the last two centuries of this period and the first century of the Christian era, a species of literature developed among the Jews which is termed apocalyptic. An apocalypse is an unveiling. The last book of the Bible bears that name. This type of writing is also found in various portions of the Old Testament prophetic books, including Isaiah, Ezekiel (38-39), Daniel, Joel, and Zechariah (12-14).

The chief noncanonical apocalyptic books are the writings ascribed to Enoch and Baruch, the Testament of the Twelve Patriarchs, and IV Ezra. They form a part of the body of ancient literature which is termed pseudepigraphal because of the fact that many of these writings were issued under an assumed name.

The apocalyptic portions of the Bible are actually a species of Biblical prophecy. They are a part of the "divers manners" (Heb. 1:1) used in the proclamation of religious truth by Israel's prophets.

During the two centuries before Christ, when the Jew was conscious of the fact that prophecy had ceased, and that the canon of Scripture was closed, he looked for no new spokesman to declare divine truth with authority — at least until the Messiah should come. Thinkers, however, felt that they had a message for their generation. Sometimes these messages contained words and thoughts which had been popularly ascribed to some ancient worthy. In order to give a production the sanctity of age, and thus to insure a wide audience, the apocalypses of the two pre-Christian centuries were pseudepigraphal. The name of some ancient man of God, like Enoch, was assigned as the author of the writing. The writers doubtless believed that they were writing in the spirit of the earlier patriarch, and much of the material which they used was really old. We should not lightly charge these writers with "pious fraud," although we cannot accept the names assigned to their writings at face value.

Apocalyptic literature was both a message of comfort in days of trouble and an effort to show how God had purposed to bring victory to His people, although they were in the midst of an apparently hopeless situation. The persecutions of Antiochus Epiphanes threatened the very existence of Israel as a people. It was in the consciousness of the sovereign purposes of God that Israel took hope.

The Old Testament prophets were largely preachers, delivering the Word of God by word of mouth to their generation. The apocalyptists wrote their messages. Their writings made frequent use of imagery. In this way they avoided possible reprisals from powerful individuals or groups attacked. Also they secured an impressive air of mystery which helped to reinforce the message.

Students of apocalyptic literature, both Biblical and non-canonical, note a constancy in the imagery. Nations are beasts which come out of the sea (Dan. 7:3; II Esdras 11:1; Rev. 13:1). There are seven heavens (Testament of the Twelve Patriarchs —Levi, iii; Ascension of Isaiah, vii-x). Frequent references are made to "horns," "heads," "watchers," and "the seven angels." In general, men are described as animals, nations as beasts, the Jews as sheep or cattle, and their leaders as rams or bulls.

The apocalyptic literature of the two centuries before Christ adapted the ideas and, in part, the imagery of the earlier prophetic literature to the needs of a new generation. An air of mystery surrounds many of these writings. They deal with the purposes of God, the "secrets" of heaven which are not known to the uninitiated. The knowledge of the divine will comes through vision or dream. The message is usually given in the first person. If Israel's prophet claimed direct revelation from God Himself, the apocalyptic writer claims to receive divine revelation mediately through an angel. The prophets had much to say about the present, but the chief concern of the apocalyptist was the future. The final consummation was regarded as imminent.

The coming Messiah is a recurrent theme for the apocalyptist. This concept finds its roots in the Old Testament. Nathan had spoken of the continuation and idealization of the Davidic line (II Sam. 7:12 ff. cf. Ps. 89). The Perfect Prince of the Apocalyptists was a scion of the house of David. The Psalms of Solomon (17:21 ff.) contain a prayer for a restored Davidic prince who will overthrow the Romans. References to a Messiah, or "Anointed One," from other lines also appear. The Testament of Reuben (6:7 ff.) speaks of a Messiah from the line of Levi, and the Damascus Zadokite fragments speak of a Messiah from Aaron (9:10). In the Similitude of Enoch, written before 63 B.C., the Messiah is called "The Anointed One," "The Righteous One," "The Elect," and "The Son of Man" (37-71). The latter title, so familiar to the reader of the New Testament Gospels, is apparently derived from Daniel 7:13. The apocalyptists frequently speak of the Messiah as the great Judge who will come in the clouds of heaven to punish the wicked and reward the righteous.

The concept of the Kingdom of God is the climax of Apocalyptic literature. Sometimes this is presented as reserved for the Jews, or the righteous Jews only. Other writers envision the Kingdom of God as including true worshipers of God from every nation.

The Kingdom of God in some writers is a period of divine rule on earth. This rule may last four hundred years, or one hundred years, or it may be eternal. If this Kingdom of God is temporary, it is followed by an eternal heavenly existence.

To those who look for a Kingdom of God in this world, the end of the present age means the end of evil in the world. The future age is earthly but not evil. Some, however, insist that the present world is inherently evil. They expect the world to be destroyed, or miraculously changed. The future age is then the heavenly world.

The glories of the Kingdom of God are described in bold language. The earth will be so fruitful that a single vine will bear 10,000 branches, each branch 10,000 twigs, each twig 10,000 shoots, each shoot 10,000 clusters, each cluster 10,000 grapes, and each grape will produce 225 gallons of wine!

To what extent were the apocalyptists influenced by outside sources? It is frequently suggested that Persian influences, particularly in angelology and the dualistic conflicts between light and darkness, account in large measure for the nature of apocalyptic. Greek and Egyptian contacts are also suggested. While the Apocalyptic writers certainly assimilated material from the various cultures which surrounded them, there is no evidence of direct borrowing. It is best to see in the apocalyptic literature an echo of the prophetic writings, given shape by the sufferings under Antiochus Epiphanes. The Christian sees in the Messianic hope expressed in the literature of the first two pre-Christian centuries a providential preparation for the advent of Christ. Behind the extravagant symbolism, exaggerated nationalism, and laborious numerical calculations, he sees a confidence in the ultimate accomplishment of the divine purposes, and the advent of a righteous "son of David" through whom the purposes of God will be realized.

EPILOGUE

In the days of Herod the Great, in an obscure corner of the Roman Empire, in the city which had been the birthplace of King David a millennium earlier, Jesus the Messiah was born. History took little note of his life. Only a few devoted disciples openly espoused his cause. The religious leaders attributed the miracles He performed to Beelzebub, the Prince of the Devils. To the Roman officials he was an insurrectionist; to the Jews, a blasphemer. In the hour of his trial, his disciples forsook Him and fled. He was crucified as a malefactor, between two thieves.

Yet His life and His death introduce a new age. From apparent defeat came the triumph of victory. The death of the cross is heralded as the divinely provided atonement for sin. The resurrection brings the assurance of life everlasting.

Time Line of Bible History

EARLY ISRAEL AND HER NEIGHBORS:

Egypt	Date	Asia Minor	Mesopotamia	Syria-Palestine
	3000 B.C.			
Old Kingdom (29th-23rd centuries) Pyramid Age (26th-25th centuries)			Early Sumerians 2800-2360	
	2500			
			Sargon of Akkad dynasty *ca.* 2360-2180 Ur III 2060-1950	
Middle Kingdom (21st-18th centuries)	2000		Abraham leaves Ur	**Syria-Palestine**
	1750			
Hyksos *ca.* 1720-1550		**Asia Minor** Old Hittite Empire 1740-1460		
New Kingdom *ca.* 1570-1310	1500	New Hittite Empire 1460-1200		Ugaritic Texts (14th century)
Amarna Letters *ca.* 1400-1350				
Exodus of Hebrews *ca.* 1280 (?)				Hebrew Conquest 1250-1200
Ramesses II 1290-1224	1250		Assyria strong under Tiglath-pileser I 1118-1078	Judges 1200-1020
End of Egyptian Empire, *ca.* 1100				Saul 1020-1000
	1000		Assyria weak until	David 1000-961
			Ashur-dan II 934-912	Solomon 961-922

THE DIVIDED KINGDOM:

Kings of Judah (Davidic Dynasty throughout)	Events and Prophets	Date	Contemporary Rulers	Kings of Israel (Italics indicate separate dynasties)
Rehoboam Abijam Asa	Pharaoh Shishak invaded Judah and Israel	925	(Assyrian) Adad-nirari II	Jeroboam I *Nadab*

THE DIVIDED KINDOM: (Con't)

	Asa allied with Ben-hadad of Syria against Baasha	900	Tukulti-ninurta II	Baasha
Jehoshaphat				*Elah*
			Ashurnasirpal II	*Zimri*
	Elijah prophesied during period of apostasy	875		Omri
				Ahab
	Battle of Karkar		Shalmaneser III	
Jehoram	Elisha	850		Ahaziah
Ahaziah				Jehoram
(Athaliah)				
Joash	Jehu pays tribute to Shalmaneser	825	Shamshi-adad V	Jehu
				Jehoahaz
	Hazael of Damascus oppressed Judah		Adad-nirari III	Joash (Jehoash)
Amaziah		800		
				Jeroboam II
Uzziah			Shalmaneser IV	
	Hosea			
	Amos	775		
	Jonah		Ashur-dan III	
	Isaiah			
			Ashur-nirari I	*Zachariah*
		750		*Shallum*
Jotham	Micah		Tiglath-pileser III (Pul)	Menahem
				Pekahiah
Ahaz	Joel (?)			*Peka*
	Obadiah (?)	725	Shalmaneser V	Hoshea
Hezekiah			Sargon II	(Fall of Samaria, 722 B.C.)
	Sennacherib invades Judah	700	Sennacherib	
Manasseh			Esarhaddon	
	Assyria fought Egypt	675	Ashurbanipal	
	Manasseh carried to Babylon	650	Ashur-etil-ilani Sin-shar-ishkun	
Amon				
Josiah				
	Nahum Zephaniah Jeremiah	625	Nabopolassar established Neo-Babylonian Empire	
	Fall of Nineveh (612)		(Babylonian)	
	Josiah killed at Megiddo (608)			
Jehoahaz	Battle of		Nebuchadnezzar	
Jehoiakim	Carchemish (605)			
Jehoiachin	Habakkuk	600		
Zedekiah				
(Fall of Jerusalem, 587 B.C.)				

THE EXILE AND RETURN:

	Date	
	575	Evil-Merodach
Nebuchadnezzar invades Egypt		
		Neriglissar
	550	Nabonidus (defeated by Cyrus the Persian)
Fall of Babylon (539)		(Persian)
Decree of Cyrus		
Zerubbabel leads a party of Jews to Jerusalem		
Haggai		Cambyses
Zechariah	525	
Malachi		
Completion of second Temple (515)		Darius the Great
	500	
Esther saved her people in Persia		Xerxes
	475	
		Artaxerxes
Ezra led a party of Jews to Jerusalem.	450	

JUDAEA UNDER PERSIANS, GREEKS, AND ROMANS:

Greece	Date	Persia	Judaea
	500		
Battle of Marathon, 490		Xerxes	
Battle of Salamis, 480		486-465	
	475	Artaxerxes (Ahasuerus)	
		465-424	
Socrates, 470-399			
			Ezra's mission
			458 (?)
	450		
Xenophon, 431-354			
Plato, 428-348	425	Xerxes II, 323-	
	400	Darius II, 423-404	
		Artaxerxes II, 404-358	
		Artaxerxes III, 358-338	
Aristotle, 384-322		Arses, 338-336	
	350	Darius III, 336-331	
Alexander of Macedon invades Asia, 334		Persia defeated by Alexander, 331	

Egypt	Date	Syria
Ptolemaic Empire in Egypt, 323-30	300	Seleucid Empire in Syria, 312-64
Egypt dominates Palestine	275	

JUDAEA UNDER PERSIANS, GREEKS, AND ROMANS: (Con't)

Translation of Pentateuch into Greek	250	
	200	Antiochus III took Palestine from Egypt, 198
	175	Antiochus IV (Epiphanes), 175-163, persecutes Jews.
Jewish temple built at Leontopolis, 161	150	Maccabean Revolt, 166 Judas the Maccabee, 166-160 Jonathan, 160-143
		Simon, 142-134
	125	John Hyrcanus, 134-104
		Aristobolus I, 104 Alexander Jannaeus, 103-76
Rome	100	
		Alexandra, 76-67
Caesar invades Britain, 55		Pompey enters Syria, 64 — Pompey conquers Jerusalem, 63
	50	Antipater, procurator
Egypt becomes Roman province, 30 Augustus, 31 B.C.-A.D. 14		of Judaea, 55-43 Herod, King of Judaea 40-4
	A.D.	Birth of Jesus, 6 B.C.
Tiberius, AD 14-37		
Caligula, 37-41 Claudius, 41-54		Crucifixion, A.D. 32 Herod Agrippa I, king of Judaea, 39-44
	50	Felix, procurator of Judaea, 52-58
Nero, 54-68 Vespasian, 69-79 Titus, 79-81 Domitian, 81-96 Nerva, 96-98 Trajan, 98-117.		Festus, procurator of Judaea, 58 Jerusalem taken, Temple destroyed, 70
	100	

Bibliography

Biblical History

Albright, William F. "The Biblical Period." In *The Jews: Their History, Culture, and Religion*. Edited by Louis Finkelstein. New York: Harper & Row, 1960. Published separately as *The Biblical Period from Abraham to Ezra*. New York: Harper Torchbooks, 1963.

————. *From the Stone Age to Christianity*. Garden City, N.J.: Doubleday Anchor Books, 1957.

Anderson, B. W. *Understanding the Old Testament*. Englewood Cliffs, N.J.: Prentice-Hall, 1957.

Baron, Salo Wittmayer. *A Social and Religious History of the Jews*. New York: Columbia University Press, 1952.

Bright, John. *A History of Israel*. 2d ed. Philadelphia: Westminster Press, 1971.

Buck, Harry M. *People of the Lord*. New York: Macmillan Co., 1965.

DeVaux, Roland. *Ancient Israel: Its Life and Institutions*. New York: McGraw-Hill Book Co., 1961.

Gordon, Cyrus H. *The Ancient Near East*. New York: W. W. Norton & Co., 1964.

Gottwald, Norman K. *A Light to the Nations*. New York: Harper & Row, 1958.

Hall, H. R. H. *The Ancient History of the Near East*. London: Methuen & Co., 1950.

Heinisch, P. *History of the Old Testament*. Translated by W. Heidt. Collegeville, Minn.: Liturgical Press, 1952.

Kaufmann, Yahezkel. "The Biblical Age." In *Great Ages and Ideas of the Jewish People*. Edited by Leo W. Schwarz. New York: Random House, 1956.

Lods, A. *Israel*. London: Kegan, Paul, Trubner & Co., 1932.

Maly, Eugene H. *The World of David and Solomon*. Englewood Cliffs, N.J.: Prentice-Hall, 1966.

Neher, Andre et Renee. *Histoire Biblique du Peuple d'Esrael*. Adrien-Maisonneuve, 1962.

Noth, Martin. *The History of Israel*. New York: Harper & Row, 1958.

————. *The Old Testament World*. Philadelphia: Fortress Press, 1966.

Oesterley, W. O. E. and Robinson, Theodore. *A History of Israel*. London: Oxford University Press, 1932.

Orlinsky, Harry M. *Ancient Israel*. Ithaca, N.Y.: Cornell University Press, 1960.

Pederson, J. *Israel*. Copenhagen: Polv Branner, 1940.

Pieters, Albertus. *Notes on Old Testament History*. Grand Rapids: Eerdmans Publishing Co., 1950.

Schwarz, Leo, ed. *Great Ages and Ideas of the Jewish People*. New York: Random House, 1956.

Ancient Near Eastern History

General

Bury, J. B.; Cook, S. A.; and Adcock, F. E. *The Cambridge Ancient History*. Vols. 3 and 4. Cambridge: At the University Press, 1953 and 1954.

Hall, H. R. H. *The Ancient History of the Near East*. London: Methuen & Co., 1950.

Meek, Theophile J. M. *Hebrew Origins*. Rev. ed. New York: Harper Torchbooks, 1960.

Moscati, Sabatino. *Ancient Semitic Civilizations*. London: Elek Books, 1957.

———. *The Face of the Ancient Orient*. London: Routledge & Kegan Paul, 1950.

———. *The Semites in Ancient History*. Cardiff: University of Wales Press, 1959.

Pareti, Luigi; Brezzi, Paolo; and Petech, Luciana. *The Ancient World*. UNESCO History of Mankind, vol. 2. New York: Harper & Row, 1965.

Pritchard, James B. *The Ancient Near East in Pictures Related to the Old Testament*. Princeton: Princeton University Press, 1954.

Rostovtzeff, M. *A History of the Ancient World*. Vol. 1. Cambridge: Clarendon Press, 1926.

Schwantes, Siegfried. *A Short History of the Ancient Near East*. Grand Rapids: Baker Book House, 1965.

Babylonia and Assyria

Budge, E. A. Wallis. *Babylonian Life and History*. London: Religious Tract Society, 1925.

Champdor, Albert. *Babylon*. New York: G. P. Putnam's Sons, 1958.

Contenau, Georges. *Everyday Life in Babylon and Assyria*. London: Edward Arnold, 1954.

Jastrow, Morris. *History of the Civilization of Babylon and Assyria*. Philadelphia: J. B. Lippincott, 1915.

Koldeway, Robert. *Das Wieder Erstehende Babylon*. J. C. Hindrichs'sche Buchhandlung, 1925.

Laessoe, Jorgen. *People of Ancient Assyria: Their Inscriptions and Correspondence*. New York: Barnes & Noble, 1963.

MacQueen, James G. *Babylon*. New York: Frederick A. Praeger, 1965.

Mallowan, M. E. L. *Twenty-five Years of Mesopotamian Discovery*. London: British School of Archaeology in Iraq, 1956.

Margueron, Jean-Claude. *Mesopotamia*. New York: World Publishing Co., 1965.

Olmstead, A. T. *History of Assyria*. New York: Charles Scribner's Sons, 1923.

Oppenheim, A. Leo. *Ancient Mesopotamia: Portrait of a Dead Civilization*. Chicago: University of Chicago Press, 1964.

Parrot, Andre. *The Arts of Assyria*. Racine, Wis.: Golden Press, 1964.

——. *Babylon and the Old Testament*. London: S.C.M. Press, 1958.

Rogers, Robert William. *History of Babylonia and Assyria*. London: Eaton and Mains, 1901.

Roux, Georges. *Ancient Iraq*. London: George Allen & Unwin, 1964.

Rutten, Marguerite, *Babylone*. Paris: Presses Universitaires de France, 1948.

Saggs, H. W. F. *Everyday Life in Babylonia and Assyria*. New York: G. P. Putnam's Sons, 1965.

——. *The Greatness That Was Babylon*. New York: Hawthorne Books, 1962.

Unger, Eckhard. *Babylon, Die Heilige Stadt*. Berlin: Walter DeGruyter & Co., 1931.

Egypt

Aldred, Cecil. *The Egyptians*. London: Thames and Hudson, 1961.

Baikie, James. *The Amarna Age*. New York: Macmillan Co., 1926.

——. *Egyptian Antiquities in the Nile Valley*. London: Methuen & Co., 1932.

Breasted, James H. *A History of Egypt*. New York: Charles Scribner's Sons, 1909.

Gardiner, Alan. *Egypt of the Pharaohs*. Oxford: Clarendon Press, 1961.

Hayes, W. C. *The Scepter of Egypt*. New York: Harper & Row, 1953.

Kees, Hermann. *Ancient Egypt: A Geographical History of the Nile*. Chicago: University of Chicago Press, 1957.

Montet, Pierre. *Eternal Egypt*. London: Weidenfield & Nicolson, 1964.

Peet, T. Eric. *Egypt and the Old Testament*. Liverpool: University Press, 1922.

Steindorff, George and Seele, Keith C. *When Egypt Ruled the East*. 2d ed. Chicago: University of Chicago Press, 1957.

Wilson, John A. *The Burden of Egypt*. Chicago: University of Chicago Press, 1951.

Archaeology

Adams, J. McKee. *Biblical Backgrounds*. Revised by Joseph A. Callaway. Nashville: Broadman Press, 1965.

Albright, William F. *Archaeology and the Religion of Israel.* Baltimore: Johns Hopkins Press, 1942.

———. *The Archaeology of Palestine.* Baltimore: Penguin Books, 1954.

———. *From the Stone Age to Christianity.* Baltimore: Johns Hopkins Press, 1946.

Barton, G. A. *Archaeology and the Bible.* New York: American Sunday School Union, 1937.

Burrows, M. *What Mean These Stones?* New Haven: Yale University Press, 1941.

Ceram, C. W. *Gods, Graves and Scholars.* New York: Alfred A. Knopf, 1954.

———. *The Secret of the Hittites.* New York: Alfred A. Knopf, 1956.

Chiera, E. *They Wrote on Clay.* Chicago: University of Chicago Press, 1938.

Finegan, J. *Light from the Ancient Past.* Princeton: Princeton University Press, 1959.

Glueck, N. *The Other Side of the Jordan.* New Haven: American Schools of Oriental Research, 1940.

———. *Rivers in the Desert.* New York: Farrar, Straus, and Cudahy, 1959.

Gordon, C. H. *Adventures in the Nearest East.* Chicago: Phoenix Books, 1957.

Kenyon, Kathleen. *Archaeology in the Holy Land.* 2d ed. New York: Praeger Publishers, 1966.

———. *Beginning in Archaeology.* New York: Praeger Publishers, 1953.

Kramer, S. N. *From the Tablets of Sumer.* London: Falcon's Wing Press, 1956.

McCowan, C. C. *The Ladder of Progress in Palestine.* New York: Harper & Row, 1943.

———. *Man, Morals, and History.* New York: Harper & Row, 1958.

Pattai, Raphael. *Sex and Family in the Bible.* Garden City, N.Y.: Doubleday & Co., 1959.

Pfeiffer, Charles F., ed. *The Biblical World: A Dictionary of Biblical Archaeology.* Grand Rapids: Baker Book House, 1966.

Pritchard, James B. *Archaeology and the Old Testament.* Princeton: Princeton University Press, 1958.

Rowley, H. H. *Recent Discovery and the Patriarchal Age.* New York: Oxford University Press, 1949.

Thompson, J. A. *Archaeology and the Old Testament.* Grand Rapids: Eerdmans Publishing Co., 1960.

Unger, M. F. *Archaeology and the Old Testament.* Grand Rapids: Zondervan Publishing House, 1954.

Woolley, C. L. *The Sumerians.* Oxford: Clarendon Press, 1929.

———. *Ur of the Chaldees.* Baltimore: Penguin Books, 1950.

Wright, G. E. *Biblical Archaeology.* Philadelphia: Westminster Press, 1957.

Biblical Geography

Aharoni, Yohanan. *The Land of the Bible: A Historical Geography.* Translated by A. F. Rainey. London: Burns & Oates, 1967.

Aharoni, Yohanan and Avi-Yonah, Michael. *The Macmillan Bible Atlas.* Prepared by Carta, Jerusalem. New York: Macmillan Co., 1968.

Baly, Denis. *The Geography of the Bible: A Study in Historical Geography.* New York: Harper & Row, 1957.

Baly, Denis and Tushingham, A. D. *Atlas of the Biblical World.* New York: World Publishing Co., 1971.

Blaiklock, E. M., ed. *The Zondervan Pictorial Bible Atlas.* Grand Rapids: Zondervan Publishing House, 1969.

Kraeling, Emil G., ed. *Rand-McNally Historical Atlas of the Holy Land.* Chicago: Rand-McNally & Co., 1959.

Orni, Efriam and Efrat, Elisha. *Geography of Israel.* Jerusalem: Israel Program for Scientific Translations, 1964.

Pfeiffer, Charles F. *Baker's Bible Atlas.* Grand Rapids: Baker Book House, 1961.

Pfeiffer, Charles F. and Vos, Howard F. *The Wycliffe Historical Geography of the Holy Lands.* Chicago: Moody Press, 1967.

Smith, George Adam. *The Historical Geography of the Holy Land.* 15th ed. New York: A. C. Armstrong & Son, 1909.

Vilnay, Zev. *The New Israel Atlas: Bible to Present Day.* Jerusalem: Israel University Press, 1968.

Wright, George Ernest and Filson, Floyd Vivian, eds. *The Westminster Historical Atlas to the Bible.* Philadelphia: Westminster Press, 1945.

Old Testament Theology

Baab, Otto. *The Theology of the Old Testament.* Nashville: Abingdon Press, 1949.

Heinisch, Paul. *Theology of the Old Testament.* Translated by William G. Heidt. Collegeville, Minn.: Liturgical Press, 1955.

Jacob, E. *Theology of the Old Testament.* London: Hodder & Stoughton, 1958.

Knight, George A. F. *A Christian Theology of the Old Testament.* Richmond: John Knox Press, 1959.

Koehler, Ludwig. *Old Testament Theology.* Philadelphia: Westminster Press, 1957.

Oehler, Gustav Frederich. *Theology of the Old Testament.* Translated by George E. Day. New York: Funk & Wagnalls Co., 1883.

Rowley, H. H. *The Faith of Israel.* London: S.C.M. Press, 1956.

Smith, J. W. D. *God and Man in Early Israel.* London: Methuen & Co., 1956.

Snaith, Norman H. *The Distinctive Ideas of the Old Testament.* London: Epworth Press, 1944.

Vos, Geerhardus. *Biblical Theology.* Grand Rapids: Eerdmans Publishing Co., 1948.

Vriezen, T. C. *An Outline of Old Testament Theology.* Newton Centre, Mass.: Charles T. Branford Co., 1958.

Wright, G. E. "The Faith of Israel." In *The Interpreter's Bible,* vol. 1. Nashville: Abingdon Press, 1952.

———. *The God Who Acts.* London: S.C.M. Press, 1952.

Jerusalem

James, E. O. "Foreword." In *Jerusalem: A History.* London: Paul Hamlyn, 1967.

Kenyon, Kathleen. *Jerusalem: Excavating 3000 Years of History.* New York: McGraw-Hill Book Co., 1967.

Kollak, Teddy and Pearlman, Moshe. *Jerusalem: A History of Forty Centuries.* New York: Random House, 1968.

Parrot, Andre. *The Temple of Jerusalem.* London: S.C.M. Press, 1957.

Pfeiffer, Charles F. *Jerusalem Through the Ages.* Grand Rapids: Baker Book House, 1967.

Simons, J. *Jerusalem in the Old Testament.* Leiden: E. J. Brill, 1952.

Vincent, L. H. and Steve, A. M. *Jerusalem de l'Ancien Testament.* Paris: J. Gabalda, 1954, 1956.

Intertestament Period

General

Fairweather, William. *The Background of the Gospels.* Edinburgh: T. & T. Clark, 1908.

Oesterley, W. O. E. and Robinson, T. H. *A History of Israel.* 2 vols. London: Oxford University Press, 1932.

Snaith, Norman H. *The Jews from Cyrus to Herod.* Nashville: Abingdon Press, n.d.

See also pertinent sections of *The Cambridge Ancient History.*

Persia

Ghirshman, R. *Iran.* Gretna, La.: Pelican, 1954.

Olmstead, A. T. *The History of the Persian Empire.* Chicago: University of Chicago Press, 1948.

Rogers, Robert William. *A History of Ancient Persia.* New York: Charles Scribner's Sons, 1929.

Greece

Bury, J. B. *History of Greece to the Death of Alexander the Great.* New York: Macmillan Co., 1922.

Carey, Max. *A History of the Greek World from 323 to 146* B.C. New York: Macmillan Co., 1952.

Kirto, H. D. F. *The Greeks*. Gretna, La.: Pelican, 1956.

Oesterley, W. O. E. *The Jews and Judaism During the Greek Period*. New York: Macmillan Co., 1941.

Hellenism

Bentwich, Norman. *Hellenism*. London: Jewish Publication Society, 1919.

Bottsford, G. W. and Sihler, E. G. *Hellenic Civilization*. New York: Columbia University Press, 1950.

Marcus, Ralph. "The Hellenistic Age." In *Great Ages and Ideas of the Jewish People*. Edited by Leo W. Schwarz. New York: Random House, 1956.

Wolfson, Harry A. *Philo*. 2 vols. Cambridge, Mass.: Harvard University Press, 1948.

Maccabees and Hasmoneans

Bevan, E. R. *Jerusalem Under the High Priests*. London: Edward Arnold, 1904.

Bickerman, Elias. *The Maccabees*. New York: Schocken Books, 1947.

Riggs, J. S. *A History of the Jewish People: Maccabean and Roman Periods*. New York: Charles Scribner's Sons, 1908.

Romans

Barrow, R. H. *The Romans*. Baltimore: Pelican Books, 1949.

Moore, George Foot. *Judaism in the First Centuries of the Christian Era*. 2 vols. Cambridge, Mass.: Harvard University Press, 1927.

Perowne, Stewart. *The Life and Times of Herod the Great*. London: Hodder & Stoughton, 1957.

SPECIAL STUDIES

Part 1: The Patriarchal Age

Alt, Albrecht. *Der Gott der Vater*. Leipzig, 1929.

Gordon, C. H. "Biblical Customs and the Nuzu Tablets." *The Biblical Archaeologist* 3, no. 1 (1940).

Hill, Dorothy B. *Abraham: His Heritage and Ours*. Boston: Beacon Press, 1957.

Lehman, Manfred R. "Abraham's Purchase of Machpelah and Hittite Law." *Bulletin of the American Schools of Oriental Research*, no. 129 (1953).

Mendenhall, G. E. *Law and Covenant in Israel and in the Ancient Near East*. Pittsburg: The Biblical Colloquium, 1955.

Part 2: Egypt and the Exodus

History of the period:

Rowley, H. H. *From Joseph to Joshua.* London: Oxford University Press, 1950.

———. "Israel's Sojourn in Egypt." *Bulletin of the John Rylands Library* 22 (1938): 243-290.

Religion of Egypt:

Hayes, W. C. "The Religion and Funerary Beliefs in Ancient Egypt." *The Scepter of Egypt.* Vol. 1. New York: Harper & Row, 1953.

Mosaic Religion:

Mendenhall, G. E. *Law and Covenant in Israel and the Ancient Near East.* Pittsburgh: The Biblical Colloquium, 1955.

The Sinai Peninsula:

Albright, W. F. "Exploring in Sinai." *Bulletin of the American Schools of Oriental Research.* no. 109 (1948): 5-20.

Rothenberg, Beno. *God's Wilderness: Discoveries in Sinai.* London: Thames & Hudson, 1961.

Jarvis, C. S. *Yesterday and Today in Sinai.* 1931.

Petrie, W. M. F. *Researches in Sinai.* London, n.d.

Robinson, E. *Biblical Researches.* 11th ed. Vol. 1. Boston: Crocker & Brewster, 1856.

Woolley, C. L. and Lawrence, T. E. *The Wilderness of Zin.* London: Palestine Exploration Fund, 1914.

Wilson C. W. and Palmer, H. S. *Ordnance Survey of the Peninsula of Sinai.* London, 1869-72.

The Nile Delta:

Cazelles, H. "Donnees geographiques sur l'exode." *Revue d'histoire et de philosophie religeuses* (1955):55.

Gardiner, A. H. "The Delta Residence of the Ramesides." *Journal of Egyptian Archaeology* 5 (1918):127.

———. "The Geography of the Exodus, an answer to Professor Naville and others." *Journal of Egyptian Archaeology* 10 (1924): 87-96.

———. "The Geography of the Exodus." In *Recueil d'etudes egyptologiques dediees a la memoire de Jean-Francois Champollion.* Paris, 1922.

———. "Tanis and Pi-Ramesse: A Retraction." *Journal of Egyptian Archaeology* 13 (1933):122-28.

Edom and Moab:

Glueck, Nelson. *The Other Side of the Jordan.* New Haven: American Schools of Oriental Research, 1940.

Balaam:

Albright, William F. "The Oracles of Balaam." *Journal of Biblical Literature* 63 (1944): 207-233.

Date of the Exodus:

Jack, J. W. *The Date of the Exodus.* Edinburgh: T. & T. Clark, 1925.
deWet, C. *The Date and Route of the Exodus.* London: Tyndale Press, 1960.

The Census Lists:

Mendenhall, G. E. "The Census Lists of Numbers 1 and 26." *Journal of Biblical Literature* 77 (1958): 52-66.

The Tabernacle:

Cross, Frank M. "The Tabernacle." *Biblical Archaeologist* 10 (1947): 45-68.

The Manna:

Bodenheimer, F. S. "The Manna of Sinai." *Biblical Archaeologist* 10 (1947): 2-6.

Part 3: Conquest and Settlement

Kaufmann, Y. *The Biblical Account of the Conquest of Canaan.* Jerusalem: Hebrew University Press, 1953.
Rowley, H. H. *From Joseph to Joshua.* London: Oxford University Press, 1950.

Part 4: The United Kingdom

Maly, Eugene H. *The World of David and Solomon.* Englewood Cliffs, N.J.: Prentice-Hall, 1966.

Part 5: The Divided Kingdom

Heathcote, A. W. *From the Death of Solomon to the Captivity of Judah.* London: James Clarke, 1959.

Thiele, Edwin R. *The Mysterious Numbers of the Hebrew Kings.* Grand Rapids: Eerdmans Publishing Co., 1965.

Samaria:

Parrot, Andre. *Samaria: The Capital of the Kingdom of Israel.* London: S.C.M. Press, 1955.

Nineveh:

Parrot, Andre. *Nineveh and the Old Testament.* London: S.C.M. Press, 1955.

Shishak's Invasion of Palestine:

Mazar, B. "The Campaign of Pharaoh Shishak to Palestine." In *Volume du Congres, Strasbourg.* Supplements to Vetus Testamentum, vol. 4. Leiden: E. J. Brill, 1957.

Part 6: Exile and Return

Whitley, Charles Francis. *The Exilic Age.* Philadelphia: Westminster Press, 1957.

The Babylonian Chronicle:

Freedman, David Noel. "The Babylonian Chronicle." *The Biblical Archaeologist* 14, no. 3, September, 1956, pp. 50-60.

Wright, George Ernest and Freedman, David Noel. *The Biblical Archaeologist Reader.* New York: Doubleday Anchor Books, 1961.

The Lachish Letters:

Albright, W. F. "The Oldest Hebrew Letters: The Lachish Ostraca." *Bulletin of the American Schools of Oriental Research,* no. 70 (1938): 11-17

———. "A Re-examination of the Lachish Letters." ibid, no. 73 (1939): 16-21.

———. "The Lachish Letters After Five Years." ibid, no. 82 (1941): 18-24.

Slavery:

Mendelsohn, Isaac. *Legal Aspects of Slavery in Babylonia, Assyria, and Palestine: A Comparative Study (3000-500 B.C.)* Williamsport, Pa.: The Bayard Press, 1932.

Babylonian Religion:

Bottero, Jean. *La Religion Babylonienne.* Paris: Presses Universitaires de France, 1952.
Dhorme, Edouard. *Les Religions de Babylonie et d'Assyrie.* Paris: Presses Universitaires de France, 1949.

Ancient Science:

Neugebauer, O. *The Exact Sciences in Antiquity.* New York: Harper Torchbooks, 1962.

Samaritans:

Montgomery, J. A. *The Samaritans: The Earliest Jewish Sect.* Philadelphia: John C. Winston Co., 1907.
Gaster, Moses. *The Samaritans.* London: Oxford University Press, 1925.

Chronology:

Parker, Richard A. and Dubberstein, Waldo H. *Babylonian Chronology, 626 B.C. - A.D. 75.* Providence: Brown University Press, 1956.

Nabonidus and Belshazzar:

Dougherty, Raymond Philip. *Nabonidus and Belshazzar: A Study of the Closing Events of the Neo-Babylonian Empire.* New Haven: Yale University Press, 1929.

Nebuchadnezzar:

Tabouis, G. R. *Nebuchadnezzar.* London: George Routledge & Sons, 1931.

Darius the Mede:

Rowley, H. H. *Darius the Mede and the Four World Empires in the Book of Daniel.* Cardiff: University of Wales Press, 1959.
Whitcomb, John C. *Darius the Mede.* Grand Rapids: Eerdmans Publishing Co., 1959.

PRIMARY SOURCE MATERIALS
Part 1: The Patriarchal Age

Translations of the Lipit Ishtar, Eshnunna, Hammurabi, Hittite and Assyrian Law Codes, the Ugaritic Epics, the Egyptian Sinuhe Story, selections from Mari and

Amarna Letters and Nuzi Legal Documents are readily available in: J. B. Pritchard, ed., *Ancient Near Eastern Texts Relating to the Old Testament* (Princeton, 1955).

Translations of the Code of Hammurabi, the Ugaritic Epics and a selection of Amarna letters will be found in: D. Winston Thomas, ed., *Documents from Old Testament Times* (London: Thomas Nelson, 1958).

Illustrations of the dress, daily life, and religious practices of the Old Testament world are conveniently classified in: J. B. Pritchard, ed., *The Ancient Near East in Pictures Relating to the Old Testament.* (Princeton, 1954).

Translations of the Amarna Letters:

S. A. B. Mercer, *The Tell El-Amarna Tablets* (Toronto, 1939).

J. A. Knudtzon, *Die El-Amarna Tafeln* (Leipzig, 1907-15). Knudtzon's work (in German) is preferred by careful scholars to that of Mercer (in English).

Translation of the Mari Letters:

G. Dossin, Charles F. Jean, and J. R. Kupper, *Archives Royales de Mari* (Paris 1950-   ). This definitive series of translations is in French.

Translations of the Ugaritic Texts:

G. R. Driver, *Canaanite Myths and Legends* (Edinburgh, 1956).

C. H. Gordon, *Ugaritic Literature* (Rome, 1949).

A popular translation of the three Epics, frequently in the form of paraphrase, is in: Theodor Gaster, *The Oldest Stories in the World* (New York, 1952).

Part 2: Egypt and the Exodus

There are no contemporary records of Israel's sojourn in Egypt. The first mention of Israel in Egyptian literature is in the Hymn of Victory of Mer-ne-Ptah, translated by John A. Wilson in: J. B. Pritchard, ed., *Ancient Near Eastern Texts Relating to the Old Testament*

Part 3: Conquest and Settlement

Pritchard, ed., *Ancient Near Eastern Texts Relating to the Old Testament* (Princeton, 1955).

Part 5: The Divided Kingdom

Translations of Assyrian and Babylonian historical annals by A. Leo Oppenheim, the Moabite Stone by W. F. Albright in: J. B. Pritchard, ed., *Ancient Near Eastern Texts Relating to the Old Testament,* abbreviated *ANET* (Princeton, 1955).

Translations of Assyrian and Babylonian historical records by D. J. Wiseman; the Moabite Stone by E. Ullendorff in D. Winston Thomas, ed., *Documents from Old Testament Times* (London: Thomas Nelson, 1958, reprint in Harper Torchbooks).

Translations of the Lachish Letters in *Lachish I (Tell ed-Duweir), The Lachish Letters* by Harry Torczyner. (London: Oxford University Press, 1938).

Part 6: Exile and Return

Translations of historical texts of Nebuchadnezzar, Nabonidus, and Cyrus by A. Leo Oppenheim in: J. B. Pritchard, ed., *Ancient Near Eastern Texts Relating to the Old Testament* (Princeton, 1955).

Translations of the Babylonian Chronicle by D. J. Wiseman; the Jehoiachin Tablets by W. J. Martin, and historical texts of Nebuchadnezzar, Nabonidus and Cyrus by T. Fish in: D. Winston Thomas, ed., *Documents from Old Testament Times* (London: Thomas Nelson, 1958).

Translations of the Lachish Letters:

D. Winston Thomas, "Letters from Lachish," in: D. Winston Thomas, ed. *Documents from Old Testament Times* (London: Thomas Nelson, 1958).

W. F. Albright, "The Lachish Ostraca," in: J. B. Pritchard, ed., *Ancient Near Eastern Texts Relating to the Old Testament* (Princeton, 1955).

The histories of Herodotus of Halicarnassus have been edited by A. D. Godley. They appear as Loeb Classical Library volumes 117, 118, 119, and 120. A popular translation by Aubrey de Selincourt appears as L34 in the Penguin Classics Series.

Translations of Business Documents:

H. V. Hilprecht and A. T. Clay, *Business Documents of Murashu Sons of Nippur Dated in the Reign of Artaxerxes I (464-424 B.C.)* (Philadelphia: Babylonian Expedition of the University of Pennsylvania, 1898).

Albert T. Clay, *Business Documents of Murashu Sons of Nippur Dated in the Reign of Darius II (424-404 B.C.)* (Philadelphia: Babylonian Expedition of the University of Pennsylvania, 1904).

Intertestament Period

For annals of Neo-Babylonian and Persian kings, consult Pritchard, J. B., ed., *Ancient Near Eastern Texts Relating to the Old Testament* (Princeton, 1955).

The writings of the Egyptian historian, Manetho, have been edited by W. G. Waddell. They appear in Loeb Classical Library volume 350.

The histories of Polybius have been edited by W. R. Paton. They appear as Loeb Classical Library volumes 128, 137, 138, 159, 160, and 161.

The writings of Flavius Josephus have been edited by H. St. J. Thackeray and Ralph Marcus. *The Antiquities of the Jews* appear in the Loeb Classical Library volumes 242, 281, 326, and 365. *The Jewish War* appears in Loeb volumes 203 and 210. *The Life* and *Against Apion* appear as Loeb volume 186.

Jewish Apocryphal and Pseudepigraphal writings were edited by R. H. Charles in conjunction with many scholars in a monumental, two volume work, *The Apocrypha and Pseudepigrapha of the Old Testament* (Oxford, 1913). The Revised Standard Version *Apocrypha* was published by Thomas Nelson and Sons, 1957.

The Behistun Inscription of Darius is readily available in *The Greek Historians,* Francis R. B. Godolphin, ed. (Random House, 1942), Volume 2, pp. 623-632.

A translation of the non-Biblical texts from Qumran is available in *The Dead Sea Scriptures* by Theodore H. Gaster (Doubleday, 1957).

The Zadokite Documents have been edited and translated by Chaim Rabin in *The Zadokite Documents* (Oxford, 1954).

Index